VAN S... R. PK.

CORT-
LANDT AV.

CITY

100

MOSHOLU

PARKWAY

BOSTON

LINE

POST

RIVER

1

1

PELHAM
PKY.

FORDHAM
RD.

HUTCHINSONS

LONG ISLAND SOUND

BRONX

BRONX RIVER EXTN.

E. 163 ST.

BLVD.

158 ST.

1A

...KNER

EAST RIVER

BRONX-WHITESTONE
BRIDGE

From
North Shor...

CROSS

NEW

From
Centr...

...RIBOROUGH
BRIDGE

WHITESTONE PKY.

ISLAND PKY.

NORTHERN

BLVD.

YORK

CITY L...

GRAND CENTRAL
BLVD

...HERN

25A

PKY.

QUEENS

GRAND CENTRAL
PKY.

QUEENS

24 25

BLVD.

HAVEN BLVD.

WOOD-

BORO

S. STA...
PKY.

YANKEES
CENTURY

YANKEES CENTURY

100 YEARS OF NEW YORK YANKEES BASEBALL

TEXT BY **GLENN STOUT**

PHOTOGRAPHS SELECTED AND EDITED BY

RICHARD A. JOHNSON

HOUGHTON MIFFLIN COMPANY

BOSTON NEW YORK

2002

For information about permission to reproduce selections from
this book, write to Permissions, Houghton Mifflin Company,
215 Park Avenue South, New York, New York 10003.

Visit our Web site: www.houghtonmifflinbooks.com.

Library of Congress Cataloging-in-Publication Data is available.
ISBN 0-618-08527-0

Book design by Julia Sedykh

Printed in the United States of America

KPT 10 9 8 7 6 5 4 3 2 1

Illustration Credits

MICHAEL ANDERSEN: 156–157, 322, 323, 328, 352, 353 left, 353 right. AP/WIDE
WORLD PHOTOS: 197, 302, 320, 388, 391, 392–393, 397, 402, 406–407, 408, 410, 412,
418, 419, 421, 425, 430, 435, 436–437, 439 right bottom, 440, 443, 444, 449, 450, 453,
454. BETTMANN-CORBIS: 208, 228. *BOSTON HERALD*: 71, 146, 186, 190, 198, 201, 202,
207, 266, 270, 290, 299, 316–317. COURTESY OF THE BRONX HISTORICAL SOCIETY:
10–11, 14–15, 80–81, 105, 110–111, 164, 192, 214–215, 237. BROWN BROTHERS: 2, 9,
10, 12–13. THE MAXWELL COLLECTION: 204. NATIONAL BASEBALL HALL OF FAME
LIBRARY, COOPERSTOWN, N.Y.: 14, 15 right, 16–17, 19, 22, 25, 28, 33, 36, 38, 42–43,
45, 49, 50–51, 52, 53, 55, 57, 59, 64, 66, 72, 73, 74, 77, 78, 89, 93, 94–95, 102, 109, 117,
118, 119, 120, 123, 127, 128, 130, 131, 134, 136, 139, 140, 141, 142, 143, 144, 149,
150–151, 153, 163, 165, 167, 174–175, 193, 212, 221, 225, 240–241, 243, 247, 253, 254,
257, 268–269, 273–274, 286, 289, 315, 333, 405. *NEWSWEEK*: 439 top right. COLLEC-
TION OF THE NEW-YORK HISTORICAL SOCIETY: 6–7, 60, 69, 112. *NEW YORK POST*: 438
top left, 438 top right, 439 top left. BOB OLEN: 222. LOUIS REQUENA: 262, 273, 279,
280, 282–283, 291, 300–301, 304, 307, 308, 310, 312–313, 318, 321, 325, 331, 334,
337, 338, 346–347, 349, 350–351, 354, 358, 363, 364, 366–367, 374, 376–377, 378, 381,
383, 384, 415, 416–417, 426–427. LOUIS REQUENA, BETTMANN-CORBIS: 265. BARTON
SILVERMAN/*NEW YORK TIMES*: 432; *SPORTING NEWS*: 160. THE SPORTS MUSEUM OF
NEW ENGLAND, BOSTON: 234, 238, 356, 398, 446. TRANSCENDENTAL GRAPHICS: 15
left, 20, 34–35, 41, 46, 82, 84, 98–99, 106–107, 114, 132–133, 145, 170–171, 173, 178,
181, 182–183, 184, 194–195, 216, 229, 230–231, 248, 258, 259, 260, 293, 296, 311, 361.

"It's Only a Game. It's More Than a Game" by Molly O'Neill. First published October
12, 1997, in the *New York Times*. Copyright © 1997 by the *New York Times*. Reprinted by
kind permission of the *New York Times*.

To my New York girl, Siobhan, and Saorla—who make these words worthwhile.

— G. S.

To the memory of my father, Dr. Robert Andrew Johnson, who served his nation in World War II as a decorated veteran of the Eighth Air Force and came to love New York while working as an intern at Bellevue Hospital and surgical resident at New York Hospital. He told me that watching DiMaggio at Yankee Stadium was like hearing "Heifetz at Carnegie Hall."

With love, gratitude, and high-fives to my unbeatable and courageous home team of Mary, Lizzy, Bobby, Minna, Amy, and Robert.

— R. A. J.

CONTENTS

Acknowledgments   xv

Introduction   xix

1902–1903   **Invasion of the Immigrant**   3

1904   **The Pitch**   23

1905–1914   **A Fine Mess**   39

1915–1919   **Two Colonels and One Boss**   65

1920–1925   **Murderers' Row**   85

1926–1928   **The Greatest Team**   115
Lardner Has Bright Idea to Help Pittsburgh Team by RING LARDNER

1929–1934   **The Pride of the Yankees**   137
Charles Devens, Yankee by CHARLES DEVENS

1935–1941   **The Clipper**   161

1942–1946   **A War on All Fronts**   187

1947–1950   **The Boston Stranglers**   205
George Weiss: Architect of an Era by DAVID HALBERSTAM

1951–1956 **The Battle of the Boroughs** 235

On Casey Stengel by IRA BERKOW

1957–1961 **57 . . . 58 . . . 59 . . . 60 . . . 61*** 263

1962–1964 **A Series of Swan Songs** 287

1965–1974 **After the Fall** 305

1975–1978 **Start Spreading the News** 329

Rivals by RICHARD A. JOHNSON

1979–1995 **Darkness at the Edge of Town** 359

Dave Winfield's Empty Afternoon by HOWARD BRYANT

1996–1997 **Top of the Heap** 389

It's Only a Game. It's More Than a Game by MOLLY O'NEILL

1998–1999 **Team of the Century** 411

2000–2002 **New York Stories** 433

Appendix A: *Yankees Century Teams* 456

Appendix B: *The Yankee Record* 460

Index 464

ACKNOWLEDGMENTS

Thanks to our editor Susan Canavan, Jaquelin Pelzer, Eamon Dolan, Gracie Doyle, Suzanne Cope, David Eber, Liz Duvall, Larry Cooper, and everyone else at Houghton Mifflin who has believed in our projects. Thanks also to Michele Lee Amundsen for creative suggestions and invaluable research assistance, Julia Sedykh, Michael Andersen, Cindy Buck, Jeff Idelson, Pat Kelley, Bill Burdick, Tim Wiles, Eric Enders, Jim Gates and the staff of the National Baseball Hall of Fame Library, the A. Bartlett Giamatti Research Center, the Bronx County Historical Society (Kathleen A. McAuley, curator), Robert Flynn Johnson, Linda Ritter, Brown Brothers, Nicole Wells, New-York Historical Society, Bill Mazieka, John Cronin, Al Lebeau and the library staff of the *Boston Herald,* Dan Friedell, Carolyn McMahon, Associated Press, Howard Bryant, Mark Rucker of Transcendental Graphics, Richard and Mary Thaler, Henry Scannell and the staff of the microtext department of the Boston Public Library, the staffs of the Uxbridge Free Public Library, the University of Massachusetts Library, the Lamont Library of Harvard University, and the New York Public Library.

Thank you to Phil Rizzuto, Brian Doyle, the late Vic Raschi, and the many other players who have spoken with us over the years, and to Max Frazee, Harry H. Frazee III, Gordon Brumm, John Dorsey, Bill Chapman, David Halberstam, Luke Salisbury, Ira Berkow, Molly O'Neill, Bill Littlefield, Mike Rutstein, Scott McElreath, Bob Leone, Philip Castinetti, John Taylor Williams of Hill & Barlow, Lisa Stout-Dean, Gary Stout, Joanie Stout, Marnie Cochran, Stephanie Peters, Kevin Hanover, Charles Devens, Sr., Charles Devens, Jr., Mr. and Mrs. William Iler, Bill Galatis, Richard Krezwick, Jim Bednarek, John Wentzel, Peter Webber, Tina Anderson, Brian Codagnone, Michelle Gormley, the Honorable Mal Graham, and the staffs of the Fleet Center and the Sports Museum of New England.

Special thanks to Louis Requena for his wonderful photographs, wealth of information, and overall support of the project, and to all the writers who have either written books about the Yankees or chronicled the club over the years, from the following newspapers: the *New York Evening Journal,* the *New York Times,* the *New York Post,* the *New York Herald Tribune,* the *Boston Herald,* the *Boston Globe,* the *Boston Post,* the *New York Daily News, Newsday,* the *Bergen Record,* the *New York Sun,* the *New York World,* and others.

To each and all, our gratitude.

INTRODUCTION

The Yankees are different. From the moment they first took the field, they have never been just another team.

The New York Yankees have won more than any other team in the game of baseball, and they have the championship banners to prove it — Yankee fans have had it easy. But it wasn't always this way; the dynasty didn't emerge fully formed. And neither has its continued success been as effortless as one might think.

When the American League's founder and first president, Ban Johnson, created the Yankees, he wasn't just creating a new franchise; he was creating a franchise for New York, and that made all the difference. While the other teams in the fledgling American League were more or less allowed to succeed or fail on their own, New York's team was held to a higher standard. The city demanded it.

Across a century the Yankees and New York have helped tell each other's story. New York took the Yankees in and over time made the club in its own image, giving the team its personality and character. And the Yankees, through their many successes and occasional failures, have come to symbolize New York's vast potential and unparalleled energy. They have helped the city celebrate when it has needed to celebrate and mourn when it has needed to mourn. The Yankees have enacted the aspirations of New York; they have made it here and, by extension, everywhere. And for a century they have made us want to be a part of it.

One hundred years ago the Yankees came to New York in virtual anonymity, an unknown immigrant. And now, a century later, the Yankees, perhaps more than any other institution, are synonymous with New York. Throughout the world the interlocking "NY" symbolizes not just a team but also a culture.

How that happened is nothing short of an epic drama. Within two decades of their birth the Yankees became baseball's ruling dynasty, a standard they have labored mightily to maintain. Their struggle tells the story of the game of baseball, for over time the Yankees have grappled with every great issue in the game. When they have reacted swiftly and with wisdom, they have succeeded. When they have failed to do so, they have faltered and demonstrated that success is not a birthright, but a product of constant change and adaptation.

Anyone writing about the Yankees is greatly tempted to write only about the team's greatest stars, greatest seasons, and greatest games. Ruth, Gehrig, DiMaggio, and a host of others are among the greatest and most compelling players in baseball history. But to focus only on the great and the well known is to miss the larger story and to lose perspective. One player doesn't make a team, and one game doesn't make a season. History is not told through championships alone.

More books are written about the Yankees than about any other team in American sports, and that vast library grows each year. Yet of the hundreds and hundreds of volumes the Yankees have inspired, most focus on the same few figures — Ruth, DiMaggio, and Mantle — and their accompanying eras, telling many of the same stories over and over again. Other figures and other periods in Yankee history have been overlooked completely, and in some instances hero-worship and myth have nearly obliterated the facts. We know Ruth far better than his slugging predecessor Birdie Cree, Gehrig more than his moral opposite Hal Chase, DiMaggio more than the equally dignified Roy White. But each has a place in the story, and what comes before always influences what comes next. Ruth, for instance, would never have come to New York had it not been for a unique set of circumstances that had nothing to do with a curse and everything to do with politics.

The full narrative history is more than just a chronology of victories, although plenty of victories are recounted in this book. But how the Yankees became the *Yankees* is the larger story. That is what attracted me to this project nearly a decade ago. My earliest baseball memories all include the Yankees. As I was growing up in the Midwest, in the dark ages before cable television and the Internet made it possible to follow any team anywhere, the Yankees *were* major league baseball. At the age of three, I had a T-shirt that featured Mantle and Maris. My mother ironed a "9" patch onto my first baseball uniform. I was thrilled to learn from the back of a baseball card that Whitey Ford and my father were born in the same year. I read the box scores religiously and prayed that Jake Gibbs would learn to hit. Every year I hoped my T-ball or Little League team would be called "the Yankees." I mimicked Roy White's batting stance in the back yard. I had a Bobby Murcer glove. I was scouted by a Yankee bird dog. I went to college upstate. I spent a summer in the hottest apartment in the world stealing cable television to watch the broadcasts of Bill White and Phil Rizzuto. After Reggie Jackson hit his second home run during game six of the 1977 World Series, I abandoned a midterm and walked a couple of miles to a bar just in time to see home run number three, thus earning my only collegiate C (and I was better for it). After college, during the strike year, I sold tickets over the phone for the triple-A Columbus Clippers. I didn't make any money, but I got to hang out at the ballpark, stand ten feet away while Dave Righetti warmed up, and sit in box seats behind home plate for free with the scouts and parents of players. I took the bus across the Bronx to see Don Mattingly. I danced to the Ramones and married a girl from 14th Street whose mother once met Babe Ruth.

Later, as a writer, I first studied and wrote about the Yankees' alter ego, the Red Sox, learning another side of Yankee history. That experience taught me that there is always more to the story, and while working on a book about Joe DiMaggio, I learned that this was also true in regard to the vaunted Yankees. I would have to write the book I wanted to read about them.

The research and conversations that supported this project were conducted over the last decade. In consultation with my partner Richard Johnson, I tried to avoid simply repeating what the reader already knows by creating this narrative principally from primary historical resources—old newspapers and microfilm—to put aside the legend of the Yankees and allow the facts to speak. My goal has been to reconstruct the events of history, for the best story is always the story of what actually happened.

The protracted birth of the Yankees immediately suggested to me that it is impossible to write about the team without writing about New York—the Yankees are as much a part of the city as the cop on the beat. The events of the autumn of 2001 underscored the real and enduring role the Yankees play in the life of the city—the Yankees matter to New York, and New York won't allow the ballclub to shirk that responsibility and slip into mediocrity. That's simply part of the deal. The advantages of New York—financial and otherwise—also come with a burden of expectations that few other teams face.

My close friend Richard Johnson gladly took up the task of selecting and captioning the remarkable photographs that accompany this book. His careful selections from a multitude of sources do not illustrate this book as much as they illuminate it. Together, we also called on friends, colleagues, and writers we admire to add their voices and perspectives.

Yankees Century covers one hundred seasons of the team and its city, its players, and its people. I feel fortunate to have had the opportunity to tell that story—the Yankees are like no other team, and New York is like no other place. I hope you find this journey through time as compelling as I have, and that it adds to your understanding of the Yankees and their relationship with the city they represent.

— GLENN STOUT

June 2002

YANKEES
CENTURY

The New York Yankees were born in 1903 in the prestigious Flatiron Building. It was here that American League President Ban Johnson relocated the league's offices from Chicago.

Water, water, everywhere,
And all the boards did shrink;
Water, water, everywhere,
Nor any drop to drink.

— SAMUEL TAYLOR COLERIDGE,
The Rime of the Ancient Mariner

1902–1903
INVASION OF THE IMMIGRANT

As he sat in his office in the Flatiron Building in January 1903, Ban Johnson, the founder of the American League and its first president, may well have pondered these words. From his perch in what was then the world's tallest building, the island of Manhattan, a place of unbounded promise, splayed out before him.

At the time Manhattan comprised 22.6 square miles, 12 major avenues, 220 consecutively numbered streets, some 2,200 city blocks, and nearly 2.2 million inhabitants. It was easily the most valuable and densely populated piece of real estate in the United States. Yet Manhattan supported only one professional baseball team — the New York Giants of the National League — and one ballpark — the Polo Grounds. And thus far, despite Johnson's best efforts, it appeared as if it were going to stay that way. The crack of bat against ball was a long way off, for the American League could find no place to play in Manhattan. Like a new boy in the neighborhood, Johnson sat on the other side of the fence, bat and ball in hand, hoping he'd one day be allowed into the game.

Two years earlier his American League had mounted a challenge to the long-established National League, becoming a second "major" league and going to war against the senior circuit. Since then Johnson had counted many successes. The AL had raided the NL of many of its best players and placed teams in direct competition with the NL in Chicago, Philadelphia, St. Louis, and Boston, supplemented by new teams in cities that the National League had ignored — Detroit, Washington, Cleveland, and Baltimore.

The new league was profitable from the beginning as fans flocked to its ballparks, where general admission cost only 25 cents, half the going rate in the NL, and players avoided the rough play that marred the NL. The NL took notice and tried — too late — to stop Johnson. In 1901 Giants owner Andrew Freedman even tried to create a trust in which all NL teams would be owned collectively. The plan failed, but that didn't stop Freedman. He had to protect his investment.

In July of the 1902 season, Freedman made a last-ditch attempt to thwart Johnson by trying to enact an unfriendly takeover by the American League's Baltimore Orioles franchise. His partner in the scheme was the pugnacious player-manager and part-owner of the Orioles, John McGraw.

Once Johnson's ally, McGraw had had a falling-out with the league founder over his own belligerent on-field behavior and a string of broken promises. Most notably, Johnson had promised McGraw a piece of a proposed New York franchise and was now backing off. McGraw contemptuously referred to him as "Czar Johnson." He demanded his release from the Orioles in exchange for forgoing a debt, and then sought revenge. He signed a contract to manage and play with the NL New York Giants, and in a complicated transaction, he facilitated a surreptitious sale of Baltimore to NL interests backed by Freedman.

With the Orioles now in their hostile possession, McGraw and Freedman pillaged the franchise. They released its best players and immediately signed them to National League contracts, sending stars like outfielder Joe Kelley to Cincinnati and pitcher "Iron Man" Joe McGinnity to the Giants. The Orioles became a major league franchise in name only.

Freedman and McGraw hoped their unfriendly takeover would weaken Johnson's league and cause its demise. For

if the Orioles couldn't complete the schedule, each team in the league would be left with a spate of open dates, and league standings would be so artificial as to be meaningless. They hoped that fans would rapidly lose interest and turn their affections back to the National League.

But Johnson was nothing if not resilient. The American League was an extension of his own personality — brash, bold, and tenacious. And it was *his.* The NL was governed by an unruly mob of owners who spent most of their time bickering and stabbing each other in the back. Johnson *was* the American League, and his rule was law.

The National League always underestimated Johnson's commitment and creativity. When the Orioles were left with too few players to field a team, Johnson invoked a clause in the team's charter that allowed him to take back a 51 percent stake in the franchise. He then forced the other AL owners to restock the franchise with their spare parts. The Orioles survived and managed to finish the 1902 season as a bad yet still competitive team. The American League remained intact.

But Johnson wasn't through. One crony once described him as "a man who always remembers a friend but never forgets an enemy." He planned to turn the Baltimore situation to his advantage and take action on his long-standing desire to move the Orioles to New York. As he later told the *New York Times,* in early August 1902 "we took our first official action toward invading New York City." That was precisely what Johnson had in mind — an "invasion." The National League, which had already repelled several earlier sorties, prepared to do so again.

For two years Johnson had led an unsuccessful assault against the National League's New York fortress, banging at the gates, alternately pleading and scheming to be allowed in. He knew that a franchise in the lucrative New York market was the greatest prize of all and the final proof he needed to convince both fans and players that the American League was indeed the equal of the National League. He had even moved the American League offices from Chicago to New York, making his intentions clear by acquiring office space in the brand-new Flatiron Building, New York's most prestigious business address. But thus far the political machinery of Manhattan had conspired to keep him offshore like an unwelcome immigrant.

At the turn of the century New York was a city of extremes.

Even as the first skyscrapers broke through the horizon and the subway system took shape underground, working farms still dotted the upper reaches of Manhattan and horses that died in the street were left to rot in the gutter. Great mansions lined Fifth Avenue, home to the scions of families named Astor and Vanderbilt, while the nameless and homeless and faceless had already found their way into the rat traps and backrooms of the Bowery. Men who made fortunes on Wall Street by day lost them in the gambling dens and bordellos of the Tenderloin by night, then were rolled and left bleeding in the alleys. Common criminals with the right political connections could become the most powerful men in the city. Anything in New York was available anytime at any price, from the finest silk, the best champagne, and the biggest steak to the youngest boys, cheapest girls, and biggest hangover. The Big Apple was at once rotten to the core and gilded in gold leaf.

Ban Johnson wanted to be a part of it. But he found Manhattan far more difficult to colonize than Boston, Chicago, or Philadelphia. Andrew Freedman stood guard at the gates.

The tactics of the Giants owner were pure New York—inspired, ingenious, underhanded, and incredibly effective. Legally, there was little he could do to keep Johnson from placing a team in Manhattan. Practically, however, there was little he could not do.

Freedman, a man of considerable political influence, was a member of Tammany Hall. After its inception as a colonial-era anti-British secret society, Tammany had evolved into the most powerful political organization in New York State and one of the most powerful such organizations in the country. In the 1850s, under William M. "Boss" Tweed, Tammany became a political machine whose power was matched only by its corruption; one observer later likened it to "the municipal equivalent of a floating crap game." Tweed himself helped fleece the public for almost $200 million before finally being brought down.

After Tweed's downfall, a wiser and more efficient Tammany machine emerged. The current boss, Richard Croker, had dodged a murder charge and developed a more sophisticated strategy for growing rich at the expense of the public. His genius was the application of so-called honest graft: shaking down all varieties of vice and making use of political power to take advantage of inside infor-

mation and secure business connections unavailable to any but those who were in the know. The concept made Croker and dozens of his cronies fabulously wealthy. The line between the criminal and the civic was so blurred as to be nearly invisible.

Tammany ran New York City regardless of who actually held political office. The machine's power came from the streets. Tammany helped out the little guy, distributing jobs, coal, cash, and other favors to New York's underclass and teeming pool of immigrants. In return, it extracted votes and kickbacks. Public policy was forged in the smoke-filled backrooms of Tammany Hall, where the public good created private fortunes for its members. But the good was always a secondary consideration, for Tammany also controlled the city's teeming vice trade — primarily prostitution and gambling—and the lucrative liquor business and licensing of taverns and hotels.

Tammany followed the money and tabbed baseball as another source of income. And there was indeed money to be made off the game, not only through ticket sales and concessions but also from gambling, ballpark leases, and other ancillary activities. The New York Mutuals, an "amateur" club that operated from 1871 to 1875 and was the forerunner of New York's original entry in the National League, had itself been a product of Tammany Hall—all its players were on the city payroll.

Freedman had been a member of Tammany since leaving City College, where he studied law before going into real estate. He made the acquaintance of Croker in the early 1880s, and the two became fast friends. True to Tammany form, the relationship soon made Freedman rich. Armed with the knowledge that a certain parcel had been selected for development, he became adept at picking it up on the cheap, reselling it for top dollar, then winning the construction contract for one of the companies that wisely paid him to serve on its board.

Although he never held elective office, Freedman was soon one of the wealthiest and most powerful men in New York City. He served on both Tammany's powerful policy board and its finance committee and in 1897 parlayed that experience into the lucrative position of treasurer of the national Democratic Party. He was also a member of the board of the Interborough Rapid Transit Company, the construction firm that was building the New York subway sys-

tem. He was thereby able to influence the placement of subway lines and stations, a power he used to his advantage time and time again to enhance the value of both his own properties and those of his friends.

In 1894 Freedman bought a small stake in the National League Giants. A year later he'd parlayed his small block into a majority interest and bullied other investors out of the picture. He then ran the club and, by association, all National League interests in New York as if they were just another offshoot of Tammany. Freedman was a strong supporter of baseball's own version of honest graft, the syndicate system, which allowed NL owners to retain a financial stake in several different clubs at the same time. It was bad for the game because it allowed one club to serve the interests of another and undercut the public's confidence in the league. But it was good for business, helping the league maintain a monopoly and keep player salaries down.

The Giants lost more games than they won, but Freedman didn't really give a damn whether they fielded a winning team. Profit was all that mattered. He fought and bickered and bullied other owners constantly, encouraged rowdy play, browbeat umpires, changed managers as often as he did shirts, berated players, and interfered with his team at every level. He was easily the most disliked owner in the National League, a perception not helped by the fact that he was Jewish and the object of anti-Semitism outside of New York. *The Sporting News* described him as a man of "arbitrary disposition, a violent temper, and an ungovernable tongue."

Freedman knew how best to stop Johnson. As a real estate man, he realized that the first requirement of any new team in New York would be a place to play. The Giants had no interest in sharing their park, the Polo Grounds on 155th Street, with anyone. Neither was adjacent Manhattan Field available. The National League leased the property for $15,000 a year just to prevent any other team from using it.

The first home of the Yankees was constructed on a rocky, barely construction-worthy plot in Washington Heights, between 165th and 168th Streets. American League Park, soon to be called Hilltop Park by fans, was built in less than two months at a then mind-boggling cost of $75,000, plus $200,000 to clear and level the site.

In theory, that still left some 22 square miles of Manhattan real estate available for a new park. At least, that's what Johnson thought. But he soon learned that in New York appearances were not always what they seemed. A different set of rules applied. What had worked in St. Louis or Boston held no meaning here.

From the moment Johnson first announced that the American League would go major in 1901, Freedman had set up his defense of Manhattan. From the Battery northward to 155th Street, he and his cronies surveyed every property in Manhattan of sufficient size to hold a ballpark. They then leased the parcel outright, took an option on it, or used their political influence either to turn the site into a city park or to split it in half with a public thoroughfare.

Thus, for two years Freedman successfully thwarted Johnson, rendering the island of Manhattan absolutely uninhabitable by another baseball team. "Water, water, everywhere, nor any drop to drink" indeed.

Johnson had run out of patience. The attempted kidnapping of the Baltimore franchise was the final insult. Near the end of the 1902 season he decided to make New York his battleground for a final assault on the National League. He first coerced the other AL clubs temporarily to foot the bill for a new New York franchise created from the ashes of the Orioles. Then, at the season's end, he turned the tables on the NL, stepping up his raids of NL stars, targeting the champion Pittsburgh Pirates, a team he'd left alone in 1901 and 1902 in the hope that he might entice the entire franchise to switch leagues. When it became clear that it would not, he attacked.

Johnson traveled to Pittsburgh, put cash on the table, and left town with the signatures of nearly every man on the team on an American League contract, save for that of star shortstop Honus Wagner, who remained loyal to the Pirates. He then assigned the best of those players — pitchers Jack Chesbro and Jess Tannehill, infielder Wid Conroy, and outfielder Lefty Davis — to the team he planned to transfer to New York.

Johnson expanded his raids to the rest of the NL. Every day the newspapers carried word of yet another defection. The strategy surprised the senior circuit. After the takeover of Baltimore, the NL had thought it had Johnson by the short hairs.

But Johnson knew that most NL teams were already in deep financial trouble. In the previous decade they'd had to fight similar challenges from the American Association and the Players' League. But their victories had extracted a heavy price. Most franchises were losing money and had become weary of the similar challenge posed by the American League. Another round of escalating salaries and increasing competition from the AL promised another season of red ink.

Johnson brought the National League to its knees. Reluctantly, NL teams sued for peace. The Giants were the final holdout in the peace plan.

In December 1902, the two leagues agreed to coexist. After some shuffling back and forth of the players whom each had recently raided from the other, they came to a formal agreement. They would respect each other's rights to players and operate under the same rules, for both wanted to hold down costs and start making some real money. The success of the American League was made almost certain.

Yet Johnson, emboldened by victory and drunk with power, wanted more. At his insistence, the price of peace between the two leagues included the ultimate prize — his right to place an American League team in New York. Placing a team in the outer boroughs was not an option, for they lacked both the cachet and the potential financial bonanza of a team in Manhattan. It was Manhattan or nothing.

The National League grudgingly agreed, and Johnson giddily signed still more high-priced talent for his new club, including former Baltimore star Wee Willie Keeler. For the good of the league, he convinced Chicago White Sox owner Charles Comiskey to give up star pitcher and manager Clark Griffith to lead the new franchise. For the time being, the press simply called the team the generic "New York Americans," to differentiate it from the National League Giants.

From the start, this new team was preordained to be the most dominant club in the game. New York was different. The city — and the situation — demanded it. As Johnson said, "It took a great deal of money to land this team, which I have every reason to believe will rank high among the leaders in the American League race." In Boston he had already employed a similar strategy, creating a powerhouse American League franchise that had quickly crushed the long-established National League team and turned the city into an American League stronghold.

Yet Johnson was still an immigrant in New York and naive in the ways of the big city. He thought that the recent accord with the NL had solved his problem of finding a home in Manhattan and expected the process to proceed smoothly. He had even paid a tithe, a donation of $5,000 — chump change — to the Tammany political machine, believing this would grease the skids. After all, Andrew Freedman was apparently out of the picture. A businessman at heart, Freedman had cut his losses in the face of competition, selling the Giants to John Brush for more than $150,000—not a bad return on his investment.

In mid-December Johnson made official his plan to move the Orioles into New York and resumed his search for a ballpark site. He quickly identified two neighboring plots of land on 142nd and 143rd Streets at Lenox Avenue. The plot was perfect—large enough, accessible to public transportation, including the planned subway, and closer to downtown than the Polo Grounds. The acquisition seemed simple. The owners were agreeable to a lease. But at the last minute the owner of the 143rd Street parcel demanded that his property be bought outright.

Things got strange fast. Johnson was directed to the Interborough Rapid Transit Company, which had won the right to both build and operate the New York City subway system, the first line of which was now inching toward completion below the streets of Manhattan. He was led to believe that the IRTC would gladly buy the land and lease it back to the AL with the expectation of turning a handsome profit once the turnstiles started spinning with fans. Transit companies in both Boston and Philadelphia even attested to the profitability of their similar arrangements with Johnson.

But Johnson had been set up. Andrew Freedman served on the board of directors of the IRTC, and Johnson might as well have asked the IRTC to buy him the entire island. According to the *New York World,* when the directors met, "the proposition was unanimously rejected on the grounds that the company was not ready to go into real

The Yankees were born into an environment of gaming, gambling, and street-corner politics. Each year Farrell and Devery helped sponsor Tammany Hall boss Big Tim Sullivan's barbecue.

Yankee co-owner Frank Farrell was known throughout New York as the Pool Room King and in 1903 controlled a politically wired gambling syndicate that raked in more than $3 million.

estate investments for the purpose of fostering the baseball business." Water, water, everywhere.

Freedman, of course, pled ignorance of any wrongdoing, commenting innocently, "Somebody has been stringing these Western men [along,] and it is time it was stopped. It is simply brutal." One could almost see him twirling his mustache as he peeked around the corner and leered at his enemy.

His intention was obvious. He would still block Johnson — any way and any how — unless he and his cronies from Tammany were cut in. If *they* could own the club, well then, "Welcome to New York City." If not, Johnson would find Manhattan inhospitable. The AL "czar" had already unwisely rejected a bid for the team from state senator Big Tim Sullivan, a saloon king, Tammany's number-two man, and a "master of the shakedown." He had also rejected Frank Farrell, known as the "Pool Room King of New York." Johnson didn't like being told whom he was going to sell the club to — that was a prerogative he retained for himself and had enforced elsewhere. But Tammany didn't like being told no. Turning down Tammany cost Johnson the Lenox Avenue site.

Johnson was appalled. He had won the war and the right to play in New York — it said so in section five of the peace agreement. Being held up by Freedman and Tammany hadn't been part of the deal.

But that was the price of doing business in New York. In early February Johnson was forced to admit that "Freedman and Brush have been and are working tooth and nail against us in New York. . . . If it were not for the necessity of dealing with them we would have announced our plans [for a ballpark] weeks ago."

Johnson kept trying. Over the next six weeks barely a day passed without another rumored site for a ballpark appearing in the papers. These included less attractive sites in the Bronx and Queens, locations that the NL announced it would block in the courts because the agreement between the two leagues allowed for a team in Manhattan and nowhere else. Meanwhile, Johnson continued to sign players for the team, and a tentative league schedule was produced with the club scheduled to play its first home games in early May — somewhere.

Johnson's search for a place to play turned into an elaborate game of cat and mouse. He would find a location, then secretly try to secure a purchase or lease. But there were few secrets from Tammany. Each time Johnson found a site, interests referred to by *The Sporting News* as "Brush's detectives" stayed a step ahead and were able to block the deal. The press even began calling Manhattan "Freedman's Island." An ever more confident John Brush announced that he had bet a suit of clothes with every other NL magnate that Johnson would be unable to find a place to play. "When Johnson shows me he has obtained land in the borough of Manhattan for his grounds, then and not until then will I believe the American League will play ball on this island," he said confidently.

By early March, as players for the new team prepared to travel to Atlanta, Georgia, for the beginning of spring training, time was beginning to run out. The new franchise was like some foreign visitor refused entry and left on Ellis Island. Even the players were running out of patience. Pitcher Jess Tannehill complained that if there wasn't going to be a team in New York, "then the American League should turn us adrift to make a deal with another team."

Johnson grew ever more desperate. Meanwhile, Freedman waited with open arms, ready to bail out the fair damsel at the right price.

But for once Freedman had overplayed his hand. Tammany wasn't operating at quite its usual strength. In the last election a reform movement had temporarily taken possession of City Hall. Croker had been ousted, and Tammany was weakened by internal battles for power. Even Freedman had lost his place at the table as chairman of the powerful Tammany finance committee, which had been abolished the previous spring. When he had concluded that there was no site above 155th Street suitable for a ballpark, he had made a critical error, one that others in Tammany were now quick to take advantage of.

Johnson was the beneficiary of Freedman's rare miscalculation, albeit most reluctantly. In January sportswriter Joe Vila arranged a personal meeting between Johnson and a competing faction of Tammany eager to do business and to stick it to Freedman in the process. They told Johnson they had a site for a ballpark. As February turned into March and the beginning of the season approached, Johnson had no choice but to deal with Tammany.

A shadowy syndicate of buyers emerged, fronted by Joseph Gordon. He operated a coal business and, until the recent election, had been New York's deputy superintendent of buildings. He'd also once owned a small piece of the Giants before losing control to Freedman. The syndicate dangled a ballpark site before Johnson's eyes.

They proposed to build a ballpark in Washington Heights, far uptown, on a plot of land between 165th and 168th Streets, bounded by Fort Washington Avenue on the west and 11th Avenue and Broadway on the east. The site was owned by the New York Institute for the Blind, but the syndicate had a lease agreement in hand.

They could not have chosen a more unlikely location, and that was precisely why the property was available and why they chose it. The locale was described as the highest point on Manhattan (although in fact it was not), leading *The Sporting News* to wax rhapsodically that it was "the most picturesque and romantic spot the white man has ever selected for a battlefield between the baseball warriors." To the east, one could see the Bronx, Long Island Sound, and Queens. To the south lay Manhattan and New York Harbor, while the northern view took in farms and meadows. The site was backed to the west by the Hudson River and the Palisades. Yet the journey from downtown still took nearly an hour by surface-bound public transportation. Although a subway station was scheduled to be built on 168th Street, the relatively remote location of the site explained why Freedman and his cronies had felt comfortable stopping their land search at 155th Street.

The location was also considered virtually unbuildable. *Sporting Life* stated that there was not "a level spot ten feet square on the whole property." The site measured nearly 800 feet by 600 feet, and the barren, rocky outcrop was dotted with massive boulders and dead trees and cleaved by deep gullies. A fetid pond ran the length of the eastern side.

But what seemed unbuildable to Freedman was precisely what made the site attractive to Gordon's men. The site offered them a consummate opportunity to indulge in honest graft in its purest form. Site preparation alone would require the rearrangement of hundreds of tons of rock and soil before a single nail could be driven to erect the stands. And Gordon had already used his political connections to acquire all the necessary permits. The project would have to be rushed to completion in less than two months, and Tammany looked forward to tapping into the huge construction contract. To make it happen, all Johnson had to do was say yes — and hand the franchise over to Tammany.

Gordon's Tammany backers treated the new team like any other immigrant. In exchange for help in finding lodging and gainful employment, Tammany would sponsor the new arrival. All Tammany wanted in return was the equiv-

alent of the immigrant's vote—undying loyalty and a percentage of the paycheck.

Johnson didn't like being held up — in essence, the offer was an act of extortion—but he disliked losing even less, particularly to Freedman. He had come too far to turn back now. If he failed to place a team in New York, he would lose face with the AL's financial backers. Quite literally, Johnson was between a rock and a hard place. Gordon's syndicate offered him his only out.

On March 11, he reluctantly awarded the syndicate the franchise and became a partner with Tammany. The price paid by the syndicate for the franchise—$18,000—was a joke and far less than the true value of the club. But the "Invaders" had a beachhead in Manhattan. The immigrant had arrived.

It was obvious to everyone who was paying any attention what had taken place. As the *New York Tribune* commented, "Politicians were standing in the way. . . . [They] not only demand that their pockets be lined, but that they be given a portion of the stock of the club." Johnson still claimed victory. He released a statement that read:

We could not fail in this undertaking, for we always had an anchor to windward, and there was never a moment when we were not confident of success. . . . In spite of the obstacles thrown in our way, of which we do not care to go into particulars, we have no hard feelings against anybody. . . . [I]t has been a long tedious affair from start to finish, but the American League has made good.

But the price Johnson and his league had been forced to pay was as steep as the island site on which the new ballpark would be built. On March 13, the press toured the site and learned that Thomas McAvoy, the ex-police commissioner and Tammany leader of the 23rd District, which included Washington Heights, had been awarded the construction contract to build the new grounds.

The cost of the sweetheart deal was mind-boggling at the time — $200,000 to clear and level the land, and another $75,000 to build the ballpark. Although Johnson claimed that no league funds would be used for the construction,

New York Police Chief Big Bill Devery, shown tossing out the first pitch on Opening Day at Hilltop Park, arrived at his co-ownership of the Yankees by a curious route: he joined with gambling syndicate partner Frank Farrell to operate the new team.

The Yankees' first manager, Clark Griffith, was a pitcher of note in the National League, where he was affectionately known as the Old Fox. He arrived from the fledgling Chicago franchise, which he had led to the first American League pennant in 1901.

it appears likely that the league was at least partially responsible for the costs, as it had been in Philadelphia and Boston. Before a single pitch was thrown, the franchise was already a license for Tammany to print money.

Five days later the front page of the *New York World* carried a story detailing a civil suit filed by Rogers L. Barstow Jr. against one Frank J. Farrell, the aforementioned "Pool Room King." In the suit, Barstow claimed that he had been swindled out of $11,000 in one of Farrell's gambling dens. With some measure of delight, the paper recounted Farrell's testimony. He professed never to have seen a roulette wheel and to be ignorant of the details of gambling in all its myriad forms. Right. That Farrell's lies were so blatant made them all the more entertaining.

On the same page a much smaller story nonchalantly reported that former NYC Police Chief William S. Devery had successfully petitioned the Tax Commission to reduce his personal tax assessment of $30,000 and noted that he

generally made such payments in cash with $1,000 bills. Not bad for a cop.

Such stories were neither shocking nor even surprising. New York was corrupt to the core, and everyone knew it. Both Farrell and Devery were familiar names to anyone who knew anything about Tammany Hall. And as the public would soon learn, Farrell and Devery were actually the owners of the new American League baseball team.

A more sordid pair can hardly be imagined. Each had made a fortune fleecing the public with absolute impunity. Buying a ballclub carried the promise of more of the same.

On March 18, with the first explosions rocking Washington Heights as construction crews used dynamite to turn 12,000 cubic yards of rock and stone into rubble, the team was officially incorporated. Farrell's status as a principal shareholder in the club was revealed to the public for the first time, although Johnson had known of his role for weeks. The announcement passed with little comment, although the *World* noted that Farrell's prominence in Tammany was thought to be enough to "overcome any influence the New York National League club may have in Tammany circles." In other words, it was business as usual in old New York.

Farrell had started out in the liquor business, pouring drinks while making friends and connections in Tammany Hall from behind the bar. He soon branched out, opening a poolroom and eventually becoming a partner in a gambling syndicate controlled by Tim Sullivan, Devery, and Richard Canfield. Together they operated hundreds of gambling enterprises ranging from poolrooms and crap games to the infamous "House with the Bronze Door." The opulent, elegantly decorated townhouse on West 33rd Street had been remodeled by the famous architect Stanford White and catered to the crème de la crème of New York gamblers. In 1900 the *New York Times* estimated that the syndicate's annual take was in excess of $3 million.

That made Farrell both very rich and very powerful, even though gambling, even then, was (technically anyway) very illegal. That's where William "Big Bill" Devery got his cut.

Like Farrell, Devery also started out behind the bar. But in 1878 he paid Tammany $200 and changed professions —he became a member of the police force. Devery wasn't drawn to law enforcement by any feelings of civic responsibility. Rather, being a police officer offered a young man in a hurry an inexhaustible opportunity to collect graft.

Devery wasn't shy. He was soon soliciting money from every gambling den and whorehouse on his beat. As soon as he could afford to, Devery bought promotions, first to sergeant, for $1,400, and then to captain for $14,000. By 1887 he was working the Tenderloin, a red-light district that ran between Fifth and Seventh Avenues from 24th Street to 42nd Street. The many nightclubs, saloons, brothels, clip joints, and dance halls in the area offered unmatched opportunities for financial advancement.

No one was better equipped to take advantage. Devery knew full well what he was getting into, announcing to his men upon his appointment: "They tell me there's been a lot of graftin' going on. . . . Now that's going to stop. If there's to be any graftin' to be done, I'll do it. Leave it to me!" He followed his motto—"Hear, see, and say nothin', eat, drink, and pay nothin'"—to the letter.

Devery soon became friendly with Farrell, for whose poolroom he provided protection, and a lifelong, mutually beneficial friendship was formed. Over time Devery provided protection for the syndicate throughout the city.

Even among the thieves of Tammany, Big Bill Devery's audacity stood out. But he always squirmed free—bribing juries bothered him not in the least. Devery's career in law enforcement flourished. In 1898 he made inspector and within six months found himself promoted once again, this time to the position of chief of police. His predecessor had made the mistake of interfering with one of Farrell's poolrooms. There'd be no similar trouble with Devery at the helm. Of his reign, muckraker Lincoln Steffens pronounced, "He was no more fit to be chief of police than the fish man was to be director of the Aquarium, but as a character, as a work of art, he was a masterpiece."

By 1901, however, Devery's brazenness had finally cost him. Although he enjoyed the full support of Mayor Robert Van Wyck—who called him "the best chief of police New York ever had"—in mid-February the legislature, desperate to be rid of his embarrassing presence, abolished his position. He "retired" with real estate holdings of nearly

The first Yankee star was former Baltimore Oriole standout Wee Willie Keeler. In nine major league seasons, first with Baltimore and then with Brooklyn, the diminutive outfielder had never hit below .333, with a high of .424 in 1897.

Standing only five-foot-four, Willie Keeler was a master of the bunt, hit-and-run, and sacrifice. He once told a reporter that the secret of his success was to "keep the eye clear, and hit 'em where they ain't."

$1 million, made plans to run for mayor, and embarked on a long, eventually successful effort to secure a city pension.

When Tammany lost in the 1901 election, Farrell had also "retired," cashing in and moving his money into more socially acceptable investments, like running a baseball team.

Meanwhile, far away from the mean streets of Manhattan, the New York Americans gathered in Atlanta for spring training. Manager Clark Griffith held the club's first practice at Piedmont Park on the afternoon of March 18. "I will give my men four hours of work every day," he announced. "While I am not strong on prophecy, you can say for me that we expect to be in the chase from the jump and can be counted on to finish in the first division."

He was being kind because, with the backing of Ban Johnson, the new ballclub was expected not just to contend but to win right away. Indeed, on paper, the club was a powerhouse. Nearly half the roster had played a key role on a team that had won a pennant in the previous two seasons.

It all started at the top, with "the Old Fox," player-manager Clark Griffith, who had already won 205 games in the major leagues, most of them with National League Chicago. He'd spent the last two seasons as player-manager of the American League White Sox, leading them to the first AL pennant in 1901. From Pittsburgh came infielder Wid Conroy, star pitcher Jess Tannehill, and spitball artist Jack Chesbro. Both pitchers had won 20 games while helping the Pirates capture the 1902 NL pennant by an astonishing 27½ games. They were joined by two of their former teammates, outfielder Lefty Davis and catcher Jack O'Connor. Second baseman Jimmy Williams, pitcher Harry Howell, and outfielder Herm McFarland remained from the 1902 Baltimore team.

Around this nucleus Griffith added former National League outfielder John Ganzel, aging former Boston star shortstop Herman Long, and outfielder Dave Fultz, who'd hit .302 and led the league in runs for the 1902 AL champion, the Philadelphia A's. But the acknowledged star

The center of American League (aka Hilltop) Park was a spartan grandstand built of spruce and pine on a stone foundation that seated 4,186 at a dollar a ticket. Bleachers down each line accommodated another 8,000 at fifty cents a ticket, and 2,500 outfield seats sold for a quarter.

of the team was diminutive outfielder Wee Willie Keeler. In nine full seasons, first with Baltimore and then with Brooklyn, he had never hit below .333, with a high of .424 in 1897.

Keeler, who stood barely five feet four inches tall, was the perfect player for the Dead Ball Era, which rewarded hitters for their ability to make contact and do the little things that move runners around the base paths. Bunts, sacrifices, and hit-and-run plays epitomized the style of play of so-called scientific or inside baseball. Keeler summed up his batting approach when he once told a reporter the secret of his success: "Keep the eye clear, and hit 'em where they ain't." A supreme place hitter, Keeler rarely struck out, was an adept bunter and base stealer, a fleet outfielder, and recognized as one of the most savvy players in the game. In New York he was expected to be the new team's first big star, the drawing card it needed to win a box-office battle with the Giants.

Griffith's job was to roll the ball out onto the field and get the disparate parts of his new club to work together. That didn't seem to be much of a challenge. The club shut out Southern League Atlanta in its first three exhibition contests as Howell, Griffith, and Tannehill all pitched spotless ball and Ganzel led the club on offense.

But while the players marched unimpeded through Georgia, Farrell, Devery, and Ban Johnson still found the going rough in Manhattan. Even as 500 men worked from dawn to dusk to turn Washington Heights into a ballpark, the immigrant invaders found their neighbors less than welcoming.

Freedman and his corner of Tammany felt betrayed by Farrell and made several last-ditch efforts to try to stop him and his associates. He rallied neighbors to sign a petition asking for a new street and sparked a strike among the workers clearing the ballpark site, but these efforts came too late. American League baseball finally had its beachhead in New York.

As work on the site continued, President Gordon held a contest to name the new park, offering a season pass for the winning entry. On April 5, he unveiled the plans for the park itself. It would be nothing more than a spare, wooden grandstand, 20 rows deep, built of spruce and pine on a stone foundation, seating 4,186 at a dollar a head. Bleachers down each line would accommodate another 8,000 fans at 50 cents apiece, and 2,500 25-cent seats would be available in the outfield. The outfield dimensions would be an imposing 365 feet in left field, 542 in center, and 400 feet in right. One observer commented that, although it would take "a mighty batsman to knock one over the fence, there is plenty of room inside the field for home runs." (Indeed, at the time most home runs were still of the inside-the-park variety.) The entrance would be on the corner of 165th and Broadway.

While hundreds of workers rushed to complete the park, which included filling a gigantic hole in what was supposed to be right field, the club broke camp in early April. They barnstormed through the South before heading to Washington to open the regular season on April 22.

On the cold, gray afternoon, the two clubs paraded into the Washington ballpark, according to tradition. They were greeted by a record crowd of 11,500 who were anxious to see the new team for the first time. Washington manager Tom Loftus opted to have his club bat first to take advantage of the brand-new baseball, which wouldn't be replaced until absolutely necessary. New York took the field as Opening Day pitcher Jack Chesbro warmed up.

The contemporary fan wouldn't recognize the team as the Yankees, for they had adopted neither that familiar nickname nor their distinctive pinstriped attire. They wore black uniforms with a large, white "NY" in block letters across the chest, black hats with white piping, white socks, and white belts. And they were called, well, "New York." As yet, the club had no other name.

This proved quite a quandary for the New York press, which somehow had to distinguish the American League club from the New York Giants. For a time they tried to get by with simply calling the team "the New Yorks," but Giants fans were accustomed to referring to their club at times by that name. Sportswriters created their own nicknames and soon started referring to the club as either the "Hilltoppers," in reference to the site of their ballpark, or the Highlanders, a name that also played on the Scottish heritage of team president Joseph Gordon. The "Americans," "Greater New Yorks," "Invaders," "Kilties," and a half-dozen other names were also occasionally used. But none really took, and most proved troublesome for the headline writers and typesetters. But within only a few months, the press began occasionally referring to the team as "the Yankees," probably in reference to the fact that they played north of the Giants. This name delighted typesetters, who shortened it to the even more manageable "Yanks." By 1904 "Yankees" was widely used, particularly by the *New York Evening Journal,* and had become the name of choice among fans.

Chesbro struggled with his control, walking the first three Washington hitters before escaping the inning by fielding a sharp ground ball himself and starting a home-to-first double play. In the bottom of the inning Lefty Davis stepped to the plate and became the first Yankee batsman in history.

He grounded one of pitcher Al Orth's serves to second for an out, but then Willie Keeler worked his magic and walked. With Keeler taking off on a hit-and-run play, Dave Fultz singled to left. Keeler slid around the tag at third with a beautiful fadeaway. Jimmy Williams followed with a ground ball to second, and Keeler dashed home to score the club's first run. It was inside baseball at its best.

And it was also the highlight of the day for the New Yorkers. After Washington scored a single run to tie the game in the fourth, an error by 37-year-old Herman Long at short helped Washington score two runs. The Senators held on to win 3–1.

The Yankees won for the first time the following day as Harry Howell went the distance in an easy 7–2 win, but the big news of the day was the public revelation that Big Bill Devery, along with Farrell, was the team's major backer.

He tried to deny it, rhetorically telling the *New York Herald Tribune,* "Me, a backer? I only wished I did own stock in a baseball club. I am a poor man and don't own stock in anything." No one was fooled, and the *Herald Tribune* went on to detail Devery's recent real estate deals that had netted him more than half a million dollars. Politically savvy Washington fans taunted the team by calling them "New York's Finest."

By the time the club arrived in New York for the home opener on April 30, it sported a disappointing 3–4 record. As Sam Crane wrote that morning, "It was a perfect day for the sport. The sun was strong and a gentle breeze blew across the stand just strong enough to make it comfortable." The good weather and curiosity about the new team combined to bring out a capacity crowd of around 16,243 fans to "American League Park," the winning entry of the young boy who won President Gordon's contest.

This was no palace of baseball. Only the bare wooden grandstand, filled with 5,000 folding chairs, and the bleachers were nearly finished. The roof existed only on blueprints. But bunting hung from the front of the stands, and every fan was given a miniature American flag, lending an

The playing field at Hilltop Park was a disaster: it contained rocks, bare baked earth, and numerous places where the ground had settled since excavation. A feature of right field was a depressed area once occupied by a pond and soon known as Keeler's Hollow because of the number of balls that disappeared behind the right fielder.

Before long the Yankees tried covering the right field depression of Keeler's Hollow with planks and sometimes roped off the field and sold tickets directly behind their Hall of Fame right fielder (note crowd and automobile at left).

appropriately festive air to the proceedings. Fans who purchased 25-cent seats were herded behind ropes down the line and in the outfield and forced to stand.

The condition of the field was appalling. A slack rope sufficed for an outfield fence. Only the infield had been sodded, and fans complained about the glare from the baked earth of the outfield and foul territory, most of which was still littered with stones and showed signs of recent settling. But the park's most distinctive, albeit unintentional, feature was in right field.

The pond that once covered the area had proven a challenge to fill. Tons of rock and dirt had only sunk in the mud. Crane described it as covering "about a sixteenth of the field." On this day, and on many others in the inaugural season, the gulch was roped off. Any ball hit into the void was a ground-rule double. Sportswriters soon referred to it as "Keeler's Hollow," for the number of balls that disappeared behind the New York right fielder.

Owing to the influence of Freedman and his cronies, the sale of alcohol was banned, but as Crane noted, fans looked at the lemonade vendors "with disgust." That response didn't stop the politicians, however, from turn-

ing out in force. The most conspicuous were Devery and Farrell, in the company of Ban Johnson. The acerbic Crane commented wryly, "There were enough diamonds in the shirt fronts of the politicians to start a fair sized jewelry store. There are three kinds of diamonds, it is said, which most politicians know much about — the diamond that glitters, the ace of diamonds, and the baseball diamond." This team was New York to the core.

A band escorted the uniformed members of both clubs from a nearby hotel, for a clubhouse had yet to be built. Ban Johnson threw out the first pitch, the home team chose to bat first, and just after 3:30 p.m. the immigrants staked their claim to the city when Lefty Davis stepped in to face Washington pitcher Jack Townsend.

He grounded out to short, but Keeler singled to left, then charged into second when outfielder Ed Delahanty bobbled the ball, turning the crowd apoplectic. He scored moments later on Jimmy Williams's double to put the Yankees in the lead.

On the mound for New York, Chesbro was all he had been advertised to be as he kept the Senators off balance. The Yankees emerged with a nifty 6–2 win to even their record at 4–4.

At the end of the short six-game home stand, the team, in the parlance of the day, looked to be a "world beater" as they took two of three from both the dismal Senators and the defending champion Athletics. Attendance was good, the team was in the race, and all looked right on the island of Manhattan.

But the protracted struggle to find a home was still having an effect. To accommodate the completion of the ballpark, the schedule makers sent the Yanks on the longest road trip in club history, a grueling 24-day sojourn that took them to every city in the league save Washington and even included a game against Cleveland played in Columbus, Ohio. The Yankees fell apart on the road and returned to New York a beaten team, an also-ran with a record of 15–18, buried in seventh place. The rejuvenated Giants, who were battling the Cubs for the National League lead, remained the unchallenged kings of New York.

Herman Long, 37 going on 57, was injured, and ground balls rolled through the left side unimpeded. Dave Fultz was also hurt. Clark Griffith couldn't pitch as often as he once had, and Tannehill was maddeningly inconsistent. The ballpark was looking somewhat better, for during the road trip the grandstand roof and left-field scoreboard and outfield fence had gone up and been painted green. Keeler's Hollow was more or less covered by planks and dirt, and grass finally began to sprout in the outfield. But field conditions remained poor, the park hard to get to, and the ballclub unfinished. When Boston dumped the immigrants three straight by a combined score of 26–5, the season was all but over. If they could have, fans would have started deportation hearings. After a loss to Cleveland on June 4, manager Griffith left the club, reportedly "out to look for players."

There was some desperation to his quest. But Ban Johnson wasn't about to allow the new club to fail. It was his league, and he ran it as he saw fit. New York had to succeed—he had invested too much to allow the team to fail.

During the previous off-season, Detroit shortstop Norman "Kid" Elberfeld had signed two contracts: one with American League Detroit, then another with the National League Giants. A fiery competitor known as "the Tabasco Kid," Elberfeld was a fine player, another student of inside baseball, and a particularly good glove man.

The Giants had wanted him badly—he was John McGraw's kind of player—but as part of the peace agreement between the two leagues, they had reluctantly relinquished their claim. Elberfeld then got off to a fine start with the Tigers, hitting .341 for the first two months of the season.

But Elberfeld wasn't happy returning to Detroit and spent much of the season feuding with Tiger manager Ed Barrow and owner Sam Angus. Like the Yankees, the Tigers weren't playing very well, or drawing many fans either. But unlike the Yankees, they didn't have the Giants playing down the street. Johnson didn't give a damn about the Tigers. If they failed in Detroit, other cities like Buffalo were waiting in the wings. So Johnson rang up Sam Angus and worked out a deal.

The Yankees weren't just another team, and soon the whole league knew it. Johnson arranged for New York to get something for nothing, sending Long, two others, and some cash to the Tigers for Elberfeld and outfielder John Deering. Elberfeld would be a star in New York for much of the next decade.

Giants owner John Brush was livid. To see the Kid in a Yankee uniform now was more than he could bear, and he sought a court injunction to ban Elberfeld from playing with the Yankees. For several weeks the dispute threatened to disrupt the peace between the two leagues, but Ban Johnson got his way. Elberfeld stayed with the Yankees.

The Kid made the Yankees one of the best teams in the league as they won 16 of their next 24. But Boston surged into first place at the end of June and kept going, while New York ran out of steam and struggled to stay above .500. A hot finish, which saw them go 19–10 in September, was enough to secure the club fourth place with a 72–62 record, but that was 17 long games behind pennant-winning Boston.

Meanwhile, the Giants won the battle of Manhattan in a cakewalk. Although they finished second to Pittsburgh in the National League, New York fans found the NL team much more to their liking. The Yankees drew barely 200,000 spectators, seventh best in the league, while the Giants paced the NL with nearly three times that amount. Of all the vaunted Yankee stars, only Keeler, who hit .318, Elberfeld, who hit .287, and Chesbro, who went 21–15, performed to their expected standard. Victories had proven as hard to come by as a site for the new ballpark.

Somewhere, Andrew Freedman was smiling.

Jack Chesbro's unfortunate epitaph lay in the infamous "pitch that got away" in the first game of the season-ending double-header in 1904 against the Boston Americans at the Huntington Avenue Grounds. Despite setting a modern single-season record of 41 victories, Chesbro tripped over the last hurdle, summed up by the stark headline "Pennant Lost by a Wild Pitch."

1904
THE PITCH

If the Yankees' failure to contend in 1903 had caused some joy among some factions of Tammany Hall, elsewhere there was only frustration. Ban Johnson, Frank Farrell, and William Devery were not happy. The new club had proven problematic, a failure in almost every way. All interested parties were determined not to let that happen again. They'd invested too much in the immigrants to let them founder.

Fans were less than impressed. American League baseball in New York, while cheaper than National League ball, hadn't been very exciting. The Yankees had failed to create their own constituency, nor had they stolen substantial numbers of fans from the Giants. Yankee rooters were foundlings who couldn't afford to attend games at the Polo Grounds, gamblers who would bet on anything, anywhere, anyhow, or Farrell's and Devery's political cronies taking a day off.

They weren't drawing fans from downtown. Getting to the ballpark was inconvenient and would be for several more seasons until the subway opened. By and large, the Yankees were fighting the Giants for the same group of fans — and losing badly.

The Giants were clearly the better team. They'd finished second in the National League in 1903. Their feisty and combative manager, John McGraw, was the toast of New York, and New Yorkers of Irish heritage turned out at the Polo Grounds to see McGraw and fellow Irish players like Dan McGann and Roger Bresnahan.

In most major league cities the majority of fans were either Irish or, in the Midwest, German, as were most of baseball's first generation or two of stars. Fans came to the ballpark more to see their countrymen succeed than to see their city represented.

The Yankees lacked both ethnic appeal and the cachet that comes with success. They would have to draw fans from elsewhere and appeal to America's next wave of immigrants, those from Italy and elsewhere in Europe. But for now the Yankees needed to win in order to give fans a reason to see them play.

Fortunately for the 1904 Yankees, the American League, like Hilltop Park, was not yet a level playing field. Nor would it ever be, a situation the club eventually would learn to exploit. For now they still needed the help of Ban Johnson, and he did everything he could to ensure a championship for the immigrants in 1904. The result would be one of the most compelling pennant races in league history and the beginning of one of professional sports' greatest rivalries.

While the Boston Americans were asserting American League superiority by besting the Pittsburgh Pirates in the very first "world's series" in 1903, the Yankees retooled. Tannehill, despite a record of success in Pittsburgh, had been a disappointment in 1903, finishing with a record of only 15–15. Meanwhile, in Boston, young Long Tom Hughes had come out of nowhere to go 20–7 for the American League champions.

To Johnson, swapping the two pitchers made perfect sense, for such a trade would serve to strengthen New York by weakening Boston, giving the Yankees a shot at a championship by sending Boston back into the pack. With one of his toadies, Henry Killilea, in charge of Boston but already looking to sell out, Johnson made the transfer in early December.

The New York press smiled broadly while their Boston counterparts screamed foul. The deal looked like a steal.

Hughes was an emerging star, five years younger than Tannehill, who had looked as if he were beginning a precipitous decline. But Johnson wasn't finished.

Cutting another deal, disguised as an outright purchase, he sent hurler Harry Howell to the St. Louis Browns and delivered Jack Powell to New York. While Howell had pitched relatively well in limited duty in 1903, sidearmer Powell was the poor man's Cy Young, one of the league's great iron men. He'd finished fully 33 of 34 games he started for the sixth-place Browns in 1903, winning 15. In essence, New York traded its fourth and fifth starters for two of the league's better pitchers — much more for a lot of less. With Chesbro anchoring the staff, and Griffith himself still valuable, the Yankees appeared to have the best pitching in the league. No less an authority than former National League great Cap Anson quickly pronounced them "a great team, one of the best."

And on Opening Day, April 14, that pronouncement appeared to be confirmed. Fifteen thousand curious fans braved the cold and saw the Yankees make the defending champion Boston Americans look like amateurs. New York erupted for five first-inning runs off Cy Young as Boston threw the ball around the infield and dropped fly balls. Jack Chesbro easily outdueled him the rest of the way, giving up only two runs on inside-the-park home runs that on another day Keeler and Fultz might well have caught. The Yankees won easily, 8–2, in a victory that seemed symbolic. They seemed to be poised to supplant the Bostonians as AL champions.

They relished the opportunity, for there was already some bad blood between the two clubs. In only their second meeting, in 1903, Dave Fultz had run down Boston pitcher George Winter in a play at first base. That set the tone. Subsequent games between the two clubs had been marred by rough play, and the trade of Hughes for Tannehill caused Boston to eye the New Yorkers warily — they knew full well that New York was Ban Johnson's current favorite. The rigged deal that cost them Hughes sparked a feeling of martyrdom in Boston that would only swell in the ensuing decades.

But after Opening Day, New York stumbled. The Yankees dropped the next two to Boston as Hughes was raked by his former teammates, and crowds were disappointing. The opening of the subway station adjacent to the ballpark was delayed as Tammany grappled over the profits. It was still little more than a hole in the ground, connecting to nothing. Fans were tiring of the long trek uptown, a journey that took them directly past the Polo Grounds, where McGraw's Giants were a powerhouse. Many chose to end their journey there. Thus far, Ban Johnson's Manhattan well was coming up dry.

By the time the two clubs met again in the first week of May, Boston led the league at 13–3, and New York seemed poised to drop even further back. Hoping to use the series to turn their season around, the Yankees gave it special emphasis. Clark Griffith told the press, "We are not afraid of the world champions." They weren't, but they weren't as good either. The Yanks lost the first game of the three-game set when Tom Hughes continued to make the Tannehill trade look bad by misplaying a series of Boston bunts into defeat.

The next day Jack Chesbro pitched and won for New York. No pitcher since has ever done what Chesbro did in 1904. It is impossible to overstate his value to the team in the 1904 season. No pitcher — not Cy Young, Christy Math-ewson, Joe Wood, Lefty Grove, Sandy Koufax, or Roger Clemens — has ever had an influence on a team and on a pennant race equal to the impact of Jack Chesbro in 1904. And none ever will.

After Powell pitched New York to a win in the series finale, Griffith bristled with confidence. "We did what we said we would," he commented. "Keep your eye on the Invaders. We took two from the world champions and can do it again." By season's end his desire would prove prophetic.

Yet not even Chesbro could stop the Boston juggernaut on his own. With the exception of Powell, no other pitcher on the staff could pitch well enough often enough to help, and injuries to key players like Elberfeld slowed the Yankees. Over the next month Boston stretched out its lead while New York struggled to keep pace.

Opening Day, April 14, 1904, at Hilltop Park. The Yankees made the defending world champion Boston Americans look like amateurs as they bombarded Boston starter Cy Young for five runs in the first inning while cruising to an 8–2 victory.

THE SPITBALLIST

In 1904 Jack Chesbro won 41 games in 51 starts, pitching 48 complete games, all still major league records. For one season Chesbro may have been the best pitcher baseball has ever seen. He was certainly the most valuable. He is also one of the more obscure.

Jack Chesbro was born in North Adams, Massachusetts, a mill town in the Berkshire Mountains. He signed his first professional contract in 1895, with Eastern League Springfield, and bounced around for several years before making it with National League Pittsburgh in 1899. After struggling for two years, he broke loose in 1901, winning 21 games, then led the NL with 28 wins in 1902 as the Pirates romped to the pennant.

In 1903 Chesbro jumped to the American League and joined the Yankees, winning 21 games. But early in the 1904 season he was inconsistent. Already 30 years old, he found that his fastball was no longer overpowering. On May 12, a 7–0 loss to Cleveland dropped his record to 4–3. In his last 35 innings, he'd given up 19 runs.

No one knew it, but he was about to become baseball's most dominant pitcher. His secret was the spitball.

The pitch derives its name from the fact that it is thrown by a pitcher who has moistened his fingertips with saliva. Thrown with a stiff wrist, the ball is squeezed upon release and leaves the hand with virtually no spin. Air creates drag on the seams of the ball, and as catcher Lou Criger once described it, the spitball "goes straight toward the batsman until he imagines he can knock it into China. Then it takes a downward shoot."

Chesbro discovered the pitch earlier that spring, when he saw it demonstrated by White Sox pitcher Elmer Stricklett. "I said to myself," admitted Chesbro later, "'Mr. Chesbro, that is something you must learn.'"

Two days after losing to Cleveland, Chesbro took the mound again and decided it was time to unveil the new pitch. He had nothing to lose.

The difference was dramatic. Using the spitball almost exclusively, Chesbro won easily, 10–1. Then he won again. And again. By July 4, he had pitched and won 14 consecutive games, during which time he gave up only 25 runs, less than half of them earned. Hitters reacted as if they were facing a pitch they'd never seen before. Most hadn't, because Chesbro had perfected the pitch. Gripping it like a curve and throwing it from three-quarters motion, he claimed he could control both the direction and degree of the drop from 2 to 18 inches. By midseason he was able to signal to his catcher just how far the ball was going to drop and later admitted, "Over the last 30 games of the season I pitched spitballs entirely. In those 30 games I didn't pitch a half-dozen balls that weren't spitballs."

Hitters were helpless against the pitch, either missing it entirely or beating it harmlessly into the ground. Chesbro found he could throw the spitball with very little rest. Not that it didn't tire his arm, for it did, but fatigue didn't affect the movement of the ball.

Chesbro's success, however, came at a cost. Not even he could control the pitch all the time, and in the end his wild pitch—the spitball that Chesbro later admitted he threw "with too much force"—may have cost New York a pennant in 1904. Moreover, the pitch may well have cut short Chesbro's career.

He was never quite the same after 1904. Late in the season he developed a sore shoulder, probably a partial tear of the rotator cuff, and never again pitched without pain. He blamed the spitball for his miseries and tried to survive without it, only to find he could not.

At the same time success went to Chesbro's head. Financially secure, he took the game less seriously. With each passing season, he became less enthusiastic and never trained properly, usually skipping spring training. Only five-foot-nine, he ballooned to well over 200 pounds.

Although he did manage to win 24 games in 1906, he was never again the best pitcher in baseball. By 1909 even his spitball was no longer effective. Cut loose by New York only three wins shy of 200 victories, Chesbro signed with Boston, pitched once, and was then set free.

Only then did he discover how much he missed baseball. He tried to come back several years later but failed. Cut by the Yankees in the spring, he returned to his farm in Conway, Massachusetts.

There he stayed, apart from a brief stint as a coach for the Washington Senators, for the rest of his life. Each time a pennant race came down to the final pitch, some intrepid reporter would find his way to Chesbro's farm and revisit the only pitch he ever threw that anyone remembered.

"It is an old, old story," he later told one visitor. "I have thought about it over and over. . . . [I]n all New York I don't believe there was a more sorrowful individual."

Ban Johnson grew concerned. Another Boston runaway could be devastating to attendance leaguewide, but nowhere more so than in Manhattan. The Giants were killing the Yankees at the gate.

The new club needed still more help. Devery and Farrell were already upset at the result of the Hughes-Tannehill trade. It had backfired and only made Boston stronger. They insisted on an adjustment. Johnson agreed.

He started by giving them some help on the mound. In mid-June he arranged the acquisition of Harvard University's Walter Clarkson, baseball's reigning phenom and brother of the great John Clarkson, who had won 327 games from 1882 through 1894. *The Sporting News* favorably compared him to the Giants' young star pitcher Christy Mathewson. But Johnson was just getting warmed up. With another big series with Boston on the horizon in late June, the Yankees needed help now.

They got it. On the morning of June 18, New York fans awoke to discover that Boston's star outfielder, Patsy Dougherty, was now the property of the Yankees, acquired in exchange for an undisclosed amount of cash and a sickly rookie infielder named Bob Unglaub. Unglaub, too ill to play, was hitting .211, while Dougherty, who could run and hit with anyone in the league, entered the season with a career batting average of .336. In contemporary terms, the transaction was the rough equivalent of getting an Ichiro Suzuki for a Clay Bellinger. It left a gaping hole in Boston's outfield and provided New York with some instant offense. Over the remainder of the year, New York had the best record in the league and, finally, a player who appealed to New York's Irish. No deal in American League history had ever been so one-sided, and few since have approached it.

Yankees fans snickered and nodded knowingly at one another as all Boston howled. The effects of the deal were immediate and dramatic.

One week later the Invaders made their initial foray into Boston, with Dougherty leading off and playing left field. He was, as *The Sporting News* described him, "the central figure of the game." New York took two of three to draw within a game and a half of Boston. Ban Johnson had his pennant race, and with the Giants running away with the NL race, there was the possibility that the New York clubs might meet in another lucrative "world's series."

That promised mind-boggling profits for Devery and Farrell, no matter which team won. After all, the house is always the biggest winner.

For the remainder of the season, Boston and New York were dance partners in a marathon whose prize neither wanted to share with the other. In early July the two clubs met again in a four-game set. Boston took the first three, defeating Chesbro twice to stop his win streak at 14. But in the finale Dougherty continued to cause Boston to rue his transfer, going four for five as New York averted disaster and won 10–1. With Boston's lead down to a still manageable three and a half games, Ban Johnson gave his favorites even more help.

Johnson traveled to Washington, where the Senators were in trouble both at the gate and in the field. "There is sure to be something doing in Ban's immediate vicinity," warned *The Sporting News,* and Johnson admitted that he was there to "strengthen the Senators whenever the opportunity offered."

It soon came knocking, led by Johnson's beckoning hand. Long Tom Hughes had fallen into Clark Griffith's deep, dark doghouse. And although Chesbro and Powell, with occasional help from Griffith, were performing yeoman service, the club still needed pitching help. Griffith had little faith in untested youngsters like Ambrose Puttman and Clarkson, whose pedigree simply hadn't translated into wins.

Pitcher Al Orth was wasting away with the last-place Washington Senators, who had opened 1–16. Orth, a crafty change-of-pace pitcher known as "the Curveless Wonder," led the National League with six shutouts in 1901 but had missed the bulk of the 1904 season with an illness. Healthy again, his return meant nothing for the hapless Senators. They already trailed Boston by more than 30 games.

That made Orth expendable, and perfect for New York. So Johnson arranged another trade, sending Hughes and another warm body to the Senators for Orth. With nearly two months before its next scheduled meeting with Boston, New York began stalking the champions.

Chesbro remained magnificent, pitching and usually winning two or three times a week and proving nearly as valuable at the plate with timely hitting; he even won one game with a ninth-inning steal of home. Powell was pitch-

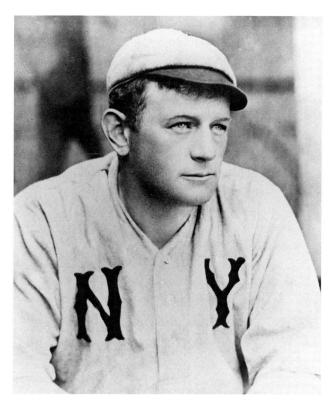

No pitcher in major league history ever enjoyed as domineering a season as Jack Chesbro in 1904. Pitching three to four times a week, he was a superior hitter who even won a game with a ninth-inning steal of home. In all, he led the league with an astonishing 55 appearances, 454 innings pitched, and 41 victories.

ing almost as often, and Orth was nearly unbeatable. Ever so slowly, the New Yorkers drew closer to Boston.

Finally, on August 5, the Yanks broke through. While Boston was losing to Detroit, Orth shut out Cleveland, 5–0, to put the Yankees in first place for the first time in club history.

Although the White Sox surged past both clubs five days later, the Chicago team soon dropped back. For the next month New York and Boston stayed in lock step with one another as New York clung to a narrow lead.

The Yankees — and Johnson — wanted still more and made one more move that they hoped would secure a New York pennant. Brooklyn pitcher Ned Garvin had long been the best pitcher on a series of bad teams. For Brooklyn in 1904, although his record was 5–15, his ERA was a spectacular 1.68 — better than Chesbro's and one of the best in baseball.

But Garvin was a drunk. In 1903 he'd been jailed for taking a shot at a bartender in Chicago. In mid-August, as Brooklyn traveled by train to St. Louis, he and a few teammates got roaring drunk. When the club secretary tried to calm them down, Garvin beat him to a pulp and then led his merry band in the near-total destruction of their Pullman car. Brooklyn released him, and no other NL club even considered picking him up.

But where the NL saw an irredeemable drunk, Johnson and New York saw opportunity. The AL president had publicly decried the "rowdyism" that he believed was endemic to the NL and positioned the AL as the moral antidote to the NL's decay, but that was all hyperbole. In true Tammany form, Johnson and the Yankees saw their opportunity and seized their chance. The New York club signed Garvin, hoping for several weeks of sobriety. He pitched for the first time on September 10 and had Washington beat before tiring in the ninth in an eventual 3–2 loss. Still, he gave the rest of the staff a needed breather.

With the pennant hanging in the balance, the Yankees were scheduled to play Boston beginning on September 14 for five games over the course of three days. The champions led New York by percentage points — 79–49 to the Yankees' 77–48. But with the acquisition of Orth and Garvin, the flag appeared to be waving in New York's direction.

The "world's series" was a non-issue. The Giants had wrapped up the NL pennant, but John Brush wanted nothing to do with a postseason meeting with either American League club. His reasons stretched all the way down his arm and into his wallet.

Brush had been the final holdout in the peace agreement between the two leagues and still held Johnson, Farrell, Devery, their ballclub, and the American League in general in disdain, believing each had cost him money. He didn't want to risk losing to any of the above parties. He arrogantly announced that the Giants were "content to rest on our laurels."

Although New York and Boston both tried to goad him into changing his mind, and several New York papers eventually presented him with petitions asking that the series be played, Brush remained steadfast. The games between New York and Boston became the next best thing to a world's series.

The Yankees were confident. Griffith told the *Evening Journal,* "My team is in the best condition it has been in all year," and bragged of his pitching rotation of Chesbro, Powell, Orth, and Garvin, saying, "I cannot see at all where the Bostons have us beaten . . . on pitchers." Hundreds of brave New York fans followed the club to Boston for the series.

They were not disappointed, but neither did they return to New York with the pennant in hand. Over the next three days New York and Boston played each other not five but six times, before some 50,000 fans. Boston emerged leading New York by all of two ten-thousandths of a percentage point, with a record of 81–51 (.6126) to New York's 79–50 (.6124). And it was even closer than that.

In a driving rain, Chesbro won the first game 3–1 over Bill Dinneen as Boston's infield made seven errors. In the second game of the doubleheader Powell and Gibson battled to a 1–1 draw over five innings before the game was called due to a combination of rain, fog, and darkness. The next day Tannehill got revenge over his former teammates and beat Griffith 3–2. Powell then pitched for the second day in a row and went the distance against Norwood Gibson, but for the second day in a row darkness ended the game with a 1–1 tie.

The two clubs tried again on Friday, September 16. The estimated 25,000 fans who had crammed into Boston's Huntington Avenue Grounds surrounded the playing field in a raucous sea of barely sane baseball humanity, sitting along the baselines, standing behind ropes in the outfield, and even perching on the outfield fence. Chesbro, pitching for the third time in five days, beat Dinneen 6–4 in the first game. Then Cy Young, who'd been too ill to pitch thus far in the series, pulled himself out of his sickbed and salvaged a tie for Boston, beating Garvin 4–2 in the final game. In 50 innings of baseball across three days, each club won two games, lost two, and tied two. Boston had scored 14 runs on 42 hits with 14 errors, while New York had scored 15 on only 36 hits — 8 by Dougherty, who continued to pound Boston — and made but 10 errors. Yet all those 50 innings had proven was that the standings were just about right — the margin between the two clubs was microscopic.

The replay of the tied contest was added to the four-game series between the two clubs that would end the season. Even as the Yankees embarked on a grueling 17-game road trip on September 18, the two teams remained joined at the hip for the remainder of the season. As September faded into October, Manhattan was half-mad with baseball fever.

YANKEE AMERICAN LEAGUE WIN PERCENTAGE LEADERS

1904	Jack Chesbro, .759 (41–13)
1921	Carl Mays, .750 (27–9)
1922	Joe Bush, .788 (26–7)
1923	Herb Pennock, .760 (19–6)
1927	Waite Hoyt, .759 (22–7)
1932	Johnny Allen, .810 (17–4)
1934	Lefty Gomez, .839 (26–5)
1936	Monte Person, .731 (19–7)
1938	Red Ruffing, .750 (21–7)
1941	Lefty Gomez, .750 (15–5)
1942	Tiny Bonham, .808 (21–5)
1943	Spud Chandler, .833 (20–4)
1947	Allie Reynolds, .704 (19–8)
1950	Vic Raschi, .724 (21–8)
2001	Roger Clemens, .870 (20–3)

THE GREATEST

Date	Wins/Losses	Opponent	Pitcher	Score	Innings Pitched	Record
April 14	W	Boston	C. Young	8–2	9	1–0
April 18	L	Philadelphia	Bender	1–5	9	1–1
April 22	W	Washington	Patten	2–0	9	2–1
April 30	L	Philadelphia	Plank	2–6	8	2–2
May 4	W	Washington	Jacobson	6–3	9	3–2
May 7	W	Boston	Dinneen	6–3	9	4–2
May 12	L	Cleveland	Donahue	0–7	9	4–3
May 14*	W	Cleveland	Rhoades	10–1	9	5–3
May 17	W	Detroit	Donovan	5–1	9	6–3
May 20	W	Chicago	White	3–2	12	7–3
May 24	W	St. Louis	Pelti	3–0	9	8–3
May 28	W	Philadelphia	Plank	1–0	9	9–3
June 1	W	Detroit	Donovan	5–3	9	10–3
June 4	W	Detroit	Mullin	5–1	9	11–3
June 9	W	Cleveland	Moore	3–2	9	12–3
June 11	W	Chicago	Patterson	6–3	9	13–3
June 16	W	St. Louis	Sudhoff	10–3	9	14–3
June 22	W	Washington	Patten	3–0	9	15–3
June 25	W	Boston	C. Young	5–3	9	16–3
July 1	W	Washington	Jacobson	8–3	9	17–3
July 4	W	Philadelphia	Bender	9–3	9	18–3
July 7	L	Boston	Gibson	1–4	9	18–4
July 9	L	Boston	C. Young	1–2	9	18–5
July 13	ND	Cleveland	Bernhard	3–16	relief	18–5
July 14**	W	Cleveland	Rhoades	21–2	9	19–5
July 16	W	Detroit	Killian	9–8	relief	20–5
July 19	W	Detroit	Donovan	2–1	11	21–5
July 23	L	Chicago	Walsh	4–5	9	21–6
July 30	W	St. Louis	Glade	3–2	10	22–6
August 3	W	Detroit	Kitson	5–2	9	23–6
August 6	W	Cleveland	Joss	4–3	9	24–6
August 10	L	Chicago	Altrock	1–5	6	24–7
August 13	T	Chicago	White	3–3	5	24–7
August 15	W	St. Louis	Pelti	3–1	9	25–7

SEASON JACK CHESBRO IN 1904

Date	Wins/Losses	Opponent	Pitcher	Score	Innings Pitched	Record
August 19	W	Chicago	White	6–1	9	26–7
August 23	W	Chicago	White	1–0	9	27–7
August 26	W	St. Louis	Howell	3–2	relief	28–7
August 27	L	St. Louis	Sudhoff	3–4	9	28–8
August 31	W	Cleveland	Hess	3–1	9	29–8
September 3	W	Detroit	Kitson	2–1	9	30–8
September 5	W	Philadelphia	Coakley	2–1	9	31–8
September 8	W	Philadelphia	Waddell	3–2	9	32–8
September 12	W	Washington	Townsend	4–2	9	33–8
September 14	W	Boston	Dinneen	3–1	9	34–8
September 16	W	Boston	Dinneen	6–4	9	35–8
September 20	W	Washington	Jacobsen	3–2	relief	36–8
September 20	W	Washington	Hughes	5–1	6	37–8
September 26	L	Cleveland	Joss	3–4	8	37–9
September 27	W	Detroit	Mullin	4–1	9	38–9
September 30	L	Chicago	White	0–4	3	38–10
October 1	W	Chicago	Patterson	7–2	9	39–10
October 4	W	St. Louis	Glades	6–0	9	40–10
October 7	W	Boston	Gibson	3–2	9	41–10
October 8	L	Boston	Dinneen	2–13	4	41–11
October 10	L	Boston	Dinneen	2–3	9	41–12

- Chesbro appeared in 55 games, starting 51, completing 48 (he failed to complete the games of August 10, September 30, and October 8), and pitching a total of 454⅔ innings. All other starts were complete games. (Several were of less than nine innings owing to rain, darkness, and defeats on the road.) He appeared in relief four times. In his 55 total appearances, he received the decision 53 times, accumulating a record of 41–12. Of the two occasions on which he did not receive the decision, his start of August 13 resulted in a tie, and he was not involved in the decision in a relief appearance on July 13.

- From May 14 through July 4, Chesbro started, finished, and won 14 consecutive games.

- Chesbro lost *every start* in which he gave up 4 or more runs. The Yankees scored more than 5 runs in only 13 of Chesbro's starts.

- Against pitchers who were later named to the Hall of Fame, Chesbro was 5–5.

* Unveils spitball for first time.

** Begins to use spitball almost exclusively.

The Yankees' pursuit of the pennant had finally captured the imagination of fans. From midseason onward the Yankees had drawn nearly as many fans as the Giants, and a rising tide of voices still called for a postseason meeting between the pennant winners. Yankee president Joseph Gordon issued a public challenge to the Giants, as did Boston owner John I. Taylor. After Brush tired of saying no, he allowed McGraw to respond. He did so in no uncertain terms, releasing this statement:

When I came to New York . . . the team [the Giants] was in last place. . . . I have worked to bring the pennant to New York [and] I for one will not stand to see it tossed away like a rag. . . . I know the American League and its methods. . . . They induced me to join them and as a souvenir of my experience they still have my money. . . . Never, while I am manager of the New York club and while this club holds the pennant, will I consent to enter into a box office grafting game with Ban Johnson and company.

For Yankee fans then, the American League pennant became everything. And for the ballclub, everything depended on Jack Chesbro.

Over the final three weeks of the season, he pitched ten games, starting nine of them. Griffith didn't trust Garvin, and on October 3 Orth hurt his arm. The Yankees entered the final five games of the season vs. Boston on the strength of Jack Chesbro's right arm.

The season-ending set began on October 7 with a single game, to be followed by doubleheaders on both Saturday, October 8, and Monday, October 10. (Blue laws prevented play on Sunday.) Boston came into New York with a record of 92–57 to the Yankees' 90–56. The winner of the series would take the pennant.

As originally scheduled, all five games were supposed to be played in New York. But Farrell and Devery had not lost sight of the reason they bought the club in the first place. Earlier in the year, when it appeared as if Boston would win the pennant going away, Farrell and Devery had looked to recoup at least a small portion of their anticipated losses: they had agreed to rent out their ballpark on October 7 to Columbia University for its football game against Williams College. Boston agreed to host the game scheduled for that day. The decision may have cost the Yankees their first pennant and a possible dynasty.

Even with Johnson's help, the pennant race had worn out the Yankees. To no one's surprise, Chesbro—with two full days of rest and in search of his 41st win in his 46th start—drew the assignment for New York in the first game at American League Park.

Such heavy use of his ace had not gone unnoticed, and Griffith had received a measure of criticism. But Farrell and Devery—and Ban Johnson—were calling the shots. A pennant for the Yankees in only their second season was an opportunity that none of the men wanted to miss. Chesbro didn't complain about his workload, at least publicly. He relished every moment he spent on the mound and was beginning to believe in his own invincibility.

On this day he succeeded again. Before 10,000 fans who braved a blustery autumn chill, the Yankees won a hard-fought struggle that, according to one Boston paper, "reminded [fans] of football." Runners and fielders contested every play and collided hard and often. Dougherty again led New York's attack. He dashed to a double in the fifth when his short fly fell between shortstop and left field, went to third on Keeler's perfect bunt, and scored on Elberfeld's fly ball to put New York ahead 2–1. Then, in the seventh, he beat out an infield single to first, stole second off Boston's vaunted catcher Lou Criger, then scored standing up on Jimmy Williams's single. Chesbro scattered four hits, and after he retired pinch hitter Duke Farrell to secure the 3–2 New York win, the *New York Herald* reported, "the rooters surged onto the field and tried to surround Chesbro. He started to sprint for the clubhouse but he had not gone far before he was grabbed and raised on the shoulders of some of the lusty lunged enthusiasts." It was the first time, but not the last, such a display would take place on the Yankees' home field. New York moved into first place needing only to split the remaining four games for the pennant.

Clark Griffith blinked away tears of joy after the game, telling the press, "There's nothing like taking the starter. We've got Boston on the run. . . . Powell and [Ambrose] Puttman are pitching tomorrow."

The two clubs immediately left for Grand Central Station to travel to Boston. Chesbro was told to remain behind and rest up for the doubleheader on Monday—if the pennant came down to one of those two games, Griffith wanted him available to pitch. But Chesbro had another notion. He followed his team to the station and confronted Griffith on the platform.

"Do you want to win the pennant or not?" he asked.

The manager looked hard into Chesbro's steely eyes.

"I'll pitch and I'll win," he said. Griffith then motioned him onto the train.

The following afternoon, as the *Boston Post* described it, "an ocean of people" poured into the Huntington Avenue Grounds for the Saturday doubleheader, with the season on the line. The 30,000 fans represented fully one-tenth of the Boston population.

Once again Dougherty reminded Boston fans of what they had lost. He singled off Bill Dinneen to open the game, and then Keeler bunted for a hit to move him to second. He went to third on Elberfeld's comebacker, and scored on Williams's fly ball for his league-best 113th run of the season, 80 in only 106 games with the Yankees. But it would also prove to be his last of the season. The clock would soon strike midnight for Dougherty.

Chesbro nursed the 1–0 lead through the first three innings as Boston went down quietly, failing to get a hit and reaching base only once. But in the fourth, Chesbro's previous 421 innings, including 12 in the previous 24 hours, started to take effect.

Boston shortstop Fred Parent reached first when his ground ball took a bad hop past Williams at second. After he was sacrificed, Boston player-manager Jimmy Collins singled up the middle, and Parent scored to tie the game. Then Buck Freeman drove the ball to left. Dougherty misplayed the ball into the overflow crowd standing in the outfield for a ground-rule double. Candy LaChance grounded to second, but instead of taking the sure out, Jimmy Williams threw home. Collins slid in safe to put Boston ahead.

Chesbro started to crack. He should have been out of the inning already, and the extra effort exhausted him. Boston started hitting him hard. Three hits and a walk gave Boston four more runs and a commanding 6–1 lead before they were finally retired. As Chesbro trudged from the mound before the jeering Boston masses, Griffith met him. His day was done. Walter Clarkson prepared to mop up.

Playing the remainder of the game as if eager to get to game two, the Yankees fell hard, 13–2. After the final out, Boston remained on the field as Cy Young took the place

of Bill Dinneen opposite Yankee starter Jack Powell. In less than a minute, game two was under way.

Determined to get a lead, Griffith had his club running from the start. But time and time again over the first four innings, Criger cut the New Yorkers down, squelching several rallies. Entering the fifth, the game was scoreless.

Boston's Hobe Ferris led off with an infield single to Williams. Criger sacrificed him to second, bringing up Cy Young.

Giants manager John McGraw dismissed the notion of playing either the Yankees or the Boston Americans in the 1904 World Series when he said, "Never, while I am manager of the New York club and while the club holds the pennant, will I consent to enter a box office grafting game with Ban Johnson and company."

1904

1904

The old pitcher, although known for his arm, was also a clutch and clever batsman. When Powell left a pitch over the plate, Young lifted it to right-center. Ferris waited, watching, as center fielder John Anderson took the fly over his shoulder. As he spun to throw, Ferris took off.

The throw and the baserunner arrived at third at the same time. Conroy dug for the ball amid Ferris's spikes, and it squirted past, rolling slowly into the mob massed only ten feet or so back in foul territory. Conroy scrambled after it, but the ball reached the roaring crowd. Ferris jumped up and trotted home, scoring what even the Boston papers described as a "cheap run." But it counted. New York fell behind, 1–0.

In diminishing light, the next two innings passed quickly. The Yankees failed to reach Young, and after the pitcher struck out to end the seventh inning, umpire Jack Sheridan called the contest because of darkness. With the sweep, Boston now needed only a single victory to win the pennant.

As the two teams embarked on the midnight train back to New York, their moods could not have been more different. Boston, having finally broken through on Chesbro, believed he was done for the year. They were confident they could beat whomever Griffith chose to pitch in either game on Monday. The Yankees, on the other hand, knew it would take a miracle to win both games.

Neither the Yankees nor their fans were deterred by the odds. The Giants' refusal to play in a postseason series had cost them, and the Yankees had picked up thousands of converts that victory could make permanent fans. Anticipation built during the off-day. On Monday afternoon nearly 30,000 zealots turned out at American League Park hoping to witness just such a miracle.

Jack Chesbro took the mound for the final time that season, and the fourth time in eight days. If it was true that he had nothing left after 445 innings of pitching, it

During the final weekend series with the Boston Americans, Jack Chesbro pushed himself to the limit and just beyond. He won the opening game of the series at Hilltop Park, then started the next day in Boston and lost the first game of a doubleheader, which New York dropped. With only a single day's rest, Chesbro started the first game of the season-ending doubleheader at Hilltop. He lost on a heartbreaking ninth-inning, two-out wild pitch that allowed Boston to capture the pennant with a 3–2 victory.

1904

In 1904 outfielder Wee Willie Keeler enjoyed the best of his seven seasons with the Yankees, batting .343 with 185 hits and 22 stolen bases.

Boston's Big Bill Dinneen had gained a reputation as a money pitcher during the 1903 World Series. He earned his salary by striking out both Dougherty and Keeler.

The contest was still scoreless, with two out in the bottom of the fifth, when Yankee catcher Red Kleinow singled to right. Chesbro was again greeted with pandemonium as he stepped to the plate.

He ripped the ball up the middle off Dinneen's pitching hand, then beat the throw to first. Dougherty followed with a single, and New York led, 1–0. Dinneen then walked Keeler on purpose to load the bases, but Elberfeld made him pay, working another walk to plate Chesbro and put New York ahead 2–0.

With a two-run lead and Chesbro on the mound, the New Yorkers were confident. But in the seventh LaChance reached first when Williams couldn't come up with his slow hopper. As he berated himself for the play, Ferris followed with a line drive that skipped between Williams's legs.

Lou Criger, no offensive threat, did as expected and sacrificed both runners. Dinneen then strode to the plate as his teammates pleaded with him to win his own game. He did the next best thing, which in this inning was to hit a ground ball to second baseman Jimmy Williams. The lumbering LaChance decided to take one and headed home. A good throw would have nailed him by 20 feet.

But this was not Williams's inning. He threw low, and the ball skidded past Kleinow. LaChance scored, and Ferris dashed in behind him as Williams's goat horns grew.

The extra pitches exhausted Chesbro. When he returned to the bench at the end of the inning, he told Griffith he was finished. The manager asked Kleinow what he thought.

"He hasn't got anything," the catcher responded, "but he's getting along all right. It's a tossup." Griffith chose to stick with Chesbro's heart, if not his arm.

Chesbro teetered through the eighth as he looked over his shoulder. Stahl, Freeman, and LaChance all cracked line drive base hits, but Elberfeld's relay cut down Stahl at home and preserved the tie. The game entered the ninth inning with the score still knotted.

Chesbro took the long walk from the bench to the mound for the 454th time that season, greeted by momen-

was equally true that he had nothing left to lose. He had told Griffith the previous day, "I'll trim 'em on Monday if it costs an arm."

After Chesbro set down Boston in the first, Dougherty worked Dinneen for a walk. Keeler bunted him over to second, but he was left stranded. Boston tallied two singles off Chesbro in the top of the second, but then the pitcher held firm. The game was still scoreless when Chesbro came to bat in the bottom of the third with one out.

As he stepped to the plate, a delegation of fans from Chesbro's hometown of North Adams, Massachusetts, broke from the stands and embraced him. They presented their hero with a sealskin coat and matching cap as the crowd stood and cheered itself hoarse. Then Chesbro really gave them something to cheer about.

He drove the ball deep to right field, past Boston outfielder Buck Freeman and over Keeler's Hollow. By the time Freeman retrieved the ball from near the exit in the

tous cheers. Criger led off with an easy ground ball to Elberfeld.

The Kid was near automatic on such plays, but on this day the Invaders failed to defend their turf. Elberfeld's throw was short, and Criger, the potential winning run, was safe. Dinneen, as expected, bunted him to second. Then, on Kip Selbach's ground ball to Elberfeld, Criger alertly dashed to third as the shortstop took the sure out at first. Chesbro was one out away from escaping the inning, but Boston was one base away from taking the lead.

Stepping to the plate was Boston shortstop Freddie Parent, already twice the strikeout victim of Chesbro's spitballs. Chesbro threw three more, getting two strikes.

There is an old baseball adage that a pitcher shall not get beat throwing anything but his best pitch. Even in 1904 that stratagem was standard fare. And the spitball, for most of the 454 innings that Jack Chesbro pitched in the season of 1904, had been not only his best pitch but perhaps the best pitch any pitcher has ever had.

Throwing a spitball is best described as akin to squeezing a seed out from between one's fingers, an act made even more difficult by the fact that it must be done in the middle of the usual throwing motion. It is a difficult pitch to learn, and nearly impossible to control precisely. No pitcher in baseball has ever been better at it than Jack Chesbro.

Yet even Chesbro, despite all evidence to the contrary, was not superhuman. He stood on the mound, wet his fingertips, gripped the ball, wound up, and threw, pulling his right arm down violently, his wrist and forearm stiff, as the ball left his hand.

But this time, perhaps because of Chesbro's fatigue, the seed squirted out wide and high. One newspaper described the pitch as "ten feet over Parent's head." Kleinow reached for the ball—too late, according to some—but he missed it. Elberfeld later said the catcher would have needed a "step ladder" to get it. The ball reportedly soared fully 75 feet in the air past him, all the way to the stands, where it was variously described as either striking the chicken-wire backstop that protected the fans or thudding against the wooden fence that supported it.

Criger trotted home as Kleinow scrambled after the rebound. Chesbro looked shocked. He turned away and wiped his face as if to remove the saliva from his hand. Clark Griffith fell prostrate in front of the Yankee bench and buried his face in the dirt. Boston led, 3–2. The New York crowd sat in silence as Boston's Royal Rooters sang and cheered and hooted for all they were worth.

A moment later Parent singled, then was forced at second. The stunned Yankees were only three outs away from the end of the season.

Chesbro returned to the bench and collapsed, alone and in tears. Over 30 years later a longtime Yankee employee, Mark Roth, told a reporter, "Someday I'll tell you how Chesbro cried like a baby after that wild pitch. But that always makes me sad. I'll save it." Chesbro barely looked up as Dinneen tried to put the Yankees away.

They didn't give in. John Ganzel led off and made Dinneen work. But after fouling off six balls, he struck out.

Now Dinneen was tiring. Conroy walked on four pitches, but Kleinow was too anxious and popped to second.

Chesbro, who already had two of New York's six hits, was scheduled to bat next. But Griffith looked at his pitcher and for the first time all year saw a beaten man. He called on 40-year-old Jim "Deacon" McGuire to pinch-hit. The veteran did his job and worked Dinneen for another walk.

Victory and defeat stood side by side as Conroy led off at second and McGuire perched on first. To the plate strode Patsy Dougherty, who had made as much of a difference in the pennant race that season as any man on the field. Boston rooters, cognizant of the way he'd beaten his old team every chance he had since the ill-advised trade, reportedly hid their eyes with each pitch, afraid to watch.

Dougherty took a strike, then a ball, then swung at a low curve for strike two before taking the fourth pitch to even the count.

Dinneen looked in at the plate and squinted. He then flashed two fingers twice to the umpire to confirm the count at 2–2. Sheridan nodded. Then Dinneen threw.

Dougherty swung. A roar came up from the third-base stands, but elsewhere there were only groans. Strike three.

The pennant was Boston's. There was no joy in Washington Heights.

The Yankees were out.

In September 1909 charges were made that Yankee manager George Stallings was cheating by stealing the signs of opposing catchers. Earlier that season, Stallings rented an apartment opposite Hilltop Park (top right center) that provided a good view of home plate. He hired a spotter to sit in the apartment with field glasses and relay the signs to batters with a mirror.

Can you imagine someone grabbing you by
the throat, tearing your heart out by the roots
and leaving you to die, suffering the tortures
of the diamond?

— CLARK GRIFFITH,
following Jack Chesbro's wild pitch

1905–1914
A FINE MESS

No one cared that the Yankees won the second game of the doubleheader, the final game of the season, 1–0 in ten innings, to finish a hair's-breadth behind Boston in the American League 1904 pennant race. They forgot about Al Orth's arm injury, Farrell and Devery's inopportune rental of their ballpark, the errors of Elberfeld and Jimmy Williams, Dougherty's strikeout, and the hundred other reasons the Yankees may have missed their first chance at a pennant. All they remembered was the one that got away—the single pitch thrown by Jack Chesbro, and in the end, the only one that mattered. The headline "Pennant Lost by Wild Pitch" defined the season and became Chesbro's epitaph.

Still, the Yankees had pushed the world champs to the limit and won a place in Manhattan. Ban Johnson was ecstatic. Farrell and Devery were making money. Chesbro was the game's best pitcher, Keeler was one of the game's most dangerous hitters, and Elberfeld and Dougherty were acknowledged stars. *Reach's 1905 Official American League Guide* commented, "No better-balanced or more powerful team exists."

Unfortunately, the Yankees had just about outlived their usefulness to Johnson. Now that the immigrants were firmly established, they were more or less left to fend for themselves. They would find lasting success elusive.

The Yankees stood pat in the off-season, believing, as many did, that only injuries had prevented them from winning the pennant in 1904. The only significant change appeared to make the team even stronger. First baseman John Ganzel owned Grand Rapids, a club in the Western League, and he paid the Yankees $3,000 for his own release so that he could play for his team. In turn, at the cost of $2,700, the ballclub drafted a young first baseman by the name of Harold Homer "Hal" Chase from Los Angeles of the Pacific Coast League. Danny Long, a former player turned scout, told Griffith: "Chase is the best young player I have seen in a lifetime."

Hal Chase, at various times in his career, was many things: a genuine phenom, a superstar, a revolutionary who literally changed the way the game was played—and an ingrate, an embarrassment, and a crook. Sometimes he was all of this at once. He would prove to be the club's dominant personality—for better or worse—for much of the next decade.

Before Hal Chase, most first basemen stood like statues only a step or so off-base. Their job was to catch the ball for putouts. No one expected the first baseman to range very far off the bag for ground balls. The first baseman was often a good hitter but the worst player on the field, installed at first because it best hid his shortcomings.

Chase was different. Relegated to playing first base because he was left-handed, Chase had the speed, instincts, arm, and reach of a middle infielder, and he played that way. He ranged far off the bag, back or in according to the situation, started double plays, chased pop-ups into the outfield, and took cutoff throws. The position is played today in much the same way it was first played by Hal Chase.

Observers were most impressed by the aggressive, almost supernatural way he played the bunt. Chase had an uncanny knack for anticipating the play. He often charged in and either caught the ball on the fly and doubled off the baserunner or forced him out at second base. On squeeze plays he sometimes fielded the ball on the run and beat the runner home, tagging him out himself. On occasion

he even made plays on the third-base side of the diamond. Bunters soon learned to stay away from Chase. Early in his career there was speculation that Clark Griffith would eschew convention and move Chase to second base, to better take advantage of his skills.

And at the plate he was no slouch. Although he topped .300 only four times in his major league career, Chase could run and in the Dead Ball Era had excellent power. Once he became an established major leaguer, he usually hit third in the batting order.

Yet the way Chase played the game served simply as an introduction to his personality, his most attractive quality. Tall, handsome, well spoken and glib, cocky and confident, the smooth-talking Chase made friends easily and quickly became the club's most popular player. The press called him "Prince Hal," and all Manhattan swooned.

That is not to say he was the best player on the team, for he rarely was, but that didn't seem to matter. Willie Keeler and Griffith were legends, but both had seen better days. Elberfeld was the most important player on the squad, but his volatile personality put people off. And Chesbro's patina of invincibility would soon wear off.

None could match Chase's charisma, style, and élan. He carried out routine plays with a flourish and made difficult plays look simple. He left the impression that he was somehow both above and beyond the game, that baseball was just the accidental beneficiary of his unique set of talents. Seven decades before Reggie Jackson came to New York, Chase saw himself as "the straw that stirs the drink." He was the Yankees' first uber-star, and in a sense, the first true Yankee, the first player of note whose major league career would become synonymous with the ballclub itself.

But he was also emblematic of the club during the Dead Ball Era. For in regard to Hal Chase, appearances were often deceiving. In time he came to be considered one of the game's crookedest players and is largely forgotten today. Yet to his contemporaries he was one of baseball's all-time greats, on par with luminaries like Cobb, Wagner, Lajoie, and Speaker — although in reality he never approached their standard of performance. So too were the Yankees of the era often a team that was better on paper than in reality, one whose performance was ultimately disappointing, and one that history has virtually ignored.

Chase was born in Los Gatos, California, and played semipro baseball before he was asked to join the Santa Clara College baseball team in 1902, where he starred as a pitcher and second baseman. But his collegiate experience was confined to the diamond. He was a ringer, and a good one, who never attended class. Yet he never corrected the impression that he was a college graduate.

On March 27, 1904, he left Santa Clara and joined the Los Angeles Angels of the Pacific Coast League. Three days later the *Los Angeles Times* prophesied, "Chase has a future before him that any ball player might look forward to." At the end of the season he was drafted by New York and joined the club in March 1905.

During spring training, as the club traveled from Vicksburg to New Orleans to play an exhibition, the train derailed. Although no one was hurt, the event became a metaphor for the 1905 season. While the Yankees opened the season on track to win the pennant, they soon strayed. Entering May with a record of 7–4, they next played Boston.

Over the next nine days they fell six times to the champions as Orth, Powell, and Chesbro all reported arm problems. Chesbro had gained 30 pounds in the off-season, skipped most of spring training to tutor Harvard pitchers,

and was telling people he'd been ready to retire for three seasons. He tried to get by without throwing the spitball but couldn't get anyone out. The press called the staff "Griffith's cripples."

Only Clark Griffith pitched well. The "slow ball" artist began pitching in relief and became one of the game's first effective relievers. He would eventually receive credit for pioneering the use of the relief pitcher.

Neither New York nor Boston was close to being the best team in the league anymore. Each struggled to play .500 baseball as Cleveland, Chicago, and Philadelphia charged into the lead. Although the subway station finally opened at Hilltop Park — a name that had caught on as a more poetic moniker — the season was over before it started. Now that it was convenient for fans to see the Yankees, they stunk.

This time Ban Johnson didn't come to the rescue — he was preoccupied with trying to keep several other fran-

The 1906 Highlanders at Hilltop Park. Led by pitchers Al Orth and Jack Chesbro, with 27 and 24 victories, respectively, the 1906 club finished in second place, only three games behind Chicago's "hitless wonders." First baseman Hal Chase led all regulars with a .323 batting average and dazzled fans with his slick fielding.

chises afloat. The team went 7–18 in May and was clearly a sinking ship. In a sense, the Yankees had served their purpose. The American League was established in Manhattan, so now the team was left to find its way on its own, without any outside help. By midseason Farrell and Devery were selling players, including pitcher Jack Powell, who was dumped for being out of shape. He'd opened a bar in St. Louis in the off-season, and he and Chesbro reportedly were drinking a case of beer a day. But the Yankees were still making money, just not quickly enough to suit their owners.

Hardly a player on the team approached his 1904 standard. Willie Keeler's batting average tumbled nearly 50 points to .302, his lowest ever. Dougherty scored only 56 runs. Chesbro was little better than average. The club suddenly had the worst pitching in the league, a fatal flaw during a season in which hitting was at a premium everywhere. They finished sixth, 21½ games behind Philadelphia, a situation made worse by the fact that, for the first time, a World Series between the American and National League champions was mandated by an agreement between the two leagues. Ironically enough, Giants owner John Brush brokered the deal. His Giants asserted National League dominance and pummeled the A's, outscoring them 15–3 and winning the Series in five games.

Chase, almost by default, became the team's acknowledged star. On August 5, he set a major league record by recording 38 putouts during a doubleheader against St. Louis, a mark for which the New York pitchers deserved much of the credit for inducing ground balls. Nevertheless, it set Chase apart. Just as pitcher Christy Mathewson, a well-spoken graduate of Bucknell, had come to exemplify the better angels of the New York Giants, Chase now served a similar role for the Yankees.

The 1906 season began in rough imitation of 1905 as the club — virtually unchanged — opened with three straight wins, then stumbled again. Just when it looked as if their season would come to a premature end, the Yankees started playing their best ball since 1904.

Hal Chase (right) coaches first base in this undated photograph at Hilltop Park. Chase had the range and instincts of a middle fielder but was relegated to playing first base because he was left-handed.

Orth did a fair imitation of Chesbro as his arm bounced back, as did Chesbro himself, who for a time discovered he could throw the spitter again. Beginning on May 15, the club won 16 of 17, sometimes with pitching, sometimes with hitting, and sometimes with hustle. The streak pulled them into first place. Sportswriter Joe Vila gushed:

Can the Yankees play ball? Well you bet they can gentle readers. . . . I do not believe there is a team on earth that has played faster ball than that shown by the Yankees. . . . Elberfeld's batting, baserunning and fielding have been the talk of the town . . . and Hal Chase! My but the boy has been hitting the ball on the nose in addition to playing first base in brilliant style.

The attention was galling to the Giants, in second place behind the Chicago Cubs, who were in the midst of setting major league records for wins and winning percentage. For the first time crowds at the American League Park consistently began to outnumber those at the Polo Grounds.

But the Yanks lost their grip on first place in mid-July and by mid-August appeared to have fallen out of the race. The pitching-rich Chicago White Sox, dubbed the "Hitless Wonders" by the press, took over first place and appeared destined to meet the cross-town Cubs in the World Series. They beat the Yanks four straight in mid-August to run their win streak to 18 and move 8 games ahead of the fourth-place Yanks, for whom the final loss was their 10th in the last 11 games. Chicago manager Fielder Jones boasted, "What's to stop us? We have the best team in the league [and] when we get home we have a string of twenty-nine games to play on our home grounds. . . . I can't dope out how we can lose."

Yet New York wasn't quite ready to quit. At a cost of $2,000, Griffith added a pitcher, West Virginian Joe Doyle, who was oddly effective. At a time when most games were played in about an hour and a half, those pitched by the ever so deliberate Doyle sometimes lasted an additional hour and earned him the nickname "Slow Joe." The Yanks took three from Cleveland and gained some momentum.

Over the next three weeks they played as if they had nearly forgotten how to lose, no matter what happened or what difficulties they faced. And in 1905 they faced plenty.

On August 27 in St. Louis, both Elberfeld and Griffith berated an umpire in front of Ban Johnson in a 2–1 win.

Both players were tossed, and Griffith was suspended for four games, a punishment he rendered moot by managing from the stands in his street clothes. After taking two of three from the Browns, the club traveled to Washington on August 30 to begin an exhausting string of five consecutive doubleheaders played over six days. After winning game one, they fell behind in game two, 8–1. Then Chase took command.

He smacked out three triples to key the club's greatest comeback to date as the Yankees won, 9–8, leading the *New York World* to comment, "Chase put up the batting record for the Hilltop Grounds if not the country." They needed him, because on the following day, on their way to winning the first game 20–5, Elberfeld pulled himself from the rout with a slight injury. As he left the field, teammate Wid Conroy made some crack that the thin-skinned Tabasco Kid couldn't let pass. According to the *World:*

Without any arguing as to the division of the purse, weighing with or without fighting togs, or the selection of a referee, the two men went at it hammer and tongs. The first round was shortened fully a minute by the interference of all the other Broadway Boys, who pulled and tugged at the fighters, and three policemen, who kept out of the way of possible wild punches. Nobody was hurt and no decision was given.

Two days and three more victories later, as the Yanks went for a win in the ninth inning of game two in doubleheader number four against Philadelphia, Elberfeld got into it with umpire Silk O'Loughlin. The two danced across the infield as the enraged Elberfeld tried to spike O'Loughlin, and the umpire hopped, skipped, and jumped free. Finally escorted to the bench by three policemen, Elberfeld broke free and tried to attack the umpire a second time, chasing him around the field before finally being caught and forcibly retired. The next day, as the Yanks won their 11th in a row and fifth consecutive doubleheader by taking two from Boston, they received word that the Kid was suspended.

It hardly mattered, for Chase had been magnificent, cracking out 14 hits in the five doubleheaders. The shortstop missed the next four games, but the Yanks still ran their win streak to 14 before finally falling to Boston on September 10. By then they led the White Sox by a full game. In 19 days they'd picked up an incredible nine games.

But now the schedule turned against them. The White Sox finished with 25 straight home games, while the Yanks went on the road for 26, including four critical games in Chicago beginning on September 21.

By the time the Yankees made it to Chicago, the Sox had regained the lead and led by a game. While 25,000 fans packed the South Side Park, a similar crowd gathered in New York on Park Row to watch the results on bulletin boards set up by various newspapers. The New Yorkers cheered mightily when the Yankees swept a doubleheader to take the lead, and then swooned as their heroes dropped the third game to fall back into a tie with the White Sox. In this important contest, Griffith turned to pitcher Billy Hogg to salvage the series.

As the *New York World* described it, "There were a bump, a bombardment and an attempt to massacre on the South Side Grounds today. The Sox got the bump, [umpire] Silk O'Loughlin was the target of the bombardment and Kid Elberfeld came near being the victim of a massacre." With the partisan crowd ringing "gongs, siren whistles and cowbells," Elberfeld scored on a hit by Chase in the first to put the Yankees ahead, 1–0. Then Hogg and Walsh settled into a classic pitchers' duel. Elberfeld and Chase, who "took them [throws] in the clouds and in the sand," protected the lead with stellar fielding. But in the eighth the game almost came apart.

Keeler was on first, and Elberfeld at bat. Keeler broke for second with the pitch as Elberfeld aimed to hit the ball in the hole between first and second. But the pitch was wide, and as he flung his bat at the ball it slipped out of his hands. It pinwheeled onto the diamond between Walsh and first base.

At least that's what the Yankees argued. But given Elberfeld's reputation, most witnesses jumped to the conclusion that, at best, he'd tried to provide a distraction for Keeler's successful theft of second. At worst he'd tried to brain Walsh.

The stands immediately erupted. After the Kid retrieved his bat and struck out, a mob of some 50 zealots charged from their seats. Elberfeld retreated toward the White Sox dugout but found no refuge. Wielding his bat as a club, Elberfeld was caught in no man's land for a few moments before cooler heads prevailed and he was allowed to make his way back to the safety of the Yankee bench.

But the crowd was ready to explode. In the bottom of the inning O'Loughlin made a call that went New York's way, and the crowd bombarded the field with bottles and other assorted missiles. The umpire was forced to retreat to the center of the field to escape the fusillade, then announced that if the attack didn't stop, he'd forfeit the game to New York. The crowd calmed, and moments later the Yankees escaped with a hard-won 1–0 victory.

The Yanks had beaten the enemy on his own turf, taking three of four, and now led by a game with only 13 left to play. But the pressure of the pennant race had caused Griffith to use the same strategy he had in 1904. With the season on the line, he had turned to his two aces, Chesbro and Orth, time and time again, even as it became apparent that each man was wearing down, a situation not helped by Joe Doyle's suddenly sore arm and the suspen-

Shortstop Kid Elberfeld stood only five-foot-five and earned the nickname the Tabasco Kid for his hotheaded nature. His attack on umpire Silk O'Loughlin in the heat of the pennant race of 1906 resulted in a suspension, which possibly cost New York its first American League championship.

sion of pitcher Doc Newton. After leaving Chicago, the club was swept by sixth-place Detroit as both Orth and Chesbro failed. They staggered through the remainder of the season as the White Sox swept to the pennant, winning by three games.

Sun reporter Joe Vila didn't pull any punches. "Griffith . . . has only himself to blame. He has made two sad mistakes. One was in permitting his team to be broken up by men like Elberfeld. . . . [T]he other was his friendship for an old play. Griffith insisted on pitching Chesbro when it had been apparent . . . that Jack is nearly all in."

But Griffith wasn't the only problem. The Yankees were not yet a team but a collection of individuals, mercenaries out for themselves. Elberfeld led one contingent, and Chase another. And already Manhattan was proving to be a temptation nearly impossible to ignore.

A planned postseason interleague series with the Giants was another casualty of the Yankees' swoon. But this time it was the Yankees who felt no compulsion to help out their rival. A subway series of any kind between the two teams remained the stuff of fiction.

Despite the Yankees' second-place finish, it was a grand time to be a ballplayer in New York City. The Yankees took full advantage of their exalted position, but none more so than Hal Chase, who found it hard to say no to anything and succumbed to nearly every temptation.

The atmosphere that surrounded the club under the ownership of Farrell and Devery was one of unbridled indulgence. The players were well paid whether they won or lost, for the ballclub was making money regardless of its record. Discipline on the club was almost nonexistent. Ban Johnson's edicts against so-called rough play and gambling held little sway in New York. Farrell treated the team like it was part of his substantial stable of racing horses. Just as he annually dropped $25,000 to $30,000 on yearlings, he spent a similar amount drafting new players, confident he'd make back his money gambling on the outcome. So far he'd been right. Touts worked the stands at the Hilltop with absolute impunity, and the taverns popping up around the park gave them more sites in which to ply their trade. In such an atmosphere it was almost inevitable that at least some members of the team, if not the entire franchise, would succumb to the dangers that surrounded it everywhere.

Card playing occupied most players in the clubhouse and on the road. None was a better practitioner than Hal Chase, who was as deft at dealing cards as he was fielding

Hilltop Park is filled beyond capacity for an early season game in 1907 against the Athletics. New York finished the season as also-rans, as the fourth-place squad featured only three regulars under the age of thirty. Even Hall of Famer Willie Keeler batted only .234 that year.

baseballs around first base. His teammates provided him with little competition, and he began to frequent Manhattan's most notorious gambling dens. In this way many Yankee salaries, in roundabout fashion, found their way back into the bank account of Farrell and Devery.

The players lived the high life in the off-season. Jack Chesbro returned to his Massachusetts farm in the fall of 1906 with a fat bankroll and hired 20 men to cut timber for him. As *The Sporting News* commented, Chesbro "has been taking on so much flesh this winter he believes he cannot reduce sufficiently," and the pitcher was pondering retirement.

Sporting Life was already referring to Chase, whose .323 batting average had been third best in the league, as "perhaps the biggest drawing card in baseball." The first baseman proceeded to act the part. When the Yankees offered him only a $2,000 raise, from $1,500 to $3,500, he returned to California. He signed a $4,000 contract to play for San Jose in the outlaw California League and moonlighted as coach for St. Mary's College, where one of his players was future star Harry Hooper. He wanted $5,500.

The whole team was acting as if they'd won two pennants, not lost them. In February a smug Clark Griffith entertained the press at Farrell's office in the Flatiron Building and announced, "The Americans will stand pat. . . . The Yankees look very good to me, gentlemen." They turned down most trade offers, including one from Boston that offered Jimmy Collins and Bill Dinneen for Conroy and Chesbro.

At spring training the players were woefully out of shape, at least those who bothered to show up. Both Chesbro and Chase stayed home. Virtually the entire team came up lame.

Chase finally signed a contract just before Opening Day, then took his sweet time to report. He missed the opener, although *The Sporting News* reported that "he was seen in Harlem. . . . He probably wanted to see a handsome young woman." Chesbro didn't bother to return until mid-May, and then had to work himself into shape.

By then it was too late. After a fair April, the Yankees soon fell far behind pennant-winning Detroit and were never really a factor. All year long everyone — the press, Griffith, and Farrell — expected the Yankees to bounce back, but all year long they fell with a thud game after

game. None seemed to recognize it, but the club was getting old. Only three regulars — Chase, outfielder Danny Hoffman, and jack-of-all-trades George Moriarty — were under the age of 30. Orth, 34, Chesbro, 33, and Keeler, 35, were ancient in an age when life expectancy was barely 50. Keeler was beginning to hit them where they was and batted a pathetic .234.

By midsummer things were starting to get strange. In a series of games against Cleveland — all New York losses — Elberfeld reportedly "made rank errors and acted like a crazy man." He wanted out, and even Farrell publicly wondered whether he'd been "tampered with" by either gamblers or another ballclub. A month later *The Sporting News* aired charges that "close observers of the Yankees games say that at least twenty games were lost due directly to the work of [Elberfeld]." The publication also discussed rumors that the season had been fixed, concluding, "If there was such a thing, don't you suppose Ban Johnson would fix it so the Yankees can win? . . . With a winning team in this city the National League would go out of business." The Giants weren't worried. The Yankees finished in fifth place, 70–78, 21 games behind Detroit. But the team still made $50,000.

The ballclub was active in the off-season, as Griffith engineered a number of trades, dumping veterans like Danny Hoffman and Jimmy Williams and adding supposed talents like Harry Niles and Neal Ball to take some of the load off Chesbro and Orth.

Everybody bought it. With the Giants training in far-off Texas, the Atlanta-based Yankees got most of the spring press coverage. On the precipice of the season Joe Vila wrote: "I have made prophecies in years gone by. . . . I have been right in some instances and wrong in others. But I have always eaten the dishes of crow with a rare appetite together with excellent humor. . . . I shall pick the Yankees to win the American League pennant."

For six weeks Vila looked like a genius. The Yankees jumped into first place and led the league as late as the end of May, winning even after losing Elberfeld. He had to be hospitalized after he was spiked from knee to ankle, an injury that effectively ended his season. The club was drawing huge crowds at Hilltop Park, and Vila once again commented that rumors "have begun to circulate again that the championship race is fixed," this time in New

York's favor. Fellow sportswriter W. R. Rankin added: "Clark Griffith goes to bed these days with a smile on his face, knowing everything is coming his way."

A month later Griffith was going to bed at his ranch in Montana, smiling only because he'd gotten out of a quickly deteriorating situation. The Yankees slumped horribly, going 6–22 from May 25 to June 23 as nearly every one of Griffith's trades backfired and nearly every pitcher came down with a sore arm. Then Farrell started interfering and telling him whom to pitch. Griffith told the owner to get another manager.

Farrell wanted Keeler to take command, but the wise old outfielder hid from his owner. So Farrell hired the most unlikely candidate of them all — Kid Elberfeld. Less than a year before Farrell had all but charged the Kid with throwing the season. Now he put the team in his hands, passing over team captain Hal Chase. After all, the still injured Elberfeld was under contract and being paid. He might as well manage.

After taking over on June 24, Elberfeld, whom the press began referring to as "the Perpetual Cripple," only made things worse. The team responded with its worst stretch of play in franchise history. From June 29 through August 18, the Yankees lost 39 of 46, going a dismal 27–91 over the remainder of the season.

And things were even worse than that. One writer noted that Elberfeld was "so unpopular that only one or two of his personal friends on the team are willing to do their best for him. Elberfeld is arrogant on the field and off, humiliates his men and in many ways rubs the fur the wrong way." Another writer called him the "opera bouffe manager . . . a joke to his men, to the fans, to the baseball world." Yet another was moved to verse, writing:

> A mighty mite that Elberfeld
> His boys were mostly girls
> The Kid was father of the team
> That swept the field in curls.

By August the team was in open revolt. "There is insubordination in the ranks," warned Vila. "Elberfeld's instructions are not obeyed. . . . Several of the overpaid stars are lolling about the hotel with big steam hammers in their hands," undermining the operation.

The major rift was between Elberfeld and Chase, who felt that he should have been named manager. Vila charged that "Chase acts at times as if his heart were not in his work. . . . [His] head has been swollen so much he has declined to run out his drives [and] has loafed after widely thrown balls." It would not be the last time Chase would be charged with giving less than his best effort on the field, but J. W. McConaughty of the *Evening Journal* noted with more than a little irony that Elberfeld himself was "leading by example, for there was never a worse case of sulky laying down than Elberfeld's . . . last year. Mr. Farrell is reaping what he sowed."

Injuries and lack of interest soon forced Farrell's hand. The Yankees weren't just getting beat; they were losing in historic fashion. Forty-one-year-old Cy Young threw a no-hitter against the club on June 30. White Sox pitcher Ed Walsh, on his way to 40 wins, beat them nine times. And Washington pitcher Walter Johnson, aged 20, shut out the club three times in four days.

Willie Keeler left the team in disgust in August. Phantom injuries became commonplace. When Elberfeld publicly questioned Chase's effort on September 2, Chase jumped overboard and signed on with Stockton in the California League. What passed for a season highlight took place on October 1 when Chesbro defeated Walter Johnson, 2–1. It would be his last big league victory.

As Vila wrote at the end of the season: "The Yankees disbanded and nobody cares." Perhaps no team in baseball history has ever fallen further, faster, than the 1908 Yankees. They finished a pathetic 51–103, in last place for the first time ever.

Elberfeld was canned, and Farrell hired George Stallings, who'd had a brief, mediocre playing career and an equally brief, mediocre managerial career, leading NL Philadelphia and Detroit without distinction. Most recently, he'd managed minor league Newark and spent most of his spare time hanging around Farrell's Flatiron Building office, which served as sort of an off-season salon for baseball men politicking for a major league job. He got it.

Stallings, the son of a Confederate general, was given almost total control of the franchise. Farrell, who never spent much time at the ballpark anyway, was now spending even less. His stable of horses had recently performed no better than the Yankees, and it was becoming harder to support his gambling habit with the profits from his ball-club. He put his faith in Stallings.

When the club reported to spring training in Macon, there were plenty of unfamiliar faces as well as the usual suspects like Elberfeld and Chase. Jack Chesbro again chose not to attend camp, preferring to run his lumber business until the season started.

Stallings instituted a near-total overhaul. Chase was the only regular to keep his spot, and even that incumbency required almost divine intervention. He first had to pay a fine to be reinstated to Organized Baseball. Then he reportedly contracted smallpox. He was put into quarantine, and when he returned to the team in early May, all was forgiven. When he made his first appearance at the Hilltop, he was greeted by his teammates at home plate, lionized in a speech by Elberfeld, and given a $600 silver loving cup.

Under Stallings, the team improved in 1909 — it would have almost been impossible not to—finishing in fifth place behind Detroit with a 74–77 record and making more money for Farrell than ever before as attendance topped 500,000 for the first time. New York was growing rapidly, and pastimes of all forms—movies, theater, boxing, bicycle racing, and horse racing—were all enjoying a boom time. Failure was nearly impossible. But some things didn't change. Elberfeld continued to be a distracting presence and was suspended again after getting into it with umpire Silk O'Loughlin. In the off-season he was sold. And Chesbro's deterioration reached its nadir. He failed to win a game and was let go in midseason. Signed by Boston, he pitched only once more and ended his major league career with 192 wins, making his final appearance against the Yankees on October 2. He lasted seven innings and gave up all six runs in a 6–5 defeat.

Two new players of note and one symbol appeared to carry the promise of future glory. Pitcher Russ Ford and outfielder William Franklin "Birdie" Cree burst onto the scene out of nowhere, and at the insistence of former cop Bill Devery, the club adopted the interlocking NY design, which had appeared on medals given to New York City police officers. Canadian native Ford, a spitball artist and curveball pitcher, made an early relief appearance for the Yankees in 1909. Sore-armed, he was drilled by Boston and soon sent to minor league Jersey City.

By 1908 the once effective Al Orth had slipped to a pitiful won-lost record of 2–13 as the Yankees finished in last place for the first time in their brief history. In six seasons with New York, the right-hander known as "the Curveless Wonder" won 72 of his career total of 203 victories.

Once his arm recovered, Ford got work on a pitch he'd discovered the previous season. By accident, he discovered that a scuffed ball curves and breaks more sharply.

Ford experimented with scuffing the ball himself with emery paper, which he sewed onto his glove, hid inside it, or attached to an elastic in his shirtsleeve. As he later told *The Sporting News,* "I discovered I could get both 'hop' and 'sail' on the ball . . . [a] double curve! Could any baseball pitcher dream of a sweeter thing than that?"

Ford's hyperbole notwithstanding (for no pitch really curves twice), it did dramatically enhance the movement

of any pitch. Ford worked on the pitch throughout the 1909 season, then was sidelined with a spike wound. After he recovered, he continued his experiment the following spring.

The new pitch would prove as effective as Chesbro's spitball had been five years earlier. Batters were almost helpless against the sharp breaking pitch. In his 1910 debut Ford beat Philadelphia 1–0 and won his next seven decisions as the Yankees and the Philadelphia Athletics fought over first place.

He was backed up by Cree's heavy hitting. Little remembered today, outfielder Birdie Cree might have been the best player the Yankees had before acquiring Babe Ruth. He'd made his debut at the end of the 1908 season and became a semiregular in 1909. Although he lacked Chase's charisma, Elberfeld's fire, and Keeler's reputation, for a time Cree displayed more talent than any of these players — and was also a near dead ringer for Derek Jeter. Over the next five seasons Cree was one of the better players in the game.

In contrast to Hal Chase, Birdie Cree was the genuine article — a player whose personal behavior was as exemplary as his play on the field. Educated and erudite, he was known to be fond of music, particularly Franz Liszt and Irving Berlin. One sportswriter commented that Cree had "an elegant and excellent command of the language, which later enabled him to call an umpire the most horrible and inhuman names without the arbiter comprehending."

The Pennsylvania native's formal education began at the California (Pennsylvania) State Normal School, where he starred as an infielder and quarterback and obtained a teaching degree. After teaching eighth grade for a year, he was offered a football scholarship to Penn State.

But that summer he dislocated his collarbone playing baseball, an injury that prevented him from playing football, so he joined the Penn State baseball team and became a star. While at Penn State, he once hit for the cycle, causing a classmate to exclaim, "He's a bird!" The name stuck.

In a ceremony at Hilltop Park in May 1909, first baseman Hal Chase (third from left) is welcomed back to the Yankees after having jumped the team the previous season and also having completed treatment for the smallpox he'd contracted at spring training. The charismatic Chase was the most popular player on the Dead Ball Era Yankees.

Like many collegiate players of the era, Birdie Cree played professionally under a pseudonym in the summer, using the name Bill Burde (a play on his nickname) in 1906 and 1907 in Burlington, Vermont, and Williamsport, Pennsylvania. After graduating with a degree in forestry, Cree was signed by Connie Mack of the Philadelphia Athletics before being passed along to the Detroit Tigers and eventually to the Yankees, for whom he was a 26-year-old rookie in 1908.

A fleet baserunner, Cree, despite standing only five-foot-six, was a surprisingly strong hitter and fine fielder. For a time he was considered one of the most complete players in baseball, mentioned in the same breath as stars such as Ty Cobb. In 1910 *The Sporting News* called him "as good a man as young Mr. Speaker. Yes, every bit as good.

Canadian pitcher Russ Ford emerged as a Yankee star in 1910 when he won 26 games and lost only 6 in his rookie season. The trick-pitch artist later told *The Sporting News*, "I discovered I could get both 'hop' and 'sail' on the ball . . . A double curve! Could any baseball pitcher dream of a sweeter thing than that?"

Perhaps better, in the long run." But while Cobb and Speaker would become two of the game's most legendary stars, Cree was destined for a more modest fate.

There was far more to the Yankee turnaround under Stallings in 1909 and 1910 than either Ford or Cree or any other player on the active roster. George Stallings had an edge. He cheated.

In September 1909, charges were made that the Yankees had been stealing the opposing catcher's signs, but not by the still-accepted method of keen-eyed coaches and players taking advantage of sloppy transfers of signs by catchers. Stallings took a more active approach.

Earlier that season the manager rented an apartment opposite Hilltop Park that provided a good view of home plate. Stallings installed a spotter in the apartment armed with a pair of field glasses. After picking up the catcher's signs, he'd signal Yankee hitters with a mirror and tell them what pitch was coming.

Thrilled with the results but frustrated by cloudy days, Stallings soon repositioned the spotter behind the outfield

fence. From there he spied through a gap in a whiskey advertisement and then opened and closed a hole in the center of the letter "O" on the sign by means of a lever. Wide-open meant a fastball, closed a breaking ball, and half-open an off-speed pitch.

The strategy was nothing new, at least to Stallings. One of his friends, catcher Morgan Murphy, who'd played for Stallings in Philadelphia in 1897 and 1898, is credited with inventing the scheme.

While a member of the 1900 Phillies, Murphy, who rarely played, stationed himself behind a hole in the outfield fence with a spyglass. He'd relay the catcher's sign by wire to a buzzer box buried just beneath the ground in the third-base coaching box. The coach then relayed a verbal signal to Phillies hitters. It apparently worked. Philadelphia was only 30–40 on the road, but 45–23 at home.

When word of Stallings's scheme first leaked out in early September, the New York press dismissed the charges as sour grapes. But the opposition was upset. Washington manager Joe Cantillon was apparently the first to figure out the scheme. Earlier in the season he sent his trainer, Jerry Ettinger, out behind the fence to have a look-see.

Ettinger told *The Sporting News* that "the man who did the tipping was an old-time pitcher, and he sat outside the fence with a pair of field glasses." Cantillon then tipped off Detroit Tiger manager Hugh Jennings.

Jennings mounted an investigation of his own and sent his trainer out beyond the fence during the Yankees' final home stand of the 1909 season. The Tiger trainer reportedly caught the spy red-handed. Upon being discovered, he dashed away from his perch in such haste that he left behind a bottle of beer and a half-eaten sandwich. Detroit then took three of four from the Yankees, their only losses in their final 16 home games. In *The Sporting News,* Joe Vila admitted to the discovery of "a couple of holes in the boards" but offered that such shenanigans were commonplace and violated no baseball rule anyway. Indeed, the ploy wasn't truly made illegal until 1961.

But American League president Ban Johnson thought otherwise. He wanted Stallings fired for the offense.

After the season the scandal was the talk of baseball. Joe Cantillon wanted something done. Hugh Jennings was reportedly told to keep quiet because the matter was being

William Franklin "Birdie" Cree came to New York from Penn State, where he'd received a football scholarship to play quarterback. After hurting his shoulder, he pursued a baseball career and ended up setting many of the Yankees' offensive records later shattered by Babe Ruth. The erudite Cree enjoyed the music of Franz Liszt and Irving Berlin.

taken care of privately — Johnson didn't want the dirty laundry aired in full view.

In December Johnson took affidavits from Ettinger and Cantillon and held a series of secret meetings with the Yankee owners. Stallings had been caught, yet was allowed to keep his job. Although the *New York World* reported that Johnson had "demanded Stallings's scalp," the Yankee owners convinced him to let Stallings finish his contract, which was due to expire on October 15, 1910. Then he'd be replaced. The matter was forgotten — for a time.

The 1910 Yankees continued their improvement, particularly in their home park, where they won two of three all year long. Indeed, the club was 49–25 at home for the season, and only 39–38 on the road. Paced by Ford and Cree, they got off to a quick start and edged into first place in mid-June. Then charges that Stallings kept "signal tippers" emerged again.

Stallings was in trouble, and he knew it. A second offense would besmirch his reputation forever and probably end his baseball career.

So he threw up a smoke screen. First baseman Hal Chase became Stallings's foil, and the manager put in motion a series of events that served to identify Chase, forever and always — and perhaps unfairly — as baseball's most corrupt player, its "Benedict Arnold," someone the baseball historian Harold Seymour called a "malignant genius." Meanwhile, Stallings's indiscretions have gone unexamined.

It was an open secret that team captain Chase wanted to manage the club and had been disappointed when Stallings was hired. In June 1910, his dissatisfaction became public when writers in Detroit intimated that Stallings was just a figurehead and that Chase, the Yankee captain, was actually running the team and should receive credit for its improvement.

Stallings was incensed. He thought Chase was behind the stories, and in fact there was an element of truth to that suspicion. At the time the position of team captain was more than ceremonial. Chase was responsible for calling certain plays in certain situations, such as the hit-and-run and steals. But after the Detroit story broke, Stallings turned all eyes on Chase, questioning every move Chase made. The signal-tipping story faded.

Each time the Yankees failed, Stallings blamed Chase and pilloried him in the press. Over the course of the season, as the Yankees slipped into second place, the club split into two camps. Stallings was hard to get along with — he was known to berate players loudly and at length in the vilest language — but those players he had brought to the major leagues remained loyal to him. Veterans tended to side with Chase.

In September, at long last, Farrell and New York Giants president John Brush appeared likely to reach an agreement for the second-place Yankees and Giants to meet in a postseason subway series to decide the championship of Manhattan. It wasn't the World Series, but it was the next best thing. For in New York the proposed matchup offered almost limitless "possibilities" for some good old-fashioned honest graft in local gambling parlors.

But just as interest in the series was heating up, Stallings dropped a bomb that threatened everyone's payday. On September 19, the club fell to the White Sox 1–0. Chase botched two hit-and-run plays, derailing rallies. A few days before, against Detroit, he'd been caught stealing third with the club down by two runs, a baseball no-no. Stallings charged that Chase was "laying down" — not putting forth his best effort.

Immediately after the September 19 game, Stallings quit the club and jumped on a train to New York to confront Farrell. Before leaving, he told the *New York World*:

I want to find out from Mr. Farrell who is running the New York American League team — Chase or myself. . . . If Mr. Farrell decides in favor of the first baseman, I will quit at once. If he upholds my regime Chase will have to step down and out. . . . Chase has refused to obey orders and has tried to disrupt the team. . . . Chase has approached several players and tried to convince them that I was unfit for the position of manager.

He also believed that while Chase was away from the team with an "illness," he'd been playing semipro ball. The move, ironically, now left Chase as acting manager.

The press didn't know that Stallings's days were already numbered. In light of this fact, the purpose of Stallings's ploy becomes clear — to smear Chase, make himself a hero, and retain his job. Otherwise, there was no point to making the charge.

But Stallings made a serious miscalculation. Naively, he had thought that the club's improving record, the support of most of its players, and the impending postseason series with the Giants would force Farrell to back him up. He may have also believed that the charge he was leveling against Chase would receive the support of Ban Johnson, who had vowed to clean up the game. But the power and authority of Johnson was hard to predict. He would prove Stallings wrong on all counts.

Johnson had never been a fan of the manager. In 1901, when Stallings had managed Detroit, Johnson believed he had cooperated with a failed National League plot to convince the team to switch leagues. Stallings also told the *New York Sun* that in 1901 Johnson hadn't backed him up after witnessing an altercation between Stallings and Joe Cantillon, who was then an umpire. The fight was sparked, according to Stallings, when "Cantillon called me 'a nigger.' That was an insult I could not stand for, so I pulled Cantillon's nose. . . . Johnson, who was present, notified me then and there he'd drive me out of baseball." The two men hadn't spoken since.

The signal-tipping scandal had grated against Johnson, for it undermined the reputation of the American League as a cleaner alternative to the rough-and-tumble National

League. And now that the Yankees were finally going to get a chance to best the Giants in the postseason and embarrass the National League, Stallings wanted to dump arguably their best player. In Johnson's view, that would not do at all.

After Stallings pled his case to Farrell, Johnson moved in and hauled the Yankee owner to Cleveland, where the Yankees were now playing, to talk to Chase. Prince Hal pled innocent to all charges, saying, "Stallings has always shown a tendency to go behind a man's back." Or behind a fence.

Stallings was the only man in baseball who was surprised when Johnson backed Chase. The league president was unequivocal in his support of the player, saying, "Stallings has utterly failed in his accusations against Chase. He tried to besmirch the character of a sterling ballplayer. Anyone who knows Hal Chase knows he is not guilty of the accusations made against him." Significantly, those accusations had not included any intimation that Chase was "laying down" to bet against his team. According to all reports, his indifferent play had been directed solely against Stallings. Besides, this was no time to air a scandal.

Unfortunately, history ended up recording the incident somewhat differently. After Chase got into trouble later over gambling, historians invariably characterized the Stallings incident as something akin to Chase's "original sin." Over time historian after historian transformed his transgressions from "laying down"—not putting forth his best effort —to "throwing games"—losing on purpose for monetary gain—two radically different infractions. But at the time there was no intimation that gambling was as yet any kind of factor in his behavior.

In Chase's first game as manager, as the *New York Sun* reported, "when he came to bat in the first inning the crowd applauded vociferously. . . . [F]our men appeared just at that moment bearing immense floral tributes. . . . [T]he players of New York and Washington took off their caps, congratulated Chase at home plate and also posed for camera men." The Yankees, under Chase, finished the season by winning 10 of their last 14 games. Stallings was forgotten as all Manhattan looked forward to the postseason matchup with the Giants. In New York that series relegated the World Series matchup between the A's and Cubs to "in other news" status.

Stallings (right) spent most of his brief tenure in New York embroiled in the signal-stealing scandal. In 1910 he compounded his predicament by falsely charging team captain Hal Chase with "laying down" and giving less than his best effort. Stallings then left the team and was later relieved of his duties when league president Ban Johnson backed Chase.

THE FIRST SUBWAY SERIES

From the moment the Yankees were born, New York baseball fans yearned to see them play the Giants. In 1910, unable to resist a certain financial windfall any longer, John Brush of the Giants and Frank Farrell of the Yankees decided there was no use waiting for twin pennants. After both clubs finished second, the two owners agreed to hold a best-of-seven postseason series to determine the champion of New York City. It was the first "subway series."

In Manhattan interest in the series eclipsed interest in the World Series between the Cubs and A's. Before the opener at the Polo Grounds on October 13, fans were reportedly approaching ticket windows in disguise to try to buy more than the allotted six tickets each. Pinkerton guards weeded out the repeaters. The Giants were narrow 10–8 favorites over the Yankees, whose chances depended almost entirely on pitcher Russ Ford. The smart money believed that Ford would be canceled out by Giants pitcher Christy Mathewson.

There was more at stake than bragging rights. Players on the winning team stood to receive 60 percent of 90 percent of the gate receipts to the first four games, a bonus that was likely to amount to more than $1,000 each. The potential to increase their take by placing bets on the side was unsurpassed. Besides, neither club was pleased to have finished second. Because victory in the series could vindicate an otherwise disappointing season, the two clubs took the

contest seriously. Mathewson himself even traveled to Hilltop Park to watch the Yankees over the final weeks, paying particular attention to Russ Ford. His "mystery ball," which no one yet knew depended on his clandestine use of emery paper, had the Giants worried.

Mathewson and Ford squared off in the opener before a nearly packed house at the Polo Grounds. The crowd got their money's worth.

The Evening Journal's Sam Crane called it "the best and most grueling pitching battle that was ever fought." Mathewson was magnificent as he mixed curves, drops, fastballs, and fadeaways on his way to 14 strikeouts, a season high. The Yankees scored a single run in the second on a dropped fly ball, but after that Mathewson took command.

Ford was nearly as good as the emery ball similarly baffled the Giants. But in one of his scouting sorties Mathewson had noticed that the opposition swung at some 40 pitches that hadn't even reached the plate. The Giants stayed patient, and in the eighth inning it paid off.

With the score tied 1–1, Mathewson led off with a single. Ford then botched a bunt, and third baseman Jimmy Austin dropped a throw. Rattled, Ford hit a batter before finally breaking down and giving up three hits. The Giants won going away, 5–1.

The Yankees got even in game two. They surged back from a three-run deficit to score twice in both the eighth and the ninth on their way to a 5–4 win as Jack Warhop beat Hooks Wiltse. But in game three, the third straight at the Polo Grounds, Mathewson came on late in relief to shut down the Yankees for a second time and beat Jack Quinn to preserve a 5–4 Giants win.

The Yankees hoped to rebound at the Hilltop. Chase called on Ford to even the

series, but for the second time his offerings proved no mystery to the Giants. He came apart in the seventh, but the Yankees scored three times in the eighth to retake a 5–4 lead.

The ninth proved crucial. Needing only three more outs, Jack Warhop was nicked for three hits, and the Giants knotted the score. One inning later the contest was called because of darkness and ended in a tie.

The Yankees had missed a fine opportunity, which became ever more apparent the following afternoon. Mathewson was again magnificent, striking out nine and scattering six hits to win easily, 5–1. The Yankees finally had a day of glory back home the following afternoon as they exploded for eight second-inning runs and won going away, 10–2. But the Giants knew they needed only one more victory to win the series and knew they had Mathewson. They were right.

For the third time Matty was the mystery while Ford, in relief of starter Jack Warhop, provided only misery. The Giants won 6–3 to take the series four games to two.

Manhattan belonged to the Giants—for a while.

The matchup was nearly as compelling as the fall classic, for it featured the season's best two pitchers in Ford, who went 26–6, and the Giants' Christy Mathewson. The two teams provided an interesting contrast: the Giants' heavy hitting was pitted against the Yankees' speed, and the experienced manager John McGraw against the inexperienced Chase.

The Yankees proved no match for their National League counterparts, and the Giants won in six games. But the series was a success at the gate, and the touts and sports that followed the team cleaned up, taking action from all comers. Meanwhile, the Philadelphia A's, who won 102 games and finished 14½ games ahead of the Yankees, swamped the Cubs in the World Series.

With Chase at the helm of the Yankees, the club was never in the race in 1911. They finished sixth, 76–76, as Philadelphia badly outdistanced the field. Connie Mack's A's were clearly the class of the league as everyone else, observed the *Spalding Guide,* indulged in a "merry scramble for position." The so-called $100,000 infield of Stuffy McInnis, Jack Barry, and eventual Hall of Famers Frank "Home Run" Baker and Eddie Collins led the league's most potent offense. Hall of Famers Chief Bender and Eddie Plank, supplemented by a team-best 28 wins from Jack Coombs, paced the A's pitching staff.

New York and every other team in the league fought to keep up. None did. The A's beat the Yankees 15 of 21. Chase's team could hit and stole 270 bases, but the pitching staff slumped badly. Ford was still effective, but his "mystery pitch" wasn't quite as mysterious anymore.

The star of the season was Birdie Cree, who emerged as one of the best players in the league. He hit .356, stole 48 bases, and knocked in 88. His slugging percentage was a robust .513, third best in the league after Detroit's twin sluggers, Ty Cobb and Sam Crawford. Before the arrival of Babe Ruth in 1920, Cree's season was easily the best in Yankee history. Even today, given the context of the era, it remains one of the best performances ever by a Yankee hitter.

Yankee history has ignored the dominance of the A's in 1911, the collapse of New York's pitching staff, and the loss of the special advantage the club had enjoyed through Stallings's use of signal tipping. Instead, the team's fall from second place in 1910 to sixth in 1911—a difference

of only 12½ games—has been blamed on the supposed evil machinations of the malevolent Hal Chase. In fact, under Chase the club was better on the road in 1911 than 1910. But at home, now without the knowledge of what pitch was coming, they lost *an additional 15 games.*

Every baseball writer who ever encountered Chase wore out the thesaurus tarring Prince Hal. Harold Seymour referred to his career as "a squalid passage" in the game's history, and revisionist stat master Bill James wrote that "something about him made wrong shine like it was right and evil smell good." Given the events of later years, when Chase was implicated in gambling scandals in both Chicago and Cincinnati, those descriptions have some credence. But when observers such as James cite the

The inaugural postseason city series between the Yankees and the Giants in 1910 came on the heels of the Stallings-Chase dispute and relegated the World Series matchup between the Athletics and the Cubs to "other news" status in the New York press. Newly hired player-manager Hal Chase (left) greets Giants manager John McGraw at the Polo Grounds at the start of the first subway series.

Yankees' fall from second to sixth under Chase as evidence of his amorality, they are dead wrong.

No one was more pointed — or influential — in his attack on Chase than Hall of Fame baseball writer Fred Lieb. In his memoir, *Baseball as I Have Known It,* he relates a story from 1911, Lieb's second year covering baseball. According to Lieb, his sports editor at the *New York Press* told him that Chase had a "corkscrew brain," saying, "He can be the greatest player in the world if he wishes. Some days he doesn't want to be. He isn't a man I would trust."

Lieb then had a revelation, a common experience for the writer, who regularly counseled Ouija boards and put his faith in spiritualism. He claimed to have checked Chase's fielding record

and discovered that for about six years running, Chase, supposedly the peerless first baseman, wound up with something like nineteen to twenty-one errors. Now I knew that was pretty unusual for a first baseman, who normally has far fewer errors than other fielders. In fact, Stuffy McInnis, while with the Red Sox, once went through a season with only one error. I made a note of Chase's suspicious error totals.

Lieb later used this as evidence that Chase was throwing games with his glove. Virtually all subsequent accounts of Chase's career have made use of Lieb's damning accusation, causing his entire playing record as a Yankee to be looked upon suspiciously.

If only it were true. Lieb, the supposedly peerless scribe, apparently lied about the first baseman's record.

Chase's fielding record does reveal some apparently high error totals. From 1905 through 1912, he annually accumulated 22 to 36 errors — even higher than Lieb's claim. But instead of supporting Lieb's assertion, these numbers actually refute it. Other first basemen of the era accumulated similar totals.

Until the 1920s, players still used small, so-called pancake gloves, and error totals were high for everyone. The best shortstops often were charged with upward of 50 errors a season. A record of 20 to 30 errors by a first baseman was not outlandish but near the norm. For example, Boston National first baseman Fred Tenney, considered by many to be the best fielder in baseball before Chase, accumulated 28 errors in 1906 — Chase had 32. Hall of Famer

Frank Chance, also considered a great fielder, was charged with 36 errors in 1903. Jiggs Donahue of the White Sox regularly accumulated over 20 errors per season. And McInnis? While he was charged with only a single error in 1921, by then glove sizes had increased dramatically and new baseballs were constantly put into play, both of which made for better fielding. In 1912 McInnis had 27 errors — *the same number as Chase.*

Modern statistical analysis does indicate that Chase's fielding prowess may have been overstated as his peers mistook flash for skill. But to believe that he was regularly throwing games with his glove is a stretch. So too is the notion that Chase's managerial strategy somehow ran the team into the ground. Run differential, the most accurate predictor of performance, reveals that the Yankees actually won *more* games than they had any right to in 1911. And the one trade Chase made, dumping Stallings supporters Jimmy Austin and Frank Laporte for Browns third baseman Roy Hartzell, was a good one. Hartzell led the team with 91 RBIs in 1911. But Lieb's charges, supplemented by some statements by players years later, after Chase's reputation had taken a well-deserved beating for his involvement in other scandals, have since cast those perceptions in concrete.

George Stallings, meanwhile, was completely unaffected. He lost his job but escaped any lasting taint from either his blatant use of signal tipping or his unsubstantiated charges against Chase. He reemerged in the major leagues as manager of the Boston Braves in 1913. The following season, with his team firmly ensconced in eighth place in mid-July, the Braves suddenly and without explanation caught fire. They won 34 of their final 44 games to surge past the New York Giants and capture the 1914 National League pennant by an astounding 10½ games, then swept the heavily favored A's in the World Series. No one ever looked behind the fence.

The real reason behind the Yankees' demise was much more mundane. Money. Farrell and Devery were almost broke.

Without the help of Tammany, each had proven to be a lousy businessman. Their addiction to gambling and the high life had squandered their fortune. They had spent millions on lame horses, broken-down ballplayers, bad real estate, and painted ladies.

Hilltop Park had also proven to be a liability. Fans had never cared for it, and as the lease on the property drew closer to its 1912 expiration date, it fell into disrepair. Its most distinguishing characteristic became the Bull Durham sign on the outfield fence. After the Polo Grounds burned on Opening Day of the 1911 season, the era of the wooden ballpark was effectively over. While Farrell had magnanimously allowed the Giants to use his park for the first two months of the season until the Polo Grounds was rebuilt in concrete and steel, his windfall evaporated in an astronomical increase in insurance on the Hilltop.

The Yankee owners had already spent thousands on a series of ill-fated plans to build a new park. On one proposed site on a streambed in Kingsbridge at 221st Street and Broadway, they planned a double-decked park seating 32,000. They wasted hundreds of thousands of dollars trying to reroute Spuyten Duyvil Creek into the Harlem Canal before political opposition forced them to abandon the project. They spilled more money in an idiotic scheme to build a floating park in the Harlem River.

Their fortunes were spinning down the drain at an increasingly rapid rate. Farrell had even been forced to abandon the racetrack. The Yankees, rather than being the plum atop his fortune, were now almost his sole source of income.

The club had virtually stopped buying ballplayers, and its thrift was starting to show on the field. More players had been sold than purchased, and as the roster grew thinner, trades for real talent became rare.

Chase knew a sinking ship when he saw it. When Farrell began making noise about a change at the top, Chase gladly stepped aside. In his stead Farrell installed Harry Wolverton, a sombrero-wearing, cigar-smoking former player cut in the mold of Kid Elberfeld, who'd recently excelled as manager of Oakland in the Pacific Coast League.

He didn't have a chance in 1912, and neither did the Yankees. The pitching collapsed as Ford, two years after winning 26 games, lost 21, and the defense was atrocious. As Heywood Broun later reported, Bill Devery "constituted himself as a board of strategy and gave Harry Wolverton daily lessons in the finer points of baseball." So the Yankees lost early, often, and in every way possible. But they looked good doing it.

As the *New York Times* first reported on February 27, "the fad for the pin stripe in baseball toggery . . . has reached the Hilltop." Several years before the Chicago Cubs had pioneered the feature. The Giants had followed suit in 1911.

On the road the Yankees wore plain gray, but at home they wore white, pinstriped in black, with a black "NY" emblazoned over the left breast, the most memorable uniform in American sports. Although the team would abandon the look at the end of the season, it would return in 1915, the pinstripes in signature navy blue.

And the team finally and officially became the "Yankees" when Farrell and Devery chose to adopt the commonly used name. Other changes were more than cosmetic.

Harry Wolverton, a rough-hewn veteran of the Pacific Coast League, managed the Yankees to a last-place finish as the New Yorkers lost 102 games. The team did make one positive move: adopting a pinstripe home uniform with the trademark "NY" logo to complement the drab gray road uniform worn here.

The mansion in which Yankee co-owner Jacob Ruppert was raised sat on the edge of the affluent frontier of Gilded Age Manhattan, at 93rd and Fifth Avenue. Ruppert's Yankee Stadium would occupy a similarly grand yet isolated location in the newly developed Bronx several generations later.

Any dim chance of the team competing that season had evaporated when a Walter Johnson fastball crushed Birdie Cree's wrist in early July. Cree, hitting .332 and proving that his performance in 1911 had been no fluke, missed the rest of the year.

The impact of Johnson's pitch lasted beyond 1912. Cree's wrist healed, but his psyche did not. Although he would return to action in 1913, as one observer noted, his "decline was swift and sudden. . . . [H]e changed overnight into a gun shy batter, who had one foot in the bucket continually."

With attendance dropping, maintenance costs rising, the lease due to expire, and plans for a new park in disarray, the immigrant gave up on its dreams of glory and opted for indentured servitude. The team abandoned the Hilltop and in 1913 became the Giants' tenant in the Polo Grounds.

Although the move relieved the Yankee owners of a gigantic headache, it reinforced the growing perception that the Yankees were a second-rate club. Even lowly Brooklyn, which had always been a distant third wheel in New York's baseball universe, was drawing more fans than the Yankees.

Ban Johnson tried to stanch the bleeding. As a tourniquet, he went after the greatest manager in the game, Frank Chance, a.k.a. "the Peerless Leader."

In seven years as skipper of the Cubs, Chance had led the team to three pennants and a combined winning percentage of .667, the best record of the century over a similar time period. But the Cubs still fired Chance after the 1912 season. The manager, who suffered from severe headaches and other health problems owing to the number of times he'd been beaned while an active player, announced that he planned to retire to his California ranch.

Instead, he was acquired by Johnson, through a complicated set of procedures, for the Yankees. Chance signed a three-year contract to manage worth $25,000 a year plus 5 percent of any profits.

Chance soon discovered that his record in Chicago had more to do with his team of all-stars than his own managerial acumen. New York's cupboard was bare, and the few talented players left on the team had given up.

By the end of spring training in Bermuda, Chance had turned over almost the entire roster, retaining only a handful of players from 1912. The manager also decided he was at least part of the solution. Despite not playing regularly since 1908, he installed himself at first base and went against baseball wisdom by moving lefty Hal Chase to second.

There were problems right away. Chase was less than enthusiastic and earned his manager's ire by repeatedly showing up late for practice. At age 35, Chance's ancient legs couldn't take the strain of playing every day, and he opened the season on the bench, but he left Chase at second.

The team opened the 1913 season on April 10 in Washington in front of newly elected President Woodrow Wilson. They scored a first-inning run off Walter Johnson on a hit batsman, a stolen base, and an error to take a 1–0 lead.

That was pretty much the high point of the season. The Yankees lost 2–1, Johnson didn't give up another run until mid-May, and the Yankees lost 12 of their first 14 games and wouldn't win in their new home until June 7. By that time all hope was lost.

There were two reasons the Yankees folded so early: injuries to the pitching staff and Chance's revolving-door roster. The press dismissively referred to the "Peerless Leader" as "P.L.," but the manager cast the blame elsewhere.

Once again Hal Chase became the bad guy, or at least one of them. He and other veterans were overtly contemptuous of the ever-serious Chance and openly mocked him. The manager was deaf in one ear, and Chase delighted in insulting him just out of earshot, then watching the manager fume as players looked his way and laughed.

The first baseman — he regained his position when Chance's legs continued to fail him — kept pushing Chance's buttons, hoping to be traded. Then in mid-May Chance charged that Chase was doing more than laying down — he was actually tossing games.

Chance went public with his charges — sort of. According to Fred Lieb, Chance told Lieb and reporter Heywood Broun: "Did you notice some of those balls that got away from Chase today? They weren't wild throws, they were made to look that way. He has been doing that right along. He is throwing games on me!"

But once again Lieb's evidence doesn't extend beyond the anecdote. To believe that Chase alone was responsible for the club's performance by botching a few catches at first base is ludicrous to anyone who has ever played baseball. Indeed, an examination of the Yankees' record that May reveals a team that not only lost but lost badly. Nei-

ther Chase's play nor that of the other Yankee infielders stands out. Indeed, from May 7 to May 13 the club actually won five of seven — their *best* stretch of play all season. Sam Crane observed at the time that "the playing of no individual stood out so prominently as that of Hal Chase. The first sacker is going like a house afire, batting and fielding right up to the handle."

But Chase, with his reputation, became Chance's convenient scapegoat. Farrell reluctantly gave him permission to seek a trade. Chance's contract made Chase expendable.

With the Yankee record a pitiful 9–28, Chance got what he wanted. The club's first star was shipped to the Chicago White Sox on June 1.

Chase moved on to the second half of his career, during which he would commit most of the offenses that have since tarnished his reputation beyond reconciliation. In nearly a decade as a Yankee, while not always the best player on the field, he was always the most popular with the fans, a position that at times gave him power and influence disproportionate to his skills. But the corrupt regime of Farrell and Devery gave him the license to indulge in behavior that wouldn't have been tolerated elsewhere and, in all likelihood, was even encouraged by New York's spineless owners. A talented player, he was not a perfect teammate by any means, yet it is impossible to separate his actions from the sordid environment that surrounded the team. And Chase became the first of many players in the team's long history whose personality would be more important than his talent. New York was a stage. Chase, the first Yankee who knew how to play it, recognized that the stage was as important as anything he did on the field.

All Chance received for Chase were two lesser talents, first baseman Baker Borton and the sore-footed infielder Rollie Zeider, aptly described by one writer as "an onion and a bunion." Both stunk in New York and caused Farrell and Devery to begin to lose faith in Frank Chance. Chase, meanwhile, hit nearly .300 for Chicago.

The club lost its first six games without Chase, extending a season-high losing streak to 13. Chance made more trades over the course of the season, picking up a few players who later proved valuable, like shortstop Roger Peckinpaugh, who was acquired just before the Chase deal, but the new personnel made little difference. The Yankees limped to the finish a pathetic 57–94, only one game ahead of the last-place Browns.

They made a small improvement in 1914, owing primarily to the absolute and utter collapse of the Cleveland Indians, who lost more than 30 games in 1914 than in 1913. New York was the main beneficiary, as the Indians helped lift them to a 70–84 record.

But their improvement was more illusion than reality. The Yankees were pathetic on offense and defense, and not much better on the mound. Even without Chase, players remained indifferent and team chemistry was pure poison. Chance tried to instill discipline, but players went behind his back to Farrell and Devery, who repeatedly rescinded fines.

Chance couldn't take it. The Peerless Leader's reputation was rapidly being tarnished. He didn't get along with team scout and Farrell crony Arthur Irwin and wanted him dismissed. Farrell refused. Then Chance suggested his own removal. "Anyone at all can manage a sixth or seventh place team," he said, "but it is ridiculous to pay a man a high salary and then not give him the proper material to work with. Mr. Farrell will not spend the money."

That's because he didn't have it. In early September the disgusted Chance asked to be released from his duties on September 15. If the club agreed to pay him until the end of the season, he'd forgo the final year of his contract.

Farrell agreed to let him go but balked at paying Chance, writing him, "I know you do not want to take money you do not earn." The irony was that that strategy was one the owner reserved for himself.

As Chance sat in the Yankee clubhouse at the Polo Grounds on September 12 after his club defeated Philadelphia 2–1, Farrell and Devery walked in. They heard Chance complaining to the press corps about the two owners. An argument ensued, and soon the manager and ex-cop-turned-owner were in each other's faces. When Devery called Chance a "quitter," the manager took a wild swing at his boss. He missed, and Chance's players soon pulled the two apart.

Chance held on a few more days, but on September 14 he and Farrell finally agreed to terms. Chance was paid through the remainder of the season and released the club from the final year of his contract.

Twenty-five-year-old infielder Roger Peckinpaugh took over as interim manager and played out the string. The Yankees finished tied for sixth in the American League, 30 games behind first-place Philadelphia, and fourth in New York behind the Giants, the Dodgers, and the Federal League Brooklyn Tip-Tops.

All baseball had looked on warily as the new Federal League took shape in 1914 and mounted a challenge to the monopoly represented by the National and American Leagues. Competition was driving up costs, and there was speculation that player raids on the two established leagues would begin in earnest in 1915.

Thus far Manhattan had escaped a Federal League challenge, but in Brooklyn the new team had cut NL attendance by nearly 70 percent. Just as Ban Johnson had chosen to make Manhattan his battleground in 1903, there was speculation that Federal League president James Gilmore would do the same in 1915.

The Yankees were in no shape to fend off a rival. Farrell and Devery were going broke as tension over Chance and Chase in 1914 caused the partnership to begin to rupture. As their wallets became strained, each blamed the other for the club's failures, but neither man realized that without a stacked deck they were utter frauds as businessmen.

Ban Johnson, still protective of his league, began casting about for new ownership. Farrell and Devery had outlived their usefulness.

Politics and baseball make strange bedfellows. Johnson found a curious ally — John McGraw. Like Johnson, McGraw and the Giants were also worried about the Feds. The Yankees weren't much of a threat to the Giants, and the rent they paid on the Polo Grounds helped keep the NL team strong. But if the Feds came into New York and the Yankees fell apart, the mighty Giants might actually be put at risk.

The Giants had a host of well-heeled fans, and McGraw knew most of them personally. He'd grown particularly close to Colonel Tillinghast L'Hommideau Huston. The civil engineer had earned a captain's commission in the Spanish American War and then made a fortune dredging Havana Harbor and building the sewer system. In World War I he would become a colonel. Through McGraw, Huston had met another big Giants fan, beer baron and Tammany politician Jacob Ruppert, who referred to himself as "Colonel" owing to his ceremonial membership in the

New York National Guard. The two became friends and even shared a private box at the Polo Grounds.

Each man had tried to parlay his friendship with McGraw into a stake in the Giants, but the team wasn't for sale. So on December 7, 1914, Huston and Ruppert met with Farrell and Johnson.

Both Ruppert and Huston were independently wealthy. Together, they were filthy rich. Their partnership offered Farrell and Devery a way out and a handsome profit, and it bucked up Johnson's New York franchise. When Johnson got a sniff of the bottom line, things moved fast, at least at first. He took Farrell and Devery by the hand and steered the franchise into the hands of Ruppert and Huston.

The deal was announced several times, but each time all parties were forced to wait while Ruppert had his lawyers go over the books. They were a mess: Farrell had misplaced most of the important paperwork covering his operation, including a mortgage he'd taken out on his now-abandoned ballpark.

For their trouble, Farrell and Devery would eventually split $460,000, a sum more than 25 times their original investment and easily enough for any reasonable persons to live on comfortably for the rest of their lives.

They barely made it. The two continued to fight and squabble and soon stopped talking to each other. Devery died in 1919 of a blood clot in the brain, leaving an estate of $1,023. Farrell did only slightly better. He lived another seven years before dying of heart failure, bettering Devery's legacy by $49 — his estate was valued at $1,072.

Their monument was a franchise in ruin.

Miller Huggins, hired by Jacob Ruppert as Yankee manager in 1918, led New York to six pennants and three world championships before his premature death from blood poisoning at age fifty, in 1929. The diminutive (5'5", 140-pound) former second baseman had managed the St. Louis Cardinals for five seasons before his arrival in New York and never finished above fourth place.

There is no charity in baseball. Every club owner
must make his own fight for existence.

— JACOB RUPPERT

1915 – 1919
TWO COLONELS AND ONE BOSS

The day Jacob Ruppert purchased a portion of the New York Yankees was the day the modern Yankees, the most recognized and successful franchise in team sports, first appeared. Ruppert actually accomplished the failed promises of Farrell and Devery and achieved the destiny of the team as originally envisioned by Ban Johnson.

Farrell and Devery's fraudulent reign had failed because of their own shortcomings. Without Tammany, they had been exposed as thickheaded thugs incapable of managing their own sordid affairs, much less those of their ballclub. The franchise they abandoned was one whose dreams and aspirations had been crushed, leaving it a team that had no home and had grown accustomed to living hand to mouth, dwelling in the ghetto of the American League, working for day wages.

The second generation would have it better under Ruppert, so much better that their forebears would be virtually forgotten. Most "historians" ignore the pre-Ruth Yankees, but

Ruppert is as important to the legacy of the franchise as the Bambino. He gave the Yankees his money and attention, quickly restoring the club's pride and promise. For the first time the Yankees cashed in on the natural advantage provided by the New York market. And it has been that way ever since. In return, the ballclub would become Ruppert's legacy and serve as a symbol of the power and influence he craved. Jacob Ruppert — not George Steinbrenner — is the Yankee owner who most deserves the appellation "the Boss."

Of course, he didn't serve alone. For a time Ruppert shared the Yankees with his partner, Tillinghast L'Hommideau Huston. But theirs was a marriage of convenience and capital that would not long survive.

Yankee co-owner Colonel Tillinghast L'Hommideau Huston made his fortune from government projects in Cuba, such as building sewer systems and dredging harbors. With his wealth he purchased not only a 30,000-acre hunting camp in Georgia but also a place in New York society with a major piece of the Yankees.

In reality the two owners were different species of men, brought together by their bank accounts and interest in baseball. Put it this way: Huston was a beer drinker. Ruppert owned the breweries.

Huston was a man's man, an engineer who at the outbreak of the Spanish-American War had led a volunteer regiment of builders. They built the infrastructure the Army needed and in return Huston gained valuable experience, government contracts, and well-placed friends.

Upon his return to the United States, Huston lived the high life and epitomized "new money." At his 30,000-acre Georgia hunting camp, he built a grotesque estate based on the Petit Trianon of Versailles. Yet at the same time he would wear the same suit for days on end and was rarely seen without his signature derby, earning him the sobriquet "the Man in the Iron Hat." New York drew him to its flame, and Huston, whom the press called "Cap" after his Army commission, did what he could to ingratiate himself into New York society.

He loved baseball and ballplayers. Buying a team became his only goal. After several aborted attempts to buy in, including an offer for the Cubs in 1913, he jumped at the opportunity to get a piece of the Yankees.

His eagerness was what made him so attractive to American League president Ban Johnson, for the Federal League was on the lookout for someone to bankroll a team in New York, and Huston had "patsy" written all over him. Better, thought Johnson, to have Huston and his money as an ally rather than have him on the other side.

In contrast to Huston, Ruppert was another kind of man altogether, someone for whom old money and old methods of making more had served well.

His Bavarian grandfather had immigrated to the United States and immediately went into the brewery business. Ruppert's father, Jacob Sr., inherited the brewery in 1867, the same year Ruppert was born. The son was raised as a young aristocrat and at age 21 began preparations to run the family business.

He proved his acumen early. At the time there was intense competition between New York breweries for business. The Jacob Ruppert Brewery, while successful, did not dominate the market. Ehret's Hell Gate Brewery brewed New York's beer of choice. Ruppert needed an edge.

So in 1888, at age 21, young Jacob Ruppert joined Tammany Hall, the quickest way to the top in New York City. His swag bought him membership in a host of private clubs where the real power lay, and he soon became one of Tammany's biggest backers, buying power and prestige and putting Ruppert beer into every Tammany-controlled tavern and saloon in the city of New York, which was most of them. Within ten years Ruppert's product dominated the market, and Ruppert himself was one of Tammany's most powerful members, serving alongside Andrew Freedman on the influential finance committee.

Ruppert was a true Tammany man and did what he was told. Richard Croker wanted to use him to placate the growing German-American vote; after first pondering a Ruppert candidacy for city council, he instead picked Ruppert to run for Congress in the heavily Republican Fifteenth District, the so-called Silk Stocking District.

Ruppert won in a mild upset and went on to serve four terms in Congress, a Tammany man all the way, voting the party line and making little mark in the chamber. All the while Ruppert's signature beer, "Knickerbocker," flowed without peer throughout the city.

After leaving Congress, Ruppert went about being a beer baron. Unlike Huston, he was no pretender to a life of wealth and privilege. Despite being a second-generation American, he affected a German accent and lived in a townhouse on Fifth Avenue and at a magnificent Hudson River estate opposite West Point, where he was always surrounded by valets, butlers, maids, cooks, and chauffeurs. He owned yachts, raced horses, bred dogs, and collected exotic animals, jade, porcelain, first editions, and, as a lifelong bachelor, mistresses, whom he usually kept anonymous and well hidden.

Although he was a genuine baseball fan, his interest in the Yankees was primarily financial. Like Huston, he had occasionally expressed his interest in buying a team. In 1912 he was offered the Chicago Cubs but said he wasn't interested "in anything so far from Broadway." When he bought into the Yankees, Ruppert became the first brewer to own a major league team. Having the Ruppert name appearing in the sports pages every day was free advertising.

As 1914 turned into 1915, the sale inched closer to conclusion. Finally, at 4:02 P.M. on December 31, Huston appeared on the grand staircase of the Hotel Wolcott and announced to the assembled press, "Boys, we've bought the Yankees." On January 1, 1915, Heywood Broun wrote in the *Herald Tribune*: "The Yankees have been sold many times during the last few weeks, but the sale yesterday (December 30) was definite and complete. . . . With a typical German love of thoroughness Colonel Ruppert applied himself to these details and 542 hours and ten minutes later the deal was settled." All that remained was the passing of papers and some checks, which took another month.

That same day another notice appeared in the New York papers, detailing the financial collapse of Cleveland owner Charles Somers, a former Great Lakes shipping magnate who had bankrolled Ban Johnson and the American League back in 1901. Somers had sunk nearly $5 million into the American League, but had now come up short as his outside investments went belly up. Eventually his failure was to have a dramatic effect on the future of the New York team.

There was a reason for Ruppert's mindfulness over the transaction. A losing team was not part of the deal. He demanded both a new, experienced manager and some quality players, and he pressed Ban Johnson hard on both issues before finalizing the deal. As the *Times* noted, "Ban Johnson is taking an unusual interest in the Yankees." The league president promised to arrange some advantageous deals and also secured former Detroit pitcher "Wild Bill" Donovan as manager. In 1914 Donovan had led Providence to the International League pennant and tutored a young pitcher named Babe Ruth.

Few observers envied Huston and Ruppert. Like the Boston Red Sox of a later era, the Yankees' reputation was that of a cursed, star-crossed franchise, one for which bad luck had been the only kind of luck at all. One reporter stepped forward and said to Huston, "Allow me to be the first one to offer you my heartfelt condolences. My sympathy goes out to you." Added Broun in his report, "'Wild Bill' Donovan has never taken a drink in his life. 'Wild Bill' Donovan has never managed the Yankees."

The reconstruction of the franchise began in earnest. Donovan's first public statement underlined the obvious. "The Yankees need building up," he said. The team had no ballpark, hardly any fans, and few players worth keeping. But they had the money. That would make all the difference.

Ruppert and Huston cleaned house, letting go virtually every club employee and letting the other owners know they were ready to buy. With the general economy in bad shape and the Federal League still raising costs everywhere, there were plenty of interested parties. Although Huston initially was the public face of the franchise, Ruppert was the one running the show.

Ban Johnson came through on his promise of players, at least at first, as he directed Detroit to release first baseman Wally Pipp and outfielder Hugh High to the Yankees on waivers and coerced a few minor leaguers under contract to other teams toward New York. But the Yankees' problems weren't going to be solved instantaneously. No infusion of cash or players could accomplish that. Donovan didn't have much to work with. Pipp and Hugh High helped, but after acquiring Ray Caldwell and Ray Fisher, he was forced to pick pitchers out of a hat.

Of course the cash did help. In contrast to their peers, most of whom were struggling financially, the Yankees had plenty of money. When other teams looked to sell, Johnson steered them to Ruppert.

In late June, with the Yankees lingering around .500, Ruppert made his first big acquisition. Connie Mack's 1914 champions had proven too expensive for him to keep. Star third baseman Frank "Home Run" Baker had even quit the club in a contract dispute. In a pique, Mack allowed him to sit out the 1915 season until his contract expired, then decided to break up his team.

Second baseman Eddie Collins was the class of the bunch. Ruppert and Huston wanted him, but Johnson allowed him to go to Chicago. Johnson promised the Yankees that the next time around they'd get first dibs on any available talent.

The A's quickly went from first to worst as Mack saved money and made plans to rebuild. On June 28, the Yankees were the beneficiaries. Mack sold pitcher Bob Shawkey, an 18-game winner in 1914, to New York for $15,000. Although Mack dismissed the fireballer as a "six-inning pitcher," for most of the next 13 years "Bullet Bob" would anchor the staff.

Shawkey was tough. Even after making it to the major leagues, he kept his off-season job in his native Pennsylvania stoking railroad engines with coal. "I thought shoveling coal would make me strong," said the fireman. He'd need his strength in New York.

But Shawkey made little difference in 1915, going only 4–7 in his New York debut. The Red Sox, Tigers, and White Sox left the rest of the league behind as the Yankees put forth the most impotent attack in the league. In August *The Sporting News* quipped, "Donovan's scouts have been instructed to go after outfielders, pitchers and catchers." That didn't leave much else.

The only consolation was that the Giants were even worse, but the landlord still outdrew the tenants by a wide margin. As the Yankees slumped to a fifth-place finish and a 69–83 record—worse than 1914—barely 250,000 fans turned out at the Polo Grounds to watch them play. They were as nameless and faceless as the teeming masses pouring into New York.

But Ruppert and Huston had plans. Lots of them. Too many in fact.

At an annual cost of $65,000, the new owners were uncomfortable renting the Polo Grounds. Every couple of weeks the press identified a new ballpark site, but it proved no easier for the club to build a ballpark in 1915 than it had been in 1903. Sites all over the city were talked about and talked about. But landowners knew the two men were flush with cash and held out for a dear price. At the same time Federal League interests took a page out of the book of Andrew Freedman and tied up several properties by taking out options on the land themselves. The league was failing, but they hoped to coerce Organized Baseball into a settlement and merger. Blocking the Yankees' new park was just part of the strategy.

The Federal League did indeed go belly up shortly after the end of season, and Organized Baseball did have to pony up in a court settlement. While the Yankees still had no luck in finding a place for their ballpark, the pool of available talent had suddenly enlarged. Federal Leaguers were up for grabs, and New York landed Brooklyn player-manager Lee Magee, who'd hit .323 for the Tip-Tops. But the Yankees lost $30,000 in 1915, a situation Ruppert and Huston did not want to repeat. Magee was a nice player, but they needed a star who would draw fans.

They turned their attention toward Home Run Baker, who'd sat out the 1915 season, playing a little semipro ball

The Ruppert brewery in Manhattan was the source of the fortune of new Yankee co-owner Jacob Ruppert, a former Tammany-affiliated congressman from New York's silk stocking district.

and farming. But working the land wasn't nearly as lucrative as working over major league pitching. Baker was itching to return, but Connie Mack still owned his contract.

Baker, age 30, was considered a great player, second only to former Boston star Jimmy Collins as the game's greatest third baseman. He'd earned his nickname by cracking two home runs in the 1911 World Series and leading the American League in home runs four years in a row from 1911 through 1914, hitting 11, 10, 12, and 9.

Baker wanted to play, but only at his price and not with Philadelphia. Ban Johnson delivered the goods and steered him to New York, which cleared a roster spot for him by releasing Birdie Cree, who had never returned to form after Walter Johnson broke his wrist. Instead of signing on with someone else, the erudite outfielder commented, "I have no plans to return to the bush leagues." Back home in his native Pennsylvania, he became a banker.

On February 15, 1916, wrote Broun, "Captain Huston and Colonel Ruppert lured Connie Mack into a brewery yesterday and before they were done with him he was induced to sell Frank Baker." For $25,000, Baker, who agreed to a three-year deal worth another $24,000, was theirs. The club announced that third baseman Fritz Maisel, whose 51 steals and .281 batting average had led the club in 1915, would move to the outfield. Baker gave the team instant credibility, and with the addition of Magee, the team appeared to have some offense. For a time it looked as if they'd have even more.

Now that the Feds had folded, every team in the league was looking to cut salaries. In Boston star outfielder Tris Speaker had upped his pay all the way to $18,000 a year as the Red Sox ponied up to keep him out of the Federal League. Now that the league had collapsed, they wanted to cut his salary in half. Speaker held out.

This was just the kind of situation Ruppert and Huston were made for. Surely, they thought, Boston would deal Speaker to the highest bidder, and surely, they thought, old friend Ban Johnson would make good on his promise to make them a winner by steering Speaker their way. After all, that's how Ban did business.

Speaker, Cobb, Joe Jackson, and Eddie Collins of the White Sox were easily the best four position players in the league. The addition of such a player could mean a pennant. But Johnson's promises often ended with his own self-interest, and he had an interest in Cleveland. When Charles Somers was forced to sell, Johnson had personally loaned part of the purchase price to the new buyer he favored, Chicago construction magnate James Dunn. On paper, in reality, and, most important, in secret, the league president was also a part-owner of the Indians. On Opening Day, Speaker was dealt to Cleveland for $55,000 and several players.

Ruppert and Huston weren't happy. They'd have loved a chance to make a bid themselves. They didn't yet know about Johnson's stake in Cleveland, but they began to look at Johnson with increasing wariness.

Shawkey got off to a strong start, however, and the team was suddenly a contender. The Yankees surged into first place at the end of June and should have been even better than that. The A's were absolutely pathetic but had somehow managed to beat New York four times. Still, all was sweetness and light in the Polo Grounds. The loss of Fritz Maisel to a broken collarbone seemed incidental, and even after outfielder Frank Gilhooly broke an ankle, the team scarcely noticed. The Yankees just kept winning.

Then one June afternoon Frank Baker went in pursuit of a foul ball at the Polo Grounds and discovered the only problem with a concrete-and-steel stadium—steel and concrete. When he ran full steam into the reinforced cement barrier separating the stands from the field, he broke several ribs and had to be carried from the field.

Yet the club somehow staggered through the next few weeks and stayed atop the league. Then, on July 18, as Grantland Rice wrote, "The Sheik's curse has descended on the hapless Yanks." As Rice reported, when pitcher Nick Cullop cut loose with a pitch in the second inning of a game against Detroit, "he dropped in a crumpled heap to the ground, face down and inert . . . like a dead man." He'd ripped a muscle in his side.

The next day it was outfielder Hughey High, wrote Rice, "who fell before the Sheik's Curse." As he dove to make a catch, he wrenched his knee.

Yet the Yankees somehow refused to fall. When Shawkey beat St. Louis 1–0 on July 22, New York's fifth victory in its last seven games, Rice offered: "If the phosphorescent Yanks can only succeed in losing three or four more steamy athletes they are liable to bust up the dad-binged league by winning the flag before September."

But then the club went on the road, accompanied, according to the *Tribune,* "by a corps of trained nurses, several field ambulances and carrying gallons of arnica and witch hazel." They lost 14 of their next 16, even falling twice on the same day to the same pitcher as St. Louis Browns journeyman Dave Davenport won a doubleheader on July 29. They soon fell from first and staggered to the finish, bloodied and beaten, ending with a record of 80–74, 11 games behind Boston.

Still, the season had been a success. Attendance had nearly doubled, and the team had apparently turned the corner. Wally Pipp emerged as a star, leading the team in most hitting categories and pacing the league with 14 home runs as left-handed hitters proved ever more able to reach the short right-field fence in the Polo Grounds. For the first time in years the Yankees approached the upcoming season with something akin to optimism.

It took a world war to stop them.

For much of the 1916 season the United States had danced around entry into World War I. Yet circumstances conspired to draw the United States ever closer to the conflict, and baseball became increasingly uncertain about the future. No one knew how a war might affect the game, either on the field or at the gate.

Even the Yankees showed caution. In the off-season they retrenched and failed to make a significant deal.

Finally, on April 6, following a spate of U-boat attacks on Allied shipping in the North Atlantic, Congress passed a formal declaration of war. One day later Cap Huston enlisted. By war's end he would be a colonel. War fueled his patriotism, not to mention the prospect in postwar Europe of finding the kind of success he'd had utilizing his engineering skills in Cuba after the last conflict.

Huston's departure marked a turning point in the team's history. Thus far Ruppert and Huston had operated the team in tandem, with Huston playing the more public role. Now Ruppert took command.

When the 1917 season opened, baseball scrambled to

adjust to the changing political climate. It wanted to support the war effort and continue business as usual. Although the Selective Service Act, passed into law in 1916, was already threatening to eviscerate big league rosters, there were plenty of loopholes. Married players, those with children or medical problems, and reservists were exempt from the draft. In 1917 most players found a way out.

Once war seemed certain, teams in both leagues mobilized and made public displays of their support of the war effort. Before joining the military himself, Huston had ordered the Yankees to begin drill practice, bearing bats instead of arms, during spring training in Georgia. An Army NCO led the maneuvers.

The club opened the 1917 campaign at the Polo Grounds against Boston on April 11. In a pregame ceremony before 20,000, the Yankees demonstrated their marching skills while shouldering bats and passed in review before Army brass. Then they lost to the Red Sox and pitcher Babe Ruth 10–3.

That was to be the pattern of the season — patriotic displays, charity games, and defeats as the club went into retreat. The Yankees hung close to the top until mid-May, then fell steadily back as the White Sox cruised to the league title. The team struggled to score runs as only Baker and Pipp hit with any consistency, although neither man approached his expected standard. Baker simply wasn't the player he'd been before sitting out 1915. The drives off his 52-ounce bat failed to fulfill the promise of his nickname.

But over the course of the season, Ruppert began to make plans. He felt Donovan had lost control of the sixth-place team. Pitchers Ray Caldwell and Urban Shocker had both been fined for failing to return to the hotel one night in Boston, and in September Baker was suspended after he refused to appear in an exhibition game. Moreover, attendance had fallen by 100,000.

Only a few days after the end of the season word leaked out that Donovan was finished. Huston — sending a letter from "Somewhere in France" — agreed with Donovan's dismissal. The new colonel wanted his buddy Wilbert Robinson for the job, but Ruppert barely knew Robinson and was cautious about appointing a Huston crony. He told the 50-year-old Robinson he was too old for the job.

Besides, Ban Johnson had other ideas. More important,

in Huston's absence he still had Ruppert's ear and his trust.

Veteran infielder Miller Huggins had recently enjoyed some mild success as manager of the St. Louis Cardinals but couldn't agree on a contract for 1918 with Cardinal president and former Yankee Branch Rickey. More significant, however, was the friendship Huggins enjoyed with J. G. Taylor Spinks, publisher of the influential *Sporting News,* the American League's house organ.

Spinks had talked up Huggins to Johnson, whose sense of competition was piqued by the idea of stealing a man-

Frank "Home Run" Baker was the first star lured to the Yankees by Ruppert and Huston. After sitting out the 1915 season over a contract dispute with Athletics owner Connie Mack, Baker was sold to New York for $25,000. Upon his arrival, the star third baseman signed a three-year, $24,000 contract.

Wild Bill Donovan, a former star pitcher for the Dodgers and the Tigers, was the first manager hired by Ruppert and Huston. In three seasons he led the Yankees to uninspiring second-division finishes, in 1915 (fifth), 1916 (fourth), and 1917 (sixth).

ager from the National League, just as it had been earlier when New York hired Frank Chance. It helped that Huggins, like Johnson, was a Cincinnati native. He also possessed a law degree. That impressed Johnson. Although most were under the impression that he was a lawyer, the Czar had dropped out of law school before finishing.

Huggins was the kind of player whom baseball people have long considered ideal managerial fodder. One of the smallest players in the league, he had gotten the most from his limited ability. A second baseman, he was a slick fielder known for his ability to draw walks, get on base, bunt, and steal.

The press compared him—unfavorably—to John McGraw. The Giants' leader was the newsmen's idea of a real manager—feisty, combative, and, after the game, gregarious, eager to share a drink and tell a story. Although Huggins shared McGraw's background and level of baseball knowledge, his temperament was much the opposite.

Huggins was hired on October 25. "Somewhere in France," Huston received the news like a "Dear John" letter. From behind the lines, where he was building railroads, he lobbed mash notes to the press complaining about the choice. But Ruppert was unmoved, and the hiring stood. Huston began to realize that while he was serving his country, Ruppert was consolidating control.

While Huston fumed and stomped around Europe, Ruppert and Huggins got right to work, politicking for a trade for St. Louis Browns second baseman Del Pratt. He was one of the league's best players but, like Hal Chase, had been charged with "laying down" by Browns owner Phil Ball. Unlike Chase, however, Pratt had decided to fight the charge and was suing Ball for libel. New York hoped to pick him up cheap.

The Yankees weren't the only team active in the market. While most clubs, scared off by the war, were retrenching and trying to save money in the off-season, flamboyant theatrical producer Harry Frazee, owner of the Red Sox, saw opportunity. He acted decisively and in December made a huge deal with the Athletics, buying star outfielder Amos Strunk, pitcher Joe Bush, and catcher Wally Schang for $60,000 and a couple of nonentities.

Ruppert was incensed. He wasn't afraid of the war either—he viewed everyone else's paralysis as an opportunity. But now, despite all Johnson's promises, Frazee had nabbed three valuable players the Yankees hadn't even known were available. First Speaker, now this. That wouldn't do. Yet in time the emerging situation would prove as significant to the franchise's future as the assassination of Serbian Archduke Ferdinand had been to the start of World War I.

The war was starting to affect everything. America had entered the conflict so confident of quick victory that many newspapers were still identifying the war by the day. Yet now it was dragging on, and dragging baseball into it, as U.S. troops proved little more adept at trench warfare than their counterparts on either side. Although the first draft the previous summer had left baseball virtually unscathed, now barely a day went by without word that another player had been lost.

The world was changing more quickly than anyone could imagine as the Victorian era began to give way to the Jazz Age. The whole world seemed about to be turned upside down — women were working and demanding the right to vote, booze was being banned, skirts were inching up, planes were filling the sky, and automobiles were filling the streets. Nothing would ever be the same, not even the game of baseball.

Ban Johnson was petrified. He was desperately afraid that the 1918 season wouldn't be played, and equally desperate to save it. A number of teams simply didn't have enough money to survive a yearlong shutdown. Johnson thought he had the solution. He made a foolish proposal that each team be able to exempt 18 men from the draft.

The public was appalled. While farm boys and clerks were dying in ditches thousands of miles from home, Johnson wanted ballplayers to have special duty. Public opinion turned. The American pastime wasn't acting very patriotic. Even when the government turned down Johnson's request, the game still suffered. Most people considered the players "slackers," little better than draft dodgers eager to shirk their duties. Interest in the upcoming season plummeted.

Johnson's miscalculation put the season at risk. Most teams became even more cautious — few wanted to spend money on a season that might be canceled. But Ruppert continued to take his cue from Frazee. Prohibition was on the horizon, and the brewer had to make the Yankees profitable. Somewhere in a period of uncertainty lay opportunity.

The Yankees and Red Sox were the only teams still buying. By Opening Day, New York had added both Del Pratt and outfielder Ping Bodie, even while it lost a number of second-line stars to the service.

Right from the start, the 1918 season was hard to figure. The season was only a few days old when the Yankees lost Bob Shawkey and outfielder Sammy Vick to the draft, departures that threw what had looked to be a set lineup and pitching rotation into disarray. Over the course of the season the Yankees lost another dozen players. Most other teams were similarly affected. No one knew from one week to the next who would be lost. Rosters were filled out with aging minor leaguers and younger players whose physical maladies left them exempt from the draft.

The Yankees were playing so-so baseball in mid-May when Provost Marshal General Enoch B. Crowder turned an already uncertain situation on its head. He ruled that

Yankee pitcher Sailor Bob Shawkey acquired his nickname when he enlisted in the Navy for nearly the entire 1918 season. On his return to New York, Shawkey started a six-year streak of winning at least 16 games per season for the rapidly improving club.

baseball was an "inessential activity," a decision that Ban Johnson had all but assured after asking for the draft exemption. Crowder's ruling, which became known as the "Work or Fight" order, meant that at some point all players would be required either to join the service or to go to work in the war industries.

Ban Johnson, the most powerful member of baseball's ruling three-member National Commission, headed back to Washington and again begged for an exclusion for baseball players. But Johnson was asking the wrong question

Outfielder Francesco Stephano Pezzolo (aka Ping Bodie) arrived from the Athletics in 1918 and was an immediate crowd favorite for the multitude of Italian-American fans at the Polo Grounds. Bodie started the Yankee tradition of great Italian-American players, among whose numbers are counted such stars as Lazzeri, Crosetti, DiMaggio, Raschi, and Righetti.

and didn't know how to play politics outside the byzantine world of baseball affairs where he enjoyed every advantage. In Washington he didn't know the players without a scorecard, and his pleas went unheeded. He announced that, "except for the cremation ceremonies," the season was dead and began to make preparations to shut it down.

In the wake of his announcement, attendance plummeted. But not everyone in baseball agreed with Johnson. The Yankees got hot, kept buying players to plug holes, and in late May were challenging the Red Sox for first place. The Yankees were one of the few teams in the game whose attendance during wartime was holding steady — they were even outdrawing the Giants. They wanted to finish the season and thought they could steal a pennant.

But so did the Red Sox. From the instant Harry Frazee had bought the team a year before — the first owner to do so without Johnson's explicit permission — Johnson had been trying to force him out. Frazee refused to kowtow

before the Czar and had no qualms about going over his head and making his own attempt to salvage the season. With the tacit support of Ruppert and a coalition of owners in both leagues, Frazee paid a personal visit to Secretary of War Newton Baker.

Frazee knew how to sell a story — he'd made a fortune on Broadway selling the same melodramas over and over. The issue wasn't about baseball — it was about America. Owners weren't trying to preserve a business — they were trying to preserve a way of life. Baseball wasn't a game for slackers — ballplayers were the ultimate patriots.

Frazee made a passionate and convincing argument that baseball, like the theater, was good for the nation's morale and provided patriotic workers with a much-needed diversion from the rigors of work and the horrors of battlefield news. The season should be allowed to continue, argued Frazee, not for the good of baseball but for the good of the country. Baseball would surely suffer under such trying circumstances but was willing to do its duty for the greater good of all.

That was an argument the government could sell to the public, and Baker bought it. In Frazee's wake, Johnson and the National Commission rushed in and made a belated plea using the same argument. For the good of the country, the "Work or Fight" order for ballplayers was stayed until October. Baseball agreed to end the season early, on September 1.

Politics turned Ruppert and the Yankees and Frazee's Red Sox into allies. Frazee had made it clear that he thought Johnson was incompetent; he wanted the three-man National Commission to be replaced with a single commissioner, a horrifying idea to the existing commission. Johnson's mismanagement of the 1918 season caused a number of teams to question their leader, none more so than the Yankees, who were beginning to wonder whether Johnson was ever going to come through on his promise of players. Frazee seemed to have Johnson pegged, and the Yankees were inclined to agree with the Red Sox owner — it helped that he was a good friend of Huston's. A schism began to form among the owners of the American League, one that eventually would change the history of baseball, deliver the best player in the game to the Yankees, and help create the game's greatest dynasty.

In the meantime, the Yankees and Red Sox did their

patriotic duty and fought it out for the pennant. On June 27, the Yankees dumped Boston at the Polo Grounds 7–5, as the *Herald Tribune* reported, "by negotiating a separate peace with Babe Ruth," holding him to a double. Because of the war, Boston's star pitcher had been making regular appearances in the field. Facing subpar pitching, his bat had been the talk of baseball. No one had ever hit the ball so far, with so much regularity.

In fact, he'd hit his first home run of the season in the Polo Grounds on May 4 as New York won 5–4. Two days later he made his first major league appearance in the field in a game against the Yankees, playing first base for the slumping Dick Hoblitzell, and hit another long home run.

Ruppert took notice. The Yankees were already one of the few teams of the era that recognized the potential importance of the home run in a team's arsenal. Since moving to the Polo Grounds, they'd stocked the lineup with left-handed power hitters who could reach the short right-field fence. Wally Pipp had led the league in home runs in both 1916 and 1917. So did the Yankee team.

According to legend, Ruppert was so impressed by Ruth's two early season blasts that he made Frazee an immediate offer for the emerging slugger. Frazee brushed him off. Ruth was one of the best pitchers in the league and too valuable to the Red Sox to deal. They were trying to win a pennant too.

Even then, Ruth flourished in New York as he did in no other place. In Boston Ruth was out of scale, too flamboy-

THE BOSTON YANKEES?

Many of the assumptions that underlie the so-called "curse of the Bambino" are simply incorrect. Boston Red Sox owner Harry Frazee was not broke and did not sell Babe Ruth to the Yankees to finance his production of the play *No, No, Nanette,* or any other. As discussed elsewhere in this book, and in greater detail in the authors' *Red Sox Century,* Ruth's sale was the result of a long and complicated political power struggle within the American League, pitting the Red Sox, Yankees, and White Sox against AL founder and president Ban Johnson and the rest of the league.

One important element of the "curse" contends that the Yankees' purchase of Ruth was dependent on the team's agreeing to loan Frazee $350,000, taking the mortgage of Fenway Park as collateral. This notion has long been offered as conclusive evidence of the alleged nefarious nature of the deal.

The truth tells a different story. When Frazee purchased the Red Sox in 1916 the press erroneously reported that he also acquired Fenway Park. But in fact he did not, and at the time Frazee sold Ruth, he still didn't own Fenway Park.

Financial documents of Frazee's, recently uncovered by the Frazee family at the University of Texas, reveal that Fenway Park was controlled by General Charles Taylor, of the *Boston Globe* Taylors, until May 3, 1920. Taylor, who owned the Red Sox from 1904 to 1911, built Fenway Park after selling the club, leasing it to subsequent owners, including Frazee, for $30,000.

Harry Frazee began negotiating with Taylor for Fenway on August 1, 1919. Ruth was sold to the Yankees, for $100,000, in late December. On May 3, 1920, Frazee bought Fenway Park. Then, just three weeks later, on May 25, Ruppert and the Yankees loaned Frazee a sum variously reported as $300,000 or $350,000, secretly taking title to Fenway as collateral. But why?

Ban Johnson was determined to bust the New York/Boston/Chicago alliance. He was threatening to revoke Frazee's franchise and install another owner in Boston. But when Frazee bought Fenway and placed it in the hands of his allies, the Yankees, a new Boston owner would not have a place to play. The ploy thwarted Johnson's scheme to take back the Red Sox.

Similarly, Johnson was also trying to get rid of Ruppert and Huston in New York. To that end, early in the 1920 season he persuaded New York Giants owner Charles Stoneham to cancel the Yankees' lease of the Polo Grounds. Johnson believed that without a place to play Ruppert and Huston would be forced to sell the team. Johnson even promised Stoneham he could handpick the competition and install a crony as the new Yankees owner.

But the Yankees *did* have a place to play: they owned Fenway Park. After being booted from the Polo Grounds, they could have moved the team to Boston and left Stoneham without a tenant. The Yankees could have shared Fenway with Frazee, throwing the American League into turmoil, perhaps creating the *Boston* Yankees and returning Ruth to the city that has rued his departure for more than eight decades.

Suddenly, and without explanation at the time, Stoneham got cold feet. He backed out of the plot, renewing the Yankees' lease of the Polo Grounds.

And, for the second time, Boston lost Babe Ruth.

ant for the stodgy old city that still gave lip service to its Puritan past. He had no anonymity, and his indiscretions were common knowledge and common gossip.

In New York Ruth fit right in, just as Hal Chase had. The Polo Grounds was a perfect stage for Ruth—in Boston's Fenway Park, his longest drives often failed to reach the distant right-field fence. But in the Polo Grounds those fly balls were home runs. And New York City was the one place, even then, where the privacy of the public celebrity was protected. The city could swallow him up, provide him with every diversion, keep his doings out of the papers, then spit him out on the ballfield each day to create a new legend. New York didn't care that Ruth didn't live with his wife, wrecked cars regularly, drank too much, or whored around. Half the rich guys in the city did the same.

New York fell hard for Ruth, where he was appreciated as nowhere else. Boston fans, for all their later protestations, simply didn't go to the ballpark to see Ruth as the slugger emerged in 1918 and 1919. Yet as the *Herald Tribune* commented later that season about another Polo Grounds appearance by Ruth, "There was more noise and commotion when Ruth struck out than there would be if any other player had poked the ball over the fence." That was New York.

Even in the midst of the war, Yankee fans were beginning to get a reputation as some of the most vocal in baseball. There was a reason for that.

The Giants had always been the team of the establishment, and Brooklyn was—well—in Brooklyn. Giants fans were older, wealthier, and more mainstream. Yankee crowds were different. They were younger, more working-class, and, most important, more ethnic.

The Yankees, the original immigrants themselves, were becoming the team favored by New York's ethnic masses. Outfielder Ping Bodie, whose given name was Francesco Stephano Pezzolo, was one of the few Italian players to play major league baseball at the time. New York Italians, a sizable and growing immigrant group, flocked to see one of their own in a major league uniform, often packing the left-field bleachers to see him play. In the Yankee victory that delivered the team into first place on June 28, Bodie's home run was the key blow. He was cheered so long and so loud that, the *Times* reported, "he had to take his cap off

so often during the afternoon he was in danger of being sunstruck." Over the next decade no team in baseball would be more ethnically diverse than the Yankees, or do a better job of appealing to immigrants and filling the stands. That appeal, however, would be but one factor in their success.

The Yankees, Boston, and Cleveland all battled for first place into midsummer, then the war got in the way. Player defections hit the Yankees hard. They finished fourth in the abbreviated season, 60–63, 13½ games behind pennant-winning Boston, which went on to capture the World Series from the Cubs. Harry Frazee was hailed as a genius.

The war ended on November 11. As players began returning from service, teams began to plan for the 1919 season. Everyone was anxious to start making some money.

Boston's returning stars left the Red Sox with a surplus of players. In the past it had been more or less standard league practice to run major trades by Ban Johnson. But after the events of the previous season, neither Sox owner Harry Frazee nor Jacob Ruppert saw much sense in doing that anymore.

Ruppert needed players and had money. Frazee had players and money never hurt. So on December 18, the Yankees acquired pitchers Ernie Shore and Dutch Leonard and outfielder Duffy Lewis from Boston for $15,000, Ray Caldwell, and three other players. It was the first of what soon would be a series of transactions between the two clubs.

On paper it looked like a great deal for the Yankees. Before the war Shore and Leonard had been big winners, and Duffy Lewis had starred on three world championship teams. Caldwell, although a talented pitcher, had been nothing but trouble for the past few years, and the Yankees were glad to be rid of him.

But the deal served several other purposes as well. In another attempt to get rid of Frazee, Ban Johnson had recently charged that he'd allowed gambling in Fenway Park. The allegation was true, but it was also true for every other park in the league. Gambling fueled interest in the game.

Frazee and Johnson were on a collision course. The deal with the Yankees helped Frazee's cause, for it gave him some ready cash in case his battle with Johnson resulted in a court case and reinforced the emerging alliance

In 1919 Frank Baker enjoyed his best season with the Yankees, batting .293 with 10 homers and 83 RBIs. It was the last great major league season for the future Hall of Famer, who retired three seasons later.

In the first inning Yankee pitcher George Mogridge, who had enjoyed a reputation as something of a Red Sox killer since throwing the Yankees' first no-hitter in 1917, gave up a leadoff single to Harry Hooper. Jack Barry forced him at second. Then Babe Ruth came to bat.

Earlier that spring, Ruth, who'd grown increasingly enamored of hitting in 1918, had told Frazee and Red Sox manager Ed Barrow that he didn't want to pitch anymore. They weren't sure if his prowess at the plate would continue when baseball returned to normal in 1919, but in the spring the Red Sox seemed to have enough pitching, so Ruth was allowed to move to the outfield. On Opening Day he played left and hit third.

He ripped a Mogridge curveball into the right-center-field gap, where it bounded over Duffy Lewis's head and rolled to the wall. Ruth scored standing up for an inside-the-park home run and a 2–0 Boston lead.

That was plenty. Submarine Boston pitcher Carl Mays, fresh off winning two games in the 1918 World Series, mesmerized the Yankees, scattering four hits as Boston won 10–0. The difference between the world champions and the Yankees appeared to be substantial.

But a week later New York took three of four from Boston, and by the end of May the Red Sox were out of the race. The reason was simple and obvious to everyone: Ruth stunk. In April and May he'd fielded poorly and after a quick start was barely batting .200, demonstrating little power and little ability to hit left-handed pitching. In the meantime, Boston's pitching had collapsed. Barrow and Frazee wanted Ruth to return to the mound.

But the Babe would have none of it. He was balking at the move and complaining about everything. Harry Hooper and other Sox were jealous over Ruth's special treatment. The Red Sox clubhouse was a mess.

Ruth finally started hitting in June and later that season set a new major league record with an incredible 29 home runs. But his slow start and reluctance to return to the mound when Boston's pitching staff collapsed were responsible for Boston's decline to also-ran status in 1919.

The White Sox had bolted out to a big lead, but the Yankees were managing to hang close. Bob Shawkey had returned to form, making up for the disappointing performance of Shore, who was lousy. And the hitting attack was surprisingly potent. The *New York World* even referred

between the Red Sox and Yankees. The transaction also served a symbolic purpose as well. It was a well-placed and very public thumb in the magnate's eye—this was precisely the kind of deal Johnson liked to arrange himself. So Johnson naturally found it galling when the Sox and Yanks acted as if he didn't exist.

The end of the war also brought the return of Huston, the captain turned colonel. He enjoyed being in command and was determined to reassert his authority atop the Yankee empire. But other concerns would soon occupy his time.

Opening Day of 1919 would prove strangely prophetic for the New York Yankees as they played the defending champion Red Sox. In ways no one could yet imagine, their future was on display.

Yankee manager Miller Huggins (left), shown here as manager of the St. Louis Cardinals, confers with New York Giants manager John McGraw and an umpire at the Polo Grounds. The two were neighbors and rivals from 1918 until Huggins's sudden death in 1929. During the Roaring Twenties Huggins's charges replaced McGraw's Giants as kings of New York and baseball itself.

world was tumbling down." Unpopular among his teammates, Mays was beset with all sorts of personal problems, and the deferential treatment of Ruth in the Boston clubhouse had made it a vat of dissension. Mays had simply had it and announced he was going fishing.

Harry Frazee was quick to act. Boston's season was over, but with four teams fighting for a pennant, Mays had value. Ban Johnson considered Mays untouchable and expected Frazee to suspend him. Until he did, Johnson wouldn't approve a trade.

Frazee didn't care. He turned down an offer of $50,000 from the White Sox and remained patient. As August approached, he knew the price would just keep going up.

Finally, on July 30, Frazee weighed all the offers and struck a deal. For $40,000 plus pitcher Allen Russell and sore-armed prospect Bob McGraw, Mays became a Yankee property.

Then Ban Johnson found out. He declared the trade invalid and suspended Mays himself:

Baseball cannot tolerate such a breach of discipline. It was up to the owners of the Boston club to suspend Carl Mays. . . . [W]hen they failed to do so it is my duty as head of the American League to act. Mays will not play with any club until the suspension is raised. He should have reported to the Boston club before they made any trades or sale.

Frazee and the Yankees disagreed. Said Frazee bluntly, "The Boston club is not interested in the action of Mr. Johnson: Pitcher Mays is now the property of the New York club, and they will have to deal with the matter. . . . The deal is closed." Ruppert was somewhat more diplomatic. Citing the unfair hardship the suspension caused his club, Ruppert telegrammed Johnson: "We respectfully ask that you raise this suspension. We make this request in the friendliest spirit. . . ." But just to make sure Johnson understood what was at stake, Ruppert continued ominously: ". . . without, however, waiving our legal rights."

Everyone understood the import of Boston's and New York's defiance of Johnson's authority — except Johnson. The baseball czar was so accustomed to getting his way that he couldn't see the mobs forming outside the winter palace. In a story headlined "Johnson's Belated Action Threatens New Ball War," W. O. McGeehan of the *New York*

to the batting order of Baker, Lewis, Pratt, Pipp, and Bodie as "Murderers' Row," a phrase a later generation of Yankee sluggers would make their own.

Into July the White Sox, Indians, Tigers, and Yankees remained bunched together. Then, in a matter of days, the pennant race, the future of the American League, and, eventually, the face of baseball all changed.

It began in Chicago, as the Red Sox and White Sox squared off against one another. Star Boston pitcher Carl Mays, who'd pitched well all year long but suffered from nonsupport, lost his composure and walked off the field. He told reporters, "I'll never pitch another game for the Red Sox. . . . The entire team is up in the air and things have gone from bad to worse."

Mays never directly addressed his reasons for jumping the team, although years later he admitted, "My whole

Tribune commented, "For some time the resentment against the rule of the Czar of Baseball has been developing. This Mays matter may mean the start of a movement that will have baseball, or at least the American League, run along more democratic lines, as befits the sport of a republic."

"There are not many Czars left."

At first, all the parties fought it out in public. Johnson announced that Mays's suspension would last until the end of the season, and five clubs — Detroit, Cleveland, St. Louis, Washington, and Philadelphia — supported his decision. The Yankees threatened to play Mays anyway and appealed the suspension. Johnson turned them down and ordered his umpires not to allow Mays to play. While Mays worked out with the team, the Yankee players threatened to strike unless he was activated.

On August 3, after a contentious and unproductive meeting with Johnson at Holland House in New York, the Yankees made plans to go to court and request that the injunction be overturned. They'd learned that Johnson owned a piece of Cleveland. That changed everything, and the Yankees knew it. Legally, Johnson was compromised. "Conflict of interest" became the most important phrase in baseball.

Ruppert now viewed Johnson in a new light, particularly in regard to his promises to help the Yankees get some players. No wonder the Yankees hadn't been given a chance to bid on Speaker. Yankee lawyers took affidavits from all interested parties and applied to the New York Supreme Court for an injunction staying the suspension and blocking Johnson from taking any action whatsoever against the club.

They won in a rout. The names Ruppert and Huston meant a lot more in a New York court than that of Ban Johnson. The temporary injunction was granted, and a hearing scheduled for September 5 to consider making it permanent. In the meantime, Mays was free to pitch.

But the delay had proven costly. Since they'd made the deal, the Yankees had played .500 ball and fallen to fourth place, six and a half games behind Chicago. The pennant was slipping away.

Mays made his Yankee debut against the Browns in the Polo Grounds on August 7. After the Yankees dropped the first game 6–3, Mays strode out to the mound to start game two. As the *New York World* reported: "When Mays walked out and started to warm up the shouting roused

the echoes around the bluffs and gave ample evidence that Ruppert's fight has struck a responsive chord in the New York baseball following." Mays then proceeded to bring down the house, striking out the first three St. Louis hitters. The Yankees won 8–2.

Although Mays pitched well, going 9–3 for the remainder of the year, the White Sox took command of the pennant race. By September the court fight between the Yankees and Johnson was all that Yankee fans had to cheer about.

Over the course of a week Supreme Court Justice Robert Wagner — who later served as Harry Frazee's divorce attorney — weighed the evidence. He eventually slapped down Johnson once more. Citing Johnson's financial interest in Cleveland, Wagner determined that the league president did not evince "a desire to do equity to all parties concerned."

The Yankees had won. To Johnson, it was the beginning of the end. Although he'd linger on as American League president for another eight years, his tenure as the most powerful man in baseball was almost at an end. As baseball historian David Voigt later commented, the ruling was "a blow from which he would never fully recover."

And baseball, in ways no one could yet imagine, would never be the same. By chance, Frazee, Ruppert, and Chicago owner Charles Comiskey were all serving their scheduled term on the American League board of directors. They took their appointments as license to strike against Johnson. Ruppert was blunt. "The time has come when the powers of Mr. Johnson should be curtailed," he said. "Ban Johnson will be put out of baseball."

While the Yankees had nudged their way into third place by season's end, the Mays incident had torn the league in two. The Yankees, Boston, and Chicago — dubbed "the Insurrectos" by the press — were united. Opposing them were Johnson and the other five clubs, termed "the Loyal Five."

The two factions battled all winter in the boardroom and in the courts as Johnson tried to deny New York its third-place money and the Insurrectos tried to dump Johnson. Old grudges received belated hearings, and decades of dissatisfaction over Johnson's despotic reign welled up to the surface. Even though the Loyal Five had the votes, the Insurrectos, owing to the happy coincidence of their simulta-

neous service on the board of directors, could control the direction of the debate, if not the precise outcome.

That's what the courts were for. In New York that was an enormous advantage, and in the end it was the only one that mattered. Decades of making campaign donations, cutting backroom deals, and currying the favor of local politicians were designed for just such moments. By the time baseball began the 1920 season, Johnson would be sitting atop a paper throne, stripped of most of his power.

In the meantime, the fallout from that political battle spread far and wide. Or at least from Boston to New York, and from 1919 until the present. For the war between the Insurrectos and Johnson and the Loyal Five would, in the end, turn Babe Ruth into a New York Yankee.

The Yankees' purchase of Ruth from the Boston Red Sox is the most famous transaction in sports, but over time the details have been distorted. In New York it is considered the birth of the Yankee dynasty, the point at which Yankee history begins. In Boston it is still blamed for all the assorted ills that star-crossed franchise has inflicted on its fans.

Both views are wrong.

From the instant the deal was made the circumstances surrounding the sale have been misconstrued, corrupted, and embellished. Myth has overridden the facts to cast Frazee as some kind of malevolent presence while elevating Babe Ruth to divine status.

In truth, there is no "curse" attached to the transaction, either real or imagined, apart from the curse of misinformation that has been foisted off as fact by generations of sportswriters who should have known better and never bothered to check. The Yankees were neither propping up Harry Frazee financially nor entering into an unholy alliance. The deal was not dependent on a loan and mortgage on Fenway Park. The Red Sox franchise was not destroyed by the sale, and it did not finance Frazee's musical *No, No, Nanette*.

The sale of Ruth was, at its core, a baseball deal, albeit a very big one, that at the time represented a considerable risk for both parties. The Yankees were gambling, betting

The site of Yankee Stadium, near the Willets Dam Bridge in the Bronx, as it appeared about twenty years before Colonels Ruppert and Huston chose it as the place to build what would become the most celebrated sports stadium since the Coliseum of ancient Rome.

After World War I, Yankee right-hander Bob Shawkey resumed his role as New York's ace starter, winning 20 games and losing 11. The 1919 season marked the first of a six-season run in which he averaged 18 wins per season while helping lead the Yankees to three pennants.

almost everything on the most intoxicating word in base-ball—"potential." Harry Frazee was simply dealing from what he believed was a position of strength in an attempt to consolidate his position.

From the Yankees' perspective, the acquisition of Ruth, while certainly central to the transformation of the franchise from also-ran to perennial power, was neither the beginning nor the end of that process, for Ruth did not immediately lead the Yankees to a string of championships. During his 15-year career in New York, the team won the World Series only four times—their reputation as base-ball's most dominant team was not truly realized until after Ruth left. In fact, the Yankees won the World Series with *more* regularity after Ruth left New York than they ever did when he was a Yankee—32 percent of the time since 1934 versus 27 percent between 1920 and 1934.

That Ruth changed baseball forever is obvious. He may well be the most important individual in the history of the game, and he is unquestionably the most dominant per-sonality in Yankee history. But Ruth, for all his prodigious

talent, was not enough, by himself, to remake the team.

In the fall and winter of 1919 the relationship between the Insurrectos—New York, Boston, and Chicago—and Ban Johnson and his Loyal Five deteriorated almost daily. Ban Johnson blamed Harry Frazee for all his trouble, refer-ring to him as "the champion wrecker of baseball." The Yankees inadvertently ended up being drawn into Frazee's campaign of resistance and reaped a totally unexpected benefit. Ruppert backed Frazee, but he was also smart enough not to lead the battle. He let Frazee lead the charge while he hung back, exposing neither himself nor his franchise to Johnson's direct wrath. It was better to let that fall on Frazee.

When Frazee purchased the Red Sox in 1917 from Joseph Lannin, he had done so with a series of notes that he planned to pay off with profits from the club. Frazee had the money—he was no small-time theatrical pro-ducer, one of the many misconceptions in his biography, but one of the Great White Way's grand success stories. By 1919 he had ingratiated himself into New York's high soci-ety and consorted with some of the wealthiest and most powerful men in the city.

He viewed the ownership of a baseball team in theatri-cal terms, calling it part of the "amusement business," just as the theater was. But Frazee wasn't stupid. He kept his theater operations separate from his baseball holdings. Each element of his portfolio had to succeed or fail on its own. So far both were succeeding. The Red Sox had made money in 1919, and on December 3 of that year he opened one of his most successful shows to date, *My Lady Friends,* which eventually ran for 228 performances and earned Frazee a weekly profit of more than $3,000.

But earlier in 1919 Frazee and former Boston owner Joseph Lannin had clashed over some disputed payments. Lannin began rattling the legal cages to get Frazee to pay up, while Frazee was distracted by his growing war with Ban Johnson, whom Frazee correctly believed "has made me his particular target."

Yet Frazee had one more concern—Babe Ruth. In spite of his talent, Ruth was a growing problem. His skills were matched only by his ability to cause trouble.

In 1918 Ruth had briefly jumped the Red Sox to join a shipyard league and had balked at pitching. Persuaded to return to the mound, he'd scuffled on the train returning to Boston from Chicago during the 1918 World Series and hurt a finger—he pitched his second game in the Series with a finger on his left hand swollen to twice its size and stained with iodine. After the season, despite having a year remaining on his contract, he'd been a holdout, leading Frazee to comment, "If Ruth doesn't want to work for the Red Sox, we can work out an advantageous trade." Ruth finally signed a new three-year deal for $30,000. But early in 1919 Ruth engaged in a celebrated battle with Red Sox manager Ed Barrow over his repeated curfew violations. His refusal to pitch early in the season had cost the club any chance it had to repeat as world champions in 1919. His subsequent politicking for the removal of Ed Barrow as manager and the reappointment of Jack Barry may have been a factor in Carl Mays's defection. Then, only a week after being feted at Fenway Park on September 19, "Babe Ruth Day," and receiving cash and gifts from fans worth several thousand dollars, Ruth jumped the club. After setting a new home run mark on September 27 by cracking two home runs for a total of 29, the Babe went AWOL, skipping the final game of the season to play in a lucrative exhibition game in Baltimore. All this was in addition to a host of less visible problems, which included car wrecks, repeated public drunkenness, and a scandal-ridden relationship with his wife. Ruth's multiple indiscretions were nearly as impressive as his batting record.

He was a helluva player—that was obvious. But he was also one helluva headache. And despite his spectacular performance in 1919—he had hit .322 and led the league with 29 home runs, 103 runs scored, and 114 RBIs—postwar attendance in Boston was soft. Red Sox fans, with four world championships since 1912, were accustomed to winning. They hadn't finished below .500 since 1908.

Until 1919. Attendance rebounded leaguewide after the war, more than doubling. But in Boston, despite perhaps the most magnificent season by an offensive player to date, attendance was up only 60 percent (and in 1920, *without Ruth,* it barely declined). Ruth alone just didn't do it for Red Sox fans. Boston didn't deserve him.

After the 1919 season Ruth went to California to cash in on some film opportunities. For the second year in a row he was complaining about the contract he'd just signed, telling the press he wanted $20,000 a year or he just might stay in California and take up a career in acting or boxing. After seeing what Ruth could get away with, other Boston players were making similar demands.

Frazee wasn't the only one who viewed Ruth as a problem. On December 31, influential Boston sportswriter Paul Shannon charged that Ruth "has hurt morale considerably. . . . If Ruth makes good on his threat and retires from the game he will be badly missed. But even as big a figure as Ruth is, the public would soon forget all about him. . . . [A] contract is a contract. Right is right in baseball as anything else."

The Boston owner had gone through this before. In the theater he knew just how to treat actors who didn't fulfill contracts. He took the motto "The show must go on" to heart—he simply canned the bad actor and found one who'd work for what he'd been promised. Now his production in Fenway Park was being threatened on two fronts—by Ban Johnson on the outside and from within by Ruth.

Well, not quite on two fronts. Although the press and public didn't know it yet, Frazee had already rid himself of the Ruth problem. On December 26, the Yankees had agreed to buy Ruth for $100,000—$25,000 in cash and three notes for the same amount payable at one-year intervals at 6 percent interest—plus "other considerations." The deal was the most lucrative cash deal in baseball history and conditional on the Yankees' getting Ruth under contract.

Boston's loss would be New York's gain. Start spreading the news.

Babe Ruth, shown here in 1921, was a star in New York even during his years with the Red Sox, when crowds swelled during his pitching appearances. His arrival in New York for the 1920 season was eagerly anticipated, and before long his home run swing had the Polo Grounds fans oohing and aahing whenever he stepped to the plate.

1920–1925
MURDERERS' ROW

Ruppert had had his eye on Ruth since first seeing him at the plate in the Polo Grounds in 1918. After watching Ruth bang the ball all over the same field in 1919, Huston shared his enthusiasm.

They were interested in more than Ruth's obvious skills as a ballplayer. The Red Sox and Giants had trained together during the spring of 1919, and the beat writers covering the Giants had fallen in love with Ruth, not only as a ballplayer but also as a subject — he was good copy, colorful and approachable. They wrote about him at every opportunity, piquing the interest of New York fans.

So when the Red Sox visited the Polo Grounds in 1919, all New York came out to take another look at a player they'd previously known as a pitcher. They fawned over him and turned out in droves to watch him play. Unlike Red Sox fans, Yankee fans didn't really care about winning — yet. Seeing Ruth swing the bat, even if he beat their team, was pastime enough. Ruppert and Huston had a similar reaction, but they also took note of the size of the crowd.

Ruth was not like any other man who had played the game. He was the first to swing from his heels and *try* to hit home runs, to do something on purpose that had always seemed accidental. He didn't give a damn if he struck out, and neither did the fans. The next best thing to seeing Ruth strike out was to see him swing and miss, his body twisting and sometimes falling to the ground as a collective "aah" spread through the stands.

But when he connected, it was a revelation. Others had hit home runs before, but no one had hit them like Ruth did. His home runs were a distinctly different kind of hit, unique enough to create an entirely different category. It took a new adjective, "Ruthian," to describe them.

Even if Ruth didn't always hit the ball very far (although he often did), his home runs seemed to take an entirely new route on their way over the fence. They *soared,* nearly disappearing from sight before dropping over the fence. Ruth's home runs were exalted, uplifting experiences that meant more to fans than any runs they were responsible for. A Babe Ruth home run was an event unto itself, one that meant anything was possible.

Babe Ruth wasn't the first guy to hit home runs. In 1884 Ned Williamson had hit 27. Buck Freeman cracked 25 for Washington in 1899. And just a few years earlier, in 1915, Gavvy Cravath had hit 24 to lead the 1915 Philadelphia Phillies to the National League pennant. But the freakish dimensions of their home ballparks helped all these players. Their home runs were unintentional byproducts of architecture that barely reached the stands. None captured the imagination of fans.

Ruth did. His home runs weren't just hits. They were events, out of scale when compared to those hit by other players. It seemed as if he could strike them at will.

Babe Ruth was the right man coming along at precisely the right time. His emergence as a hitter coincided with changes to both the rules of the game and the manufacture of the ball, factors that at first only he was able to use to advantage. In February 1920, a host of "freak" pitches were outlawed, such as Russ Ford's signature emery ball, the shine ball, and the spitter, although practitioners of the spitter were allowed to use the pitch until retirement. In short, hitters gained a considerable advantage when

pitchers were no longer allowed to doctor the baseball in any fashion.

In regard to the baseball itself, there was and still remains considerable debate about whether a livelier so-called jackrabbit ball was put into use, either in 1920 or shortly thereafter. While that debate can never be resolved definitively, anecdotal evidence suggests that it was so—from 1918 to 1921 total home runs more than quadrupled. Ruth wasn't the only guy hitting them.

New York City was precisely the right place for Ruth. The dual tragedies of the war and the recent plague of Spanish influenza, which killed half a million Americans, had left the nation saddened and pessimistic. But now society was on the rebound, the postwar economy was booming, lifestyles were changing, and Americans were ready to cut loose and have some fun.

New York City emerged in the 1920s as the nation's commercial and cultural center. And Ruth was New York incarnate—uncouth and raw, flamboyant and flashy, oversized, out of scale, and absolutely unstoppable. He towered over baseball like the Manhattan skyline. Compared to Ruth, all else was in shadow.

His doughy face, dark, broad features, and massive torso drew fans toward him. The simple fact that he was neither English nor Irish made it easy for fans of other ethnicities to identify with him, and New York City, more than ever before, was still a city of immigrants, a place they had made their own. Manhattan was more than Fifth Avenue and Wall Street. The heart of the city was where the people lived, in dozens of ethnic enclaves such as Little Italy, Hell's Kitchen, and Chinatown.

Ruth was one of them, a street urchin raised in a Baltimore orphanage. His behavioral incorrigibility somehow made him even more endearing, because Ruth, despite his many personal faults, was never cruel. There was no malice in his behavior, simply unchecked enthusiasms run amuck.

When New York permitted Sunday baseball for the first time in 1919, the makeup of the crowd was forever changed. One reporter noted that the fan base changed from the "semi-idle" to "the men from the dock and factories . . . their wives and children . . . thousands of fans who never in their lives had been to a big league game." They adopted Ruth. Italians in the neighborhood around the Polo Grounds dubbed him "Bambino," and even African Americans claimed him as one of their own. From the moment Ruth emerged as a star the black press wrote about him matter-of-factly as a "Negro" and "sepia star." Decades after Ruth's death the black press still made frequent references to Ruth's "secret" black heritage. While the best Ruth scholarship thoroughly refutes this belief, it still has some credence in the African-American community today.

Ruth was baseball's "Everyman." He belonged to everyone. But he would play for the Yankees in New York.

For better or worse, Babe Ruth created the essential character of the team, the template against which all other Yankees would be measured, and the standard of both performance and personality. While the Yankees would often have players who embodied one or more of Ruth's traits — Mickey Mantle's unmatched, raw power, Reggie Jackson's ability to seize both the moment and the headlines, Derek Jeter's cross-ethnic appeal — no one in baseball, whether for the Yankees or any other team, has ever been like Ruth.

When you say "New York Yankees," Ruth is the player you see. He is the reason children grow up not just wanting to be a baseball player but, like Derek Jeter, wanting to be a New York Yankee.

Since the end of the 1919 season Boston owner Harry Frazee had been quietly making it known that Ruth was available. The White Sox had offered Joe Jackson and $60,000 for Ruth, but Frazee had to see what the well-heeled Yankees would offer.

The standard account of the transaction appeared some 30 years later. In his ghostwritten autobiography, *My Fifty Years in Baseball,* 82-year-old Ed Barrow, who had fallen on hard times and was being supported in his retirement by Red Sox owner Tom Yawkey, repeats the fiction that Frazee was broke. Barrow claims he advised his boss to take money over players because "there is nobody on that ball club I want." That's an odd statement about a team that had just finished 13 games ahead of Ruth's Red Sox. Pipp, Pratt, Peckinpaugh, Bodie, Duffy Lewis, Muddy Ruel, and Bob Shawkey were among the best players in the game and could have played for any team in baseball.

Barrow's account simply doesn't square with a number of known facts and contradicts stories he had told others years before. Frazee would tell the press that he took money

instead of players because "no club could give me his equivalent in players without wrecking itself." He claimed he would have had "three or four stars in exchange for him. What club could stand a drain like that?" Good question, because none could. Ruth's outlandish performance was off the scale. Only the Yankees could meet his price.

One hundred thousand dollars was a lot of money in 1920. Measured against the consumer price index, it would be the equivalent of nearly $1 million today. But according to another standard, measuring wealth in comparison to the gross national product, Ruth's sale price is equivalent to almost $4 million. Few baseball owners could afford that.

As soon as Frazee and the Yankees agreed to terms, the Yankees sent Huggins to California to meet with Ruth, get his name on a contract, and make it official. After some haggling, and some admonitions from Huggins to behave himself, Ruth agreed to fulfill his existing contract, and the Yankees agreed to give him a $20,000 bonus, payable over the next two seasons.

With Ruth on board, all parties could now go public. Ruppert and Huston announced the deal late on the afternoon of January 5, 1920, and Ruppert indicated that the political problems he and Frazee had been having with Johnson were a huge factor in the deal. As soon as he made the official announcement, he hurried to add: "This is our answer to those who would like to drive us out of baseball. We are no longer afraid of Johnson or care what he thinks. Ruth will be with the Yankees when the season opens. That fact is settled."

But there were other reasons Ruppert pulled the trigger that went beyond the close relationship between the two clubs, their alliance against Johnson, and Huston's personal friendship with Frazee. On January 16, Prohibition was scheduled to go into effect. Ruppert already had his millions, but his brewery had to go into mothballs. His other pursuits — yachting, art, and dog breeding — were costly pastimes. Baseball had become his business.

Owning the Yankees would take on a larger role in his life. To the public, he was no longer Jacob Ruppert, beer baron, but Jacob Ruppert, baseball baron. His ballclub would soon dominate the local market just as his beer had. The Ruth deal, an investment in infrastructure, reflected his commitment to the enterprise. Just as joining Tammany

Hall had given him an edge in selling beer in New York, acquiring Ruth gave him an edge in selling baseball.

Contrary to common belief, reaction to the trade of Ruth in both Boston and New York was mixed. In Boston the deal was both applauded and derided in the press, as many were willing to admit that Ruth, for all his ability, had become difficult to deal with. A cartoon in the *Boston Post* entitled "The Bull in Frazee's China Shop" showed Ruth wreaking havoc and Ruppert holding the door open, waving a bag of money, and saying, "This way out, Harry." Players from both teams were surprisingly close-mouthed over the deal. No one on the Red Sox made a public comment. Yankee reaction was tempered—Bob Shawkey offered only a lukewarm but optimistic "Well, I guess we're headed for a pennant."

The New York press was more positive about the deal, but their enthusiasm was dampened by the feeling that in regard to the Yankees something always seemed to go wrong. There was a consensus that Ruth should be enough to deliver the 1920 pennant to the Yankees, but the emphasis was on the word *should*. The press was thrilled, however, with the theatrics of the deal. In the wake of Johnson's interference in the Mays deal, acquiring Ruth rubbed Johnson's nose in it. Nevertheless, many questions about the team and about Ruth himself remained unanswered.

Few of those questions were answered in the spring of 1920. Although Ruth hit well and drew huge crowds, he was still a problem child, and his acquisition still represented a significant risk. His New York career would mimic his experience at Baltimore's St. Mary's Industrial School for Boys—Miller Huggins and Ed Barrow would have to take turns playing Brother Matthias, Ruth's mentor at reform school.

On March 20 in Jacksonville, the Yankees fell to the Dodgers 5–1. Ruth had a bad game and struck out twice. Local fans razzed him, and after the game Ruth, who'd been playing left field, decided he'd had enough.

He scaled the wall in front of the bleachers and went after a fan. Others scattered as Ruth's target, a small man just over five feet tall, held his ground. As the Babe drew near, his antagonist drew a knife. Ruth pulled up but didn't back off.

Fortunately, teammate Ernie Shore was sitting in the stands in his street clothes. Shore got between the two men, and while he held Ruth at bay told the man with the knife to get lost. A possible tragedy was averted.

Huston had watched the proceedings from his box, and he didn't like it. Ruth was a big investment who wasn't worth anything dead. "That kind of stuff will have to be stopped right away," he said. "If criticism down here gets under Ruth's skin, what will he do in the big league parks?" That remained an open question.

There were other problems that spring too as Ruth's arrival coincided with the traditional run of Yankee bad luck. Frank Baker's wife had passed away in the off-season, and he voluntarily retired. Utilityman Chick Fewster was beaned and almost died. Ping Bodie was in Huggins's doghouse and would eventually jump the team. While the addition of Ruth should have guaranteed a pennant, the loss of those three players made that unlikely, no matter how well Ruth played.

And Ruth was already making demands. He knew the Polo Grounds well enough to know that left field was the sun field and that right, owing to its short porch, was difficult for a novice outfielder. Ruth "asked" to play center field, and Huggins agreed.

He had little choice. Few did when it came to the Babe. The relationship between the player and the manager, although romanticized in many later accounts, was problematic. Both were stubborn and keenly aware of just how far they pushed the other. Ruth knew he didn't really answer to Huggins—his bosses were Ruppert and Huston. The manager was caught in between, somehow trying to control the incorrigible slugger without sending him crying to the front office.

The situation was made worse by Huggins's own precarious position. Knowing that Huston wanted to fire Huggins, Ruth had an ally against the manager, at least for a while. And during spring training Huggins gave the players ample reason to ask for his scalp.

The Yankees' third-place finish in 1919 had earned the club a cut of the World Series money. Huggins divvied up their take and gave full shares to the groundskeeper, the trainer, and the two club secretaries. As *The Sporting News* noted, "As soon as the allotments were made known, shrieks of distress came from the players." They threatened to strike until Ruppert and Huston eventually quieted the discontent by writing out checks for $35 to every man on the team to make up the difference, but Huggins's authority remained tenuous.

The Yankees opened the season on April 14 in Philadelphia. By game's end it was clear that Ruth alone would not be the answer to New York's problems.

Playing center and batting cleanup, Ruth was on deck when Wally Pipp blasted a first-inning home run to give New York a 1–0 lead. Ruth singled in his first Yankee at bat, off the A's Scott Perry, but was left stranded.

The game turned in the bottom of the eighth. With the score tied at 1–1, the A's put two on with two out. Then A's second baseman "Jumping" Joe Dugan lifted a fly ball to center field.

The highest-paid player in the game drifted back with the ball—and drifted and drifted as the routine fly kept carrying. By the time he realized the ball was going over his head, it was too late. As the *Tribune* described it, Ruth then "set himself in an artistic pose," and the ball bounced

Manager Miller Huggins (left) views a spring training game with owner Jacob Ruppert (right) in St. Petersburg, Florida, in 1925. Huggins's tenure with the Yankees was both tempestuous and glorious. He led New York to six pennants and three world championships while locking horns with Babe Ruth for most of his dozen years at the helm.

out of his glove. Running hard with two out, both baserunners scored. Error on Ruth. The A's won 3–1.

Ruth struck out three times in his second game as a Yankee, although New York won. Then Ruth made his return to Boston for a three-game set against the Red Sox.

Boston fans hardly broke down the gates to get a glimpse of their newly departed star. Only 10,000 fans welcomed him back. And while Ruth received an ovation when he stepped to the plate for the first time, he did little damage as Boston shut out the vaunted Yankees and won 6–0.

In contrast, Fenway Park was filled to the brim the next day for the return of Carl Mays. One Boston paper said he was "roasted unmercifully" upon his return, and Boston won again, 8–3. The Red Sox went on to sweep the Series, as Ruth remained quiet. Early returns on the big deal favored Boston.

Ruth made his New York debut on April 22 against Philadelphia before 22,000 fans—13,000 of whom paid a dollar and the rest 50 cents. It was a big crowd, but only slightly over half the capacity of the Polo Grounds.

As W. O. McGeehan noted in the *Tribune*, "A load of hard luck landed on their necks." During batting practice Ruth tried to wow the crowd with some tape-measure home

YANKEE AMERICAN LEAGUE
RBI LEADERS

1916   **Wally Pipp, 99**

1920   **Babe Ruth, 137**

1921   **Babe Ruth, 171**

1923   **Babe Ruth, 131**

1925   **Bob Meusel, 138**

1926   **Babe Ruth, 145**

1927   **Lou Gehrig, 175**

1928   **Babe Ruth and Lou Gehrig, 142**

1930   **Lou Gehrig, 174**

1931   **Lou Gehrig, 184**

1934   **Lou Gehrig, 165**

1941   **Joe DiMaggio, 125**

1945   **Nick Etten, 111**

1948   **Joe DiMaggio, 155**

1956   **Mickey Mantle, 130**

1960   **Roger Maris, 112**

1961   **Roger Maris, 142**

1985   **Don Mattingly, 145**

runs. So far in the young season those had been the only home runs he'd been able to hit.

On one big swing he not only missed the ball but fell to the ground in obvious pain and had to be helped to the bench. He'd separated his ribs. But the show had to go on. Wrapped in tape, Ruth trotted out to center field to begin the game.

He came to bat in the bottom of the first, struck out on three weak swings, then nearly collapsed and had to be half-carried to the dressing room. Some debut. *The Sporting News* couldn't help but comment, "The Yankees' ancient hoodoo is still on the job." Ruth missed several games as Ping Bodie conveniently returned to take his place. On May 1, the Yankees were a rather pathetic 4–7, and Ruth had done nothing. Meanwhile, the ruthless Red Sox were leading the league with a 10–2 mark.

Then Ruth finally got on track. He cracked his first home run of the season against Boston on May 1, a stupendous drive that cleared the right-field roof in the Polo Grounds.

It was like a dam breaking, both on the field and at the turnstiles. For the next three months Ruth rarely went more than three or four games without smacking out another home run, and fans began to pour into the Polo Grounds. Despite a capacity of nearly 39,000, on some days another 15,000 fans or more had to be turned away. On the road the frenzy was nearly as intense.

One reason for Ruth's turnaround, apart from his good health, was the emergence of Bob Meusel as an offensive threat. When Ruth hit fourth, usually behind Pipp, pitchers soon learned that it was safer to walk Ruth, or at least pitch around him, than it was to give him anything to hit.

But Huggins started doctoring his lineup and eventually moved Ruth up to third, after Peckinpaugh and Pipp, with Meusel hitting fourth after Ruth. Meusel flourished in the role. While he was no Babe Ruth (no one was), Meusel instantly became one of the top six or eight sluggers in the league. Ruth reached base more than 300 times in 1920. When the opposition pitched around him, Meusel made them pay.

The change in the batting order coincided with a Yankee surge and a Ruth hitting streak. Beginning on May 25, the Yanks won 18 of 20 to pull into first place just ahead of

Chicago as Ruth embarked on a tear, eventually hitting in 26 consecutive games and lifting his average to nearly .400.

That got everyone's attention, including Ban Johnson and the New York Giants. Johnson, still smarting from his losses in court, now tried to extract revenge with one final ploy to retain his power. He encouraged Giants owner Charles Stoneham to cancel the Yankees' $60,000 annual lease of the Polo Grounds, effective at the end of the season. In return, Johnson offered to take over the lease in the name of the American League, boot the Yankees, and allow Stoneham to handpick a new ownership group and select a new member to the National Commission.

Stoneham was intrigued. The Yankees were outdrawing his team, and he disliked divvying up the lucrative Sunday dates. He announced that the Yanks would have to find new headquarters for 1921.

But Johnson had overplayed his hand. The Yankees held the mortgage to Fenway Park and apparently threatened more legal action. Stoneham didn't want to get dragged into Johnson's lost cause and lose a tenant. Within days a new lease was signed through 1922, but the two colonels knew the time had come to finally get their own park.

The Yankees, for all their potency, couldn't keep hold of first place. The White Sox, still several months away from the revelation over the 1919 World Series that would rock baseball to its core, pulled ahead. With a batting attack led by Eddie Collins and Joe Jackson and a pitching staff that featured four 20-game winners, the Sox were simply deeper than the Yankees.

Then what *The Sporting News* called their "Old Jinx" reemerged. In mid-July, Lewis, Peckinpaugh, Aaron Ward, Bob Shawkey, and George Mogridge all went down for a few days with injuries. Ruth nearly kept them afloat by himself. He tied his own home run mark of 29 on July 15, broke it the next day, and then kept going, finishing the month with a total of 37. But new injuries, this time to Carl Mays and Hank Thormhalen, gave Chicago and surging Cleveland an edge.

Huggins became the scapegoat, at least in the minds of some, as every move he made and every one he didn't was criticized. And then the Old Jinx took effect in ever more creative and tragic ways. Ruth escaped injury in a car accident, then was forced out of the lineup for a few days when a bee sting caused an infection to his arm. He "slumped" along with the rest of the club in August, resuming mere mortal status. Then Ping Bodie broke his ankle, and Yank fans received a healthy scare in early September when an erroneous report was aired that Ruth had been killed in a car accident, a rumor eventually credited to gamblers.

All that paled in comparison with a genuine tragedy. On August 16 in the Polo Grounds, Carl Mays unleashed the pitch that killed, striking Cleveland shortstop Ray Chapman in the head and fracturing his skull.

It was a hot, muggy August day aching to rain. Both clubs were in the thick of the pennant race. Carl Mays was in search of career victory number 100. Entering the fifth inning, Cleveland led 3–0. Shortstop Ray Chapman led off, coming to the plate for the third time that day.

His first two times up he'd bunted, for a sacrifice in the first — his 34th sacrifice of the year — and he popped up in the third.

Mays was thinking bunt again, thinking up and in, for such pitches are the most difficult to bunt. He wound up, turning and bending at the waist so that his upper body was parallel to the ground, whipping his right arm up and back, perpendicular to the ground. As he stepped forward, his arm whipped down and forward, knuckles nearly scraping the ground, releasing the ball from about the seven o'clock position.

Mays was the only so-called submarine pitcher in the game at the time, and part of his success was due to the extreme angle at which the ball came toward the plate. He threw hard. His fastball rose, but he could also take something off and make the ball sink, or make it curve sharply. Since reaching the major leagues in 1915, he'd become one of the best pitchers in the game. Mays was earning his money in New York.

He was also one of the most disliked players in baseball, a person with few friends in the game, even among his own teammates. Physically imposing, Mays's temperament had always left him ostracized. On the field he was belligerent, argumentative, and ultracompetitive. He berated teammates for errors and showed them up on the field. In the clubhouse the articulate, intelligent pitcher had little in common with his teammates, who considered him something of a Simon Pure. He didn't drink, smoke, or sleep around and held those who did — virtually every other man on the team — in haughty contempt. In baseball he was a social misfit.

Yet he had a reputation as a pitcher who would do anything to win, including pitching inside, as all pitchers must. Mays regularly led the league in hit batsmen, owing in part to his unique delivery, which hitters were not accustomed to.

Mays was well aware of his reputation. He didn't deny occasionally throwing at hitters, and he knew how his teammates felt about him, once telling an interviewer, "I have always wondered why I have encountered this antipathy from so many people wherever I have been. And I have never been able to explain it, even to myself."

Mays's pitch rose from his hand toward catcher Muddy Ruel. Chapman crouched over the plate. The ball rode up and in as Chapman leaned in ever so slightly.

There was a crack, and Mays saw the ball bounding toward him. He fielded it and threw to first baseman Wally Pipp, who made the putout and started to throw the ball around the horn, then froze and stared toward home. Chapman was on his knees, blood coming from his left ear, struggling to stand.

The pitch, which catcher Muddy Ruel had thought was a strike and that Mays later claimed was a curve, had hit Chapman squarely on the left temple.

Everyone knew Chapman was hurt, but no one knew how badly. The umpire called into the stands for a doctor. Chapman finally stood and, with some assistance, made his way off the field. The game resumed. Cleveland won 4–3.

Chapman lost consciousness shortly after leaving the field and underwent emergency surgery to relieve pressure on the brain caused by bleeding and swelling from a three-and-a-half-inch depressed skull fracture. He died the next day. Mays became known forevermore as the man who threw the pitch that killed.

Such a thing had never happened before in the major leagues, although deaths from thrown balls in semipro and minor league baseball were not unknown. A ball thrown from the pitcher's mound to the catcher travels that distance in only three-tenths of a second, giving the hitter precious little time to get out of the way. Most do. Chapman didn't.

Had another pitcher been on the mound, the incident would have been viewed as the tragic accident it probably was. But Mays's reputation cast it in a different light. Already ostracized, he became a pariah.

The incident shook the Yankees, who lost not only that game but also five of the next seven as all baseball and much of America debated Mays's intent. When the Yankees went on the road in mid-September, Cleveland threatened to boycott the games if Mays played. But Ban Johnson wisely quelled the threat, and the Yankees wisely skipped over Mays's turn in Cleveland. He remained effective for the remainder of the year, but in the end both Chicago and Cleveland pulled ahead as the Yankees fell off the pace.

The pennant looked as if it were headed to Chicago once more, but Cleveland surged after losing Chapman, and on September 28, the Black Sox scandal, a conspiracy to fix the 1919 World Series at the behest of gamblers for financial gain, broke wide open. Eight players, including Joe Jackson, were indicted by a Cook County grand jury. Comiskey immediately suspended all eight. Over the closing days of the season, the depleted White Sox dropped two of their final three games while the Indians won four of six to capture the pennant. The Yankees finished third behind both clubs, three games back with a record of 95–59. Although the Black Sox scandal didn't help the Yankees in 1920, and certainly didn't help baseball, the exposé had a tremendous impact on the fortunes of the club. The White Sox were an emerging dynasty. Yet the suspensions that resulted from the scandal castrated the club. Chicago wouldn't contend for a pennant for another 20 years. No team would benefit more from the White Sox demise than the Yankees. Chicago's withdrawal from the marketplace left New York as Boston's only viable trading partner, a position the Yankees would soon take advantage of.

It had been one helluva season, featuring two of the game's most regrettable tragedies amid the greatest offensive season by a player to date. In the final weeks of the season Ruth had surged again and resumed hitting home runs at a record pace. He finished with an incredible 54 and led the major leagues with 158 runs and 137 RBIs as well. He wasn't quite a one-man team, but he was the closest thing to it baseball had ever seen.

He helped lift attendance leaguewide. The Yankees alone gained more than 600,000 fans for a total of nearly

Babe Ruth became such a big star in New York that he eventually signed a $100,000 movie contract. America fell in love with Ruth's home runs and personable style and couldn't get enough of the Bambino, on or off the field.

1.3 million, the first team ever to draw seven figures, and league attendance jumped 1.2 million as fans everywhere came out to see Ruth.

Many baseball historians have since credited Ruth with "saving" baseball in the wake of the Black Sox scandal. He didn't. Baseball didn't need saving after the scandal broke because Ruth had already inoculated baseball against any lasting taint caused by the Black Sox. Fans were far more excited by the prospect of Ruth hitting home runs than they were upset about a few ballplayers throwing games.

As soon as the regular season ended, the battles off the field commenced anew. The war with Ban Johnson resumed and reached its inevitable conclusion.

The final battle centered on the so-called Lasker Plan, which proposed to replace the ruling three-man National Commission, from which Johnson gained his authority. The Insurrectos, in consort with the National League, put a

figurative gun to Johnson's head over the issue. If he didn't go along, they'd break off and form their own 12-team league.

The threat was more bravado than anything else, but it had its desired effect. On November 15, the Lasker Plan was adopted, and in a final display of power, the Insurrectos and the National League installed their own candidate, Judge Kenesaw Mountain Landis, as the first commissioner of baseball. Johnson would linger on as AL president, but the Czar had been toppled.

Meanwhile, the Yankees kept pressing on with on-field issues. Earlier in the year Harry Sparrow, the club's long-time business manager (roughly the equivalent of today's general manager), had passed away. In the interim, Miller Huggins had done both jobs, neither to the satisfaction of Huston, who was still hoping to install his own guy. That's where Ed Barrow came in.

No one in baseball could match Barrow's background and experience, which ranged from field manager duties in Detroit and Boston to the presidency of the International League. He had been a consummate wheeler-dealer, running dozens of players through the Boston organization. Barrow knew everybody in baseball, from the players to the front office. For over two decades he had proven he knew how to win, spot talent, and make money.

He'd also just made a major screwup, which he was anxious to put behind him before anyone realized what he'd done. Earlier in the year he'd spotted a hot prospect and loaned the player to the Portsmouth club in the Virginia League, working out a gentleman's agreement with Portsmouth owner Ed Dawson, who agreed to return the prospect to Boston at the end of the year. Instead, the player —all-time great Pie Traynor—was sold to the Pittsburgh Pirates.

Barrow howled and went running to Ban Johnson, who still served as league president. But the Czar was in no mood to do Boston any favors and allowed the sale to stand.

Barrow saw the writing on the wall. Johnson was going to screw the Boston franchise any chance he had. The next few years were not going to be fun. Barrow wanted out while the getting was good and his reputation was still intact. When the Yankees asked Frazee for permission to hire Barrow, Frazee told Barrow, who lived in New York, to go.

Barrow and Huggins made the perfect team. Huggins already had his hands full keeping Ruth on track and handling a ballclub known for its rowdy behavior. Barrow's presence freed him from a host of administrative duties, and Barrow had no problem playing the bad guy on disciplinary matters. Moreover, Ruppert and Huston gave Barrow an almost limitless budget. The last time he'd been given carte blanche, with Boston in 1918, he'd worked out a purchase and trade with the A's that had delivered the pennant to Boston.

He got right to work for the Yankees. In an age-old baseball tradition, he knew the personnel and needs of his old club best and set out to work out a deal with Boston. On December 15, he talked Boston manager Hugh Duffy into a trade, sending catcher Muddy Ruel, Del Pratt, Sammy

Yankee Stadium under construction in the summer of 1922. Jacob Ruppert rejected a site at 163rd Street and Amsterdam Avenue for a ten-acre plot in the Bronx, across the Harlem River from the Polo Grounds. Osborn Engineering Company of Cleveland, the firm that built Fenway Park and Braves Field in Boston, was hired to build the new stadium.

Let WHITE Build it of CONCRETE

1925

Vick, and pitcher Hank Thormhalen to Boston for catcher Wally Schang, infielder Mike McNally, and two pitchers, Waite Hoyt and Harry Harper.

The deal was so one-sided that it was almost beyond belief—for Boston. Ruel was the best young catcher in baseball, Pratt was second only to the A's Eddie Collins as a second baseman, Vick was a solid regular, and Thormhalen had star potential. Schang was all right, but McNally was a backup, Harper hadn't yet proved he could win, and Hoyt, although only 21, had performed poorly in 1920, been hurt in 1919, and still threatened to become a holdout. Some members of the press openly wondered whether Barrow was still doing Frazee's bidding. One Boston paper offered that the real reason behind the trade was "a few inside family matters on the Yankee club. . . . [T]here are wheels within wheels here and it seems that they rotate to the greater glory and team strength of the Red Sox."

But Barrow knew what he was doing, as he would prove again and again in several subsequent deals with Boston, many of which initially appeared to benefit Boston. Barrow was a consummate evaluator of talent. He knew that Fenway Park, even then, was hard on young pitchers, though it was a great place for a young hurler to learn how to pitch, if not win. Freed from Boston and pitching in the relative spaciousness of the Polo Grounds (and later, Yankee Stadium), pitchers with talent thrived. Barrow had seen what Mays did after coming to New York. He expected the same from Hoyt and Harper.

While Huggins and Barrow focused on the team on the field, Ruppert and Huston were concerned with the field itself. Being a tenant of the Giants' was uncomfortable at best. But the two colonels' search for a place to play had been almost as difficult as that of their two predecessors. Tammany still pulled the strings.

In February they announced with great fanfare that they had finally secured a location for their own ballpark. After turning down a site at 163rd Street and Amsterdam Avenue, they purchased a 10-acre plot for $500,000 in the Bronx just across the Harlem River from the Polo Grounds. Occupied by a lumberyard, the land was owned by the estate of William Waldorf Astor. Cleveland's Osborn Engineering Company, the same firm that built Fenway Park and Braves Field, had already drawn up plans for the ballpark.

The new park, similar in design to the Yale Bowl, was designed to be fully enclosed, although Ruppert admitted that at first he would build on only three sides, leaving the outfield open for temporary bleachers. Nevertheless, the park would easily be the biggest in baseball, seating over 55,000 fans. They hoped to begin construction in May.

Despite Ruppert's close connections with Tammany, he still had to pay homage to the machine. A series of delays, including procrastination by the city over the closing of Cromwell Avenue and 158th Street, eventually pushed groundbreaking back a full year, until May 1922, when, to no one's surprise, a well-connected New York firm, White Construction, was named contractor. After that, things went smoothly.

With Chicago out of the way, New York's task in 1921 got a whole lot easier. Only the Indians seemed capable of keeping a pennant away from the Yankees. Or the Yankees themselves.

Although Prohibition had taken effect the previous year, it hardly dampened the public's taste for alcohol. Before Prohibition, New York supported 18,000 saloons. Afterward there were 35,000 speakeasies. It was still easy to get a drink anywhere, particularly if one had a little money and a little notoriety.

For the Yankee players, who had both, Prohibition mattered not at all. During spring training in Shreveport, Louisiana, the team was reported to be out and about town virtually every night, usually quite late, usually quite drunk, and usually led on their raucous parade by Babe Ruth.

The Yankees served notice on Opening Day that nothing could dampen their prospects. The Polo Grounds was filled to capacity, and another 15,000 fans were turned away. Carl Mays, who showed an amazing capacity to continue his stellar career after Ray Chapman's death, scattered three hits and even knocked out three of his own. Ruth went five for five, and the Yankees romped to an 11–1 win.

They were much improved. Hoyt gave them another dependable arm. Frank Baker was still valuable, if not a star. And hitting behind Ruth, Bob Meusel gave the Yankees the most powerful one-two punch in baseball.

The Yankees hit stride in May, locked arms with Cleveland, and the two clubs never looked back. The pennant would reside in either Cleveland or New York.

THE STADIUM

There ought to be a sign out front that says, "Baseball History Made Here."

Yankee Stadium is the Babe Ruth of ballparks, the unforgettable, oversized, off-the-scale standard that changed everything. Even the name made it clear that this place would be unlike any that preceded it. While concrete-and-steel ballparks had been in vogue for nearly two decades, Yankee Stadium, with an eventual capacity of more than 70,000 — nearly twice that of any other park — was an exponential leap in form and scale. Babe Ruth was the biggest drawing card in baseball, in the biggest city, at a time when baseball teams derived virtually all their revenue from ticket sales. The Stadium provided the Yankees with a source of income that no other team could match. It would have been out of scale in any other city, but the Stadium fit New York.

The design and construction of the Stadium was a group effort. Ruppert's only admonition was to make it big. The enormous yet essentially utilitarian plan is credited to Cleveland's Osborn Engineering Company, yet the name of no single architect is attached to the facility. Its parentage, like Ruth's, is communal.

The contract to build Yankee Stadium was awarded to the White Construction Company on May 5, 1922, for a flat fee of $2.5 million, with the directive that it had to be finished by Opening Day of 1923. This deadline caused the design to be scaled back, for in the original the triple-decked stands were supposed to enclose the park completely. The more modest version still required the removal of 45,000 cubic yards of earth, 3 million board feet of lumber used for concrete forms, 20,000 yards of concrete, 800 tons of re-bar, 2,200 tons of structural steel, 13,000 yards of topsoil, 116,000 square feet of sod, 950,000 board feet of lumber for the bleachers, and 1 million brass screws — numbers as awe-inspiring as 714 home runs and 26 world championships. Completed in a remarkable 284 days, the Stadium opened on April 18, 1923. Baseball would never be the same.

Every other park in baseball had been built for the Dead Ball Era, with fences either so far away they were nearly impossible to reach or so close they provided little challenge to a slugger like Ruth. Yankee Stadium was not built for the game that was, but for the game that baseball was becoming, the game of power and offense. It was the first modern ballpark.

It is no coincidence that the Yankees won their first championship in their first year in the Stadium, and that the Stadium is the only constant in every world championship the team has won. It provides an unmatched home-field advantage. While Yankee sluggers skilled enough to pull the ball hard down the lines can reach its fences, its expansive outfield enables pitchers to succeed by keeping the ball in the middle of the park. Both skills, once learned, are just as useful elsewhere. The Yankees have never had to retool their game or style of play on the road. But many other clubs (the Red Sox in Fenway Park being the most notorious example) have found themselves caught in between, shackled by a ballpark that demands a particular style of play that doesn't always travel well.

The Stadium has evolved with the game. Fences were moved in and out, seating was increased, the scoreboard was changed, lights were installed in 1946, and various other improvements were made. Its adaptability to other uses has made it an even more valuable financial asset. Some 30 championship fights have taken place in the Stadium, as well as college and professional football, Negro League baseball, conventions, political rallies, and religious ceremonies, including visits by Pope Paul VI in 1965 and John Paul II in 1979 and even a mass wedding ceremony held by Sun Jung Moon's Unification Church.

The 1974–75 renovation changed the Stadium dramatically — by altering the dimensions and moving the monuments off the field — but retained its advantages. It helped spark a rejuvenation of the franchise, and in subsequent seasons the wisdom of the reconstruction has been proven over and over again.

But beyond all this, Yankee Stadium also provides the perfect stage for this team. The stands wrap around the field like some updated Globe Theatre, and on the field below, everything baseball seems enhanced. Yankee Stadium, despite its name, is still at heart a ballpark, made for the game in New York. When one thinks of the greatest players in the game, and the greatest moments, one sees them in Yankee Stadium. Looking across the field, it somehow still seems possible to witness the grace of DiMaggio, the power of Gehrig and Ruth, even though they departed long ago.

Ruth was, well, Ruthian. More than 80 years later his performances in 1920 and 1921 are still the standards against which any subsequent offensive performance in baseball must be measured. Although many players have hit for a higher average, scored more runs, collected more RBIs, and cracked more home runs, none has ever come close to Ruth's aggregate performance over those two seasons.

Physically, Ruth was at his peak, a strapping six-foot-two and 220 pounds of still mostly muscle. His youth and exuberance burned off the extra calories and alcohol—he had the constitution of a Clydesdale and had yet to gain the weight that would later make him look cartoonish. In fact, during Ruth's first three or four seasons on the Yankees, Huggins claimed that Ruth was the second-fastest man on the club, behind only Bob Meusel. True. For in addition to his slugging, Ruth outperformed such renowned fly boys as Tris Speaker and Eddie Collins by cracking 16 triples in 1921 and stealing 17 bases—tied for tops on the Yankees and eighth best in the league. W. O. McGeehan of the *Tribune* believed he was "the best bunter of all the Yankees"; the sportswriter even politicked for Ruth's return to the mound, offering that he was "no worse than a half dozen Yankee hurlers." Even Ruth claimed he could win 30 games if he was allowed to take a regular turn on the mound. He was a monster, and the closest thing to unstoppable that baseball has ever seen.

Not that pitchers didn't try; they walked him 144 times in 1921. But when they did, that brought up Meusel, who in only his second big league season cracked 24 home runs of his own to Ruth's new record of 59. As Grantland Rice observed in September:

More than two pitchers have discovered that passing Ruth to get at Meusel was no way to kill an afternoon. . . . Cobb and Crawford, Cobb and Heilmann, Lajoie and Jackson, Baker and Collins—these have all been great batting pairs, but none of them carried as much high explosive as Ruth and Meusel, who have more extra base hits than any other pair in baseball history.

The adjective "Ruthian" was coined during the early twenties when Babe Ruth dominated the game like no player before or since. In 1921 Ruth was at his physical peak, carrying 220 pounds of muscle on his six-foot-two frame. In addition to his slugging, Ruth hit 16 triples in 1921 and stole 17 bases and was also the best bunter on the Yankees.

True again. Meusel and Ruth formed the game's first back-to-back home run–hitting tandem.

Under Huggins, the Yankees were often ahead of baseball's evolutionary curve, for even though he was an old-style baseball man, schooled in so-called scientific baseball, he was quick to recognize the changes in the game, perhaps quicker to do so than any other man. Huggins put up with Ruth's and Meusel's relatively high number of strikeouts without complaint. And he was already beginning to create a rudimentary bullpen, designating certain pitchers to pitch in certain situations.

Cleveland and New York had left the rest of the league behind, but neither club could quite shake the other as they passed first place back and forth. The Yankees held first place by percentage points when Cleveland came to New York for a four-game set on September 23 that local scribes touted as "the series of the century." But the Indians were crippled. Although they had scored runs all year long as easily as the Yankees, player-manager Tris Speaker was out with a bum knee. Pitching would prove to be the difference. Ruth would make it so.

In the first game all he did was go three for three — all doubles — and score three times as Hoyt outdueled Cleveland ace Stan Coveleski. But the next day Speaker returned to the lineup, and George Uhle shut out the Yankees 9–0.

In game three the Indians were vanquished. "For the most part," wrote Jack Lawrence in the *Tribune,* "the contest looked like a game between married men and single men at a College Point clambake with a keg of Pilsner on third base." To no one's surprise, the Yanks proved better at quenching their thirst and battered Cleveland for 20 hits to win 21–7 as Mays won his 26th game of the year. The next day Ruth crushed two home runs, and Mays stopped Cleveland in relief as the Yankees won again, 8–7, to open up a two-game lead. The Indians never recovered, and the Yankees swept to the pennant a week later.

Meanwhile, John McGraw and his New York Giants had overtaken Pittsburgh and rushed to the National League title. The best-of-nine-game World Series of baseball would be a world championship confined to the Polo Grounds, not a "subway series" but a much cozier one that would require the two teams merely to switch dugouts. After 18 years, the Yankees were finally in it.

And they were big favorites to win. Although the Giants matched up well with the Yankees at virtually every position, and in McGraw were thought to have the edge in leadership, Ruth was the one player the Giants couldn't account for, at least on paper.

The city of New York was in a baseball frenzy, which would eventually result in a gate of nearly $1 million. Yet for game one attendance at the Polo Grounds was some 10,000 fans short of capacity. Speculators had scooped up tickets in bunches, some of which were selling for over $10 each, ten times their face value. Rumors of a sellout swept through the city and kept the crowd down, although 10,000 fans packed Madison Square Garden to watch a re-creation of the game, following tokens around a diamond-shaped board as announcers followed the action by telegraph.

Huggins selected Mays to pitch the opener, and McGraw countered with "Shuffling" Phil Douglas, a fine pitcher when sober, which was not always the case. Earlier in the year he'd been suspended and sent away for a few weeks to dry out.

The Yanks struck first as Elmer Miller singled, went to second on Peckinpaugh's sacrifice, and scored on Ruth's single. That was enough, because Carl Mays held the Giants to only five hits, and the Yanks won 3–0.

Hoyt drew the assignment next and came away with a similar result, defeating Art Nehf 3–0. McGraw made it clear what he thought of Ruth, walking him three times, which so frustrated the slugger that in the fifth he stole both second and third. Although he was stranded, the final theft proved to be the most important play of the Series.

When Ruth barreled into third base, he twisted to his left to avoid third baseman Frankie Frisch's tag. His left elbow took the brunt of his effort and was scraped raw. Ruth shrugged it off.

But when he awoke the next morning and went to the ballpark, his elbow began to swell. Dirt and grit had worked into his skin, and the wound was infected. It was sore, but not sore enough to keep him from playing.

In the third inning the Yankees appeared to put the game, and the Series, in their back pocket. Ruth's two-run single was the key blow as they erupted for four runs off Fred Toney. No team had ever lost a Series after taking the first two games. And now they had a big lead in game three.

But Shawkey lost command in the bottom of the inning,

and the Giants tied the score. Then the NL team exploded for eight runs in the seventh and won going away, 13–5. To make matters worse, Ruth scraped his elbow again on a third-inning steal and was forced from the game in the eighth.

By the time game four rolled around, Ruth's elbow was a swollen mess, discolored and oozing pus. It had to be lanced, and the club announced that he'd be unable to play. He stayed on the Yankee bench while his teammates took batting practice and warmed up. But when the game began, he popped out of the dugout and made his way to left field, his arm heavily bandaged and held stiffly at his side.

Swinging almost one-handed, he somehow managed to get two hits, including his first-ever Series home run in the ninth inning, but it wasn't enough as Douglas got revenge on Mays and won 4–2. Now the Series was tied.

Before game five doctors had to insert a tube into Ruth's elbow to help drain the wound. He gamely played on but could barely swing the bat and was reduced to bunting for his only hit — when he swung away in his other three at bats, he struck out.

But the bunt was important: Ruth scored on Meusel's double, giving the Yankees a 2–1 lead. Hoyt made it stand up, and the Yankees won 3–1 to take a 3–2 lead in the Series.

But that was it for Ruth — his elbow had deteriorated from the grotesque to the dangerous. His Series was over.

The *Sun*'s Joe Vila, the dean of New York baseball writers, demonstrated that Ruth's psyche was as delicate as his elbow. When he wrote of Ruth's "alleged injury," Ruth went ballistic. He had a photographer take a picture of his arm and challenged Vila to put it in the paper.

He didn't, but he also didn't criticize Ruth anymore. Without Ruth, the Yankees were lost and found it hard to score. The Giants curved Meusel to death and exposed the Yankees as a club overly dependent on their big slugger.

The Giants stormed back to take a 4–3 lead in the Series. In game eight the Yankees trailed 1–0 in the ninth inning when Huggins called on Ruth. He grounded out weakly for the first out.

Then the Series ended in the worst possible fashion. After Ruth, infielder Aaron Ward walked. Then Frank Baker sent a ball scooting between second and first. Giants second baseman Jimmy Rawlings ranged to his left, sprawled over the ball, twisted, and threw out Baker. But Ward, thinking the ball was going into right field, kept running.

Giants first baseman George Kelly made a strong throw to Frankie Frisch at third. Ward slid hard, spikes high, in an attempt to dislodge the ball, but Frisch had the World Series in his grasp and refused to let it go. He put what one reporter described as a "Jack Dempsey tag" on Ward — hard and to the jaw. Ward was out on the unusual 4–3–5 double play. Game and Series to the Giants.

There was no small measure of delight around the baseball world at the Yankees' demise. McGraw and the Giants weren't very popular either, but the Yankees, whose dependence on power eschewed convention, were considered arrogant, a team that had bought a pennant with cash. The Giants' victory sent the message that old-fashioned inside baseball still had a place in the game. As *The Sporting News* sniffed:

The fans who shrieked their heads off last summer every time the Yanks knocked the cover off the ball had their eyes opened to the fact that it wasn't real hitting and it wasn't the lively ball that enabled the Hugmen to break all home run records during the American League race. Punk pitching was the real reason. . . . But when the Bambino and his ball smashing companions went up against the Giants' pitchers . . . the light was turned on and thousands of deluded fans suddenly realized how badly they'd been fooled by the so-called supermen wearing Yankee uniforms.

Huston was upset as well, although he placed the blame where he usually did and began pressing once again for Huggins's removal.

Before the end of the season Ruth had signed a lucrative contract to barnstorm around the country with a few teammates and semipros on the "Babe Ruth All-Stars." Such exhibition tours fronted by stars were common, and Ruth stood to earn $25,000. As soon as his elbow healed, he made plans to begin his tour, taking Bob Meusel, Carl Mays, Bill Piercy, and Wally Schang with him.

But since 1911 baseball had banned such tours by World Series participants, allegedly to prevent anything from taking away from the Series, such as an out-and-out replay between the two league champions. In reality, the rule was about a greater concern — gambling.

Nearly every World Series to date had been marred by

charges that called into question either the entire Series or one or more games. Players had an incentive to make sure the Series lasted as long as possible—their take was dependent on the gate. Barring Series participants from barnstorming increased the players' dependence on Series money and, theoretically, provided incentive to win and keep the Series on the up and up.

But everyone wanted a piece of Ruth, who was going through money even faster than he could make it. He often picked up the tab for the constant party that surrounded him, and gamblers had learned that Ruth was an easy mark in a card game or at the racetrack. He needed the extra income just to stay even for the year.

Judge Landis decided to enforce the rule—which Ruth had broken with impunity back in 1916—and warned him

Outfielder Bob Meusel started his Yankee career in right field before moving to left when Hall of Fame center fielder Earle Combs joined the team in 1925. After the 1921 season, Meusel joined teammates Babe Ruth and Bill Piercy on a barnstorming tour that resulted in each player's receiving a suspension for the first six weeks of the 1922 season.

not to go, saying, "I have warned Ruth that he need expect no light penalty if he appears." But Ruth rarely paid attention to anything anyone told him not to do. Ruth, Meusel, and Piercy decided to ignore Landis, although Mays and Schang reluctantly withdrew.

When crowds proved disappointing, Ruth eventually cut the tour short and told the press he planned to apologize to Landis, but that was as close to "I'm sorry" as he got. After all, now he had a vaudeville tour to take part in.

On December 5, Landis weighed in on the matter. He fined the barnstormers $3,362 each—the amount each earned in the World Series—and suspended them for the first six weeks of the 1922 season.

The Yankees' greatest fear when they'd acquired Ruth was coming true. Ruth, despite being the best and highest-paid player in the game, was also almost impossible to depend on. Looking ahead, the Yankees were suddenly lacking—six weeks without Ruth could ruin the 1922 season.

But the colonels' money made up for Ruth's indiscretions. It always did. Time and time again over the course of his career, Ruth's suspensions and self-induced health problems were rendered moot because the Yankees could afford to spend the money to make up for his absence.

Barrow and Huggins got busy. Since the end of the season Huggins had been eager to make a change at shortstop. Roger Peckinpaugh would soon turn 31 and, in Huggins's view, hadn't set an example as team captain. A small trade soon became a big one.

Barrow again turned to the Red Sox, who were willing to gamble because they were still being frozen out by the Loyal Five. Boston shortstop Everett Scott was a clone of Peckinpaugh, but three years younger. New York packaged Peckinpaugh with aging spitballer Jack Quinn, two younger pitchers of unfulfilled potential, Bill Piercy and Rip Collins, and some cash, rumored to be as much as $100,000 but in all likelihood quite a bit less. In return, Boston sent the Yankees Scott and two pitchers who had won a combined 39 games in 1921, "Sad Sam" Jones and "Bullet Joe" Bush.

Reaction in Boston was predictable, although fans were mollified somewhat when Frazee made a few more trades, including one that sent Peckinpaugh away in a three-way deal that landed them Joe Dugan. In New York most of the press fell all over itself praising the deal. There was some consternation at the loss of Peckinpaugh, who was considered Scott's superior, but Bush and Jones, who'd had a hard time winning behind Boston's anemic offense, were expected to thrive in New York — particularly when Ruth returned.

The Yankees moved their spring training camp in 1922 to New Orleans to take advantage of the crowds turning out to see Ruth, who despite his suspension was allowed to work out with the club.

Yet New Orleans proved too great a temptation for the Yankees. Huggins completely lost control of the team — he cut workouts back to one a day, leaving some 20 hours a day available to the players to sample the many and varied wares of the French Quarter, as they did to excess. Even the press, which usually looked the other way or made only veiled references to ballplayers' behavior, couldn't ignore what was going on. One spring training headline read "Yankees Train on Scotch."

As if it really mattered. Even with Ruth and Meusel sidelined, the Yankees were the team to beat in the American League. Whenever the club seemed lacking in any area, Ruppert filled the breach with cash. In mid-April, when Huggins and Barrow decided they needed a center fielder, they bought fleet young outfielder Whitey Witt from the A's. When Frank Baker began to show his age in late July, another trade and cash deal was made with Boston, delivering Joe Dugan for the home stretch. This trade was made so late in the season that Ban Johnson later put in place the trading deadline.

The Yankees' only problem, apart from the St. Louis Browns, who hung with New York all year long, was themselves. On the field they were all business, but as soon as the game ended, they were a holy mess. Almost every week there were reports of internal battles — Ruth fought Pipp, Aaron Ward clashed with Braggo Roth, Carl Mays and Al Devormer squared off, and there were numerous other smaller incidents. When the players weren't fighting, they were carrying on as if they were still in New Orleans. When the Yankees were on the loose, every street was Bourbon Street, and Huggins had all the effect of a sidewalk preacher. As *The Sporting News* commented, "Huggins finds it hard to enforce his orders. . . . [T]he treatment that Huggins has received from some of his players is a shame."

Ruth was a continuing problem. He'd returned out of shape, but that didn't stop him from becoming involved immediately in a series of scrapes — going after a fan in the stands and getting fined, battling umpire Bill Dinneen and earning a five-day suspension from Landis and another fine. Ruth blew hot and cold all year long — on the field. After the game he kept the candle burning on both ends. Huggins would try to admonish him, but Ruth treated his manager like a minor annoyance.

Ruppert, Huston, and Barrow even hired a detective who ingratiated himself with the players and got the goods on everybody, but it had as much effect on their behavior as their behavior had on the way they played the game. In the end talent won out, albeit by the narrowest of margins, for Ruth "slumped" to only .315 with 35 home runs, second to the Browns' Ken Williams, who hit 39. While the performance would have been spectacular for anyone else, for Ruth it represented a major slide. Yet the Yankees still won 94 games, edging the Browns for the pennant by a single game despite losing four of their last five.

Only the Giants, once again, stood between the Yankees and their first world championship. After the Series, they still did.

The Series returned to the now-familiar seven-game format, but all that did was shorten the Yankees' period of suffering. They were never in it.

"I have never seen a team representing our organization in the World Series play worse ball than the Yankees," said Ban Johnson later. "The Giants have humiliated the American League in a way that cannot be forgotten. . . . [T]he mistakes of the Yankees were abominable." Indeed. The Giants outplayed the Yankees in all facets of the game as the Yanks squandered leads in every contest, losing four games and managing only a tie in game three, which was inexplicably called because of darkness with the sun still high in the sky. They fielded poorly, failed to hit, ran the bases like amateurs, and gave up the big hit at every opportunity.

Ruth was a particular disaster in the Series, as were pitchers Joe Bush and Carl Mays. The Giants razzed Ruth to distraction, and McGraw ordered his pitchers to throw the slugger plenty of curveballs in the dirt, which Ruth was unable to either resist or hit. He went a woeful 2–17, leading Joe Vila to refer to him as "an exploded phenomenon." W. O. McGeehan concurred, calling Ruth a "tragic figure. . . . The Babe flashed like a comet over all baseball fields. . . . [T]he most universal comment that he hears as his flaming star seems about to sink is 'Ya big bum, ya.'"

The play of Bush and Mays had a different taint, as each coughed up late leads in a manner that raised suspicion. Years later Miller Huggins reportedly expressed the belief that each man had lost on purpose, a charge that Fred Lieb also leveled against Mays in the 1921 World Series. In the annals of Yankee history, the World Series of 1922 represents a low point.

Off-season criticism of the Yankees in general and Ruth in particular was heavy. Huston laid the blame squarely on Huggins, claiming that his inability to enforce discipline had cost the team the pennant. Ruppert disagreed, and just a few days after the end of the Series announced that Huggins would return in 1923.

The announcement precipitated a front-office crisis. Barrow had tired of having two bosses and threatened to quit. Ruppert offered to buy out Huston, who initially agreed, then backed off. But he returned as very much a second fiddle. From then on Barrow took his orders from Ruppert. And in the meantime, Ruth was put in his place.

It was a setup, a planned repentance cooked up by Ruth's agent and with the tacit support of the Yankees, but it had its desired effect. At the baseball writers' Elks Club banquet, at which Ruth was a guest, speaker after speaker admonished him on his behavior, culminating in a tear-jerker by New York state senator Jimmy Walker, who later would become mayor of New York. He called Ruth a "fool," saying that while Ruppert makes "millions of gallons of beer, Ruth is of the opinion that he can drink it faster than the colonel can make it. . . . You have let down the kids of America. . . . [They] have seen their idol shattered and their dream broken." Publicly humiliated, a tearful Ruth promised to make amends. Then, rather surprisingly, he actually did.

He returned to his Massachusetts farm and spent the winter working. By the time he hit Hot Springs for his annual round of steam baths before training camp, he was in the best shape of his life, down to around 210 pounds. All the while, work on Yankee Stadium continued at a frantic pace, and in January Barrow made two more deals with Harry Frazee, who had finally decided to sell the Red Sox but was determined to leave nothing behind for whomever Johnson decided would become the next owner. For a few warm bodies and some cash, the Yankees came away with rookie pitcher George Pipgras and veteran Herb Pennock. Pipgras hadn't played an inning in the majors, and Pennock had pitched for ten years without distinction, but each flourished on the best team in baseball, pitching in the largest park in the majors. They gave the Yankees the deepest pitching staff in baseball.

Spring training was relatively uneventful, and by the time the Yankees inaugurated Yankee Stadium on Opening Day, April 18, another Yankee pennant was all but assured.

No ballpark ever opened to more fanfare or higher expectations. Yankee Stadium represented a grand leap forward in ballpark design, for it was not just a ballfield surrounded by stands, but a building that contained a ballpark, grander and more ostentatious than any built before or since. Fred Lieb dubbed it "the House That Ruth Built," but that appellation was something of a misnomer. While Ruth certainly sparked the attendance revival that helped Ruppert and Huston finance the park, Yankee Stadium was also "the House Built for Ruth." Nothing else was to have a greater impact on his career, and ever since that day the Yankees have sought sluggers for whom Yankee Stadium has been similarly suited.

The Yankees ensured that Ruth would have little trouble reaching the fence in right field. They kept it short down the line at 295 feet — not as short as the Polo Grounds' 256, but significantly smaller in the power alley. In fact, Ruth benefited from similar dimensions in most American League parks, save Comiskey in Chicago and Fenway in Boston. In effect, the dimensions of Yankee Stadium mimicked the average dimensions of the average American League ballpark — short in right, very deep to center, and, compared to right field, somewhat deeper in left. This factor made Ruth equally dangerous at home and on the road.

They also eschewed baseball tradition and made left field the sun field. Ruth had settled in right, and the Yankees didn't want him staring into the sun. That honor went to Bob Meusel, who would soon suffer chronic headaches from the late afternoon glare.

Yet Ruth was later quoted as saying, "I cried when I left the Polo Grounds." Surprisingly, given the success he was to have there, Ruth hated hitting at the Stadium, which he complained provided a poor background. Had he stayed at the Polo Grounds, he believed, he would have hit even more home runs.

The gates to the new park opened at noon, and by two o'clock were locked shut. Although the Yankees announced a crowd of 74,000, only some 60,000 fans had poured in, the largest crowd ever to see a game at the time, leaving another 10,000 to 15,000 milling around outside the park.

Beginning at one o'clock, the obvious rituals took place involving marching bands, politicians, and the other usual suspects. John Philip Sousa himself directed the band, and before the game the 1922 pennant was raised.

Bob Shawkey drew the starting assignment against Boston, and almost everything went according to plan. Boston's George Burns collected the first hit in the new Stadium, a second-inning single, and Aaron Ward struck first for New York, with a third-inning single. But the blow everyone remembered came in the fourth.

After Bob Shawkey scored the ballpark's first run on Joe Dugan's single, Ruth came up with Dugan on first and Whitey Witt on second. With 60,000 fans roaring, Ruth worked the count to 2–2, then hit Howard Ehmke's next pitch ten rows deep into the lower right-field stands. He toured the bases to prodigious applause, a scene he would repeat at the Stadium more than 250 times.

That home run virtually clinched the pennant. Shawkey scattered three hits for the day, and New York won, 4–1. The Yankees soon took over first place, a spot they would never relinquish. Ruth, slim, trim, and generally under control, hit "only" 41 home runs to tie Cy Williams for the big league crown, but he set a host of other records, including reaching base a major league record 379 times and reaching a career high in batting average (.393) and doubles (45).

Yankee Stadium proved to be a continuing success, although the Yankees' romp to the pennant held attendance down, and they actually drew fewer fans than they

When Yankee Stadium opened in April 1923, it stood like a concrete island in the Bronx. Soon a neighborhood would grow up alongside a park that was more "the House Built for Ruth" than "the House That Ruth Built."

had the previous year at the Polo Grounds. In May Huston finally agreed to a buyout, leaving Ruppert as the sole owner of the Yankees, legal confirmation of what reality had been for several seasons.

The New York Giants again stood between the Yankees and a world championship. And Ruth was again considered the key. If he could approach his regular season performance in the fall, a Yankees championship seemed certain.

John McGraw oozed confidence before the Series began. He'd never liked Ruth, predicting back in 1918 that if Ruth ever played regularly, "he'd hit into a hundred double plays." The Giants had kept Ruth in check in the last two Series, and McGraw confidently predicted: "I believe the same system which nullified his presence in the batting order in 1921 and 1922 will suffice."

In McGraw's "system" the manager called all the pitches, usually breaking balls off the plate. But this year the smart money was betting on Ruth. His time had come, most observers thought, even though thus far his World Series performance was not unlike that of Mighty Casey in Ernest L. Thayer's poem. This year they were betting on Casey to finally come through.

And in game one, Casey did come through — outfielder Casey Stengel of the Giants.

In something of an October tradition, the Yankees jumped out to a quick 3–0 lead. But then the flip side of that coin turned up, and the Giants stormed back in the third, routing Waite Hoyt for four runs to go ahead 4–3.

Ruth finally got off in the fifth inning, after a fashion. With one out, he sliced a drive down the left-field line. Giants left fielder Emil "Irish" Meusel, Bob's brother, ran it down and was surprised to see Ruth heading for third. He beat the throw with a beautiful hook slide. Then Bob Meusel lofted a short fly into center. Giants second baseman Frankie Frisch raced back and made what Grantland Rice called "a catch replete with magnificent splendor." Ruth broke for the plate in an attempt to tie the score, but Frisch followed with a throw that Rice termed "as deadly

In game one of the 1923 World Series at Yankee Stadium Babe Ruth makes a great hook slide while legging out a fifth-inning triple. On Bob Meusel's short fly to center, Giants second baseman Frankie Frisch made a running catch and a perfect throw to nail Ruth at home.

as Sergeant York ever knew." This time Ruth tried to vault over the tag, but catcher Snyder tagged him out.

Joe Dugan later tied the game with a triple, and the two clubs entered the ninth tied. Then up stepped the soon-to-be-Mighty Casey.

Stengel drove a liner to the gap in left center between Meusel and Witt. It rolled all the way to the bleachers in the deepest part of the stadium as all three men sprinted for the finish line. But that is mere description.

Damon Runyon provided the narration:

This is the way old Casey Stengel ran running his home run home. . . . This is the way — His mouth wide open. His warped old legs bending beneath him at every stride. His arms flying back and forth like those of a man swimming the crawl stroke. His flanks heaving, his breath whistling, his head back. . . . The warped old legs, twisted and bent by many a year of baseball campaigning, just barely held out under Casey until he reached the plate, running his run home. Then they collapsed.

Runyon was almost as tired as Casey was by the time he made it home safe, sliding in ahead of the relay from Meusel. The Giants led 5–4, and a few moments later the game ended with Ruth on deck swinging three bats in anticipation of an at bat that never came.

Ruth extracted revenge in game two, leading Grantland Rice to new shades of purple prose as he noted afterward, "The ancient slogan still rides down the ages — Ruth crushed to earth, will rise again." And rise he did, twice, cracking two home runs, one to the roof in right in the fourth, and the second a low liner in the fifth. He barely missed another in the ninth as Pennock collected the win, 4–2. Added John Kieran after the game, as New York's finest sportswriters slugged it out, "Ruth is not only original, he is sometimes positively aboriginal." The Giants concurred. Giants pitcher John Bentley suggested that the only way to pitch to Ruth was to use a "change of direction — throw the ball to second base."

Rice wore out the "Casey" theme in game three as Stengel came through again, breaking a scoreless tie with another home run, this time over Ruth's head and into the right-field bleachers, to win the game 1–0. The Giants' Art Nehf followed Bentley's advice, in spirit anyway, as he wisely walked Ruth twice.

But that was about it for the Giants. The Yankees won game four going away with six second-inning runs to win 8–4, then repeated the pattern in game five, scoring seven runs in the first two innings. Ruth was proving to be the difference, as Stengel's magic had evaporated. As one scribe noted, the McGraw system in regard to Ruth had come down to two options — either walk him or watch him "sliding into third."

Art Nehf, who had shut out the Yankees in game three, got the ball from McGraw for game six. But game six would prove different.

In the first inning Ruth homered into the upper deck of the Polo Grounds, just fair, to put the Yankees ahead, setting a Series record with his third home run. The Giants then chipped away at Herb Pennock and led 4–1 entering the eighth. Then the rest of the Yankee lineup and the Giants defense exploded as the Yankees strung together three hits, three walks, and an error. Ruth struck out with the bases loaded, but Meusel, as he had done so many times before, backed him up with a key single and the Yankees plated five runs. One inning later the Yankees walked off the field with a 6–4 win and their first world championship.

That evening at a party at the Hotel Commodore, Ruppert announced that Huggins would return for the 1924 season. Both men thought the club was in fine shape to repeat as champions.

Ruth, in his fourth season as a Yankee, had finally delivered. Although he'd gained back much of the weight he'd lost over the course of the season and had begun to drift back toward his usual lifestyle, the club was confident that he'd finally accepted Huggins as manager and that he'd also matured, as much as he could. Ruth had even given a little speech celebrating Huggins at the celebration party, saying, "Boys, we owe a lot to Hug," before presenting him with a diamond ring from the players.

Ruppert was ecstatic, calling it "the happiest day of my life," quite a statement for someone who had every possible resource for happiness at his disposal. "Now I have the greatest ballpark and the greatest team!" The Yankees felt invincible. After winning the pennant by nearly 20 games and dumping the Giants, it seemed as if nothing could stop them. Before the 1924 season got under way, they even sold Carl Mays, who had fallen out of favor with Huggins,

Only seven years after this picture was taken of a thirteen-year-old Lou Gehrig (front row, second from right) and his sandlot teammates, the Washington Heights native was playing in Yankee Stadium. By 1925 he'd won the first-base job, and soon established himself as baseball's "Iron Horse" over fourteen seasons, which included a streak of consecutive games played, which was broken by Cal Ripken, Jr., six decades later.

to the Reds. Two youngsters seemed about ready to burst on to the scene.

Outfielder Earle Combs had been the most talked about player in the minor leagues in 1923, when he hit .380 for Louisville in the American Association. A fast runner and powerful gap hitter, Combs's only weakness was an average arm, which his speed helped make up for. He was also the anti-Ruth, a quiet, clean-living ballplayer who'd be immune to the Yankees' usual bag of misbehavior. In the off-season the Yankees outbid several other clubs and purchased Combs for $50,000. The idea was to break him in slow and have him eventually take over in center for Witt.

The other player was a strapping but awkward first baseman from Columbia University, Lou Gehrig. When Yankee scout Paul Krichell saw him blast a long home run, he told the top brass that he'd found "another Babe Ruth." They didn't believe him—until they invited Gehrig to try out at the Stadium in 1923 and saw him launch the ball into the upper deck. The club signed him, then optioned him out to Hartford so he could learn to field and hit more consistently. Gehrig got a few at bats at the end of the 1923 season after Pipp sprained an ankle, and he got the Yankees' attention during spring training in 1924. He came north with the club for the experience but was soon sent back to Hartford to resume his tutelage.

His education continued during spring training, when he witnessed the Yankees' usual camp shenanigans, which included more work off the diamond than on. No one was really worried, however, until the season started.

They opened the season at Fenway Park in Boston with a lineup identical to that of the previous season. And despite the fact that much of the team was still feeling the effects of a party at Babe Ruth's Sudbury, Massachusetts, farm the night before, they collected the expected result, another Yankee win.

But the woeful Red Sox beat the Yanks the next two days, and when Washington followed with two more victories, the Yankees found themselves in alien territory—last place. In a sense, the pennant race was already lost, for those two losses to Washington would eventually prove to be the difference in the pennant race.

Although the Yanks immediately ripped off an eight-game winning streak, over the first two months of the season the club was strangely out of sync, often winning big when they did, but losing close games as their pitching, apart from Pennock, slipped back. The answer to those woes was in Cincinnati, where Carl Mays went 20–9 with a 3.15 ERA.

Huggins shook things up, benching Witt and inserting Earle Combs into the starting lineup. He was hitting .400 and providing a much-needed spark when he broke his ankle on June 15 and missed the rest of the season. By the end of the month the Yankees found themselves in a three-team race for the pennant with Detroit and Washington.

The Tigers, behind player-manager Ty Cobb, eventually slipped back, but the Senators, with Joe Judge, Sam Rice, and Goose Goslin, finally had an offense to back up the pitching of Walter Johnson. The Yankees just couldn't shake them, and after taking three of four from New York in the final meeting between the two teams at the end of August, the Senators moved into first place.

The Yankees closed with a rush, winning 18 of their final 26, but the Senators were even hotter and won the pennant by two games. The Giants won the National League pennant, and just one season removed from a world championship the Yankees were second fiddle in New York again.

Ruth was blameless, as he had won his only batting title with a .378 average and cracked a league-best 46 home runs. But as if not believing what had happened, the Yankees again did little in the off-season apart from trad-

A full house enjoys Yankee Stadium in this undated photograph from the twenties. Note the exaggerated warning track with pathways leading to the stands. These paths allowed fans to leave the Stadium after a game by walking on the playing field and heading toward the large exits near the grandstand and box seats. Only the elevated tracks and apartment houses still exist today; the Stadium was entirely rebuilt in 1974 and 1975.

Yankee Stadium during the 1923 World Series, captured from the last row of the bleachers, looking down toward Babe Ruth. The Stadium was America's biggest and best in the country's largest metropolis. The income generated by its 55,000 seats allowed the Yankees to maintain the solid financial footing needed to build a dynasty.

ing Joe Bush to the Browns for veteran pitcher Urban Shocker.

The wheels fell off early in 1925. Ruth, emboldened by the success of his reform efforts over the last two seasons, tumbled off the already listing wagon.

His weight ballooned to nearly 260 pounds, which no amount of steam during his annual pre–spring training stay at Hot Springs could melt off, for every moment Ruth spent out of the sauna he spent painting the town. He got sick and hadn't recovered completely by the time he showed up in St. Petersburg for spring training. When he felt well, he played well and then went out carousing. He'd suffer a relapse, play poorly, and take it easy until he felt better. Then the cycle would repeat itself.

On the train back to New York to start the season, Ruth collapsed outside a train station in Asheville, North Carolina, feverish and deathly ill. Rushed to New York the next day, he was hospitalized, half-delirious and suffering from convulsive fits.

The incident was dubbed "the bellyache heard 'round the world," and protective sportswriters blamed it on too many hot dogs and too much soda pop. That fooled no one but kids and rubes in the hinterlands. Those who ate hot dogs and drank pop knew better.

The true nature of Ruth's illness has always been something of a mystery. A number of teammates intimated that his problem was venereal disease, while others have speculated that he may have been felled by a combination of exhaustion, influenza, and a poor diet. Doctors eventually performed a 20-minute operation for what they termed an "intestinal abscess," but he'd reportedly injured his groin sliding during spring training, and the brief operation would have been more in line with repairing a hernia rather than any invasive intestinal procedure.

Ruth's illness may have been all of the above, none of the above, or a combination. Nearly 60 years after his death, the Ruth legend is still one of the most sheltered in sports, and none of his various biographers have noted what was most likely the root cause of this "mysterious" ailment. Taking into account Ruth's behavior, lifestyle, and symptoms, it seems likely that alcohol, directly or indirectly, was the cause of his malady.

Growing up in his father's Baltimore saloon, Ruth himself admitted to drinking regularly while still a child. And as an adult, if there was any constant in Ruth's life apart from baseball and women, it was booze. He often drank at breakfast, and he always drank at night. In fact, about the only time he didn't drink was during a game. While he may not have been a classic "shakes and pink elephants" alcoholic, living from one drink to the next, in today's parlance he would be classified as a binge drinker whose episodes were beginning to evolve into the classical definition. The circumstantial evidence suggests that the well-documented alcoholic assault Ruth inflicted on his body in the winter and spring of 1925 may well have finally caught up with him, leaving his immune system weakened and barely functional. Those problems may have been exacerbated by the additives in illegal Prohibition spirits, which were often laced with all sorts of other substances, including poison and drugs.

Treatment of alcoholism at the time could be as dangerous and debilitating as the disease itself, often consisting of forcible stomach-pumping, hot baths, massive sedation by narcotics, and injections of substances such as "double chloride of gold," the main ingredient in the popular "Keeley Cure." Such cures often lasted weeks and left patients weakened and dazed.

Ruth's extended hospitalization is in line with such treatment. He remained in St. Vincent's nearly six weeks following his operation, including a week in which he indulged in supervised workouts at the Stadium only to return to the hospital each day. That suggests that at some point his stay had more to do with enforcing behavioral discipline than with any urgent medical treatment.

At any rate, it didn't take. Ruth returned to the team on June 1, weak and 30 pounds lighter, but significantly, he almost immediately resumed his previous pattern of behavior, slowing his full recovery.

By that time any chance the Yankees had to regain the pennant was long gone. The club collapsed in every way possible in 1925. By the time of Ruth's return, they were already a dismal 15–25, already in seventh place, barely ahead of the Red Sox. There they would stay.

Ruth was part of the reason for their demise, but the fault was not his alone. In fact, his replacement, Ben Paschal, hit .360 and slugged .611 for the season.

The Yankees got old in 1925. Shortstop Everett Scott was released on May 6, halting his record consecutive-games-played streak at 1,307. Pee Wee Wanninger, who played about as well as his name, replaced him. Second baseman Aaron Ward and Wally Schang slowed noticeably, and Joe Dugan got hurt. Combs returned to hit .342, and Meusel led the league in home runs and RBIs, but the highlight of the year was when slumping Wally Pipp got beaned.

On June 2, he stepped in to take batting practice against a prospect out of Princeton named Charlie Caldwell. Trying to impress, Caldwell was throwing hard. An errant pitch hit Pipp on the temple.

He went down and stayed down. The semiconscious first baseman was hustled off to the hospital, where he stayed for the next two weeks.

When he returned, the Yankees had a new first baseman. Huggins used Pipp's injury to make a move he'd been contemplating for several weeks. The season was over, and it was time to experiment. He told Lou Gehrig, "You're my first baseman." Gehrig, who'd played sparingly thus far, including a pinch-hit performance the day before, took over at first base on June 2. He wouldn't relinquish the spot for 13 years.

But not even Gehrig could help the Yankees in 1925. Ruth returned to the lineup weak and out of shape and stayed that way all season, warring with Huggins over his behavior and, for Ruth, not hitting, finishing with only 25 home runs, 66 RBIs, and a .290 batting average. The best minds in baseball assumed that at age 30 the Yankees' oldest regular was finished, at the beginning of a slide from which few returned. So were the Yankees. They finished seventh — and deserved to with a record of 69–85 — as the Senators took the pennant for the second year in a row.

It was the best thing that ever could have happened to them.

In 1927 the Murderers' Row Yankees had a formidable infield. From left: first baseman Lou Gehrig, second baseman Tony Lazzeri, shortstop Mark Koenig, and third baseman Joe Dugan.

What necessity is there to say much about a team that can
make a record like that? It is the equivalent to the performance of Othello by suffocating Desdemona. The Yankees
spread their hands over the remainder of the American
League face when they began in April and their hands were
still over the face when they finished in October.

— *Spalding's Official Base Ball Guide*

They just beat our brains out.

— AL SIMMONS,
Philadelphia Athletics

1926–1928
THE GREATEST TEAM

The 1927 Yankees were a force of nature, like a tidal wave or a hurricane, immense,
irrefutable, brutal, and at the time almost beyond the capacity of the English language to
explain. They just were — a law of baseball physics, obvious and immutable.

To all who saw them, the 1927 New York Yankees were the greatest team in baseball history. While all manner of statistical analysis and logic has since been used to question that
statement and strip them of their crown, none of it has really succeeded in doing so. The
phrases "'27 Yankees" and "greatest team" still go together as naturally as "Babe Ruth" and
"60 home runs."

The reason that remains true extends beyond the field, although it was on the field that
this ballclub revealed a brand-new game. No other team, before or since, has been covered
by the collection of writing talent that was employed by the New York press corps in 1927.
They supplied the competition that was lacking on the field. As the season unfolded, each

sportswriter strove to outdo all the others in trying to describe the exploits of this remarkable team.

There was no radio, not for the Yankees, not yet, not until the World Series. There was only the game on the field and the words on the page and Babe Ruth hitting 60 home runs, outdoing everyone and everything. But the '27 Yankees were much, much more than Babe Ruth alone. One can trace the story of the 1927 Yankees to the waning days of their demise in 1925. It starts with Babe Ruth.

On August 29 in St. Louis, Ruth arrived at the ballpark late—no big surprise, since he had arrived at the hotel late earlier that morning. He had been late several times in the last week and had ignored various orders from his manager. Huggins suspended him and fined him $5,000. Ruth threatened Huggins and used every word in his considerable vocabulary to ream him out, ending by telling Huggins something like, "If you were half my size I'd punch the shit out of you." Huggins got right in Ruth's face and responded that if he were, he'd do the same to Ruth. The slugger stormed off.

Ruth got no support from his teammates, the press, or, more significantly, the only person in his life apart from himself who really mattered.

That wasn't Mrs. Ruth. Unable to take his womanizing, his drinking, his everything, she'd been hospitalized earlier in the year with a nervous breakdown. When asked what it was like having Ruth for a roommate, Ping Bodie had answered, "I don't know. I room with his suitcase." Helen Ruth knew exactly what he meant. She was just another piece of the Babe's luggage.

Her husband had hooked up with a strong-willed and attractive divorcée, Claire Hodgson. While their relationship began according to Ruth's usual pattern, Mrs. Hodgson got to Ruth.

So did his agent and ghostwriter, Christy Walsh, who had visions of his cash cow checking out. Ruth's behavior and habits had put everything at risk—he was one more poor season away from being somebody who used to be somebody. The two laid down the law: Ruth had to reform—or else.

The Yankees concurred and in the off-season put Ruth in the hands of trainer and gym operator Artie McGovern. Ruth dried out and got back into shape, losing all the weight he'd put back on since midsummer. Mrs. Hodgson

took care of the rest, and over the winter Ruth separated from Helen.

While Ruth remade himself, Huggins and Barrow focused on the rest of the team. The Yankees' pathetic 1925 performance gave them license to make changes, and Ruppert's bank account gave them the means to do so. That's an advantage the Yankees have almost always enjoyed over the competition. Time and time again cash has made it possible for them to rebuild before collapse.

Gehrig and Dugan, who was healthy again after being hurt, were secure at the corners, and the outfield was set as long as Ruth held up. But second baseman Aaron Ward had slowed down, and rookie shortstop Pee Wee Wanninger had been overmatched.

One answer was in hand, and the other was available. The year before the Yankees had signed shortstop Mark Koenig out of the American Association. And out in the Pacific Coast League, Salt Lake City shortstop Tony Lazzeri was the talk of minor league baseball.

All he'd done in 1925 was hit .355 and crack 60 home runs in the PCL. That made him the top prospect in the minor leagues, to a point.

There were all sorts of questions surrounding his performance, none of which had anything to do with Lazzeri's raw talent. Recent PCL alumni such as Jimmy O'Connell, Willie Kamm, and Paul Strand, all of whom cost more than $70,000, had failed in the major leagues. None had come close to justifying their cost. Strand, like Lazzeri, had played for Salt Lake City and put up remarkable numbers at the higher elevation. His failure at sea level caused some to discount Lazzeri as another product of thin air.

But that wasn't all. Lazzeri was Italian. At the time only a handful of Italians had played major league baseball, and baseball wasn't particularly eager to increase that number.

Italians were among the least desirable immigrants. Accepted only slightly more than American blacks, they were subject to all forms of vicious stereotyping and prejudice. Italians were considered greasy, hotheaded thieves on a par with gypsies, Slavs, and other "unwashed," suited only for the most menial labor. Sportswriters, even in New York, would refer to Italians in unflattering terms until after World War II, often calling them "Fascists," "Wops," and "Dagos."

But the Yankees were unique. The team that had come

to the city itself as an immigrant was then one of the few major league teams that reached out to immigrants, including Italians. It was good business. By the 1920s one out of every seven New Yorkers was Italian — more than a million people. Italians had followed the team since they played at the Polo Grounds with Ping Bodie — Francesco Pezzolo — in their outfield. While the Yankees' record in regard to the integration of baseball by African Americans would be as appalling as that of most other major league teams, their foresight in accepting players of Italian descent gave them a tremendous advantage over the next decade. They became the de facto favorites of Italian Americans throughout the country, increasing their road appeal, for which they received one-third of the gate receipts. Even in an anti-Yankees enclave like New England, the Yankees remain the favored team in the Italian sections of such cities as Worcester, Providence, and Boston.

The Cincinnati Reds reportedly had the first crack at Lazzeri, whose fellow Italians nicknamed him "Poosh 'em Up" for his uncanny ability to push runners around the bases and knock in runs. But the Reds passed on him, and Yankee scout Bob Connery then told Ed Barrow bluntly, "Buy him — he's the greatest thing I've ever seen." Barrow did. Lazzeri cost the Yankees $65,000, $10,000 more than Combs several years before. The versatile Lazzeri anchored the Yankee infield for more than ten years and was one of the first middle infielders in the game to demonstrate power.

That spring Huggins sorted through his choices. Ruth was in shape again, on his best behavior, and hitting with his usual prowess — *The Sporting News* noted that "the big boy seems to be infected with a determination that will not be denied." Veteran Pat Collins won the catcher's job, Koenig was installed at short, and Lazzeri moved over to second base.

Still, no one expected much from the team in 1926. Syndicated baseball writer Hugh Fullerton predicted that the A's and Pirates would meet in the World Series. Of the Yankees he offered that they "are reviving a little after the explosion of last year. Ruth is back in form but it is doubtful whether he can last through a hard season."

The club got off to a quick start, scoring runs in bunches. With Gehrig improving, Ruth back to form, Meusel his usual steady self, and Lazzeri as good as advertised, the

Babe Ruth, shown here being carried off the field at Fenway Park after twisting his ankle, rebounded from his worst season, in 1925, to reestablish his credentials as the biggest star not only in baseball but in all of American sports. From 1926 to 1928 Ruth averaged nearly 54 home runs per season, including his record-breaking 60-home-run season in 1927.

club had four players capable of hitting the ball out at anytime. In mid-May they won 16 in a row to effectively put the pennant away.

They cruised through the second half but remained on the lookout for talent. Barrow noticed that a journeyman named Wilcy Moore on a Class B team in Greenville, South Carolina, had won 17 games in a row and was on his way to a 30–4 mark for the season. Yankee scout Bob Gilks was unimpressed, stating bluntly, "He can't pitch," and questioning his age, believing the balding pitcher was at least ten years older than his stated age of 28. But numbers impressed Barrow, and in late August he purchased Wilcy Moore for $3,500.

Moore might have made his Yankee debut in 1926 had it not been for a misdiagnosed case of appendicitis. Veteran Washington pitcher Dutch Reuther, bedridden with abdominal pain, was cut loose and acquired on waivers by the Yankees a week after they had acquired Moore. Yankee doctors determined that the problem wasn't appendicitis but a slight hernia, which wouldn't even require surgery.

Yankee executive Ed Barrow rebuilt the team after its disastrous 1925 season to win three consecutive pennants and back-to-back world championships in 1927 and 1928. His purchase of second baseman Tony Lazzeri for $65,000 before the 1926 season was instrumental in the team's transformation.

Reuther, who had feared going under the knife, suddenly pronounced himself fit and resumed pitching.

He helped the Yankees limp home as they outlasted Cleveland by three games to win the pennant. In the National League the St. Louis Cardinals pulled a surprise of their own to win the National League pennant.

But the Yankees' late season woes drew caution. Most observers agreed with Grantland Rice, who believed the Cardinals to be "a trifle better."

The result was a memorable Series that swung back and forth several times, marked by spectacular performances, capped by one that has since become legendary, and finished by one long forgotten. The Yanks won game one, and the Cardinals came back to take two and three. In game four Ruth appeared to take over.

He had already cracked two home runs to tie his own single-game Series record. When he stepped to the plate in the sixth, radio broadcaster Graham MacNamee seized the moment, saying, "Babe's shoulders look as if there's murder in them."

Ruth worked the count to 3–2 against pitcher Hi Bell. Then, as MacNamee described it, "the Babe hits it clear into the center-field bleacher. For a home run. For a home run! Did you hear what I said? Oh, what a shot!" *The Sporting News* estimated that the blast carried nearly 600 feet, the first ever to that part of the ballpark. The Yankees went on to win 10–5.

But the Cardinals sloughed off Ruth's histrionics. When aging legend Grover Cleveland Alexander beat the Yankees for a second time in game six on October 9 at Yankee Stadium, the Series was tied. It all came down to the seventh game the next day.

The Cardinals nursed a 3–2 lead into the seventh, but then pitcher Jesse Haines developed a blister. Even though he'd pitched a complete game the day before, Alexander had told Cardinal manager Rogers Hornsby that he'd "had it easy in there." If the manager needed him for another inning or two, he'd be ready.

Precisely how he prepared himself for the game is still the subject of debate. Alexander had both epilepsy and a drinking problem, which combined to make him look much older than his 38 years and made the word "griz-zled" the standard adjective placed before his name. He may or may not have been hung over when he took the mound with the bases loaded and two outs. Lazzeri was up.

With the count 1–1, Lazzeri turned on the ball and lashed a long drive down the left-field line. The crowd gasped, thinking it was a home run, but the ball curved foul by several feet. (In subsequent retellings over the years, it has moved ever closer to the foul line.) Then Alexander blew a fastball by Lazzeri at the letters for a strikeout, ending the threat.

It all came down to Ruth and Alexander, two out, none on, in the last of the ninth, and the Cardinals still clinging to a 3–2 lead. Alexander worked Ruth carefully, not want-ing to put him on but not wanting to risk a home run either. As W. O. McGeehan noted: "The count went to three and two, Ruth was swaying eagerly. The soupbone creaked again. The ball seemed a fraction of an inch from being a strike. Ruth paused for a moment. Even he was uncertain. Then he trotted down to first."

That brought up Meusel, he of the .315 batting average and 81 RBIs in just over 100 regular season games—not quite Ruth's standard, which had translated into a .372 average and 47 home runs, but still among the best in the game. Meusel was hot. He already had one hit in the game and had doubled and tripled off Alexander the day before. And if he got on, Gehrig stood in the on-deck circle, await-ing his chance.

Ruth, on first, had made a career of careening between incredible and incorrigible. He now added the inexplica-ble to his résumé.

Representing the tying run in the last inning of the final game of the World Series, with Bob Meusel at bat, Gehrig on deck, and two out, Ruth tried to steal second.

He didn't get a good jump. Cardinal catcher Bob O'Far-rell took Alexander's pitch and gunned the ball to second base, where Hornsby, playing near the bag, was already waiting.

The result was as ordinary and dramatic as a spring train-ing drill. Hornsby caught the perfect throw and dropped the tag to the bag. Ruth slid right into it, out by ten feet.

Hornsby couldn't believe it. Stunned, he later recalled that Ruth "didn't say a word. He didn't even look around or up at me. He just picked himself up and walked away."

Ballgame over. Series over. The Cardinals were world cham-pions.

Ruth's failed steal, not an understandable physical error but an inexplicable mental one, is easily the worst play ever to end a World Series. Yet because he cracked four home runs in the Series and Alexander provided the Series' signature moment, Ruth's gaffe has since been overlooked. His only comment about the play later was that he was "trying something."

The gaffe raised some suspicions. Over the next month *The Sporting News* dropped hints that some people thought the Series hadn't been quite on the level. In fact, only a week after the Series ended, Joe Vila noted the Yankees' "surprising indifference" when the Series had returned to New York and noted that all the betting had "swung to the Cardinals."

He then noted "an incident at the Stadium during the final game that escaped the vigilance of the scribes. Sitting in a field box, near the Cardinals bench, was a notorious gambler from Boston, who, it is recalled, was charged dur-ing the trial of the Black Sox in Chicago seven years ago with handling some of the 'tainted money.'" Vila went on

With two outs in the bottom of the ninth inning of the seventh game of the 1926 World Series, Babe Ruth made the inexplica-ble mistake of attempting to steal second. Cardinal catcher Bob O'Farrell fired Grover Cleveland Alexander's pitch to Rogers Hornsby, shown here making the easy out.

to state that the gambler was spotted by Ban Johnson and escorted from the Stadium.

The gambler in question was Sport Sullivan, the only Bostonian implicated in the scandal, and the man who first approached Chick Gandil in a Boston hotel and set the whole scam in motion. Sullivan had disappeared after being indicted and subsequently was thought to have

Manager Miller Huggins executed a masterstroke in 1927 when he batted Babe Ruth in front of Lou Gehrig, thereby allowing a slowing Ruth the protection of the budding superstar. Huggins also discovered a thirty-year-old rookie pitcher named Wilcy Moore, whom he used to maximum effect as both a starter and reliever.

been killed or to be hiding out in Mexico. Yet here he was. A month later Vila wrote of the "enormous sums" that had been bet on the Cardinals, citing one individual bet of $250,000.

He didn't implicate Ruth or any other player directly, but he did allude to problems with Meusel—who didn't do anything until game six—and pitcher Urban Shocker, who was awful twice in the Series. Yet Ruth's attempted stolen base was easily the most questionable play of the entire Series.

Major League Baseball leveled a final warning on gambling later that winter, airing the news that some of the game's biggest stars—Joe Wood, Dutch Leonard, Tris Speaker, and Ty Cobb—had all been involved in a plan to fix a game between the Tigers and Indians at the tail end of the 1919 season. Their guilt was obvious, but all involved were given a virtual pass. The incident was Major League Baseball's last major gambling scandal until the Pete Rose affair in 1989.

The Yankees' second-half slump and Series loss caused many to question the ballclub during the spring of 1927. A couple of minor trades delivered a handful of backup players, like outfielder Cedric Durst and catcher Johnny Grabowski, and Ruth, despite spending much of the winter in Hollywood demonstrating that his acting skills were nonexistent, showed up at camp in shape. But they did little else to rectify the situation beyond setting a new record for team payroll, which now stood at $350,000 per annum, $70,000 of which went to Ruth. In all baseball, only the Giants' payroll of more than $250,000 approached that of the Yankees. Ruth's salary alone eclipsed the player budget of several clubs.

For a defending league champion, expectations in 1927 were low. Most observers cited New York's aging pitching staff as reason enough to pick Philadelphia to win the crown. A straw vote of 100 American League players concurred, as did the oddsmakers, who installed Philadelphia as 9–5 favorites to win the pennant. New York was at 3–1.

But the spring revealed some subtle signs of change. In 1926 Lou Gehrig had emerged as a legitimate power hitter—his 16 home runs were fourth best in the league, and he'd become an adequate fielder. His improvement continued. And Wilcy Moore surprised everyone by demonstrating that he was almost as effective facing major league hitters as he had been in the minors.

Yankees fans got an early opportunity to gauge the strength of the club when they opened the season on April 12 at the Stadium against Philadelphia. Waite Hoyt outpitched Lefty Grove as the Yankees won 8–3 despite losing Ruth in the middle of the game with "indigestion" and dizziness. Gehrig picked up the slack, making up for an error by smacking a double to deliver two runs. That was a hint of what would follow.

In spring training Huggins had made a subtle but important change in the Yankee batting order. For most of the 1926 season Ruth had hit third, followed by Meusel and then Gehrig. But in 1927 Huggins reversed Meusel and Gehrig. Gehrig became the Yankees' cleanup hitter, batting between Ruth and Meusel, a change that would have a profound impact.

Ruth was 32 years old and at a stage in his career when his age was beginning to show. Placing Gehrig behind him in the batting order protected Ruth. As Ruth's skills began subtly to erode, the presence of Gehrig forced pitchers to pitch to Ruth. As a result, from ages 32 to 39, with Gehrig behind him, Ruth was a greater home run threat than he had been in his physical prime. And Gehrig, with Ruth on base before him nearly 50 percent of the time, became an RBI machine. Significantly, the Yankees would win more world championships with Ruth and Gehrig in tandem than with Ruth alone. For at this point, despite more than 300 New York home runs, the Babe's Yankees had won only a single world championship.

The Yankees got off to a quick start, taking three of four from the A's, with one tie. In the *Times,* James Harrison noted that "the apathetic A's have displayed nothing that should cause a Yankee fan to walk the floor restlessly at night. Connie Mack, at first blush, appears to have an interesting but not highly valuable collection of antiques." Stars Eddie Collins, Ty Cobb, and Zack Wheat were all in the twilight of their illustrious careers and would pose no threat.

Barely a week into the season Huggins unveiled what would become the Yankees' secret weapon that season, the x-factor that no other team in baseball could match. Wilcy Moore had been the Yankees' most effective pitcher all spring, but he couldn't crack the New York rotation. Huggins began using Moore almost exclusively in relief.

He was perfectly suited for the job. The veteran pitcher had been headed nowhere in the low minors until breaking his arm in 1925. When it healed, he couldn't throw overhand and was forced to drop down and throw sidearm.

The effects were dramatic. Now he couldn't throw the ball straight. His ball had a natural sink, moving down and away from lefties and down and in to right-handed hitters. One visiting writer wrote: "Moore's pitch sinks so rapidly the Yankee catchers have to get closer to the plate to keep from picking the ball from the dirt and to prevent umpires from misjudging the pitches. Moore's sinker may pass the batter above the knee but drops so fast before the catcher gets it as to be only ankle high." The result was usually a harmless ground ball. The press dubbed him "Doc," for as one writer noted, "he specializes in treating ailing ball games and putting them back in a healthy condition."

Huggins quickly recognized Moore's unique curative powers. When a Yankee starter looked weak and the game was within reach, he turned to Moore for healing. Moore wasn't a closer, a pitcher put in to hold a lead, but an old-time fireman, a far more valuable and now almost extinct commodity. A fireman comes in with men on base in a close game, gets out of the inning, and then finishes the game. As Moore did his work, the Yankees caught up and went ahead. "Wilcy Moore must think there are always at least two men on the bases in the American League," wrote one observer. "There always are when he enters a game." He thrived in his role and had the perfect disposition for the job. Moore said of himself, "I ain't a pitcher, I'm a day laborer."

It was almost revolutionary. In fact, Moore was only second in line, not first, of a new order. In 1924 and 1925 Washington manager Bucky Harris's use of pitcher Firpo Marberry as a relief specialist had helped the Senators win back-to-back pennants. For the Yankees, Moore strengthened a veteran starting staff whose strength was its depth, not its stamina. Urban Shocker, for instance, had a heart condition and was risking his life every time he took the mound. Waite Hoyt and George Pipgras were the only two starters under the age of 30, and over the last half of 1926 every man on the staff had faded. Huggins's decision to use Moore in relief made strength of a weakness and put the Yankees light-years ahead of the competition. It was almost as if the Yankees—already the most potent team in the game—had an extra player. In effect, they did.

And then there was Lou Gehrig. Ruth started slowly, yet it hardly mattered. Although Gehrig was Ruth's opposite in virtually every other way, beginning in 1927 he was Ruth's near-equal at the plate. And when Ruth started hitting — which he did as April turned into May — the Yankees took another exponential step forward.

Ruth and Meusel had earlier formed one of baseball's first power-hitting duos, but the pairing of Gehrig and Ruth was an evolutionary leap. In 1927 Ruth, who would hit a record 60 home runs, outhomered every other team in the American League. Gehrig, with 47, the highest number in baseball history hit by anyone not named Ruth, outhomered four of them. Together, their 107 home runs were nearly twice the number hit by the A's, whose 56 home runs in 1927 were second to New York's 158.

No pair of hitters had ever been so powerful, and they gave the Yankees an enormous advantage. Today the equivalent would be for two sluggers on one team to crack 70 or 80 home runs each. The Yankees were a first-place team already, and a good one, but Gehrig and Moore made them legendary. The Yankees began playing baseball like no team that had ever come before it. Baseball was never the same.

The great unveiling took place slowly, as Ruth warmed and Moore settled into his role. Moore picked up his first win on April 21, giving up only one hit to the A's after relieving Hoyt in the fifth inning as the Yankees rebounded to defeat Philadelphia 13–6. Ruth was quiet, singling and walking twice, but Gehrig lashed the telling blow, banging the ball off the upper tier of the left-field stands. And the Yankees won a game when both their starting pitcher and Ruth had failed to deliver, a game they surely would have lost before 1927. Despite the fact that Ruth had but one home run and one RBI, they were already 7–2.

That soon changed. Over the remainder of the month Ruth hit three more home runs, and the Yankees entered May with a 9–5 mark, tied with the A's. Gehrig had been the key to their success so far, but now that Ruth was hitting, the club began to show itself.

On May 1, the A's came to New York to make up an earlier rainout, and Yankees fans turned out in force, filling the Stadium. They witnessed a vintage performance.

In the first inning, after Koenig walked, Ruth homered to right to put the Yankees up 2–0. Ty Cobb didn't even turn around as the ball sailed over his head. Gehrig dupli-

cated Ruth's feat in the sixth, and Ruth cracked a solo shot in the eighth. New York won 7–3, despite collecting only five hits. First place was theirs alone.

Now Moore made his showing count. On May 2 in Washington, he squashed a late threat by the Senators as the Yankees won 9–6. The next day he came on in relief of George Pipgras with the score tied 4–4. He shut down Washington again, and the Yankees, hitting way over .300 as a team, scored twice to win 6–4. Both contests easily could have gone the other way, yet they tilted to the Yankees. In 1927 they always did.

By midmonth the Yankees had taken command of the American League and were starting to cause their opponents to shake their heads in wonder. After beating the Browns 4–2 on May 12, St. Louis pitcher Milt Gaston, despite pitching rather well, offered: "I would rather pitch a doubleheader against any other club than one game against the Yankees. There isn't a moment's mental rest for a pitcher in that batting order." As June approached, only the A's and White Sox seemed capable of keeping pace with New York.

The Yankees then went to Philadelphia, and before 4,000 fans in the first game of a separate-admission doubleheader, they gave the A's some faint hope as they fell 9–8. The A's then pressed the second game into extra innings. It was 5–5 entering the eleventh.

Then came Ruth. The Yankees shed their challenger with a flick of his powerful wrists. He sent the ball into the left-field stands, and Moore collected the win.

The A's never recovered. The next day the Yankees swept another doubleheader, 10–3 and 18–5. Ruth, as James Harrison noted in the *Times*, "went crazy and [ran] amuck," cracking two "festive bunts," his fourth and fifth home runs in the last four days. Gehrig, Pat Collins, Lazzeri, and even Mark Koenig chipped in with similar blows to go along with 4 triples, 4 doubles, and 23 singles. The defeats left the A's "drawn, quartered, cooked in boiling oil and otherwise slaughtered," observed Harrison, already beginning to grapple with new ways to describe the club. By the end of game two Ruth even went to bat right-handed. Philadelphia was humiliated.

In the finale of the five-game set, the Yankees teased Philadelphia again, as the score was tied 1–1 in the ninth. But with Ben Paschal on second, Joe Dugan put the A's out

The 1927 Yankees discovered a working-class hero in rookie pitcher Wilcy Moore. The former minor league sensation and railroad worker thrived as the Yankees' fireman, causing one observer to remark, "Wilcy Moore must think there are always at least two men on the bases in the American League."

of their misery with a single to win the game and complete the destruction of the A's. Only Chicago remained.

The White Sox came to New York on June 7 trailing by only a single game. White Sox pitcher Al Thomas shut down the Yanks early, but the second time around Ruth and Gehrig launched back-to-back home runs to give Waite Hoyt the only runs he needed in the 4–1 win. "Folks," wrote Paul Gallico in the *Daily News,* "the existence of Santa Claus can not be denied."

It remained Christmas in New York the following afternoon. Despite two Tony Lazzeri home runs, the Yankees trailed 11–5 in the ninth. But four base hits produced three runs and brought up Lazzeri once more. The result was home run number three and a tie game, which the Yankees won 12–11 two innings later.

The insult was completed the following day, as the Yankees won again, 8–3, erupting for six seventh-inning runs. Ruth tripled in the midst of the rally, and then, as if pissed

off that the ball didn't go over the fence, he topped it off by stealing home. Chicago left New York trailing by three games and fully aware that the Yankees were a much better team. Three days later the Yankees began a nine-game winning streak, capped by a three-home-run performance by Gehrig against the Red Sox, and the pennant race was effectively over.

In the *Herald Tribune,* Grantland Rice asserted at the beginning of his column "The Sportlight" that "any argument concerning the best ballclub of the last thirty-five years, which might be taken as all-time, includes at least five clubs": the 1897 Boston Nationals, the Cubs of either 1906 or 1908, the Athletics of 1910 and 1911, and the White Sox of 1919. Then, added Rice, "there is another ballclub that must be added to the list . . . the New York Yankees." He cited an unnamed writer from another city who had assessed the team point by point and concluded, "You can class the Yankees with five or six of the best clubs baseball has shown and not go wrong."

Rice was the most influential sportswriter in the country, and his column was distributed nationwide. With the pennant race virtually decided, the New York press had to turn its attention away from the simple details of the games, which increasingly lacked any drama, and look elsewhere for interesting copy. For the remainder of the season the story of the 1927 Yankees concerned itself with two questions: Just how good was this baseball team? And would Ruth, already running ahead of his record home run pace, hold off teammate Lou Gehrig and set a new home run record?

The competition to tell these two stories among New York's storied cast of baseball journalists was fierce. The *Times* had editor and columnist John Kieran, and James Harrison and Richards Vidmer covered the Yankee beat. The *Herald Tribune* featured Rud Rennie and W. O. McGeehan. Paul Gallico and Marshall Hunt were with the *Daily News.* Fred Lieb wrote for the *Post,* and Ford Frick and Bozeman Bulger were with the *Evening Journal.* Veteran Joe Vila and Frank Graham manned the *Sun* sports desk, and Dan Daniel and Joe Williams held court for the *Telegram.* Heavyweights who'd cut their teeth on sports and then moved on to a wider literary landscape, such as Damon Runyon and Ring Lardner, also occasionally weighed in. They combined to push each other to ever-greater heights of rheto-

LARDNER
HAS BRIGHT IDEA
TO HELP PITTSBURGH TEAM:
WHEN PIRATES ARE PERFORMING,
HE WOULD HAVE ETIQUETTE OF TENNIS AND GOLF PREVAIL

RING LARDNER

PITTSBURGH, OCT. 4 —(SPECIAL)— In a last minute effort to be of assistance to the friend of my youth, Donnie Bush, in his ball club's impending brawl with the big bruisers from the Bronx, this handsome writer gained audience tonight with Judge Landis and presented a scheme which, if put into effect, may change the entire complexion of the series and probably of all future baseball.

It would be clearly unfair to pit these two teams vs. each other on even terms. The Yankees won the pennant the day before the season opened and the only thing they have had to worry them since was the remote possibility that one of the other American League [teams] would trade itself in bulk for Casey Stengel's Toledo nine and thus introduce the element of competition into what has long been laughingly known as the Ban Johnson circuit. This didn't happen and the Yanks are entering the World Series as carefree as a vegetable dinner. Whereas on the other hand, the Pirates are nervous. If they ain't nervous, they ain't human. I didn't mean to imply that they are scared. If they were the kind of boys that gets terrorized they would have jumped right out of the league just listening to the Giants talk. But you can't go through what they have been through and not feel kind of shaky and for that reason I have figured they ought to be given some little handicap to kind of counterbalance the advantage of the Yankees' "sang froid."

TRUE SPORTSMANSHIP

Well, I suggested to the judge that regular baseball rules and customs prevail only when the New York players are doing something but that when the Pittsburgh Athletics are performing either in the field or at bat, the game be played according to the etiquette observed in tennis and golf, the two outdoor sports whose exponents appear to be very sensitive. Judge Landis, who was now dozing off, asked me to jot down a few of the regulations I had in mind so they might be submitted to Messers Dreyfuss and Ruppert before game time.

I have kept a copy of same and here they are:

1. The umpire shall request that while a Pittsburgh pitcher is pitching or a Pittsburgh fielder fielding or a Pittsburgh batter batting, the spectators maintain absolute silence.
2. There shall be no booing of any Pittsburgh player at any time.
3. The spectators shall not applaud Pittsburgh errors.
4. When a New York batter hits a ground ball or a fly ball to any Pittsburgh infielder or outfielder, there shall be no demonstration of any kind until the play is completed.
5. If a Pittsburgh player is called out when a New York player thinks he is really safe, or when a safe hit by a Pittsburgh player is called foul and a New York player thinks it is fair, the New York player shall purposely strike then turn to the press stand and smile as much as to say, "This is true sportsmanship, typical of France."
6. No spectator shall be allowed to arise to his feet except between innings.
7. New York players, whether running bases or running after batted balls, shall stop and replace each divot made by their spikes before making another one.
8. In the game called golf it is annoying to most high-class players to leave anyone stand close to them or directly behind them while they are making a stroke. Therefore, when Pittsburgh players are about to swing their bats, the New York catcher and the home plate umpire shall betake themselves to one or the other of the two benches and remain there quietly until the Pittsburgh player has swang.

"Well, K. M.," I said to the Judge, when I had read the above aloud to him, "will you see that these ideas are carried out?"

"Yes," he replied. "Just toss them in the basket there and the maid will tend to them in the morning."

"Is everything jake with you, Judge?" I asked.

"Oh, no," the Judge answered.

"I like Barney just as well."

"Which reminds me," said I, "that I haven't seen much liquor around here."

"No," agreed the judge.

"It looks as if this was to be a Dreyfuss."

Deciding that the high commissioner of baseball was growing a trifle ribald, I ventured downstairs to the crowded Schenley lobby and ran into Jimmie Sheckard, who played left field for Methuselah's club in the days when fly balls had to be caught in the beard.

"What do you think of the series, Sheck?" I shouted in his good ear. "It ought to be a short series," he said. "Both the managers are short. If you took Bush and Huggins and laid them end to end, the game warden would make you throw them back in the brook."

"I never thought about both of them being so little," I said. "It may be their success will influence the owners of other major league clubs to hire brief managers."

"Hardly," said Mr. Sheckard, lifting his skirts and beginning an old-fashioned quadrille. "Look at Dave Bancroft and Ray Schalk. They are both midgets, too. But if you took them and laid them end to end, or even side by side, it would be at least a week before you would have to apply for tickets to a World Series between the White Sox and Braves."

At the end of the dance he asked me who I was picking to pitch tomorrow's game.

"Aldridge and Pennock," I replied.

"Just those two," said Sheck.

"I think we Wilcy Moore."

(COPYRIGHT 1927)

From 1908 to 1913 **RING LARDNER** was a sportswriter covering baseball. In 1914 he published his first fiction, and his collection of baseball-inspired stories, *You Know Me Al* (1916), made him a celebrity. The 1927 World Series was the last he covered writing for the Bell Syndicate. Lardner died in 1933 at age 48.

ric and hyperbole. Yankee games would not be broadcast to the New York audience for another decade. The often-exalted observations of these writers were the final and only words on their subject.

These men did not conform to the "Oscar Madison" sportswriter stereotype. The genre was still relatively new — sportswriting was in its adolescence. And while much of their work today appears arch and ridden with clichés and wordplay, today's clichés were then brand-new. True, most of these men indulged in hero-worship and hagiography and could be described as proponents of either the "Gee whiz" or "Aw, nuts" school of sportswriting, but in their day they were the best, and their work was often the best writing in the paper.

Well educated and accomplished, many were the products of prep schools and prestigious private colleges. Many later left sports and made their mark in other genres. John Kieran, for example, won the Burroughs Medal for his writing on natural history, Paul Gallico wrote popular fiction, Vidmer served under General Eisenhower in intelligence, and Frick became the American League president. Even one Ed Sullivan of the *New York Graphic* later found fame as the noted host of the television program that bore his name. The stable of writers covering the Yankees in 1927 was their literary mirror image — a Murderers' Row of reportage.

Two days after Rice's laudatory column, Dan Daniel weighed in and interviewed Dodger manager Wil Robinson, who'd played for the powerhouse 1896 Orioles. Robinson called the contemporary Yankees "the greatest club ever got together," citing not only their prodigious hitting but their speed and defense as well.

He was right: the Yankees were more than unbridled power grossly unleashed. Their baserunning was superb, and Combs, Meusel, and Lazzeri were constant threats to steal. If not for their power, the Yanks could have easily led the league in that category. The club could still play "little ball" when the occasion called for it, pushing across runs with sacrifices, steals, and the hit-and-run.

Defensively, they were more than adequate. Combs and Meusel made up for Ruth's increasing lack of range in the outfield, but when the Babe got to a ball, he knew what to do with it. Koenig, while erratic, was still one of the league's better shortstops, as was Dugan at third, and second baseman Lazzeri, who also spent time at short and

third filling in for the injured, had great range and a powerful arm.

On June 30, the Yankees beat Boston 13–6 to enter July with a record of 49–20, 10½ games ahead of the nearest challenger. In the *Times,* James Harrison underscored their invincibility, writing: "There was a ball game at Yankee Stadium yesterday, but nobody paid the slightest attention to it. Everybody knew that the Yankees would beat the Red Sox. It wasn't the ball game that drew the customers to the ball yard; they had come to see the great home run derby between G. Herman Ruth and H. Louis Gehrig." The fans weren't disappointed: both men cracked their 25th home run of the season, which Harrison described in excruciating detail before adding, "Oh yes, the ball game. It was a very nice game."

There were a couple of other nice games on July 4, when the Yankees entertained the Washington Senators at Yankee Stadium for a holiday doubleheader. The second-place Senators, pennant winners in 1924 and 1925, had beaten the Yankees the day before to draw to within nine and a half games of first place and still held to a faint hope of making a pennant race.

Before a crowd announced at 72,641 — their largest ever at the time — the Yankees, as if turning around and noticing the Senators for the first time all season, first swatted them off their shoulder, then used their bats to beat them senseless. As the *Tribune* noted: "They put all they had into hitting the ball and made a total of 37 hits and a total yardage of 300 miles," winning the first game 12–1 and the second 21–1. Gehrig hit two home runs to go two up on Ruth, and Pipgras and Moore, in a rare start, both went the distance. Jaded Yankee fans took the wins in stride: "A home run seemed to be the only thing that mattered . . . nothing else aroused the crowd."

So it would be for the remainder of the season. Ruth and Gehrig were the only race that mattered.

Gehrig led Ruth 28–26 in the home run derby, but few expected Gehrig, who'd never hit more than 20 before, to retain his lead. He was more of a gap hitter, and some of his longest drives went to the deeper parts of the ballpark for doubles and triples.

Yet for the next six weeks the two sluggers traded home runs. Ruth took the lead on July 26 against St. Louis, cracking two to Gehrig's one in a 15–1 and 12–3 doubleheader sweep, but Gehrig seized the lead back four days later when he smacked two home runs in Cleveland. He would hold that lead for the next three weeks. Meanwhile, the Yankees' lead over the rest of the league grew ever wider. By the end of July even Miller Huggins was willing to admit that the Yankees' 13–5 record on their last road trip virtually guaranteed the pennant. "When booking your World Series reservations in New York," wrote Vidmer in the *Times,* "pick a nice place in New York to stay part of the time for the Yankees are what the boys call 'in.'" Washington had won nine of its last eleven, yet the Senators' Joe Judge moaned to Vidmer, "We win and we win, yet the Yanks don't even pause for breath. How can you jump a team when you can't even catch up to it?" Judge already knew the answer, and so did everyone else.

"The Yanks are coming," wrote John Kieran. "In fact, they are here . . . out in front so far the other teams are keeping track of them by radio."

By September they were 89–37, 25 games ahead of second-place Philadelphia. Yet despite the runaway, attendance throughout the league held steady. Only Cleveland, which had collapsed after finishing second in 1926, suffered a significant drop in attendance.

The Yankees were good for business. Interest in Ruth buoyed attendance everywhere. Apart from holidays, many teams enjoyed their biggest crowds while hosting New York. The Yankees, with Ruth, were the only club in baseball with a national constituency.

The closest thing to a seasonal low point for the Yankees took place on September 3 in Philadelphia. In the first inning, after Grove retired Combs and Koenig, Ruth singled sharply to left before Gehrig flied out to end the inning. Over the next six innings the remarkable happened. No Yankee reached base.

Grove struck out the side in the second on ten pitches, easily the best-pitched inning against the Yankees all year long. And for the next five innings his fastball proved to be sufficient as batter after batter went meekly back to the bench. Only Lazzeri managed a hit, and he was quickly put out on a double play.

The Yankees made a passing threat in both the eighth and the ninth, managing a hit in each frame, but that was all. When Lou Gehrig struck out to end the game, John Drebinger noted in the *Times:* "Those 25,000 staid Philadel-

phians became so many frenzied souls when they howled a mighty paean. There could not have been a greater demonstration had these Mackmen clinched the pennant and the World Series title all on the same afternoon." The league had learned to take what it could get from the Yankees. One Philadelphia scribe likened Grove's performance to that

Eddie Bennett, a hunchback, was the Yankees' mascot and batboy for much of the twenties. Baseball superstition of the time held that such men brought teams good luck, and in countless photos Bennett is shown congratulating Ruth and Gehrig when they hit home runs.

of Sergeant York when he "took a hundred Germans and spiked a dozen menacing machine guns single handed." He had managed to do something no other pitcher had done all season long—shut out the New Yorkers.

But for the Yankees of 1927, even in defeat there was a silver lining. Wilcy Moore got a rare start opposite Grove. He needed the work, for over the previous eight games, all Yankee wins, his teammates had scored at least eight runs in each contest, giving him precious little to do. He proved nearly as effective as his rival, giving up only five hits and a single run and giving manager Miller Huggins an idea, which he filed away for use in October.

All was soon back to normal. Playing a doubleheader in Boston on September 5, the Yankees split but left the Red Sox fat and happy. Thirty-eight thousand fans punched their way into Fenway Park. Not bad for a Tuesday. And in another doubleheader split the next day, they drew 20,000 more. The two-day total was fully 19 percent of Boston's home attendance for the entire season. Thanks, Yanks.

After battering the Red Sox in the season finale, the Yankees returned to New York to play out the string . . . er, complete the schedule . . . finishing the regular season with 21 consecutive games at home. It hardly seemed fair. When the Yankees clinched the pennant on September 13, John Kieran was moved to write dryly, "On a golf basis, the Yankees won the league championship by 18 up with 17 to play, a rather large margin." With that, Huggins moved to give his regulars a little rest and take aim at the 1912 Red Sox record of 105 victories. Everyone else settled in to watch Ruth's assault on history. He already had 52 home runs.

It was a big story, but not a *big* story. The *big* story was the upcoming heavyweight fight between Gene Tunney and Jack Dempsey, which pushed Ruth and the Yankees below the fold for much of the next week. After all, Ruth had already smacked 54 in 1920 and 59 in 1921. While 60 home runs was, like the Babe himself, a nice, round, satisfying number, hitting that many did not yet seem insurmountable. It was simply a pleasant diversion, a reason to

In 1927 the best player ever led perhaps the best team ever as the nation delighted in the antics of Babe Ruth and his unbeatable team. Never shy, Ruth took every opportunity to ham it up for photographers, as when he posed with the American Legion marching band at Yankee Stadium.

keep paying attention to something other than the pennant race in the National League, where the Pirates were beginning to settle in comfortably ahead of the Giants.

Ruth benefited when the whole league started packing it in, since over the final weeks he didn't exactly face the best pitching. But then again, baseball has never had a showman quite like Ruth. He was never better or more entertaining than when he knew all eyes were on him, and over the final weeks they were and he knew it.

Ruth hit another home run nearly every other game or so until hitting number 56 on September 22. It was an important one, not only because it came in the ninth inning and beat Detroit, 8–7, but because the victory, the Yankees' 105th of the season, tied them with the 1912 Red Sox. An entourage of idolaters accompanied Ruth around the bases, and he carried his bat with him, holding it with both hands, for many of his followers tried to relieve him of his burden. But just as Ruth appeared to have the new record in his grasp, he went four games without a home run, his longest drought in a month. With only three games remaining, his task seemed almost impossible.

On September 28, Philadelphia manager Connie Mack didn't make it easy. He emptied his bullpen in an effort to thwart Ruth and the Yankees.

Rube Walberg shut down New York for three innings, then gave way to Jack Quinn, who gave up a home run to Gehrig, his 46th of the year. Sam Gray and then Lefty Grove followed him, making Ruth's task harder still. He hadn't homered against Grove in 1927, and only 17 of his home runs had come against left-handed pitching.

Ruth came up in the sixth with the bases full of Yankees. It was the perfect situation. The Yankees led 2–1, and Grove had no place to put the Bambino. He had to pitch to him.

As though hoisting a sack of laundry, Ruth lifted the ball to right and dropped it over the fence—a grand slam, and only the third in his Yankee career. Number 57 and an eventual 7–4 Yankee win.

He still needed three for sixty, and after an off-day Ruth took aim at the Senators' Hod Lisenbee. He wasted no time, lining an 0–2 curveball into the stands in the first inning for number 58.

Thus began the onslaught. In the second inning New York chased Lisenbee as Ruth tripled to center. He was

YANKEE AMERICAN LEAGUE
BATTING
CHAMPIONS

1924 **Babe Ruth, .378**

1934 **Lou Gehrig, .363**

1939 **Joe DiMaggio, .381**

1940 **Joe DiMaggio, .352**

1945 **George Stirnweiss, .309**

1956 **Mickey Mantle, .353**

1984 **Don Mattingly, .343**

1994 **Paul O'Neill, .359**

1998 **Bernie Williams, .339**

replaced by Paul Hopkins, a 22-year-old rookie making only his second appearance of the year, and one of only 11 in his career. Hopkins got Ruth to fly out in the fourth, but in the sixth he loaded the bases, "arranging things," as the *Herald* noted, "in such a fashion as to bring his fame in that direction if no other." Ruth worked the count to 3–2 and then connected.

Once more the ball went on a line into the right-field stands, halfway up the bleachers. The blast gave New York a 15–4 lead, which was also the final score, as all parties seemed to rush the game to a finish from there. The drama, after all, was over, but as the *Herald* accurately commented, "In order that Ruth might make home runs a ball game was necessary." That's what it had come down to.

There was a ballgame the next day as well, against Washington, and Ruth once again overwhelmed the proceed-

On September 30, 1927, Babe Ruth smacked two home runs against the Washington Senators at Yankee Stadium, including a grand slam, for his fifty-eighth and fifty-ninth homers of the season. The sight of Lou Gehrig greeting Ruth with extended hand was almost a trademark for the '27 world champions.

ings. Yet only 10,000 fans, an average crowd, turned out for the Friday afternoon contest to witness Ruth's assault on the summit. Those not in attendance undoubtedly hoped he'd wait a day and break the record on Saturday, when it would be easier to make the game. Ruth had other ideas.

Washington veteran lefty Tom Zachary pitched well, and the game was tied 2–2 entering the eighth inning. Ruth had already had a good day, collecting two hits and scoring both Yankee runs, as if any of that mattered at all, and it did not.

All that mattered was his next at bat. Koenig tripled with one out, bringing Ruth to the plate for what would probably be the last time that game.

He took a fastball for a strike. He watched a pitch sail high for a ball. Then Zachary threw once more.

He tried to cross Ruth up and threw what Babe later described as "a slow screwball." The pitch broke down and in. Ruth saw it all the way. As W. B. Hanna wrote in the *Tribune,* it was a screwball "until it met Ruth's unruly bat. Then it was a minie ball," a type of rifle bullet.

It was an accurate description, for Ruth chopped down hard on the pitch, caught it out front, and sent it on a line toward the bleachers. It had the distance but started to curve foul, and plate umpire Bill Dinneen straddled the line to make the call. As the ball rattled into the bleachers some 15 rows shy of the back wall, he waved his hand over his head. Number 60 had just settled into the hands of 40-year-old Joseph Fortner.

As Ruth took a glowing circuit around the bases and 10,000 fans roared and waved handkerchiefs, Zachary stomped around and halfheartedly protested that the ball was foul. The hit won the game, 4–2, the Yankees 109th victory.

It is important to note, however, that Ruth did not mince around the bases in the energetic shuffling trot with which we are familiar from the newsreels, or from John Goodman's imitation in a recent movie. That curious gait is the result of film shown at the wrong speed. Ruth's home run trot was similar to that of other players.

The press fairly slobbered all over itself attempting to record the proceedings and lend the occasion the appropriate gloss. "Succumb to the power and romance of the man," pled Paul Gallico. "Drop your cynicism and feel the athletic marvel that this big uncouth fellow has accomplished." John Kieran reprinted his poem "Was There Ever a Guy Like Ruth?" and added, "Put it in the book with letters of gold. It will be a long time before anyone else betters that home run mark."

Ruth himself was absolutely giddy. He told the *Evening World*, "Will I ever break this again? I don't know and I don't care." Added reporter Arthur Mann, "If the world ever forgets a guy named Ruth lived, it will be due to universal amnesia."

The Yankees wrapped up the season the next afternoon, winning 4–3 as 20,000 pled for one more Ruthian blast. They got their wish, only Gehrig struck it, his 47th of the season and league-best 175th RBI. The victory was number 110 for the Yankees.

"The performance of the Babe rather seems to dwarf the impending World Series," wrote W. O. McGeehan. "The baseball season ended in a way when the Babe drove his sixtieth home run." Pittsburgh won the National League pennant, but after the histrionics of the last few days, the World Series was something of an afterthought. Pittsburgh had to struggle mightily to edge out the Giants and Cardinals, winning 94 games, to win the pennant by a game and a half.

The Yankees were the heaviest of favorites, as the odds opened at 7–5. Pittsburgh's chances rested with the notion espoused by Rud Rennie that "any team composed of nine major league players is capable of winning ballgames, especially in a short series." But he also noted "there is popular belief that the World Series will be over after the fourth game."

Not that the Pirates were without talent. Pie Traynor and the Waner brothers, Lloyd and Paul, all hit above .340 and would eventually make it into the Hall of Fame, and the club hit .305 for the season. The pitching staff was paced by journeyman Carmen Hill, who had the year of his life and won 22 games, backed up by veterans Ray Kremer, Lee Meadows, and Vic Aldridge.

But the Pirates did not inspire fear. Before the start of the Series, the Waner brothers introduced themselves to Ruth at the Yankees' hotel. After they left, Ruth told a writer, "Why, they're no bigger than a couple of little kids. If I was that size I'd be afraid of getting hurt."

At least according to legend, the Yankees did inspire fear. Shortly after the Yankees arrived in Pittsburgh, they took several rounds of batting practice, and Ruth, Gehrig,

and the other members of Murderers' Row sent balls over the fence in impressive numbers.

The mythic performance reportedly left the Pirates open-mouthed and defeated. Actually, New York's first such workout was rained out, and most of the Pirates never left the clubhouse and saw nothing more than their own lockers. Although a handful of Pirates players watched from the stands, nothing they saw was unexpected. New York's power was no mystery, and after all, the Pirates had

The 1927 Yankees won 110 games, and in the 109th win Babe Ruth hit the two-run homer that set the single-season home run record of sixty. Paul Gallico joined a journalistic chorus when he wrote, "Succumb to the power and romance of the man. Drop your cynicism and feel the athletic marvel that this big uncouth fellow has accomplished."

beaten the defending world champion St. Louis Cardinals to win the NL pennant.

Both clubs were confident. "I don't care what they do," said Huggins. "We'll beat them." His counterpart, Pirates manager Donie Bush, was similarly certain of victory. "Naturally I think we'll win," said Bush. "I figure it will go six games and that we'll win." Pirates owner Barney Dreyfuss, expecting to play four games in Pittsburgh, even built extra stands behind the left-field fence and added boxes down the foul lines to increase the capacity of Forbes Field. The dimensions of the park were larger than those of Yankee Stadium. It was 360 feet down the left-field line and 462 feet to the deepest part of the park, just left of center. While the right-field line was only 300 feet, the fence angled back sharply — it was over 400 feet to the power alley. Pitching loomed as more important than raw power.

And in that regard the Yanks were worried. Backup outfielder Cedric Durst lined a ball off Herb Pennock's leg in practice, breaking a blood vessel. His availability was uncertain.

But speculation was soon replaced by reality. Before 43,000 fans in game one, the Yankees slowly exerted their superiority. Pitcher Ray Kremer kept the ball in the ballpark, but the Yankees found another way to win, parlaying two errors, two walks, one hit — a Babe Ruth single — and a double steal into three runs. Hoyt pitched into the eighth, then turned the ball over to Moore. The Yankees won 5–4.

They won again the next day in much the same fashion. Pipgras spotted his fastball and scattered seven hits, and the Yankees used a series of seeing-eye singles to spark two three-run rallies to win 6–2. Grantland Rice accurately described the Pirates as "listless," noting that the contest "was not by any means a thrilling ball game." A *Tribune* headline even called it "the World's Dullest World Series." New York was simply beating Pittsburgh with the passionless and efficient precision of a machine that stamped out "W's"— about as thrilling as an assembly line.

The 1928 season and the World Series to follow were very much a continuation of the Yankees' 1927 campaign. Their four-game series sweep over the Cardinals was sparked by this fourth-inning two-run homer by Bob Meusel (running behind Babe Ruth), in the first game at Yankee Stadium.

1928

In 1927 there was no more beloved sports hero in America than Babe Ruth, shown here with children at an orphanage in Bangor, Maine.

called Cedric Durst up to his office and said, "Your duties will be to burst one of Pennock's blood vessels twice a week." He then added, "Colonel Ruppert himself is to pitch today. And why not?"

He was referring to the rumor of the moment. There was rampant speculation before game four that the Pirates would be allowed to win. A third game played in New York would be worth $200,000 to Jacob Ruppert. No American League team had ever swept a Series, a fact that most observers believed said more about greed than talent. "If the Yankees make it four straight today," wrote McGeehan, "some of the insinuation . . . will be refuted."

Huggins started Wilcy Moore in game four, but it was Ruth who left his mark on the game. He gave the Series its only memorable moments, knocking in a first-inning run with a single and cracking a two-run homer in the fifth to put New York ahead 3–1.

But Pittsburgh tied the score, and it remained that way when the Yankees came to bat in the ninth. The Yankees loaded the bases with none out, but then reliever Eddie Miljus fanned Gehrig and Meusel, bringing up Tony Lazzeri with the game on the line and everyone in attendance recalling his failure against Alexander in the previous World Series. Here was an opportunity for redemption.

But the dullness of this World Series was not to be denied. As Paul Gallico wrote: "The slapstick is mightier than the bludgeon and for that reason the New York Yankees are the baseball champions of the world, and if ever a dramatic ball game came to a sillier ending, I would like to be informed."

With the crowd roaring and Lazzeri at the plate and Earle Combs only 90 feet away from home, Miljus threw a wild pitch. It bounced off the catcher's glove and rolled away. Combs loped home, and the Yankees were world champions.

They hadn't even broken a sweat. They had simply won with the same cool efficiency with which they'd won all year long, knocking the opposition to the ground, then keeping them there. From all appearances, they seemed able to continue to do so for the foreseeable future.

The Yankees took that approach in 1928, making only cosmetic changes to their roster, counting on their reputation and considerable momentum to vanquish the opposition.

Back in New York for game three, New York asserted itself against Hill with two first-inning runs, capped by Gehrig's triple, in which he was thrown out trying to make home. Hoyt, feeling no effects from his leg injury, shut down the Pirates, and the Yankees chased Hill back to mediocrity in the seventh. Ruth capped the six-run outburst with the first home run of the Series, a rather meaningless blast that put the Yanks up by the eventual final score, 8–1. Yankee fans were so blasé they didn't even bother to fill the bleachers.

The Series was a laugher. Ring Lardner, weighing in for the Bell Syndicate, "reported" that after the game Ruppert

It worked — not perfectly — but it worked. The Yankees kicked off the 1928 season by winning 34 of their first 42 games to open up a seemingly insurmountable lead over Philadelphia. But the Yankees were not quite the same team that had romped to the 1927 pennant.

Eighteen-game winner Urban Shocker's heart gave out, and he was forced to retire. He would die in September, the first of many members of that fabled team to die before their time. The Yankees relaxed in the second half and fought off injuries that knocked Dugan, Koenig, Meusel, Lazzeri, and Pennock out of the lineup for significant periods of time and saw Wilcy Moore crash back to earth with a so-so season and a sore arm. The Athletics, buoyed by the addition of young slugger Jimmie Foxx, made a late charge and even took the lead for a few days in early September. Then the Yankees awoke and took three of four from the A's and rolled to another pennant as Ruth hit 54 home runs, Gehrig tied him for the league lead in RBIs with 145, Pipgras won 23 games, and Hoyt 23. Ho-hum.

The World Series brought on the Cardinals, who, like Pittsburgh the year before, had been forced to fight out a close pennant race and entered the Series spent and exhausted. But so were the Yankees. The smart money was all going toward St. Louis at odds of 5–3. W. O. McGeehan was referring to New York as "the Hypochondriacs." On the eve of the Series he cautioned, "There is one bright spot to it all. If it goes as predicted, the post-mortems will be brief. The alibis for the Yankees were in months ago."

They didn't need them. Even though they played without Combs and Pennock, both of whom were hurt, the Yankees were hardly tested — St. Louis led for all of three innings in the Yankees' four-game sweep. McGeehan offered that the Cardinals were obviously "handicapped by being too healthy." Manager Bill McKechnie was more succinct, saying, "We are terrible."

Ruth set record upon record by hitting .625 with three doubles and three home runs — all three in the final game. It was enough to upstage Gehrig, who hit four home runs himself but hit "only" .545. Together, the two men scored more runs than the entire Cardinals team and accounted for more bases. As Richards Vidmer noted, "The Yankees said it with homers. The conventional way is to say it with flowers, but the flowers today were for the Cards. They were funeral wreaths."

For the Yankees, "wait till next year" took on an entirely different meaning. They could hardly wait for it to come.

Babe Ruth epitomized the confidence and hedonism of pre-Depression New York. His city was the biggest and best, and his team were champions. He was the most photographed man in America, and his paycheck exceeded that of the President and many captains of industry.

1929–1934
THE PRIDE OF THE YANKEES

In less than a decade Ruth, the Yankees, and New York City had expunged their past and created an apparently boundless future. He was King, and New York his empire.

The city was almost unrecognizable. New York had been remade into its modern form. Where once the Flatiron Building had looked serenely over a sleepy Manhattan, dozens of skyscrapers now dwarfed it in shadow, and the city hummed 24 hours a day. New York was the acknowledged capital of American culture, business, and industry. The beacon that beamed from the Statue of Liberty had successfully guided millions of immigrants to the shores of the city, a place they had made their own.

Everything was jumping. Harlem set the rhythm of the street, Wall Street created fortunes by the fistful, and the bright lights of Broadway beckoned everyone. Even the mayor of New York, the flamboyant Jimmy Walker, moonlighted as a songwriter. The Yankees epitomized the era. No one mentioned their dismal past or humble beginnings anymore;

few even knew the history of the club. The names Chesbro, Chase, Cree, and Elberfeld meant as much to most New Yorkers as the place names the Munsee natives had once given to Manhattan's physical features.

Babe Ruth stood atop the Yankee dynasty. In his nine years as a Yankee they had won six pennants, including the last three, and three world championships, including the last two, in which they had won eight World Series games in succession. And now, with Gehrig as his consort and Ruppert's millions supplying the armaments, there seemed no reason to expect that streak to end, just as there seemed no reason for the building of New York City to cease. One architect was already planning a skyscraper some 7,000 feet tall. The Yankees seemed fully capable of reaching similar heights.

It was, of course, all an illusion, a gigantic group hallucination of the Jazz Age. That future was as spurious and unobtainable as a mirage, and the signs were everywhere.

In New York the economy was starting to falter as fortunes built on paper began to sag. The endless party grew ever more frenetic, oblivious to the inevitable hangover. For the Yankees, the 1928 season had not been quite the frolic it now seemed.

The club's late season pillaging of the A's and subsequent romp over the Cardinals in the World Series had masked some real problems. Both the club's offense and pitching had slipped in 1928, while the A's, with an influx of younger talent best represented by Al Simmons, Jimmie Foxx, and Mickey Cochrane, were on the rise.

Ever so slowly, the Yankees — even Ruth — were beginning to slip. Injuries had masked that fact in 1928, but Dugan, Meusel, and Pennock, all in their thirties, were on the decline, and Moore had proven to be a one-year wonder. Ruth, entering his 15th year in the major leagues, was now the second-oldest man on the team. Although he'd played in all 154 games in 1928, his workload and his lifestyle had extracted a toll. He still hit home runs like no one else, but he didn't run very well anymore, and he was beginning to be a defensive liability. Over the next few seasons would come a slow acknowledgment that Gehrig, not Ruth, was the club's best player. But Ruth, to the end, would remain the most beloved.

In the wash of their recent success, the Yankees didn't recognize their problems. Since retooling in 1926, Barrow

had hardly made a trade, acquiring minor league talent instead. While some of these players had come through — witness Lazzeri, Gehrig, and Moore — in recent years the return had been more modest. In 1928 the only notable additions were backup infielder Leo Durocher, a fine talent but not an impact player, and veteran pitcher Tom Zachary, whom they'd picked up from Washington on waivers.

After nearly a decade at the helm, Barrow simply didn't have the same intimate knowledge of Organized Baseball he had had when he joined the Yankees, and other major league clubs had grown wary of dealing with him. When Barrow showed interest in a player now, the price went up.

At the same time Ruppert no longer had the cash flow from his breweries to back his baseball operation. He was still one of the wealthiest magnates in the game, but baseball had become his primary business. Although the Yankees were successful — they'd drawn over eight million fans since acquiring Ruth, far more than any other team — they were also the most expensive team in baseball. Ruth was now in the final year of a three-year contract that paid him $70,000 a year, and the construction of Yankee Stadium had been costly. The club was making money, but attendance had stayed flat at just over one million fans a year, and the two World Series sweeps had cost Ruppert hundreds of thousands of dollars. His margin was growing thinner, and he was a little less eager to take on heavy salaries or throw money at unproven minor leaguers like Lyn Lary and Jimmy Reese, two disappointments who had cost him more than $100,000.

The end of Prohibition was yet another factor. Ruppert was preparing to take his brewery operations out of mothballs and start making beer again. That was going to take money. The Yankees would have to share the wealth. Standing pat was beginning to look like the Yankee way.

Only Huggins seemed to realize that trouble lay ahead. Responding to calls to break up the Yankees, he said, "It won't be necessary. . . . [T]he law of averages will take care of us . . . the time will come when we will crash."

Off-season news was dominated by off-season events. Ruth and Helen were still living apart, and the public would soon learn just how far apart that was. On January 11, 1929, the home of dentist Dr. Edward Kinder in Watertown, Massachusetts, a Boston suburb, burned. A woman's

In January 1929 Babe Ruth attended the graveside service of his estranged wife, Helen. Regarding the circumstances of her death, in a fire at the home of Dr. Edward Kinder of Watertown, Massachusetts, the tabloid press called the arrangement a "love nest" before the Yankee slugger asked the press to "leave my wife alone. Let her stay dead."

body was discovered on the second floor, and over a period of days it was revealed that the woman the neighbors knew as Mrs. Kinder was actually Mrs. Ruth.

It was a messy and sensational scandal, with hints of drug abuse and foul play and references to Mrs. Ruth's living arrangement as a "love nest." While there was nothing truly scandalous about her arrangement from today's perspective — she had simply sought the companionship and devotion her husband hadn't been willing to give her — at the time it was news.

A subdued Ruth said, "I hold nothing against my wife. She was the victim of circumstances, I still love her. I have fine memories of her." He then asked the press to "leave my wife alone. Let her stay dead."

They did. The scandal passed quickly, and Ruth got a virtual pass from the press. Such a scandal may have destroyed another player. Yet no matter what Ruth did, the press either forgave him or let it pass unnoticed.

He paid for their understanding. Through his press agent and ghostwriter Christy Walsh, Ruth spent nearly $10,000 a year entertaining the press, buying their goodwill and occasional silence. Incidents like auto accidents, paternity suits, and fights were almost always hushed up. Teammate Billy Werber even reported that a disgruntled paramour once shot Ruth through the lower leg, yet it never made the newspapers.

At the same time the press played up Ruth's visits to sick kids, gifts to charity, and other acts of kindness, providing him with a bottomless reservoir of goodwill. As with a handful of other public figures, nothing one ever learns about Ruth ever diminishes him. People loved him, and his considerable foibles only made him more lovable. That's just the way it was. His athletic accomplishments were superhuman, but his human weaknesses made him entirely sympathetic.

The Yankees played unimpressively in the spring as the confident club took considerable time getting in shape for the upcoming season. Ruth hit only one home run during

Second baseman Tony Lazzeri enjoyed a career season in 1929, with a .354 batting average and 106 RBIs. His achievement was one of the few bright spots in a season that saw the Yankees lose Miller Huggins and finish sixteen games behind the Philadelphia Athletics.

the Yankees' extensive and lucrative barnstorming trip through the South. But their popularity was at its peak. During one exhibition in Oklahoma City, "the greatest crowd to ever witness a ball game in the state of Oklahoma," according to the *World*, the crowd rushed the field in the eighth inning, surrounding Ruth "in a circle of two thousand fans," ending the game prematurely. Ruth had to fight his way out of the park and beat a hasty retreat in a cab.

Not until the Yankees played Brooklyn in a preseason contest on April 13 did they begin to resemble world champions. The sloppy 10–8 win was nonetheless described as "their best exhibition game of the year." Ruth homered

for only the second time that spring, a massive blast that landed on the roof of a house on Bedford Street, "probably the longest home run ever hit at Ebbets Field," at least according to the *Times*.

But Miller Huggins told *Spalding's Official Base Ball Guide,* "It is not reasonable to believe that this team is not going to lose some time. The thing to do is to prepare as best as possible to put off defeat to the farthest date that we can."

To that end, where once there were only answers, Huggins now found himself with questions. Dugan had been let go on waivers, and Huggins shifted Koenig to third, while installing Durocher at short. Young Bill Dickey, a promising but unproven prospect, prepared to take over behind the plate. Herb Pennock still had a sore arm, and Huggins admitted, "The Babe is getting along in years." He offered that the Athletics would provide the biggest challenge to his club and that "nearly every club has been strengthened in one way or another."

Yet the players remained confident, fully expecting to resume their usual standard of play once the season started. On Opening Day it appeared they would. Ruth, who had married Claire Hodgson several days before, hit a home run in the first inning, Meusel and Gehrig each collected two hits, including a homer by Gehrig, pitcher Fred Heimach shut down Boston in relief of Pipgras, and the Yankees won 7–3. Business as usual.

The only obvious change was made to the Yankee uniform. The players wore numbers on their back for the first time, with the starters identified by their position in the batting order. Other clubs soon followed suit.

The Athletics soon proved Huggins right. In two early season series they played the Yankees to a draw, gaining confidence, and when the Yankees dropped five in a row in mid-May to Detroit, Cleveland, and lowly Boston — their longest such streak since 1925 — the A's slipped into first place.

For the next two and a half months the Yankees stayed close, but they were unable to catch up to the A's. Ruth was doing his usual slugging, as were Gehrig, Combs, and Lazzeri, and Bill Dickey emerged as a star-in-waiting, but the pitching was woefully inconsistent. Swingman Tom Zachary, who went 12–0, was the best pitcher on the team as Pipgras, Pennock, Moore, and Hoyt all struggled to win. The left side of the infield gave the team trouble all year long as Huggins shuffled Durocher, who couldn't hit, Koenig, who couldn't field, Gene Robertson, and rookie Lyn Lary between third and short. Even with the race still close in mid-June, the Yankees seemed to throw in the towel, selling off several spare parts.

The A's put the pennant away in August as the humbled Yankees tumbled, going only 13–18 for the month, their first losing record in such a period since 1926. Any faint hope the Yankees had of winning the pennant again passed on the first three days of September when the A's took three straight from them, outscoring them 26–10. The A's made it official on September 14, writing New York's obituary and clinching the pennant with a shutout win over Chicago while the Yanks split a doubleheader with St. Louis.

On the following day, September 15, the Yankees played Cleveland in a doubleheader at the Stadium before a surprising 40,000 fans. Midway through game one, a 1–0 Yankee win on a Zachary shutout, manager Miller Huggins turned the team over to coach Art Fletcher. For the last ten days he'd been annoyed by a small boil that had formed under his left eye. Now it began to give him real trouble. As the Yankees dropped the second contest, Huggins stayed in the clubhouse, baking the malignancy under a heat lamp, then the accepted treatment.

Over the next few days Huggins made only brief appearances at the ballpark as his eye worsened. The wound was now clearly infected. The heat treatment and all manner of poking and prodding had only made it worse.

Huggins looked terrible, but he and Barrow made plans for next year, as Barrow told the press, "Huggins is aiming at a young club next season. . . . There isn't a position on the club, except right field, that we can't fill with a fine upstanding youngster." It was time to rebuild. The Yankees released infielder Gene Robertson to that end, and Barrow indicated that at least five more players on the roster would discover that their contracts would be assigned elsewhere in the off-season.

Wherever he went, Babe Ruth played to capacity crowds. He appealed, it seemed, to all kinds of people. In particular, some blacks embraced the Yankee superstar in their steadfast belief that he was part African American.

1934

When Huggins awoke in his hotel room on September 20, he felt feverish. His eye was virtually swollen shut, and the side of his head throbbed. He contacted his doctor, Edward King, who had him admitted to St. Vincent's Hospital. "Nothing serious," King reportedly told Ed Barrow, "but we must have him under observation." But in the days before antibiotics, any infected wound was dangerous, particularly those on the face, for the blood vessels there also serve the brain.

Huggins's malady underscored the medical risks of playing ball. Strawberries and spike wounds, if left untreated, could end careers. Team "trainers" were often old-timers who prescribed such primitive treatment as rubbing dirt in a wound. Doctors were expensive and didn't have the answers either. Injured players were often released. There was no players' union, and if you couldn't play, you didn't get paid for long. Those who succeeded in the majors were often those who managed to stay healthy. In a crude kind of baseball Darwinism, it was survival of the fittest.

Huggins's condition quickly deteriorated. As the Yankees traveled by train to Boston on September 23, he became delirious, calling for his brother and sister, who were already present, and a business partner. His temperature soared to 106 degrees as the doctors tried first one blood transfusion, then a second and a third. The *New York World* reported, "Hope, while not high, is not yet gone." Late that night he lapsed into a coma.

As the *World* reported the next day from Fenway Park, where the Yankees were playing Boston, "few on the field noticed when the flag in distant center field fluttered and started its low descent from the top of the staff. Half way down it stopped and drooped in a dying breeze, a mute signal that one of the greatest leaders of the game had passed on." Huggins had died at 3:15 P.M. of blood poisoning.

After the fifth inning the players were told of his death, and members of both teams gathered around home plate for a minute of silence as word of Huggins's death was

Lou Gehrig (left) and Babe Ruth (right) with manager Miller Huggins. The trio were the pillars on which the first great Yankee dynasty was built. All three died before their time and were the first uniformed Yankees honored with monuments at the Stadium.

announced to the crowd. Then the game resumed, and the Yankees, who had led comfortably 7–3, immediately gave up seven runs before fighting back and winning the game.

"It's one of those things you can't talk about much," said Ruth, who served as one of Huggins's pallbearers. Coach Art Fletcher took over as the ballclub played out the string, losing four of its last five to finish 88–66, 18 games behind the A's, who slumped at the end to win "only" 104 games.

Ruppert and Barrow quickly turned their attention to the matter of Huggins's replacement. The job was a plum, and the two men fully expected to fill the position quickly. But they were shocked when first Donie Bush, then Eddie Collins, the legendary second baseman of Connie Mack's A's and former White Sox manager who finally retired as an active player at age 42, turned down the post.

Barrow then decided to give the job to Art Fletcher. But Fletcher stunned the Yankees by turning them down as well. He was happy coaching third and didn't want the headaches that came with the top spot. Didn't anyone want the job?

Well, the only man the Yankees knew they *didn't* want to hire did. Babe Ruth openly politicked for the position in his ghostwritten newspaper column, which made Ruppert and Barrow uncomfortable. True, Ruth *was* the Yankees and felt he deserved the post, but Barrow and Ruppert didn't agree—Ruth still had problems managing himself. They strung him along with a vague promise that perhaps he'd be considered in the future. Ruth was hurt, but before the start of the season he was mollified with a new contract worth $80,000 annually. That was more than the salary paid to President Herbert Hoover, an observation that reportedly led Ruth to utter his famous quip that he deserved the money because "I had a better year than he did." Yet the Yankees' refusal to name Ruth manager was the first faint sign that the club was beginning to ponder a future that didn't include Ruth at all. They found the prospect curiously refreshing, for Ruth, despite his prodigious talent, was still a handful.

In the context of their recent success, the organization was clearly foundering. So was the U.S. economy, which was shaken by Black Tuesday, the infamous stock market crash of October 29, 1929. In one day some $11 billion of paper wealth was wiped out, and the U.S. economy thrown

Former Yankee pitcher Bob Shawkey, here shaking hands with Athletics manager Connie Mack, was selected to manage his old team following Miller Huggins's sudden death in September 1929. Shawkey's tenure lasted only a season, in which the Yankees slipped to third place.

into a depression. Within months there were bread riots on the streets of New York. Ruppert, who'd been a conservative investor, was still rich, but the Yankee well was no longer overflowing. Bob Meusel, who had slumped in 1929 and after Ruth was one of the better-paid players on the team, was let go on waivers and not really replaced.

Finally, in December, the Yankees hired a new manager: former pitcher Bob Shawkey, who'd served as a Yankee coach in 1928 and 1929. He didn't have any experience, but he was a Yankee, and after all, with Ruth and Gehrig, the Yankees didn't really need much managing. At least that was the theory. Shawkey even subscribed to it himself, saying before the start of the season that since "a ball player has only his own services to sell," that was motivation enough to stay in shape and perform. Besides, he was cheap, and the Yankees seemed resigned to the fact that the A's were the better team. In the off-season they stood pat again.

Ed Barrow (left) and Joe McCarthy may have joked for photographers in this 1939 photograph, but when Barrow hired McCarthy, before the 1931 season, he told him Ruppert would understand if McCarthy finished second that season, but expected a pennant in 1932.

The club opened the season with two rookies in the lineup, outfielder Dusty Cooke and fleet third baseman Ben Chapman, both of whom later became notorious for their racial attitudes. As manager of the Phillies, Chapman would lead the heckling of Jackie Robinson, and Cooke was charged after striking two African Americans with his car in North Carolina, taking them to the hospital, and then fleeing.

The Yankees lost to Philadelphia on Opening Day and then kept losing. At the end of April the vaunted Yanks were a desultory 3–8. They knew they were in trouble and, too late, tried to retool, getting pitcher Red Ruffing from Boston and dumping Koenig and Hoyt, who were both costly and, in Hoyt's case, clashed with Shawkey over his pitch selection. They sent both players to Detroit for outfielder Harry Rice and a couple of prospects.

The new players helped, but Shawkey scrambled all year to put together an infield, a pitching staff, and a pecking order. Chapman could hit but not field, and eventually he traded spots with Lazzeri and Lyn Lary took over at short. Cooke didn't cut it. The opposition scored 10 or more runs 27 times. And Ruth and most other vets, save Gehrig, barely listened to Shawkey. He'd been one of the boys, and they ran roughshod over him.

The Yankee offense scored runs at a record pace, however, and that kept them in the race — for a while. They entered July in a virtual dead heat with the Senators and A's. But on the rare occasions when they didn't hit, they didn't win. Over a six-game period against the two clubs above them in the standings, they didn't hit and lost all six to fall back and leave John Kieran of the *Times* writing about cricket and tennis.

They won only 86 games and tumbled to third place as the A's won 102 games. Sure, they hit .309 as a team and scored 1,062 runs as Dickey emerged as a star, Combs hit .344, and Ruth and Gehrig hit 49 and 41 home runs, respectively, but the pitching staff was the second-worst in the league.

Shawkey took the fall. Ruppert and Barrow strung him along while not so secretively shopping for his replacement. Once again, Ruth thought he deserved the job. Ruppert and Barrow disagreed. They had their eye on Joe McCarthy.

After nearly five years as manager of the Cubs, who won a pennant in 1929, McCarthy had been cut loose in the final days of the 1930 season. Rogers Hornsby, who had helped undermine him, became the new manager. But given McCarthy's reputation, he knew he wouldn't be without a job for long. In fact, the Red Sox were already courting him. They wanted him badly, but McCarthy knew Boston simply didn't have the resources to win.

And that was important, for thus far that's all McCarthy's teams had done. In 1921, after a long minor league career, McCarthy had become the Louisville manager, a job in which he earned a reputation as one of the best minor league managers around. His players were well schooled — McCarthy insisted on discipline on and off the field and drilled his players relentlessly in the fundamentals. There was a right way to play the game, and McCarthy expected his players to know it. At Louisville Earle Combs had been the most successful of his protégées.

But McCarthy also had his quirks. He didn't think much of Polish players or southerners, whom he thought were hotheads and drunks, or pipe smokers, who were too complacent. At the same time he was focused entirely on baseball, an attitude that suited Ruppert and Barrow. The Yankee players didn't need a friend; they needed someone who commanded respect.

Shawkey learned that he'd been fired when he went to the Yankee offices on 42nd Street to sign a contract for the 1931 season, only to find McCarthy on his way out, carrying a five-year contract in his pocket worth $30,000 a year. Ruppert had told him he would understand if the Yankees finished second in 1931, but in 1932 he expected a pennant.

McCarthy was no Miller Huggins, who sat quietly on the bench directing his charges from afar. McCarthy took control and spent his time in the third-base coaching box. "All I ask," he said at the news conference announcing his appointment, "is that my men go out there and hustle."

McCarthy quickly put his stamp on the team. He liked putting the same names in the lineup every day, an approach that eventually earned him the reputation of being a "push-button" manager. That didn't include the way he handled his pitching staff, however, because McCarthy didn't really trust pitchers and rarely settled on a set starting rotation. One or two men might find themselves pitching every fourth day, but after that McCarthy went with hot hands, hunches, and whoever hadn't pitched his way into the manager's doghouse. The strategy often got the most out of the talent he had, but it wasn't very popular with the pitchers themselves.

To McCarthy, the game started the instant his team reached the clubhouse, which in recent years had been

Babe Ruth did everything in a larger-than-life manner, including umpire-baiting. Here he's shouting at umpire Brick Owen following the call of a third strike on Yankee pitcher Red Ruffing. Ruth (at right, standing next to Lou Gehrig) was ejected for his comments.

CHARLES DEVENS, YANKEE

CHARLES DEVENS

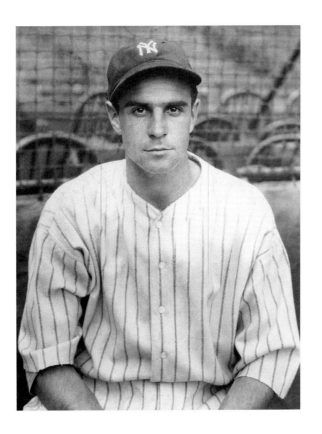

It hardly seems possible that 70 years have passed since I went directly from Harvard University to Yankee Stadium following my graduation. It was only recently I lost my old teammate Frank Crosetti. Back in '32 we arrived as rookies and finished the season as champs. Until the end he never failed to call me at World Series time, especially if the Yankees were playing, and when I heard his voice it seemed like yesterday that we were rubbing shoulders with men like Ruth, Gehrig, Lazzeri, Rolfe, and the others.

I was born on New Year's Day in 1910 and was named for my great-uncle General Charles Devens, who had the hell beaten out of him by Stonewall Jackson at Chancellorsville, where he was also wounded. Growing up in Boston, I played all sports and at Groton was a three-sport captain of football, hockey, and baseball. I am almost certain I am the only major leaguer to come from Groton, a school more famous for producing Franklin D. Roosevelt than anything.

From Groton I went to Harvard, where I was fortunate enough to play for two wonderful coaches: Arnie Horween in football and Fred Mitchell in baseball. In football we played the likes of Michigan, where on one memorable occasion we reacted to the placement of anti-Semitic posters directed at Coach Horween and nearly beat them at Ann Arbor. Before 100,000 fans our All-American Barry Wood had one of the only bad days of his career as he missed the point after on both our touchdowns and also missed two field goal attempts within their 20-yard line as we lost 14–12.

I am proud to say I was never licked by Yale in any sport during my college career. On the day before graduation I beat Yale and my future Yankee teammate Johnny Broaca, whom I'd also faced when he pitched at Philips Andover, by a score of 6–0. We had other great times, including a game against another of my future Yankee teammates, Red Rolfe, and his Dartmouth baseball team in Hanover on a weekend that included several fraternity parties. I seem to recall a few of us broke training that night and Coach Mitchell literally had to drag us to the station and deposit us on the Boston-bound train the next morning.

A week following my graduation I signed a Yankee contract with scout Paul Krichell that called for a $6,000 bonus and a salary of $1,000 a month. In the depths of the Depression I felt rich. The money also allowed me to help my younger brothers go to prep school.

Ever since I first saw the Yankees in the early twenties at Fenway Park I liked everything about them, from their uniforms, their many star players, and the way they seemed to win all the time. After playing for winning teams in prep school and college, I found the Yankees' offer too good to refuse.

I was mostly a fastball pitcher, and it was that pitch that caught the Yankees' interest. If they'd had radar guns in the thirties, I know my fastball was in the nineties. Despite some control problems, I also had a decent curve and change of pace. In New York I was lucky to work with Hall of Fame catcher Bill Dickey, who was always one pitch ahead of the batters. He not only called a great game but had the best arm I'd ever seen. It seems funny now, but I remember that in street clothes Dickey almost appeared awkward.

In New York I lived with the parents of my Groton and Harvard friend Saint John Smith. They lived on East 70th Street, and I'd take the subway from their home to Yankee Stadium. On game days I'd get there by 11:30 or noon for a 2:00 P.M. start — in time to watch the away team take batting practice and then pitch some batting practice myself to warm up.

God, I loved the fun and comradeship of that clubhouse. I'll never forget how long a walk it was to the dugout. I also remember Babe Ruth, poetry in motion in the batter's box and always a law unto himself while coming and going pretty much as he pleased. We had several college men on the team: Gehrig, Joe

Sewell, Rolfe — all gentlemen, as was most everyone associated with the club. Manager Joe McCarthy's office was located just off the main dressing room, and everyone respected him tremendously for his unmatched won-lost record, even when he took the occasional drink.

Jacob Ruppert rarely visited us at Yankee Stadium but loved to watch us at spring training in Florida, where he enjoyed introducing us to his friends. We all knew he treated us better than any owner in baseball.

I am often asked about the famous called shot by Babe Ruth in the 1932 World Series in Chicago. I can still see him pointing to center field in what I thought was a gesture indicating his intention to hit the home run. Frank Crosetti was there as well and thought Ruth was telling Cubs pitcher Charlie Root he needed one more strike. It makes for a great story in any case.

After the 1934 season I decided to retire and get married. Baseball wasn't much of a life for a young bride, and I couldn't leave her for half a season each year. When I signed in 1932, I promised to give myself three seasons and was proud that I'd played on a world champion for the greatest team in baseball.

In 1935 I had the chance to play in my hometown of Boston for the Red Sox after their general manager, Eddie Collins, called and asked me to come to spring training. After initially saying yes, I called him back within hours and said no.

To this day I still think of myself as a Yankee.

CHARLES DEVENS pitched for the New York Yankees from 1932 to 1934, going 5–3 with a 3.73 ERA in 82 innings. He lives in Milton, Massachusetts.

exactly that, a place to play cards and kibbutz. Under McCarthy, the only talk tolerated was about baseball, and he had a clubhouse attendant take an ax to the team card table. Players were expected to act like Yankees at all times. He instituted a dress code on the road, and instead of a nightly curfew he made an 8:30 A.M. breakfast mandatory, accomplishing the same purpose.

Although the Yankees opened the season with virtually the same lineup they had employed in 1930, they got off to a slow start as the A's won 17 in a row in May, then ended the month by taking five of six from the Yankees. Next year was just around the corner for New York.

McCarthy didn't sit back. Even when the Yankees won, he was rarely content. He moved Ben Chapman to the outfield to take advantage of his speed and picked up Cleveland veteran Joe Sewell to play third, moving Lazzeri back to second base. Rookie pitcher Vernon "Lefty" Gomez, who had been purchased two years before from the PCL, started strong and soon became the ace of the staff.

Ruth and Gehrig still provided the punch, although Gehrig was beginning to supplant Ruth as the Yankees' main power threat. Both men cracked 46 home runs, but Gehrig bettered Ruth in the RBI department and led the league for the second straight year.

But the A's rendered the Yankees' improvement moot, for the 1931 A's were one of baseball's greatest teams. Foxx, Simmons, and Cochrane were in their prime, and Lefty Grove was an astounding 31–4, while George Earnshaw and Rube Walberg won 21 and 22. New York's pitching just couldn't match them, and the A's won an incredible 107 games to finish 13½ games ahead of the Yankees.

Despite the results, the players weren't entirely happy under the new regime. Ruth, for one, was dismissive of McCarthy, who he thought had stolen a job that was rightfully his. But each man knew better than to challenge the other. They engaged in an uneasy, unspoken truce as McCarthy allowed Ruth to set his own rules and Ruth, who was still trying to prove he had the mettle to become a manager, generally took fewer liberties than in the past.

That said, he was still the most important man on the team. While the Depression was hard on baseball—major league attendance fell by one-third from 1929 to 1932—it only made the Yankees stronger. Even as the A's had taken over the top spot in the standings, the financial gap between the Yankees and the other teams in baseball grew wider. Although ticket prices and revenue dropped and even Ruth took a pay cut as his skills diminished, Yankee Stadium attendance held more or less steady, and the club remained the league's major attraction of the road. The Yankee organization also continued to add to its revenues by renting out the Stadium for all sorts of other activities, such as boxing and, beginning in 1930, Negro League games.

In contrast, Connie Mack was having a hard time paying his team full of stars. While he was smart enough not to deal with New York, the financial pressure on him to begin to break up his team lifted the Yankees. At the same time the structure of the game began to change.

Traditionally, young players had been procured directly from minor league teams, who found amateur talent, nurtured it, then sold it off to major leagues at a dear price. But beginning in 1921, major league teams began purchasing minor league teams, enabling them to control minor leaguers who were not yet on the major league roster. The result was cheaper ballplayers.

The practice went counter to the desires of the baseball commissioner, Judge Kenesaw Landis, but it was not technically illegal. The St. Louis Cardinals, under Branch Rickey, had been the most aggressive in the acquisition of minor league teams. Now with the Depression in full swing, there was added incentive to acquire players as cheaply as possible.

The Yankees entered the minor league business in 1929, buying Chambersburg in the Class D Blue Ridge League. At the end of the 1931 season they became more active, buying International League Newark for $600,000. And in February 1932, Barrow hired a man who reminded him of himself, 32-year-old George Weiss, to be the Yankees' assistant secretary and general manager of their minor league interests. As much as any player they subsequently acquired, the hiring of Weiss would have a huge impact on New York's future.

Weiss grew up in New Haven, Connecticut, where he was a high school teammate of Joe Dugan's. Forced to leave Yale before graduation, he began operating a local semi-pro team, then bought the Eastern League New Haven Profs. Weiss fielded a winning team and proved adept at making money by signing, developing, and then selling players. He then moved on and did the same thing for the International League Baltimore Orioles, taking over after the death of Jack Dunn, who'd first signed Babe Ruth. In his 13 years in the minors, Weiss had sold players for a total of more than half a million dollars while keeping his teams competitive. Dozens of his progeny had made the majors.

He would do the same for the Yankees, developing talent, retaining the best, and selling off the surplus to finance the club's next acquisition. He immediately began stocking Newark with talent.

With Weiss scouring the hinterlands for players, Barrow and McCarthy focused on the 1932 season. New York set the tone early. On Opening Day the Yankees trounced the A's 12–6 as Ruth and Sammy Byrd, who temporarily had beaten out Combs for the center-field spot, each thumped two home runs and Gehrig added another and even stole home on the front end of a double steal. But in the long run the most important number that day was the attendance figure at Shibe Park. Despite the draw of Ruth and the Yankees, the defending world champion A's drew only 16,000 fans. Mack was running out of money and soon would have to start over.

That pattern has been repeated ever since. Over the years a number of teams have challenged the Yankees for supremacy, but few can long afford the high cost of that competition. The lucrative New York market has always been the Yankees' greatest friend.

The Yankees got off to a quick start, winning this time with pitching, not hitting, as the A's struggled on the mound even as they mounted a superb offensive attack. The 1932 season would signal the end of Ruth's reign as baseball's premier power hitter. His replacement wasn't Gehrig, but the A's Jimmie Foxx, who erupted for 58 home runs, while Ruth hit only 41 and Gehrig 34. But it was Gehrig who provided the most memorable moment of the regular season and convincing evidence that 1932 would be the Yankees' year.

On the first day of June the A's appeared ready to make a charge as they won a doubleheader in Philadelphia against the Yanks to open a five-game series, raising their record to 25–18, still within range of New York's league-best 28–13 mark. But the Yankees won 5–1 on June 2. Now the A's desperately needed to win the next two games,

For most of his illustrious career, Lou Gehrig toiled as the Yankees' quiet hero and was outshone early in his career by Babe Ruth and later by Joe DiMaggio. The New York native was overshadowed by another local baseball legend when the story of his four-homer game against the Athletics in 1932 was relegated to "other news" by the death of John McGraw.

which would enable them to pick up three games in the standings. If New York captured either of the remaining games, the series would essentially be a wash.

Gehrig opened the contest with a two-run home run to right in the first inning off Earnshaw to give the Yankees a quick 2–0 lead. But the A's Mickey Cochrane one-upped him in the bottom of the inning, cracking a three-run homer to put the A's ahead. Gehrig then came to bat in the fourth and smacked another home run, a solo shot, as

New York took a 4–3 lead. But the A's came back again, scoring four times in their half to take the lead again.

The Yankees were not to be denied, however; they scored in every subsequent inning. Gehrig smacked a third home run to right off Earnshaw in the fifth, driving him from the game. By the time Gehrig came to bat in the seventh, the game was out of hand and most of the crowd rose to its feet to cheer his attempt to hit home run number four. Mack even admonished Earnshaw to pay attention to how reliever Leroy Mahaffey worked Gehrig, implying that Earnshaw hadn't been pitching the slugger correctly.

This time Gehrig went with a fastball over the outside part of the plate and drove it the opposite way and over the wall in left. "I understand," snapped Earnshaw to his manager. "Mahaffey made Lou change direction."

The blast put Gehrig in the company of two stars of a previous generation, Bobby Lowe and Ed Delahanty, the only players at the time ever to hit four home runs in a game. But the Yankees were scoring at will. He'd have two more chances in the game to set a new standard.

In the eighth Gehrig grounded out, but he came up once more in the ninth. This time he gave the ball the longest ride of the day. Unfortunately, it was a solid 450 feet to center at Philadelphia's Shibe Park. Al Simmons, filling in at center, raced back and, according to one account, "captured the ball only a few steps from the farthest corner of the park."

The Yanks romped to a 20–13 win, but Gehrig's feat was only the second-biggest baseball story in New York that day. John McGraw's death dominated the headlines, and Gehrig's feat was almost ignored.

Poor Lou. At nearly every step in his career, he always seemed to be overshadowed, first by Ruth and later by DiMaggio. As the upcoming World Series would demonstrate once again, no matter what he did, there always seemed to be someone else stealing his thunder.

In part that fate was a product of his personality. He wasn't as well equipped for the spotlight as others — when

On October 2, 1933, Babe Ruth made his final major league pitching appearance against the Red Sox at Yankee Stadium. He pitched a complete game, scattered twelve hits, and walked three with no strikeouts as he beat his former team by a score of 6–5.

The Pride of the Yankees

1934

it turned his way he withdrew. He always seemed to be at his best when attention was focused elsewhere, and he lived in the sheltering arms of Mom and Pop Gehrig until age 31. He was, in many ways, Ruth's opposite, a player whose temperament and personal behavior were so different from the Babe's that each player stood out in greater relief in comparison to the other. But in the batter's box their performances were nearly identical.

The inevitable contrast also worked to Gehrig's advantage. Had it been the other way around, Gehrig might not have been able to maintain the daily grind of excellence exemplified by his growing streak of consecutive games played. Ruth's greatness was explosive and intermittent, but it appeared with uncanny regularity — he rose to the occasion like no one else. Gehrig's talent lay in his unyielding consistency. He was always there.

While Ruth set the Yankees' standard of performance, Gehrig exemplified the Yankee way, epitomizing the "Pride of the Yankees," a standard of behavior and bearing beyond and above wins, losses, or statistics. As much as Ruth, Gehrig created the Yankee prototype. The ultimate Yankee player would be the one who could encompass the best of both men. No one yet knew it, but this prototypical Yankee was already beginning the journey that would soon land him in New York.

Gehrig's bravura performance demonstrated that the A's, for all their talent, couldn't quite match New York's offensive output. Neither could they do much of anything with the Yankees' Lefty Gomez, who won that game in relief and ended the season with seven wins in eight decisions against Philadelphia. The Yankees took control of the American League with the win and weren't seriously challenged thereafter as they finished the season matching the A's 1931 win total of 107.

They won the right to play McCarthy's old club, the Chicago Cubs, in the World Series, giving the Yankee manager plenty of incentive. He still felt the sting from his release two years before and relished the thought of defeating his old club. The Cubs were all right, but 1932 was a year of parity in the NL as the top six clubs all finished within 18 games of each other. Had the Cubs been in the AL, their 90 wins would have barely qualified them for fourth place.

The Yankees, as usual, were huge favorites entering the World Series. Even Chicago's Wrigley Field seemed better suited to the Yankees than the Cubs, its short fences wholly incapable of containing Ruth and Gehrig. Cub pitchers already appeared overmatched against the duo — only reliever Jakie May was left-handed.

In the first two games in New York the Yankees toyed with Chicago. In game one the Cubs scored twice in the first inning before Ruffing settled down. Then, in the fourth, Ben Chapman quashed a rally with a superb catch, and Gehrig homered to right. "Chicago never overcame the blighting effect of Gehrig's hit," commented the *Spalding Guide* later. The Yankees cut loose and romped to a 12–6 win. Game two unfolded in similar fashion. The Cubs scored one in the first off Gomez, but Chicago's Lon Warneke struggled with control. The Yankees quickly responded with two runs of their own, then cruised to a 5–2 win.

With that, the Series moved to Chicago. Game three provided one of the most storied moments in World Series history, although in truth it never happened and its significance, at least in terms of the Series, has been overstated.

In the first inning the Yankees raked Cub starter Charlie Root, and Ruth cracked a three-run home run on the first pitch he ever swung at in Wrigley Field to put New York ahead. But the Cubs fought back against Pipgras, and the game was tied 4–4 entering the fifth.

This much is certain. With one out and the bases empty, Ruth stepped to the plate against Root.

Thus far in the Series the real action had been taking place off the field. The Yankees were upset that former Yankee Mark Koenig — he was picked up by the Cubs in midseason and his .353 average had been a key factor in their drive to the pennant — had been shortchanged by his teammates: they had voted him only a partial share of World Series swag. Ruth led the Yankees' bench-jockeying brigade, calling the Cubs "cheapskates" in the most profane manner.

The Cubs responded in kind. They knew how to get under Ruth's skin, calling him a wide variety of epithets that compared him to apes and questioning his racial background. After the first two games the Series outcome was virtually decided, and the razzing got uglier and louder in game three. The fans had picked up on the debate and added their voices to the fray.

Richards Vidmer described Ruth's at bat best in the *Tribune:*

Ruth grinned in the face of the hostile greeting. He laughed back at the Cubs and took his place supremely confident. A strike whistled over the plate and joyous outcries filled the air, but the Babe held up one finger as if to say, "That's only one. Just wait."

Two balls went by, then another strike. The stands rocked with delight. The Chicago players hurled their delight at the great man, but Ruth held up two fingers and still grinned, the super showman.

On the next pitch the Babe swung. There was the responding report like the explosion of a gun. Straight for the center field fence the ball soared on a line. Johnny Moore went racing back with some vague idea of catching it, then suddenly stopped short and stared as the ball sailed on, clearing the farthest corner of the barrier and dropping out into the street, 436 feet from home plate.

Before Ruth left the plate and started his swing around the bases he paused to laugh at the Chicago players, suddenly silent in their dugout.

All true. As Ruth toured the bases, he gestured at the Cubs and taunted them at every turn, ending his sojourn with one final burst of invective toward the Cubs bench before reaching home plate, where he couldn't conceal a huge smile. New York led 5–4.

The home run became known as the infamous "called shot," a perception first offered the next day in the *New York World Telegram.* In a story headlined "Ruth Calls Shot as He Puts Homer No. 2 in Side Pocket," Joe Williams wrote: "Ruth pointed to center and punched a screaming liner to a spot where no ball had been hit before."

Those were keystrokes of brilliance if not accuracy, for they elevated Ruth's home run to legendary status and raised Williams's profile among New York writers. Yankee fans, who often read several papers during the Series, responded to the drama of his story and took it as the definitive account. Within days other writers who'd made no mention of a "called shot" in their game stories, and a few who hadn't even been there in the first place, now weighed in with their version of the episode. Most mir-

Earle Combs was a mainstay of the great Yankee teams of the twenties and thirties, first as a center fielder and later as a left fielder. On July 24, 1934, he fractured his skull and clavicle after running into the concrete outfield wall at Sportsman's Park in St. Louis. He made a slow recovery and was never the same after the injury; he played only part of the 1935 season before retiring.

rored Williams's account, and none debunked it as pure hokum. The question of what Ruth actually did would be debated for the next 66 years.

What really happened is precisely what Vidmer and a host of others described at the time — Ruth responded to the taunts with gestures, then hit a home run. He'd done the same thing while at bat on numerous other occasions during his career — Ruth couldn't stand for anyone to intimate that he was black, and he always responded. But this time it was the World Series. This time he hit a home run. And this time a writer embellished the story.

The camera, however, doesn't lie. In 1999 a definitive film account finally emerged. Shot by a fan named Harold

AMERICAN LEAGUE
MOST VALUABLE PLAYER

1936 Lou Gehrig, 1B

1939 Joe DiMaggio, OF

1941 Joe DiMaggio, OF

1942 Joe Gordon, 2B

1943 Spud Chandler, P

1947 Joe DiMaggio, OF

1950 Phil Rizzuto, SS

1951 Yogi Berra, C

1954 Yogi Berra, C

1955 Yogi Berra, C

1956 Mickey Mantle, OF

1957 Mickey Mantle, OF

1960 Roger Maris, OF

1961 Roger Maris, OF

1962 Mickey Mantle, OF

1963 Elston Howard, C

1976 Thurman Munson, C

1985 Don Mattingly, 1B

Warp with a 16mm camera at the only major league game he ever attended, the film clearly demonstrates that Ruth didn't point to center and he never called his shot. That event has as much to do with reality as the mistaken belief that Red Sox shortstop Johnny Pesky held the ball on Enos Slaughter's mad dash home in the final game of the 1946 World Series. Film proves that wrong too.

Ruth, who spent thousands each year currying the favor of the press, was savvy enough not to deny the story, and in subsequent retellings and movies the home run has loomed ever more magnificent. The called shot under-scores his unique place in the game's history. And in the end it matters little that the event never took place. The mere fact that so many found it possible that Ruth *could* have hit a home run at will demonstrates that he reached a level that few players in the history of the game have ever approached. But while Ruth's home run put New York ahead, 5–4, on Root's next pitch Lou Gehrig struck the telling blow, hitting a home run of his own that provided the winning run in the Yankees' 7–5 victory.

That sealed it, and in game four the Yankees won just as they had won the first three, giving up an early lead and then pounding the Cubs into submission. Gehrig, who led all players in the Series with a .529 batting average, three home runs, 19 total bases, and 8 RBIs, keyed the Yankees' final comeback as Lazzeri added two home runs and Combs one. But all anyone would remember was a called home run that not only didn't win the game but didn't even happen.

That's the Yankee way. Myth, particularly in regard to Ruth and other Yankee stars, has often been more important and better known than the nearly as remarkable facts of their history. Winners always write the history, and the Yankees have written more than their share.

Another reason the incident later became so well known was that the blast represented Ruth's last World Series home run and provided a final fabulous moment in the biography of his Yankee career. Although he would play another two seasons in New York, he would approach his established standard on fewer and fewer occasions.

Babe was slowing down. His weight was back up, and he looked as if he wore a balloon inflated under his shirt. Opponents rarely bothered to hold him on at first base anymore — he was no threat to steal — and McCarthy, like Huggins, didn't even bother to give him the signs. Ruth knew what his job was. Just before the start of the World Series he'd had some intestinal trouble, and there had even been some speculation that he'd be unable to play. As it was, although he hit well, he fielded poorly, bobbling several balls and not reaching some fly balls that appeared catchable.

Gehrig's performance at the plate underlined the passing of the torch — the Yankees were *his* team now. Yet even as he took over as the team's most important player, Gehrig would still labor under Ruth's shadow. He was loved, but Babe Ruth was *beloved*. Over the next few seasons the dominant story of the franchise would not be Gehrig and his prodigious slugging, but a far more uncomfortable experience. How does a team retire a legend, particularly one who is bigger than the game itself?

Despite 107 victories, the 1932 Yankee team was not the juggernaut of the 1926–28 edition. True, the A's were already passing, but with the rapid demise of Ruth, so was New York. By standing still, they would soon slip back.

In the off-season between 1932 and 1933, the equation of baseball began to change. In March 1933, a young, virtually unknown scion of a timber and mining fortune named Thomas A. Yawkey turned 30 years old and took control of his considerable fortune, which came to somewhere between 20 and 40 million Depression-Era dollars — in all likelihood, more than Jacob Ruppert's. Days after taking control of the family fortune, young Tom Yawkey purchased the Boston Red Sox.

That would change the balance of power in the American League — sort of. For many of the next 45 years and beyond, the Red Sox would be the Yankees' virtual equal in terms of wealth. Although the Red Sox would rarely outdraw New York, Yawkey's personal fortune rendered that inequity almost insignificant. While Connie Mack's A's receded, Yawkey's Red Sox would often provide the Yankees with their most significant challenge, if not always on the field, at least in the marketplace for talent.

Shortly after taking over as Red Sox owner, Yawkey attended his first meeting of American League owners and after being approved abruptly announced, "I'm here to buy ballplayers and the money is on the table." The other owners could hardly believe their ears. During a depression, Yawkey was a Messiah, turning loaves and fishes — empty seats and warm bodies — into cash.

Even Ruppert couldn't resist his largesse. The Yankees were overstocked and planned to cut aging pitcher George Pipgras and infielder Billy Werber, a fine player who couldn't crack the Yankee lineup and didn't have the proper makeup to sit on the bench.

Ruppert and Barrow took Yawkey to the cleaners, getting $100,000 for two players he could have picked up for virtually nothing in a few more days. Compared to the other AL clubs, the Yankees didn't really need the money, but hell, if Yawkey was gonna *give* it away . . . well, Weiss could always use it on some prospects.

Although the Yanks opened the season with seven straight wins, they struggled on the road, giving hope to the opposition, particularly Washington. The club run by boy manager Joe Cronin lacked the Yankees' star power, but they were solid at every position. During a mid-June road trip the Yankees slipped badly. In a 13–5 loss to lowly Boston on June 14, the Yankees' sixth defeat in their last eight games, they finally showed the strain as both McCarthy and the normally restrained Lou Gehrig were tossed by ump Bill Summers. The Senators moved into first place a few days later.

It wasn't anything specific, it was everything. Hardly a man on the team was playing as well as he had in 1932. With Ruth falling off badly, opponents could now pitch around Gehrig. The Yankees slowly fell even further behind and never challenged for first place after early August, as Washington won the pennant with 99 wins to New York's 91.

Meanwhile, however, Weiss's efforts to build the farm system were finally beginning to pay off as the Yankees began a slow influx of talent in the spring of 1934. The Yankees had shed aging stars Pennock, Pipgras, and Moore, and Johnny Murphy and Johnny Broaca emerged to give the club two dependable arms after Gomez and Ruffing.

There had been some speculation that Ruth would retire, but he decided to stick around, at least for one more season. He still had his eye on the manager's job and in recent years had turned down entreaties from both the

Tigers and the Red Sox. Ruth still hoped to outlast McCarthy and believed that in the end Ruppert and Barrow would give him a shot at the top spot.

The Yankees opened the season in customary fashion, moving smoothly into first place while the rest of the field sorted itself out. This time the Tigers, bolstered by the emergence of pitcher Schoolboy Rowe and slugger Hank Greenberg, stepped forth to provide a challenge. The two clubs broke away from the field in June, and Detroit edged ahead just after the All-Star break when the Yankees lost three out of four in Detroit.

Detroit was a powerhouse, scoring runs like the Yankees once had while New York struggled at the plate. Ruth was now a liability in the field and barely a threat at the plate. He tired easily and was hampered by all sorts of nagging injuries. He was only nominally a starter as Sammy Byrd and Myril Hoag made ever more frequent appearances in the Yankee outfield alongside Chapman and Combs. New York's vaunted power now resided solely in the formidable arms and shoulders of Lou Gehrig, who was on his way to a career-high 49 home runs.

But on July 24, the season turned. Trailing Detroit by only a game and a half after winning four straight, the Yankees looked to make it five in a row in St. Louis against the Browns. Entering the seventh, New York led 2–1, and with one out, Johnny Murphy walked the bottom two hitters in the Browns lineup, bringing up outfielder Harland Clift. He drove the ball deep to left.

Earle Combs, playing left field, took off after the ball, which was headed toward the bleachers. Running at full speed, he reached out for the ball, and it struck his glove just as he crashed into the concrete barrier before the stands.

Combs crumpled to the ground as the ball rolled free. Chapman retrieved the loose ball and threw it in as Clift made third and the Browns took the lead. Then Chapman attended to his fallen teammate.

Combs was out cold and had to be carried from the field. Rushed to the hospital, doctors discovered a broken clavicle and a skull fracture that ran along the left side of his

By 1934, forty-year-old Babe Ruth, shown with teammates Red Rolfe (left) and Don Heffner, had reached the end of his days in New York. When the season ended, Yankee owner Jacob Ruppert gave the slugger his unconditional release.

head from the orbit to just behind his ear. "He is a very sick man," reported Dr. Robert Hyland. Anesthetized by morphine, Combs slipped in and out of consciousness for several days before beginning a long, slow recovery. But his season was over. He returned to play in 1935, but he would never again be the player he had once been.

The Yankees never recovered from his loss. They hung with Detroit into mid-August, and then the Tigers put them out of their misery. The pennant race was over, and the Yankees limped to the finish, winning 94 games to finish 7 games behind Detroit.

Gehrig won the Triple Crown, something Ruth never did, by hitting .363 and knocking in 165 to go with his 49 home runs. But Ruth found one final way to hold on to the spotlight just a little bit longer. While it was a foregone conclusion that his career was over, at least to everyone but the Babe, he still had his eye on the manager's job, and McCarthy's contract was about to expire.

But Ruppert had no intention of making a change, and he told Ruth at the World Series that he had no plans to replace McCarthy. Ruth came to the abrupt conclusion that he was through with New York, announcing that he had no plans to return as a player. He wanted to manage. McCarthy didn't want Ruth around anymore, and the Yankees made it known that they'd give Ruth his release whenever he wanted it.

Instead of sticking around to politick for a position, he embarked on a world barnstorming tour. Meanwhile, the usual shuffle of managers took place around baseball, and Ruth, while often mentioned in the press for PR value, wasn't treated as a serious candidate anywhere.

By the time he returned to New York in February, only the Boston Braves were interested in Ruth. He had always been popular in Boston, and Judge Emil Fuchs, owner of the team, needed something to counteract the effect of Tom Yawkey's millions. Ruth was still a draw in any capacity.

Even Fuchs didn't want Ruth as a manager—he was happy with Bill McKechnie. But he knew that was the job Ruth wanted, so he created a deal that seemed to give Ruth a role beyond the box office.

Fuchs offered Ruth a deal as player/"assistant" manager/club vice president, an amorphous position that Ruth soon learned included few duties beyond pinch-hitting, standing in the coaching box, and pulling in the crowds for the lowly Braves. Ruth thought the job was going to be more than that, and Fuchs let him think so.

Ruth formally agreed to the deal on February 26, 1935. He made no grand speech but simply appeared at an awkward press conference with Ruppert and Fuchs at Ruppert's brewery.

Ruppert spoke first and outlined everything that had taken place since the World Series. "Today I hand Ruth his unconditional release. The American League clubs have all waived on him. . . . There are no strings on the release I give him. I get not a penny in return, not a promise, nothing. Ruth is a free man." The Yankees released the greatest player the game has ever seen for nothing.

And at that precise instant Ruth seemed to shrink and withdraw. The legendary Ruth remained in New York, a memory and a myth, while the man who bore his name went off to Boston. Without the "NY" emblazoned on his chest, he was suddenly just another aging ballplayer.

"Well," wrote John Kieran, "he's gone."

Something had ended that had helped make him great, and now, with Ruth gone, it suddenly became visible. During Ruth's reign in New York the game, his team, and the city of New York had all changed and been transformed. Because of Ruth, baseball was now a game of offense, the New York Yankees were its best-known, most successful, and most popular franchise, and New York City, more than ever before, was viewed as the ultimate stage, the only place where true greatness was possible. Despite competition from vaudeville and the movies, baseball was bigger than ever. Radio broadcasts now brought the major leagues to every corner of the country. And in the midst of the Depression, Ruth, of all Americans, had seemed immune to the atmosphere of fear and poverty that gripped the country. Whenever one of his blasts cleared the fence, spirits had been lifted and troubles temporarily forgotten. The miracle cures he was credited with delivering to little boys in hospitals took place for real for millions who saw him play.

In his 15 years in a Yankee uniform, Ruth cracked 659 of his 714 career home runs and hit .349, both of which remain club records, although at the time he also held team marks for games played, at bats, walks, hits, strikeouts, doubles, RBIs, games, hits, hot dogs, hangovers, whores, and just about everything else imaginable. In his

15 seasons as a Yankee, he earned nearly $850,000 in salary, and the club won seven American League pennants, four world championships, built a ballpark, and drew nearly 14 million fans. And that's not the half of it.

No one yet knew what the future held for the New York Yankees, but while the ballclub and Ruth underwent their drawn-out divorce, the club began a new relationship, one with a player who would prove to be almost as important to the club's future as Ruth had been to its past. On November 24, 1934, while Ruth was touring the Far East, the Yankees took a flyer on a young prospect turned suspect because of knee problems. They dealt five spare parts named Dinsmore, Norbett, Powell, Farrell, and Newkirk, none of whom had any chance of reaching the major leagues, to the Pacific Coast League San Francisco Seals for an option on an outfielder with a bum knee. The Yankees even agreed to let the Seals keep the player in 1935 to see whether the knee would hold up. If it did, and they liked what they saw, the Yankees agreed to take him for another $25,000. If not, the Seals could keep the five players and the damaged prospect. They weren't taking much of a chance.

His name was Joe DiMaggio.

.25

GGIO.5

By July 1936 attendance at Yankee Stadium had increased by more than 200,000 over the previous season because of Joe DiMaggio. At one contest a reporter noted that "Italian fans dominate," and, "There can be no doubt that Joe DiMaggio is fast taking the place of the one and only Babe Ruth as a drawing card."

1935–1941
THE CLIPPER

With the passing of Ruth, the Yankees moved quickly to turn the page and look forward. Compared to other major league clubs, save perhaps Tom Yawkey's Red Sox, the Yankees were the wealthiest team in the game and growing ever more wealthy. Shedding Ruth's salary gave them even more flexibility. In essence, the money New York saved by dumping Ruth had already been invested in DiMaggio.

Over the last decade the Yankees had solidified their place as one of baseball's best organizations. They alone had been virtually immune to the effects of the Depression. George Weiss's farm system was not only profitable but coming into harvest — flagship Newark had started dominating the International League and was already providing players to New York. Steady Red Rolfe had been brought up in 1934 and would take over at third in 1935, and outfielder George Selkirk was poised to play in Ruth's stead, if not replace him, in right field. By 1937 the Yankee farm system included 15 teams and had begun to send a stream of talent to the Yankees that would flow unchecked for the next 25 years. The club made relatively few significant trades for major league players over that time period. The farm system provided either the talent itself or the prospects to acquire what the club lacked. While other teams shuffled the deck, the Yankees rolled out more or less the same teams for years, plugging in new recruits only when age or injury made it necessary.

But for the time being, DiMaggio and the next generation of Yankee stars were still unknown quantities. To emphasize the new beginning in 1935, McCarthy announced when the team arrived in New York to start the season that Lou Gehrig would be the Yankee captain, a post that had gone unfilled since Miller Huggins stripped Ruth of the title a decade before. It was a none-too-subtle message that McCarthy was now fully in control and that Gehrig, not Ruth, was the exemplar.

Even Gehrig seemed to recognize this. He and Ruth, who had never been particularly close, had had a falling-out during the barnstorming tour through the Far East. Claire Ruth took offense at a comment Mrs. Gehrig made on the way she dressed her children, and the two husbands gave each other the silent treatment. One day before the start of the season Gehrig told the *Times,* also none too subtly, that he believed the 1935 squad was "a greatly improved ballclub in every department. . . . Selkirk in right will strengthen our defense and will help us, too, with our hitting." Gehrig certainly wasn't pining for the old days.

Still, it was a strange experience for Yankee fans when the club opened the season on April 16 at the Stadium against Boston with Selkirk, not Ruth, in right, and Selkirk, not Ruth, hitting third in front of Gehrig. That difference was driven home dramatically in several ways. Only 29,000 fans turned out for the opener, the smallest opening crowd since the club had left the Polo Grounds for the Stadium. Then Wes Ferrell shut out the Yanks 1–0 on two hits. Meanwhile, the Babe cracked a home run and drove in three in his debut with the Braves. He was through, but still capable of the occasional explosion.

Although the Yankees soon moved into first place, they slowly fell away in midseason as the Tigers once again proved to be the class of the league. Only an inconsequential late fade by Detroit made it seem close as Detroit won the pennant by three games with 92 wins.

The Yankees missed Ruth. Not so much the Babe Ruth of 1934, for Selkirk, while demonstrating little power, did hit .312 with 94 RBIs. No, the Yankees missed the Ruth of 1932, his last great year and their last championship. Gehrig was pitched around all year, hit only 30 home runs, and set a career high in walks. When Combs failed to return to form, he retired, and the club simply didn't have enough offense to back up the league's best pitching. The end result was not only second place but also a home attendance mark of less than 700,000, the second year in a row they'd been outdrawn by Detroit. The Tigers, Giants, and even the last-place Philadelphia A's hit more home runs than the Yanks. The former Bronx Bombers were more the kind of bomb one found on Broadway. The reviews weren't good.

By midseason it was apparent that the answer to both problems was in San Francisco.

Yankee scout Bill Essick had been watching various DiMaggio brothers play semipro ball for years. Tom and Mike, the two oldest, had given up the game to work on the family fishing boat, but Vince was a solid pro and Joe had some skills. In 1932 he'd made a brief appearance with the San Francisco Seals, and in 1933 the shortstop-turned-outfielder blossomed, saving his fledgling baseball career by embarking on a record hitting streak. Batting only .249 and in danger of being released, DiMaggio came out of nowhere to hit in his next 61 games, during which he hit .405 to finish the year at .340. But he was still only 18 years old, and in the offense-minded PCL, a .340 batting average barely put DiMaggio in the top 20. He could run and had a strong arm, but he was still learning to play the outfield. Nevertheless, Bill Essick and fellow scout Joe Devine began watching him more closely.

They weren't alone, but there wasn't a great frenzy around DiMaggio either, partially because of his age and inexperience, but also because he was Italian. To some big league clubs, that was still a strike against him.

It wasn't for the Yankees. Next to Ruth, Tony Lazzeri had been their most popular player, an idol of New York's one million Italians. Now shortstop Frank Crosetti was similarly revered. The Giants and Dodgers were improving, and the Yankees were fighting both teams for fans. Another Italian star could be a huge draw, and the Yankees knew it.

DiMaggio grew up in 1934, and scouts started to salivate. He learned to harness his arm, judge fly balls, and make use of his speed on the bases. And he was beginning to show some power. All this added up to something new. In a sense, DiMaggio was the first postmodern ballplayer, the first so-called five-tool player — someone with not only the traditional skills of hitting, running, throwing, and fielding but also the ability to hit with power that Ruth had made indispensable.

Seals owner Charlie Graham sat back and awaited New York's bid for his prize, which the press speculated would be as much as 100,000 much-needed Depression-Era dollars. A few years before the Yankees had paid nearly that much for Crosetti, but that was before the Depression, and shortstops were always in short supply. The market for DiMaggio was smaller, but Graham still stood to make a nice killing.

Early on the morning of May 22, Graham's dreams of wealth nearly evaporated on a dark San Francisco street. Earlier that day Joe and his brother Vince had been feted with a "Family Day" at Seals Stadium. Afterward they celebrated with some wine. Returning home, DiMaggio, according to the police, slipped off the running board of his car while climbing in and sprained his knee.

That wasn't the way DiMaggio and a host of sportswriters later told the story. They sanitized the incident into a freak accident that occurred after DiMaggio's leg fell asleep in a cab, with no mention at all of the day at the park or the postgame party. The New York press had been schooled by Ruth and knew how to protect their meal ticket. It didn't take them long to treat DiMaggio the same way. Unlike Ruth, however, who paid for his press, DiMaggio would get it all for free, in exchange for the status that came with his company.

DiMaggio sat out for a while as the Yankees tempered their interest. Graham, watching his fortune slip away and worried about the gate, rushed DiMaggio back into the lineup. But he was clearly diminished, and in early August the knee gave out again when he chased after a fly ball. He made it back to the bench but collapsed in full view of everyone and had to be carried away. He missed the rest of the season, and interest in him waned.

But the Yankees were sandbagging. They kept tabs on DiMaggio in the off-season and arranged for him to travel

Twenty-one-year-old Joe DiMaggio arrived in New York in 1936 as the highly touted heir to the legacy created by Ruth and Gehrig. As a rookie he batted .323 and led the league with 22 outfield assists. In the Yankees' World Series triumph over the Giants, DiMaggio hit .346, highest in the Series.

After the sale of Babe Ruth, Yankee manager Joe McCarthy named Lou Gehrig team captain in 1935, thereby asserting his authority over the club. The following season the Yankees were champions once more, creating a dynasty that would capture five world championships in the six seasons from 1936 to 1941.

to Los Angeles, where they paid a specialist to examine his knee. The doctor found no lasting damage. Armed with that bit of inside information, the Yankees cut a deal with Graham, gambling $25,000 that DiMaggio wasn't damaged goods.

He proved the opposite in 1935, hitting nearly .400, leading the Seals to the PCL championship, and being named league MVP. That kind of performance would have been worth $100,000, but the Yankees exercised their option and took their prize for a cut-rate price.

Though Gehrig had been a great player, he was lousy copy. In the winter of 1935–36, the New York press, still missing Ruth, began touting DiMaggio as the second coming. By the time spring training began, no rookie in baseball history had ever faced higher expectations.

But DiMaggio, after a good start in the spring, sprained an ankle and then burned it taking treatment under a heat lamp. New York opened the 1936 season with the phenom on the bench. And the Yankees started the season just as they had a year before, losing 1–0, this time to Washington.

Even without DiMaggio, the 1936 Yankees were already a much better team. Rolfe and Selkirk were a year older and a year better, and Crosetti was finally starting to hit, while Bill Dickey became a star. Two off-season deals by Barrow delivered two valuable pitchers, Bump Hadley and Monte Pearson, as well as veteran outfielder Roy Johnson.

Dickey's importance to the team over the next few seasons, while easy to overlook, is hard to overestimate. Like Lazzeri, he gave the Yankees potent offense from an unexpected source, and he was one of the game's best defensive catchers — years later he would be brought in to tutor Yogi Berra.

But of even more significance is the way he handled the pitching staff. For more than a decade Dickey was the common thread that turned previously mediocre pitchers into winners for New York. Apart from Gomez and Ruffing, McCarthy treated his pitching staff as interchangeable parts. A manager on the field, Dickey roughly massaged egos and guided them to performances beyond their talent. Few pitchers who left New York ever got better. Dickey was the glue that held them together, leading one writer to comment, "He isn't just a player; he's an influence."

So was DiMaggio, and his influence became apparent

when he made his big league debut on May 3, playing right field. The Yankees were 11–6, in second place behind Boston. To make room for DiMaggio, New York sold Dixie Walker to Chicago. Walker was hitting .350, but the Yankees had seen enough of DiMaggio in Florida to be sure. He'd been the best player on the field, and even the normally restrained Gehrig had offered, "DiMaggio will develop into one of the grandest right handed hitters of all within three years." He was wrong — by three years. DiMaggio was already one of the best.

His first game as a Yankee drew over 25,000 fans to the Stadium, the club's biggest crowd since Opening Day. He didn't disappoint. Hitting third, playing left field, and sending Roy Johnson to the bench, DiMaggio keyed New

York's biggest offensive outburst of the young season, collecting two singles and a triple against the Browns as New York romped to a 14–5 win.

He was the missing piece on a team that wasn't missing much to begin with. On another club his contribution might have been muted, but in New York, on this team, and in this lineup, what DiMaggio added to the team was enhanced, for he filled a void, figuratively and literally, that had been empty since the release of Ruth.

DiMaggio almost made the Yankees forget Ruth, for as soon as he entered the lineup they began to pull away. They took over first place on May 10 with a 7–2 win over the A's as DiMaggio cracked his first home run, a line drive to left off George Turbeville. The Yankees were 6–1

THE FIRST FIREMAN

According to the National Baseball Hall of Fame, the first print reference to a relief pitcher as a "fireman" appeared in a June 15, 1939, article about Yankees pitcher Johnny Murphy in the *New York World Telegram.* Murphy was the standard by which all relievers were judged.

Before Johnny Murphy, the relief pitcher rarely commanded respect. Pitching skill was equated with the ability to start and finish games. Relievers were generally trick pitch specialists or failed starters nursing an injured arm, angling for innings, and trying to extend their careers. Only Washington's Firpo Marberry and former Yankees great Wilcy Moore had escaped that definition.

Then came Murphy. After he won 14 of 20 starts in 1934, his first major league season, Joe McCarthy asked Murphy to move to the bullpen. At first the pitcher protested. He accepted the move only when the Yankees agreed to pay him on

a scale commensurate with that of a starting pitcher. Within three seasons, Murphy's array of pitches made him the best reliever in baseball. In 1937 his 12–4 record and ten saves (a statistic created and calculated later) led the league while helping lead the Yankees to a world championship.

Between 1935 and 1943, Murphy set an American League record by leading the league in relief victories six times while also leading the league in saves four times. In five World Series appearances Murphy was dominant, winning twice while saving three games, including two Series finales in 1936 and 1939.

But after World War II, Murphy enjoyed only mixed success. He ended his career in 1947 with the Red Sox. After more than a decade as Boston's minor league director, he returned home to guide the New York Mets as chief scout, as vice president, and finally, as the general manager who molded the 1969 "Miracle Mets." He died of a heart attack only weeks after the Mets clinched their incredible world championship.

When asked how he felt prior to one of his many World Series starts, Yankee Hall of Famer Lefty Gomez remarked,

"How I feel isn't important. The important thing is how Murphy feels." Gomez later paid further homage to his teammate, crediting his own success to "clean living, a fast outfield, and Johnny Murphy." Joe McCarthy was more succinct when he called Murphy "my pennant insurance."

with DiMaggio in the lineup and never looked back. The press fawned over him, ignoring the fine performances of teammates Gehrig and Dickey to lavish DiMaggio with praise.

They weren't alone. Fans turned out in droves to see the new star. Attendance jumped by 200,000 in the first half of the season. Entire sections of the stands at the Stadium were reportedly populated by the Sons of Italy cheering their hero. One reporter noted at one contest that "Italian fans dominate," and that "there can be no doubt that Joe DiMaggio is fast taking the place of the one and only Babe Ruth as a drawing card." Those fans elected him to the All-Star game with more votes than any other player as he outpolled established stars and eventual Hall of Famers Gehrig, Dickey, Foxx, Gehringer, Appling, and Simmons.

He also earned the respect and deference of his teammates. In one early game in Cleveland he went into second hard several times to break up double plays. In retaliation, Cleveland second baseman Billy Knickerbocker tried to take off his head with a throw. DiMaggio was oblivious to the ploy, and as a frustrated Knickerbocker tried to goad the bewildered young man into a fight, the entire Yankee team, led by Lazzeri, came to his defense. They knew the value of a meal ticket.

But the Yankees weren't satisfied. In mid-June they picked up Jake Powell from Washington for center fielder Ben Chapman, who had been a holdout in the spring and whose volatile personality didn't fit in. The deal wasn't made to accommodate DiMaggio. Powell took over in center, Selkirk went to left, and DiMaggio moved into Ruth's old spot in right field to make better use of his arm. Although there had been some speculation that DiMaggio might one day play center—the Seals had occasionally played him there in 1935 at the Yankees' request—New York's brain trust seemed to have decided that right field would be DiMaggio's final destination.

All that changed in Detroit on July 28. Powell slumped upon arrival, and Myril Hoag was playing center. In the sixth inning Goose Goslin drove a ball into the right-center gap.

It was Hoag's catch to make, since the center fielder always has the right of way, but DiMaggio saw only the ball as he ranged far to his right. He and Hoag cracked heads running at full speed. Both went down and stayed there as Goslin scored on an inside-the-park home run.

After a few tense minutes each rose and finished the inning, but then Hoag, still groggy, had to leave the game. Two days later he collapsed in the team's hotel with a blood clot on his brain. He underwent emergency brain surgery and would miss the rest of the season.

Now the Yankees made the change. On August 1, with little fanfare, DiMaggio moved into center field, and Powell shifted to right.

DiMaggio finally had his stage, for in center field he was able to fully display his prodigious talent, eating up ground in huge strides as he glided after fly balls. His reputation as a player, already outsized in regard to his experience, expanded exponentially.

The Yankees clinched the pennant on September 10, the earliest date ever at the time, and cruised to a 102–51 record, 19½ games ahead of Detroit. DiMaggio, who slumped over the final weeks to drop his average from above .350 to a more mortal .323 with 29 home runs and 125 RBIs, was one of six Yankee starters to hit above .300 that year, paced by Dickey's .362 and Gehrig's MVP-worthy .354 with 49 home runs and 152 RBIs. Gehrig was one of five Yankees to knock in more than 100, the Yankees hit .300 as a team (no starter finished below .287), and they outscored the opposition by more than 300 runs.

The Giants swept to the National League pennant as New York resumed its place atop the baseball world for the first time in more than a decade. Fans called it the "nickel series," after the price of a subway ride from the Stadium to the Polo Grounds.

Giants hopes rested on the left arm of Carl Hubbell, permanently twisted from throwing his signature screwball. But DiMaggio and the Yankees weren't intimidated. Or at least they wouldn't admit it. After Hubbell beat them in game one at the Polo Grounds, scattering seven hits to win 6–1, a reporter asked DiMaggio what he thought of Hubbell. "Well, I didn't think he was so tough," he said. "He wasn't invincible, anyway."

After a day of rain the Yankees made a statement in game two. With two on and no out in the first, DiMaggio dropped a bunt to load the bases for Gehrig. He knocked in a run with a fly ball, and the Yankees jumped out to a 2–0 lead. They rolled to an 18–4 win as Lazzeri hit a grand slam, only the second in Series history. The game ended when Hank Lieber flew out to DiMaggio in deep center field.

DiMaggio then stood at attention as President Roosevelt left the ballpark by car through the center-field exit, waving to DiMaggio as he passed.

The Yankees then swept the next two games at the Stadium to put the Giants on the ropes as Gehrig hit home runs in each game and New York beat Hubbell in a rematch. But DiMaggio went hitless against the screwballer.

After dropping game five, the Yankees returned to the Polo Grounds for game six. They nursed a 6–5 lead into the ninth, then seemed to grow suddenly bored with the prospect of playing a seventh game. They sent 13 men to the plate and scored 7 runs. DiMaggio singled twice in the inning to put the game and the Series away.

It was a gratifying win for everyone. McCarthy, whom the press had started calling "Second Place Joe," proved his mettle as manager, and Gehrig won his first title with-

Tony Lazzeri (left), Lefty Gomez (center), and Joe DiMaggio, after Gomez beat the Giants in the first game of the 1937 World Series by a score of 8–1. Gomez secured his complete-game triumph with help from Lazzeri, who socked the game's only home run, and DiMaggio, who struck a bases-loaded single.

out Ruth and his first MVP Award. DiMaggio hit .346 in the Series, the best of his career. All was right with the world as the Yankees looked unstoppable again. Apart from Gehrig and Lazzeri, the entire starting lineup was still in their twenties. And Gehrig, the oldest man on the team, was only 33. DiMaggio seemed capable of doing for Gehrig what Gehrig had once done for Ruth—extending his career at a higher level for a few extra seasons. The Yankees again owned New York and the American League.

The 1937 season proceeded in a rough imitation of 1936. The pennant race, what there was of it, ended on May 25 when Detroit catcher Mickey Cochrane was beaned and fractured his skull, an injury that ended his career. The Tigers, who along with Chicago and Cleveland had more or less kept pace with the Yankees thus far, fell back, and by the time New York lost its third game in July—on July 23—the race was over.

The Yankees even managed to win the All-Star game, sort of. With five players on the team—Gehrig, Rolfe, DiMaggio, Dickey, and Gomez—the Yankee players were dominant in the AL's 8–3 win as Gehrig drove in four and

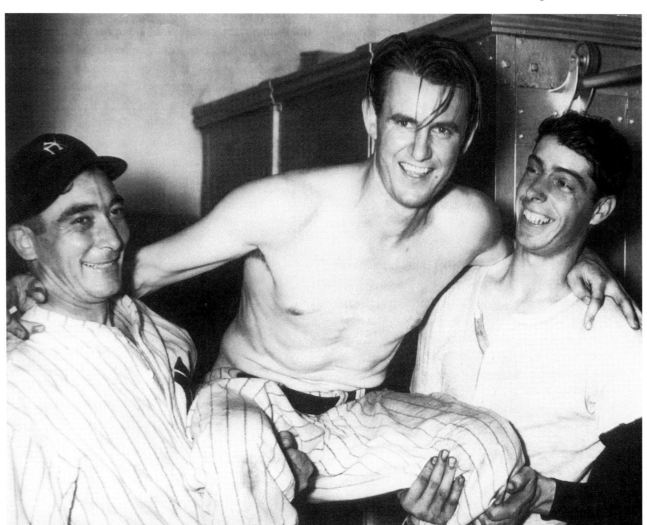

LEADERS IN SAVES

1916	Bob Shawkey, 9
1921	Carl Mays, 7
1927	Wilcy Moore, 13
1928	Waite Hoyt, 8
1936	Pat Malone, 9
1938	Johnny Murphy, 11
1939	Johnny Murphy, 19
1941	Johnny Murphy, 15
1942	Johnny Murphy, 11
1945	Jim Turner, 10
1949	Joe Page, 27
1954	Johnny Sain, 22
1957	Bob Grim, 19
1958	Ryne Duren, 20
1961	Luis Arroyo, 29
1972	Sparky Lyle, 35
1976	Sparky Lyle, 23
1978	Rich Gossage, 27
1986	Dave Righetti, 46
1996	John Wetteland, 43
1999	Mariano Rivera, 45
2000	Mariano Rivera, 50

Gomez picked up the win. That moved Stanley Woodward to write in the *Herald Tribune*, "I was only fooling a few days ago when I suggested that Joe McCarthy might as well select the Yankees en masse for the All-Star Game . . . there were other players filling in other positions, but their names might as well have been Stanislaus."

DiMaggio was immense all year. He'd filled out and now carried a solid 190 pounds on his six-foot-two frame. He'd also made some adjustments, spreading his stance and generating more power than many observers ever expected him to. On August 2, he cracked his 31st home run of the year, putting him ahead of Ruth's pace in 1927 and leading Arthur Patterson to comment, "They said there would never be another Babe Ruth, [but] there is another babe at Yankee Stadium." With the pennant race decided, the press fawned over DiMaggio for the rest of the year, just as they had fawned over Ruth in 1927—there was nothing else to write about.

Ruth, as Patterson noted, had had "the indefinite thing called color." DiMaggio did not. But that didn't stop the writers.

They took him in, coddled him, showed him around town, and taught him how to live, if not act, like a star. DiMaggio himself was never particularly giving off the field. Ruth created headlines wherever he went no matter what he did, but DiMaggio was more like Gehrig. Off the field he wasn't very interesting.

It was too late for them to create a persona for the already established Gehrig—his continuing streak of consecutive games played had already done that. But DiMaggio was malleable, a blank slate marked only by base hits, home runs, and great catches. The press took those talents and created an image to fit, extrapolating from DiMaggio's play a whole series of laudatory personal qualities. DiMaggio didn't resist. He realized early on that the press could make him rich. In only his second year he was already making almost as much as Gehrig.

DiMaggio—quiet, taciturn, suspicious, and surly, supremely confident on the field but socially awkward—became something else, a hero. His reserve was translated as humility, his public reticence as a reflection of his commitment and drive, his lack of dimension as a sign of an unmatched ability to focus on the task on the field.

None of it would have worked if he had not been a genuinely remarkable player and if his actions on the field had not backed up those assumptions. As it was, the results seemed to reinforce his image. Even Ruth's team didn't win all the time. But DiMaggio's did. He wasn't the only reason, but after a string of second-place finishes, it sure seemed that way. As a Yankee, he would match Ruth in world championships in only four seasons.

While in time DiMaggio would become both isolated by that image and enslaved by it, for the present it served him well, relieving him of the responsibility to take care of himself. All he had to do was play the game. And that, of all things, was something he could do.

Of course, he didn't hit 60 home runs in 1937. As a right-handed hitter, he found himself robbed of many home runs in Yankee Stadium, and Ruth in 1927 had hit 17 homers in September alone, but DiMaggio finished with 46 (still a club record for a right-handed hitter), 167 RBIs, and a .346 batting average. Gehrig was nearly as good, topping DiMaggio only in batting average and giving the Yankees another unparalleled one-two punch. And in other news, punch number three, Bill Dickey, hit .332 with "only" 29 home runs and 133 RBIs — only third-best on the Yankees but a better all-around year than every other player in the league except Detroit's Hank Greenberg.

The pitching wasn't bad either, as Gomez and Ruffing continued to forge Hall of Fame careers, each winning 20 games as the club led the league in ERA. Once again, the Yankees met the Giants in the World Series.

This time they beat Hubbell in game one, 8–1, behind Gomez, beat 20-game winner Cliff Melton in game two by the same score with Ruffing on the mound, and beat Hal Schumacher 5–1 behind Monte Pearson in game three. The Series was essentially over. Hubbell picked up a win in game four despite a home run by Gehrig, his last in a World Series, but the Yankees ended the Series quickly, winning game five 4–2 as DiMaggio cracked his first Series homer off Melton, a towering drive that hit the flagpole on the Polo Grounds' left-field roof.

It was a tour de force performance: no one on the team had a really great Series but no one had a bad one either. DiMaggio helped win two games with a bases-loaded single and the home run. Selkirk, who'd taken over for an injured Jake Powell in midseason, keyed another win, and Tony Lazzeri hit .400. But the Giants were completely outclassed. As one writer put it, "The Giants won one game and the Yankees won the Series and that's the way it should have been."

The rich continued to get richer. The Yankees had picked up another PCL star, shortstop Joe Gordon, in 1936. They decided that, after one year of seasoning and a switch to second base at Newark, he was ready. Once that decision was made, the Yankee brain trust didn't mess around. Sentiment counted for nothing. Lazzeri, only 34, was let go. He signed with the Cubs.

Although he had often been overlooked on a team with Ruth and Gehrig, Lazzeri, a middle infielder with power in an era when few other middle infielders had any, had been central to his teammates' success. But what a player did yesterday has rarely played much of a role in Yankee personnel decisions, not then and not now, not in regard to Ruth and not in regard to David Cone. Lazzeri's release was prescient, however, a classic case of getting rid of a player a year early rather than a year late, for Lazzeri was just about finished, and Gordon was ready.

They needed him, because in 1938 Gehrig began to fade. They were prepared and had already acquired prospect Babe Dahlgren from the Red Sox a year before to serve as Gehrig's understudy. There was also speculation that another youngster in Newark, Tommy Henrich, might also take over at first one day.

In the spring the big news was DiMaggio. Beginning to realize his value, DiMaggio was a holdout, something New York fans, accustomed to Lou Gehrig's more stoic compliance, found disquieting. When he finally signed for $25,000 — $15,000 less than he had wanted — and made his debut on April 30, a bit of the shine had come off the young star. Richards Vidmer wrote, "It appears that DiMaggio is more a businessman than a ballplayer." The fans agreed and greeted DiMaggio's home debut with boos. But Vidmer also noted, accurately: "Give him a few good days in the sun, a sprinkling of base hits and a couple of homers and all will be forgiven." He was right, for without DiMaggio the Yankees went 6–5 at the start of 1938. He returned to the lineup and they won eight of nine. That pattern would be repeated time and time again over the remainder of his career. The bottom line on DiMaggio, and the only one that ever really mattered, was that anytime he was out of the lineup, the Yankees had trouble winning. With him, they did not. It was that simple.

McCarthy took advantage of DiMaggio's return to make a change in his lineup. Gehrig had been terrible all spring, and over the first ten days of the season he showed no signs of improvement. Never the most gifted athlete, to many observers it appeared as if Gehrig had aged overnight. He seemed slow and was even having trouble in the field. Writer Jim Kahn later noted what McCarthy had already sensed. "For some reason that I don't know," he wrote, "his old power isn't there. . . . [H]e is meeting the ball time after time but it isn't going anywhere."

So on May 1, McCarthy made a change, shaking up the batting order, in the words of one writer, "as he might a medicine bottle." He moved DiMaggio from his accustomed third spot in the batting order to fourth, dropping Gehrig from the cleanup spot to sixth, after Dickey.

When the weather warmed in July, the Yankees, save Gehrig, finally got going, surging past Cleveland to take command of the pennant race. And in August, facing the weaker sisters of the American League, their bats came to life as even Gehrig started to hit a little, pushing his average up toward the .300 mark.

The Yankees capped their two-month spree, which saw them win 48 and lose only 13 in July and August, with a memorable doubleheader sweep of Cleveland on August 27, sealing the Indians' fate to finish the year fighting Boston and Detroit for second place.

In the first game the two clubs traded the lead back and forth, but the Indians took a 7–5 lead into the ninth and were one out away from a win before the Yankees woke up. DiMaggio capped the comeback with his third triple of the day as the Yankees won, 8–7.

The victory was a dagger to the heart of the Indians. In game two pitcher Monte Pearson twisted it even deeper. He no-hit the Indians, the first no-hitter ever at the Stadium and the first for a Yankee pitcher since "Sad Sam" Jones did it in 1923. No one came close to getting a hit, and

Hardly a collection of regular Joes, the 1939 Yankees featured (left to right) Joe Gordon, Joe Gallagher, Joe Beggs, Joe DiMaggio, and Joe McCarthy.

the Yanks won 8–0. Fans mobbed Pearson after the game, and police had to escort him off the field.

The Yankees won the pennant by nine and a half games even as they slumped late and DiMaggio hit only .324 with 32 home runs. Gehrig tumbled to a .295 mark with 29 home runs and 114 RBIs. That would have been great for anyone else, for he was still seventh in the league in RBIs and home runs, but far below his usual standard. Gordon and Henrich had picked up the slack, however, each hitting more than 20 home runs and 90 RBIs.

The Cubs won the National League in a hard-fought battle with Pittsburgh, New York, and Cincinnati, but no one considered them in the same league as the Yankees, and the World Series proved that. Dizzy Dean, his arm shot, put in a courageous performance in game two, but the Yankees won in four games and seemed to play hard only when they had to and to do just enough to win. Afterward Joe McCarthy said, "I believe we are the greatest ballclub ever assembled. . . . We have the pitching, the power, the defensive play."

Lou Gehrig was strangely reserved the whole Series. As the team celebrated after Lefty Gomez's game-two win, which gave him a Series record of 6–0, Gehrig was observed "over in one corner . . . quietly puffing a cigarette, his cleated feet up on another chair, his head rested against a radiator. . . . Today's victory was the twenty-fifth World Series triumph he has celebrated. 'But boy, I still get a bang out of it. So I'm just sitting over here, seeing everything, hearing everything and enjoying it all.'" It was as if he already knew this would be his last World Series.

It was the last one for owner Jacob Ruppert as well. His health had been slowly failing for several years, and he'd suffered from phlebitis throughout the 1938 season. In the off-season his condition deteriorated.

He knew he was dying. Ruppert had never married and had no direct heirs. His brother George had no interest in running the team, so in January 1939 Ruppert made arrangements to transfer 300 shares of team stock to Ed Barrow, ensuring that he would serve as team president, the reward for his long service. Although Barrow would never technically "own" the Yankees—the club would eventually become the legal property of one of Barrow's long-time lady friends and his two nieces—as far as the day-to-day operation was concerned, Barrow was the man.

On January 13, Ruppert's doctors knew the end was near, and Ruppert made a final request to see Babe Ruth, who hurried to his bedside in his Fifth Avenue apartment. He referred to him as "Babe" for the first and only time in his life—he'd always been plain "Ruth" before—and passed away later that day.

Just as Ruth had set the template as the quintessential Yankee player, so did Ruppert as Yankee owner, for in the future the team would prove successful only when the front office recognized the inherent natural advantage of the New York market and milked it unmercifully. That's precisely what Ruppert had done, selling baseball like he sold beer. To do anything less squandered that advantage.

And Ruppert had also been wise enough to continue investing in the club, building Yankee Stadium, and starting a farm system. These forward-thinking moves would be echoed later in the ballclub's renovation of Yankee Stadium (albeit with civic funds) and, after the team failed to take advantage of integration and initially missed the boat on Latin ballplayers as well, its focus on baseball's emerging talent pools in the Far East and Latin America in more recent years. Unlike other wealthy owners, such as Boston's Tom Yawkey, Ruppert was continually ahead of the curve.

He needed to be, for after his death it was revealed that his estate, which most believed to be in the $40–70 million range, was in fact much smaller—only some $7 million, one-third of which was represented by the Yankees. In recent years he had apparently invested heavily in Depression-Era real estate and lost heavily. This revelation made his achievement with the Yankees even more impressive.

Ruppert's stock transfer to Barrow ensured a seamless transition and business as usual in the Yankee front office, which did little in the off-season because, well, there wasn't much to be done.

In fact, many expected the Yankees to be even better, for Gordon and Henrich would have another year under their belt, DiMaggio would have the benefit of spring training, there were several promising arms in the farm system, and rookie Charlie Keller had completed a recent devastation of the International League with Newark and was scheduled to make his Yankee Stadium debut. There was even some optimism that Gehrig might bounce back.

That final wish, however, was not forthcoming. Gehrig, as puzzled by his performance in 1938 as everyone else, worked out hard in the off-season. But he took several falls that worried his wife, Eleanor, and worried Gehrig himself enough that he went to see a doctor, who diagnosed him with gall bladder trouble and recommended a change in diet. Meanwhile, Gehrig got weaker and weaker, despite increasing the frequency and duration of his workouts.

At spring training in St. Petersburg it was clear to everyone that Gehrig was done. Had it been any other Yankee player, the reaction would have been swift, sudden, and sure — he'd have been gone. But Gehrig's streak of consecutive games played, which now numbered over 2,000 and was an increasing source of admiration among the press and the public, made him bulletproof. Neither Barrow nor McCarthy was about to mess with that. They all just watched and hoped Gehrig would somehow snap out of it even when it became apparent he wouldn't.

He was horrible all spring. As the Yankees barnstormed north playing mostly minor league competition, Gehrig barely hit .200 and was overmatched by pitchers who had no chance of ever playing in the major leagues. One day in Norfolk he did hit two home runs, but McCarthy noticed that each had barely made it over an abnormally short fence in right. McCarthy dismissed them as "fly balls."

Rain stopped the Yankees for the first three days of the season, but then Ruffing shut out the Red Sox 2–0, holding their West Coast phenom Ted Williams to one hit, and the Yankees were off. Yankee fans finally had the opportunity that fans in other cities had had for a number of years. For the first time Yankee games were broadcast on the radio.

New York City's three baseball teams had been the lone holdouts against the technology, except during the World Series. All three had worried that if baseball were available for free on the radio, fans might stop coming to the park. That hadn't been the case in other cities, but then again, no other city offered fans three major league options, plus the continuing presence of Negro League baseball.

Maverick Larry MacPhail had taken over as president of the Dodgers, and he broke the gentleman's agreement between the three clubs that had resulted in the citywide blackout. The Giants and Yankees were forced to follow suit, and Arch MacDonald, joined a few weeks later by Mel Allen, became the voice of the Yankees on WABC. It was MacDonald who gave DiMaggio his nickname, "the Clip-

per," for the way he roamed the Yankee outfield, graceful as a clipper ship moving across the sea. Despite all the rain and the radio, more than 30,000 fans still turned out for the opener.

But even the Yankees were mortal. Over the first ten days of the season injuries started to peck away at the club. Joe Gordon hurt his thumb, Monte Pearson had a bad wrist, and on April 29 DiMaggio caught his spikes and tore some muscles in his lower leg. He had to be hospitalized.

In 1936 Lou Gehrig, shown in a 1939 photo, won his second American League Most Valuable Player Award, as he batted .354 with 49 home runs and 154 RBIs. At thirty-three, Gehrig was the oldest player on the world champions' roster.

DON'T QUIT

And then there was Gehrig, whom John Kieran had recently described as looking "like a man trying to lift heavy trunks into the back of a truck." Even Yankee opponents had noticed; they were afraid he couldn't get out of the way of a ball pitched inside and were having no trouble blowing the ball past him over the heart of the plate. In 28 at bats he had only four hits, all singles. He struck out only once, though, as he pushed at the ball with his bat, desperate just to make contact.

He was going rapidly from bad to worse. He knew it, and so did everyone else. His teammates started praising him for making routine catches, for making contact with pitches he knew he should have crushed. But now, with DiMaggio out for at least a week or two, his teammates, particularly those younger teammates who had never seen him at his best, started to grumble. Gehrig was a liability. Gehrig was costing them games. Gehrig was hurting the team.

Gehrig couldn't take that because he knew in his heart they were right. So on May 2, as the Yankees prepared to play Detroit, Gehrig approached manager Joe McCarthy at the team hotel. Gehrig had been up all night and looked awful.

"I'm not helping the team any. I know I look terrible. This streak of mine means nothing to me. It isn't fair to the boys for me to stay in there. I want you to take me out of the lineup today."

McCarthy didn't try to talk him out of it. When the club arrived at the ballpark, coach Art Fletcher told Babe Dahlgren his time had come, and word of Gehrig's decision filtered through the clubhouse. When Dahlgren manned first during the Yankees pregame workout, Gehrig ran right past him and headed to the outfield where he shagged flies, not even bothering to take batting practice.

And on that day the Yankees crushed Detroit, 22–3, as Dahlgren made his bid to turn Gehrig into Wally Pipp by cracking a home run and a double. With Boston's game rained out, the Yankees moved into first place and became the best team in baseball again.

On July 4, 1939, the Yankees held Lou Gehrig Appreciation Day to honor their stricken star. He led off his remarks by saying, "Fans, for the past two weeks you have been reading about what a bad break I got. Yet today, I consider myself the luckiest man on the face of the earth." He died on June 2, 1941.

Gehrig stayed with the team for a little over a month, and his condition rapidly deteriorated. He never asked to go back into the lineup, and McCarthy was never tempted to put him back in. In mid-June, worried that he might have a brain tumor, Eleanor Gehrig made an appointment to have her husband examined at the Mayo Clinic. The verdict, which Gehrig learned of on his 36th birthday, July 19, and made public two days later, was sudden and direct. He was afflicted with amyotropic lateral sclerosis (ALS), since known popularly as "Lou Gehrig's disease," a progressive disease of the nervous system for which there is no known cure. Ever so slowly, the nerves that controlled his muscles would cease to function; that had already been taking place for more than a year. He now began a countdown far more important than his streak of games played, which stopped at 2,130. Now began the countdown to the end of his life.

Gehrig did not yet know, definitively, that the disease would kill him, for in the next two years he would take a variety of experimental treatments. But he soon sensed that it was so.

With Dahlgren at first, the club lost only four times in May, their best full month ever. Another pennant loomed.

The season paused on July 4 when the Yankees held "Lou Gehrig Appreciation Day" at the Stadium between games of a doubleheader against Washington. After the first game a microphone stand was placed near home plate, and Gehrig's former teammates—Ruth, Lazzeri, Meusel, Combs, and others—joined the current squad in a semicircle around Gehrig.

Sportswriter Sid Mercer served as master of ceremonies, and after McCarthy gave a brief speech, Mercer distributed gifts to Gehrig from his teammates, the writers, and others. Gehrig approached the microphone, then turned to Mercer and spoke softly. Gehrig had prepared some remarks, but now felt incapable of delivering them. The writer then announced, "Lou has asked me to thank all of you. He is too moved to speak."

From every corner of Yankee Stadium came a calm, slow, strong chant—"We want Gehrig! We want Gehrig!"—as his fans implored him to make a final unforgettable appearance on a ballfield. Gehrig heard them and stepped slowly to the microphone before home plate, his uniform hanging loosely from his once-robust frame, as Dahlgren, at McCarthy's urging, got into position to catch him if he faltered.

Nothing is quieter than a silent crowd. Yankee Stadium was never more silent. Gehrig then summoned all his strength and spoke from memory, mixing his prepared remarks with the observations and emotions that now washed over him in a torrent:

Fans, for the past two weeks you have been reading about what a bad break I got. Yet today, I consider myself the luckiest man on the face of the earth. I have been in ballparks for seventeen years and I have never received anything but kindness and encouragement from you fans. Look at these grand men. Which of you wouldn't consider it the highlight of his career just to associate with them for even one day? Sure I'm lucky. Who wouldn't consider it an honor to have known Jacob Ruppert? To have spent six years with that wonderful little fellow, Miller Huggins? To have spent nine years with that outstanding leader, that smart student of psychology, the best manager in baseball today, Joe McCarthy? Sure I'm lucky. When the New York Giants, a team you would give your right arm to beat, and vice versa, sends you a gift, that's something. When everybody down to the groundskeepers and those boys in white coats remember you with trophies, that's something. When you have a father and a mother who work all their lives so that you can have an education and build your body, that's a blessing. When you have a wife who has been a tower of strength and shown more courage than you dreamed existed, that's the finest I know. So I pause in saying, I might have had a bad break, but I have an awful lot to live for. Thank you.

With that the crowd roared, and even Ruth, who had been estranged from Gehrig for several years, was so moved the past was forgotten. He threw his arms around Gehrig's once-powerful shoulders in a memorable embrace.

Gehrig, who had always been overshadowed, first by Ruth, then by DiMaggio, now stood apart, squinting away tears in the bright sunshine of a baseball field, and with words alone created a moment more memorable than anything he ever did in any of those 2,130 games. Yankee fans seemed to realize, at last, that Gehrig had made them the luckiest fans on the face of the earth, for he had been a player and a man like no one else they had ever seen. And in his last at bat, his last game, he had done more than strike the winning hit or smash a home run—he had given them his greatest gift, the lesson of his life. For when one thinks of the Yankees, one may see Ruth or DiMaggio or Mantle at bat, but one hears the voice of Gehrig echoing through the Stadium, "the luckiest man on the face of the earth."

The season resumed. The Yankees were, in a word, magnificent, easily the equivalent of the 1927 team and probably better, for in 1939 they faced far better competition. In any other season the Red Sox, Cleveland, Chicago, and Detroit, all of which finished far above .500, would have contended for a pennant. But in 1939 they fought only to retain interest in a season already lost by the end of May.

DiMaggio led the way, hitting .381 as every member of the starting lineup, even light-hitting Frank Crosetti, cracked at least 10 home runs. Four—DiMaggio, Selkirk, Dickey, and Gordon—knocked in more than 100. Dahlgren hit only .235, but even he hit 15 home runs with 89 RBIs.

With that attack, it didn't matter who McCarthy pitched, and he pitched everyone as eight different pitchers started at least ten games and seven won ten or more, paced by Ruffing's 21. Apart from the loss of Gehrig, it was a season wholly without drama as the Yankees finished 106–45, 17 long games ahead of Boston, a team with five eventual Hall of Famers—Williams, Doerr, Cronin, Foxx, and Lefty Grove—on its roster. Boston actually won the season series with the Yankees, but none of their 19 meetings meant a thing to the pennant race, and three late September rainouts were simply canceled and never made up.

With apologies to Joe McCarthy, the 1939 Yankees may well have deserved the title "greatest" that he lavished on the 1938 edition. For as good as they were, one cannot help but wonder just how much better the 1939 Yankees might have been had Gehrig not been cut down by disease. Might they have won another 10 or 15 games? Would a record of 120–34 have been possible? 125–29? As it was, 14 of their 46 losses were by only one run. Would DiMaggio, with a potent Gehrig hitting behind him, have hit .400? Without him, DiMaggio was hitting as high as .410 in early September before being felled by a bad cold and a wrenched knee. He continued to play anyway.

And what numbers would Gehrig have put up for his career, which halted on 493 home runs? Might he have played until age 40 or 41 and challenged Ruth's record 714? Those are questions with no answers.

The Cincinnati Reds had the task of stopping the Yankees in the World Series, and they proved no more successful than the Cubs of 1938 or the Giants of 1936 and 1937. Once again it was New York in a walk, four and out. Ruffing outpitched Paul Derringer to win game one 2–1, and it was never close again. Pearson came within five outs of a no-hitter in game two to win 4–0. Although the Reds held the Yankees to only five hits in game three, four of them were home runs, which translated into another 7–3 Yankee win.

The finale provided the most memorable moment of the Series, Reds catcher Ernie Lombardi's infamous "snooze." In the tenth inning, with the score tied and runners on the corners, DiMaggio singled to right, knocking in one, and then Reds right fielder Irval Goodman misplayed the ball. Keller came home just ahead of the ball, which smacked Lombardi in the cup and nearly knocked him unconscious. All the while DiMaggio kept running like some possessed kid in a sandlot game, finally sliding in safe at home with a great scissors slide as Lombardi crawled after the ball and tried to make the tag. The Reds then went out, and New York won 7–4 to take the Series.

Richards Vidmer compared the 1939 Yankees to Joe Louis: both the Bronx Bombers and the Brown Bomber ended up in the "same place—on top." They were, noted Vidmer accurately, "a team that has won four American League pennants in a row; a team that has won four successive World Series, the last two without a loss of a single game, a team that won the pennant this year by a margin of seventeen games over their American League rivals and has won sixteen of nineteen World Series games from the National League, whoever they may be, in the last four Series."

Another pennant in 1940 seemed almost certain. Other teams had taken note of New York's dominance and were doing what they could to imitate them. The Red Sox, who under Tom Yawkey had tried to buy a pennant, abruptly shifted gears. Yawkey stopped buying and started building the farm system. Fortunately for the Yankees, those two strategies didn't quite overlap on the field, and the club that seemed most likely to provide a challenge missed its opportunity.

For the 1940 Yankees stumbled badly, winning 18 fewer games than the 1939 team as little problems added up to

In 1939 Red Ruffing was thirty-five and had already staked his claim as the greatest right-hander in Yankee history. That year Ruffing led the staff in victories with 21 and added another in New York's four-game sweep of the Reds in the World Series.

losses. Trying to stretch a single into a double in the Yanks' final exhibition game against the Dodgers at Ebbets Field, DiMaggio caught his spikes sliding and wrenched his knee.

The club got off to a terrible start, losing eight in a row in early May as DiMaggio tried to play his way into shape. Veterans Rolfe, Selkirk, Dickey, and Ruffing all began to show their age, and Frank Crosetti forgot how to hit.

They finally got on track in August, going 21–3 from August 9 to September 3 to nudge into the pennant race, but the effort exhausted the team. After New York momentarily pulled into first place on September 11 by beating Cleveland in the first game of a doubleheader, the Indians grabbed a lead in game two. When it started raining in the sixth inning, Cleveland's groundskeepers helped things along by putting the tarp down late and in the wrong place. Cleveland won the rain-shortened contest to knock New York out of first, and the Yanks lost five of their next six. Detroit edged out the Indians for the pennant, and New York finished two games back. DiMaggio won another batting title, hitting .352, but only he and Joe Gordon had approximated their 1939 performance. Ruffing, after winning 20 or more for four straight years, won only 15. DiMaggio sat out October for the first time in his career.

The Yankee front office used the finish as an excuse to retool. Down in Kansas City, diminutive shortstop Phil Rizzuto had been named the American Association MVP and hit .347. At the beginning of the season he was thrust into the shortstop spot and hit leadoff while Crosetti moved into a utility role. KC second baseman Jerry Priddy moved Gordon to first.

Rizzuto's promotion to the majors demonstrated that New York's dominance was based on more than money. The Yankees had the best scouting crew in the game and weren't afraid to take chances.

Rizzuto, who stood only five-foot-six and described himself as "not very big for a little guy," was a throwback, a player better suited for an earlier era, a master of the bunt and hit-and-run. He'd starred at Brooklyn's Richmond Hill High and then played semipro ball. In 1937 his high school coach begged New York's three big league teams to give him a tryout.

Manager Casey Stengel of the Dodgers took one look at Rizzuto, told him to get a shoeshine box to stand on, and said, "You'll never make it in the big leagues." The Giants' Bill Terry had a similar reaction.

But the Yankees let Rizzuto play, and he worked out for them for almost a week, making a better impression on scout Paul Krichell each day. New York signed him for what Barrow later claimed was "20 cents," the cost of his lunch at the tryout.

Even though Rizzuto didn't represent a big investment, once he started playing in the minors, the Yankees allowed his performance to determine his future. He moved up quickly, passing a dozen other shortstops in the system to reach the majors in his fifth year as a professional. He would play a key role in New York's success for more than a decade as he gave the club a dimension it had lacked since Earle Combs patrolled center field. He was the quintessential "table-setter," the guy who got on base and let DiMaggio and the other Yankees hit him in. And in 1941 Joe DiMaggio hit like no one else has in the history of the game.

It didn't seem possible for DiMaggio to get much better. In five years his .343 career batting average was already the sixth-best all-time, and his 168 home runs were in the top 20. Apart from Rogers Hornsby, he was the best right-handed hitter the game had ever seen, and easily the most complete player in baseball's era of power. But in 1941 DiMaggio, or at least his reputation, rose to new heights.

New York got off to a quick start, then DiMaggio slumped and hit only .194 as the Yanks stumbled and lost eight of ten, including five in a row, to fall to fourth place with a 14–13 record on May 14. The bottom was rushing to meet them.

The next day the *World Telegram*'s Dan Daniel looked into the future and wrote: "Once the bellwether shows the way, a whole club will often follow him. It is possible that when DiMaggio begins to hit again he will pull the other Yankees with him." Remember those words.

New York hit rock bottom in a 13–1 loss to the White Sox the next day, but DiMaggio showed signs of life with a single off Edgar Smith, and he hit the ball hard in two subsequent at bats. McCarthy used the loss as an excuse to shake up his lineup, moving Gordon from first back to second, benching second baseman Jerry Priddy, putting Johnny Sturm on first, and temporarily benching Rizzuto.

DiMaggio hit in each of the next four games as well,

and on May 20 New York finally started to put together a streak, coming from behind to beat the Browns and start a five-game winning streak to lift them permanently above the .500 mark.

Subtle improvements continued over the next two weeks as the Yankees improved by increments and McCarthy kept tweaking his lineup, batting order, and pitching rotation. DiMaggio, quietly, had hit in every game since May 15, a streak that the press finally noticed on June 1 in a doubleheader sweep of Cleveland. He wasn't exactly tearing the cover off the ball, for his average had risen only 30 points. In 14 games of the 18-game streak, he had collected only one hit. The next day, June 2, he collected another hit to push his streak to 19 games.

Lou Gehrig died later that night. The Yankees lost to the Tigers the next day in Detroit, where Gehrig had taken himself out of the lineup just over two years before. McCarthy and Bill Dickey left the club to attend the funeral in New York. The rest of the club remained behind. There was business to attend to.

But Gehrig's death hit them hard. There is no greater trial for a team than the loss of a teammate, even one whom many of the younger Yankees didn't know and whom many of his older teammates hadn't seen in months. They lost again in Detroit on June 5, their third defeat in a row, and the season seemed about to slip away. Their record stood at 25–22.

The next game, in St. Louis on June 7, may have been the most important of the season. After New York jumped ahead 6–1, the lowly Browns roared back and took a 7–6 lead. Only a great throw by DiMaggio, nailing a runner at third, kept it from being more.

The throw seemed to awaken New York. In the top of the ninth the Yankees exploded for five runs to win 11–7, a lucky number. DiMaggio had kept the rally going with an infield hit after the Yankees tied the game.

It was a portent of what was to come. Over the next six weeks, as if to honor their fallen teammate, the Yankees played as well as any Yankee team ever has, winning 41 of 47. And DiMaggio, each and every day, kept hitting. Incredibly, as his streak grew and the pressure increased, he hit even better.

He started hitting the ball hard in a doubleheader sweep of the Browns on June 8 to run his streak to 22 games, collecting four extra-base hits and knocking in seven runs. On that same day another streak ended. Boston's Ted Williams had started a hitting streak of his own on May 15, but it ended on June 8 at 18 games, the longest of Williams's career.

The end of Williams's streak drew attention to DiMaggio's. And as DiMaggio's streak grew and the Yankees kept winning and drawing ever closer to league-leading Cleveland, even more attention began to be paid to DiMaggio. Writers took note that the start of his streak coincided with New York's low point. Since he'd started hitting, the team had started winning.

DiMaggio broke Roger Peckinpaugh's team mark of 29 on June 17, and the press began to follow his performance in earnest. George Sisler held the modern major league record of 41 games, while Wee Willie Keeler held the all-time mark of 44, set in 1897.

The Yankees finally passed Cleveland with a 7–5 win over St. Louis on June 25. Rizzuto was back in the lineup and starting to make good, and DiMaggio cracked his 16th home run.

DiMaggio's closest call took place the next day. Elden Auker held him hitless, and although New York took a 3–1 lead into the ninth, DiMaggio was due up fourth — there was a chance he would not receive another at bat.

But Rolfe walked with one out, bringing up Henrich. He knew that if he hit into a double play the streak would end, so he asked McCarthy whether he could bunt. The manager nodded his head. The lead was only two runs, and an insurance run would help. Besides, the way DiMaggio had been playing he deserved the chance.

Henrich successfully sacrificed Rolfe to second. And DiMaggio plated him with a double to stretch his streak to 39. He tied and then broke Sisler's mark in Washington.

Thirty-one thousand fans turned out to see him do it, for DiMaggio's streak had captured the attention of the nation. While the first weeks of the streak had taken place in relative anonymity, now that he had tied Sisler it became something of a national obsession. Fans began to track his progress daily, and the story of his streak became the background music of the summer of '41.

Keeler's mark fell against Boston on July 2 when DiMaggio cracked his 18th home run and the Yankees completed a sweep of Boston that effectively put the Red Sox out of the race. Lefty Gomez quipped, in reference to Keeler, that DiMaggio, who had homered, had "hit one today where they ain't." After the game even Ted Williams was over-heard muttering, "I wish I could hit like that guy DiMaggio." Although Williams was out-hitting DiMaggio — his average was well above .400 — DiMaggio had outperformed the Red Sox slugger in their first meeting that ever mattered.

DiMaggio was now in pursuit only of himself, for in the entire history of professional baseball, only two men had ever hit in more games — DiMaggio's 61 with the Seals, and Joe Wilhoit of Wichita, who hit in 69 straight games in 1919. No one was better prepared for his quest, for only DiMaggio knew what it was like to be in his position.

The streak was at 48 games when baseball broke for the All-Star game in Detroit. Although DiMaggio didn't need a hit in the contest to continue the streak, if he failed to do so there is no question that any subsequent discussion of his accomplishment would carry that caveat. He rendered the question moot with an eighth-inning double, scoring brother Dom, then beat out a double-play ball in the ninth to bring up Ted Williams, who cracked a home run to give the American League a win.

Meanwhile, the Yankees were on the best possible roll. They went into Cleveland on July 16 the winners of 15 of their last 16 games. It was a do-or-die series for the Indians, who now trailed the Yankees by five games and were the only team close. They died.

The Yankees put them away in the first game of the set. DiMaggio hit in game 56 in the first, keying a rally with a single and scoring the Yankees' second run by racing home from second on a ground out. The Yankees cruised to a 10–3 win.

The game of July 17 is one of the most scrutinized in baseball history, one surrounded by equal proportions of legend and myth. A cabby supposedly jinxed DiMaggio. In another version, it was a shoeshine boy. But in the end it wasn't any measure of magic that stopped DiMaggio — it was the compelling odds against any such streak at all and the glove of Cleveland third baseman Ken Keltner.

The Yankees already led 1–0 when DiMaggio came up in the first against Indian right-hander Edgar Smith. He pulled a curve sharply down the line. Keltner, playing DiMaggio deep and to pull, backhanded the ball, and his

The 44-game hitting streak of Wee Willie Keeler fell on July 2, 1941, as DiMaggio cracked his eighteenth home run of the season to beat the Red Sox at Yankee Stadium.

momentum carried him into foul ground. DiMaggio got out of the box slow, for the base paths were soft with rain from the day before. Keltner threw. Out by a step.

He came up again in the fourth and walked; then in the seventh he grounded the ball to Keltner's backhand again, and the third baseman again threw him out. Keltner wasn't doing anything extraordinary. He was easily the league's best third baseman in 1941. He made such plays all the time.

With the Yankees leading 4–1 and a man on, DiMaggio came up one last time, this time against Jim Bagby Jr., son of the major league pitcher of the same name. Oddly enough, eight years before Ed Walsh Jr., whose father had also been a major league pitcher, had stopped DiMaggio's 61-game streak with the Seals.

He took a ball, swung through a strike, and then hit a hard ground ball right at Lou Boudreau at short. The ball almost skipped up his arm and over his shoulder, but he grabbed it and flipped to second. Barring a miracle, the streak had ended the instant second baseman Ray Mack turned the double play.

No miracle took place. New York held on to win 4–3, and DiMaggio never got another at bat. The streak was over at 56 games, but New York's lead over Cleveland was up to seven games.

DiMaggio wasn't happy—his ego loved the record— but he was politic with the press and said, "I'm glad it's over," meaning that he was glad he wouldn't have to deal with as many reporters and photographers as he had in the last few weeks. When he left the park that night, he borrowed some money from Phil Rizzuto, ducked into a local bar, and decompressed, alone with his thoughts.

The streak became DiMaggio's defining achievement, and many of the qualities later ascribed to him all resulted from the streak, but none more so than his reputation as a winner, the ultimate team player, someone whose myriad skills were not always best reflected by statistics. The streak seemed to provide definitive evidence of DiMaggio's inimitable talent, for it was a unique record, unlike any other in sport. The streak represented both longevity and the sustained individual achievement that took place alongside the team's best stretch of sustained play in its history. And DiMaggio, of all players to ever play the game, was the only one who hit in at least 56 consecutive games twice, or who even came close to doing so.

His legacy needed the streak, for the second half of his career would lack the statistical magnificence of his first six seasons. DiMaggio never had a truly standout World Series, like Reggie Jackson did in 1978 or even Bobby Richardson in 1961. DiMaggio's .346 batting average in the 1936 World Series, his first, was the best of his career. Every October rule number one was "pitch around DiMaggio."

In contrast, another remarkable achievement occurring at the same time took on an entirely different character. Ted Williams hit .406 in 1941, the singular accomplishment of his career. Yet Williams's not inconsiderable achievement took place divorced from the performance of his team — his early season streak coincided with a Red Sox losing streak, and Williams's enduring reputation is that of a player for whom team performance was secondary.

Indeed, Williams would stand in contrast to DiMaggio for the next decade as the Yankees and Red Sox formed a rivalry that at times would be as contested as any in sports. Just as the stature of each team would grow in comparison to the other, so did DiMaggio and Williams, for each stands out in greater contrast when compared to the other. Even the two players themselves recognized this: DiMaggio always gave Williams the nod as the "greater hitter," while Williams always said, "DiMaggio is the greatest player I've ever seen." And that's precisely what each man wanted to be.

DiMaggio and the Yankees suffered no letdown at the end of the streak. DiMaggio immediately embarked on another hitting streak of 16 games, while the Yankees won 9 of their next 11, ending any dreams of a pennant in Chicago and Detroit, just as they had done in Cleveland. By that time their lead was 12½ games, and their record since May 15 — the start of DiMaggio's streak — was a gaudy 55–16.

The league collapsed in their wake, and the Yankees bettered their earlier mark by clinching the pennant on September 4. In the end the Yankees went 101–53 to finish 17 games ahead of second-place Boston while every other team in the league finished closer to last place than first. DiMaggio ended the season hitting .357, third best in the league, with 30 home runs and 125 RBIs, while Charlie

DiMaggio strokes a single off Indian southpaw Al Milnar in his first at bat at Cleveland's League Park to reach the 56-game mark in his record-breaking streak.

1941

Yankee second baseman Joe Gordon is tagged out at home by Dodger catcher Mickey Owen in the second inning of the second game of the 1941 World Series at Yankee Stadium. In game four Owen's dropped third strike with two out in the ninth inning cost the Dodgers a victory and any chance of defeating the Yankees in the Series.

Keller lived up to his nickname "King Kong" by hitting 33 home runs and chipping in 122 RBIs. No Yankee pitcher won 20 games, but seven of them, paced by Gomez and Ruffing with 15 each, won 9 games or more.

This time, however, there was a challenger to their title as the Baseball Kings of New York. The Brooklyn Dodgers, with Pete Reiser hitting .343, Dolph Camilli putting up an MVP season, and Whit Wyatt and Kirby Higbe each winning 22 games, won 100 games to take the National League pennant. Fiery former Yankee Leo Durocher had created a team that was a mirror image of himself, a hard-fighting, feisty club that blended speed, power, defense, and pitching. They would provide a better test for the Yankees than many of their recent World Series opponents.

Nevertheless, the Yankees were still installed as 2–1 favorites, for they had the opportunity to get their pitch-ing set for the Series, and the Dodgers did not. Time and time again over the years the Yankees entered postseason play with just such an advantage, which enabled them to prove that winning a pennant big is better than just winning.

That is why Red Ruffing started in game one against Dodger swingman Curt Davis. Ruffing tossed a six-hitter, and as Rud Rennie noted, "McCarthy's men simply moved out in front and stayed there." But Wyatt bettered Gomez by the same score in game two, and game three, which matched Marius Russo and Freddie Fitzsimmons, was scoreless through six innings. The Yankees were in danger of falling behind in the Series.

In the seventh Russo took matters into his own hands, literally. With Joe Gordon on second, Russo lined the ball straight back at Fitzsimmons. The ball struck him on the left knee and careened in the air, where the shortstop caught it on the fly for the third out.

But Fitzsimmons was hurt. He limped off the mound with a chipped kneecap that ended his season. That was the only break the Yanks needed.

Russo worked out of a jam after Reiser doubled to lead

off the Dodger half. Dodger relief ace Hugh Casey took the mound in the eighth for Brooklyn. With one out, Rolfe singled. Then McCarthy called for a hit-and-run.

Rolfe took off with the pitch, and Henrich hit a weak ground ball wide of first. Camilli had no chance at second and made a move to throw the ball to first, but Casey was late to the bag.

DiMaggio then singled to center on a 3–2 pitch to plate one, and Keller knocked in another to score New York's second run. Russo gave up a run in the eighth but held on, and the Yankees won 2–1.

New York effectively won the Series in game four. In the ninth inning, with the Yankees trailing 4–3 with two out, Tommy Henrich stepped in against Casey. He'd been almost untouchable since entering the game in the fifth, more than making up for his performance in game three.

With three balls and two strikes on Henrich, Casey threw. The bottom dropped out on the pitch, and Henrich tried to check his swing, but failed. He looked over his shoulder to see the umpire raising his right arm to indicate strike three, and then saw something else.

The ball was free. The pitch had glanced off catcher Mickey Owen's glove toward the first-base dugout as a contingent of police burst out, anticipating the end of the game.

Henrich ran as Owen scrambled through traffic after the ball in what the *Herald Tribune* called "a vivid imitation of a man changing a tire . . . grabbing for monkey wrenches, screwdrivers, inner tubes and a jack and he couldn't find any of them." Henrich was safe at first, and the Yankees were still alive.

In all likelihood, Casey had thrown a spitter, although at the time Owen called it a low curve, but that doesn't really matter. Owen had stayed back on his haunches and stabbed at the ball with a downturned glove instead of col-lapsing on his knees and blocking the pitch. His error was a fundamental mistake.

That was precisely the kind the Yankees never seemed to make when it mattered. DiMaggio, up next, singled to left with two strikes, as did Charlie Keller to tie the game. Then Dickey walked on a full count, and Gordon doubled with two strikes. All of a sudden the game that the Dodgers could have won 4–3 was 7–4 in New York's favor.

The stunned Dodgers went out quietly in the ninth, having lost a game they should have won.

"It was a bad pitch—I mean a ball—but it had me fooled completely, I'll admit that," said Henrich later. Casey drawled, "I've lost a lot of ball games in some funny ways, but that is the first I've lost by striking out a man." Owen took the blame, saying, "I shoulda caught the ball," but in his defense he simply gave New York a chance; Casey got two strikes on each of the next four batters, but all of them reached base.

But the catcher took the fall. Richards Vidmer began his column the next day shadowing the mythical night watchman of "the Gallery of Goats" as he pushed the goats of World Series past aside to make room for Owen, writing, "This way, young fellow."

The Dodgers had handed the Yankees two of their three wins, but the Yanks took the fourth on their own. Ernie "Tiny" Bonham scattered four hits, Henrich homered, and the Yankees won, 3–1, to take their fifth World Series in six years. Joe DiMaggio filled a hand with rings in record time.

Once again the question around baseball became: "Was there anything on the face of the earth that could stop the Yankees?" It was already clear to everyone that both the American and National Leagues seemed lacking in that department.

Then, on December 7, 1941, the Japanese bombed Pearl Harbor, and the United States entered World War II.

Pitcher Atley Donald (left) and manager Joe McCarthy (center) greet Private Marius Russo before a Yankee-Dodger exhibition game in Trenton, New Jersey, on April 4, 1944. It had been less than a year since Russo, then a Yankee starter, beat the Cardinals in game four of the 1943 World Series at Sportsman's Park.

To hell with Babe Ruth!

— COMMON TAUNT OF JAPANESE SOLDIERS

1942–1946

A WAR ON ALL FRONTS

With the onset of World War II, baseball became a distraction. That was the only thing that saved it.

Baseball has always survived war — changed by it, to be sure, but nevertheless serving as a sign that life goes on. But in an instant, questions such as who would or wouldn't win the pennant didn't seem so important anymore. With news of real battles on the front page, box scores and baseball wars seemed strangely out of place. A world championship was a curiously empty title.

Baseball looked to the past for guidance. At the onset of American involvement in World War I, baseball had made the successful argument that the game was important to the nation's morale, for while millions of Americans would enter military service, millions more would remain at home, their lives essentially unchanged. Baseball could provide a much-needed diversion from the anxiety caused by the war.

Baseball had been proven correct then, for the day-to-day pace of the baseball season had indeed served as a calming influence, a reinforcement of normality, a sign that while the world might be going to hell, the American way of life continued to thrive. News of the baseball season also reassured the American military man that the passage of time could still be measured in ways other than by troop movements and body counts.

That argument resonated once again in the halls of power. President Franklin Delano Roosevelt was a baseball fan, and most baseball owners enjoyed the political access that comes with fabulous wealth. These men were not strangers to the president, and though baseball stayed silent in December as the war effort geared up, in January 1942 Judge Landis wrote Roosevelt and asked, "What do you want it [baseball] to do?" Roosevelt gave the game the green light, writing back, "Honestly, I feel it would be best for the country for baseball to keep going." But he was careful to emphasize that professional players would be treated no differently than other men eligible for the draft.

From the very beginning of the war, however, most ballplayers were treated quite differently from other soldiers. Many major leaguers spent the bulk of their military service playing ball. Although a number of big league stars like Bob Feller saw heavy combat and became military heroes, most did not, and only two players, Harry O'Neill and Joe Gedeon — with a combined six games of major league experience — lost their lives in combat.

So baseball went on. It would be different, but it would continue. Road trips became more difficult, for the military had priority on trains and in hotels. Spring training camps had to be moved because of travel restrictions, and baseball equipment became hard to come by. As were baseball players. Over the next few seasons, the Yankees fought a number of skirmishes on several fronts, most of them caused by the war. By the time it ended, the postwar Yankees bore little resemblance to their prewar dynasty and were changed in ways few could have imagined.

After Roosevelt's go-ahead, baseball feared the loss of talent more than anything else. As players entered military service, either as volunteers or through the draft, who would remain to play the game? Even the Yankees had no ready answer to that. Their recent dominance on the field didn't make them immune to world events. But

their ability to adapt would provide a measure of their strength.

The Yankees suffered one of the first losses when Johnny Sturm enlisted in January, leaving a hole at first base. But Barrow and Weiss proved surprisingly adept at adjusting to the loss of players to the service. Barrow, after all, had been through this before, when World War I had played havoc with baseball. Then, most clubs had remained passive, tossing off the 1918 season and simply filling their rosters with the aged, infirm, and inexperienced, trying to get by on a shoestring.

Barrow's Red Sox had taken a different tack. He and Boston owner Harry Frazee had acted aggressively, acquiring players and taking on salaries and trying to win. They had bet heavily on their belief that in an economy fueled by the war industries, attendance and revenues would hold relatively steady. Under Barrow's guidance, the Boston Red Sox had won the pennant and the World Series — their last of the century — in 1918.

These Yankees would take a similar approach. Compared to other teams, their farm system still provided a huge pool of talent. While the minor leagues shrank dramatically during the war — the Yankees went from twelve teams in 1941 to nine in 1942, and then only five for the duration of the war — most clubs cut their farm systems to only two or three teams. And after years of relative inactivity, New York suddenly got active in the trade market. The Yankees planned to keep winning.

The Yankees were one of the few big league teams that still had a surplus of players available. Throughout the war they made full use of that advantage — filling gaps with players from the farm system, trading when they had to, selling off the excess, and reinvesting the money. Before the 1942 season they even splurged on DiMaggio, giving him a new contract worth $43,500. In return, he all but promised a batting title over Ted Williams. "Don't misunderstand me about Ted," he said at the signing. "He's the greatest hitter I ever saw. . . . But with all that he can still be caught."

They also moved quickly to make up for the loss of Sturm. Center fielder Tommy Holmes was running in place in Newark — with DiMaggio ahead of him, his career in the organization had hit the ceiling. So on February 5 he was dealt to the Boston Braves for the veteran first baseman and Bronx native Buddy Hassett, a slick fielder and occasional .300 hitter with little power. In one sense, it was a lousy trade, one of the few poor ones Barrow and Weiss ever made. Braves manager Casey Stengel later called Holmes "the best leadoff man I ever had." He became a star in Boston while Hassett played only one year in New York before entering the service, never to return. But for 1942 it worked. Hassett gave the Yankees what Sturm had and a bit more. He caught the ball at first and ran around the bases when the other Yankees hit the ball.

Sturm's enlistment was unique; relatively few ballplayers volunteered for military service, particularly in the war's early months. Married players and those with children or other dependents were routinely bypassed by draft boards, which focused on young men unfettered by families. DiMaggio, for instance, had married actress Dorothy Arnold in the off-season and was classified 3-A. Rizzuto received a similar classification because he helped support his parents and younger brother — his father earned only $20 a week as a night watchman. And a fair number of ballplayers had physical maladies that prevented them from serving but didn't affect their play. Tommy Holmes was classified 4-F owing to a sinus condition.

In the spring of 1942 the war's full effects on baseball were still unknown as the American war effort geared up. By the start of the 1942 season relatively few players had been lost and little had changed. But it was war, and the Yankees opened the season in Washington amid an orgy of patriotism. Players from both clubs wore patriotic patches on their left sleeve, and the Army Band presented the colors and played the national anthem. Throughout the war, baseball eagerly cooperated with war bond efforts and put on patriotic displays whenever called on. Gate receipts for select games and exhibitions were often turned over to war charities. Ballpark promotions to sell war bonds and promote conservation and rationing were common.

The Yankees opened the season considerably diminished. Rolfe, after a decade of steady service, was slipping and hurt, and Frank Crosetti and Jerry Priddy would both split time with him at third. Age and injury also caught up with Bill Dickey. He was in and out of the lineup all year long.

The Yankees were lucky, but their luck, to paraphrase Branch Rickey, was the residue of design. Boston had been

YANKEE AMERICAN LEAGUE
STOLEN BASE LEADERS

1914 Fritz Maisel, 74

1931 Ben Chapman, 61

1932 Ben Chapman, 38

1933 Ben Chapman, 27

1937 Ben Chapman, 35*

1938 Frank Crosetti, 27

1944 George Stirnweiss, 55

1945 George Stirnweiss, 33

1985 Rickey Henderson, 80

1986 Rickey Henderson, 87

1988 Rickey Henderson, 93

1989 Rickey Henderson, 77**

* tied
** played part of the season with the Oakland Athletics

the only other AL team to finish above .500 in 1941, and they were in transition — Grove had retired and Foxx would soon be cut loose. They were all leaving while a new generation of stars like Bobby Doerr, Johnny Pesky, and Tex Hughson were just stepping forth. Boston's two generations of stars just missed each other by a season or two. Detroit might have provided a challenge, but slugger

Forkballer Ernest "Tiny" Bonham dances with a showgirl after his victory in the fifth and final game of the 1941 World Series. During the war years, the right-hander was a consistent performer, winning 21 games in 1942 and 15 the following season.

Hank Greenberg had been drafted in 1941. New York's depth cleared the way for another pennant.

After beating Washington 7–0 on Opening Day, the Yankees won eight of their first ten to move into first place. But all was not smooth sailing.

The Clipper, for one, seemed to have a hard time finding the wind. DiMaggio started slow, struggling except for the occasional explosion, such as the one he had against Chicago on May 5 when he hit two home runs and a tenth-inning triple to personally turn a possible 4–0 defeat into a 5–4 Yankee win. Charlie Keller, hitting behind him, also got off to a bad start, and without much of a supporting cast, DiMaggio was looking awful ordinary. Entering June, he was batting only .253.

But "awful ordinary" was a way of life in the American League in 1942, and the Yankees' "awful ordinary" was several notches above the rest of the league. DiMaggio was being booed by the New York crowd, but the pitching, paced by Tiny Bonham, had rarely been better, and Joe Gordon and Phil Rizzuto were playing the best ball of their careers.

The jeers for DiMaggio were for more than his batting average and the size of his contract. Just as World War I had resulted in a backlash against German players, World War II fostered some similar anti-Italian sentiment. In 1942 native-born Italians were designated as aliens, as were Japanese Americans, although Italians would avoid being relocated to internment camps. And as the war continued, fans were beginning to look on ballplayers, particularly stars, in a new light. Why weren't they fighting?

But DiMaggio earned back the cheers with a July surge, hitting nearly .400 for the month, including an 18-game hitting streak. The Yankees, as had become customary, took his cue and went on a bender, putting the league away with their best sustained stretch of play all season, winning 18 of 21 from July 5 through July 28.

The fight for the American League pennant ended early: the Yankees clinched the title on September 14 as Ernie Bonham notched win number 20 in an 8–3 win over Cleveland. New York won 103 games. Boston finished nine games back. The margin may as well have been 90, for the Red Sox never provided a serious challenge.

The Cardinals won the National League pennant, passing Brooklyn in a rush. St. Louis lost only four games in September to beat the Dodgers by two games with 106 wins. Like the Yankees, St. Louis, with its massive farm system, was well armed during the war. The 1942 NL pennant winners were the youngest team in history to make it to the World Series. Center fielder Terry Moore, at age 30, was the oldest man in the starting lineup.

In retrospect, they were also better armed entering the Series. For in August New York had suffered its first significant loss. Tommy Henrich, whose nickname "Old Reliable" illustrated his value, had been ordered to join the Coast Guard in late August.

But what had New York done? On August 31, the Yankees picked up the veteran Roy Cullenbine from Washington. He'd made the All-Star team in 1941, and over the last month of the 1942 season he hit .364 for New York and outslugged every man on the team, even DiMaggio. Despite his July reawakening, he finished the year hitting only .305 with 21 home runs and 114 RBIs. But Cullenbine was still no Henrich.

Normal life in America seemed to require another Yankee world championship. New York's recent legacy of dominance made the team 2–1 favorites entering the Series.

In game one in St. Louis that certainly seemed to be the case. McCarthy, foreshadowing some curious pitching choices in key games later in his career, pulled a surprise. He passed over Bonham, who'd led the league in ERA and went 21–5, and started Red Ruffing, in pursuit of his seventh World Series win.

Ruffing made McCarthy look like a genius. He took a no-hitter into the eighth, and DiMaggio started an eighth-inning rally that was good for three runs. New York led 7–0 with two outs in the ninth.

Then Ruffing hit a wall, and the feisty Cardinals took advantage, pushing across four runs, chasing the pitcher, and bringing the winning run to the plate in Stan Musial. Facing reliever Spud Chandler, he hit a hard ground ball to first, but Hassett did what he was paid for and scooped it up for the final out.

The Yankees shrugged off the comeback, but it gave the young Cardinals some much-needed confidence. In game two Johnny Beazley outpitched Bonham. After New York tied the game 3–3 in the top of the eighth on hits by Cullenbine and DiMaggio followed by a Keller home run, Musial came up in the bottom of the inning with another chance to win a game in the World Series. This time he did, singling in Enos Slaughter. New York then blew a chance to go ahead in the ninth when pinch runner Tuck Stainback was foolishly thrown out at third. The Cardinals emerged with a 4–3 win.

That loss seemed to break the Yankees. The two clubs traveled to New York for game three, and Ernie White

shut out New York 2–0, the Yankees' first whitewash in Series play since 1926. As John Drebinger noted in the *Times,* the Yankees were left "stumbling to their locker room stunned and bewildered." Trailing in a World Series was an experience that Joe DiMaggio, for one, had never before experienced.

The Yankees' bewilderment soon turned to utter incomprehension. The Cardinals, behind timely hitting and a series of great catches by center fielder Terry Moore, rolled to a 9–6 win in game four. Someone tried to provide some motivation for the Yanks before game five, writing on the blackboard in the clubhouse: "TRAIN FOR ST. LOUIS LEAVES AT 8 O'CLOCK TONIGHT." But it left without the Yankees. St. Louis beat Ruffing 4–2 and took the world championship.

The loss was a heavy blow to New York. McCarthy was testy afterward, snapping at the press and asking, "What's the matter? . . . What do we have to do, win all the time?" Well, in New York the answer is yes, and always has been, ever since the arrival of Ruth. That's something that makes the Yankees different from every other team in baseball. Performing above expectations, coming close, or making the postseason with a wild card or division championship is enough for other teams, but for the Yankees anything less than a victory in the World Series is considered a failure. New York demands it.

The war was starting to get to McCarthy. For all he knew, the 1942 Series might be his last chance to win a championship. The war had been only a minor distraction in 1942, but no one knew who would still be around in 1943 and how long the war would last. In fact, if the 1942 Series had gone beyond five games, the Yankees would have been forced to play without Phil Rizzuto. Having been reclassified, he enlisted in August, knowing that most enlisted men were given several months to get their affairs in order. Rizzuto had hoped that would allow him to complete the season, but he had been ordered to report to the Navy at Norfolk, Virginia, immediately after game five.

The war wasn't waiting anymore. McCarthy knew he would have to manage under an entirely new set of conditions. He would have to adapt, just as millions of New Yorkers already had. World War II lifted the city out of the remnants of the Depression. Work was plentiful for the first time in a generation as factories that had been sitting empty hummed with new life, churning out whatever the war demanded. The city teemed with people, and the streets were full again. The Brooklyn Naval Station and Army Terminal played a central role in the war effort—over three million American troops passed through New York on their way to Europe, as did an incredible 63 million tons of military supplies.

The war was anything but a party, of course. New York's nightlife didn't shut down, but it did dim as double shifts and overtime left most workers with few opportunities to cut loose. That's where baseball came in: the Yankees, Dodgers, and Giants provided a happy escape, and radio broadcasts carried the game to every street in the city. New York would adapt, and baseball played a part in that. It did that summer at least.

During the winter of 1942–43, the daily newspapers delivered ever-larger doses of bad news. This would be no quick war for the United States, which was fighting on two fronts—holding Germany at bay in Europe and Africa while regrouping with the routed Allies, rebuilding the Pacific Fleet, and trying to halt Japanese aggression in the Pacific. These military efforts took bodies, lots of them. When baseball fans turned to the sports page that winter, the only stat that mattered was the one that designated a player 1-A. More players were joining the service every day.

Yankee losses were heavy, but no heavier than those of other teams. The war was blind to batting averages. Stars and scrubs were treated alike, at least at the time of induction. Boston lost Ted Williams and Dom DiMaggio, Detroit lost Gehringer, and the Indians' Bob Feller enlisted. Even Joe DiMaggio, who was being threatened with a divorce from his wife, had been reclassified. They patched things up—sort of—and DiMaggio, like many other ballplayers, asked permission to enlist and retain some nominal control over his future rather than wait for the draft. He joined the Army on February 17, the eighth Yankee to change uniforms, his salary dropping from nearly $4,000 a month to 50 bucks. Before the start of training camp, Selkirk, Ruffing, Hassett, and several spare parts also departed. Ruffing's loss dramatically illustrated just how dire the American military considered the situation. He was 39 years old when he was drafted, and he had lost four toes on his left foot in a childhood accident.

Barrow didn't wait around. He needed another first baseman with some power, and he traded for the best available candidate, Nick Etten of the Philadelphia Phillies. Etten had hit .311 in 1941 but slipped in 1942 to .264, and every NL team passed him through on waivers. Barrow gambled that Etten, who had shown some power in the minor leagues, would feast on wartime pitching. He became a Yankee for $10,000 and two players. For some depth, he added the veteran outfielder Roy Weatherly.

Owing to wartime travel restrictions, major league baseball was ordered to hold spring training closer to

At spring training in 1943 manager Joe McCarthy tried several experiments, including moving utility man Snuffy Stirnweiss to shortstop. The Bronx native batted only .219 in his rookie season.

home in 1943. This wasn't much of a hardship for teams in warmer climates, like the Cardinals, but for clubs like Boston and New York it meant starting baseball season with snow still on the ground. That spring the Yankees sent their preseason greetings from Asbury Park, New Jersey, a resort town on the Jersey Shore.

It was a fine place to spend the summer, as 100,000 summer residents proved, but the 90,000 who left every September knew it was a lousy place to live the rest of the year. In March the wind blew in off the water almost constantly, delivering little snow but a near-constant damp, bone-chilling cold. The club worked out as best it could on the high school field and in the gym, bunking in the frigid Albion Hotel, where a fuel shortage kept the furnace turned down low when it was turned on at all. Calisthenics often took the place of batting practice, and outdoor workouts were often limited to an hour or two of rushed activity in sweaters and long johns.

McCarthy found the situation frustrating—it was impossible for him to gauge just how good his team was going to be, for in other years many of them would never have been qualified to step onto a big league diamond. A few bona-fide major leaguers like Gordon and Keller remained, as did pitching stalwarts Ernie Bonham, Spud Chandler, Hank Borowy, and reliever Johnny Murphy, but after that there were only questions. For the first time since he'd become a big league manager, McCarthy knew he was undermanned. He had to write names in the lineup he normally wouldn't have even bothered learning. Rookie infielder Billy Johnson spent two weeks at camp in virtual anonymity as McCarthy worked out the vets before the manager abruptly approached him and asked, "Do you think you can play third base in the majors?" Johnson said he could, and that was it—the job was his.

McCarthy didn't like to platoon or juggle his lineup—even under these conditions—so he handed out other starting jobs to other unknowns. Coming out of camp, he made George "Snuffy" Stirnweiss his shortstop and Johnny Lindell his right fielder.

On Opening Day it became obvious just how much had changed. Taking a day off wasn't acceptable during the war. Barely 7,000 people turned out at the Stadium as the Yankees edged out Washington, 5–4.

Second baseman Joe Gordon greets pitcher Spud Chandler after the right-hander won the first game of the 1943 World Series, 4–2, over the Cardinals. Chandler not only won two games in the five-game series, but also won twenty during the regular season.

The Yankees weren't the Bronx Bombers of old, but in 1943 they didn't have to be. New York's edge on the pitching mound held the opposition to a league-low 542 runs, the fewest for the club since the Dead Ball Era, as Spud Chandler went 20–4 with a league-best 1.64 ERA. Etten made Barrow look like a genius, leading the team in RBIs with 107, Keller hit 31 home runs, and Bill Dickey bounced back against subpar pitching to hit .351 in part-time duty.

The Yankees' quick and sudden march into first place and their ability to stay there made a look at the box score a comforting experience. They captured the pennant—again—by winning 98 games and finishing 13½ ahead of Washington.

For the second year in a row, the Cardinals provided the opposition. They'd lost a ton of players too, including the 1942 Series heroes Johnny Beazley, Earl Moore, Terry Moore, and Enos Slaughter. But like New York, their farm system provided new players, and what it didn't provide general manager Branch Rickey did.

But 1943 was a pitcher's year, and the Cardinals couldn't match New York's pitching. Wartime travel restrictions gave New York another advantage, for the first three games were played at the Stadium.

That's all the Yankees needed. Chandler won twice, and the New York pitching staff shut down the Cardinals. New York won in five games, losing only game two when the Cardinals' battery of Mort and Walker Cooper, motivated by the death of their father the day before, won 4–3. Otherwise, it was a quiet, workmanlike win for New York, capped off by Dickey's two-run home run to back Chandler's shutout in the finale. The Yankees' win seemed to provide evidence that the war hadn't changed everything. Not quite, not yet.

By 1944, it would. The draft cut ever deeper into rosters, and even the Yankees couldn't make up for all the losses. Abandoning Asbury Park for Atlantic City made spring training a bit more comfortable for the team. They practiced inside an armory for a few weeks until permission to use it was withdrawn because it was needed to house wounded soldiers. The team moved to an abandoned air hangar. Their outdoor field, converted from football, wasn't bad, but the weather was atrocious — they practiced outdoors only six days all spring. McCarthy was so discouraged that by the end of camp he was holding potato sack races to keep up morale. Gordon, Keller, Dickey, Johnson, Russo, and virtually every other recognizable name was gone. Chandler lasted only a week into the regular season before he joined them. More than 350 major leaguers were now in the service. Even Ed Barrow couldn't fill all the gaps.

All over baseball, rosters were now stocked with 4-Fs, the aged and infirm, turning the season completely upside down. Has-beens and who's-thats? became stars. The result would be the first pennant race in the American League in years.

But on Opening Day the Yankees would not have Joe McCarthy on the bench. He was a war casualty of another kind.

The wartime Yankees featured lineups that blended stars and rookies, such as this contingent before the start of the 1943 World Series. From left: Frank Crosetti, shortstop; Bud Metheny, right field; William Johnson, third base; Charlie Keller, left field; Bill Dickey, catcher; Nick Etten, first base; Joe Gordon, second base; John Lindell, center field; and Spud Chandler, pitcher.

McCarthy was one of baseball's true believers, a man who lived and breathed the game 24 hours a day. But the grind and the insecurity of the war were beginning to get to him. He drank more than he should have, and his health was beginning to suffer. He missed the first three weeks of the season with gall bladder trouble and other health difficulties. Coach Art Fletcher managed in his stead.

George Stirnweiss, a native New Yorker who was nicknamed "Snuffy" because it was the only form of tobacco he didn't use, became the team's de facto star. Designated 4-F owing to ulcers, Stirnweiss was a good fielder and fast baserunner whom the war turned into a great hitter. In 1944 he led the league in hits, runs, triples, and stolen bases.

Etten, Stirnweiss, and Lindell, backed by the pitching of Borowy and Bonham, kept the Yankees close all year as they battled for the pennant with the Red Sox, the Tigers, and the surprising St. Louis Browns.

The Browns, long the doormat of the American League, were the only team the war actually helped. They'd been so bad and so underfinanced for so long that their prewar roster was already fleshed out with 4-Fs and those otherwise unfit for either military service or major league play on any ballclub. Thirteen players on the St. Louis roster — more than on any other team — were unfit for service, making them perfect for the Browns. As one writer later noted, "Their strength was in their superior weakness." In 1944 it earned them a pennant. The Yankees finished third.

While it was "business as unusual" for baseball stateside, the best baseball in the world was being played in the military. A disproportionate number of major leaguers served their time running military conditioning programs as recreation specialists, and they had plenty of time for baseball. Military bases created their own baseball teams, which did battle against similar teams from other bases and other branches of the service as ultracompetitive commanders schemed to build the best ballclub. These games provided much-needed entertainment for the troops, but the public found it disquieting that so many men were spending much of their service time throwing baseballs instead of hand grenades. To be fair, the players by and large didn't request such duty, and they still had to live under the same conditions as other servicemen. Life wasn't easy, and overzealous commanders abused some players, particularly pitchers. The players were just following orders, and the orders of the day were often "play ball!"

The Norfolk Naval Training Station team was an absolute powerhouse that generally featured an all-big-league starting lineup. When Phil Rizzuto beat out Pee Wee Reese for the shortstop position, Reese was transferred to another base to play for another team. Joe DiMaggio was assigned to Special Services and played baseball for the Santa Ana (California) Air Base, playing exhibitions against local colleges, the PCL, and semipro teams. The best of these wartime teams, like the Great Lakes Naval Station team, regularly defeated major league teams in exhibitions.

In the spring of 1944 a small scandal erupted when it became public that of the 350-plus major leaguers who had completed basic training, nearly 300 were still stationed in the United States and many were playing ball. Embarrassed Army Chief of Staff George Marshall ordered their dispersal overseas, but the powerhouse teams were simply re-created elsewhere. The Army's Seventh Air Force team, headquartered in Hawaii, became the military's reigning dynasty. Former Yankees Ruffing, DiMaggio, and Joe Gordon all played for the team, as did Phil Rizzuto, who was obtained on loan for an important series of games, then returned to the Navy. Red Sox pitcher Tex Hughson spoke for many players when he later said, "I fought World War II with a bat and glove."

The success of military squads against major leaguers undercut the superiority of major league ball during the war, but attendance held steady — for many workers the war was providing their first steady income in years. At Roosevelt's request, most teams added a number of night games to their schedule, making baseball available to those who otherwise would have been unable to attend. The Yankees, however, remained a holdout until after the war and did not install lights until 1946.

But there was no shortage of baseball fans in New York. Attendance at Yankee games held relatively firm even when the level of play did not. And in 1945 it did not, because in 1945 everything changed. The Yankees were sold and the war ended.

Before the war the Brooklyn Dodgers franchise had been rebuilt by general manager Larry MacPhail. He'd made money, won, and turned New York City into a three-team town, taking the also-ran Dodgers and making them contenders. He'd resigned in 1942 to join the military, and now, as the war finally showed signs of reaching its conclusion, MacPhail wanted back in the game. He'd burned his bridges to Brooklyn, where Branch Rickey now held sway, so he set his sights on the Yankees.

He was an operator, a brash, flamboyant bon vivant and hyperactive dilettante who had dabbled in a half-dozen disconnected occupations before meeting up with Branch Rickey in law school. A rich kid, MacPhail talked his father into investing $100,000 in Rickey's Cardinal franchise in Columbus, Ohio, with the understanding that MacPhail would be allowed to run the team.

He decided to make baseball his career. After turning around the Columbus Redbirds, he was hired as general manager by the Reds. Getting fans into the seats was his number-one priority. To fill the ballpark, MacPhail instituted night baseball in the big leagues, embraced radio broadcasting, and pioneered the use of promotions. Impressed, and desperate for a new approach, the Dodgers hired him in 1938.

But MacPhail's talents came with a price, for he was also a drunk, a boor, and a bully who took delight in spending other people's money. He was a micromanager who didn't recognize any barrier between the front office and the field. He was not above giving his manager suggestions, even in the midst of a game. Someone who combined the traits of Frank Farrell, Bill Veeck, and George Steinbrenner would give one a rough idea of the personality of Larry MacPhail. As Leo Durocher, who managed for MacPhail in Brooklyn, noted, "MacPhail was a genius . . . but there is a thin line between genius and insanity and in Larry's case it was so thin you could sometimes see him drifting back and forth."

This was the man who wanted to own the greatest franchise in American baseball. He was no Jacob Ruppert, not in any aspect except, Yankee fans hoped, the final standings. As a GM, MacPhail was a rarity in baseball at the time: not a baseball man trying to run a business, but a business guy trying to operate a team. There was a difference. The game — and the Yankees — would soon change as a result.

MacPhail wanted to run the whole show. But he had no intention of spending all his own money. He didn't have enough, for one thing, but beyond that he enjoyed spending other people's fortunes far more — that's what he'd done in Cincinnati and Brooklyn. And he knew lots of guys with money. The cultivation of the wealthy and connected was something of a MacPhail trademark. He set his sights on two men in particular.

Dan Topping was a country club guy, a prep school kid who went to the Hun School, then got a degree in business from Wharton. He played the role to the hilt, keeping up memberships in 14 golf clubs and flying off to Florida every few weeks to maintain his permanently tanned appearance. He was a playboy who enjoyed squiring beautiful women and hanging around Hollywood, a man whose eventual six marriages included one to his current wife, actress and figure skater Sonja Henie. He had earned his money the real old-fashioned way — inheriting it from

Joe DiMaggio at a service game with Brooklyn Dodger shortstop Harold "Pee Wee" Reese (third from left). DiMaggio lost three full seasons to the war, from 1943 to 1945.

his father, who owned a steel company. Topping dabbled in banking and advertising, was a scratch golfer, and enjoyed the limelight and the company of the rich and famous, actresses, starlets, and their male equivalents, athletes. He had first become acquainted with MacPhail in 1934 when he purchased the NFL Brooklyn Dodgers.

MacPhail knew that owning the Yankees would appeal to Topping's considerable vanity. For despite his wealth, Topping wasn't really accomplished in anything. Sitting atop the Yankees, even if he had to share the seat, would appeal to his ego and provide proof of his success.

But MacPhail didn't want only one partner, for that might mean he would have to share power more or less equally. Under a division of power among two partners, he was confident that his personality would prove dominant. He wanted a quieter, more acquiescent behind-the-scenes guy for the third spot.

That was Del Webb, who next to MacPhail and Topping was a veritable wallflower. An understated, taciturn former semipro ballplayer, Webb had built a construction company in true Horatio Alger fashion. He was as bland as Topping and MacPhail were flamboyant, yet Webb was also smart and politically astute. In the 1930s he cultivated his political connections and during World War II made a fortune as a government contractor, best known for his ability to get massive projects done on time and at the agreed-on price. He won over $100 million worth of government contracts and employed 25,000 men building bases, camps, airfields, hospitals, and other facilities, including the Japanese Relocation Center in Parker, Arizona.

All three men were acquainted with one another, and in 1944, while still serving in the military and pondering his future, MacPhail heard that Ruppert's heirs, worried about their taxes, were thinking about selling. He tapped Topping and Webb, both of whom agreed to ante in. Own-

Dan Topping with his wife, the former Olympic skater Sonja Henie, was a country-club guy who sported a permanent tan while spending his inherited wealth. Larry MacPhail enlisted him in 1945 as a co-owner of the Yankees, along with MacPhail and Del Webb.

ing a baseball team like the Yankees was a nice toy and would give Topping and Webb added visibility in their myriad other businesses. Webb would stay in the background while Topping and MacPhail became the more visible heads of the Yankees.

MacPhail spent a year lining up his ducks and made his move at the conclusion of the 1945 season. Ed Barrow proved his greatest challenge. When he first heard that MacPhail wanted to buy the Yankees, he vowed it would be "over my dead body," for Barrow, an old-time baseball guy, had no respect for MacPhail's credentials or his style. When the three women who owned the team decided to sell, however, there was little Barrow could do, even though he served as Yankee president and executor of the Ruppert estate. So for $2.8 million, on January 28, 1945, the triumvirate of MacPhail, Topping, and Webb bought not only the Yankees but also Yankee Stadium and the entire Yankee farm system. It was a steal, for baseball would experience a boom after the war and quickly increase the value of the team several times over.

MacPhail's first act was to move the club offices from 42nd Street to swanky new Fifth Avenue digs, an early sign that he valued style over substance. Barrow stayed on, a figurehead with the title of Chairman of the Board, but he was left far out of the loop, a former giant in the game given a comfy chair in the corner of the room. MacPhail became general manager.

Under the leadership of MacPhail, Webb, and Topping, the character of the franchise changed. Under Ruppert, the Yankees had been a baseball team, a family business with but one goal—winning. Ruppert had never complained, for instance, when the Yankees swept a World Series even though every game they didn't play cost him a windfall of $200,000 or more. But under the new regime, the ballclub took on the character of a corporation that was beholden to other interests. What success the team enjoyed over the next decade or so would in many respects be due primarily to the residue of the Ruppert era still in place. Its failures would be the product of the new order.

Initially, however, MacPhail, Topping, and Webb pursued a do-nothing policy in regard to their new toy. Their influence on the team was not in anything they did but in what they didn't do. Even though the United States was on the precipice of victory in both Europe and the Pacific, in 1945 more players than ever before were stuck in the service. The new owners saw little sense in spending good money on bad ballplayers, and in 1945, for the first time since the days of Farrell and Devery, the team was allowed to founder.

But Opening Day provided evidence that change of a different kind was just around the corner: Yankee Stadium was the target of a group of 20 or so people walking a picket line. Led by James Pemberton, a member of the state assembly representing Harlem, a group of African Americans carried signs that asked, "If We Can Pay, Why Can't We Play?" and, "If We Can Stop Bullets, Why Not Balls?" From the time of Ruth, African Americans had always been a small but significant part of the crowd at the Stadium, yet the club employed no blacks in any capacity and, like every other major league team, no black players. In the wake of the war, in which African Americans had shed blood like all other citizens, black Americans had a new and ultimately persuasive argument for making changes that recognized their civil rights, including the integration of baseball.

The Yankees had never dealt with the issue in the past, and they didn't now, choosing to ignore the protesters, but over the next few years the issue of race and the integration of baseball would affect the game like no other issue. The Yankees' slow realization that change was inevitable would eventually have a damaging impact on the future of the team.

McCarthy and the Yankees beat Boston 8–4 on Opening Day and went with what they had, which wasn't much. In 1945 the Yankees' starting lineup often included players like third baseman Oscar Grimes, outfielders Bud Metheny and Hersh Martin, catcher Mike Chartak, and other names of little note in Yankee lore.

By juggling the pitching as best he could, McCarthy kept the team, which could hit a little, in the race for the first half of the year. But in midseason the volatile and impatient new general manager vented to a sportswriter, criticizing several players, including Nick Etten, who was among the league leaders in RBIs. MacPhail charged that Etten wasn't earning his salary. Etten, who had once described the Yankee organization as one "that specializes in harmony," was stunned by the public attack. So was McCarthy.

Such a thing never would have happened under Ruppert or Barrow. MacPhail's public criticism was an indirect swipe at McCarthy himself—he was doing the best he could with what he had, and MacPhail hadn't been any help at all in that regard. But MacPhail was just getting started.

The Chicago Cubs were locked in a battle for the NL pennant. In late July, with the Yankees only four games out of first, MacPhail asked for waivers on pitcher Hank Borowy, who led the pitching-short Yankees with ten wins. It was a not-uncommon procedure, often used to gauge the needs of other clubs. A team that claimed the pitcher, for example, would be revealing their need for pitching, which might later be reflected in a trade. Most players put on waivers are withdrawn.

But when Borowy passed through the American League unclaimed, MacPhail was free to deal him to the National League, and MacPhail sold him to the Cubs for $97,000. Then MacPhail made a bad deal even worse by offering the excuse that Borowy was a lousy second-half pitcher whom the Yankees wouldn't miss anyway. McCarthy hadn't even been consulted.

The manager couldn't take it. Ruppert and Barrow had always given him the means to win and then left him alone. He repaid their confidence with world championships, and McCarthy was proud of the fact that no manager in baseball history had accumulated a better record. Throwing away a potential pennant and selling the staff ace in the midst of the race was something he couldn't understand.

MacPhail ignored his manager, and McCarthy turned inward. Baseball was everything to him. Even in 1945 wins and losses mattered. His drinking problem grew worse.

Claiming he was ill with "gall bladder trouble," McCarthy left the club and went home to his farm. He stayed away three weeks and then offered to resign, but MacPhail held him to his contract, which ran through 1946. He didn't want to hire a new manager—not yet.

The Yankees fell further back. In mid-September DiMaggio, whose final year of military service had been marred by physical problems, including ulcers, was mustered out of the Army, and he volunteered to play the rest of the season. Against 1945 pitching, even a diminished DiMaggio might have made the difference, but MacPhail threw away whatever chance for a pennant remained and told DiMaggio to rest up and get ready for 1946. The Yankees, with a

late charge, finished a respectable 81–71 in fourth place behind Detroit. But had they retained Borowy, who won 11 games for the Cubs in August and September, and activated DiMaggio, they might have stolen a pennant themselves.

The new regime didn't care—there was no cachet in winning the pennant in a war year, and besides, the $97,000 they got for Borowy made the books look good. There was backslapping all around the front office and utter bewilderment elsewhere.

The war was over, which made everyone happy, but MacPhail wasted little time in letting the Yankee players know that they were returning to a much different organization. Under MacPhail, the bottom line was always money. Wins were nice, but money mattered more.

So on the heels of their return from military service, Yankee players were greeted with a notice that in 1946 the ballclub would hold a special pre–spring training workout session—in Panama. That was just where everyone wanted to be after getting out of the service. Then they learned that spring training would take place not just in St. Petersburg, the team's traditional home, but in Bradenton, Florida, as well.

It was a weird spring for everyone as players returned from the war anxious to spend time with their families, only to pack a duffel bag and be shipped out. When they finally got to Florida, they spent barely any time on the field before MacPhail, realizing that the country was hungry for baseball again and the Yankees were the biggest drawing card around, took them on tour. They embarked on the most ambitious exhibition season in baseball history, playing 50 exhibitions before 250,000 fans against minor league teams throughout the South and Midwest. Red Smith of the *Herald Tribune* termed it MacPhail's "weird Chataqua tour."

Nevertheless, New York played well that spring, particularly DiMaggio, who hit .370 with 19 home runs, but it was an exhausting experience that left the Yankees less than ready for the start of the season. They needed to see major league pitching, not a bunch of minor leaguers. Still, as Smith noted before a final exhibition against Brooklyn, "you'd have thought the joint was full of Yankee fans to hear the cheering . . . but it wasn't Joe [DiMaggio] they were cheering. It was the return of big league baseball."

In January 1945 a syndicate including Dan Topping, Del Webb (left), and Larry MacPhail (right) purchased the Yankees, Yankee Stadium, and the team's farm system for $2.8 million. Longtime team executive Ed Barrow (center) continued to serve as chairman, but MacPhail soon ran the show as general manager.

New York opened the 1946 campaign in Philadelphia before a capacity crowd. Spud Chandler shut out the A's, and DiMaggio cracked a long two-run homer to pace the club to a 5–0 win. It looked for all the world as if the Yankees were ready to resume their stranglehold on first place.

But the score was as deceiving as their record on the "Chataqua tour." New York was still awaiting the return of Gordon and Rizzuto. A number of wartime players like Stirnweiss, Etten, Grimes, and Lindell remained in the starting lineup. The simple truth was that the prewar Yankees had all grown old during the war, spending their peak years in the military. Old vets like Red Rolfe had retired, but almost everyone else either was pushing 30 or had celebrated that birthday with K-rations. And the pitching staff had turned over almost completely. It would take more than Nick Etten returning DiMaggio's number 5 jersey to him for the Yankees to resume championship form.

They weren't a team of stars anymore. For years the Yankee trademark had been that three or four positions were always manned by great players. The championship Yankees hadn't been Ruth alone, but Ruth, Gehrig, and Lazzeri, then Gehrig, DiMaggio, and Dickey, all supplemented by others who could have played every day for virtually any other team in baseball.

But after the war the only star was DiMaggio, and even he wasn't shining quite as bright anymore. The other Yankees were either role players or otherwise solid performers, but not the best in baseball.

The stars were elsewhere, and the Yankees soon learned exactly where that was. On May 10, with a stellar record of 16–8, the Yankees played Boston for the first time since the war, and from a unique position. They were looking up. Way up.

The Red Sox were loaded. Tom Yawkey's millions were finally paying a dividend. Ted Williams, Bobby Doerr, Johnny Pesky, and Dom DiMaggio were several years younger than their Yankee counterparts, and all returned from the war in their prime. They had won 14 in a row and their record of 20–3 had put them four and a half games ahead of New York when the two clubs met for the first time.

Sixty-four thousand fans packed Yankee Stadium for the first game of the already important series—the Yan-

Joe DiMaggio (far right) signed autographs at one of the few World Series in which he wasn't a participant, in 1946. Joining him at Fenway Park are Dodger manager Leo Durocher (second from left), actor–bad boy George Raft (center), and saloonkeeper to the stars Toots Shor.

kees could not afford to fall much further behind. Mac-Phail chose that date to hold his first big promotion — Ladies Day. He distributed more than 100,000 free passes before the game, gave away 500 pairs of nylons, and held a pregame fashion show in which models were paraded around the field in jeeps painted in pastels.

The incredulous Yankee players watched open-mouthed from the dugout. They'd been schooled by Ruppert, Barrow, and McCarthy to look and act like Yankees on and off the field. Coats and ties on road trips were mandatory. Now they were a sideshow.

DiMaggio cracked a grand slam, but the Red Sox won the game, 5–4, for their 15th consecutive win. "The only thing familiar in Yankee Stadium yesterday," wrote Red Smith, "was the national anthem." Although the Yankees snapped Boston's streak the next day, they lost the third game to fall five and a half games back. Over the next week they fell even further behind.

The return of familiar faces had not made things easier on McCarthy. The game according to MacPhail was one he

barely recognized, and McCarthy emerged from the war a full-blown alcoholic. Isolated and estranged from the front office, and watching any hope of a pennant slipping away, McCarthy was losing his grip.

On May 21, as the Yankees flew from Cleveland to Detroit, the manager lost it. McCarthy didn't like flying, which was another MacPhail innovation, and before the plane took off he had one or two too many. He decided this was the time to confront Yankee pitcher Joe Page, a prodigious talent who hadn't performed to McCarthy's standards and whom McCarthy suspected of living the high life.

He began lecturing Page, and with each word he lost control, his voice getting louder and louder, until he was screaming uncontrollably at the pitcher. His embarrassed teammates tried to ignore the altercation and looked away. That only made McCarthy angrier, and his invective soon spread to include others, including MacPhail, as several years of frustration poured forth in a torrent.

When the plane landed, McCarthy was still beside himself, almost paralyzed with rage and alcohol. He went to the team hotel but failed to show up at the ballpark for the game the next day. Instead, he jumped the club and went home in shame, a pattern that, sadly, he would repeat several years later when he managed Boston. A great manager and a good man ground down, McCarthy was a basket case, mentally and physically exhausted. Three days later he resigned, and this time MacPhail accepted the resignation. He was going to fire McCarthy anyway. Bill Dickey reluctantly took over.

The McCarthy era was over, and with it went a certain stage of Yankee innocence. The players, particularly the veterans who played every day, had respected McCarthy's professionalism, and for the most part it had been returned. DiMaggio called him "the best manager I ever played for," a sentiment echoed by most of his long-time teammates. McCarthy had made being a Yankee something special — he had insisted on it. He had been among the first to recognize the existence of a Yankee tradition, and he had demanded that it be maintained. But under MacPhail, the New York Yankees were just another business. From that moment on, the players and the front office were not always on the same page. Playing baseball for the Yankees would never be quite the same.

DiMaggio carried the team into June, cracking 20 home runs in the first 41 games, but then he slumped and the Red Sox drew away. Then, just before the All-Star break, DiMaggio tore some cartilage in his knee.

The Yankees were ordinary, and after DiMaggio returned, so was he, hitting only 5 home runs in the second half and finishing with only 25. Dickey soon feuded with MacPhail as well, and he resigned in September. Coach Johnny Neun managed out the season.

The Yankees were left to play out the string. They finished 87–67, 17 long games behind Boston. The Red Sox lost the World Series to the Cardinals in a Series best remembered for Enos Slaughter's "mad dash": the Cardinal outfielder scored the winning run in game seven by running all the way from first base on a hit by Harry Walker that was generously scored a double.

Still, on the basis of their 104 regular season wins — including a 14–8 mark against the Yankees — and their near wire-to-wire romp to the pennant, the Red Sox, not the Yankees, were designated baseball's next dynasty. Boston missed setting an American League record for wins and winning percentage, held by the 1912 Sox, by only a single game, leading Fred Lieb to term their pennant romp "almost ridiculous." For the next five seasons a preseason survey of baseball writers would make the Red Sox odds-on favorites to win the American League pennant.

The Yankees were a much different club from the one that had won the World Series in five of six seasons from 1936 to 1941. Nevertheless, over 2.2 million fans responded to MacPhail's string of promotions and set a new major league attendance record, although fans were so hungry for baseball they probably would have come out in record numbers anyway, even without the nylons.

The war was over, but not without a certain cost. The price of finishing in second place would prove costly to the Yankees.

Left to right: Ted Williams, Dominic DiMaggio, Joe DiMaggio, and Tommy Henrich at Fenway Park in 1942. After the war both clubs took their long-standing rivalry to new heights, as Joe DiMaggio and Henrich helped lead the Yankees to memorable World Series victories in 1947 and 1949. The Red Sox managed only a pennant in 1946 and near misses in '48, '49, and '50.

We are tired of eating New York's dust.

— RED SOX OWNER TOM YAWKEY

1947–1950
THE BOSTON STRANGLERS

Since the Yankees had first joined the American League, a rivalry between New York and the Boston Red Sox seemed somehow predestined. The two cities were natural geographic and civic rivals, representing the American struggle of the past and the future, the entrenched and the immigrant, the civil and the coarse. Boston had dominated American life during the 19th century, as both a commercial and cultural center, only to be toppled and overwhelmed in the next century by New York.

In baseball a similar evolution had taken place. In the game's infancy, a version of baseball known as the "Massachusetts game" had, for a time, been dominant. But a variation evolved in New York that quickly toppled its predecessor and gave birth to the modern game. The Massachusetts game became extinct.

When the Yankees first joined the American League, it took only one year for them to become a threat to the defending champion Boston Americans. They battled Boston for the

American League pennant down to the final pitch in the 1904 season, one of the great pennant races in baseball history.

But the emerging rivalry stalled when the Yankees tumbled into mediocrity and Boston remained dominant for much of the next two decades. Then, as the Yankees—with Boston's Babe—emerged as baseball's dominant team in the 1920s, the Red Sox had foundered. In the 1930s Boston's new owner, Tom Yawkey, said, "My main purpose in buying the Red Sox is beating the Yankees." He spent millions trying, only to fall short.

But Boston's pennant in 1946 seemed to signal a change. Suddenly it looked like the Red Sox had every advantage—more talent, more money, and more resources to remain on top—and the Yankees found themselves in the unfamiliar position of the underdog trying to keep pace with Boston. Over the next few seasons the rivalry would finally fulfill its promise.

It was always more important in Boston than in New York, for in recent years Boston had developed a considerable inferiority complex in regard to New York, one that would only increase over the next few seasons. The relationship between the two clubs helped to define each team, making the Yankees perennial champions and the Red Sox a team known for only coming close.

After winning the 1946 pennant, the Red Sox were absolutely giddy over their prospects, particularly when they compared their roster to New York's. In Fenway Park they boasted that their own DiMaggio, Dominic, was, if not better than Joe, a remarkable player in his own right—at least Joe's equivalent in the field and, unlike his older brother, a hitter who was still improving. After Joe, the Yankees didn't have many players whose better years still lay ahead—and even Joe seemed like yesterday's news.

Only a year before there had been some speculation that Tom Yawkey would sell the Sox and acquire the championship he so desired by purchasing the Yankees from the Ruppert estate. MacPhail had beaten him to the punch, yet now Yawkey seemed to have gotten the better of the deal. For the first time in decades Boston didn't fear the Yankees.

In the winter of 1946–47 MacPhail was a tornado cutting through the torpor of the game. No one and no thing was safe from his touch. He used New York's second-place finish behind Boston to justify a series of sweeping changes as he tried to reshape the club in his own image. To Mac-Phail, New York's record in 1946 provided license to erase the past 25 years. Almost everyone with any connection to the Ruppert regime would be affected. MacPhail's purge took on an almost Stalinist edge, and he didn't limit his reign solely to the Yankees either: among the men who ran baseball, MacPhail quickly became one of the most influential members.

He first took aim at the Yankee roster. Joe Gordon was the first to go.

Gordon hadn't played particularly well in 1946, hitting only .210, but then again, he hadn't had the benefit of spring training. No matter, he was sent to the Indians in exchange for fastball pitcher Allie Reynolds, whom DiMaggio had urged MacPhail to acquire. But Reynolds's acquisition was counteracted a few days later when MacPhail sent Ernie Bonham to Pittsburgh for Cookie Cuccurullo. Bonham had 89 wins as a Yankee and an ERA under 3.00, and he would win another 25 games for Pittsburgh over the next three seasons. Cuccurullo never appeared in a Yankee uniform and never added to his career victory total of three.

MacPhail was just getting started. He needed a manager. There was some speculation that he wanted Brooklyn manager Leo Durocher, who had succeeded under MacPhail in Brooklyn but whose ego matched MacPhail's. Durocher, however, was still under contract. In early November MacPhail finally settled on Bucky Harris, the one-time "Boy Manager" of the Washington Senators. He had won pennants in his first two seasons at the helm, but in 18 subsequent seasons as manager in outposts like Detroit, Philadelphia, and Boston, then Washington again, Harris had never finished higher than fourth. Harris, whom a Boston sportswriter aptly described as someone "who was just there, like a flag in the corner of an auditorium," was MacPhail's kind of guy—easily swayed. To help him out, MacPhail hired away Dodger coach Charlie Dressen. Durocher was incensed.

Two weeks later, on November 21, Ed Barrow submitted his letter of resignation, ending his 51-year career in baseball. He wasn't well and, at age 79, was wise enough to see the writing on the wall. Red Smith provided his baseball obituary, writing that Barrow's departure was a mere formality. . . . [T]he club had long ceased to resemble, either on the field or in the office, the Yankees as we have known them. . . . He [Barrow] had a program that seems curiously archaic in a day when the sport is administered by a song-and-dance man, when a fan dropping in for a ball game finds himself in a swish saloon ogling bathing beauties in a fashion parade. . . . [M]aybe nylons and night clubs are symbols of progress. But the product that bore Ed Barrow's brand was something you could buy with confidence and remember with pleasure.

MacPhail's brand was demonstrated by his treatment of DiMaggio. He thought the Clipper was taking on water and offered him straight up to Washington for first baseman Mickey Vernon, who had led the American League in hitting in 1946 with a .353 average but had few other skills. Fortunately for New York, the Senators turned him down. MacPhail signed 38-year-old George McQuinn to play first base instead.

This wasn't the first time DiMaggio's name had come up in trade since the arrival of MacPhail, nor would it be the last. On the precipice of the 1946 World Series, Boston newspapers had reported that Ted Williams would be traded, perhaps for DiMaggio, for Tom Yawkey liked collecting ballplayers—he'd once paid $250,000 for Joe Cronin. The Yankees didn't refute the rumor, and oddly enough, neither did the Red Sox for nearly a week, leaving Ted Williams twisting in the wind during the Series, wondering whether he was playing his last games in a Boston uniform.

But the deal wouldn't die. At some point during the off-season—or perhaps, according to other reports, as late as April—Tom Yawkey, noted for his fondness for hard liquor and inability to hold it, had spent an evening in the company of either MacPhail, Dan Topping, or both. He emerged with a deal scrawled on a cocktail napkin trading Ted for Joe. But when he awoke—sober—he apparently got cold feet and backed out of the deal.

Yankee owners Del Webb (left) and Dan Topping (center) chat with rival owner Thomas Austin Yawkey of the Boston Red Sox at baseball's 1947 winter meetings at the Waldorf-Astoria in New York. The trio remained cordial even as their teams battled furiously in the late forties. In one legendary chat over drinks they even discussed a possible trade involving Ted Williams and Joe DiMaggio.

DiMaggio was damaged goods anyway. Late in the 1946 season he had developed a bone spur on his heel, probably caused by his troublesome knee, which caused him to change his stride. In January he underwent surgery.

MacPhail, meanwhile, found himself embroiled in several other battles. Branch Rickey wanted to promote Jackie Robinson and break the color line. He announced his intention to the other 15 owners in a secret meeting in January at the Waldorf-Astoria Hotel. All 15 clubs, including the Yankees, opposed the move.

Yogi Berra arrived in New York in 1946, just as Joe DiMaggio's career was winding down in glorious fashion. Like DiMaggio, Berra won three American League MVP Awards and played on 10 Yankee world championship teams in a playing career spent exclusively in the Bronx.

MacPhail was a key member of the opposition. Six months earlier, in the middle of the 1946 season, he had chaired a steering committee of owners to consider the race question and authored their report. The document was an artistic masterpiece in its convoluted logic, which tried to mask its "segregation forever" message in an insincere, and grotesquely paternalistic, concern for the future of the Negro Leagues. MacPhail also wrote a similar report entitled "The Negro in Baseball" as a member of a similar committee appointed by Mayor Fiorello La Guardia. He employed the same moral gymnastics, simultaneously arguing that no blacks were capable of playing major league baseball and that integration would permanently damage the Negro Leagues.

What MacPhail really wanted was for Organized Baseball to take over the Negro Leagues. He was, after all, renting out Yankee Stadium to the Negro Leagues, just as he had once rented out Ebbets Field. As black sportswriter Wendell Smith observed in the spring of 1947, MacPhail "makes thousands of dollars off Negro Baseball each year [and] can't stomach the thought of the lily-white color line being broken." MacPhail's actions over the next year would indicate that Smith was right.

Already at loggerheads over the race issue, in the spring MacPhail and Rickey started sniping at each other over the hiring of Dressen. Then MacPhail and Dodger manager Leo Durocher got into a public pissing contest. MacPhail denied Durocher's claim that he'd been offered the Yankee job, and soon the two were hurling insults back and forth. The battle escalated in the spring when first Rickey and then Durocher claimed that MacPhail attended a Yankees-Dodgers exhibition in Havana in the company of gamblers. MacPhail considered that libel and at length convinced commissioner Happy Chandler to suspend Durocher for the 1947 season. He himself had to pay a $2,000 fine for signing Dodger coach Charlie Dressen.

Larry MacPhail had already made more news in a year than Jacob Ruppert had in more than twenty. And in the end nothing much had really changed. The Red Sox were still favored to win the American League pennant, and by an even greater margin than before.

DiMaggio's postsurgery wound wouldn't heal. He eventually checked into Johns Hopkins Hospital and had to have a two-by-one-and-a-half-inch flap of skin grafted from his hip to close it. He didn't even join the Yankees for spring training—held that year in Puerto Rico, Venezuela, and Cuba before commencing in St. Pete—until March 26.

New York opened the season without DiMaggio and Henrich, who had a bad wrist, and Bill Dickey, who'd retired. Rookie Larry Berra—the press had yet to pick up on his nickname—had hit well in the minors but was a defensive liability behind the plate. He joined Lindell and Keller in the outfield. The infield of McQuinn, Stirnweiss, Rizzuto, and Johnson hardly inspired awe, while Aaron Robinson reminded no one of Dickey.

DiMaggio missed the first ten days of the season as the Yankees struggled to score runs, a point driven home on April 27, "Babe Ruth Day," when New York entertained Washington.

The Bambino was dying, ravaged by throat cancer, and he looked at least a decade older than his 52 years as he took the microphone in a pregame ceremony to address the crowd of nearly 60,000. His haggard and drawn appearance seemed to mirror the condition of the franchise. The mighty had fallen.

In a hoarse whisper, Ruth addressed the fans: "The only real game, I think, is baseball. . . . You've got to start all the way down at the bottom, when you're 6 or 7 years of age. You can't wait until you're 15 or 16. You've gotta let it grow up with you, and if you're successful and you try hard enough, you're bound to come out on top."

He stayed seven innings, leaving after DiMaggio grounded out in the 0–0 tie. The Yankees lost, 1–0, their second defeat by that score in the last four games, over which they'd scored a total of only two runs. These were not the Bambino's Yankees.

Fortunately, the vaunted Red Sox were also struggling, since most of their top pitchers in 1946 had come down with a sore arm. In mid-May, although the Yankees lingered under .500, they weren't yet out of the pennant race.

Enter MacPhail. On May 22, as the Yankees prepared for an important four-game series with Boston in which both teams hoped to turn their season around, MacPhail levied fines ranging from $25 to $100 on half a dozen Yankee players. DiMaggio took the biggest hit.

The players were not fined for breaking training, indifference, insubordination, or anything they did or did not do on the field. They were fined for refusing to participate in one of MacPhail's endless promotions, a newsreel shoot for one of the owners' Army buddies.

The Yankees were livid. MacPhail had kept them busy almost every night appearing at two-bit banquets and other events that, beyond the time they took, the players felt ran counter to the Yankee tradition. At the same time a number of players had rebelled against flying. MacPhail told them to pay their own train fare. It was a helluva way to try to win a pennant.

Red Smith captured the mood, writing, "The Yankees upstairs office is promotion-happy. A seal that can play Beethoven's Fifth on an oboe is more beautiful to L. S. MacPhail than a twenty-game pitcher." Battered by the press, MacPhail soon rescinded the fines, but the incident brought the team together—they all hated MacPhail equally. Thus inspired, they went into Boston and played their best baseball of the year, dumping the Red Sox four straight—9–0, 5–0, 17–2, and 9–3—in the first "Boston Massacre" of the emerging rivalry. DiMaggio announced that he wasn't through, going nine for sixteen in the series, while Ted Williams did nothing of significance. DiMaggio went on to hit nearly .500 over the next two weeks.

The Red Sox were dead and learned a bitter and lasting lesson (or they should have): the Yankees could never be taken for granted. Time and time again over the ensuing decades, just as Boston appeared to have the Yankees by the neck, New York would use Boston to disprove the rumors of their demise. The Red Sox would never, ever be able to drive a stake through the heart of New York. For just as Boston would bend over New York's prostrate body to check for breath, New York would rise and seize the Red Sox by the throat. And even when the Yankees ultimately didn't win themselves, they often proved capable of playing havoc with Boston's psyche. In time New England's obsession with the Red Sox would inspire a similar, near-pathological obsession with the Yankees, a fixation often shared in both the dugout and the front office.

Having dispatched Boston, New York took aim at front-running Detroit and swept a four-game series in late June to take command. DiMaggio was hitting like it was 1941 again, and the Yankees were making their customary surge in his wake, inspiring Joe Williams to write in the *World*

Telegram: "There used to be a saying, 'As goes Ruth, so go the Yankees.' . . . You can say that about DiMaggio these days. . . . DiMaggio has been the answer since the first day he joined the Yankees."

As if they couldn't be bothered with the tension of a pennant race, the ballclub ended the month by embarking on a 19-game winning streak. By the time the streak ended on July 19, the Yankee record was 58–27, 10½ games ahead of Detroit and 12½ in front of Boston. Take that.

They cruised to the pennant in the second half despite losing several key players to injuries. Charlie Keller had a back operation, and both Spec Shea and Spud Chandler were sidelined with arm woes. Even DiMaggio went down as injuries to his elbow, neck, shoulder, and left knee kept knocking him out of the lineup—and knocked his average down from over .340 at midseason to just over .315 by the season's end. But it didn't matter. His work was done, and the Yankees clinched the pennant on September 15.

In the National League, Jackie Robinson keyed a Dodger pennant, giving MacPhail an opportunity to thump his chest and best his former club, although he'd had little to do with the Yankee pennant. But Robinson's success was a herald of great changes to come.

Brooklyn's pennant proved that breaking the color line wasn't just morally correct but good business, both in the final standings and at the gate: the Dodgers had drawn 1.8 million fans, the all-time franchise record in Ebbets Field and nearly as many as the Yankees had drawn to the much larger Yankee Stadium.

Robinson, who had played only a single year in the Negro Leagues before being signed by Rickey, wasn't the only African-American player with major league ability. Neither was he the best. A tremendous pool of talent, the greatest ever available to major league baseball at one time, was there for the taking.

No team was in a better position to capitalize on this than the Yankees. Because of Ruth, the Yankees were, before Robinson signed, the de facto favorites of black America. Few teams could match their financial resources, and in Newark, Kansas City, and New York the Yankees already rented their ballparks to Negro League clubs. The Yankees had an inside track signing Negro League players from these teams if they chose to. Owner Tom Baird of the Kansas City Monarchs even went so far as to write MacPhail

and say, "I feel as though I am a part of the Yankee organization and I want to give you first chance at any players that your organization might want." Effa Manley, owner of the Newark Eagles, gave New York the first shot at both Larry Doby and Monte Irvin, who were signed by the Indians and Giants, respectively. The Birmingham Black Barons, put off by the racism endemic within the Red Sox organization, from which they rented their ballpark, were also predisposed to send their players to New York—and beginning in 1948 their roster included Willie Mays.

But the Yankees signed none of these men, and the Yankees did not return the loyalty of Baird and other black Americans. In fact, they squandered it.

One can only imagine what the consequences would have been of adding a Larry Doby, Monte Irvin, or Ray Dandridge to the postwar Yanks. And what if former Kansas City Monarch Ernie Banks, Hank Aaron, or Willie Mays had been in a Yankee lineup with Mantle, Berra, Maris, and the next generation of Yankee stars? As it was, the size and breadth of the Yankee farm system and the skill of Weiss's scouts in ferreting out white prospects covered for their reluctance to hire black players. The Red Sox, by way of comparison, had a much smaller farm system and fewer scouts and would pay a much steeper price, much sooner, for their reluctance.

The Yankees were the best-known franchise in sports, as they remain today. Had they not turned their back on black players, the consequences might well have been more significant than a string of world championships. By their example they could have played a leading role in helping to usher the nation into a new awareness of civil rights and racial equality, creating a lasting legacy beyond sports. But they blew it.

Of course, the Yankees still dominated baseball like no other team ever had, and most of the other AL teams found themselves playing for second place anyway, but the Yankee dynasty that lasted through 1964 could have been even more dominant and continued ad infinitum. Only when the club allowed its farm system to deteriorate in the 1960s would its failure to sign significant numbers of black players finally be reflected in the final standings, a fall from grace the ballclub deserved.

MacPhail did start scouting Negro Leaguers in 1947, but it was a halfhearted effort designed to appease political pressure groups, one that George Weiss did not support. The Yankees would be one of the last major league franchises to integrate, and one of the more reluctant.

The 1947 World Series was a classic, a thriller that provided as many memorable moments as any Series in history, most of them favoring the Dodgers. Yet while the Dodgers would win on style, the Yankees still prevailed.

New York didn't have the benefit of its usual glut of power—DiMaggio's twenty home runs had led the team—but the club still depended on the home run: seven Yankees had hit ten or more. The Dodgers, paced by Robinson, were a scrappy, energetic club that worked for every run. If the Yankees' ideal inning included a three-run homer, Brooklyn's included a stolen base, a hit-and-run,

and a forced error from a baserunner taking an unexpected chance.

But there was more at stake than the Series. Rickey and MacPhail hated each other, and the Yankees didn't want the Dodgers to get a leg up in the New York market either. The Giants were improving and had led the major leagues in home runs in 1947. The Yankees might not have been the most entertaining of New York's three teams, but they could still prove they were the best.

The Yankees were favored, but then again, they always were. Tradition—and DiMaggio, who was again being lauded as the greatest player in the game—made it so.

If the Yankees failed to recognize the impact that Robinson had on the game in 1947, they got a quick lesson

A DESERVING MVP

The season of 1947 took its toll on Joe DiMaggio. For the second time in his career he had to undergo surgery, this time for bone chips in his right elbow. But his off-season was brightened somewhat by word that he'd been selected by the Base Ball Writers Association of America (BBWAA) as American League MVP. He won by one vote over Ted Williams, outpolling Boston's triple crown winner 202–201.

Although DiMaggio hit only .315 with 20 home runs and 97 RBIs to Williams's league-best .343, 32 home runs, and 114 RBIs, his selection inspired little debate at the time. Yet as time passed it became more controversial. Ted Williams has long thought he was robbed and has complained that he lost the award only because *Boston Globe* sportswriter Mel Webb left him off the MVP ballot altogether. Williams's discontent is a measure of just how much all things

Yankee have a way of working their way into the Boston psyche.

Although his allegation made an interesting story, Williams was dead wrong. Webb didn't vote for the MVP in 1947 and fellow *Globe* sportswriter Harold Kaese later revealed that the three Boston writers who did vote all gave Williams a first-place vote, the only three first-place ballots he collected. Kaese identified the voter who left Williams off the ballot as a midwesterner.

Williams apparently never noticed that DiMaggio, who collected eight first-place votes, suffered an even more egregious omission. He was left off the ballot entirely by three writers.

Voting results reveal a suspicious pattern. Berra, who played in only 85 games, somehow received two second-place votes, and Eddie Joost, who hit only .206 for Philadelphia, received two *first-place* votes, only one fewer than triple-crown winner Williams. Something was rotten with the BBWAA.

Two years later *The Sporting News* ran a front-page story by Dan Daniel revealing that over the past several seasons voting results had been released to the media a week in advance of their public

announcement. Armed with inside information, a number of writers were betting large sums with bookmakers on the outcome, which Daniel estimated in 1949 totaled at least $500,000 in New York alone. The inequities of the 1947 vote were probably the result of writers trying to skew the outcome to tilt the odds even more in their favor. Baseball commissioner Happy Chandler soon forced the BBWAA to change its voting procedure.

But Williams's "woe is me" tale, later propagated in his autobiography and spread far and wide by a legion of sportswriters who should have done their homework, has since been taken as gospel and places the legitimacy of DiMaggio's award in doubt. But in fact DiMaggio deserved his honor. Williams's Triple Crown had virtually no impact on the fortunes of the Red Sox, and in Boston's critical mid-May series with New York in 1947, he'd been shut down while DiMaggio almost single-handedly knocked Boston out of the race. DiMaggio then keyed New York's 19-game win streak, which put the pennant away. Williams had the better numbers, but only if one chooses not to consider wins and losses.

Floyd Clifford "Bill" Bevens makes the final fateful pitch of the fourth game of the 1947 World Series. Dodger pinch hitter Cookie Lavagetto not only broke up Bevens's no-hitter with two out in the bottom of the ninth, but also drove in the tying and winning runs of Brooklyn's 3–2 victory.

in game one. With one out, Robinson worked Spec Shea for a walk. Before the Series Berra had bragged that in 1946, when he'd caught for Newark in the International League, Robinson hadn't stolen a single base against him.

Despite Berra's bravado, he was not yet a very good defensive catcher. His arm was erratic, and he had a hard time stopping balls in the dirt. He was in the lineup for his bat, and after the Series Robinson would say that if he ran against Berra every day he'd steal 60 bases a year.

Robinson didn't hesitate. He immediately stole second, and then broke for third on Reiser's tap to Shea. Mistake Robinson. But he managed to dance back and forth in a rundown long enough to allow Reiser to make second. Mistake New York. Dixie Walker then singled the run home to put Brooklyn ahead.

The Dodgers' Ralph Branca took a no-hitter into the fifth, when DiMaggio beat out a ground ball into the hole at short, the first of many subtle yet significant plays he made in the Series. Branca, only 21, then fell apart, loading the bases on a walk and a hit batsman before Lindell doubled home two runs. The Yankees went on to plate three more and held on to win, 5–3. New York then won game two in a rout, 10–3. So far it was business as usual. As the Series moved to Brooklyn, the Yankees were up two games to none.

But the Yankees lost game three, 9–8, as the Dodgers routed starter and former Dodger Bobo Newsom with six second-inning runs. They faced Bill Bevens in game four, looking to tie the Series. No one could have predicted that this beautiful mess of a game would be one of the most memorable in World Series history.

Bevens, who'd made the Yankee roster during the war and then held on, was 31 years old, a well-traveled pitcher whose middle name could have been "Journeyman." Yet he was still valuable, particularly after Chandler went down. He ate up innings and saved the bullpen, even if he lost, which he had done 13 times in 20 decisions in 1947.

Bevens's problem was control—he gave up more than a hit an inning in 1947 and walked too many men on top of that to win consistently. The Yankees were depending on Shea and Reynolds to carry them through the Series. Their hope with Newsom and Bevens was that they would keep things close until they could turn the game over to ace relief pitcher Joe Page.

Brooklyn was in similar straits, for after Branca and Joe Hatten, the Dodger pitching staff was also suspect. Harry Taylor was the Dodgers' version of Bevens, another journeyman who struggled with control and who bore the added burden of a sore arm that had limited him to four innings pitched over the last six weeks.

The Yankees started the game as if they were prepared to end things early. Stirnweiss singled on the first pitch, Henrich followed with another hit, then Pee Wee Reese botched the transfer on Berra's double-play ball to load the bases with no out. Taylor then walked DiMaggio to force in a run. Dodger manager Burt Shotton, hired as a one-season replacement for Durocher, had seen enough. He pulled Taylor for Hal Gregg.

Gregg got out of the inning but found himself in trouble in the third. DiMaggio singled with two outs, and when Dodger catcher Bruce Edwards threw away George McQuinn's squib in front of the plate, DiMaggio kept running. Charlie Dressen, coaching third, sent him home, but Dixie Walker's throw beat him by 15 feet—DiMaggio didn't even bother to slide, and the Yankees squandered another scoring opportunity.

They scored another run to go ahead 2–0 in the fourth, when Johnson tripled and Lindell followed with a double, but then Gregg settled down.

Meanwhile, Bevens was all over the place in what Rud Rennie called "the most strangely beautiful performance ever seen," walking two in the first and one more batter in the second and third. Yet the Dodgers couldn't manage a hit, for Bevens was just wild enough to keep them off balance, and New York's defense kept making the plays.

But that didn't stop Brooklyn from scoring. In the fifth Bevens walked Spider Jorgensen and then committed the pitcher's ultimate sin, walking his counterpart, Hal Gregg.

An Eddie Stanky sacrifice and a ground ball by Reese plated a run without a hit.

On the game went, Gregg suddenly dispatching the Yankees with ease while Bevens continued to flail about on the rubber, never falling, but causing most Yankee fans to hide their eyes in fear. Harris's hands were tied—Joe Page had pitched three innings the previous day. Entering the ninth, the ballgame was Bevens's to win—or lose.

He hadn't given up a hit, but at the same time he'd been hit hard—DiMaggio and Henrich had both bailed him out with fine running catches, precisely the kind that a pitcher generally needs to collect a no-hitter. No pitcher in Series history had ever thrown a no-hitter—not Christy Mathewson, not Cy Young, not any of the game's immortals. Journeyman Bill Bevens was only three outs away from pulling it off.

But in the top of the inning Shotton pulled Gregg and inserted Hank Behrman, the first of a series of inexplicable moves he was to make in the final inning. The Yankees promptly loaded the bases. With one out, Shotton then called on Hugh Casey despite the fact that, like Page, he'd thrown three innings in game three.

And there he was, facing Henrich again with the game on the line, 1941 all over again. This time the veteran wound up and threw one pitch, a low curve. Henrich reached out and hit a wicked comebacker right at Casey. He stabbed at the ball, caught it, and then converted the home-to-first double play.

Now Bevens trudged out to the mound for the ninth time, already more than 120 pitches into the game and needing even more to reach baseball immortality—or at least a World Series win. Both were in sight as Bruce Edwards stepped in to lead off the inning for Brooklyn.

Hearts leapt in Ebbets Field as he drove the ball deep to left. But Lindell drifted back and back—and caught the ball at the wall. Two outs away.

Now Bevens's control again deserted him. Carl Furillo walked. After Spider Jorgensen fouled out, Shotton called time and sent backup outfielder Al Gionfriddo in to pinch-run. The Dodger manager was emptying his gun, playing to win, not just tie, at home. Gionfriddo was faster than Furillo, and Furillo had earned his manager's ire on several occasions earlier in the year by missing the bag while running the bases. Bevens was one out away.

Now Shotton gambled. With Reiser pinch-hitting for Casey and the count 2–1, Gionfriddo lit out for second. He got a good jump off Bevens, but wasted it, slipping on his first step. Berra, for once, made an accurate throw, waist high to Rizzuto, who applied the tag as Gionfriddo disappeared in a cloud of dust, sliding headfirst.

Umpire Bill McGowan hesitated, then signaled safe. The Dodgers were still alive. The pitch was called a ball, and now Yankee manager Bucky Harris, as Red Smith later noted, "violated all ten commandments of the dugout" and signaled for Bevens to put Reiser, the winning run, on first. It would come back to haunt the manager.

Shotton now gambled yet again. He sent 21-year-old Eddie Miksis in to run for Reiser, hobbled with a broken ankle, as Eddie Stanky started to step to the plate. Shotton called him back to the bench.

Stanky stopped in his tracks and looked at his manager incredulously before slamming his bat to the ground. Shotton hadn't pinch-hit for Stanky all year and had no left-handed hitters available. And Stanky had handled Bevens as well as anyone else, walking twice, sacrificing, and popping up. Although he had little power, he'd walked 103 times in 1947 and rarely struck out. Instead, Shotton called on the veteran Cookie Lavagetto.

It made no sense — none — to put another right-hander up to pinch-hit for Stanky, not even Lavagetto. True, Lavagetto had made a few key pinch hits earlier in the year, including one to beat the Cardinals on September 11 in what many Dodger fans considered the critical game of the season, but he was cold, with no hits in two at bats in the Series so far.

The Bronx and Brooklyn both paused as Bevens wound up and threw. Lavagetto swung through a fastball on the inside corner. Then Bevens aimed a pitch up and away. He didn't want Lavagetto, a pull hitter, to turn on the ball.

It was right where he wanted it, and Lavagetto was a little late. But he still got the fat of the bat on the ball, slicing it to right field. Miksis and Gionfriddo broke with contact.

The bleachers, Yankee Stadium, at the first game of the 1947 World Series. Note that the monuments (at left) to Miller Huggins and Lou Gehrig, as well as the adjoining flagpole, are in the field of play.

1950

GEORGE WEISS
ARCHITECT OF AN ERA

DAVID HALBERSTAM

George Weiss, the architect of much of the New York Yankees' success in the Forties and Fifties, and even the early Sixties, was important in baseball history for two reasons. In the first place he was self-evidently very good at what he did — he created a formidable scouting network which brought the Yankees the best talent available year after year, and he knew how to maximize the leverage of a rich New York team against weaker major league teams in order to pick up just the right player to protect any vulnerability that the farm system might have created. Was he short a pitcher or two? Then he always had a good many middle infielders, and the great Joe Gordon (three times over 100 RBIs at second base before the war) could be dealt for Allie Reynolds — in a trade which worked well for both clubs, but probably better for the Yanks. Was he still short a pitcher? Well a young catcher named Larry Berra seemed ready to bloom, and therefore Aaron Robinson could be traded to the White Sox for Eddie Lopat, a trade which helped the Yankees a great deal more than the White Sox. The Yankees were always deeper in talent than most of their American League opponents, always able to make the two-for-one trade that guaranteed getting the one player they needed.

In addition Weiss was an immensely important man in the history of baseball's labor relations. He never dealt with the players' union, but because of his relentlessly parsimonious — indeed virtually inhumane — treatment of his players, his instinct to turn the ratchet a few notches tighter than was needed in order to minimize their salaries, he helped set the stage for very different laws governing freedom of movement among today's athletes. He became Exhibit A of a now discredited era. He had operated with great skill in an era when the economic laws of baseball were truly draconian, completely favoring the owner over the player, and the players had no recourse. Negotiations in any real sense were a sham:

in the late Fifties if the Yankees wanted to sign one of their star pitchers for another season, they could go through the charade of negotiation, but a facade it always remained. Knowing that the final figure would be, say, $16,000 a year, Weiss could send a player a contract for $14,000, leaving him the illusion—and it was little more—that he had managed to fight his way back for two thousand more dollars.

But in truth the players had no alternative, they could not trade themselves to another team, and if George Weiss really wanted to, he could send a player a contract, and the player had to sign it. If he turned it down, his only other option was to retire. No wonder then that Weiss was truly hated by most Yankee players who had any serious dealings with him. No one made the coming of Marvin Miller and the end of what might be the nation's most archaic labor laws—few professionals in any field had less freedom and greater restraints—more inevitable than George Weiss and a handful of men, owners and general managers all like him. There was a time when they held all the cards, and they badly overplayed their hand, leading to a very different new era, where in baseball the players now hold almost complete control of their own future.

Weiss was efficient but not very lovable, almost completely devoid of charm. He was an almost perfect reflection of a certain kind of success in business in an old fashioned era, before labor laws were modernized, where a very few people were rich, where a great many people were poor, and a relatively small number of people were middle class, and where therefore his job, as a part of that still small middle class, was solely to please the people above him. He felt no obligation to those underneath him— the players. He operated coldly, shrewdly, and without mercy, protected by totally one-sided labor laws. Baseball was always a business for him; it might be a sport to the players at first, but he taught them as

well—and often very quickly—that it was always business.

He was a hard man. He had a Darwinian view of life—it was an act of faith on his part that a well-paid baseball player was a lazy one. Therefore it was his job to protect the players from their lesser selves, and the best way to do that was to limit their salaries, guaranteeing that they would always be hungry. Many of the best Yankees of that era who were driven by pride more than hunger raged at that view, but had no alternative. Nearly 35 years after he had thrown his last pitch for New York, Vic Raschi, one of the great Yankee pitchers of the Forties and Fifties, a member of the great Raschi-Reynolds-Lopat staffs, a truly tough and honorable man, could barely bring himself to talk to this reporter because his rage against George Weiss was still so great and so palpable.

In the minds of the players, Weiss's sins against them were unusually egregious. In the Fifties, when a given player's salary was perhaps $15,000, and a World Series check was about $5,000, Weiss literally counted the Series check as part of the salary during negotiations, and he would tell a player that they had in fact paid him $20,000 the previous year.

What made it worse, and more bitter, was the fact that he had a considerable financial incentive for being so cold and stingy. He was given a budget of say $1 million a year by the owners for the entire payroll. To the degree that he kept the sum total of the salaries under that—say, it reached $600,000— then he got, in addition to his salary, 10 percent of the $400,000 he had saved, or $40,000. When some of the more senior players discovered this fact, the idea that he was profiteering from his miserliness, Eddie Lopat, one of the great Yankee pitchers of the era noted, it was almost too much.

Baseball was never about popularity for Weiss. He was a businessman with roots in a Dickensian era, when generosity to employees was more often than not considered a weakness. He sought no approval save from the people he worked for. He was disliked by most working reporters, and he disliked them in turn—in an age when the press was a great deal less iconoclastic, and accepted all too many favors from the ball club, he viewed reporters with open contempt. He once looked around a room filled with beat reporters who were helping themselves to sandwiches and drinks in a part of the Yankee clubhouse, turned to a friend and said, "I can buy all of these sons of bitches for a five-dollar steak." As such, always cold, treating the writers much like he treated his ballplayers, he was nonetheless somewhat irate when Jimmy Cannon, one of the most important columnists of the era, called him "Lonesome George."

After some of those "Lonesome George" columns began to appear in the *New York Post,* Weiss showed up one day at Toots Shor's, which was the main watering hole for sports figures in those days. He put several of them down on the table, began to complain about them to Shor and then said, "But what the hell, Toots, who reads that guy anyway?"

"You do, George," Shor answered.

No one was to get anything for free, not at his ballpark. Weiss hated the idea of televising baseball games, sure in the beginning that he was giving away his product, that television would ruin baseball and that the crowds would decrease, rather than as happened, the audience would in the long run, if the product was good, expand. He was always on the lookout for anyone getting any unnecessary freebie. Once during a big Sunday doubleheader with the always competitive Cleveland Indians, with some 60,000 people in the stands, Red Patterson, who handled the press relations for the team, got a telephone call from Weiss. Weiss had been checking the free ticket list, and there was a name he did not recognize. Who was it? he demanded of Patterson. It was,

explained Patterson, the elevator operator from the downtown office. *The elevator operator from the office!* Weiss exploded—free tickets for people like that should never be given to big games like this. The elevator operator, if he wanted to see a game free, could go during the week against the St. Louis Browns.

He managed to cast a constant shadow over what should have been a very happy place to work. If you won, then you had to fight for your next year's salary increase. If you negotiated with him—there were no agents in those days—he came armed with all your weaknesses from the previous season, remembering the days when you were knocked out of the box, not the 21 complete games you had pitched, as Vic Raschi noted. Even your strengths were used against you. Famously, after the Yankees had swept the Phillies in four games in the 1950 World Series, he had dampened the celebration in the winning clubhouse by getting up and giving a speech. The coda of the speech was that because the Series had been so short, four games instead of seven, they had not made as much money as they should, and therefore salaries would have to be held down in the coming year.

Because he spent so much time snookering other people over money, Weiss was sure that others were always out to exploit him in return. He paid excruciating attention to detail, watched the expense accounts of his scouts like a hawk, sure that the scouts, paid miserable wages in those days, were padding their expenses. He once complained bitterly to Lee MacPhail, one of his assistants, about a scout who claimed that he had driven 300 miles in one day to see a game. It was impossible, Weiss said, to do that. "What I realized," MacPhail told me years later, "was that this was a test, and that Weiss was trying to see if I was on the side of the poor scout in the field, or the Yankee organization in New York—he wanted to see if I was made of stern enough stuff to work for him." Years later Weiss was in California and went over the Golden Gate Bridge with one of his scouts. The fee was 25 cents. He was not pleased. "I just want you to know that you've been billing me 50 cents for each trip all these years," he told the scout.

On another occasion when Lee MacPhail was running the Yankee minor league team in Kansas City, Weiss came to visit his minor league park in Lake Wales, Florida. For MacPhail it was a big day — he was going to find out which players he was going to get from the major league club. But that was not on Weiss's mind. What was on his mind was that as he arrived at the park he had seen two kids climbing the fence in right field. "These kids," he complained angrily to MacPhail, "were going to watch a Yankee farm team play in spring training for free!" All other activities stopped. The prime order of business was now the assault upon local urchins who could sneak into a baseball game and were thereby depriving the New York Yankees of their rightful revenues. "Lee," he had said, "this sort of thing must stop at once!"

At the core of his success was his scouting system. It was very good — along with that of the Cardinals, and the Dodgers, the best in baseball. He had good scouts and the entire operation was well systematized. The Yankees had the luxury of multiple farm clubs, they could, like a few other teams, overstock, and they could always trade two or three marginal prospects who had good minor league statistics but whom they felt were never going to be that good for one first rate prospect. Weiss did not, of course, pay his scouts well, but he left them alone — except of course, when he came to his greatest failure, the crude racism which blocked him from going after the great black ballplayers of the new generation.

Here he was limited by his own deeply ingrained prejudices, biases which represented the worst prejudices of a generation just about to fade from holding power. Despite all kinds of evidence in front of him — the ascent of players like Jackie Robinson, Mays, and

Aaron — Weiss for more than 15 years essentially clung to the ignorance of the past rather than the striking new evidence of the future. Black ballplayers were not Yankee types, he decided, and he always wanted a Yankee type. A Yankee type was not merely to be a great ballplayer, but he was to look like a Yankee and behave like a Yankee as well. Yogi Berra, notwithstanding — "the Yog" did not look like a Yankee but he certainly played like one — there was a Yankee look that scouts were to pay attention to. A prototype Yankee was big, and he was clean cut. Paul Krichell, the great Yankee scout, once spoke at a staff meeting about a prospect he had seen: "You're going to love him — good hitter, good fielder, great jaw — he really looks like a Yankee." In addition to being clean cut with a good jaw, it should be added, the jaw was supposed to be white. He let the scouts know that.

Where Weiss floundered therefore, as the world changed around him and he paid no attention, was on the issue of race. Here his prejudices simply blinded him. In the early Fifties it was obvious that Vic Power was the most talented first baseman in the farm system, but senior management did not like him—he was Puerto Rican, he was black, he was flashy, and he was said to like white women. ("I'm the original showboat hotdog," he once said.) In 1952 in Triple A at Kansas City Power had hit .331 and driven in 109 runs. But Weiss wanted no part of him. He started pushing the idea through friendly beat reporters that Power was not very bright. Not only did Power never play for the major league club, but the Yankees virtually gave him away.

At almost the same time the Yankees had a shot at signing an immensely talented young infielder from the black Kansas City Monarchs named Ernie Banks. Banks, who played shortstop, was hitting .350 in the Negro League in 1950, had heard that the Yankees were interested in him, knew that Phil Rizzuto was aging (he was 32 that year, and Banks was only 19 — a perfect age gap under which to break in a younger player) and was excited because that was the team he wanted to play for. But the Yankees never moved on Banks — no one up top was interested in him. That meant that the Mantle-Maris years were not, as they might have been, the Maris-Mantle-Banks years.

In truth the Yankees — and it led to the great drought of the mid to late Sixties and much of the Seventies until the rules were changed with free agency — missed the boat on the great black ballplayers. It was not until Derek Jeter and Bernie Williams flowered in the Nineties, more than 40 years after Jackie Robinson broke in, that the team could showcase great black ball players who had come up through its own farm system.

The cracks in the system, the looming empty cupboard of talent, the fatal flaws caused by his prejudice, might have shown up earlier except for the Roger Maris trade. It was Weiss's last hurrah, the last great snookering of a weak team when he could still leverage New York's wealth and muscle against a poor, insecure franchise — Kansas City was by then a major league team, but it was still a de facto Yankee farm club, and the trade was something of a steal. It bought an otherwise aging team three more years.

But it also covered up the fatal weakness in the farm system, and the damage done by Weiss's prejudice. Weiss had always been blinded in two ways by his prejudices. First, he did not think that his prime customers, the white middle class gentry from the suburbs whose support he coveted, would pay to see black ballplayers. He was, of course, wrong about that. But even more tragic and pathetic was the degree of his own human miscalculation. He thought black players were not as good as white players, and even worse, he thought they lacked heart and toughness. This was the irony of ironies. He did not see that the classic Yankee type — a tough, hungry kid with

talent who also played very hard — was now as often or more often black, because he and his people had been denied so much for so long, and was out to settle a score. Weiss did not deign to see what had been in front of him for more than 15 years, that the black kids coming into the majors were very hungry and very tough, the embodiment of what a Yankee type had been. It was only when the Yankees met the Cardinals in the 1964 Series and ran into Bob Gibson, Lou Brock, Curt Flood and Bill White that what had happened began to dawn on people in the Bronx.

DAVID HALBERSTAM is one of America's most distinguished journalists and the author of two baseball titles, the best-selling *Summer of '49* and *October 1964*.

Tommy Henrich, playing Lavagetto to pull, was stationed squarely in the middle of the scoreboard in right center. He turned and ran back and to his left—the ball was going to reach the wall, and Henrich went after it. He could have played it safe and tried to field the carom, but if he caught the ball, the Yankees would win and Bevens would have a no-hitter. He went after the ball.

He jumped for it, eight feet shy of the wall, but the slicing drive was over his head, hitting squarely in the middle of the Gem Blade sign. The no-hitter was gone.

The ball then caromed back, glancing off Henrich's chest then dropping to the ground and rolling between his legs as he tried to stop. That was the game. By the time his relay reached first baseman George McQuinn, Gionfriddo had scored and Miksis was crossing the plate. Brooklyn erupted with joy. The Dodgers had won, 3–2.

Lavagetto was mobbed, and broadcaster Red Barber described the scene for the rest of the country: "Friends, they're killing Lavagetto . . . his own teammates . . . they're beating him to pieces." All of them but Stanky anyway. He was still steamed.

But for all the histrionics, all Brooklyn had done was tie the Series. And New York had Spec Shea ready for game five.

Shotton was suddenly enamored of his hunches. Instead of throwing game-one starter Ralph Branca, a 21-game winner during the regular season, he started Rex Barney, whose last starting assignment had come on the Fourth of July.

That was a mistake. Barney had one of the best fastballs in baseball but struggled with his control. DiMaggio homered, and entering the ninth New York led 2–1 as Shea worked on a three-hitter. The Dodgers threatened, but this time Lavagetto, batting for Casey, struck out to end the game. The Yankees returned to the Stadium needing only one more win to take the Series.

The Dodgers had one more magic moment in their pocket. As Brooklyn nursed an 8–5 lead in the sixth inning of game six, DiMaggio came up with men on first and second. He hit the ball on a line deep to left.

Al Gionfriddo, in the game as a defensive replacement, was out of position—he was playing DiMaggio shallow. But in this Series the baseball gods deemed that if nothing

In the sixth inning of game six of the 1947 World Series, Dodger left fielder Al Gionfriddo, a late-inning defensive replacement, made one of the greatest catches in baseball history off a liner by Joe DiMaggio. The catch, made with Yankees on first and second, protected Brooklyn's 8–5 lead and ultimately saved an 8–6 victory.

else the Dodgers would at least walk away with wonderful memories.

Gionfriddo raced back and back and back, then twisted around and stuck out his glove and caught the ball before the low wall at the corner of the bullpen, just in front of the "415" marker on the wall, preventing DiMaggio from collecting a three-run homer and the Yankees from tying the game. DiMaggio even kicked the dirt between first and second at Gionfriddo's catch, one of the few times DiMag-

mactic. Brooklyn got to Shea early but couldn't keep the Yankees off the board as Bevens pitched two and two-thirds scoreless innings and Page closed things out with five innings of one-hit ball.

"We were beaten by a darn good ball club," said Rickey. "Any team with Henrich and DiMaggio is a darn good team. Better put DiMaggio's name down first, incidentally. But here's to 1948 and I'll bet we beat the Yankees more often in the next ten years than they'll beat us." Well, that's what the Red Sox were thinking too. Another season ended with a world championship in the Bronx.

Meanwhile, the real celebration was going on in the Yankee clubhouse, and they were celebrating more than their Series victory. Moments after the final out, MacPhail, drunk and blubbering, burst into tears and announced his retirement.

The players hardly believed their good fortune, and even as Red Smith was writing that "interviewers sought to ascertain (a) whether MacPhail meant it, (b) whether the statement was 'authorized for publication,' and (c) whether he would insist later that he was misquoted," MacPhail tried to back off. At the team victory party he lost control, trying to renege on his plan to retire, getting into a fistfight with a writer, threatening to punch out Webb and Topping, and trying to fire George Weiss. But in the end it was MacPhail who went. Topping and Webb bought him out, ending one of the most tempestuous periods in club history. Weiss, his long apprenticeship at an end, finally took over as Yankee general manager.

In the off-season both Boston and New York tried to retool for the 1948 season. In February Weiss traded Aaron Robinson and a few others to Chicago for pitcher Ed Lopat, a 16-game winner in 1947, giving the team another solid starter. Gus Niarhos and Berra would take over behind the plate.

But the Red Sox trumped the Yankees. GM Eddie Collins retired, and Yawkey bumped manager Joe Cronin upstairs. He'd tried to hire Joe McCarthy in 1947, but the former Yankee manager wanted to take a year off. When Yawkey and Cronin asked again after the 1947 season, McCarthy said yes. Baseball's most successful manager was now leading the opposition.

That wasn't all. For nine warm bodies and $375,000, the Red Sox landed St. Louis Brown slugger and shortstop

Yankee president and co-owner Larry MacPhail greets Joe DiMaggio just after his team won the seventh game of the 1947 World Series. A few minutes later MacPhail resigned his position.

gio ever showed his emotions on the field. Brooklyn won 8–6, and the Series was tied once again.

But this was a Series that Red Smith later termed "the most implausible, most disheveled and one of the most exciting . . . a series that began with two dreary games, included two horribly blowsy but gloriously exciting games, produced two of the finest played on any field and closed with one that was relatively routine." Compared to what had come before, game seven was entirely anticli-

Vern Stephens and two valuable arms—Ellis Kinder and Jack Kramer. Boston was wild with optimism, and the Sox were again odds-on favorites to take the pennant.

Boston got off to a slow start, however, while the Yankees battled Cleveland and Philadelphia for first place through June. Lopat had solidified the rotation, and Vic Raschi emerged as a topnotch starter as well. And DiMaggio, finally healthy again, bounced back with his best power numbers in a decade.

In July McCarthy, true to form, finally settled on a starting rotation. The Red Sox caught fire at last, Philadelphia fell back, and the Yankees, Boston, and the surprising Cleveland Indians, behind an MVP season by manager and shortstop Lou Boudreau and the knuckleball of pitcher Gene Bearden, battled it out for first place.

On August 16, the season paused for a moment when Babe Ruth died. He'd made his final Yankee Stadium appearance on June 13, managing a team of old-timers and wearing the pinstripes for the last time. He looked terrible and felt worse. The Yankees learned of his death in, of all places, the Polo Grounds, Ruth's old home and favorite park, where they were playing the Giants in an exhibition game.

The next day Ruth's body lay in state in the Yankee Stadium rotunda. An estimated 100,000 fans—or perhaps twice that number—filed past his body over the next two days. His funeral, held at St. Patrick's Cathedral on August 19, drew thousands more who stood in silence on the surrounding streets.

Entering September, the Yankees, with eight games remaining with Boston, controlled at least a portion of their own destiny, for they had only one game remaining with the Indians. Not since the final month of the 1904 season had any series of games between Boston and New York been more important.

They met the Red Sox in Boston for three games beginning on September 8, trailing Boston by a game and a half. Each team hoped to deliver the knockout blow with a sweep, and each knew it couldn't afford to be on the wrong end of the broom.

The Yankees jumped out in the first game, scoring four first-inning runs off Joe Dobson, but Boston battled back and won, 10–6. Then the next day New York squandered another lead and lost 9–4.

The Yanks now trailed the Red Sox by three and a half games. They absolutely had to win the series finale on September 10 to stay alive.

With the score tied 6–6, the game entered extra innings. Boston's Earl Caldwell loaded the bases with two out, bringing up DiMaggio.

He was a mess. His heel was giving him trouble, and his left leg was heavily taped. He later admitted, "I feel like a mummy."

With the capacity crowd at Fenway screaming itself hoarse, DiMaggio fouled a pitch back, then connected. The crowd, wrote Red Smith, "made a noise like a fat man punched in the stomach." But the drive curved foul into the net in left field.

Three pitches later DiMaggio hit another ball hard, this time to center, this time sending brother Dom first racing back, then slowing, then looking up. The ball landed a half-dozen rows up in the center-field bleachers, just to the right of the flagpole. "That," wrote Smith, "is the end of the story." New York won 11–6 and stayed alive.

The three clubs staggered to the finish, unable to put each other away, and on September 24 all three teams were tied for first place with identical 91–56 records. But as the Yankees took two of three from Boston at the Stadium, the Indians edged ahead.

The season came down to the final two days, October 2 and 3, New York against Boston in Fenway Park, each team trailing the Indians by a game after Cleveland lost to Philadelphia, each team needing a sweep and some help from the Indians' final opponent, the Detroit Tigers.

Boston was baseball-crazy. Across town the Braves were sweeping to the National League pennant, and Boston salivated over the prospect of a streetcar World Series. "Stay with me, boys," pleaded McCarthy the day before the first game against New York. "Cleveland gets knocked off by Detroit. We take the Yankees. That's the ending. That's my dream. You can't take that away from me." Bucky Harris wasn't quite as inspirational; both DiMaggio and Tommy Henrich were subpar and held together by tape and gauze. "I didn't think Cleveland would blow it," he sighed. "Maybe it's a good sign."

For once, Williams bettered DiMaggio. In the first game of the Series he cracked a two-run homer off Tommy Byrne in the first inning, and Jack Kramer slammed the door, scattering five hits. DiMaggio gave the Yankees their last chance in the seventh, cracking a double and, as one scribe noted, dragging his left leg behind him "like a wounded animal." Despite the 5–1 lead, no one left Fenway until Kramer retired DiMaggio in the ninth. Boston won and knocked New York from the race.

After the game there was some grumbling over Harris's decision to start Tommy Byrne. He'd been pitching well recently, but Allie Reynolds was rested and had shut down the Red Sox the last time he faced them.

Now it didn't matter. As far as the pennant was concerned, the final game was meaningless for New York. But Boston, with a win and a Cleveland loss, could still tie for the pennant.

There was no real reason for DiMaggio to play in the final game — he belonged in bed, not in center field, but relations between the Red Sox and Yankees had hardened over the past three years. The presence of McCarthy in the Boston dugout, Dom DiMaggio in center field, and Williams, DiMaggio's only rival, in the Red Sox lineup meant there was more at stake than just the pennant. The rivalry between the two clubs was beginning to take on an added dimension not always reflected in either the box score or the final standings. The Yankees had lost the pennant, but they could still have a say in who would win. Joe spent the night in his brother's suburban Boston home, and as the two DiMaggio brothers rode together to the ballpark on the morning of October 3, Joe threw down the gauntlet. He told Dominic the Yankees would win and knock the Red Sox out, adding, "I personally guarantee it." Ticked off, Dominic fired back, "I might have something to do with that."

Boston would not be denied. After falling behind 2–0, the Red Sox exploded for five runs in the third and pushed on to win, 10–6. Dom DiMaggio proved prophetic, cracking a home run in the sixth to help put the game — and some champagne — on ice.

But Joe DiMaggio still made good on his promise. He was magnificent, going four for five and keeping the Yankees in the game all by himself, ending his season with a ninth-inning single and then leaving the game because he could barely run. Even the Boston crowd was impressed and gave him one of the greatest ovations they have ever given an opposing player. As Red Smith wrote afterward:

"Sometimes a fellow gets a little tired of writing about DiMaggio; a fellow thinks 'There must be another ballplayer in the world worth mentioning.' But there isn't really, not worth mentioning in the same breath as Joe DiMaggio."

For all the while, in fear of what DiMaggio might inspire, Joe McCarthy had kept his bullpen working, and swingman Denny Galehouse throwing six long innings in the pen. When McCarthy pitched Galehouse against Cleveland in the playoff the next day, he was bombed, beaten by the six innings he spent throwing to a phantom the day before.

In New York reaction to the Yankee loss was swift. Weiss, with the blessing of Topping and Webb, fired Harris. He was too remote and too reserved. Besides, he was MacPhail's hire; Weiss wanted his own man. The manager was stunned, saying later he felt as if he'd been "socked in the head with a steel pipe." Yankee observers felt the same way a few days later when they learned that Weiss was considering hiring Casey Stengel as the team's new manager.

Everyone thought it was a joke. Stengel, despite a fine career as a player, had a managerial résumé that hardly inspired envy. He had served as manager of the Brooklyn Dodgers from 1934 to 1936 and the Boston Braves from 1938 to 1943, finishing above .500 only once (barely) and never topping fifth place. Of course, he hadn't had much to work with in either place. The press in both cities had considered him something of a clown, for Stengel, a man who as a player had once carried a sparrow onto the field beneath his cap and then released it with a flourish, made people laugh even when he was trying to be serious.

Boston writer Harold Kaese had noted that when Stengel managed the Braves, it had been "more fun losing with Stengel than winning with someone else." But others thought Stengel's comedic mix of malaprops and misdirection was an act, and a tired one. When Stengel was hit by a cab during his last year in Boston, broke his leg, and missed the first two months of the season, columnist Dave Egan named the cabby the "man who did the most for Boston in 1943."

George Weiss, who had known Stengel since his days in the Eastern League, had hired him to manage New York's Kansas City farm club in 1945. After being let go when

MacPhail took over, Stengel went on to manage Oakland in the PCL. He won a championship in 1948 — his first ever as a manager — with a veteran club that local writers referred to as "the Nine Old Men." Which made Stengel, already 58, well, ancient.

Yet he'd proved his managerial mettle in Oakland. His players loved him. The Yankees had a working agreement with Oakland, and Stengel had played a role in the development of Spec Shea, taught Gene Bearden the knuckler (only to watch the Yankees sell him to Cleveland), and made a young infielder named Billy Martin his special project. There was nothing funny about any of that.

Rumors that Stengel was going to be hired swirled around New York for several days before Weiss made it official and formally introduced Stengel to the New York press at the 21 Club, 25 years to the day after he'd hit two home runs against the Yankees in the 1923 World Series.

Most of the New York press contingent knew Stengel from his tenure at Brooklyn and personally liked him. He was great company, didn't mind a drink or two, and had seen it all during a lifetime in baseball. He could tell stories all night, and often did.

But they didn't think he was right for this job. The beat writers liked to think of themselves as part of the club, carriers in their own way of the Yankee tradition. If Stengel was now part of that, what did that make them? Most thought Stengel had been hired as a pleasant caretaker to keep the seat warm until Weiss rebuilt. Then he'd hire a real manager.

But Weiss, who liked to say that the press could be bought "with a five-dollar steak," didn't care what they thought. He'd done his homework on Stengel. Those who'd played for him or managed against him knew he had a shrewd baseball mind.

In Boston news of Stengel's hiring caused a near-celebration. Egan wrote giddily that "the Yankees have now been mathematically eliminated from the 1949 pennant race." Put off by that reaction, Stengel said, "This is a $5 million business. They don't hand out jobs like this because you're a friend."

History would prove him correct, for Stengel's baseball genealogy and intelligence was equal to that of anyone in the game. He'd been a better player than many gave him credit for, had made a fortune in the stock market, and

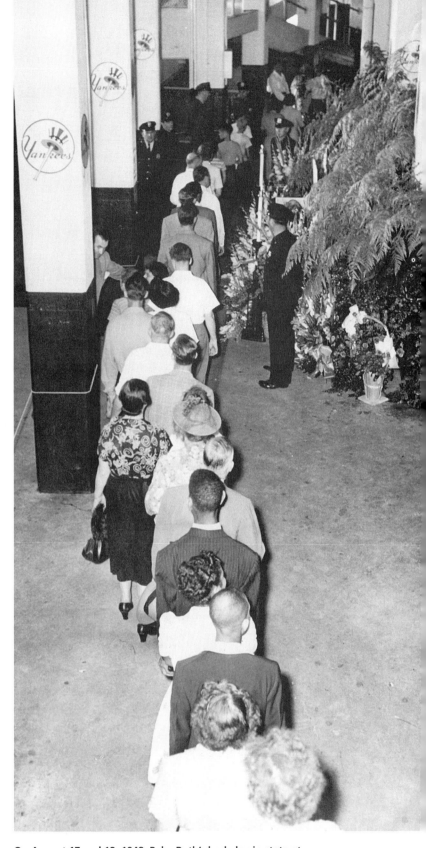

On August 17 and 18, 1948, Babe Ruth's body lay in state at Yankee Stadium, and more than 100,000 fans paid their last respects. His funeral was held on August 19 at St. Patrick's Cathedral on Fifth Avenue, where thousands also gathered.

YANKEE AMERICAN LEAGUE
STRIKEOUT LEADERS

1932 Red Ruffing, 190

1933 Lefty Gomez, 163

1934 Lefty Gomez, 158

1937 Lefty Gomez, 194

1951 Vic Raschi, 164

1952 Allie Reynolds, 160

1964 Al Downing, 217

comes a time in every man's life, and I've had plenty of them." And each had a story attached.

Stengel's task wasn't going to be easy, though, a point made clear to him when Joe DiMaggio went under the knife in November, this time to remove spurs on his right heel. Doctors claimed that he'd be fine by spring training, but that's what they'd said the last time.

Weiss made only one significant move in the off-season, at least only one that ever made it to the field. In December he paid the Browns $100,000 and some names for hard-luck pitcher Fred Sanford and catcher Roy Partee. Former Brown Jack Kramer had come through for the Red Sox in 1948, and Weiss hoped Sanford would prove similarly successful.

The Yankees also made their first excursion into the Negro Leagues. Pressure was mounting on the club to sign a black player, and that's precisely the approach they took.

An unsigned Yankee scouting report in the files of the National Baseball Hall of Fame mentions both Piper Davis and Artie Wilson. While it identifies them both as "good ball players," the report also states:

There isn't an outstanding Negro player that anybody could recommend to step in[to] the big leagues and hold down a regular job. . . . I know of not one that would stick. If they come up with certain players please advise me and I will give you the low down on them. . . . I am aware of how these committees apply pressure on the big leagues to hire one or perhaps two players. If you hire one or two, they will want you to hire another one.

Wilson, then a 28-year-old shortstop with the versatility to play other infield positions, had hit .402 for Birmingham in 1948. He was a left-handed line-drive hitter who went the opposite way to such a degree that opponents sometimes pulled a shift on him. In January scout Tom Greenwade reached an agreement with Black Baron president Tom Hayes to purchase Wilson's contract and reportedly spoke to Wilson in Puerto Rico. Wilson agreed to play in Newark for $500 a month.

At least, that's what the Yankees claimed. Because when it came time for Wilson to sign on February 4, he balked. He'd made $750 a month in Birmingham and was no fool—he didn't intend to take a pay cut or, as he put it,

he'd been taught the game of baseball by the best, John McGraw, who in turn had learned the game from Ned Hanlon, the legendary manager of the Baltimore Orioles in the 1890s. Stengel had learned baseball in the Dead Ball Era and been active as a player when Ruth had turned the home run into a national institution. He'd seen the game change and had more than a few ideas about how it should be played. This was, he knew, an incredible opportunity, one that, at close to age 60, he had not expected to be offered. He was determined to make the most of it. After all, he had nothing to lose, no reputation to protect. And he knew that for the first time in his life he actually had some players. That had never been the case in Brooklyn or Boston.

But Stengel also served another purpose. He became the public face of the franchise, leaving Webb and Topping and even Weiss free to stay behind the curtain and pull the levers. As long as Stengel was around, the three-man Yankee brain trust was rarely under much scrutiny. Weiss bought off the press, not with a steak but with Stengel's storytelling ability. As Stengel himself said, "There

"go through what Robinson did" while playing in Newark. Hayes and Wilson then cut a deal with Cleveland, where Bill Veeck had followed Rickey's lead, signing Larry Doby in 1947 as the second African American to play in the majors.

The Yankees appealed to baseball commissioner Happy Chandler to settle the dispute, and he ruled in the Yankees' favor, assigning Wilson to New York. But Wilson still balked at going to Newark, and the Yankees eventually sold him to PCL Oakland, where, as the Oaks' first black player, he became a star and eventually the roommate and close friend of Billy Martin.

The Yankees quickly moved to sign two other Negro Leaguers, Frank Austin and Luis Marquez, but they would quickly sell off these players as well. Later that year the Yankees signed two Monarchs for Newark, Bob Thurman and Earl Taborn, but when the Yanks sold the franchise at the end of the 1949 season, their pathetic experiment in integration went on hiatus and they considered the matter closed.

At spring training in 1949, Stengel wasted little time demonstrating that he was his own man, initiating two workouts a day and dividing the veteran club into groups for work on fundamentals. That kind of practice miffed Yankee veterans, who felt they were beyond such things. In a celebrated exchange, DiMaggio asked a writer what he thought of Stengel. When the writer responded that he didn't think Stengel had a clue, DiMaggio responded, "That's what a lot of the fellows think too." DiMaggio would never change his estimation of Stengel either, for Stengel would have the unwelcome task of managing DiMaggio in the winter of his career.

Only a few days into camp the tenor of the season changed. DiMaggio thought his heel was fine, but after one day of wearing spikes he began experiencing excruciating pain. On March 2, he left camp to have the heel reevaluated.

That changed everything. Without DiMaggio, Stengel was even freer to do what he wanted. All spring long he experimented, shuffling players between positions and trying out rookies. When it became apparent that DiMaggio was going to miss not only Opening Day but also a significant portion of the regular season, most observers gave New York little chance in the upcoming pennant race. But Stengel was unruffled. When one writer offered

that the best New York could hope for was a third-place finish behind Boston and Cleveland, Stengel quipped, "Third ain't so bad. I never finished third before. That's pretty high up."

DiMaggio's injury forced Stengel to freelance, and on a team made up of primarily role players and good starting pitching, that's just what he had to do. A set lineup would only expose New York's weaknesses, so Stengel used the only strength the club had — depth.

He moved rookie Jerry Coleman from short to second. With Coleman paired with Rizzuto, the Yankees suddenly had their best double-play combo in years. At third Stengel platooned right-handed hitter Billy Johnson and lefty-swinging rookie Bobby Brown, getting the most out of each man and milking more than 100 runs and 100 RBIs from a position in which the Yankees appeared weak. He saved Henrich's legs and filled a hole by moving him to first. Berra, whom Stengel had handed to Bill Dickey in the spring, was finally coming around behind the plate, and in the outfield he mixed and matched Gene Woodling, Cliff Mapes, Hank Bauer, Lindell, and Keller according to who was pitching, who was hot, who was healthy, and where the Yankees were playing.

It all worked. The players griped, and even Stengel characterized his approach as "new and baffling," but it all worked. New York got the jump on Boston and started the season 10–2, then ran their record to 25–12 by the first of June. The rotation of Raschi, Reynolds, Byrne, and Lopat was one of the strongest in team history, and it was backed up by Joe Page and his blazing fastball, which had rarely been more effective.

After a slow start, Boston began making a push in June. They trailed New York by only five games when the Yankees came into Boston on June 28. DiMaggio was finally without pain and chose to make his return.

Thirty-six thousand Boston fans found it memorable, but for all the wrong reasons. DiMaggio singled to start a rally in the second, cracked a two-run homer in the third, wiped out Vern Stephens on a force-out at second in the eighth, and ended the game underneath a Ted Williams fly ball with the tying run on third in the ninth.

He was even better the next two days, hitting two home runs to lead New York on a comeback from a 7–1 deficit and stopping Dominic's 34-game hitting streak with a

Rookie manager Casey Stengel (center) leads the cheers in the Yankee Stadium clubhouse, his team having just completed a two-game season-ending sweep of the Red Sox to capture the 1949 American League pennant by a single game.

tough catch in New York's 9–7 win, then homering again in the Yankees' 6–3 win in the finale. When a plane circled Fenway Park trailing a banner that read "the Great DiMaggio," one dour observer noted, "Although there were two DiMaggios present, one was only very good." The sweep sent Boston reeling, and by July 4 they were 35–36 and 12 games out.

But the Yankees couldn't pull away, and by late August their lead was down to one and a half games. Weiss did what he could to help, sending $40,000 to the Giants for first baseman Johnny Mize, an all-star and a career .323 hitter, which gave Stengel either another hitter off the bench or the option to move Henrich back into the outfield. Mize won two games with his bat soon after joining the club, and then hurt his shoulder. New York would have

to go the rest of the season with what it had. The Red Sox and Yankees entered September alone on the stage.

But in midmonth DiMaggio was knocked out of the lineup by pneumonia. He was bedridden as the Red Sox swept the Yankees three straight to pull ahead in the pennant race by one game with only five to play.

The Yankees still trailed by one when Boston entered Yankee Stadium on October 1 for the final two games of the season. The club chose that date to celebrate "Joe DiMaggio Day." DiMaggio was weak and had to be held up by Dominic during much of the hourlong ceremony, which he ended by saying, "I'd like to thank the good Lord for making me a Yankee," bringing down the house. Then he went out and played, telling Stengel before the game, "How far I'll be able to go, I don't know."

Boston was ultraconfident. Tom Yawkey had a train waiting in Boston to bring the Red Sox wives in for an expected pennant celebration. When the Sox jumped ahead 4–0 off Allie Reynolds, they started loading the train.

But New York scratched and clawed, scoring two in the fourth as DiMaggio hit a ground-rule double, then two more in the fifth off Mel Parnell. Johnny Lindell hit his first home run in two months in the eighth inning, and Page, in his 60th appearance of the year, throttled Boston with six and two-thirds innings of scoreless relief work. The Yankees won, 5–4. The season would be decided on its final day.

The game matched two 20-game winners, Massachusetts native Vic Raschi and Ellis Kinder of Boston. On this day both men were ready.

In the first inning Rizzuto hit the ball down the line and dashed all the way to third as Ted Williams first lost the ball in the sun and then lumbered after it in the corner. Rizzuto's teammates had come to expect such play. Henrich, "Old Reliable," then gave himself up with a ground ball to second and New York led, 1–0.

But that was it. For the next seven innings neither team budged.

Then Joe McCarthy blinked, and just as significantly, Casey Stengel did not. Stengel had worked his roster all year long, while McCarthy depended almost entirely on the same 12 or 14 players. With one out, McCarthy pinch-hit for Kinder, and the Yankees breathed a sigh of relief.

McCarthy, who'd lost faith in his bullpen, called on Parnell to pitch the ninth despite the fact that he'd started and lost the day before. He was cooked. Henrich homered, Berra singled, and McCarthy admitted the obvious, bringing in Tex Hughson. After DiMaggio hit into a double play, Lindell and Johnson singled. Hughson then walked Mapes to face Jerry Coleman.

Coleman popped a flare off the end of his bat down the right-field line. Bobby Doerr and Al Zarilla raced after the ball, and Zarilla dove for it but couldn't hold on. Coleman's hit cleared the bases, and the Yankees led 5–0.

Boston tried a comeback and came close, scoring three runs. DiMaggio pulled himself from the game when he misplayed a drive by Bobby Doerr into a triple. But Stengel didn't flinch. Joe Page wasn't available after his long relief stint the previous day, and the manager stuck with what got him there. When Henrich approached Raschi to settle him down, the pitcher barked at him and shooed him away. Then he got Birdie Tebbetts to pop up to Henrich at first, and the Yankees were champions. Again. A headline in a Boston newspaper the next day read: "No Joy in Mudville." But that was in Boston. New York's Casey overflowed with joy.

The Dodgers, with Shotton back in charge after Durocher fired himself and jumped to the Giants in 1948, edged out the Cardinals for the NL pennant. They were a much deeper, much better, much more powerful team than the one that had faced the Yankees in 1947. Rickey had continued to mine the Negro Leagues better than anyone else and had come away with two stars, catcher Roy Campanella and pitcher Don Newcombe.

After each team traded 1–0 wins in games one and two, as Reynolds beat Newcombe and then Preacher Roe bettered Raschi, the Series was decided in game three. With the score knotted 1–1, Johnny Mize pinch-hit in the ninth

Ty Cobb once said he believed that of the postwar major leaguers, only Yankee shortstop Phil Rizzuto and Stan Musial would have been stars in the rough and tumble of the Dead Ball Era. In 1950 Rizzuto (throwing) won American League MVP honors with his usual blend of defense and inside baseball skills (bunting, baserunning), bolstered by a .324 batting average and 200 hits.

with the bases loaded and drove in two runs as the Yankees took a 4–1 lead. Page then held on for the 4–3 win.

The next two games went to the Yankees early. They won 6–4 and 10–6 to take the Series, Stengel's first.

DiMaggio tried to retire in the off-season, but Topping talked him out of it—DiMaggio was, for all intents and purposes, the only big star the Yankees had. But Stengel's profile was rising rapidly.

The 1949 Manager of the Year entered the 1950 season far more secure. Results tempered the dissatisfaction that some players had felt about the lack of playing time, but Stengel got no grief from the Yankee front office. Platooning players kept salaries down, and Weiss had rapidly gained a reputation as a tough negotiator. Getting a significant raise from him was next to impossible—Weiss always factored in the World Series money when he talked contract.

Stengel didn't change much in the spring. He added a few youngsters for depth, but that was about it. And by Opening Day you could already see it coming—the pace and tenor of the 1950 pennant race was already set.

New York opened in Boston, at Fenway Park, and the Red Sox were eager for revenge. They battered Allie Reynolds and jumped out to a 9–0 lead.

"So what?" said New York. In the eighth inning the Yankees skewered five Boston pitchers, sent 14 batters to the plate, and scored nine runs.

The shell-shocked Red Sox already knew it was over. Detroit surprised early, and the Yankees kept pace as Rizzuto played the best baseball of his career on his way to earning an MVP Award, Berra became a bona-fide star, and Stengel continued to hone his new and baffling approach.

He was never more baffling than on July 3, when he moved Joe DiMaggio from center field to first base. Of all the Yankees, only DiMaggio had been immune to Stengel's machinations. But DiMaggio was now 35 years old. The wear and tear of the last few seasons had taken effect, and the Great DiMaggio was great considerably less often in

Rookie southpaw Edward "Whitey" Ford (center), with Joe DiMaggio and Gene Woodling, was a sensation in 1950, winning nine of ten regular-season decisions followed by a World Series clinching victory in the fourth game against the Philadelphia Phillies.

1950. Sometimes he wasn't even very good. And Stengel was the only guy who could tell him so.

The experiment lasted only one day — an injury to Hank Bauer forced DiMaggio back into the outfield — but Stengel made his point again later in the year by benching a slumping DiMaggio in August. The ploy worked, for when DiMaggio returned, he turned back the clock for the remainder of the season and was Joe DiMaggio again for the last extended period of his career.

Boston, meanwhile, struggled early, and McCarthy lost control, both of himself and of his team. When he missed a game on Father's Day because he was drunk, he was allowed to resign a few days later. Under new manager Steve O'Neill, Boston, for the third season in a row, mounted a late charge. But the Red Sox still had to play the Yankees in two critical games in late September. The Yankees won, 8–0 and 9–5, taking over first place from Detroit and pushing to another pennant.

The 1950 World Series, in a sense, marked the end of an era, not for the Yankees or their opponents, the surprising Philadelphia Phillies, but for baseball. The 1950 World Series would be the last in the history of the game to feature two teams without a single African American on the roster.

Weiss had kept criticism at bay in 1950 by signing three more black players — Elston Howard and Frank Barnes from the Monarchs and Puerto Rican slugger Vic Power. But the club was in no hurry to bring any of these men to the majors. Outside observers, particularly in the black press, later speculated that they had been signed not so much to help New York but to ensure that other clubs didn't get them. Besides, once Weiss had them under contract, they could always be used as trade bait. He still played that game better than anyone else in baseball.

What made the Yankees' reluctance to acquire black players even more distressing was the fact that more than a decade earlier co-owner Dan Topping had signed Buddy Young for his football team, the first black player in the NFL in decades. Yet in regard to the Yankees, Topping and Webb were strangely quiet on the race issue. They deferred to Weiss on everything, and Weiss saw no reason to change. In 1950 he didn't even feel the need to address the question or admit that there was any kind of problem. Thus far, Stengel's peculiar genius and a string of pennants had kept the criticism on the fringes.

The Phillies were even worse. Under former manager and ex-Yankee Ben Chapman, they had led the NL in the harassment of Jackie Robinson. Philadelphia had yet to sign any black players, even to minor league contracts.

They'd won the NL pennant because of one man — relief pitcher and MVP Jim Konstanty, who allowed the Phillies to get by with only two credible starters, Robin Roberts and Curt Simmons. Their starting lineup was a collection of young unknowns, paced by center fielder Richie Ashburn and slugger Del Ennis, known as the "Whiz Kids." As it was, they still had to beat Brooklyn on the final day of the regular season to secure first place, which they did when first baseman Dick Sisler cracked a home run.

The Phillies entered the Series on fumes. Simmons had been lost to the Army a few weeks earlier, and Roberts had pitched three of the last five games, including the finale against Brooklyn. There was no sense in saving Konstanty to protect a lead that might never come, so manager Eddie Sawyer didn't. He shocked everyone by picking Konstanty to start game one, his first start of the season.

Konstanty held the Yankees to only five hits in Philadelphia in game one, but one of them was a double by Bobby Brown, who moved around and scored on Jerry Coleman's fly ball. Vic Raschi gave up only two hits to the Phillies, and the Yankees won, 1–0.

Sawyer handed the ball to Roberts in game two, and he and Allie Reynolds matched each other for nine innings. After the Series Philadelphia catcher Andy Seminick said, "Roberts could handle DiMaggio — he could get him out with a pitch inside, but Roberts had to get the pitch in the exact spot inside. If it was a speck off, DiMaggio could put it in the seats on you."

And when DiMaggio came up in the tenth, Roberts was a speck off. DiMaggio drove the ball into the upper deck in left-center, and New York won 2–1 to lead the Series two games to none. The Yankees, wrote Harold Rosenthal afterward, "practically invented the World Series," and they were playing like it.

Back in New York for game three, Rud Rennie wrote in the *Herald Tribune*: "The Yankees, the big champions got tired of them and slapped them into the corner for the third time in succession." Trailing 2–1, the Yankees tied the game in the eighth when Phillies shortstop Granny Hamner booted a ground ball, and they won it in the ninth when Coleman's third hit of the game singled in Gene Woodling with the bases loaded.

With a sweep at hand, the Yankees made quick work of game four, scoring two in the first, then waiting for Konstanty, who came on in relief in the first, to tire. He did in the sixth as Berra homered and Brown tripled in a three-run rally. Twenty-one-year-old rookie Whitey Ford, who had gone 9–1 down the stretch, pitched like "a kid on a boy's errand," in the words of Red Smith. He carried a thoroughly carefree shutout into the ninth before Allie Reynolds helped him carry it over the line as the Yankees won, 5–2, to take the Series.

In three of the last four years the Yankees had vanquished most opponents, and even when they hadn't in 1948, they'd still made the difference in the pennant race. Stengel's peculiar genius, combined with Weiss's savvy work behind the scenes, DiMaggio's occasional brilliance, and the best starting staff in baseball, had helped the team overcome the Red Sox and their own institutional conservatism to emerge from a group of contenders as the best team in baseball again, a crown the Yankees hadn't worn comfortably since before the war.

Over the next few seasons the only challenge to their reign would come from themselves and from their own back yard.

Casey Stengel not only led the Yankees to five straight world championships, from 1949 to 1953, but also won a total of seven world championships and ten American League pennants in his thirteen seasons as Yankee manager.

1951–1956
THE BATTLE OF THE BOROUGHS

In the 1950s New York was it, the center of *everything*.

The city came alive in the years after the war. People had money again. Bebop bounced Harlem. The Beats found the wonder of words and cheap rent in Greenwich Village. Jackson Pollock splattered abstract expressionism all over the art world. Madison Avenue put a price on everything and wrapped it in a nice package, and television brought it into everyone's home, ushering in an age of conformity.

New York was also the center of the baseball world. At no time before or since has one city enjoyed the concentration of talent, championships, and drama that New York experienced from 1951 through 1956. In those six seasons the only games that mattered were all played in New York. New York's three teams won eleven of twelve available pennants and all six world championships. The three best center fielders in baseball called Yankee Stadium, Ebbets Field, and the Polo Grounds home. So did the game's best all-around players, best managers, best pitchers with the game on the line, best broadcasters, best beat writers, best ballparks, best bullpen catchers, best . . .

You get the idea. That's what everyone in New York believed, even if it wasn't entirely true, for success masked most sins, and in New York, like nowhere else, perception is reality. But from 1951 through 1956 the final standings confirmed it in black and white year after year. The rest of Major League Baseball was just out there, like the rest of America in Saul Steinberg's famous *New Yorker* cover, "The View from 9th Avenue"—an undefined, immaterial elsewhere whose only role seemed to be to usher the Yankees, Dodgers, and Giants toward their appointed roles in October.

For the Yankees, the pennant race during these years was like the exhibition season for most other clubs—a necessary evil. They were the organization men—playing by the rules, putting in their time, and at the end of the day receiving their just reward. Not that the Yankees had a particularly easy time winning the American League five out of six seasons, but it took a near act of God—the Indians' remarkable 111 wins in 1954, trumping the Yankees' equally impressive 103 victories—to stop them.

The Yankees never panicked—they just did what they had to do to get ready for October and whomever they would play, just as Brooklyn and the Giants prepared to battle only each other and then endure the inevitability of the Yankees. And of the three New York franchises, the Yankees were supreme, winning five pennants and four world championships on their own. Meanwhile, baseball's other clubs, the unlucky 13, looked forward only to April and then another season of playing out the string in a supporting role, next to anonymous.

New York even dominated baseball in spring training. In 1951 the Yankees traded sites with the Giants and trained in Phoenix. Just two days after they opened camp, DiMaggio made a rare misstep. One day after telling reporters, "I'm out to surprise those who believe I'm finishing up my career," he kicked the dirt and said, "This year may be my last."

The Yankees were caught off guard. DiMaggio's play at the end of the 1950 season had led them to believe that he'd play several more seasons. Weiss released a terse statement that read, "We regret to hear anything like this,"

while Stengel quipped, "What am I supposed to do? Get a gun and make him play?"

On any other team the potential loss of a player of DiMaggio's magnitude might well have created a gap that would take a generation to fill. But no team has ever been more adept than the Yankees at replacing the apparently irreplaceable. They'd survived—even thrived—after the loss of Ruth, and then Gehrig. DiMaggio's eventual departure would also be overcome. In the Yankees' vast pool of talent, removing one player, even DiMaggio, didn't change the water level. They were still full to the brim.

Besides, the *next* great one was already in camp.

Yankee scout Tom Greenwade had signed Mickey Mantle after he graduated from high school in rural Oklahoma at age 17 in 1949, an acquisition emblematic of New York's strength. Saying he felt like "Paul Krichell when he first saw Lou Gehrig," Greenwade thought Mantle had as much talent as any prospect he had ever seen. Yet the Yankees were still able to sign Mantle for only $1,100 because most other teams hadn't seen him at all. And the few that had, like the Cardinals, saw nothing but a scrawny teenager who stood only five-foot-seven and weighed barely 150 pounds. Greenwade saw the future, a player with unmatched speed and power potential who was so eager to play that he'd learned to switch-hit under the tutelage of his father and grandfather. While the Yankees' scouting efforts in the Negro Leagues and the black, rural South remained virtually invisible, they beat the proverbial bushes for prospects elsewhere. Mantle was their greatest prize.

He was raw, but raw in all the right ways, a budding physical talent whose skills had yet to emerge within the confines of the game. All he needed was time.

Mantle kept growing and blossomed in his second season of minor league baseball in Joplin, Missouri, leading the league in hits, runs, batting average (.383). . . and errors—55 at shortstop. Greenwade saw him in midseason and believed that his bat was almost ready for the big leagues. The Yankees brought him up to New York at the tail end of the 1950 season, not to play but to watch and learn how to act. In February 1951, Stengel got his first good look at Mantle in an illegal pre–spring training camp that commissioner Happy Chandler soon forced the Yankees to close. But by then Stengel had seen enough. When regular camp opened, he moved Mantle to the outfield, something the organization had been considering for more than a year. "His speed is big," said Stengel, and in the outfield "he can use it. . . . His arm is so strong that he won't have to think out there."

It didn't take the press long to discover Mantle. With DiMaggio on his way out, Mantle became the designated heir. And like DiMaggio a generation before, Mantle's background gave the press a similar opportunity to indulge in some mythmaking. Just as they'd used DiMaggio to tell the "Everyman" story of the immigrant family, Mantle's background—his father was a zinc miner—became a parable of the Depression. Here, they intimated, is the product of survival, the indefatigable American spirit. Everyone ate it up. The press touted Mantle like no Yankee rookie since DiMaggio.

The Yankees were oozing with young talent that spring. In addition to Mantle they'd brought up former football All-American and outfielder Jackie Jensen, infielder Billy Martin, Texas League MVP Gil McDougald, and pitcher Tom Morgan, who'd won 17 games for double-A Binghampton. Stengel didn't hesitate to give his new charges playing time either—two straight world championships had made him almost immune to criticism, and rookie Whitey Ford's 9–1 record over the final two months of the 1950 season had been a huge factor in the Yankees' championship. Ford had since been drafted, but Stengel hoped to find some similar help from the farm in 1951.

Mantle, Jensen, Martin, and McDougald all played well during camp. Morgan ended the spring with 25 consecutive scoreless innings, and Mantle was absolutely magnificent. He hit .402 that spring with 9 home runs as the Yankees went 22–12. All but Martin made the Opening Day roster. Stengel loved the way Martin played, but the infielder was a victim of the numbers game.

The four rookies were all in the starting lineup for the scheduled opener in Washington on April 16, an incredible turnaround for the defending champions. But the game was rained out, and when the Yankees opened at home the next day against Boston, only Jensen in left field and Mantle in right remained in the starting lineup. The veterans on the team had gotten the message—this was a new team. Under Stengel, you had to produce to play.

Boston, again the paper favorite to win the American League, was spanked by the Yankees, 5–0. On the field the

Gil McDougald joined the Yankees in 1951 along with fellow rookie Mickey Mantle and toiled in the superstar's shadow his entire ten-year career. McDougald captured American League Rookie of the Year honors in 1951 and was one of the most versatile players in team history, playing third, second, and shortstop with equal skill on five world championship teams.

Red Sox were no match for New York. Vic Raschi, who'd gone 70–28 since making his debut, threw a shutout. Jensen cracked a two-run homer, and DiMaggio's running catch of Ted Williams's liner was miraculous enough for him to double Dominic off first for a double play, ending Boston's only threat. A headline in the *Herald Tribune* spoke the truth—"Stadium Setting Again Proves Waterloo to Hapless Red Sox." They weren't the favorites anymore.

The only thing that slowed the Yankees that year was the Yankees. A series of nagging injuries pecked away at DiMaggio, and this time there would be no second-half surge. His bat had noticeably slowed. Pitchers were getting him out with fastballs inside, a place they'd previously been afraid to go.

Mantle emerged as DiMaggio faded. He cracked his first career home run on May 1 in Chicago off Randy Gumpert, and over the first month of the season he seemed nearly unstoppable. Then in late May Mantle began to be exposed. Like most youngsters, he couldn't lay off fastballs up and in. His average dropped as his strikeouts went up.

On May 30, in a doubleheader against Boston, he hit bottom, striking out five times in a row against Mickey McDermott and Willard Nixon before being pulled by Stengel. Mantle was crushed and broke down in tears on the bench.

Five strikeouts in one day were a lot in an era when few players struck out as often as 100 times per year, but Stengel overreacted. Pulling Mantle from the second game turned what might have been just a bad day into something more. Mantle, who was hitting around .300 at the time and leading the team in RBIs, was humiliated. He began to press and swing at everything.

Stengel lost faith, and soon Mantle was in and out of the lineup, platooning with Jensen, a situation that Mantle, only 19, new to New York, and new to right field, couldn't handle. The Yankees foundered behind the White Sox, and Boston and Cleveland were both breathing down their necks.

Allie Reynolds twirled a no-hitter against Cleveland on July 12, but the Yankees couldn't seem to make a move. So Stengel, never shy about making changes, shook things up some more.

On July 16, he sent Mantle down to Kansas City, bringing up pitcher Art Shallock. It was a gutsy, risky, even dangerous move. Since Mantle's five strikeouts against Boston,

the Yankees had played barely .500 baseball. And Mantle, despite his slump, was still hitting .260 and leading the club with 45 RBIs. Yet he was being sent down. That kind of move could destroy a young player forever and get a manager fired. In contrast, earlier that same year, when Willie Mays opened his major league career going one for twenty-three, Giants manager Leo Durocher told him, "You're my center fielder." Mays soon started hitting and never stopped.

To his credit, Stengel tried to soften the blow, telling Mantle he just needed to get some at bats, and telling the press, with some exasperation: "We wouldn't be in second place without this kid . . . [but] he's got to cut down on his strikeouts. He's got to learn to bunt better. He's got to get on base more. That's all, and then he'll be back, and I'll bet you that when he does he won't go down anymore."

Hank Bauer is embraced by Joe DiMaggio after the Yankees' dramatic come-from-behind 4–3 victory in the sixth and decisive game of the 1951 World Series. Bauer's sixth-inning triple drove in three runs to cap the victory in DiMaggio's last game.

Mantle's demotion and subsequent return has since been cast as the most critical event of his career, the transcendent legend-making moment. It could just as easily, however, have been the cause of his demise and turned him into a Ruben Rivera—a footnote in Yankee history.

Stengel kept working the roster, putting Bobby Brown on third and temporarily platooning McDougald, who was in a minor slump, with Jerry Coleman, who was in a major one, at second. The move could have backfired, but instead it woke the team up. With everyone battling for his job, the Yankees won 19 of their next 24, leaving Boston and Chicago behind.

Mantle teetered on the brink of collapse in Kansas City, starting out one for twenty-three. Jolted by a visit from his father, who started packing his bag and told him that if he didn't want to play to come back home, Mantle finally started hitting. The Yankees brought him back up on August 20. On the final day of the month, at the cost of $50,000 and pitching prospect Lew Burdette, the Yankees also picked up veteran pitcher Johnny Sain from the Braves.

The rejuvenated Yankees faced Cleveland in the Stadium on September 16, trailing the Indians by one game. In the first contest Stengel shook up his lineup, according to one scribe, "as thoroughly as an electric fan shuffles papers." Mantle led off, Rizzuto hit eighth, McDougald hit third, and DiMaggio, for the first time all year, was moved from cleanup to fifth, behind Berra. Bob Feller pitched for Cleveland.

And of course, according to the genius that was Stengel, it worked out fabulously. Mantle led off the fifth with a drag bunt hit, then moved to second, and with two out, Feller walked Berra to face the aging DiMaggio. He promptly smacked a triple. The Yankees won, 5–1, to move into first place by .003, a position they made permanent the next day by beating Cleveland 2–1 as DiMaggio scored on a squeeze bunt by the displaced Rizzuto. The Indians were finished.

On September 28, Allie Reynolds punctuated the season by tossing his second no-hitter since April, this time in the first game of a doubleheader against Boston. It was a bravura performance, one made memorable when Berra dropped Ted Williams's foul pop-up, which could have ended the game, and Reynolds was forced to get Williams

out twice—on another pop-up that this time Berra caught. In the second game DiMaggio crashed a home run off Chuck Stobbs, his 361st and the last regular season blast of his career, as the Yanks won 11–3, clinching the pennant.

But the casual fan in New York can be forgiven if the Yankees' surge left no lasting memory. The Dodgers and Giants were engaged in one of the great pennant finishes in NL history. When the Giants made a late charge to tie Brooklyn, the end of the regular season found all three New York teams still playing.

The Dodgers and Giants squared off in a best-of-three playoff to decide who would play the Yankees. As the Yankees waited, many players went to one or more games on something of a personal scouting mission. They were already confident of eventual victory no matter who won the NL pennant. They'd had time to prepare for the Series and knew that whichever team they eventually faced would probably be exhausted by the ordeal.

The Giants won the pennant on Bobby Thomson's game-winning blast off Ralph Branca in game three at the Polo Grounds. The home run blast is one of baseball's most enduring moments, made even more notable by the recent claim that the Giants' late-season charge and Thomson's home run benefited from some illegal sign stealing.

The Giants' momentum carried them into the World Series. In the fifth inning of game one they became the prohibitive favorite when Willie Mays lofted a routine fly ball to right-center field.

Mantle took off after the drive as DiMaggio drifted over. He called for the ball, for the center fielder always has the right of way. Mantle pulled up sharply to avoid interfering with the catch, and his spikes caught on the rubber cover of an outfield drain. He dropped as if shot.

The ligaments of his right knee were torn apart, the first of a series of debilitating injuries that would cast a "what if?" pall over the remainder of his remarkable career. Mantle, despite suffering from osteomyelitis, a bone disease, was blessed with incredible speed. The Yankees claimed that they had timed him from home to first in 3.0 seconds from the left side, and 3.1 from the right side. While those figures are certainly exaggerated (world-class sprinters, even today, don't approach those numbers), it is equally true that Mantle could turn routine grounders into hits. After the injury, Mantle's vaunted speed would never fully return, and subsequent injuries to his knees would eventually rob him of his speed altogether.

Dependable Hank Bauer took over for Mantle, but his loss was huge. DiMaggio, by all accounts, just wasn't DiMaggio anymore, a point driven home by a cruel but essentially accurate scouting report by Dodger scout Andy High that appeared in *Life* magazine before the Series. DiMaggio's reflexes, he wrote, "are very slow and he can't pull a good fastball at all." The Giants swept to victory in game one of the Series at the Stadium, 5–1, before losing game two, 3–1. Crossing over the Harlem River to the Polo Grounds for the next three games, the Giants still oozed with confidence. All the signs — in every way — pointed to a National League victory.

But games three through five demonstrated that if any club was stealing signs in the Polo Grounds, it was the Yankees. After the Yankees dropped game three 6–2 to fall behind in the Series, Giants pitching was suddenly no mystery. With the score 2–1 in the Yankees' favor in game four, DiMaggio finally emerged, cracking a two-run home run — pulled to left — to put New York up 4–1.

DiMaggio relished the hit, which came on a slow curve and with a 34-ounce bat in his hands, one ounce lighter than the bat he generally used. His hit was even more significant than the score indicated, for the entire Series turned at that point. Mantle was gone, but DiMaggio, suddenly and inexplicably, was back.

In game five the Yankees hit like they knew what was coming, while the Giants appeared clueless against Reynolds. The Yanks won 13–1 to take command. Back in the Stadium for game six, Raschi stood tall and the Yanks held on for a 4–3 win. DiMaggio, in the last at bat of his major league career, doubled to right-center.

In the end all the Giants had won was, like the 1947 Dodgers, an enduring place in history. The Yankees were world champions again, their ninth title with DiMaggio in the lineup.

October in New York City in the fifties meant baseball at Yankee Stadium. Here, television cameras perched in the press box train their lenses on action between the Dodgers and the Yankees in the 1952 World Series. The television exposure helped the Yankees attract suburban fans in a time of changing demographics in New York.

1956

After the game his teammates gathered around him, asking him to autograph all sorts of equipment, guessing that he wouldn't play a major league game again. After participating in a postseason tour of Japan, he made his retirement official on December 11 at the ballclub's Fifth Avenue offices, closing his prepared statement by saying simply, "I've played my last game of ball." Moments after he finished the press conference, a power outage cut the lights. DiMaggio was off the stage, and the curtain drawn on his career.

Joe DiMaggio may not have been a happy man, or even a very pleasant one most of the time, but for nine innings of every game of the baseball season DiMaggio was often, in the estimation of his teammates and opponents, the best player on the field, the best player in the game, and the one they most often credited with making the difference between winning and losing. Moreover, he had the record to prove it. If winning is the best measure of a player, the Yankees' nine world championships and ten pennants in DiMaggio's thirteen seasons speak volumes, as does the Yankees' 1,272–724 record, a .637 winning percentage, during his tenure. Few players in baseball history, not even those with the gaudiest personal statistics, have approached those figures.

But these were the Yankees. Just as they had moved on after losing Ruth and after losing Gehrig, they would do the same after losing DiMaggio.

Mantle's knee injury left open the question of who would take over in center field — no one was certain how his knee would hold up. Today he would probably have undergone arthroscopic surgery and then a closely monitored program of rehabilitation. Back then, Mantle had to undergo a much more invasive operation, after which doctors put his leg in a cast, took it off after six weeks, gave him some exercises to do, and let him be.

Mantle never bothered to do the exercises, and the Yankees never checked to see whether he did. While Mantle's legacy of injuries is one tragedy, a greater one is his cavalier attitude toward his own health, stemming from his morbid belief that he would die young. And the Yankees' failure to monitor his recovery, while not unique in baseball at the time, was just stupid. But under Weiss, players were merely products, replaceable and interchangeable.

In spring training Stengel decided to open the season with Jensen in center, but when the Yankees got off to a slow start, he became impatient. The club made a rare bad trade in early May, sending Jensen, Spec Shea, and a couple of prospects to Washington for veteran Irv Noren, who gave the team nothing more than Jensen had but who lacked Jensen's power and potential. Entering June, the Yankees were barely playing .500 baseball, and little was going their way. Jerry Coleman had been drafted into the service. Bobby Brown was right behind him.

Thank God for Gil McDougald. The 1951 AL Rookie of the Year would prove to be perhaps the most valuable Yankee of all during much of the next decade. McDougald could play third, second, and short with equal facility and provide enough offense at each position. He gave New York a huge advantage — whenever they lost a player at any infield position and there was no one ready to take over in the farm system or available in trade, McDougald filled the position and the Yankee machine chugged forward without missing a beat. Signed off the San Francisco sandlots for $500, he was another example of the strength of the Yankee scouting system. In 1952 he split time between third and second, rendering the loss of Brown and Coleman insignificant.

And then there was Billy Martin. A favorite of Stengel's since their days together in Oakland, Martin brought some fire to New York's normally steely mode of play. After Martin recovered from an ankle injury, Stengel put him in at second base, allowing McDougald to return to third.

All the pieces were in place, but Stengel kept tweaking the lineup, looking for the right mix. On May 22, he moved Mantle to center field. Mantle started hitting, and as pitchers became more concerned about him, Yogi Berra also started to hit.

Berra's nickname had nothing to do with being Hindu — when he was growing up, other kids thought he looked goofy and thought "Yogi" was a goofy word that fit. But there was nothing goofy about the way he played baseball. He was unique for more than his appearance. He was a catcher who could hit, giving the Yankees some offense where few other teams, apart from the Dodgers with Roy Campanella, received much of a boost. In mid-June he went on a power surge, hitting 10 home runs in 12 games. He and Mantle were answering the question Stengel had posed earlier in the year, "Whose gonna hit the home runs now that Joe DiMaggio is gone?" No catcher in the American League came close to his production, or his value, and he had evolved into a better-than-average receiver.

The Yankees opened June by winning 15 of 18 and pulling ahead of Cleveland. But in September the odds seemed to favor Cleveland, for the Indians would play 20 of 22 at home while the Yankees spent most of the month on the road. The two clubs had only one game remaining against each other, on September 14, a critical makeup game for an earlier rainout.

The Indians trailed by only one and a half games, and manager Al Lopez had earmarked the game for weeks by going with a three-man rotation so that the Yankees would face Mike Garcia, who had already beaten them four times. When a reporter asked Stengel what he thought of Lopez's strategy, Stengel responded, "I always heard it couldn't be done, but sometimes it don't always work." Exactly.

That was the difference between the Yankees and everyone else. Other teams panicked and the Yankees didn't. They always had an answer. While there's a tendency to view the Yankees of this era solely in terms of their power and their dependence on Berra and Mantle, they were more than that. New York also excelled at the little game—

"A STRANGE FELLOW OF REMARKABLE ABILITIES"

Yogi Berra is best known for his patented "Yogi-isms"—"It ain't over till it's over," "It's like déjà vu all over again," "We made too many wrong mistakes"—but his comic comments obscured his on-field accomplishments. As a ballplayer, he was unique and memorable. It was Casey Stengel who summed up Berra best when he described the catcher as "a rather strange fellow of remarkable abilities."

Berra grew up in an Italian ghetto of St. Louis known as Dago Hill. Even as a child, he was odd-looking, his ears, hands, and arms out of proportion to his body. Only five-foot-eight, he was squat and stocky and looked awkward and slow.

Yet he was neither. Like Honus Wagner, his appearance belied his talent. He was quick and, for his size, remarkably powerful. The ability of Yankee scouts to see beyond his appearance is yet another instance of their acumen. He signed for only $500 after both the Cardi-

nals and the Dodgers passed on paying so much.

He paid the Yankees back a thousand times over. Berra was that rare commodity who was invaluable in Yankee Stadium— a catcher who hit left-handed. The Yankees loved his bat, which earned him a promotion to New York in 1946 at age 21, but they weren't sure whether he'd ever develop into a good catcher. He couldn't block pitches in the dirt, his arm was erratic, and he couldn't call a game. But he had the raw skills. The Giants once offered MacPhail $50,000 for Berra, and according to some reports, the Yankees backed off a proposed trade of DiMaggio for Ted Williams when the Red Sox insisted that Berra be added to the deal.

Bill Dickey, to paraphrase Berra, "taught him what he didn't know." Dickey took Berra to school, taking his raw talent and turning him into a catcher. By 1949 his instruction and Berra's work ethic had created one of the better catchers in baseball. He just kept getting better and, like Dickey, helped a host of pitchers achieve career years with the Yankees.

On offense he was the bridge between DiMaggio and Mantle, one of the best-slugging little men in the history of the game, cracking a total of 358 career home runs. He was even named American League MVP in 1951, 1954, and 1955, albeit by slender margins. Some later criti-

cized his awards as examples of the press simply finding someone on the Yankees to reward, and in 1954 he also benefited from some split votes for a number of Cleveland Indians and latent racism in regard to Larry Doby. Nevertheless, a player doesn't win three MVP Awards by accident. On the short list of baseball's greatest catchers, Berra belongs right up there with Dickey, Mickey Cochrane, Josh Gibson, Johnny Bench, Ivan Rodriguez, and Mike Piazza.

There's nothing funny about that.

YANKEE AMERICAN LEAGUE
ROOKIES
OF THE YEAR

1951 Gil McDougald, 3B

1954 Bob Grim, P

1957 Tony Kubek, IF-OF

1962 Tom Tresh, OF-SS

1968 Stan Bahnsen, P

1970 Thurman Munson, C

1981 Dave Righetti, P

1996 Derek Jeter, SS

land error resulted in another run. When Lopat tired, Stengel handed the ball to Allie Reynolds, and the former Indian — who was also Native American — stopped the rally and gave up only one hit the rest of the way. The Yankees won definitively, 7–1, without a home run, beating Cleveland with basic fundamentals. With a lead of two and a half games and only eleven to play, the pennant was New York's to lose, and they didn't, going 9–2 the rest of the way to finish two games ahead of Cleveland.

The baseball world turned its attention to New York once again. Although the proliferation of television coverage and migration to the suburbs were starting to cut into attendance, the three teams still drew more than three and a half million fans. The Dodgers, taking advantage of the loss of Giants outfielders Willie Mays and Monte Irvin to military service, jumped out to an early lead and survived a late charge by New York to capture the pennant. Brooklyn was near its peak. Robinson, Campanella, Reese, Duke Snider, and Gil Hodges were all in their prime.

But the Yankees weren't intimidated. "Once you took them out of Brooklyn and put them in Yankee Stadium," said Billy Martin of the Dodgers, "they were just another ballclub," a fact the Yankees would have reason to remember for the next several seasons.

The oddsmakers made the Yankees 8–5 favorites. The Dodgers didn't help their cause when they provided the Yanks with some bulletin-board fodder in the days before the Series. "The younger fellows have beaten the Yankees in the chains," said Jackie Robinson. The game-one starter, rookie Joe Black, was so confident, claimed Robinson, that "the Yankees don't mean anything to him."

Yet the Yankees won just as they had won all year. Although the Dodgers did win a moral victory or three and provided the Yankees with a serious challenge, New York's depth proved once again to be the difference.

Every time the Dodgers had an opportunity to put the Series away, they didn't. Black won game one, but in game two the Yanks battered Carl Erskine, and Martin cracked a three-run homer after Hodges left the door open with an error, proving that even in Ebbets Field the Yankees were more powerful than their Brooklyn counterparts. They weren't just another team — they were the Yankees, no matter where they played. Raschi scattered three hits in the 7–1 win.

playing defense, running the bases, and capitalizing on the mistakes of the opposition. Stengel's relentless focus on fundamentals and juggling of the lineup to match the situation gave the Yankees an edge not unlike the one they have enjoyed under Joe Torre in recent years. Unlike his Cleveland counterpart, Stengel made use of his depth, particularly the Yankees' pitching depth, which had recently been bolstered even further by the acquisition of Ray Scarborough and Ewell Blackwell.

In the critical game against Cleveland, Stengel's style and impact were on full display. Early on, although neither team scored, the Indians played nervous baseball while the Yankees put on the squeeze, making plays while Cleveland didn't. The Yankees then put the game away in the third, starting with a single by pitcher Lopat. Two more hits pushed him across, and with no out, Stengel had Mantle try a safety squeeze play. It didn't work — Garcia nabbed Rizzuto at home — but the play rattled the pitcher and the Yankees rallied to score two more. Then a Cleve-

Brooklyn won game three and game five as well, each time going a game up on the Yankees. But in game four Stengel inserted Johnny Mize into the lineup. As Red Smith noted, "The sweet ineffable mystery of Casey Stengel's mental processes were made clear," for Mize, who'd done little more than pinch-hit all season, cracked a home run and the Yanks won 2–0. Meanwhile, his Brooklyn counterpart, Hodges, was hitless, causing clergymen throughout Brooklyn to ask parishioners to pray for him.

Brooklyn entered game six with a chance to win the Series, but Stengel went for broke, bringing scheduled game-seven starter Allie Reynolds on in relief of Raschi and shutting down Brooklyn late after Mantle and Berra both homered off a tiring Billy Loes. That brought it all down to game seven, and there has never been a team better in game seven than the Yankees.

They proved it in the seventh inning. Nursing a 4–2 lead in the seventh, Brooklyn loaded the bases with one out, and Stengel took out Raschi, who'd gotten in all the trouble in relief, and put in reliever Bob Kuzava. He got Snider, who had four Series home runs—three in Brooklyn—to pop up.

That brought up Jackie Robinson, who got the attention of Billy Martin at second. Martin had made the World Series a personal mission—he was determined to outperform his more notable Brooklyn counterpart. With the count 2–2, Robinson lifted a weak pop-up.

The Yankees sighed in relief. The Dodger threat was over.

Except that Yankee first baseman Joe Collins lost the ball in the low October sun, and Kuzava simply watched, for the pitcher is supposed to defer to infielders on pop-ups. Meanwhile, Robinson streaked down the line, and the Dodgers, sensing the ball was in trouble, dashed around the bases.

"For what seemed like a full week," wrote Red Smith, "nobody moved." Then one Yankee did—Billy Martin.

He looked at Collins, saw the puzzled first baseman frozen, and took off in a mad sprint, charging toward the ball, desperate, gaining speed with each step, his hat falling off and his arms outstretched as the ball fell from the sky.

Then, with a final lunging step, he grabbed the ball at his shins. Out. The inning was over and disaster averted. The Yankees mobbed Martin in the dugout for his heads-up play. He'd even had the foresight to make the catch with two hands in case he collided with anyone else on the play. The Dodgers went quietly in the final two innings, and the Yankees emerged with their fourth straight Series win. "Every year," moaned Roger Kahn, writing in the *Herald Tribune*, "is next year for the New York Yankees."

Unless you were African American. Then next year was not next year at all, but far ahead in some indeterminate future. The Yankees' continuing dominance still left them, if not immune from criticism, at least immune from feeling as if they had to respond. Had Brooklyn, with a number of black players, beaten New York, the club might have felt some pressure to answer the growing call that it was now time to enter the modern age and integrate. Yet the team continued to give the topic the thousand-mile stare and refuse to admit the obvious.

The Yankees didn't hide the way they felt. George Weiss had the power and authority, and he stood at the gates, keeping one foot of the franchise securely in a part of the past it should have abandoned long before. According to Roger Kahn, Weiss once told people that the club's increasingly suburban fan base would be offended "to sit with niggers," and that if the Yankees brought up black players, they'd draw black fans. But they were the best-drawing team in baseball and weren't looking for new fans of any stripe, another error for which they would later pay a dear price.

Down in Kansas City, the Yankees had one of the best prospects in all of baseball, black Puerto Rican Vic Power, who'd hit .331, stolen 18 bases, hit 16 home runs, and knocked in 109 in 1952. But the Yankees made no move to bring him up. Instead, they not only denigrated his abilities but also moved him out of position—he played more at third base and in the outfield in 1952 than at his best position, first base. Dan Topping dismissed him as "a poor fielder," even though, statistically, he'd been one of the better third basemen in the American Association that year; indeed, he was much better than prospect Andy Carey, who was handed a starting job in 1954. A whisper campaign in the press alluded to Power's lack of intelligence and his personal flamboyance and womanizing, particularly with white women. The press wrapped it all up in a nice evil package that held that Power didn't have the "right attitude" to be a Yankee. But if intelligence, fidelity, and restraint were required to play for the Yankees, they wouldn't have been able to field a team. Similar indiscretions by white Yankees were continually overlooked and had been for years.

The press rarely pushed the Yankees on the issue, and some reporters were complicit in the policy, touting the party line. Few Yankee writers were willing to rock the boat and do anything that might cause waves or cost them access. Covering the Yankees carried a certain cachet in New York—it was almost like being a member of the team and carried all sorts of perks. For most writers, the race issue was either unimportant or not worth the risk to their careers.

And besides, in a way, the Yankee press corps already had a black player to tout. The influx of black talent had changed the style of play: Negro League players combined speed with power and provided evidence that one style did not necessarily preclude the other. The Dodgers were evidence of that, and New York Giants center fielder Willie Mays epitomized the new hybrid style.

The Yankees had someone who could play that game—Mantle. Inadvertently, he was the Yankees' great white hope. The press wasn't even aware of it, but they assigned qualities to Mantle that elsewhere were recognized and valued in the first generation of black stars. In a sense, the presence of Mantle and his myriad skills provided the Yankees with an excuse, for because of him the Yankees weren't missing out on the evolution of the game on the field. The Yankees weren't missing anything.

And that he was white made Mantle, in the eyes of many, even better. Nowhere is this made more obvious than in the way the press wrote about Mantle's myriad injuries. When he played hurt—and to his credit, he often did—the press always viewed him as courageous and selfless. But Mantle didn't take care of himself off the field and rarely followed doctors' instructions in terms of rehabilitation. Had he been black, reporters undoubtedly would have modified their view of his "courage."

While political groups and the black press had kept up a steady din of complaint, it was left to Jackie Robinson to point the finger in public. When asked on a kids' television show in November 1952 whether the Yankees were prejudiced, Robinson bluntly and accurately responded, "I

think Yankee management is prejudiced," and cited not only the team's major league roster but the paucity of blacks in the Yankee farm system. His comments made no difference to the Yankee front office; Weiss called them "silly" and said haughtily, "If Robinson can get me a free agent who can take the job of a Yankee regular, I would only be too glad to establish a Negro player on our club." That answer was telling, for it was also an admission that as far as the Yankees were concerned, no such black player existed in their farm system and the Yankees wouldn't even consider a trade.

Nevertheless, next year still came early for the Yankees in 1953. With virtually the same roster, supplemented by the return of Whitey Ford, the Yankees played the entire season as if it were a simple exercise of their various ways to dominate their opponents, for they had the best pitching and best hitting in the American League.

In April in Washington, Mantle was canonized. On April 17 at Griffith Stadium, Mantle, hitting right-handed, cranked a home run to left-center off Chuck Stobbs, where it ticked off the scoreboard a full 515 feet from home and disappeared. Yankee publicist Red Patterson claimed to have found a boy who saw where the ball landed and paced it off at an incredible 565 feet, the longest home run ever hit. Patterson later admitted the story was a lie, for he never found a boy and never paced it off, although the ball was hit far, rolled into a back yard, and was found by a boy. Although the story has no more credence than Ruth's called shot, it stuck, and a legend was born.

In late May and June the Yankees won 18 in a row almost effortlessly as their pitchers gave up more than four runs only twice. They took command in the race, and when the White Sox began making some noise in early August, they took care of business. "It's an old Yankee custom," noted Rud Rennie. "In the clutches they beat the teams they have to beat." They took three of four from the White Sox and checked the subway schedule for Brooklyn.

The Dodgers had an even easier time in the National League. Roy Campanella had the season of his life with 41 home runs and 142 RBIs, and Snider hit .336 and cracked 42 home runs. Dodger fans touted him as better than Mantle or Mays, who was still in the service. Brooklyn won 105 games and ran away from the league. The Dodger

On April 17, 1953, Mickey Mantle, batting right-handed, slugged a home run at Griffith Stadium in Washington that was erroneously reported to have traveled 565 feet. The telling of the tale as much as the blast itself immediately placed the Yankee center fielder in the same legendary landscape as Babe Ruth and his "called shot." This photo, taken in Mantle's next (left-handed) at bat, shows the path of the homer.

writers, desperate for their club to best the Yankees, were calling them the greatest team in baseball history. All they needed to assume that title was a win in the World Series.

But the Dodgers couldn't run away from the Yankees, who popped that balloon and took the first two games of the Series at the Stadium. Brooklyn seemed on the verge of collapse, but then Carl Erskine set a Series record at Ebbets Field in game three, striking out 14 Yankees, including Mantle four times, in Brooklyn's 3–2 win. The Yankees hit bottom in game four when Billy Martin was thrown out at the plate in the ninth inning of the 7–3 defeat. The Dodgers were cocky after the win, laughing at Martin, whom Crosetti had foolishly sent home. Out by a mile, he'd tried to crash through Campanella, who flipped him aside like a doll and sent him hurtling through the air. "That boy," laughed Campanella after the game, "ought to learn how to slide."

Brooklyn's flippant confidence lasted precisely one batter into game five. Gene Woodling led off with a home run off Johnny Podres, one of four Yankee home runs, including a grand slam by Mantle. New York emerged with an 11–7 win.

And in game six Billy Martin cashed in his chips. Despite the baserunning gaffe, Martin had been magnificent all Series long, sparking rally after rally and already collecting ten hits. He saved the best for last.

The classic contest went down to the bitter end. The Yankees led 3–2 going into the ninth, but Reynolds, in relief of Ford, walked Snider. Carl Furillo then cracked a dramatic home run to silence the Yankee Stadium crowd. All Dodger pitcher Clem Labine needed was three outs to force a game seven.

But he walked Bauer to open the inning. Berra then lined out, bringing up Mantle.

There was no home run this time. Instead, Mantle made use of the other part of his game, hitting what was described as "a silly half-swing dribble hit" down third. He beat the throw, and Bauer moved to second.

That brought up Martin, cocksure and confident as ever, burning over the Dodgers' comments after game five. He smacked a base hit up the middle, his 12th of the Series,

ON CASEY STENGEL

IRA BERKOW

A lot of people don't know this, but Casey Stengel almost became a Broadway star instead of one of the most successful and unsuccessful managers in the history of baseball, winning ("you can look it up," as he used to say) ten pennants in twelve years with the Yankees from 1949 to 1960, including an unprecedented five straight World Series championships in his first five years with the Bronx Bombers—and earned him election to the Baseball Hall of Fame, which is upside down from his first years as manager when from 1934 to 1936 with the Brooklyn Dodgers and from 1938 to 1943 with the Boston Braves he never finished higher than fifth place in the National League, and in his last years as manager from 1962 to 1965 with the New York Mets in which he never finished higher than tenth and dead last, and which led Warren Spahn, who was with the Braves as a rookie in '42 and with the Mets in the last season of his career in '65 to say, "I played for Casey before and after he was a genius."

Now, if the above sentence is suspect in the august halls of academe for certain run-on qualities, among other grammatical irregularities, it may be excused as simply a meager attempt to imitate a language that has come to be known as Stengelese, and spoken truly by only one person, now deceased, one Charles Dillon "Casey" Stengel.

"Students of Stengelese, which is a live language only superficially resembling Sanskrit," wrote Red Smith, "have endeavored for years to capture in print the special quality, the pure body and flavor, the rich, crunchy goodness of his speech.

"They have not succeeded. The human ear is a wonderful instrument, but not so wonderful as the Stengel larynx."

Smith then observed that a recording is "required for proper reproduction."

How true. I once took it upon myself, in a private conversation in a Manhattan hotel room, to record the Ol' Perfesser himself, in which he discussed his brush with Broadway. It began, however, when I innocently asked him about Henry Aaron. This was in February of 1974, when Aaron was bearing down on Babe Ruth's all-time home-run record. Following, in part, was Stengel's reply:

"Even though Babe Ruth ran me out of vaudeville, I still can't knock him. Now this fella in Atlanta is amazin'. He hits the ball the best for a man of his size. But I can't say he hits the ball better than Ruth. Ruth could hit the ball so far nobody could field it. And that's even with the medicinal improvement today. They come along now with the medicinal cup and it improves players who only used to wear a belt and it's better for catching ground balls."

Stengel jumped up from his chair and, with his bowed, lumpy, but still spunky 84-year-old legs, hounded down an imaginary ground ball that bounded under the coffee table.

"I got an offer from Van and Skank, the biggest names in vaudeville—they were from Brooklyn—to go on the stage after the 1923 World Series.

"I hit two home runs to win two games in that Series. I hit one in the first game and one in the third game. And this was when I was with the Giants and the Yankees were already the Yankees with Babe Ruth.

"Now, I remember Ruth when he was a young pitcher with the Red Sox. I batted against him, and this was before he grew the barrel on his belly but he always had those skinny legs. Well, they figured they could make more money with him in the lineup every day instead of every fourth day so they moved him first to first base but they had a good fella there so then moved him to outfield.

"In that Series I hit an inside-the-park homer to win the first game. I was 33 years old. And I had a bad heel so I wore a cup—in my shoe. The cup started comin' out when I was roundin' the bases. All the pictures show me like this"—head with hunk of white hair thrust back in the hotel room—"and like this"— head flung forward, rheumy blue eyes wide, tongue thrust out from his deeply stratified face—"and puffin'.

"So then the vaudeville guys asked me, could I sing. 'Sure I can sing'"—his voice sounds like cracked stained glass—"'and I can dance?' 'Sure.' They wanted to pay me a thousand dollars for a week. And I wasn't making but five thousand—maybe six thousand—for a season playin' ball.

"I was riding high. But the Yankees and Ruth said, 'Better watch out,' after I got the home run. It was a threat to brush me back. In the third game I hit a homer over the fence to win the game. And I ran around the bases and I made like a bee or a fly got on the end of my nose and was bothering me. I kept rubbing it with my thumb and sticking my five fingers in the direction of the Yankees' bench—Commissioner Landis fined me for that.

"So I began to practice my dancing and I thought I'd be the new Fred Astaire. But then Ruth hit three home runs in the last game and the Yankees won the Series and vaudeville forgot about me and nobody heard about me again for ten years.

"So now Ruth, he could have gone on vaudeville. Hell, he coulda gone to Europe! It was near the end of my career and pretty soon I commenced managing."

There was more, to be sure, but let us leave Casey for the moment and return to the narrative.

Stengel's major-league playing career, as he indicated, more or less, ended in May of 1925 when the owner of the Braves, Judge Emil Fuchs, recognizing Stengel's unusual and brilliant baseball mind, offered him the job of president, general manager, and player-manager of the Braves' new Worcester, Massachusetts, minor-league team in the Eastern League. Stengel accepted but moved up the next season to manage the Toledo Mudhens in the American Association—winning a pennant in 1927. In 1932 he returned to the major leagues as a coach with the Dodgers and two years later replaced Max Carey as manager.

After being fired by the Braves in 1943, Stengel returned to the minors to manage Milwaukee in the American Association, winning a pennant in 1944. He managed Kansas City in the same league the next year, and Oakland in the Pacific Coast League from 1946 to 1948—winning another pennant the last season. Then the Yankees called.

In 1949 Stengel's comical language and his incorrigible clowning (some of his antics, such as when he doffed his cap to jeering opposing fans and a sparrow flew out, were already legendary), as well as his relatively dismal record as a major-league manager, hardly seemed the proper credentials to manage the most famous and fancy franchise in the history of American sports. He was also said to be too old— he was then 58. But George Weiss, the general manager of the Yankees, understood and appreciated that beneath the playful Stengel veneer ground the wheels of a superb baseball mind.

"I didn't get the job through friendship," Stengel said at the Yankee press conference. "The Yankees represent an investment of millions of dollars. They don't hand out jobs like this just because they like your company. I got the job because the people here think I can produce for them. I know I can make people laugh. And some of you think I'm a damn fool." End of speech.

Joe DiMaggio, aloof and strait-laced, had difficulty accepting Stengel. "So what if DiMaggio doesn't talk to me," said Stengel. "He's getting paid to play ball, and I'm getting paid to manage. If what I'm doing is wrong, my bosses will fire me. I've been fired lots of places before. He doesn't get paid to talk to me, and I don't either."

The first time I saw Casey Stengel in person was in a dugout before an old-timers' game at Shea Stadium, in July of 1968. Someone asked him about the lack of hitting in the major leagues then. He said, "They ask you, you ask yourself, I ask you, it's them good young pitchers between 18 and 24 that can throw the ball over the plate, and don't kill the manager, isn't it?"

I was then a young sportswriter, age 28, and was startled and delighted by Stengel's expression and taken by the good sense he made when you parsed through the thicket of his verbiage.

I listened to his insights on baseball and beyond, gleaned from a vast professional experience that began in the minor leagues as an outfielder with the Kankakee, Illinois, club in 1910. Stengel advanced to the major leagues in 1912, with Brooklyn, and enjoyed his best full major-league season in 1914, hitting .316 for the Dodgers. He also played for the Pirates, the Phillies, the Giants, and the Braves, finishing his 14-year big-league career with a respectable .284 lifetime batting average.

Some of Casey's aphorisms, axioms, and wisecracks have become national treasures:

"The trick is growing up without growing old." "Now there's three things you can do in a baseball game. You can win, you can lose, or it can rain." "You make your own luck. Some people have bad luck all their lives."

But his baseball knowledge was impressive, as much to Mickey Mantle as anyone. When Mantle came up to the Yankees as a 19-year-old outfielder in 1951, after having recently been shifted from shortstop, the team was playing an exhibition game in Ebbets Field. Mantle recalled this to my friend, the superb baseball writer Jim Kaplan, and me, when we were working on a book about Stengel.

"Casey took me out to the short right-field wall," Mantle said, where Stengel gave him this advice: "'If the ball's hit at all good, it'll hit the wall or screen, so you might as well play shallow and catch the balls that aren't hit too good. Also, if you're not too close to the wall, the carom will come back to you and you can hold the batter to a single. If you're too close to the wall, the ball will bounce over your head.'"

"I couldn't believe how much Casey knew about Ebbets Field. 'Did you ever play out here?' I asked him.

"'Hell, yes,' he said. 'I was a good outfielder, too.' I'll never forget what he told the press the next day: 'The kid from Oklahoma thinks I was born at age 62 and started managing immediately.'"

In 1974 I published an offbeat instructional book with the Knicks' star guard Walt "Clyde" Frazier, *Rockin' Steady: A Guide to Basketball and Cool.* I thought it would be a terrific thing if I could do the same with Casey. We met in that hotel room where he related his near-debut on Broadway. I showed him the book, which he said he liked, and explained my intentions. He said he'd let me know. About two weeks later a letter from him arrived. It was written in a firm but uneven hand on lined notebook paper. The letter was in blue ink, though the addresses on the envelope were written in green ink. The envelope, which was personal stationery, announced at left:

"Casey Stengel
1663 Grandview
Glendale, California 91201"

The letter read exactly as follows:

"Dear Ira,

Your conversations; and the fact you were the working Writer were inthused with the Ideas were Great but frankly do not care for the great amount of work for myself.

Sorry but am not interested. Have to many propositions otherwise for this coming season. Fact cannot disclose my Future affairs.

Good luck.

(signed) Casey Stengel

N.Y. Mets & Hall of Famer"

Casey died on September 29, 1975, and in time I interested Kaplan in working with me on the book without, unfortunately, Casey's direct help, but with interviews of scores of people in Casey's life, as well as the great printed record of his quotes. The book was published in 1992, with the title *The Gospel According to Casey: Casey Stengel's Inimitable, Instructional, Historical Baseball Book.* It contains also perhaps my favorite response to a question by Casey.

Shortly before his death, Casey was asked if he was ever going back to managing. "Well," he said, "to be perfectly truthful and honest and frank about it, I am 85 years old, which ain't bad so to be truthful and honest and frank about it, the thing I'd like to be right now is . . . an astronaut!"

IRA BERKOW is a columnist for the *New York Times* and author of more than a dozen books, including *The Minority Quarterback and Other Lives in Sport.*

breaking the existing record of eight. Bauer scored, and all the air went out of Brooklyn. The Yankees were champions again for the fifth consecutive time. As Whitey Ford quipped after the game, "I felt bad when Casey took me out. Then I thought, 'Well, he hasn't been wrong in five years.'"

No kidding. No team in baseball history—except perhaps the Yankees of recent vintage, who have had to win their championships through three rounds of playoffs—has ever been more successful, and no manager in history has ever had more to do with his team's winning ways than Stengel. These Yankees were talented, without question, and the pitching staff, although it lacked a prototypical number-one starter, was the deepest in baseball—Reynolds, Raschi, Lopat, and Ford would have started on any club in the game. But during these seasons DiMaggio was diminished and then gone, and Mantle and Berra were just beginning to develop.

They weren't a team of stars—Boston and then Cleveland had the stars. Instead, with Stengel working the roster to perfection, milking production from positions that seemed undermanned and squeezing out as many wins as possible, the star was the team. The players didn't always like it, and they didn't always like Stengel, but they liked the extra check they received at the end of the year.

So did George Weiss. He used the annual Series swag as a bargaining tool to keep salaries down, just as he used the effects of Stengel's platoon system to argue that certain players, like Joe Collins, McDougald, Bauer, and Woodling, weren't regulars and didn't deserve to be paid as such. Stengel's managerial style, the depth and breadth of the roster, Weiss's motivational penny-pinching, and the economic advantage afforded by the largest market in all baseball combined to create a monster.

Their only threats came from within, and in the off-season that began to show. Weiss expected gratitude from the players, and when he didn't get it, he took action. Pitcher Vic Raschi had slumped to only 13 wins in 1953 and returned his 1954 contract unsigned. Weiss abruptly sold him to the Cardinals, making him an example to any other players who decided to argue terms. Vic Power was also sent off, traded to the A's for Eddie Robinson and Harry Byrd, while fellow prospects Andy Carey and Bill Skowron were elevated to the varsity. Mantle's knees required more

surgery, and once again he did little to rebuild his strength. When he arrived at spring training, his legs were weak and atrophied.

In 1954 the American League was divided firmly into the haves and have-nots. Boston, Detroit, Washington, Baltimore, and Philadelphia definitely did not have. The White Sox had some, and the Yankees, despite all the changes, had a little more.

But the Cleveland Indians had the most.

New York's 103 wins in 1954 were the most that any Stengel team would ever win, and the most won by a Yankee team since 1942. But that year it was nowhere near enough.

Cleveland, with the best starting pitching in baseball and the power of third baseman Al Rosen and outfielder Larry Doby, started strong and got stronger, while the Yankees, as Mantle played his way into shape, got off slow, finishing April 6–7. By the time they hit stride, they trailed both the White Sox and the Indians, who were playing as if they'd forgotten that winning baseball games was supposed to be hard to do.

To the Yankees' credit, they kept the streaking Indians within sight if not reach. Their last slim chance to head off the Indians came in mid-September. Cleveland, with 102 wins already, led the Yankees by six and a half games with only twelve left to play.

Fully 86,585 fans packed Cleveland's Municipal Stadium for the doubleheader, and all 86,585 went home happy. For the first time in five seasons one of Stengel's teams lost, and lost badly, when they had to win. The Indians swept the Yankees 4–1 and 3–2 to put the pennant in their back pocket.

But New York would not be without a pennant in 1954. The return of Willie Mays from the Army propelled the Giants to a pennant. At age 23, he hit 41 home runs, knocked in 110 runs, hit .345, and played the best center field ever seen. In the World Series the Giants exposed the Indians, not only beating them but beating them four straight. For the first time since 1948 the Yankees watched.

Then they reacted. Most clubs would have sat pat after more than 100 games—the Indians, for instance, made few changes in 1955. But the Yankees were not like any other team and rarely have been. After finishing second,

103 wins meant nothing, particularly when another New York team was calling itself the world champion.

It's hard to underestimate the degree to which the three New York clubs motivated each other in the years after the war. They weren't fighting for fans, for the constituency of each club was well defined. Brooklyn fans lived in Brooklyn and Queens. The Giants had the edge in Manhattan, while the Yankees' strength was in the Bronx and the growing suburbs in New Jersey and Westchester. The Dodgers and Giants weren't fully aware of it yet, but the Yankees' strength in these areas — built through the power of television and expanding each year — was slowly strangling them both.

They were still fighting it out, however, in the newspapers and in the ego department. For the Dodgers and Giants, winning a World Series was nice, but beating each other was nearly as important. Actually beating the Yankees in the World Series was almost beyond imagination. And the Yankees, while pretending not to care who they faced in the Series, also knew that when they were up against a New York team, the stakes were infinitely higher.

The Yankee pitching staff, apart from Ford and Rookie of the Year Bob Grim — who won 20 games in 1954 — was getting old. Weiss was concerned that it might fail overnight. Raschi was gone, Reynolds had retired, and Weiss needed replacements.

Over a two-week period in November and early December, he engineered a massive trade with the Baltimore Orioles, the former Browns who changed addresses in 1954. In all, 18 players were swapped, 11 players going to the Orioles and 7 going to the Yankees.

The trade rid the Yankees of a surplus of marginal prospects and fading veterans, and the club added pitchers Bob Turley and Don Larsen — both top prospects in their early twenties — and shortstop Billy Hunter. The pitching staff got younger overnight, as did the infield. Phil Rizzuto, at age 36, had hit only .195 in 1954.

Those were not the only changes to take place in 1955. Eight long years after Jackie Robinson made his debut, the Yankees were about to integrate.

Elston Howard, whom the Yankees had originally switched from the outfield to catcher, had been switched back to the outfield in 1955. He wasn't very fast, but he had a strong arm and was fundamentally sound. Besides,

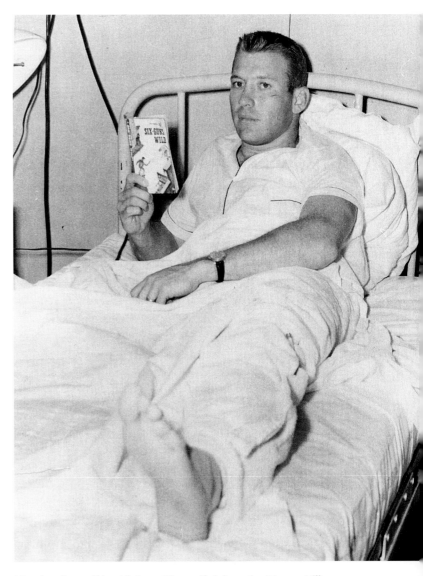

Mantle, after striking his leg with a golf club, rests at Lenox Hill Hospital, 1957. During the fifties he suffered far greater injuries but recovered and played brilliantly as the Yankees reached the World Series in seven of his first eight seasons. In 1956 he won the MVP Award and the Triple Crown, batting .353 with 52 homers and 130 RBIs.

with Berra ahead of him, he had little chance to crack the Yankee lineup behind the plate. The ability to play another position gave him the kind of flexibility that often translated into playing time on the Yankees.

Howard forced his way into New York's plans in 1955 by hitting .330 with Toronto in 1954, leading the International League in triples, and earning league MVP honors. The Orioles had originally wanted Howard to be part of the deal the previous fall, offering to sweeten the pot by some $100,000 and a couple more kid pitchers.

Weiss was tempted, but there was increasing pressure on him, particularly in cosmopolitan New York, where Willie Mays was now the biggest star in baseball. The Yankees were not the only team in baseball without a black player, but the list was getting shorter. The Tigers, Red Sox, Cardinals, and Phillies were all still holdouts, and all, by 1955, were paying the price in the standings.

Ultimately, however, what got Howard on the team was not his talent but his demeanor. In the prejudicial parlance of the day, there were still "good" blacks, who knew their place and stayed there, and "bad" blacks, who were hotheaded and confrontational. In the view of the Yankees' front office, Howard was a "good" one — black but not too black, soft-spoken and reserved, and squeaky clean in his personal behavior, particularly in regard to white women. Even Weiss grudgingly had to admit that if he had to have a black player on the team, Howard was the one to have.

Whitey Ford (left) listens to Casey Stengel in this undated photograph. The left-hander dominated the World Series like no other pitcher in history, prompting writers to dub him Chairman of the Board. Teammate Jerry Coleman called him "the oldest young player I ever saw."

Of course, Howard was savvy enough to know that as the first black Yankee, it behooved him not to stand out or make waves, and that wasn't his nature anyway. Yet he was not blind to the racism all around him. At camp in St. Petersburg and on the road with the Yankees when they played exhibitions elsewhere in the South, he had to stay apart from his teammates. In St. Petersburg, where the Cardinals also held camp, Howard roomed with the Cardinals' young black prospects.

For the most part, his Yankee teammates welcomed him. Skowron and Carey had played with Howard in Kansas City, and a number of Yankees acquired in trade had played with blacks in other organizations. When he arrived in St. Pete, Skowron even met him at the train station.

Other players accepted him because he was a teammate or simply because that was their nature. Phil Rizzuto had served as the Yankees' unofficial goodwill ambassador since he first joined the club, and he went out of his way to make Howard feel welcome, making sure to include him in activities away from the ballpark. Howard jokingly referred to Rizzuto as his "Great White Father." As far as most players were concerned, the question of blacks in baseball had been answered, definitively, long before.

Some of Howard's teammates were more open-minded than others — Gil McDougald and his wife, for instance, later adopted several mixed-race children. But by and large, the players' response to Howard was similar to the response that most people have when given the opportunity to meet an individual — the barriers of prejudice slowly drop away with familiarity. Any Yankee player would have had to be blind not to see the contribution of black players on the teams that had provided their stiffest competition — the Indians and the White Sox in the AL and the Dodgers and Giants in the NL. Larry Doby, Minnie Minoso, Jackie Robinson, Roy Campanella, Monte Irvin, and Willie Mays were not easily dismissed. The Yankees knew that *any* talented player could help them win, and the Yankee players depended on those World Series checks. Their motives may not have been completely altruistic, but the result was the same.

But Howard still had a difficult time. As the team's only black player, he was often isolated. For his first five years with the team Howard was the only Yankee who didn't have a roommate. And he was subject to the unintentional but no less stinging racism of Stengel and the Yankee coaching staff — all men of an earlier era. Stengel's language was peppered with epithets — "eight-ball" and "nigger" — and he would occasionally address Howard in these terms, oblivious to their effect. The gentlemanly Howard never complained. In his own way, Howard turned the other cheek just as Jackie Robinson had done and carried himself with a similarly transcendent dignity.

The presidential opener against Washington was pushed back a day by rain. Howard's impending appearance in a Yankee uniform received little attention, but the *Herald Tribune* did illustrate the rain-out with a picture of Howard, poncho draped over his head, standing with one foot on the field and the other in the dugout, communicating a subtle message — he was almost there.

Most eyes, however, were on Mantle, who was ready to begin his fifth season in the major leagues. Although he'd provided some moments — cracking 84 home runs so far — fans were beginning to run out of patience with their injury-prone young star. Willie Mays, only a year older, was already the best player in baseball, or at least the National League. They expected the same from Mantle. Very good just wasn't good enough.

The next day the Yankees announced loudly and clearly that they were prepared for Cleveland. Mantle, Berra, and Skowron all homered as New York pounded out 19 runs, dumping the Senators 19–1. Despite the blowout, Howard didn't play.

That had to wait until another day, April 14, in Boston. In the sixth inning of the Yankees' 8–4 loss to Willard Nixon and the Red Sox, Irv Noren was thrown out at the plate trying to score from second on Jerry Coleman's single. Umpire Bill McKinley called him out, and when Noren bumped the umpire arguing the call, he was tossed from the game. Howard replaced him in left field and came to bat for the first time in the eighth inning, but his appearance went virtually unnoticed by the fans and the press. He singled to collect his first major league hit and went on to become a valuable part of Stengel's outfield rotation, while occasionally spelling Berra behind the plate, another cog in the Yankee machine.

The Indians didn't run away in 1955, they simply found their level. Too many guys who had great years in 1954 returned to their usual standard — for example, second baseman Bobby Avila's batting average dropped from .341 to .272. Not even the emergence of star pitcher Herb Score was enough to prevent a fall.

Of course, after winning 111 games in 1954, the Indians could fall pretty far and still be looking down at most of the league. But the Yankees rose to meet them.

New York passed Cleveland with a late May spurt, and the two clubs stalked each other into September, when they broke away from Chicago and a surprising Boston team. Mantle, despite battling continuing knee problems, quieted the fans with his best performance to date, Turley's fastball found the plate often enough to provide the club with a solid number-two starter behind Ford, pitcher Tommy Byrne found new life after a tour in the minor leagues, and Stengel excelled at his usual lineup card magic.

The Yankees won the pennant over a three-day period in mid-September. As the Indians were dropping three in a row to Detroit, the Yankees did their usual number on Boston. Stengel said, "It's nice to see the Tigers so wonderful."

The sweep brought them from one game back of Cleveland to two games ahead, and they went on to sweep to victory, winning eight in a row when they absolutely had to as the Indians collapsed. Cleveland had to return $3 million worth of applications for World Series tickets, all accompanied by a note that read, "We're sorry." New York's performance was even more notable considering that it was done without Mantle — he'd ripped a hamstring in his thigh and spent the season's final weeks on the bench.

But the real excitement that season took place in Brooklyn. Time was running out for this group of Dodgers. The heart of their club — Robinson, Reese, Campanella, Hodges, and Furillo — was all on the wrong side of 30. After they clinched the pennant, more than 300,000 fans turned out on September 16 for a parade celebrating their pennant. All were hoping this would not be the last hurrah.

With Mantle still sidelined at the beginning of the Series, Brooklyn appeared to have a good chance. Irv Noren would have to play center field and bat in Mantle's spot in the lineup. Noren could catch the ball, but New York was giving up a .300 hitter who led the league with 37 home runs and a .611 slugging percentage for a .250 hitter with no power.

The Series opened at the Stadium, and New York won, as Harold Rosenthal noted, "because Casey Stengel, an old percentage player, went with the left-handed-hitting [Joe] Collins against the right-handed offerings of [Don] Newcombe." It was a classic Stengel move. He sat Skowron, who led the Yankees with a .315 average, and Collins, who hit only .234, responded with two home runs, knocking in four as the Yankees won, 6–5.

That the two teams didn't like each other became apparent after the game. In the sixth inning Billy Martin tried to steal home and was put out by Campanella with a hard tag to the jaw. Martin jumped to his feet and for a moment looked as if he would throw a punch at the catcher. And in the eighth inning, as the Dodgers trailed 6–4, Robinson, on third, caught Whitey Ford napping and took off for home looking for some revenge. Pitch and player arrived at home plate at the same time, and Berra applied the tag. Robinson was called safe, sending Berra into hysterics as he jumped up and argued the call. Berra still insists Robinson was out, and Robinson, to his death, was just as certain he had scored.

Berra wouldn't let it go afterward. He told the *Herald Tribune* the play was "'lousy showboat strategy,' which cleans up the words Yogi actually used." Robinson responded in kind. "Tell Berra that any time he wants to give me a run I'll take it. . . . [Y]ou can write something about Berra's lousy tag." They shook hands for photographers the next day, but the tone was set.

When the Yankees won game two handily, 4–2, behind Tommy Byrne, the Series appeared over—no team had ever won the Series after losing the first two games. But Martin's comment several years before was cogent. In Ebbets Field, before the home crowd, the Dodgers were a different team. This Dodger team anyway.

Despite the return of Mantle to the Yankee lineup, the Dodgers took three straight. Insult was added to injury on several occasions, as Robinson deked Elston Howard into throwing behind him on one play and then took third, and Yankee owner Del Webb was knocked silly by a foul ball off the bat of Don Larsen. The signs weren't good.

Yet back in the Stadium the Yankees exploded for five first-inning runs and Ford won game six, 5–1, setting up game seven. Stengel turned to game-two starter Tommy Byrne, while the Dodgers went with 22-year-old Johnny Podres, who'd gone the distance winning game three.

This was next year for Brooklyn. The Yankees squandered several scoring opportunities—Rizzuto slid into a slow-rolling ground ball at third in the third inning—but in the sixth it became clear that, in 1955 anyway, God had finally decided to become a Dodger fan.

The Dodgers led 2–0 after Byrne, in the words of one writer, was "beaten to a pulp by butterfly wings." The Dodgers had scored their two runs, one in the fourth and one in the sixth, on fist hits, infield rollers, bunts, and bobbles.

In the bottom of the inning, with two on and no out, Berra sliced the ball into the left-field corner. Dodger left fielder Sandy Amoros had entered the game at the start of the inning because Jim Gilliam moved to second after Dodger manager Walt Alston pinch-hit for Don Zimmer. Unlike Gilliam, Amoros, a lefty, wore his glove on his right hand. And that made all the difference.

As the crowd roared, praying the ball would both stay fair and find the stands, Amoros raced toward the corner, following the ball and fighting the sun. As he headed into the corner, he braked to keep himself from running headlong into the crowd, then stuck out his right, gloved hand.

The ball stuck in the webbing. Amoros then had the foresight to spin and throw the ball back to the infield. The relay doubled McDougald off first for a double play.

There was no way—no way—he should have caught the ball, for Berra was a pull hitter, and a ball hit that far into the corner shouldn't have been caught, but as Podres said later, "It seemed to hang up there forever." For fans of the Dodgers, it still does.

There were three innings left to play on the scoreboard, but the Series was over. Podres made the lead hold. And when he induced Howard to hit a ground ball to Reese in the ninth, the Brooklyn Dodgers, at long last and for the first and only time ever, for all time, were the champions of the world.

It was a stunning victory, one that moved Red Smith to write: "One has to pause a moment and consider, before the utter implausibility of the thing can be appreciated." He concluded, "That's how it went because that's how it was meant to go." And they had beaten the Yankees.

A healthy Mantle might have made a difference, but the Dodgers were destined, and the Yankees' cool efficiency, while nearly unstoppable over the long haul, was not immune to magic. The world title stayed in the city, but the Yankees got little satisfaction from that.

The musical *Damn Yankees* was a hit on Broadway in 1956. In the play the Yankees lose the pennant to the woeful Washington Senators, but Broadway has always been a place of dream and fantasy. Reality was Yankee Stadium, and while the opposition would still refer to them as "those damn Yankees" all year long, no Joe Hardy emerged with a pact with the devil. If anyone made a pact with the devil in 1956, it was Mantle. He finally became the uberstar that so many had long predicted he would become. Enjoying a year of rare health, Mantle was the best player in baseball in 1956 at age 24. Having the best player in baseball on a team that was already better than nearly everyone else hardly seemed fair, but that's precisely the way it was.

Casey Stengel and Yogi Berra express the frustration that marked the Yankees' 1955 season. Despite recapturing the American League pennant after their 103-victory runner-up season in 1954, the Yankees finally lost to the Dodgers in the sixth subway series against their bitter Brooklyn rivals.

Mantle began to make good on the legendary promise of his apocryphal 565-foot home run. Instead of swinging hard all the time at almost everything, he matured as a hitter and became more discriminating—still swinging hard but at better pitches, finally learning which ones he could drive, and then doing so.

He did just that on Opening Day in Washington in his first at bat against Camilio Pasqual. With two out, he took two balls as Pasqual worked carefully. Looking for a fastball next, he got one on the next pitch.

Mantle blasted the ball to center field, where it cleared Griffith Stadium's 31-foot fence, crossed Fifth Street, landed on the roof of a house, and bounced onto the street.

As Billy Martin (foreground) watches, Jerry Coleman stretches for a throw as Jackie Robinson slides back toward second in action from the 1956 World Series. The Dodgers won the first two games at Ebbets Field, then the Yankees dug in to win four of the next five to win the Series.

Mantle home run after another—Mantle, Mantle, and more Mantle, chasing Ruth into September. He didn't catch Ruth but still finished with 52 home runs, a number that had been reached by only seven men before him. Mantle did edge out Ted Williams for the batting title by hitting .353 and led the league with 130 RBIs to win the Triple Crown, not only of the American League but of all baseball. He was near-perfect, as were the Yankees. That word would be used a lot before the season ended.

Only Mantle in the next several seasons and Mark Mc-Gwire in 1998 have ever hit so many tape-measure home runs in one year. Mantle left writers digging through the thesaurus for new phrases describing distance. Perhaps no Mantle home run ever went farther—or would have—than the one he hit off Pedro Ramos of Washington on May 30. With two on and a 2–2 count, Mantle, hitting left-handed, got it all.

The arc of the blast towered over the roof of Yankee Stadium's upper deck before the ball began its descent. Most balls hit that high expend their energy and don't travel for much distance, but this ball was an exponential leap in home run physics.

As it began its trip back down, the Stadium got in the way—the tallest, most distant corner of the Stadium, the filigree atop the upper deck in right field. The ball missed leaving Yankee Stadium by no more than two feet. Engineers and physicists later estimated that the ball would have traveled between 550 and 600 feet had it not been impeded. No one will ever know for sure, but Yankee first-base coach Bill Dickey was uniquely qualified to rate the blast. He had seen Ruth, Gehrig, Foxx, Greenberg, and every other slugger of note up close. He said simply, "Mantle has more power than any other man I've ever seen."

The 1956 World Series was a rematch of the 1955 Series; Brooklyn had edged out Milwaukee to win its second consecutive pennant. And although the Dodgers were a year older and had lost Johnny Podres to the draft, pitcher Don Newcombe's 27 wins got them into the Series. The Yankees were a 3–2 favorite at the start.

At first, the Dodgers seemed to have solved New York. In the first two games they kicked around a series of Yankee pitchers at Ebbets Field to win both games, 6–3 and 13–8, coming back from a 6–0 deficit in game two. The Yankees were reeling.

Then he did it again in the sixth inning, this time hitting the ball just to the left of center where, after clearing the fence, the ball landed in a clump of trees outside the park.

The crowd was nearly stunned into silence: each blast carried—legitimately this time—over 500 feet. Even Stengel was impressed. "They tell me the other feller which hit that tree was Ruth. When his ball landed, it shook some kids outta the tree. The tree's got bigger in twenty-five years."

That's the way it went all year long. The Yankees toyed with Cleveland for a few weeks before surging in mid-May and loping out to a big lead, after which they were never seriously challenged. The season was just one prodigious

But Stengel didn't panic, for now his club was back at the Stadium, and the Yankees knew that the Dodgers had overcome a similar deficit in 1955. He brought back first-game pitcher Whitey Ford on two days' rest in game three — Ford hadn't pitched long in the opener and had had a week's rest entering the Series — and late-season pickup Enos Slaughter cracked a three-run homer as Ford went the distance, giving up only eight hits in the 5–3 win. Then Tom Sturdivant gave up only six hits in game four, another Yankee victory, this time by a score of 6–2 as Mantle smacked his second homer of the Series.

Stengel had several options to pitch game five — none of whom looked very promising, for Don Larsen, Johnny Kucks, Tommy Byrne, Bob Turley, and Tom Sturdivant had all been knocked around in game two, and Larsen, who'd started, had been staked to a 6–0 lead that he couldn't hold. But Stengel went with Larsen again, saying, "Maybe he was just thinking too much about those fences [at Ebbets Field]. He can pitch better, you'll see."

That would prove to be an understatement, even for Stengel.

Larsen, despite a 20–7 record since arriving in New York, was perceived as a typical underperformer, a player with all the stuff in the world who never quite seemed able, or willing, to put it all together. He'd lost 21 games for Baltimore in 1954, and in two seasons with the Yankees he'd never been consistent enough to win a full-time job as a starter. Stengel used him as a swingman, and he'd earned the ire of the front office for his attraction to the nightlife.

But still, of all the Yankee pitchers in 1956, only Ford had a better ERA. In September, while pitching at Fenway Park, Larsen had had a flash of inspiration and adopted an abbreviated wind-up. "That day in Boston I learned that without pumping, just keeping the ball and glove in front of me, throwing with no preliminaries, I didn't get tired," he said. The change seemed to help his control, and it helped him to four straight September wins, but after his performance in game two, no one knew whether that really meant anything.

The Dodgers countered with veteran Sal Maglie, who'd been their nemesis when he starred for the Giants. Since coming over to Brooklyn after a trade with Cleveland, he'd won 13 games and had a well-deserved reputation as one of the best money pitchers in baseball. All the smart money was on the Dodgers to win game five, particularly if they knew where Larsen had been the night before.

For three innings both pitchers were perfect as hitters on both teams seemed anxious, swinging early in the count. The closest thing to a hit was a line drive by Jackie Robinson that Andy Carey deflected toward McDougald, who picked it up and threw out Robinson by half a step. On another day Carey would have missed the ball, and in another year Robinson would have beaten it out, but he

Don Larsen is mobbed by teammates following his perfect game at Yankee Stadium in the fifth game of the 1956 World Series. Not only was Larsen's 97-pitch masterpiece the first perfect game in Series history, it was also the first in the majors since 1922 and only the fourth in modern baseball history.

Yankee left-fielder Enos Slaughter chases pitcher Clem Labine's eighth-inning double in the sixth game of the 1956 World Series at Ebbets Field. Two innings later Jackie Robinson hit a ball to the exact same spot to drive in Jim Gilliam for the only run of the game, which tied the Series at three games apiece.

was 37 years old, in the final season of his career. It was the kind of play nearly every no-hitter requires.

In the fourth Maglie tried to sneak a fastball by Mantle inside. He hit it down toward the trademark but got enough of the ball to pull it into the stands in right, his third home run of the Series. The Yankees led 1–0, and Maglie had lost his chance for both a no-hitter and a shutout.

But Larsen hadn't, and he kept getting help. Mantle ran down a drive by Hodges in the fifth, making a fine back-

handed running catch, and Amoros's drive curved just foul. The crowd started paying attention to the "0" under the hits column of the line score opposite Brooklyn on the scoreboard.

In the sixth Larsen helped himself. After Carey singled, he bunted with two strikes, and Carey was safe on the attempted force. Bauer then singled the run home to make the lead 2–0.

Larsen wasn't challenged in the seventh, when he got three outs on a roller and two flies. In the eighth Robinson grounded out, then Hodges hit a sinking liner to Carey, who caught it at his shoe-tops and threw to first anyway in case the umpire missed the catch. Amoros then flied out, and Larsen was three outs away.

Furillo led off the ninth. He fouled off four pitches, tension rising with each one, and then flew out to right. One out.

That brought up Campanella. He pulled the first pitch deep but foul. Then he rolled a ground ball to Martin. Two outs.

Maglie was due up, but everyone knew Alston would pinch-hit. He settled on veteran Dale Mitchell, who'd joined the club in August and collected six pinch hits over the final week of the season.

Larsen threw a ball, then got a called strike, sticking with fastballs. Mitchell then swung through a pitch and fouled the next one off.

For the 97th time that game Larsen stood there, stared in, and took the sign from Berra. He hadn't shaken Berra off all day, and he didn't now.

Fastball. Berra reached for the ball, which came in letter high and tailed from the left-handed Mitchell, who started to swing but stopped.

Umpire Babe Pinelli's hand shot up in the air, a called strike, and the final memorable gesture in a long career, for he was retiring after the Series. Mitchell was out. Don Larsen had pitched not only a no-hitter, the first and only in World Series history, but also a perfect game, one of only four in the modern history of the game, and the first since 1922.

Stunned, he almost fell over when Berra jumped into his arms and his teammates and a smattering of fans who scrambled onto the field swarmed him. The moment remained frozen in time, not only for the Series but forever. Larsen was almost speechless later, saying, "I don't believe it happened to me. I don't believe it." As Berra said later, "People have asked me what I did in that game. . . . I don't remember what any of us did. I just remember Larsen."

And that was it. Nobody remembers much of what happened next, although the Dodgers tied the Series back in Brooklyn with a 1–0 win as Clem Labine, pitching just as well as Larsen and Maglie the day before, shut out the Yankees and Bob Turley, who was nearly as good. And in game seven Johnny Kucks gave up only three hits, and the Yankees raked five Dodger pitchers, and Berra cracked two of New York's three home runs. Kucks struck out only one

man, Jackie Robinson, in the last at bat of his career, for the final out. The Yankees won, 9–0, to take the Series.

Over the last four games Sturdivant, Larsen, Turley, and Kucks all pitched complete games, giving up only 3 runs and 13 hits in 36 innings as the Yankees became only the second team ever to come back from two games down to win the World Series and resume their place atop baseball. They were the best team in the city of New York, and that meant they were the best in all of baseball. When Brooklyn organist Gladys Gooding played "Auld Lang Syne" while the crowd rapidly emptied out of Ebbets Field, no one knew she was playing a dirge for an era of baseball that would never be seen again.

Mickey Mantle, posing near the on-deck circle at Yankee Stadium before the third game of the 1958 World Series, was the embodiment of the Yankee dynasty of the fifties and sixties.

1957–1961

57...58...59...60...61*

The only noises coming from the Yankees' front office in the winter of 1956–57 were those that come from the counting of cash, the counting of championship rings and assorted other items of good fortune. The rich — which the Yankees were in every accountable way — were getting richer. And their embarrassment of riches seemed likely only to increase with the passing of each season. Eight pennants in ten years and seven world championships set a standard that, to paraphrase Stengel, was new but not very baffling.

The battle for New York was just about over. The Dodgers and Giants, for all their combined efforts, had not been able to break the Yankees' stranglehold in the standings, at the turnstiles, or at the bank. In fact, over the previous decade the Yankees' advantage had become even more pronounced.

Pouring into Yankee Stadium with the predictability of a migrating herd were a million and a half fans, a number nearly equal to the annual attendance at Ebbets Field and the

Polo Grounds combined. There seemed no end to that trend, even as the Dodgers and Giants both operated farm systems that were more extensive and ambitious than the Yankees'. The simple fact remained that the Yankees had the money to sign more of the best young talent, despite their continuing reluctance to sign black players. The Dodgers and Giants were running as hard as possible and still falling behind.

Compared to Yankee Stadium, Ebbets Field and the Polo Grounds were falling apart. Both the Dodgers and Giants, forced to cut financial corners, gave up on their physical plants and drooled as modern stadiums were built or maintained by municipal governments in cities like Milwaukee, Kansas City, and Baltimore. Their fans, for all their passion and eloquence, simply weren't coming to the ballpark. The sticky nostalgia that many would later express for the two teams simply wasn't reflected in attendance figures. Oh, they loved their Dodgers and Giants, Jackie and Willie and the Duke and the rest, but they loved them from afar. Dad took the kids to the ballpark, but only once. The rest of the time he sat on the davenport at home watching the game on television or listening to the radio.

There were several other reasons for the falloff in attendance, not the least of which was the changing makeup of the urban population. The traditional, mostly white, fan base for both the Giants and Dodgers was abandoning the city for the suburbs, and newer neighborhood residents — many of whom were black — didn't have the same long-standing relationship to the clubs and weren't made particularly welcome. The Yankees didn't welcome new fans either, but the combination of a winning team, a more attractive facility, and easier access by car kept the seats relatively full.

Dodger and Giant fans may have loved their team more than Yankee fans loved theirs, but there simply weren't as many of them. Baseball was a numbers game, and the most important numbers of all were those preceded by dollar signs. Passion counted for pennies — pennants raked in the paper.

The Giants in particular were in serious trouble. In 1956 home attendance dropped to just over 600,000, the worst gate in the National League. Already Giants owner Horace Stoneham and Dodgers owner Walter O'Malley were mak-

ing plans to abandon New York for the supposedly cash-rich, sun-drenched environs of San Francisco and Los Angeles.

The Yankees were looking west as well — to their triple-A farm team in Denver and the next best thing, their triple-A farm team masquerading as the Kansas City Athletics of the American League.

After the 1954 season the A's had been sold by Connie Mack's sons to Arnold Johnson, a Chicago real estate man and a buddy of both Dan Topping's and George Weiss's. In 1953 they'd sold Yankee Stadium to Johnson and his brother, then leased it back. Johnson moved the A's to Kansas City after Topping magnanimously sold him the rights to Kansas City and moved the Yankees' triple-A team to Denver.

Johnson made money in Kansas City and showed his gratitude by accommodating the Yankees with trades, all the time thinking he was getting the better of the deal as Topping and Weiss raped his farm system and strung him along with a series of has-beens and never-would-be's. The end result was the closest thing to syndicate ownership that baseball had seen since Ban Johnson created the American League. Although Arnold Johnson eventually divested himself of the Stadium in 1955, selling it to Chicago banker John Cox, his relationship with the Yankees was clearly compromised.

A series of relatively minor deals in 1955 and 1956 had already caused observers to refer to the A's as the Yankees' "cousins." But on February 19, 1957, the incestuous relationship was fully consummated.

Other major league teams had become wary of dealing with the Yankees, leaving the A's as New York's only willing trading partner. The situation was not unlike the relationship between the Yankees and the Red Sox in the 1920s, only this time there was no pretense that things were equitable.

The two clubs announced a massive deal that took several months to be completed. When all was said and done, the Yankees netted the valuable young pitchers Art Ditmar and Bobby Shantz, bonus baby infielder Clete Boyer, and several others. The Yankees gave up Irv Noren, Tom Morgan, Billy Hunter, and others who weren't in their plans for 1957. Lee MacPhail, Larry MacPhail's son and a Weiss assistant, explained: "We've got too many big leaguers and had to cut down. And we were not going to let them go for the $10,000 waiver price," which was exactly what the Yankees would have had to do. Kansas City could have acquired the players for virtually nothing without giving up anything. As Stengel quipped when asked what he thought about the deal, "They didn't put a gun to my head."

The opposition was not amused. Chuck Comiskey of Chicago said the deal "will cost the American League at least 500,000 in attendance, due to the lack of competition." One anonymous New York scribe later accurately described the situation in verse:

> When the Yankees meet the Athletics
> One thinks back to the days
> When half the A's were Yankees
> And half the Yankees A's.

Baseball commissioner Ford Frick, who had succeeded Happy Chandler in 1951, could have and should have looked into the cozy situation and put an end to it. But Frick was in the Yankees' corner. The onetime New York sportswriter had been Babe Ruth's ghostwriter for a time, and baseball's most powerful franchises—the Yankees and Dodgers—pulled all his strings.

The Yankees were dripping with talent again. In addition to the former A's in camp, the farm had provided them with youngsters Tony Kubek, Bobby Richardson, Woodie Held, Marv Throneberry, and Ralph Terry, all of whom seemed ready for the big leagues. There wasn't room for them all, but Kubek played his way into the starting lineup by leading the team in RBIs. Stengel liked the Yankees' chances.

"Never had so many [pitchers] in my life," he told the *New York Daily News.* "Not so many good ones anyway. When I had bad clubs I had fourteen or so but had trouble finding nine who could pitch. . . . I should win. If I have injuries, I can replace the men."

"What purports to be the American League race is a joke," wrote Dick Young of the *Daily News* in his influential "Clubhouse Confidential" column. "The seven teams who do seasonal business with the Yankees should be ashamed. . . . [I]n any other racket, say selling beer, if the competitors marketed such an inferior product the Yankees could move into their area, flood it with the genuine product and quickly put the competition out of business." That was already about to happen in New York, for in the

Once New York became a one-team town in 1958, Yankee manager Casey Stengel practically needed a lecture hall to accommodate the media who hung on his every word.

In 1955 Elston Howard became the first African American to play for the Yankees. In time Howard shared catching duties with Yogi Berra (left) and also played outfield.

NL Young looked for "the Dodgers to lose the flag and New York to lose the Dodgers."

In Las Vegas the Yankees were 2–5 favorites to win the pennant, the heaviest favorites in baseball history. In all ways, shapes, and forms, they were loaded. And that would prove to be about their only problem.

The Yankee players were increasingly taking advantage of their place atop the sports world and were both more than a little drunk with their fame and often more than a little drunk. Alcohol, far more so than drugs, has always been baseball's dirty little secret. Life on the road and players' celebrity status add up to a standing invitation to a more or less endless party. If you were a Yankee in 1957, the drinks were often free and flowed without cessation. It would be hangovers, not hanging curveballs, and brawls, not beanballs, that got in the Yankees' way that year.

They started the season a little slow. Whitey Ford hurt his arm in his second start and was forced to sit out until midseason. Then on May 7 in Cleveland, as the Yankees looked to extend a six-game winning streak and head off the streaking Chicago White Sox, Gil McDougald, batting second in the first inning, stepped in against Indian pitcher Herb Score.

Score, only 24, had won 20 games in 1956 and led the American League in strikeouts for the second consecutive year. He looked for the entire world like the second coming of Bob Feller.

McDougald, only 29, was in his prime. In 1956 he'd hit .311 and taken over at shortstop, leading the Yankees to unceremoniously release Phil Rizzuto. McDougald seemed poised to take over as the premier shortstop in the American League.

Score cut loose a fastball, and McDougald hit it square, sending it back through the box. The line drive exploded in Score's face, striking him flush in his right eye and breaking his nose.

Score had to be carried off the field, and for the next 24 hours doctors worried that he might lose his eye. Fortunately, his eye was eventually saved, but Score's career was essentially over. Gun-shy, he'd never recapture his form.

McDougald was crushed and felt responsible, telling the press afterward, "If Herb loses the sight in that eye, I'll quit this game." He eventually recanted, realizing he bore no responsibility for the injury, but McDougald became a secondary victim of the tragedy. His progress as a ballplayer stalled precisely when he appeared to be ready to emerge as a star. Although he remained a fine player, he never developed further, a subtle element of aggressiveness gone forever.

A week later the Yankees made headlines again. It was Billy Martin's 29th birthday, and Martin, along with Hank Bauer, Mickey Mantle, Yogi Berra, Johnny Kucks, and their wives, went club hopping, ending at the Copacabana, where they watched Sammy Davis Jr. It was nearly 2:00 A.M., and there was a game the next day, but they were the Yankees.

According to the ballplayers, someone in a group of bowlers, out for a night on the town, yelled a racial epithet at Davis. According to the bowlers, several of the Yankees blocked their view and wouldn't move. The argument escalated, and the two groups got up to go and settle things, but bystanders tried to keep them separated. That's when everything that was already a little hazy got a little woozy.

A few minutes later the Yankees scrammed, and one of the bowlers got up with a broken nose and jaw, plus other assorted bruises. He claimed Bauer did it. Bauer claimed a bouncer did the damage. The end result was a big splash in the newspapers and a big headache — both figurative and literal — for everyone involved.

In an earlier era the press probably would have either decided not to report the story or left it in agate type. There was a newspaper war in New York, however, fueled by the tabloid excesses of the *Post* and *Daily News* and the aggressive, iconoclastic reportage of a new generation of sportswriters, best represented by Dick Young and the *Post*'s Leonard Shecter and Leonard Koppett. They were less reverential toward the players and more critical of the franchise, the first generation of New York sportswriters who worked their craft with the knowledge that the all-seeing eye of television loomed over their shoulder. Since their readers already knew the details of the game, they were forced to explore previously unreported territory — off-field incidents, background, and machinations of the front office. Slow erosion of the Yankee myth was the result.

Although a grand jury eventually refused to hand down an indictment, judge George Weiss and court officer Casey Stengel leveled their own punishment. Berra and Ford, who was hurt anyway, were benched. Kucks and Martin weren't scheduled to play the next day anyway — Martin had just lost his second-base job to Bobby Richardson, who was hitting .381. Weiss, who blamed Martin for starting the fracas, fined Mantle, Bauer, Martin, and Ford $1,000, and Kucks, who didn't make as much, $500. But when Stengel was asked why he didn't bench Mantle or Bauer, he said, "I'm not mad enough to take a chance on losing a ballgame."

So of course, the day after the fracas, the Yankees went and shut out the A's, 3–0. Mantle even cracked a home run.

But Weiss wasn't done. Martin was already a spare part, and even though he was one of Stengel's favorites, somebody had to take the fall. Joe Trimble of the *Daily News* reported that Martin was on the trading block. Two weeks later, on June 5, the Yankees made another deal with Kansas City, sending Martin, Ralph Terry, and minor league outfielders Woodie Held and Bob Martyn to the A's for out-fielder Harry Simpson, minor league reliever Ryne Duren, and a few others.

How mad was Weiss? He traded Martin for a black player, Harry Simpson. He was a steal, or should have been. The outfielder was an all-star in 1956, knocking in 105 runs in 1956 and hitting .293.

But Stengel didn't want Simpson. When Weiss indicated that Simpson would play left field, Stengel said, "I'll play who I want." He barely spoke to Weiss for the next three years. Martin had been like a son to the Yankee manager, and the trade was directed as much at Stengel as it was at the players. Weiss thought Stengel was losing control. Stengel rarely played Simpson, who never duplicated his 1956 performance.

The trade's major impact was symbolic, for it let everyone know that off-field actions would have consequences, particularly if the individual involved wasn't a big star. Big stars, like Mantle and Ford — and Stengel of course — were immune from direct discipline. But trading Martin, who was not only Stengel's favorite but also Mantle's constant companion, sent a message to everyone else.

Thus awakened, the club soon went on a tear. Bobby Shantz and Tom Sturdivant picked up the slack while Ford recovered, and Mickey Mantle was putting up MVP numbers again. The Yankee lead over the White Sox was approaching double figures in mid-August and Mantle was hitting .385 when trouble worked its way into the Yankee lineup once again. Mantle showed up at the park with his shin cut to the bone. He told Stengel he caught his leg on the edge of a car door. The club announced he had shin splints. Actually, Mantle had hit himself with a golf putter while fooling around on the golf course with Tom Sturdivant.

He played hurt for several weeks but eventually had to be hospitalized. Although he'd return before the season was over, the leg bothered him throughout the World Series. Mantle, who still finished with a .365 average, 34 home runs, and 94 RBIs, had ruined yet another season for himself.

But stopping the Yankees in 1957 was like trying to stop the flow of water, for Stengel, as he knew at the beginning, "could replace the men." Tony Kubek hit .297 as a rookie and filled in everywhere, even taking Martin's

1957

place as Stengel's designated surrogate son, while Jerry Coleman and Jerry Lumpe plugged holes in the infield. Every pitcher on the team had a good year as the club finished with a team ERA of 3.00 and in first place again.

The Milwaukee Braves followed a similar tack in the National League, hitting more home runs and scoring more runs than the Yankees, as 23-year-old outfielder Henry Aaron hit 44 home runs in his first great season. Pairing Aaron with Eddie Mathews, the Braves had the best 3–4 punch in baseball, and starter Warren Spahn, former Yankee farmhand Lew Burdette (who'd been traded for Johnny Sain in 1951), and Bob Buhl gave the team three starters who were equal—or better—than anyone Stengel had. The Braves didn't have the Yankees' depth, but in a short series depth can be less important than raw talent. The Braves had that and more, including the fans.

Since moving from Boston in 1955, the Braves were the big story in Major League Baseball. Ensconced in a brand-new ballpark built by the county, the Braves drew more than two million fans annually. Every other team in baseball—except the Yankees—looked to the Braves and saw the future.

That included the Dodgers and Giants. On August 19, Horace Stoneham of the Giants pronounced, "We're going to San Francisco in 1958," and Dodger stockholders made their move to Los Angeles official on October 8. California beckoned. "Untapped market" was suddenly the most potent phrase in baseball. The Yankees hardly looked up as their longtime rivals started packing, and Dodgers and Giants fans couldn't bear to acknowledge the Yanks either.

New York was an 8–5 favorite to win it all, and the odds went up when the Yankees and Ford—finally healthy—beat Spahn 3–1 in game one at the Stadium. Although the Yankees lost Bill Skowron in the contest when his chronically sore back started acting up again, a win over the great Spahn twisted the odds dramatically in the Yankees' favor.

But heroes are made in October. Even though the Yankees have had more than their share of Series supermen,

On July 23, 1957, Mickey Mantle enjoyed one of his greatest games as he hit for the cycle against the White Sox. Not only was his feat the first in the majors since 1952, but his inside-the-park home run won the game in the bottom of the ninth.

Yankee general manager George Weiss and manager Casey Stengel confer following the Yankees' loss to the Milwaukee Braves in the 1957 World Series. Within a year they regrouped, and Stengel won his final world title against the Braves in 1958.

even they haven't managed to corner that market. In game two Lew Burdette shackled the Yankees and the Series started to turn.

Milwaukee native Kubek made his hometown bid for renown in game three, leading a Yankee onslaught with two home runs to key a 12–3 win. Milwaukee fans taunted him with chants of "Traitor" and dumped garbage on his parents' lawn, leading Dick Young to sniff, "They [Braves fans] are provincial people out here [with] an illusory feeling of being 'Big League.'" But that one game did not make the Series.

The next one did. The Yankees trailed 4–1 with two out in the ninth against Spahn, but then Berra and McDougald singled, bringing up Elston Howard.

Howard worked the count to 3–2, then, wrote Young, "Real Merriwell stuff. Spahn fired a screwball. Howard lashed with his full sweep and the ball soared well into the left field for the score-snarling circuit."

Then, in the tenth, Bauer doubled over Aaron's head to score Kubek and put the Yankees ahead. New York needed but three more outs for a 3–1 lead in the Series.

Nippy Jones pinch-hit for Spahn. Tommy Byrne's first pitch was low and in, and Jones tried to skip away from

the ball as it passed, then started jogging to first before being stopped by ump Augie Donatelli. Jones argued that he'd been hit with the pitch. "Look at the ball," he pleaded.

Donatelli did and discovered a black streak — shoe polish — where it had struck the toe of Jones's shined shoe. He waved Jones to first. Stengel pulled Byrne and inserted Bob Grim. Red Schoendienst bunted pinch runner Felix Mantilla along, then Johnny Logan doubled into the left-field corner, tying the score. Eddie Mathews came to bat and delivered the crushing blow, homering deep to right. The breweries of Milwaukee did prime business for the rest of the day and long into the night.

But it was not Kubek or Howard or even Jones or Mathews whom the Series would elevate to new status. It was Lew Burdette. The Yankees found his spitball — which Burdette laughingly called a sinker — nearly unhittable, and he won game five, 1–0. Although the Yankees won game six back in New York, they were hurting. Mantle had injured his shoulder diving into second in game four and couldn't throw. He sat out game six and played game seven with one arm.

Burdette came back on two days' rest in game seven only because Spahn had the flu. He was magnificent again, holding the Yankees to only seven hits and winning 5–0 to beat Larsen, who was less than perfect this time. Afterward Burdette, whom the Yankees had ridden mercilessly during the Series, dismissed his former club, saying, "I'd like to play them again next year. We'll win the pennant, but I'm not so sure about them." Spahn chimed in: "The Yankees couldn't finish fifth in the National League." Happy to agree with them were the 750,000 Braves fans who turned out on the streets of Milwaukee to celebrate.

But it was the Yankees' institutionalized arrogance as much as the performances of Jones and Mathews and Burdette that had cost them the Series, arrogance and their condescending view of the competition. Too many wins, too many late nights, too many women, and too many people telling them how great they were led to overconfidence.

Weiss's strategic approach was beginning to show some cracks, although it would be several years before they would become obvious. Depth in the farm system kept the Yankees competitive, and recent trades with the

A's had managed to fill the gaps. But the Yankees hadn't developed a real star since the arrival of Mantle and Ford. And the steady flow of cash from "untapped markets" was beginning to enable other franchises, such as Milwaukee and Baltimore, to outbid the Yankees for the best amateur talent.

Another example of Yankee arrogance was exposed in the off-season. The Yankees now had New York all to themselves. The departure of the Giants and Dodgers had cast free millions of potential fans, and while it would be naive to think that the Yankees could have co-opted these fans overnight, they were still baseball fans and the Yankees were the only game in town. Even if they had shown up at the Stadium to root against the Yankees at first, their dollars still would have found their way into Yankee coffers and a new generation of fans could have been developed.

But the Yankees ignored the recently emancipated and did absolutely nothing to court Giants and Dodgers fans. Incredibly, despite the absence of competition for the baseball dollar in New York, Yankee attendance actually went down in 1958 and stayed relatively flat for several seasons thereafter.

They forgot the great lesson that has always been the foundation for the Yankees' success—the unapologetic and ruthless milking of the New York market. In the end it would cost them.

Yet for the time being the club viewed the loss to Milwaukee and other assorted troubles in 1957 as temporary bumps in the joy ride. Just after the Series Stengel expressed confidence in his club in 1958. Although he claimed the Yankees wouldn't stand pat, that just meant they'd follow their usual pattern. Triple-A Denver, said Stengel, "won 23 of their last 29, so somebody on that club has gotta be pretty good."

Indeed, in the spring of 1958 the Yankees displayed their usual embarrassment of riches. The 1956 and 1957 minor league Players of the Year—farmhands Marv Throneberry and Norm Siebern—were deemed ready for the majors. Throneberry entered Stengel's platoon system, and Siebern more or less became a regular in the outfield. Kubek took over at short while McDougald and Richardson shared second. Howard took on a larger role behind the plate, leading Stengel to comment, "You can substitute, but you can rarely replace." In Howard, said Stengel, "I have a replacement, not a substitute." The losses of Jerry Coleman, Tommy Byrne, and Joe Collins to retirement were inconsequential. Mantle, Skowron, and Ford were all healthy again. At only 33, Yogi Berra was the oldest man on the team.

When the bell rang, the Yankees took off. On May 25, they swept Cleveland in a doubleheader, raising their record to a gaudy 25–6. "Sure, complacency could set in here," admitted Stengel, "but it ain't goin' to." He might as well have started thinking about setting up his pitching rotation for the World Series.

Complacency did set in, however, supplemented by a series of nagging injuries over the final two months of the season to Ford, Skowron, Kubek, and McDougald. The Yankees played only .500 baseball over August and September, but by that time they were so far ahead it didn't mean a thing. They clinched the pennant on September 14.

The Braves, as Burdette had predicted, won the NL again in a similar romp. About the only apparent difference in the Series was that it opened in Milwaukee. The Yankees were still favored, this time by 13–10 odds.

But after the first two games Warren Spahn's estimation of the Yankees as a "fifth-place team" seemed accurate. The Braves thumped New York two straight in Milwaukee, winning game one 4–3 behind Spahn in ten innings and crushing the Yankees 13–5 in game two behind Burdette, who hit a first-inning home run as the Braves exploded for seven runs.

The Braves were cocky and oozing with confidence. In a ghostwritten magazine article, Burdette quipped that the Yankees "couldn't play in the National League."

The bulletin board fodder woke the Yankees up. When the Series moved to New York, they sent two dozen unsigned baseballs back to the Braves, violating the protocol that called for the two teams to exchange signed balls. And when a radio reporter asked Stengel, "Do you think your Yanks are choked up?" Stengel blew up, ending the interview by saying, "If there's any choking to be done, it might come right on this mike." It was one of the few times in his career that the reporter, Howard Cosell, would be rendered speechless.

Hank Bauer saved the Yankees. He collected three of New York's four hits and knocked in all four runs as Don

Larsen shut out the Braves, keeping them off balance by switching back and forth between a full wind-up and his no-wind-up delivery. For Bauer, it was his 17th straight World Series game in which he'd had a hit.

Bauer, who had won a purple heart on Okinawa, was Stengel's ideal player. He played hard, played when and where he was told, didn't complain, and almost always came through, making Stengel look like a genius. On any other team a player like Bauer might well have been the man, the big star. Several AL teams had standing trade offers for his services. But Bauer knew his role on the Yankees and relished it. "When you're walking in a bank in November with that World Series check, you don't want to leave," he said.

After Spahn shut out the Yankees in game four, 3–0, it appeared as if Bauer might not make such a hefty deposit, but the scales soon tipped toward the Yankees. Milwaukee manager Fred Haney got greedy. Instead of maintaining his rotation and bringing back game-three starter Bob Rush, who'd given up only three hits in his first start, Haney tried to rush to victory. He brought back Burdette on three days' rest, and the Braves lost 7–0. Then, back in Milwaukee, he turned to Spahn, on two days' rest, and the Braves lost 4–3 in ten innings when Gil McDougald popped a home run. In game seven Haney turned once again to Burdette, again on two days' rest. He tired late, and Turley, in relief of Larsen, shut down the Braves. The Yankees won 6–2 to take the Series.

There was ecstasy and relief in the visitors' clubhouse in Milwaukee's County Stadium, for as Dick Young noted, "They said it couldn't be done. They said a team down 3 and 1 in the World Series . . . couldn't win the next three." Stengel relished the win and was uncharacteristically churlish — at least in public — when he snarled at a reporter, "Well, I guess that we showed them we could play in the National League." The difference, he said, was "the two days of rest. They had those two big pitchers and they pitched too much." Stengel knew that while the players had done the work, the key to the Yankees' victory was that he hadn't panicked and Haney had. Stengel's players knew that too. On the plane trip back to New York the Yankees burned cork and painted each other's faces. On Stengel's cheeks they drew dollar signs. That's what Stengel meant to them.

Ever so slowly, however, the gap between the Yankees and the competition was becoming smaller. Although the Yankees had won 92 games and won the pennant by ten games in 1958, six of the eight other teams in the AL ended the season around .500, bunched within nine games of each other. That made the Yankees vulnerable, for if they faltered at all, there were several candidates to knock them off.

Weiss was considering retirement, and Stengel was also pondering his future. Dan Topping was beginning to look ahead toward a future without either man. But as yet, there was no excuse or real reason to make any changes.

Topping soon had one. In 1959 the Yankees were the same team that had played .500 baseball for the last two months of 1958. It wasn't any one thing but a lot of little things and a few injuries, made worse by the organization's utter disbelief that the Yankees could lose. They started slow, and the "Go-Go" White Sox, a team that featured good pitching, defense, and small ball, keyed by their double-play combo of Luis Aparicio and Nellie Fox, bolted out front. On May 21, following a 13–6 loss to Detroit, New York hit bottom. Splat. For the first time in 19 seasons, the Yankees were in last place.

They started scrambling. Weiss rang up Kansas City and traded Sturdivant, Kucks, and Jerry Lumpe for Ralph Terry and outfielder Hector Lopez. It helped a little — Lopez could hit some, and that gave some protection to Mantle, who started to produce — but it wasn't enough.

On June 29, Jimmy Powers wrote in the *Daily News* that "there was a certain amount of forgivable hysterical prose written from the turbulent ringside of Yankee Stadium. Words like blast, detonation, berserk attack, explosion, eruption and maniacal fury." He wasn't referring to the Yankees — he was commenting on Ingemar Johanson's recent pounding of Floyd Patterson to win the heavyweight title. But he might as well have been writing about the Yankees, for the day before in Chicago the White Sox blasted the Yankees with maniacal fury and swept a doubleheader, knocking New York to the canvas and back into the second division, just a game over .500. The losses effectively ended Yankee pennant hopes. They then lost to the Braves the next day in an exhibition in Milwaukee, 8–3, committing five errors. Spahn had been right after all. They were a fifth-place team. He'd just been off by a couple of years.

The Yankees ended their desultory season somewhat better, 79–75, in third place but closer to the seventh-place A's than the first-place White Sox. They hadn't finished so poorly in 34 seasons, not since Ruth's infamous and apocryphal bellyache.

Topping wanted to can Stengel. As the long season dragged on, the aging manager seemed to lose interest, sometimes falling asleep on the bench as the team fell further out of the race. Yankee players were paying more attention to what they were doing after the game than to what they were doing on the field. Mantle hit only .265 with 75 RBIs. Topping didn't agree with who Stengel was playing when, where, why, and how, but he also didn't want to eat the last year of Stengel's contract, and Stengel wasn't going anywhere willingly. Not yet.

Weiss had one more deal up his sleeve. For the past two years the Yankees had been following Kansas City outfielder Roger Maris closely. When the A's acquired him from the Indians in 1957, there had been some speculation that KC had been acting at the Yankees' behest. That was probably the case, but it couldn't be proved. KC owner Arnold Johnson died in 1960 and took that information with him.

Maris was a good left-handed hitter and a fine fielder who was learning to pull the ball, something Stengel wanted. Stengel thought another bat with home run potential would help protect Mantle.

The deal was made on December 11, the 15th transaction between the two clubs since March 1955, involving the transfer of 59 players, an incredible number. New York sent Larsen and a suddenly aging Hank Bauer along with Norm Siebern to the A's for Maris, Joe DeMaestri and Kent Hadley.

The rest of the league howled. Maris had been leading the AL in hitting in May 1959 before having his appendix removed. Everyone had pegged him as a future star, a player the A's had refused to deal to others. White Sox owner Bill Veeck called the relationship between the two teams an "unholy alliance," and Cleveland GM Frank "Trader" Lane complained that the cozy relationship tied up fully 25 percent of the players in the league.

The Yankees laughed—not too loudly—but they laughed. If the deal worked, they were suddenly players again.

That was a big if, but Weiss provided some inspiration by cutting nearly everybody's contract. Mantle held out when Weiss tried to cut him $17,000. Mantle finally slunk into camp with only a $7,000 cut.

Apart from the eventual elevation of third baseman Clete Boyer to the starting lineup, necessitating a move of Hector Lopez into the outfield, the Yankees were little changed in 1960. It was still the same old faces: McDougald,

In 1959 Mickey Mantle led the league with 126 strikeouts, and the defending world champions slipped to third place behind the "Go-Go" White Sox and the Cleveland Indians. The 15-game margin between Chicago and New York was the largest the Yankees had suffered since finishing 17 games behind Boston in 1946, and their won-lost record of 79–75 was their worst since 1925.

Skowron, Richardson, and Kubek divvied up the rest of the infield, and Howard split time with Berra behind the plate.

On Opening Day Maris went four for five in the leadoff spot and hit a home run as the Yankees beat Boston 8–4. Virtually everyone else bounced back at least a little, and some a lot more. Maris was all he'd been advertised to be. His short left-handed stroke was made for the short porch in right field at Yankee Stadium. He didn't hit them as far as Mantle did, for his typical home run landed only six or eight rows back in the stands, but he hit them just as often.

Casey Stengel turned 70 on August 1, and the Yankees were in second place, only one and a half games behind the White Sox. On August 23, Chicago came into the Stadium for a key two-game series.

The first game got off to a wild start and quickly got wilder. Yankee starter Eli Grba gave up three first-inning runs as the Yankees made three errors. Chicago manager Al Lopez then tried to pull a fast one—at least Stengel thought so. Instead of using announced starter Billy Pierce, Lopez pulled him before he'd thrown a single pitch, claiming he was hurt, and inserted right-hander Early Wynn.

It was a clear violation of the rules, which state that the starting pitcher must throw a pitch before he is replaced, and it conveniently screwed up Stengel's lineup. The Yankee manager filed the first protest of his long career.

Another protest took place in the fourth inning. As the Yankees took the field, a squad of nine Cuban anti-Castro partisans stormed the field holding banners that read "Cuba Yes, Russia No" and "Revolutionary Recuperation Movement for Camile Ciengfuegos"—a reference to the mysterious disappearance of one of Castro's army commanders on the eve of an attempted defection. Stadium guards tackled the protesters while the crowd cheered.

The Yankees had no more luck with their protest than the anti-Castro contingent with theirs, but they beat the White Sox the next day to start a string of eight wins in nine tries. Then, as the White Sox collapsed, they went 20–7 in September and finished eight games up on the sec-

In 1960 Mickey Mantle recaptured his old form with a league-leading 119 RBIs while batting in front of Roger Maris. After he made this late season catch against the Red Sox, Stengel was moved to remark, "It's amazing what he has done this year. And him a cripple, playing on one leg, and a bad shoulder. He's twice as good a fielder as he was last year."

ond-place Baltimore Orioles — the old Browns — with a record of 97–57. Maris, whom Stengel had moved to cleanup, earned an MVP Award with 39 home runs and 112 RBIs, helping Mantle bounce back with 40 home runs of his own and a league-best 119 runs.

Late in the season a background story by Joe Trimble in the *Daily News* focused on the probability that any hitter would ever top Ruth's home run record of 60. Maris had briefly sparked that debate earlier in the year by hitting 25 home runs through June 30. But his pace slowed in August, and then his chance was ruined when he was knocked from the lineup for several weeks with some cracked ribs. Trimble noted, "What kills off hopefuls is that Ruth belted 17 in September." He also asked several baseball men for their opinion on who had the best chance to break the record, and most of them named Mantle, Mays, Mathews, Ernie Banks, and Harmon Killebrew. But, wrote Trimble, former Yankee turned broadcaster Phil Rizzuto "accords Maris the best chance."

In short, Maris made them the Yankees again, or at least a reasonable facsimile of the team that had dominated the previous decade like no other. He was the piece that had been missing, a second star to pair with Mantle, a player whose presence elevated both men, just as Gehrig had once lifted Ruth.

But baseball was changing, and as it entered the 1960s it soon became clear that the conditions no longer existed that would allow one team to be as dominant as the Yankees had been in the 1950s. The 1960 World Series, almost by accident, would provide the first evidence of that.

In the National League the Pittsburgh Pirates won their first pennant since 1927, and most observers thought they had about as much chance to win the Series as the '27 Pirates had. They were a good club, anchored by pitchers Vern Law and Bob Friend. Players like shortstop Dick Groat and third baseman Don Hoak were valuable, lunchbucket performers, and outfielder Roberto Clemente was a star-in-waiting. The Pirates, however, lacked the Yankees' firepower.

Mantle and Maris and Skowron and Berra were scary. When manager Danny Murtaugh said, "We respect everybody, we fear nobody," the mere acknowledgment of fear as a factor seemed a recognition that the reverse was true. It all added up to make the Yankees 6½–7½ favorites.

There was no way, absolutely no way, the Yankees should have lost the 1960 World Series, for no team has ever been more dominant than the Yankees in their three Series victories, games two, three, and six, with scores of 16–3, 10–0, and 12–0. After game two Red Smith even wrote, "The football teams may now proceed according to plan. . . . Certain formalities remain to be disposed of . . . but the illusion of competition for the world rounders championship died a swift, untidy death in yesterday's bright, Bronx sunshine." Yet, as the *New York Post* later editorialized about Smith's pronouncement, "Beware of certitude forecasting human behavior." Within a few days those words would serve as the Yankees' epitaph.

The Pirates played the tortoise to New York's hare in the Series, plodding on, oblivious to the odds, to take games one, four, and five, winning when they did with pitching and defense and timely hitting. Meanwhile, the Yankees alternately napped and surged, flicking the power switch like a kid who has just discovered he can reach the light fixture.

Game seven in Pittsburgh's Forbes Field was the first six games of the Series replayed in miniature. "If I'm not mistaken," said Murtaugh before the game, "the score is 3–3 right now." And that was the only score that mattered.

The last few innings rendered the first several almost meaningless, for they had only served as the setup for one of the more unlikely finishes in Series history. Pittsburgh went ahead 4–0 early, blasting Turley before the Yankees woke and scored a single run on Skowron's fourth-inning home run, then plated four more in the fifth to chase Vern Law. In the eighth New York appeared to put the game away, collecting two more runs on three hits, capped by Clete Boyer's double. Six outs from victory, the Yankees led 7–4, and reliever Bobby Shantz walked out to the mound looking for his sixth scoreless inning in relief.

Gino Cimoli opened the Pittsburgh eighth with a simple, soft, quiet single. The Pittsburgh outfielder Bill Virdon followed with a hard ground ball right at Tony Kubek, a double play only two quick throws from being put in the book.

"One hop . . . two hops . . ." noted the *Herald Tribune,* "and then a third outlandish hop that sailed above Kubek's cupped hands and squarely into his throat. He dropped as if he were pole-axed." Instead of two outs, there were two on, and Kubek, coughing up blood, went first to the dressing room and then to the hospital. The game entered the realm of legend.

Shantz hadn't pitched longer than four innings all year, and after Dick Groat singled to make the score 7–5, Stengel called on reliever Jim Coates. Bob Skinner laid down a bunt, moving the runners over. After a short fly out, Roberto Clemente stepped in.

Coates jammed him, and Clemente's half-swing chopper bounced toward Skowron. Playing back to protect the lead, he couldn't make the play himself but fielded the ball and looked to flip the ball to Coates.

He wasn't there. Clemente beat him to the bag, and Pittsburgh scored another run. Then, angry with himself, Coates fired a pissed-off fastball to a bad spot, and Pittsburgh catcher Hal Smith put it in an even worse place, over the wall in left, and the Pirates were suddenly ahead. After reliever Ralph Terry got the final out, Pittsburgh took a 9–7 lead into the ninth. The tortoise was ahead again.

But Coates's ill-timed nap woke the Yankees. Bobby Richardson and Dale Long singled to open the ninth. Harvey Haddix, called in to relieve Bob Friend, got Maris on a pop-up, but Mantle crushed a single, plating one and sending the tying run to third.

Then came what the *Daily News* called "the screwiest play of the Series." Berra lined a one-hopper down the first-base line. Rocky Nelson grabbed it and stepped on first for the out and started to throw to second for the double play.

But Mantle wasn't running to second. Afraid that Berra's smash had been caught in the air, he stopped in his tracks ten feet off first. Dick Young wrote that Mantle and Pirate first baseman Rocky Nelson then "stood in a strange tableau, staring at each other no more than ten feet apart as though saying, 'Whose move?'"

Then both moved simultaneously, Mantle diving back to first and Nelson reaching for the tag. Mantle dove and twisted and lurched and got there first. Meanwhile, McDougald, pinch-running, scored the tying run. Then Skowron hit into a force-out, and it was Pittsburgh's turn again in this World Series of turn, counterturn, and turn.

It ended fast. Ralph Terry knew how the Yankees wanted to pitch Pittsburgh second baseman Bill Mazeroski — down. But his first pitch was up, and Yankee catcher Johnny Blanchard yelled at him, "Get it down."

He did, but only by a few inches. Mazeroski swung, and the ball sailed to left, and in left field Yogi Berra turned and took a few steps, then did not move any farther. The ivy-covered wall in deep left was 12 feet high and a full 406 feet from home plate. Mazeroski was a tremendous fielder but not much of a hitter. That was just about as far as he could ever hope to hit the ball.

The ball traveled just over 407 feet, 12 feet high and a little more, passing over the ivy at the top of the fence and disappearing into the trees, just enough to make the Pittsburgh Pirates world champions and leave the disbelieving Yankees short of the finish line.

While Mazeroski floated around the bases, the first and only player ever to win game seven of a World Series with a walk-off home run, the stunned Yankees staggered off

YANKEE OWNERS BY THE NUMBERS

Owner	Years	Record	Percentage	Championships
Farrell/Devery	1903–14	861–937	.479	0
Ruppert/Huston	1915–21	553–475	.538	0
Ruppert	1922–38	1,604–1,103	.593	7
Ruppert estate	1939–44	579–342	.629	3
Topping/Webb/MacPhail (1945–47)	1945–64	1,916–1,329	.590	10
CBS	1965–72	636–649	.495	0
Steinbrenner	1973–2001	2,525–2,039	.553	6

the field. For about the first time ever the mighty Yankees had lost when they should have won.

"Great is a tired word," wrote Young, "but great great great is the only word to describe the ballgame." Swan song was another, for while they celebrated in Pittsburgh, the fate of Stengel hung in the balance in the Bronx. Clearly, the Yankee advantage was starting to erode. After Art Johnson passed away, the Kansas City pipeline had been cut off when the A's were sold to the flamboyant Charles O. Finley. Baseball was preparing to expand. The loss to Pittsburgh should have caused the franchise to take a step back, look at the changing situation, and change its approach. Instead, the Yankees became increasingly myopic.

"Somebody up there hates sentiment," wrote Red Smith. So did Dan Topping and Del Webb. For several seasons they had thought Stengel was too old and had cited the policy of Webb's construction company, which mandated retirement at age 65. But Stengel's record and contract status had extended his fate. Now, finally, they had their excuse. They'd grown fond of former Yankee third-string catcher Ralph Houk, who'd caddied for Stengel for several seasons and turned down offers to manage other teams. It was his turn.

Stengel went, but not quietly. On October 18, Topping held a press conference and announced that Stengel had resigned due to his advanced age. While Stengel bristled at his side, Topping tried to smooth things over by citing Stengel's $160,000 severance package and proposing his immediate induction into the Hall of Fame.

But at a press party immediately afterward the old manager exploded. When a reporter asked whether he'd been fired, he thundered, "Goddamn right I've been fired," and then launched into a tirade, shouting, "I'm not a yes man. I've never been a yes man!" Then Stengel launched into a vintage description of his numerous complaints, which he said included orders on who to play and who not to play. He finished quietly, saying, "The results speak for themselves."

Casey Stengel may not have been the greatest manager ever, for he certainly had more talent at his disposal than many others, but then again, no one did as much with it as he did. It is hard to imagine another manager this side of Joe Torre who has ever been more adept at getting the most out of his roster, at taking players and making them

a team, or at outmanaging his opponent in the postseason, nearly always selecting just the right pitcher and just the right hitter in every situation. In twelve years he won ten pennants and seven world championships. And even in the three World Series he lost, Stengel pushed the contest to seven games. That wasn't any Stengelese, his signature double talk that was mostly just an act to entertain reporters. That is simply the truth. Yet over time winning became so common to the organization that it lost sight of Stengel's contribution.

Topping and Webb were pilloried in the press. "We were ridiculed when we hired him," whined Topping. "Now we're ridiculed for letting him go."

Weiss went next. Two weeks later, at age 65, Weiss announced that he had "decided" to step down. He was replaced by his 58-year-old sidekick Roy Hamey, who had already failed as GM in Philadelphia and Pittsburgh. Weiss took the high road, as Young noted, "for having made the mistake of being 65 years old."

Like Stengel, Weiss was someone whose record spoke for itself, but for all the Yankee victories he had helped engineer, it still contained one sizable blemish that would grow larger in his passing. In a franchise that hadn't experienced too many failures, Weiss's failure to sign black players was a significant one. And in the end it would be an important factor in the demise of the reigning Yankee dynasty.

Now that Topping and Webb were in charge, the organization stopped taking any risks at all and simply preserved the status quo, both on the field and off. Topping and Webb were thinking about selling the club and wanted to bolster the bottom line. They stopped spending big money on prospects and pared back their acquisition of young talent. The farm system, once one of the largest in baseball, was down to only eight teams—average for the era, but the Yankees had never been average in anything before.

The American League added two teams in 1961, one in California and the other in Washington, for the original Senators were moving to Minnesota. To accommodate the additional teams, the schedule was expanded from 154 to 162 games, a decision that would soon be the cause of one of the most controversial rulings in baseball history. Just two days before Stengel was let go, the National League

Roger Maris (left) and Mantle being interviewed by Red Barber. In 1961 Maris became the most famous man in America. Beginning on May 17, he socked an incredible 23 home runs in his next 36 games on his climb toward Babe Ruth's single-season home run mark of 60.

announced that it would expand in 1962, adding two teams, one in Houston and one in New York. Eventually there would be more competition than ever for talent, although for the time being the addition of two expansion teams in the American League made it even easier for New York to win.

When the Yankees learned that there would be a new New York franchise, the organization hardly noticed. Even though they hadn't picked up a fan since the Giants and Dodgers headed west, they remained indifferent. The team was losing sight of the fact that its success started on the field, with the players. Stengel's record led to the false impression that Yankee success was due to some inherent organizational magic. Neither the players nor the makeup of the front office were as interchangeable as the organization believed. A player did not become great simply by putting on the pinstripes, and the Yankee logo was no guarantee of anything.

Houk and Hamey stayed the course in the off-season. But when spring training started, the players discovered that Houk was not Stengel.

He'd been one of them, having served as a backup catcher from 1947 through 1954. He was a players' man-

ager, strategically more like McCarthy, preferring a set lineup. It was a wise course at the time, for the club's vast depth was already starting to erode. A set lineup now made more sense.

Pitching was Houk's only concern, and in April and May he struggled to find the right mix to back Ford at the top of the rotation. Lefty reliever Luis Arroyo kept the staff afloat while Houk sorted things out.

Hitting was not a problem, for the specter of Maris, who hit third, followed by Mantle, was beginning to send a shudder through the rest of the league. The lineup had power from top to bottom. Howard and Blanchard platooned behind the plate and would combine for more than 40 home runs, Berra would eventually hit another 21 as a part-time outfielder, and Skowron would chip in with another 28 home runs. They were scary.

No one could have predicted what transpired in the summer of 1961. The events of the next few months would become a part of baseball lore. And while the day-to-day details of Maris and Mantle's combined assault on Babe Ruth's home run record of 60 are well known, the larger context — why it happened the way it did, particularly in regard to Maris — is a subject less often explored.

In a sense it was 1927 all over again, a spectacular performance that the media spoon-fed the public. But there were also significant differences. In 1927 the performance had been delivered by the game's greatest star, Babe Ruth, and recorded by perhaps the best group of working journalists who ever covered a major league team, at a time when America believed there were no limits and recognized no barriers. But in 1961 the performance was delivered by the wrong man, a player who was merely very good, not great, and recorded by a group of journalists who spanned the full spectrum from the best to the most pedestrian, all doing the same story every day. And it took place at a time when America was beginning to question its heroes and during a season that some found artificial.

Roger Maris, like the rest of the Yankees, had started the season slowly. By mid-May he had hit only three home runs. But when the Yankees returned to the Stadium on May 14 and the weather began to warm, so did Maris. This was his second year in New York, and he was 26 years old and in his prime. He'd learned not only how to hit in the Stadium — how to pull the ball to take advantage of right field — but what the Yankees expected of him. Mantle, with Maris before him, could carry the load. Maris's job was to take advantage of the good pitches he was destined to see, hitting in front of Mantle, and send them over the wall.

Beginning on May 17, Maris hit an incredible 23 home runs in the next 36 games — one of the greatest home run hitting streaks in baseball history — and the Yankees won 23 games out of the next 36 to vault into a virtual tie with the Tigers. Apart from this remarkable span, Maris would strike only 38 home runs in the other 137 games that season — very, very good, but not particularly awe-inspiring. By mid-June, however, the pennant race had become a sidebar. Roger Maris was hitting home runs at a faster pace than Babe Ruth.

For that matter, so was Mantle. Ruth's record was made for such comparisons. Like Maris, in 1927 Ruth had been only very, very good for much of the year before putting together one tremendous surge: 17 home runs in 27 Sep-

Maris pays homage to Babe Ruth at Yankee Stadium's monument park in the midst of his assault on Ruth's home run record. By July media pressure mounted and soon became almost unbearable for the 26-year-old slugger.

tember games to reach his final number of 60. Ruth had been more mortal before September — he'd hit only 43 in the previous 127 games.

Ruth's surge coincided with the end of season, when every other team was so far out of the race that they were merely playing out the string. In a sense, so did Maris's. From May 17 through June 22, the Yankees played only five games against the only two teams over .500 at the time, Detroit and Baltimore. Everyone else was already waiting for next year. Their pennant race was over. Maris never went more than two games without a home run during this stretch, belting them out at a rate that, sustained for a season, would have given him more than 100.

Phil Rizzuto's optimistic prediction aside, there was absolutely nothing in Maris's past that could have predicted his surge. He'd never had such a streak before, and he never had one remotely like it ever again. But it was enough to vault him into a race with immortality, to create a set of expectations that were completely unrealistic, and to participate in a frenzy over which he had no control.

The only reason players hit a lot of home runs in the first place is that some pitchers aren't very good and make mistakes. The ability to take advantage of pitching mistakes is what makes one a major league hitter. This observation doesn't diminish what Maris did. But it does offer some perspective on his pursuit of Ruth over the rest of the season. By the time the press began to notice that he had a chance to hit 60 home runs, Maris's inexplicable, early season streak had ended. For 36 games he had been Babe Ruth in September 1927, but for the rest of the season — and in fact for the rest of his career — he was Roger Maris again, a disparity both obvious and inexplicable.

Maris hit his first 27 home runs in virtual anonymity. Just as his task began to be recognized, it instantly became harder, for now it took place in the spotlight. In late June, Joe Trimble of the *Daily News* was the first to form the question, asking Maris, "Do you think you can break Ruth's record?" Maris answered with profane and profound honesty, saying, "How the [bleep] should I know?"

Exactly. Maris didn't know why or how he'd hit 23 home runs in 36 games to begin with, he didn't know the stir it would cause, and he sure as hell didn't know how to deal with it. Neither did the Yankees. Or the press.

Over the next few months the media made Maris's attitude toward the record as much a part of their coverage as the question of whether he would better Ruth's mark. They were as uncertain about how to report on Maris's quest as he was in answering their questions. Eventually, after the press decided that Maris lacked personal appeal, they became more interested in his reaction to the surrounding hoopla than to the record itself. In a sense, the media made itself, not Maris, the story.

The role of media had changed dramatically since 1927. Then, New York's newspapers had had the home run story to themselves, and the writers played a supporting role to both Ruth and the Yankees. They competed with each other, not so much in content as in style.

But in 1961 the New York press was competing not only with each other but with the national media — guys from other papers and magazines — plus a growing group of television and radio reporters. And newspaper coverage had changed, particularly in New York. A new, younger generation of writers, dubbed "chipmunks" by Jimmy Cannon and exemplified by Dick Young, didn't recognize the cozy old relationship that baseball writers of the past had maintained with their subject. At their best, they gave fans insights and honest appraisals that would have been impossible in the earlier era. But at their worst, they took Red Smith's caution not to "god up" the ballplayers to the extreme — they ripped away without caution.

The New York press also missed the Giants and Dodgers. A number of New York writers had changed beats after 1958, and the Yankees were the only game in town. They weren't happy about that. Since 1958 coverage of the team had been increasingly critical and mean-spirited.

They now had Maris in their sights, and he paid the price. He wasn't Ruth and he wasn't Mantle, both of whom knew how to deal with the press. Maris was just a guy from North Dakota with a singular talent who liked to be left alone but who had suddenly found himself in the middle of something over which he had no control.

As soon as the press started looking at Maris, they found him lacking. The comparisons to Ruth stopped before they even started, and the comparisons to Mantle weren't very flattering. Maris was hitting only .255 in late June. Mantle was over .300. Maris had never hit more than 39 home runs, while Mantle had hit as many as 52 and topped

40 on two other occasions. Mantle's home runs were predictable and hit with regularity. He ran faster, played a more difficult position, played hurt, was better-looking, and made better copy. Maris, the press soon concluded, was the wrong man.

The scrutiny built slowly through June and into July. The Yankees, who hardly seemed to lose anymore, particularly at home, were pulling ever closer to Detroit as both teams pulled away from the rest of the league. Then commissioner Ford Frick got involved.

Baseball had given no thought to the impact of an expanded 162-game schedule on the record book. Maris and Mantle caused baseball to start mulling that question, and before the debate had hardly began, Frick ended it abruptly and awkwardly. On July 17, he announced, "Any player who may hit more than 60 home runs during his club's first 154 games would be recognized as having established a new record." But if the record was set after the 154th game, "there would have to be some distinctive mark to show that Ruth's record was set under a 154-game schedule and the total of more than 60 was compiled while a 162 games season was in effect."

Frick still hadn't thought things through. If he had, he'd have realized that any such edict needed to be comprehensive and include all seasonal marks. But Frick—Ruth's old ghostwriter—was thinking only about Ruth's record.

The press further distorted the ruling, which, as stated, really only created the possibility of two records. Dick Young was the first to use the word "asterisk," writing, "Maybe you should use an asterisk for the new record. Everybody does that when there's a difference of opinion." His interpretation stuck. The press gave it the infamous asterisk and determined it would affect only Maris's mark, although baseball's *Official Record Book* would simply list the two marks on separate pages. They ignored the diminishing element it brought to Ruth's mark if it went unbroken. And that made all the difference.

As July turned into August, the Yankees, who went 20–9 in the month, began to pull away from the Tigers and

Roger Maris hit his record-tying sixtieth home run on September 26 off Oriole pitcher Jack Fisher. It was Maris's 159th game, before a below-average crowd of 19,000 at Yankee Stadium. On the last day of the season, he broke the record with a solo blast off Red Sox righty Tracy Stallard.

Maris and Mantle hit home runs at a more or less regular pace and stayed ahead of Ruth. Mantle drew even with Maris on August 2. Both men had 40 home runs.

The fact that two players on the same team were pursuing Ruth in the media capital of the world increased the scrutiny of both players. From today's perspective, formed as it is by cable television, the Internet, ESPN, and the 24-hour news cycle, the level of press attention on Mantle and Maris in 1961 seems subdued. But in 1961 it was revolutionary. The electronic media in particular was new to this game. The borders and restrictions on coverage and access that would be commonplace during Cal Ripken's consecutive game streak and the dual assault by Sammy Sosa and Mark McGwire on Maris's mark were unknown. The Yankees made little effort to control the press. Maris and Mantle found themselves at the center of an uncontrolled feeding frenzy. Both players became virtual prisoners of the clubhouse, their hotel rooms, and their homes. Mantle was used to it and could laugh it off and relax with a drink or two or three. Maris couldn't.

He tried to say the right things. "A season's a season," he said about Frick's ruling, but, "If Mick breaks it, I hope he does it in 154. The same goes for me." Of Ruth he was respectful, saying, "I admire Ruth and all he stands for."

But the questions just wouldn't stop. When Maris didn't answer, he was ripped. When he did answer, he sometimes was made to look foolish. If he talked to one reporter, 10 others expected him to talk to them too. Either way, Maris made headlines. The New York papers fought over him. TV and radio people swooped in, took their sound bites, and swooped away. On radio Maris sounded disinterested. On TV he looked either bored or angry. His image took a beating. The closer the public got, the more absurd the comparison to either Ruth or Mantle appeared. When he hit a home run, he was cheered. When he didn't, he was booed, particularly on the road, where the Yankees were already evil incarnate. But as the season wore on, he was even booed in New York.

The story should have been that in spite of it all Maris kept hitting. Pitchers, pressure, and the pennant race couldn't stop him. But the story became, not the record or the chase, but what Maris wasn't and what the record, if set by him, was not.

Mantle and Maris hung close into mid-September, and then Mantle went down. Bothered by a cold, on September 11 he went to a quack doctor recommended by Yankee broadcaster Mel Allen and received a shot in the thigh that got infected and developed an abscess. He dropped out of the race a week later, stuck on home run 53, and hit only one more the rest of the season to end at 54. Maris hit his 57th home run on September 16, and his 58th on September 17. It came in the 12th inning and beat Detroit. The Yankees' magic number to clinch the pennant was two. So was Maris's.

Maris's task became exponentially harder. Mantle wasn't hitting behind him—he'd end the season in the hospital. Maris had to move from right field to center. The Yankees were about to clinch the pennant. Game 154 was only three days away, and Maris was the only story.

September 18 was an off-day. But it was no day of rest. The Yankees flew in to Baltimore—Babe Ruth's birthplace—from Detroit the night before. No one missed the connection.

On September 19, the Yankees played a twilight doubleheader, games 152 and 153. It was hard to see. With Hurricane Esther looming off the coast, the wind was blowing in and it was spitting rain. Steve Barber shut out the Yankees on four hits in the first game, a 1–0 Baltimore win. The Yankees won game two, 3–1, but Maris managed only a single off the two knuckleballers Skinny Brown and Hoyt Wilhelm.

He had one chance left. He needed two home runs to tie Ruth, three to pass him. He told Dick Young, "You'd almost have to be Houdini to do it." He was only Roger Maris.

Baseball fans were ambivalent. A good crowd, 24,382, turned out for a chance to witness history on a Wednesday night, but it wasn't a tough ticket. This wasn't McGwire or Sosa in the summer of 1998, or Bonds in 2001.

In the first inning he lined out hard to right, just missing hitting the ball flush. In the third he homered off Milt Pappas for number 59, and hope stayed alive. In the fourth he struck out. In the seventh he blasted the ball three-quarters of the way up the right-field bleachers but 15 feet foul. He flew out on the next pitch.

He came up again in the ninth against Hoyt Wilhelm's knuckleball, perhaps the hardest pitch in baseball to hit square. Acting Baltimore manager Lum Harris threatened to fine Wilhelm if he threw anything but a knuckleball or grooved one. Maris fouled one off, then checked his swing at the next dancing pitch.

It hit his bat and rolled 40 feet down the line, where Wilhelm scooped it up and tagged him. Maris turned and jogged slowly back to the bench. Ruth's encumbered record was safe.

The Yankees won the game, 4–2, won the pennant, and celebrated with champagne. Maris stayed dry, sat alone, and tried to breathe as the press pinned him against the clubhouse wall. "I tried," he said. "I tried."

"Now that the ghost-hunt has ended," wrote Red Smith, "the most striking aspect of it all seems, in retrospect, to be the way everyone got emotionally involved.... Perhaps the individual who preserved the sense of proportion best of all was Maris himself.... 'Of course you were under pressure,' said a fellow when it was over. 'Of course,' he said, simply."

But home run number 60, maybe more, was still possible. Over the next few days it stayed out there in the future as Maris failed to hit a home run. That was the story now — not what Maris had done, but what he failed to do. When the Yankees went to Boston, the headline in the *Daily News* told the story: "Maris Fails."

The crowds of newsmen around him slacked off, and the Yankee Stadium crowd was almost blasé. But the pressure was still there, for now Maris still wanted to show what he could do, to prove to those who questioned his fortitude and his talent that he could meet the challenge. "It's worse than ever now," he said.

Number 60 came on September 26, off Baltimore pitcher Jack Fisher in the third inning of game 159 before a crowd of just over 19,000, less than the average that year. It crashed into the empty third deck in the Stadium and bounced back onto the field.

But they cheered him when he hit it, and they cheered him when his teammates pushed him out of the dugout for a quick, embarrassed tip of the cap, for the 19,000 who were there cared, even if the millions who weren't did

not, or did not care as much. "There was," wrote Joe Trimble, "only one ballgame. Maris at bat."

Oriole right fielder Earl Robinson retrieved the ball, and when Maris received it after the game, he held it tight in his hand. "I wanted that homer badly," he said. "I'd like one more too."

Exhausted, he took the next day off, and the press snarled. "Ask yourself," wrote Leonard Shecter in the *Post,* "you've got sixty home runs and four games to become the first man in baseball history to hit 61.... Do *you* take a day off? Roger Maris did." And a few days later another *Post* headline screamed: "Maris Has Changed—And He Admits It."

But despite it all — who he was and who he wasn't, what the phantom asterisk meant and what it did not, what happened to him and the Yankees later, and how it would take Mark McGwire to really make the record Maris's after all — on the last day of the season, against 24-year-old Boston right-handed pitcher Tracy Stallard, in the fourth inning of the last game of the year, he did it. He knocked the ball six rows deep into right field before 23,154 fans and into the hands of a 19-year-old man named Sal Durante, the only run in the 1–0 Yankee win, their 109th of the year. Some gave him his due and some did not, but his teammates did, and the players on the field, and his family. And in time each of those 61 home runs and Roger Maris became the story of the season.

The Yankees, of course, did go on to the World Series and play the Cincinnati Reds. Mantle was still hurt and barely played, and Maris hit only one home run — in the ninth inning to win game three — but Joe DiMaggio came back and threw out the first pitch, Whitey Ford twirled two shutouts, Clete Boyer fielded everything at third, Bobby Richardson hit .391, and the Yankees won in five quick games.

And after the fifth game, Roger Maris, the first man to hit 61 home runs, was the first man off the field, the first man into the shower, the first man dressed, the first man out of the locker room and onto a plane and on his way back home.

Manager Yogi Berra watches his 1964 Yankees lose to the Red Sox in extra innings on the forty-second Opening Day in Yankee Stadium history. Boston owner Tom Yawkey helped the Yankee great secure his job by attempting to hire Berra as Red Sox manager after the 1963 season.

1962–1964
A SERIES OF SWAN SONGS

Ralph Houk spent most of spring training in 1964 confidently chomping on the end of his cigar. The Yankees had moved training camp from sleepy old St. Petersburg on Florida's Gulf Coast to Fort Lauderdale. Spring training reports focused on the difference between the two cities. There was precious little else worth reporting.

Life was good. The Yankees were a sure thing.

They had earned the right to stand still, and they did just that, making no trades and simply adding the usual complement of prospects to the already powerful club. The only difficult question facing Houk was how to replace Tony Kubek, whose National Guard unit had been activated. Even that quandary was more pleasant than problematic, for the top two candidates, rookie infielders Tom Tresh and Phil Linz, led the Yankees in hitting that spring. Two more highly touted rookies, first baseman Joe Pepitone and pitcher Jim Bouton, also joined the club, the latest in a long line of presumed stars-in-waiting ready to assume their place in the Yankees' championship conga line. It was a great time to be young and a Yankee.

The obsession with Roger Maris and his pursuit of 60 home runs in 1961 had obscured a season that, even without Maris, had been one of the greatest in franchise history. The Yanks' 109 wins were second in team history only to the 110 wins accumulated by the 1927 team. Mantle, with 54 home runs and 128 RBIs to go with a .317 batting average, had rarely been better. In any other season he would have been a shoo-in for the MVP Award, which rightly went to Maris for the second straight year. Elston Howard busted out from Berra's shadow and hit .348. Arroyo saved a club record 29 games, and Whitey Ford was a spectacular 25–4. In the World Series he'd even broken Babe Ruth's record of 29⅔ consecutive scoreless innings pitched, running his streak to 32 with 14 shutout innings. It had been, noted one observer, "a bad year for the Babe."

None knew it, but this edition of the Yankees was at its peak, for Maris, Mantle, Arroyo, Ford, and Howard would never again reach the heights they scaled in 1961. Yet at first the unavoidable slide would be so subtle as to be nearly invisible.

There was a sense of inevitability to the 1962 season, even as the Yankees got off to their customary slow start. After dropping a doubleheader to Cleveland on June 17 — their fourth loss in a row and seventh in their last eight games — to fall three games back of the surprising Indians, the Yanks, far from being worried, were completely unconcerned. Noted Leonard Koppett in the *Post,* the Yankees "were laughing it off and the Indians were almost on their knees apologizing."

"We got 100 games to play," said Houk. "We ain't gonna quit." Ford was temporarily sidelined with a muscle strain, and on May 18 Mantle suffered his semiannual leg injury, tearing his right hamstring while running the bases and simultaneously pulling the ligaments behind his left knee as he tried not to fall. As soon as Mantle and Ford returned, everyone expected the Yankees to make their customary move. They always had.

Mantle's leg injuries were becoming as predictable as world championships. At age 30, Mantle, who once described himself by saying, "All I have is natural ability," was beginning to see the erosion of those natural physical gifts, precipitated by his continuing failure to take care of himself. Muscle pulls can be caused by a host of factors, among them chronic joint injuries, the failure to stay in shape, and dehydration precipitated by alcohol abuse. Mantle was three for three. While he still looked like the Blond Bomber, he no longer resembled the player they once also had called "Mick the Quick," as the injuries had stripped him of much of his speed. When he played he played hard, and with his legs wrapped in tape like a mummy, his teammates sometimes couldn't believe he was taking the field. Over the next few years, however, it would become clear that Mantle's greatest seasons were behind him.

Other Yankee hitters could still make up for the loss of Mantle. At this point Ford was more important to the team's success. Elston Howard had nicknamed him "Chairman of the Board." The moniker referred not only to his Sinatra-like presence as a card-carrying member of the Yankee rat pack but also to his central role on the Yankee pitching staff and as the club's elder statesman.

With Berra starting to fade at age 37, Ford, at 33, was the oldest regular on the club. A native of Manhattan raised in Queens, Ford thoroughly understood New York and what it meant to be a Yankee. With his cocky confidence, he gave the team its swagger, the arrogance they carried on the field, which was never more pronounced than when he was standing on the mound.

Stengel had affectionately called Ford his "Banty rooster" and recognized early on just what he meant to the team. On a club that often had no true ace, Ford was the best in club history.

He would do anything to win and often did, such as using a specially made ring to cut and scuff the baseball in critical situations. For apart from his curveball, his stuff was rather ordinary. He survived on control and guts, once telling a reporter, "It's amazing how many outs you can get by working the count to where the hitter is sure you're going to throw to his weakness, then throw to his strength instead."

But Stengel had always been cautious with Ford, who was only five-foot-ten and weighed 180 pounds. He'd been afraid that if he overworked the diminutive pitcher during the season, he might break down or lose his effectiveness.

Most teams used a four-man starting rotation that gave top starters as many as 40 starts per season. But Stengel saved Ford for big games, keeping him strong, and rarely wasted the pitcher in meaningless contests against teams the Yankees were probably going to beat anyway. Throughout the 1950s, for instance, Stengel rarely used Ford in Boston's Fenway Park, which was a tough place for left-handers to pitch and where the Yankees could win without him. Under Stengel, Ford had started more than 30 games only once. The hurler appreciated the treatment and repaid his manager with a series of high-profile wins.

Only Stengel could afford to worry about October in June and July. In October Ford had been virtually untouchable. While other pitchers were often looking for their second wind in October, Ford was still strong. Through 1961 his Series record was a stellar 9–4, and he was still looking to increase his streak of consecutive scoreless innings.

Houk increased Ford's workload. The manager took a militaristic "take no prisoners" approach to the game. In 1961, for the first time, Ford had pitched every fourth day, making 39 starts and pitching nearly 300 innings. For all the Yankees' posturing in the first half of the 1962 season, they needed Ford back on the mound now as they never had before. In his absence, Ralph Terry was carrying the load.

Ford tossed a three-hitter in his first game back and won nine of his first ten. Mantle returned on June 22 even though his legs weren't close to being healed. But Houk was more concerned than he was letting on. The Yankees needed him, and if Houk didn't see blood, he didn't see any reason for a player not to play. Mantle was less than enthusiastic about coming back so quickly, saying, "They [the Yankees] say I can't hurt it anymore by playing." So he played.

Still, for the first time the Yankees began to accommodate his deteriorating skills. When he came back, Mantle played right field for the first time since 1954. He delivered the desired effect, for the Yankees won 29 of their next 40 to put the pennant in their back pocket. Yankee fans took note and, in an interesting turnaround, cheered Mantle wildly for the remainder of his career. They saved all their boos for Maris, whose struggles they seemed to enjoy as much as Mantle's successes. For as Mantle rebounded, Maris found his more customary level, hitting around .250 and hitting home runs only half as often as he

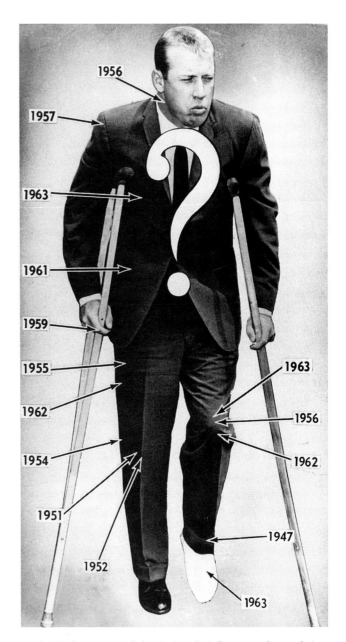

As the Yankees entered the sixties, their fate rested on a dwindling corps of decent prospects such as Tom Tresh and Mel Stottlemyre as well as the aging knees of Mickey Mantle. His injuries were depicted in the press like battlefields on a map.

had in 1961. Leonard Koppett reflected the general feeling when he wrote in the *Post* in September, "One really can't compare him to Mantle in real value." The fans and the press seemed to take some delight in that, and the taciturn Maris started to withdraw even further. When he was benched in early September, Koppett wrote, "Maris didn't seem upset by this. In a strange sort of way he feels a kind of vindication. . . . [H]e has always insisted he is not a 'super-star' [and] has resented being treated like one."

The Yankees won the pennant by five games over the Minnesota Twins, then sat back to watch the Dodgers and Giants square off in a best-of-three playoff to decide the NL title. Time and time again they were able to enter the World Series fresh while their NL opponent always seemed to be engaged in either a playoff or an equally exhausting pennant race that went down to the season's final day.

The Giants won, but little was made of the fact that the team would be returning to its former home. Most old Giants and Dodgers fans still resented the loss of their teams and had cut their ties. Besides, both clubs had already returned to New York during the regular season to play

Manager Ralph Houk remained true to his military background with his "take no prisoners" approach to the game. Nicknamed the Major in honor of his rank during World War II, Houk increased the workload of the Yankee pitching staff to one start every four days. When it came to injuries, if the Major didn't see blood, you weren't hurt.

the expansion New York Mets, managed by Casey Stengel, in the Polo Grounds. The Mets were terrible, but with Stengel at the helm that somehow didn't seem to matter much. "We are a fraud," he said of his club, and the fans just laughed and cheered and bought more tickets. The new club drew nearly one million fans to the rickety Polo Grounds while their new home was being built in Queens. That was half a million less than the Yankees drew, but what Met fans lacked in numbers they made up for in passion.

Without even trying, the Mets, not the Yankees, had won the next generation of New York baseball fans. Part of the reason was the "anybody but the Yankees" syndrome of old Dodgers and Giants fans, and part of it was allegiance to National League–style baseball, but there was another factor. When blacks, Latinos, and younger, more politically aware fans took a look at the Yankees — all white except for Howard and Lopez — they didn't see an organization worth rooting for. Met crowds looked and acted like New York — Yankee crowds looked and acted like Westchester.

The San Francisco Giants provided a similar contrast to the Yankees. One of baseball's most integrated teams, the Giants sometimes featured as many as six or seven blacks and Latinos in the starting lineup. Willie Mays, coming off a season in which he had cracked 49 home runs, was still in his prime, and he was supported by slugger Orlando Cepeda, Felipe Alou, youngster Willie McCovey, and veteran Harvey Kuenn. The pitching staff featured three veterans, 24-game winner Jack Sanford, Billy O'Dell, and Billy Pierce, and young Dominican Juan Marichal, enjoying his first great year. These Giants knew all about the Yankees. Manager Al Dark had been a key part of the Yankees-Giants rivalry in the 1950s, and former Series hero Don Larsen was a valuable member of San Francisco's bullpen.

The two clubs split the first two games in San Francisco, Ford winning the opener despite seeing his record-breaking streak end at 33 innings in the second inning, and Jack Sanford twirled a shutout in game two. Back in New York, Bill Stafford put the Yankees up 2–1 with a four-hitter, despite taking a line drive off his shin. "I didn't see any blood," quipped Houk, explaining his decision to leave him in the game. But Stafford would be unable to pitch again. Injuries were starting to mount up. Berra was playing with a broken finger.

Hall of Fame pitchers Whitey Ford (left) and Juan Marichal square off before the fourth game of the 1962 World Series at Yankee Stadium. Ford left the game for a pinch hitter in the sixth inning with the score tied at two. The Giants came back to win, 7–3, on Chuck Hiller's grand-slam home run, the first by a National Leaguer in Series history.

The Giants knotted the Series with a 7–3 win in game four when Chuck Hiller drilled a grand-slam home run after Houk pinch-hit for Ford with the score tied 2–2. Then the rains came. The final three games would be played across eight days as rain pelted first New York and then San Francisco in the form of Typhoon Frieda.

The delay helped the Yankees immeasurably. With Stafford hurt, New York was short—the fourth and fifth starters had been troublesome all year. Now, because of the rain, Houk didn't have to use them. Terry would pitch twice over the remainder of the Series and Ford once. It would prove to be the difference.

The repeated delays were agonizing for the players and robbed the Series of much of its drama. Meanwhile, the writers were left twiddling their thumbs, which led them to explore topics usually ignored.

In one profile of Giants manager Al Dark, Milton Gross of the *Post* riffed on the Giants' racial makeup, noting that elsewhere in the NL the team was nicknamed "the Jungle Bunnies." He credited Dark—a southerner—for overcoming his own prejudices and getting the multinational, mul-

tiracial team to play together. Later in the Series Leonard Shecter also touched on the theme, contrasting the styles of Houk and Dark and mentioning matter-of-factly that "both [managers] have been known to refer to Negroes in terms not generally considered polite," then adding parenthetically, "This does not mean they dislike Negroes, just that they don't understand the power of words which generate prejudice." But the difference was that Dark, apparently, had adapted. With the Yankees, Houk didn't really need to.

While they waited out three days of rain in San Francisco, both clubs eventually skipped town for a day to work out in Modesto, where Del Webb owned a minor league team. Still, three helicopters had to be employed to dry the field at Candlestick Park.

The Series came down to the final game on October 16, played in a sun-drenched Candlestick Park with a gale blowing in at 35 miles per hour. The Yankees scored a run in the fifth on Kubek's double-play grounder off Sanford, and Ralph Terry was simultaneously torched yet untouched—time after time the Giants hit the ball on the nose, only to have the wind knock it down and into the hands of the Yankee outfielders.

Terry nursed the lead into the ninth, but Matty Alou bunted for a hit, and after two failed sacrifice attempts, Mays doubled. There were now runners on second and third with two out and Willie McCovey up at bat.

The powerful McCovey laced a screaming line drive that he later called "the hardest ball I ever hit." But before the Giants fans could even let out a roar, second baseman Bobby Richardson took their breath away. The sinking line drive was hit right at him, and he snagged it while dropping to his knees.

Many had long believed it would take an act of God to beat the Yankees, but times were changing. Now it was taking some divine intervention for the Yankees to prevail. Had McCovey's drive been hit a foot in any other direction, the Giants would have won the Series. New York won by the narrowest margin, assisted by the rain, the wind, and the glove of the devoutly religious Richardson.

Thus far general manager Roy Hamey had proven to be no dummy. Not that he did anything. His talent so far had consisted in doing very little. But in the off-season he made the only big trade of his tenure, sending Skowron to Los Angeles for pitcher Stan Williams. Pepitone was deemed ready to take over at first, and Williams, only 25, had won 14 games for the offensively anemic Dodgers. With New York he was expected to blossom.

The 1963 season opened in rough imitation of 1962. The Yankees were hurting as nagging injuries chipped away at Kubek, Ford, and Maris, but no other team in the American League was any better. Jim Bouton pitched his way into the starting rotation and over the first two months of the season kept the club afloat.

On June 6, New Yorkers picked up the afternoon papers and saw a *Post* headline that screamed: "Mantle Out at Least a Month." The night before he had caught his spikes on the chainlink fence in Baltimore and broken his foot.

By now the Yankees were accustomed to playing without Mantle. To replace him on the roster they brought up fireballing left-hander Al Downing, the first African-American starting pitcher in club history and, some 17 years after Jackie Robinson broke the color line, only the fifth African-American player in the history of the team.

Downing threw a two-hitter in his first start. The rotation of Ford, Bouton, Terry, Williams, and Downing would become one of the deepest in club history. In Mantle's absence, the club started to win and pull away.

This was a different Yankee team. The Bombers of old were getting old, and while Tom Tresh and Joe Pepitone supplied some power, this team couldn't wait for the three-run homer anymore because most of the time it never came. Neither did these Yankees have a running game. The offense hadn't been this anemic since 1959, when the Yankees finished third.

But they won again because of their pitching, their defense, and their reputation, for the league's bottom feeders in Boston, Washington, and Kansas City rolled over before them. Mantle returned in August and hit a dramatic home run in his first at bat, but he still suffered through his least productive season. Maris was also sidelined for much of the year and ended 1963 with only 53 RBIs.

Despite carrying the load when Mantle was hurt and hitting .360 for the first three weeks after Mantle's injury, Maris had become the whipping boy. The fans and the press blamed him for the team's offensive struggles, although that responsibility rightly should have been handed to Mantle, for he was the player who simply couldn't stay healthy enough to win. Maris didn't help himself. On the top shelf of his locker was what Milton Gross described delicately as "a cast of a closed fist except for the middle finger." Maris told Gross that the sculpture was "for when I have a good day and the writers come looking for me." Of course it also didn't help Maris that Gross wrote about it.

Nevertheless, the Yankees were still favored against the NL champion Los Angeles Dodgers. The Dodgers' offense, described best by one writer as "pitty-pat," made the '63 Yanks look like the '27 Yanks in comparison. But then again, the Dodger pitching staff, paced by Sandy Koufax and Don Drysdale, made even the Yankees' staff seem ordinary. Houk was unconcerned. The Yankees were finally healthy and able to field the team that Houk had envisioned in the spring.

Privately, the Yankees dismissed the anemic Dodgers, believing that their pitching would shut them down. They were certain that they'd pound enough home runs off Koufax and Drysdale to make the difference. They'd heard all about Koufax, who had led the NL with 304 strikeouts, 25 wins, and a 1.88 ERA, but the Yankees thought they'd have little trouble with him. They were a fastball-hitting team.

Their confidence lasted all of about five minutes. For as Joe Trimble noted after game one at the Stadium, "The Yankees thought Sandy Koufax was human. 'Taint so."

Kubek opened the game and struck out, bringing up

Bobby Richardson, one of the best bat control artists in the league. In 630 regular-season at bats, he'd struck out only 22 times.

But Koufax blew him away for strikeout 23. The Yankees now knew they were in trouble, just as surely as the Dodgers knew that with Koufax on the mound they only needed to score one or two runs.

They got five off Ford, and Koufax struck out 15, a new Series record. The Yankees were completely overmatched. In game two Houk went with Downing, passing over both Terry—a proven commodity in the Series—and Bouton, who'd won 21 games. He was afraid of the Dodger running game and thought the left-hander could keep Maury Wills and the other Dodger speedsters from stealing.

But the Dodgers ran early and often. Downing picked off Wills, but he beat Pepitone's poor throw to second to start things off, and the Dodgers scored two first-inning runs. Pitcher Johnny Podres, who as a member of the Dodgers in 1955 had said confidently of New York that "I can beat them any day of the week," proved that was true in L.A.'s 4–1 win.

The Yankees were reeling, and it didn't get better in Los Angeles. "It's enough to make a guy lock himself in a closet with a bottle of booze," wrote entertainer Jackie Gleason, whom the *Post* employed as a columnist for the Series. "The Yankees look like they forgot their Geritol. The Dodgers look like they took too much."

The Yankees were as tired as Gleason's jokes. The Dodgers made the Yankees look old and slow. Whitey Ford even admitted as much to old friend Toots Shor, saying, "We're playing like old men." Drysdale twirled a three-hitter, and the Dodgers won game three, 1–0. "The standard joke on the Dodgers," wrote Dick Young, "is this: They get a run in the first or second inning then say to the pitcher, 'There's your run; now hold it.'"

That's just about the way game four went, although the Dodgers waited until the fifth to get that run, when Frank Howard crushed a home run. Mantle did the same to tie it, and then Pepitone lost a throw from Boyer in the crowd and the Dodgers walked off with a 2–1 win. "I see how Koufax won 25 games," said Berra. "What I don't understand is how he lost five."

"The fall from the top is long," wrote Young afterward, "and when you hit bottom it makes a big noise." The sweep shook the Yankees, but not the way it should have. They didn't hear what was obvious to everyone else. The 1950s were over, and the game was starting to pass the Yankees by. When Houk and Hamey looked at the Yankee roster, they still saw the Yankees of seasons past. And although they should have known better, when they looked to the farm system they saw promise where there was none.

For most of his nine-year Yankee career, shortstop–utility man Tony Kubek placed second or third in fielding percentage for his position. He injured his back in a touch football game in 1962 and was forced to retire at age 29 in 1965.

YANKEE AMERICAN LEAGUE
GOLD GLOVE AWARDS

1957 Bobby Shantz, P

1958 Bobby Shantz, P
Norm Siebern, OF

1959 Bobby Shantz, P

1960 Bobby Shantz, P
Roger Maris, OF

1961 Bobby Richardson, 2B

1962 Bobby Richardson, 2B
Mickey Mantle, OF

1963 Elston Howard, C
Bobby Richardson, 2B

1964 Elston Howard, C
Bobby Richardson, 2B

1965 Joe Pepitone, 1B
Bobby Richardson, 2B
Tom Tresh, OF

1966 Joe Pepitone, 1B

1969 Joe Pepitone, 1B

1972 Bobby Murcer, OF

1973 Thurman Munson, C

1974 Thurman Munson, C

1975 Thurman Munson, C

1977 Graig Nettles, 3B

1978 Chris Chambliss, 1B
Graig Nettles, 3B

1982 Ron Guidry, P
Dave Winfield, OF

1983 Ron Guidry, P
Dave Winfield, OF

1984 Ron Guidry, P
Dave Winfield, OF

1985 Ron Guidry, P
Don Mattingly, 1B
Dave Winfield, OF

1986 Ron Guidry, P
Don Mattingly, 1B

1987 Don Mattingly, 1B
Dave Winfield, OF

1988 Don Mattingly, 1B

1989 Don Mattingly, 1B

1991 Don Mattingly, 1B

1992 Don Mattingly, 1B

1993 Don Mattingly, 1B

1994 Don Mattingly, 1B
Wade Boggs, 3B

1995 Wade Boggs, 3B

1997 Bernie Williams, OF

1998 Bernie Williams, OF

1999 Bernie Williams, OF
Scott Brosius, 3B

2000 Bernie Williams, OF

2001 Mike Mussina, P

Just after the Series the Yankees elevated six young players to their major league roster, presumably the next wave of talent waiting in the wings to carry the dynasty for the next decade. Of the six players — Elvio Jimenez, Roger Repoz, Pete Mikkelsen, John Chambers, Chet Trail, and Tom Dukes — only Mikkelsen would have any kind of sustained major league career, and even that would be modest.

Had Ruppert or Barrow or Weiss or even Stengel been on board, they'd have made some decisive changes. That's why they'd remained on top for so long. But this regime was living in the past. Houk and Hamey made changes without changing direction.

A year before, while the Yankees waited out the rain in San Francisco, Hamey told Houk he would retire after the 1963 season and offered him the job as Yankee general manager. Houk, who was far better suited for the field, wasn't sure he was qualified. Hamey asked him to think it over; when Houk arrived at Fort Lauderdale in February, he had decided to take the job. His first task, with the input of Hamey and Topping, was to select a manager for 1964.

True to form, he stayed in-house. Yogi Berra was a Yankee to the core and nearly ready to retire as an active player. Throughout the 1963 season he had huddled at Houk's side, learning the job. The Yankee players knew the change would take place, but they kept silent.

It was an organizational decision made by organizational men for organizational reasons. But nobody in the organization understood that what really needed to change was the organization itself.

Hamey's retirement and Houk's promotion were announced simultaneously on October 22. Topping called Houk "the only logical candidate," the youngest GM in Yankee history, and the first with field experience in both the majors and minors. Not true, for Ed Barrow had managed in both the majors and minors, but Topping was trying to justify the change. Houk was not only the youngest but also the least experienced GM in club history. He would be new to every administrative task and taking over at a time when business as usual was about to change. Baseball would soon adopt the free agent draft of minor league players, bringing an end to the Yankees' long-standing advantage in that area.

And there was still the lingering problem of the Yankees and race. Houk was a company man, and the status quo had been just fine with him. Thus far the Yankees, incredibly, had hardly paid a price for their outdated approach.

Berra was officially named manager three days later. Reaction in New York was positive, but tempered. On the one hand, he'd never managed anything, unless one counted the Yankee pitching staff. On the other hand, he'd been a helluva player, and over the last few seasons several teams in love with the Yankee mystique, including Tom Yawkey's Red Sox, had approached the club and asked to speak with Berra about managing their team. If others thought he was managerial material, what reason was there for the Yankees to think otherwise?

Besides, Berra's cartoonish appearance and verbal gymnastics caused everyone to recall Stengel. All Stengel had done with the Yankees was win, but as manager of the Mets he'd somehow made losing not only palatable but also wildly popular. Berra was nearly as entertaining in print as Stengel, and public relations played a huge role in his hiring.

Leonard Shecter accurately predicted that "this will be a big season for Yogi Berra's wit," repeating many of the malaprops that are even better known today. Such coverage thrilled the Yankees — Berra hadn't managed a game yet, and he was already getting good press. He got more at his first news conference. According to Dick Young's account, Berra was a veritable joke machine, saying he hoped "to stay in the same shoes as Houk did" and that he'd learned how to manage from Stengel and Houk because "you can observe a lot just by watching." Asked if he could be harsh enough to enforce discipline, he said, "In anything you do, you have to put your foot down somewhere along the line."

Shecter called Berra's line about observing by watching a "cuddly line" that was merely part of the "Berra myth. Reliable witnesses said he never said it." Although some of Berra's famed malaprops were genuine, many others were mostly shtick, misstatements gussied up by writers for public consumption — as one alleged Yogi-ism admits: "I never said most of what I said." Stengel, on the other hand, really said what the press reported, but he used the convoluted logic of Stengelese for entertainment purposes

Mickey Mantle enjoyed his last great year in 1964, batting .303 with 35 homers and 111 RBIs. The Yankees forged the last link of a forty-year dynasty, although they barely won the pennant and lost the World Series to the St. Louis Cardinals in seven games.

employed him as a spokesman and vice president. Not bad for a guy with an eighth-grade education.

But the Yogi-isms served their purpose, for they displaced more serious discussions over his qualifications. Shecter was one of the few writers to look closely at that question. He wondered whether the players would take Berra seriously. Mantle and Ford had responded to the news by sending their new manager a telegram informing him that they were retiring to become pro golfers. That cavalier treatment, Shecter thought, was worrisome. Berra had long been the butt of jokes from Yankee players. "The kidding Berra has taken around the clubhouse sometimes came dangerously close to ridicule," warned Shecter. And stripped of the public relations shtick, Berra was sensitive about the way he spoke and his lack of education, particularly around the press. He could be surly, suspicious, and evasive. He was being handed a first-place team, and the feeling was, noted Shecter, that "Berra could read his comic books on the bench and still win." The Yankees hoped that was true.

From the very beginning of the 1964 season, the Yankees didn't take Berra seriously. Houk hadn't acquired any players of consequence in the off-season, reinforcing the notion that the Yankees could and should win with what they had. Yankee veterans, who knew Berra as a teammate, ran roughshod over his tentative efforts to enforce any kind of discipline, and younger Yankees like Pepitone, Bouton, and Linz, who were less respectful of authority to begin with, looked at the behavior of the veterans as tacit permission for them to virtually ignore him. It was a loose camp, as players practiced indifferently and partied hard. They all knew they'd be in the lineup anyway, and with Mantle relatively healthy again, they expected to be better without even trying.

But when the Yankees got off to their usual slow start, the number of nagging injuries began to mount. As players who never got into shape in the spring now tried to do so, they started to blame Berra for their own poor performance, and the veterans went over his head to whine to Houk about every decision he made.

They were right, to a point. Berra managed just as he had caught when he first came to the major leagues — cautiously. He didn't inspire confidence by sometimes wondering out loud whether he should bunt, steal, change

only. When he had to say something important, he used the king's English. Berra's verbal foibles were accidents made popular by the former major leaguer turned broadcaster Joe Garagiola, who was also his childhood friend. In later years those foibles were milked for their commercial potential and helped make Berra rich. He had always been popular with fans and was a near-millionaire already owing to a favorable relationship with Yoo-Hoo soft drinks, which

pitchers, or take some other action in the midst of a game. But it wasn't entirely his fault either.

All the talent that had once been funneled toward the Yankees was now signing elsewhere. The Yankee roster, which had once been the deepest in the game, now included a number of players they had no faith in and were afraid to use. Ralph Terry, Bill Stafford, and Stan Williams all struggled in the fourth-starter spot, and the bullpen was ordinary, a situation Berra didn't help by warming guys up and then not putting them in, wasting their best stuff.

For the first time in generations the best young talent in the league didn't reside in New York but in Minnesota, where Cuban outfielder Tony Oliva was becoming a star, in Los Angeles, where young Dean Chance was already the best pitcher in the league, and in Chicago, Baltimore, and Detroit. While New York's top 15 players were the class of the league, the rest of the roster was below average.

First Baltimore and then Chicago controlled first place while the Yankees lingered a few games back, expecting to catch fire but never quite doing so. The club nudged into first place on August 6 and then played 15 straight games against Baltimore and Chicago. It was a great opportunity to put the pennant away, the kind of opportunity the Yankees always seemed to take advantage of. But this edition of the Yankees went a listless 5–10.

Meanwhile, a series of events were setting up the last hurrah. On August 11, the Yankees brought up rookie pitcher Mel Stottlemyre. He'd gone 13–3 at triple-A Richmond and in the spring had impressed pitching coach Johnny Sain. For a young pitcher, he wasn't just a thrower. Stottlemyre had a good curve and a sinking fastball, and he knew, even then, how to pitch, working the corners and getting ground balls. For the remainder of the season he was the Yankees' best pitcher.

Then, on August 13, word leaked out that the team was being sold. Their suitor was as surprising as the fact that they were being dealt in the middle of the season, a sign many saw as an admission by the club that next year had already arrived. The Columbia Broadcasting System (CBS), the so-called Tiffany network, was buying the Yankees.

At first blush, it looked like the perfect match, the number-one television network and baseball's number-one team, the best pairing since Joe and Marilyn. It would prove to be just about as successful and as well thought out beforehand — plenty of sizzle and sex but damn little substance.

Baseball had concluded its annual summer meeting of owners only two days before, and there had been nary a word about the sale. Then AL president Joe Cronin polled American League ownership by telegram and hastily approved the sale. Owners Arthur Allyn of Chicago and Charlie Finley of Kansas City howled. It smelled like the inside deal it was. Finley called it "another example of the shenanigans of the American League president and the New York Yankees."

CBS, obviously, was interested in the Yankees for their profit potential as a TV and radio commodity. Broadcast revenue already earned the team an easy $2 million annually, most of which they didn't have to share then and still don't now. Although CBS didn't have rights to broadcast the World Series in 1964, they had broadcast a *Game of the Week* for a number of years. They made the Yankees as much a part of their regular lineup as *The Ed Sullivan Show* and sent more than half a million dollars a year the Yankees' way. The hot television topic du jour was cable technology, which carried the promise of forcing consumers to pay for what they had once received for free. CBS was the first to envision "America's team," and they were named the Yankees.

CBS paid $11.2 million for 80 percent of the team. Topping and Webb each retained 10 percent, but CBS had an option to purchase the remaining shares in the future. Topping would stay in place as Yankee president until that day came.

But instead of gaining the inside track in regard to broadcasting rights, the opposite happened to CBS. Finley and Allyn continued to raise questions about the deal and complained to the Justice Department. One government lawyer termed the marriage of broadcaster and ballclub "an incipient monopoly. . . . I don't like the looks of the whole thing." One of the keys to baseball's economic health, at least from the perspective of ownership, was its long-standing exemption from antitrust legislation. There is no more sacred cow in the game, and once baseball saw that Washington was willing to go there, CBS got the message and backed off before ever revealing its plans. CBS was left with a team, but there was nothing the broadcasting company could do with it.

Topping and Webb had hoodwinked them anyway. As attractive as the Yankees' bottom line appeared, the vat of cash that CBS envisioned amounted to so many figures on paper. The well of talent was dry, and the organization was ready to go into an extended drought. CBS would be left chewing on straw.

In the midst of all this Houk reportedly made some ill-timed, racially charged remarks to *Newsday.* Houk denied making the statements, but nevertheless the issue had been raised at a most inopportune time. Then the club lost four in a row to Chicago. As they traveled by bus to the airport on August 20, Phil Linz pulled out of his pocket a two-dollar harmonica that he'd bought the day before and tried to teach himself how to play "Mary Had a Little Lamb."

Berra was testy after his club's fourth straight defeat. There was rampant speculation that he was about to be replaced. Had it not been for the sale to CBS and Houk's run-in with *Newsday,* he probably would have been. From the front of the bus he yelled, "Hey, Linz, shut that thing up!" Linz didn't hear him. Mantle thought it was funny, and told Linz the manager wanted him to play louder. He did, and Berra yelled again. This time Linz heard him. Pissed off about not playing, and dismissive of the manager anyway, Linz yelled back, "I didn't lose the game," and kept playing.

Berra bolted from his seat. Standing over Linz with his hand raised, he told Linz to put his harmonica in a place it couldn't be played. The two started yelling back and forth, and Linz finally tossed the harmonica at Berra. He swatted it away. It struck Pepitone on the knee, and he started howling in mock pain. While Berra steamed and stormed off, the rest of the Yankees laughed.

Many subsequent observers later cited the incident as the day Berra asserted his authority and the Yankees turned the season around. Not true. Their slide continued as the team lost four of the next seven to fall further back. Linz was fined $200, but he also got a $20,000 endorsement contract from Hohner Harmonica.

The Yankee surge was more the product of the schedule than the harmonica. New York was finally done playing Baltimore and Chicago, who had to play each other at the end of August. They beat each other up and then slumped, as each club played barely .500 baseball in September against teams they had beaten handily all year. Meanwhile, the Yankees finally started getting healthy, or at least close to it. Mantle's legs were a mess — he'd jammed his knee in mid-August — but he went out there every day in spite of it. "The Yankee pennant hopes," wrote Maury Allen in the *Post,* "rest on Elasticfoam," the commercial name for the bandages wrapped around Mantle's knees and thighs. They moved him to right field again, putting Maris in center, and padded the outfield walls at the Stadium to protect their star in the unfamiliar position. He still wasn't hitting as expected, but his daily presence in the lineup gave the other Yankees some good pitches to hit. Howard hit near .350 for the month, while Pepitone and Maris knocked in nearly 60 runs between them.

There was also, finally, a trade. Houk had stood pat all year as he pondered Berra's fate and watched the standings before finally deciding to do nothing and let him fall. But Dan Topping and CBS were under fire over the sale and eager to curry some favor. So on September 5, with the Yankees still four games out, and over the objections of Houk, Topping acquired veteran pitcher Pedro Ramos from Cleveland for $75,000 and some players to be named later (eventually Ralph Terry and Bud Daley). Ramos, who threw hard, had long been a valuable starter for Washington. The Indians had put him in the bullpen, and he was having a terrible year. But he'd long dreamed of pitching for New York — he'd been telling the Yankees that for years.

Although he wouldn't be eligible for the postseason because he was acquired after August 31, Ramos was immense in relief the rest of the way. He pulled down eight saves and gave up only 13 hits and no walks in 22 innings spread across 13 games, shoring up the Yankee pen at a critical time. Had they acquired him a week earlier, they might have won a world championship.

Still, for the last time in a long time the Yankees were the Yankees again. They pulled into first place on September 17, beating the Angels 6–2 as Mantle got his 2,000th hit in the sixth inning and his 450th home run in the seventh. New York went 22–6 in September, despite losing Kubek to a sprained wrist, and clinched the pennant in game 161 on October 3 with an 8–3 win over Cleveland.

Pitcher Jim Bouton (left) and infielder Tom Tresh react to the news of August 13, 1964, reporting the sale of the controlling interest in the Yankees by Dan Topping to CBS.

They finished one game ahead of Chicago and two games in front of Baltimore.

They were more relieved than anything. Despite New York's 99 victories, it was not so much that the Yankees had won this pennant as that Baltimore and Chicago had lost it. Mantle admitted that he had figured the Yankees were out of it "around the middle of the season." Yankee fans had concurred, and attendance dropped for the third season in a row, down to only 1.3 million. In contrast, the Mets, playing with no expectations of victory, moved into brand-new Shea Stadium adjacent to the World's Fair. They won 53 games, finished 40 games out of first place, and outdrew the Yankees by more than 400,000 fans. For the first time since the end of World War II, the Yankees weren't the most popular team in New York.

While the Yankees fought for their pennant, National League contenders underwent one of the closest pennant races in major league history. On September 21, the Philadelphia Phillies, with a record of 90–61, seemed to have the pennant in hand: they led the Reds by five games,

the Cardinals by six, and the Giants by seven. But the Phillies collapsed, going 2–9 the rest of the way. The Cardinals went 10–3 to steal a pennant.

The contrast between the Cardinals and the Yankees was dramatic. The Yankees had won, finally, with what had always worked for them before, pitching and power. But the Yankees represented the past, the end of a long tradition of success that had begun in the era of Babe Ruth and was based on the home run. The Cardinals were the future—better balanced, deeper, younger, faster, and like every Yankee opponent in recent years, considerably blacker. Four members of the starting lineup—outfielders Curt Flood and Lou Brock, first baseman Bill White, and shortstop Julian Javier—were black or Latin, as was pitching ace Bob Gibson. The Cardinals had power, but it was the kind of power that led to doubles and triples and kept the pressure on. While the addition of Stottlemyre gave New York an edge in starting pitching, the Cardinals had the deeper bullpen, and the Yankees would have neither Kubek nor Ramos for the Series.

Almost by habit, the Yankees were again installed as 2–1 favorites in the Series. Like the Yankees themselves, most observers still looked at the Yankees and saw the

1962

dynasty that had been rather than the fading collection of stars and half-talents they were becoming.

In a sense, the Yankees lost the Series in game one. Ford's eight or ten extra starts each season since 1960 had caught up with him. He'd pitched under increasing pain over the course of the year, and his arm gave out. He couldn't hold a 4–2 lead and had to be pulled from the game as the Yankees lost, 9–5. An artery in his shoulder no longer carried blood to the rest of his arm, leaving his fingers numb and cold. Without Ford, whom one observer accurately called "a walking Series record book," the Yankees were seriously disadvantaged.

But that description pointed out the Yankees' problem. Ford had once been nearly unbeatable in the World Series, but since setting the new scoreless innings mark, he'd lost four Series games in a row. He wasn't that guy anymore. The same could be said of many of his teammates.

In truth, the Yankees lost the 1964 Series owing to a number of bad decisions that had been made over the last 20 years. Their failure to integrate, the increase in Ford's workload, the recent sale of the team, their loss of dominance in the New York market, and a dozen other poor choices all added up and came due at about the same time. It was remarkable that they'd stayed on top as long as they did, and equally remarkable that they pushed the Cardinals to seven games. Stottlemyre and Bouton were both magnificent in the Series, Richardson collected 13 hits, and Mantle, playing on one leg, hit three home runs and led everyone in total bases. But in the end the Cardinals were simply better, a team coming into its prime as opposed to one searching for a last hurrah.

Bob Gibson's victory in game seven was emblematic. Stottlemyre, pitching on two days' rest, ran out of steam, and the Cardinals pulled ahead 6–0. The Yankees battled back on Mantle's three-run home run, and in the ninth Clete Boyer and Phil Linz hit solo home runs, but Gibson had just enough to finish. The Yankees, wrote Tommy Holmes in the *Herald Tribune*, "tripped over the last hurdle and sprawled inelegantly on their red faces. They were still driving at the finish, but in vain."

Rookie pitcher Mel Stottlemyre arrived midway through the 1964 season and won nine of twelve starts. In the World Series he beat Cardinal ace Bob Gibson in game two, then lost to Gibson in game seven, pitching on two days' rest.

Bob Gibson throws a strike to Phil Linz of the Yankees, the first pitch of the seventh game of the 1964 World Series. Gibson pitched a complete game and the Cardinals won, 7–5, ending five decades of dynastic Yankee glory.

Not until the Series ended did the New York press begin to recognize that the Yankees' defeat had been no accident. "These Yankees don't make the play," wrote Dick Young.

These Yankees made nine series errors and a few other goofs that escape the boxscore. . . . People used to talk about the invincible Yankees and how homers won pennants and the World Series but that was only partially the truth. The whole truth is that the old Yankees knew how to stop the other guy from scoring, too, and these Yankees don't.

The old Yankees. That was a phrase that hadn't been heard before. The whole team was now in the past tense.

Young went on. "They run on Mantle because they know the arm has gone along with the legs, so they take liberties they wouldn't have dared a few years ago, when

Mantle was a whole ballplayer, and great." He might as well have been describing the franchise itself, for the Yankees were now neither whole nor great, and their aura of invincibility had been thoroughly shattered. He then warned: "The last Yankee manager to lose a World Series in seven got fired."

Milton Gross piled on in the *Post.*

The blow that struck the Yankees as they lost the World Series to the Cardinals is only the first which may fall on Yogi Berra's shaky crew before they play baseball again next spring. Many are thinking this is the end of the Yankee dynasty as we've known it. . . . [T]he once lordly Yanks, pressured at the gate by the Mets . . . will have to scuffle like ordinary mortals. . . . Pride did not go before the fall, but what comes after could become the most frantic juggling act in show biz history.

On October 17, a few days after the Series ended, Berra bounced into a meeting with Topping and Houk expecting to be handed a contract for the next season or two. Instead, he stumbled out stunned: he'd been bounced upstairs to a job amorphously titled "special field consultant." Berra, Houk and Topping had concluded, couldn't control the team.

But the Yankee organization still didn't get it and still didn't understand that changing managers wasn't going to fix anything. It wasn't that they were no longer the Yankees of old, but simply that they were old Yankees. Houk had made the decision to fire Berra back in August when it looked like neither the Yankees nor the Cardinals would be playing in October. His choice then was Cardinal manager Johnny Keane, a no-nonsense guy who was more compatible with the corporate image the Yankees were trying to project. Keane was feeling unappreciated by St. Louis and had let the Yankees know he was interested. Winning the World Series hadn't made him change his mind. At about the same time Berra was walking out of the Yankee front office, Keane was walking into the Cardinal front office and tendering his resignation. The Yankees hired him on October 20.

Nobody had ever seen anything like it. There'd be a lot of that in the Bronx over the next few years.

The 1965 Yankees, shown here in formation on Opening Day, started the season as defending American League champions and ended the season in sixth place, 25 games behind the Minnesota Twins. The dynasty had crumbled, and the following season it collapsed as the Yankees slipped another four places in the standings— to dead last.

1965–1974
AFTER THE FALL

During a paralyzing transit strike in 1966, with the streets in gridlock and millions forced
to walk for miles just to get to work, New York Mayor John Lindsay said of New York, "I
still think it's a fun city." Few New Yorkers agreed. *Herald Tribune* columnist Dick Schaap
picked up on the phrase and used "Fun City" as an ironic description of a city that was
becoming just the opposite, a place known more for its poverty than its wealth, for its
crime rather than its creativity, for its past rather than its present, and certainly not the
near future.

By the mid-1960s the postwar boom was over in New York. People and industry had left
the city in droves, and the tax base had collapsed. City services suffered. No one in power
wanted to admit that grime and garbage had replaced the glitz and glamour that had long
been New York's trademark. The city spent money it didn't have to prop up a fading image,
initiating a decade of deficit spending that nearly sent the city into bankruptcy.

New York was rapidly becoming a place that used to be something. Just like the Yankees. Over the next decade they became as tawdry and worn as the city they represented. In 1965 forty years of dominance by the New York Yankees came to a sudden end. Johnny Keane had been hired to manage a team that simply didn't exist anymore. The problems the Yankees had on the field and in the front office came to a head just as the structure of baseball was changing. Baseball's signature franchise became one of its sorriest, and the franchise suffered through its most frustrating seasons since Babe Ruth played in Boston. While the collapse wouldn't last very long, compared to what had come before it seemed like forever. But even worse, hardly anyone would seem to care. The Yankees were yesterday.

"I know this is a sound and powerful ballclub. . . . A man would be a fool if he started changing things around," said Keane at the press conference announcing his appointment. He hadn't been on the job 15 minutes, and he was already clueless about the team's troubles. Seduced by the Yankee name, he had walked blindly into a situation for which he was thoroughly unprepared. From the players on the field to the front office and the roundtable of CBS executives who liked seeing the Yankee logo on their stationery, nearly everyone connected to the franchise suffered from the same delusion. They all thought the Yankees just had to start playing like the Yankees again.

It wasn't that simple. The gaps in the Yankee roster during the 1964 season widened in the off-season as everyone got a little older. In the front office Houk's do-nothing approach kept the focus on the bottom line, holding down salaries. He didn't make a single trade of consequence. Keane was on his own.

The manager tried to lay down the law in spring training. A baseball lifer who'd once studied for the priesthood, Keane was stern and serious. The fast and loose Yankees didn't want to hear it. Although Keane had promised to make no changes, as he familiarized himself with the out-of-shape veteran team he did just that.

The players blanched. They were the Yankees, for crying out loud, and Keane expected them to work on fundamentals, adhere to a curfew for the first time in their careers, and win during spring training. When he pushed, the Yankees first pushed back, then stood back and let him fall on his face. It wasn't pretty. They didn't try to hide their disdain for the manager either on or off the field. When Keane tried to sweat the alcohol out of Mantle one humid morning by making him chase fly ball after fly ball, the Yankee star fired a baseball past Keane's head. When the manager's daughter came to visit, Joe Pepitone tried to pick her up.

In the 1964 World Series Keane's Cardinals had run the Yankees ragged, and he wanted the Yankees to play the same aggressive style, but the Yankees weren't buying it. They didn't know how. Since the days of Ruth, the Yankees had, as one player noted, "just hit and play[ed] defense." They felt they knew how to play that game and had the rings to prove it.

When the usual injuries started piling up, the aging team became unsound and not very powerful. They grunted their way through spring training and into April, and this time there was no depth to fall back on, no Gil McDougalds available to fill in wherever needed, no Roger Marises available in trade, no more Mel Stottlemyres or Al Downings ready to win right away. There were only the unknown and unproven, names like Roger Repoz, Ross Moschito, and Jack Cullen, pretenders whom the Yankees had signed not for their talent but for their affordability.

That wasn't likely to change. In their lust to improve the bottom line, the Yankees forgot that their success had always come from pouring their resources back into the team. The best young players had always signed with the Yankees because New York outbid everyone else, and when they didn't, all they had to do was ask, "Do you want to play for the Yankees, kid?" But when Topping and Webb had cut back, the new, more aggressive owners of other clubs raised the bidding past the point where that romantic plea made sense.

The Yankees first blinked, then closed their eyes entirely. In 1964 the Los Angeles Angels had paid $200,000 for collegiate outfielder Rick Reichardt. That summer and fall the A's Charlie Finley had spent $634,000 for 80 players, signing nearly every other talented amateur player of consequence. At the same time the Yankee free agent budget was under $200,000. In 1966 it would drop to only $75,000.

The poorer franchises had been howling over escalating player costs, and in the off-season baseball adopted the free agent draft, assigning rights to amateur free agents in reverse order of each team's finish in the standings, a football idea designed to keep bonuses down and level the playing field. The Yankees meekly signed on and slit their competitive throat. Playing in New York had always provided a huge advantage. The last thing the Yankees needed was a level playing field.

On Opening Day of 1965 the Yankees lost to the Twins, 5–4. Mantle, who couldn't run anymore, played left field. Tresh took over in center, but little else had changed.

After their usual slow start, the Yankees kept losing, first by a little and then by a lot, as the injuries added up. Bouton had a sore arm and didn't pitch well. Maris, who'd rebounded nicely in 1964, pulled a hamstring. Mantle's legs came undone. Elston Howard needed surgery for bone chips. Kubek's shoulder started bothering him.

In other years the Yankees had stayed calm and waited for everyone to get healthy. But Keane quickly lost patience. By May he was in panic mode and started pressuring his players. He questioned small injuries, played guys who were hurt, and made their injuries worse. He squandered rallies by playing for the single run. Stottlemyre, Ford, and Downing provided adequate starting pitching, and Ramos remained effective in relief, but that wasn't enough.

In mid-May Houk looked at the nameplate on his office door, remembered he was general manager, and figured he'd finally better get busy. He picked up the phone and called the usual suspect, Kansas City. But under new owner Charlie Finley, the A's had changed, and Houk was no George Weiss. He gave up two proven major leaguers, pitcher Rollie Sheldon and catcher Johnny Blanchard, for part-time veteran catcher Doc Edwards, a .224 hitter in 1964. It had always been the other way around. Edwards hit .190 with New York in 1965 while Sheldon led the A's in wins. The deal made the Yankees weaker.

One of the few highlights of the 1965 season was pitcher Mel Stottlemyre's inside-the-park grand-slam home run against the Red Sox at Yankee Stadium. Attempting to tag the sliding Stottlemyre is Boston catcher and future team co-owner Haywood Sullivan.

Brooklyn native Joe Pepitone possessed tremendous potential but squandered what could have been a great career with personal problems and a social life worthy of the swinging sixties. His best season as a Yankee was 1964, when he drove in 100 runs while socking 28 homers.

By mid-July the Yankees were in seventh place, already nearly 20 games behind the first-place Twins. The season was over. The veterans didn't know how to play on a losing team and had quit. Desperate, Keane and Houk brought up some rookies and started playing kids. Roy White, Bobby Murcer, and Horace Clarke all made their debuts in 1965. But they weren't ready yet, and the others couldn't play. The expected surge never came.

In August the Mets let Stengel go, and the local press began advocating his return to the Yankees, even though they knew that by now he really was too old for the job. On September 8, after losing seven straight, the Yankees ended such speculation by announcing that Keane's contract had been extended through 1966. "We cannot blame our present position on the manager," said Houk. Well, not all of it. The fault lay with everyone on the payroll. They finished sixth, 77–85, Yankees in uniform only, with a team batting average of .235. And it wasn't about to get better.

Houk continued to demonstrate his lack of front-office acumen, and Webb and Topping continued to demonstrate that they didn't care — Webb wisely sold out. CBS continued to demonstrate that it knew more about running a television network than a ballclub. At least the network canceled failing TV shows. CBS had made this team the centerpiece of the nationally broadcast *Yankee Game of the Week.* "Game of the Weak" would have been more accurate.

The off-season provided one last chance to stop the slide. Houk could have traded some big names and received equal value in younger talent, but the GM still thought 1965 had been an anomaly, not the norm. He didn't make any significant trades, and the team entered the 1966 season unchanged apart from an additional year of deterioration. "We expect to win the pennant," said Houk. He didn't say in what year.

Keane brought up more kids in 1966, such as pitchers Fritz Peterson and Dooley Womack. They weren't enough. In early May the Indians beat the Yankees three straight to run their record to 15–1. The Yankees were 4–15 and next year was already here. The only thing the Yankees were leading the league in was boring baseball and acts of defiance. When Joe Pepitone skipped an exhibition game at West Point, Keane fined him $250. Pepitone, whose life was coming apart at the seams and whose salary was already going straight to an attorney to pay off debts, had been fined so much he'd lost track of how much he owed. He was well on his way to blowing what could have been a fine career.

Keane, a good man in an obviously bad situation, was fired on May 7. Someone had to be sacrificed, and Houk wasn't going to fire himself. He continued to misread the situation. Instead of rebuilding, he simply switched suits and returned to the field. Dan Topping's son, Dan Topping Jr., became general manager. Milton Gross called the move a "scapegoat for Houk's failure" and termed the junior Topping "scarcely qualified." Houk stayed the course. "I still think we can win the pennant."

The Yankees stayed above water for about a month and a half because for about a month and a half Mickey Mantle was Mickey Mantle for the last time. That was enough — almost — to make the Yankees the Yankees again. He couldn't run anymore, but when he was healthy he could still hit. He hit his first home run of the year on May 9 and over the next two months hit 17 more and even moved back to center field. The team went 36–29 over the stretch — almost respectable.

Then the Yankees lost their tenuous hold on respectability when Mantle tore a hamstring. Ford was almost done, and Maris had a bad wrist. Houk, who'd been everybody's friend during his first tenure as manager, found upon his return that he'd lost the respect of many of the veterans. When he was GM, he'd torn them apart during contract talks. Now, when he told them how good they were, they didn't believe him and thought he was a phony. The club quit again.

They fell into last place on September 7. The *Daily News* started using headlines with the name "Yanks" in smaller typeface in reference to the Yankees' shrinking record. Dan Topping quit and sold out on September 19. CBS vice president Mike Burke became team president.

The news kept getting worse. On a drizzly afternoon on September 21, the Yankees lost 4–1 to the White Sox. Only

YANKEE AMERICAN LEAGUE
ERA LEADERS

1920	Bob Shawkey, 2.45
1927	Wilcy Moore, 2.28
1934	Lefty Gomez, 2.33
1937	Lefty Gomez, 2.33
1943	Spud Chandler, 1.64
1947	Spud Chandler, 2.46
1952	Allie Reynolds, 2.07
1953	Eddie Lopat, 2.43
1956	Whitey Ford, 2.47
1957	Bobby Shantz, 2.45
1958	Whitey Ford, 2.01
1978	Ron Guidry, 1.74
1979	Ron Guidry, 2.78
1980	Rudy May, 2.47

413 fans sat in cavernous Yankee Stadium and watched — 413 people in a market that approached 10 million. Between the vendors, the players, and assorted other staff members, there were almost as many people on the payroll at the Stadium as there were paying customers.

The Yankees ordered the television cameras not to show the empty stands. When announcer Red Barber told the radio audience, "I don't know what the paid attendance is today, but whatever it is, it is the smallest crowd in the history of the Stadium, and this crowd is the story, not the game," Burke called him into the front office and fired him. The box score took up more room in the *Post* than the game story. Most obituaries were longer.

Yankee Stadium was starting to scare people, or at least the dwindling group of suburbanites who considered themselves Yankee fans, for most city dwellers had jumped to the Mets. The neighborhood around the ballpark had started to deteriorate as rent control gave landlords an excuse to let their buildings fall apart and displaced residents of Manhattan housing projects flooded the Bronx. Black and Puerto Rican faces on the streets around the park frightened xenophobic fans, and as the poverty in the neighborhood increased, so did the crime rate, real and imagined. Now that the Yankees weren't winning anymore, fans had an excuse to stay away. It was easier and more comforting to go to Queens and see the Mets.

All the Yankees had left was Mantle, a relic of an earlier age. Fathers still brought their sons out to see him play, but they came only once and scurried away as fast as possible.

The Yankees had never had to market themselves; they had simply opened the gates and people streamed in. Now that they needed to, they didn't know how. On T-shirt day, they didn't give them away but charged fans 25 cents. Except for holidays and weekends, crowds stayed small.

The franchise had hit bottom, finishing in last place at 70–89, 26½ games behind Baltimore. And they were not bouncing up but sitting there, unable and unwilling to do anything about it. The only cheers the Yankees heard came from those who followed every other team in every other city in baseball, everybody who'd ever felt slighted or slammed by the long-standing Yankee dynasty and the club's famed arrogance. The new national pastime became dancing on the grave of the Yankees.

Even the players were starting to bail. Tony Kubek had retired after the 1965 season. Bobby Richardson followed

Whitey Ford pitches in a nearly deserted Yankee Stadium in 1966. On September 21 of that season, the last-place Yankees reached their nadir when only 413 fans showed up to watch them lose, 4–1, to the White Sox. On the team's broadcast of the game, cameramen were ordered not to show the empty seats.

him in 1966. Mantle, Maris, Ford, and Elston Howard, all of whom were older than Richardson and Kubek, were all thinking about doing the same.

Burke finally had to admit it—the Yankees stunk. A few weeks after the end of the season Burke jettisoned pretend-GM Dan Topping Jr. and hired Lee MacPhail, Larry MacPhail's son. After leaving the Yankees in 1959, he'd served as both GM and president of the Baltimore Orioles, turning the former Browns into an annual contender. Rebuilding the Yankees would be just as daunting a task.

There was nothing to build on but memories. Attendance had dropped almost to the one-million mark for the last-place team. The farm system was virtually empty. Mantle was untouchable, as was Stottlemyre, but few of the remaining Yankees had any trade value. Bouton's arm trouble made him a has-been, and Maris's wrist injury stripped him of his power and desire. Howard and Ford were preparing to retire. Still, the club had to start somewhere, and MacPhail did what he could to start the rebuilding process.

The vaunted Yankees became the equivalent of the old Kansas City A's, sending players to contenders while contenders sent pretenders back. First to go was Clete Boyer, one of the best third basemen in baseball and the only player left with any value. He was sent to Atlanta for two prospects, pitcher Chi Chi Olivo and outfielder Bill Robinson.

The deal was telling. Trading for two players of color provided evidence that desperation was forcing the organization to change. Robinson was considered a top prospect—he'd hit .312 with 20 home runs in triple-A in 1966—and scouts liked him better than either Reggie Jackson or Reggie Smith, two players on the verge of becoming stars. Robinson was expected to be "the black Mickey Mantle."

That wish was a holdover from an earlier era and an example of just how hard it was for the organization to break with the past and look forward. The era of Ruth had flowed seamlessly into Gehrig's, then into DiMaggio's and Mantle's, and the Yankees and the New York press still expected that pattern to hold: another major star, a savior, would arrive and pull them from the doldrums. Almost without fail, any remotely promising prospect would be touted in terms of the deposed dynasty and rushed in before he was ready. Outfielders were always the next Mantle or Maris, catchers the next Berra or Howard, infielders

Shortstop Bobby Murcer arrived in New York as a teenager in 1965 and was touted as the next Mickey Mantle. Like Mantle, Murcer was from Oklahoma and was also hurried through the minors. Unlike Mantle, his talents, while considerable, weren't prodigious, and he enjoyed a solid but unspectacular 18-year career.

the next Kubek or Richardson, pitchers the next Whitey Ford. Prospect Roger Repoz, who'd done nothing in his minor league career to warrant a comparison with Mantle except look the part, had already collapsed under the weight of such expectations. Robinson would be the next.

Robinson and Steve Whitaker, who made the mistake of hitting three home runs in a week in 1966, were both thrown into the Yankee outfield in 1967, platooning with each other. Together they became the next Roger Repoz. Whitaker never became more than a fourth outfielder. Robinson eventually succeeded, but only long after the Yankees gave up on him and he rebuilt his confidence and his game with the Pittsburgh Pirates.

Bobby Murcer narrowly avoided a similar fate. One of the last notable players signed by New York before the draft, the parallels between Murcer and Mantle were too obvious to ignore. Both came from similar backgrounds in Oklahoma, and like Mantle, Murcer was a shortstop who excelled in his first professional year, a potential five-tool player. So as they had done with Mantle, the Yankees rushed Murcer to the majors.

He failed in brief trials in both 1965 and 1966. But his notoriety resulted in a change in his draft status, and he was forced into the service before his confidence was thoroughly destroyed. Murcer had two years to mature before being thrown to the wolves again. By that time he was better prepared.

Even veterans Tom Tresh and Joe Pepitone, whose modest achievements made the Yankees expect even more, fell into the trap. They'd been fine players in the early 1960s, role players on a team of stars. But now Tresh and Pepitone were the two most productive Yankees, each of them good for 20 or more home runs and—on a team increasingly challenged offensively—60 or 70 RBIs a year. But that was never enough. Because neither player was Mantle, each ended up looking like a failure as his production dropped year by year.

Boyer was the last player the Yankees had with any trade value. Since 1961 Roger Maris had been hurt much of the time and never met expectations. He was as disgusted with the Yankees as they were with him. A week after the Boyer deal, he was dealt to St. Louis, where he got healthy and resurrected his career. In exchange, all the Yankees got was Charlie Smith, a third baseman with skills as common as his name.

The 1967 season was over almost before it started. Injuries, age, and desperation led to an almost complete turnover of the starting lineup. Mantle was moved to first base in an attempt to save his knees, and Pepitone became the center fielder. The Yankees peaked on Opening Day with an 8–0 win over Washington as Stottlemyre twirled a

Basking in the sunlight late in his career, Mantle (bottom left) is joined by teammates Fritz Peterson (bottom right), Reuben Amaro (top left), and Mel Stottlemyre (top right) at Yankee Stadium. Following the 1968 season, in which he batted .237 with 18 homers, Mantle retired with seven world championships and the undying admiration of a generation of Yankee fans.

1974

two-hitter. But in the home opener on April 14, Boston rookie Billy Rohr no-hit New York for 8⅔ innings before Elston Howard broke it up. The crowd booed. In his next start in Boston, Rohr beat the Yankees again. And the Red Sox had finished ninth in 1966.

Attendance continued to drop. Ford retired in May when he lost circulation in his arm again. He walked away with 236 career victories and 106 losses, all with the Yankees. In August the club traded Elston Howard to Boston for minor league pitcher Ron Klimkowski. Boston's "Cardiac Kids" became the darlings of baseball in the midst of their "Impossible Dream" season. Desperate for fans, in late August the Yankees even held a day at the Stadium for Boston outfielder and Long Island native Carl Yastrzemski. "Yaz" should have been a Yankee. He had wanted to sign with New York, and the Yanks were prepared to outbid Boston, but a Yankee scout had ticked off Yastrzemski's father when he threw a pencil in the air during contract negotiations. He won the Triple Crown in 1967 and led the Red Sox to their first pennant since 1946. The Yankees finished ninth, 72–90.

As difficult as it was for the Yankee organization to handle the franchise's demise, it was equally hard on the press. From what seemed like the beginning of time, the Yankees had been the top franchise in all of sports. Covering the Yankees was the most coveted job in sportswriting. But now the Yankee beat was the worst in the city. The Mets, the AFL Jets, the basketball Knicks, the hockey Rangers, and even the NFL Giants were all more popular.

Even when the Yankees began to claw their way back to respectability in 1968, finishing 83–79, the press found their mediocrity as difficult to handle as their abject failure had been. Win-one-lose-one baseball was boring and would be made even more so by the Mets' stunning world championship in 1969 and 1973 pennant. In regard to the Yankees, respectability wasn't enough. The writers hated their loss of status, hated the team, hated going to work every day. It showed in their coverage; often cruel and unfair, the writers took delight in tearing down players who were doing the best they could—it wasn't their fault it wasn't 1955 anymore. Onetime young guns like Dick Young became curmudgeons before their time.

The targets they chose spoke volumes about how much had changed. Mantle, the heroic lion in winter, was still protected and considered above criticism. The once-great star was allowed to age gracefully. But the press ripped into players who didn't act like old Yankees, like Pepitone, or younger players who didn't seem to fit the Yankee mold.

Mantle decided to retire just after the start of spring training on March 1. "I've had three or four bad years in a row," he explained. His skills had been eroded by six knee operations, innumerable muscle pulls, and too many nights on the town. "I just can't hit anymore, and there's no use trying." In 1968 he had hit only .237, dropping his career batting average to .298, below .300, a figure that left him ashamed. He came to the realization—too late—that he had squandered what might have been a career of no known limits.

Yet it is hard to imagine that he could have done much more, for he still put up numbers equal to those of any player in the game and played more games in a Yankee uniform—2,401—than any other Yankee. In addition, he hit a record 18 home runs in 12 World Series and helped the Yankees win even more than Ruth had. Mantle had cracked his final home run, the 536th of his career, on September 20, 1968, against Boston pitcher Jim Lonborg at the Stadium. His home run total was the third best in history at the time, trailing only Ruth and Willie Mays. His withdrawal went unnoticed as he came to bat for the last time a week later at Fenway Park, flying out to left before leaving the game in favor of Andy Kosco. He left the game quietly, embarrassed by what he had become.

Beyond the numbers, Mickey Mantle had been the Yankees. For a generation of fans, Mantle and the Yankees—like Ruth and the Yankees, Gehrig and the Yankees, and DiMaggio and the Yankees before him—were synonymous. He represented the club's unbridled, brawny, raw power and a period of time when invincibility seemed to be the norm. The Yankees would always win again, and Mantle would always hit another home run longer than the last one. His sudden departure caused everyone to look up and wonder how he or she had gotten so old so fast. Sportswriter Jerry Izenberg put it in verse:

Where is the magic that was Mantle?
Kubek to Moose, a double play.
I don't recall getting any older.
When did they?

The press vented at the "lesser" Yankees, men they felt fell below the now-imaginary standard. A favorite target became second baseman Horace Clarke. They referred to the time disparagingly as "the Horace Clarke era" and vilified the infielder, who was actually one of the better and more productive members of the team. In fact, about the only thing that was wrong with Clarke was that he wasn't a typical Yankee — whatever that was. Typical Yankees just didn't exist anymore.

The Virgin Islands native was a natural shortstop who had served a long apprenticeship in the Yankee farm system before being moved out of position to take over at second base for Bobby Richardson. He was black and fast, a switch hitter whose game was built around his glove and his speed, a rarity in the Yankee system. Yet over the next five or six seasons he was regularly ripped, even as he led the league in fielding chances and assists at second and paced the team in runs and stolen bases. The writers focused only on what he wasn't, which was Bobby Richardson, and what he could not do gracefully, which was turn the double play.

Yankee outfielder Bobby Murcer faced a similar problem. He too became known more for what he couldn't do and who he wasn't than for what he could do and who he was. Upon his return from the military in 1969, he was thrust into the lineup and responded by hitting 26 home runs in what was essentially his rookie season. Despite becoming by far the most successful "next Mickey Mantle," even moving into center field, Murcer's career plateaued below expectations. He became a star on a team that needed a superstar, a player who teased observers by hitting .331 in 1971, a standard he would never approach again. He was just another reminder that the era of Mantle was over.

Only two players of the era escaped the stigma of the past. Pitcher Mel Stottlemyre, almost by himself, first kept the Yankees from utter collapse and then spearheaded their return to respectability. When he was on the mound, they could still beat anybody, and often did. If he had played either in another era or just a season or two longer, he might well have made the Hall of Fame. But he was a great pitcher on a bad team, and when his arm gave out midway through the 1974 season, he left the game as suddenly as he had arrived. Yet from 1964 until that day, year

after year and start after start, Stottlemyre held the Yankees together, taking the ball every fourth day and giving the otherwise undistinguished team a chance to win as his sinker induced ground ball after ground ball. He somehow managed to win 164 games, including 20 or more three times, on teams that struggled to win 80 games a year.

Second baseman Horace Clarke bore the brunt of blame when his name was affixed to the last-place Yankees of the late sixties. While addressing the mediocrity of the "Horace Clarke Era," the tag failed to acknowledge the fact that Clarke was a decent player and hardly the reason the once proud Yankees had slipped to the second division.

Outfielder Roy White also escaped the Yankee ghosts. A slender five-foot-ten, White wasn't big enough to be saddled with the "next Mantle" nonsense. Signed in 1962 as an infielder, the Compton, California, native, who overcame polio as a child, spent five full years in the Yankee system — primarily as a second baseman, slowly maturing as a hitter, using his speed, and hitting with power to the gaps — before finally getting a chance in the Yankee outfield.

After failed trials in 1966 and 1967, the switch-hitting White moved into the Yankee outfield after Joe Pepitone hurt his arm in 1968. For much of the next ten years he would be one of the few constants in the Yankee lineup. White could hit anywhere and play in all three outfield spots, and he was one of the first ballplayers to work out year-round, becoming a black belt in karate. A decade ear-

Yankee president Mike Burke's fielding prowess was only slightly better than his skill at running the dilapidated juggernaut that was the Yankees of the late sixties and early seventies. The former OSS officer led a management team that included general manager Lee MacPhail and manager Ralph Houk.

lier he'd have been the perfect addition to the Yankee dynasty and probably would have been viewed as a star. As it was, he was still almost the perfect Yankee — a thorough professional and one of the few players on the team a kid could pretend to be in sandlot games and not get laughed at.

These four players kept the Yankees afloat while the triumvirate of Houk, MacPhail, and Burke worked patiently to try to rebuild. They finally had some success. Helped by baseball's adoption of the divisional system in 1969, in 1970 the club finished a surprising second in the AL East, winning 93 games. That was still 15 games behind first-place Baltimore, and they had never really been in the race, but it was a sign of progress.

The highlight of the season was "Mickey Mantle Day," celebrated on June 8, 1969, between games of a doubleheader. As soon as Mantle poked his head from the dugout, the crowd of more than 61,000 fans let loose with all the pent-up affection they still retained for the old Yankees and started chanting, "We want Mickey! We want Mickey! We want Mickey!" over and over again.

After eight or nine minutes Mike Burke gave up trying to introduce the Yankee star. He simply waved Mantle to the microphone. Only then did the cheering stop.

Mantle was surprisingly eloquent. "I never knew how a man who knew he was going to die could say he was the luckiest man in the world," he said in reference to Lou Gehrig's farewell, "but now I understand." After his death Mantle would join Ruth, Gehrig, Huggins, and DiMaggio as one of five Yankees immortalized with his own monument in Yankee Stadium.

The first Yankee of the next generation had arrived in 1970. Top draft pick Thurman Munson, a catcher, won Rookie of the Year honors. Munson wasn't an athlete but a ballplayer, a chunky guy who looked like he'd been born with stubble on his face and dirt on his uniform. Drafted out of Kent State, Munson spent two impatient years in the minors, telling everyone he was ready. He was right, and for the next decade Munson would be one of the premier catchers in baseball, a determined clutch hitter, and the heart and soul of the Yankees. Stan Bahnsen also emerged in 1970 as a legitimate third starter behind Stot-

tlemyre and Fritz Peterson. And Lee MacPhail was proving far more adept in the trade department than Ralph Houk —at least MacPhail was trying. But attendance at Yankee Stadium remained a problem as Yankee fans proved slow to respond to the "new" Yankees.

CBS had dumped several million dollars into the Stadium, replacing seats and sprucing up the place with paint, but there wasn't very much the team's owner could do— the Stadium itself was still owned by Rice University and the land by the Knights of Columbus, both of which were acting like every other absentee owner in the South Bronx. And the Yankees were powerless to do anything to the area surrounding the Stadium. Many fans didn't feel safe parking nearby or taking the subway to the Bronx. And despite their improving record, the Yankees still hadn't been in a pennant race since 1964. Many of their recent wins and much of their respectability had come in the second half of seasons lost, after the division title had long been decided. Compared to the Mets, the Yankees were boring.

They slumped back to .500 in 1971 as the bullpen collapsed. In the spring of 1972 MacPhail made the first in a

series of key moves over the next several seasons that would eventually result in a new era.

For some reason, the Boston Red Sox fell in love with Yankee first baseman Danny Cater, a thoroughly mediocre player with no power. When they offered MacPhail lefty reliever Sparky Lyle in exchange, he jumped at the offer.

The timing couldn't have been better, because a few months earlier MacPhail had made probably the worst deal of his tenure. Desperate for a third baseman, he traded Bahnsen, who looked like an emerging ace, to the White Sox for Rich McKinney, a part-time player whom the

Albert "Sparky" Lyle arrived from Boston in 1972 in a trade for first baseman Danny Cater and soon became a Yankee superstar. Not only did he possess a hard slider, he also brought unity to the Yankee clubhouse with his madcap sense of humor. On one memorable occasion, Lyle greeted the locker room presentation of a birthday cake by sitting on it while nude.

Yankees thought, incorrectly, could play third. The move probably cost the Yankees a chance to win a pennant—Bahnsen won 21 games for Chicago, while McKinney, after a horrific three-error performance in one early season game, spent much of the year in Syracuse. As it was, Lyle almost got the Yankees a pennant anyway. In a season cut short by labor strife he saved 35 games and gave the team some much-needed swagger.

The Yankees entered September still in the race, battling Baltimore, Boston, and Detroit for the division lead, a new experience for nearly every man on the club. On September 13, they faced Boston at the Stadium with a chance to take over first place for the first time since 1964. But as Larry Merchant noted the next day in the *Post,* "The Yankees gave a party last night at the Stadium and almost nobody came." Only 15,000 fans braved the Bronx.

And the Yankees gave them little reason to. In the fifth inning of a scoreless tie, the Red Sox hit four straight balls to third baseman Bernie Allen, one of several unsatisfactory solutions to the hole left unfilled by McKinney. He caught the first but had no play, and then the Red Sox bunted. On consecutive plays Allen had to eat the ball. He then bobbled a fourth ground ball for an error, and Boston ended up scoring four runs and going on to win, 7–2. "I just plain stunk," Allen admitted later.

The loss ended Yankee pennant hopes, but in the long run it also helped the franchise move forward. CBS finally realized that the Yankees were not ready for prime time and pulled the plug.

Over the previous several years virtually every New York sports franchise, save the Mets, had been politicking for a new facility. The state of New Jersey was planning to build a multi-use facility at the Meadowlands and hoped to lure as many New York teams as possible across the Hudson. Burke was able to use the threat to wrangle a deal from the city, which feared the loss of prestige that would come with the loss of the Yankees.

The ensuing political battle was nearly as complicated as the one that had first brought the Yankees to New York, for many New Yorkers believed that the last thing the financially strapped city needed to do was provide welfare to a large corporation like CBS. But the network brought a lot of money into New York, and the city didn't want to alienate it. New York Mayor John Lindsay backed a plan to designate the Stadium and the surrounding area an urban renewal district, which would free the plan from a number of fiscal and political constraints. The city purchased the Stadium and the land it sat on for $24 million from Rice University and the Knights of Columbus, and on

March 24, 1972, the Yankees agreed to a 30-year lease. In exchange, the city promised to embark on an ambitious two-year plan to renovate the Stadium and provide key infrastructure improvements that would make it possible for fans to drive to the Stadium without feeling like they were putting themselves at risk. While the renovation was taking place in 1975 and 1976, the Yankees would share Shea Stadium with the Mets.

The plan satisfied CBS president William Paley. The network had been taking a bath as the owner of a ballclub, losing as much as $1 million a year in real money, although CBS corporate accountants were able to make it look better than that. Far from developing the Yankees as a broadcast entity, CBS had seen broadcast revenue for the failing club actually drop, to only $200,000. The Yankees, incredibly, even had to *pay* to have their games broadcast on radio. The Mets had become far more adept at milking the New York market. The Yankees were a poorly rated show in a lousy time slot.

Paley wanted to sell, but he also wanted to make sure the Yankees stayed in New York before the network got out from under the team. He feared the PR fallout if the Yankees left town under his watch, and without the Stadium deal, the value of the franchise would be diminished. Now he gave Burke the go-ahead to sell the team.

A lot had changed since CBS took over. Baseball's flagship was now one of its weakest franchises. No New Yorkers made a serious offer to buy the team. At first only one party expressed real interest.

Former New York Giants catcher and San Francisco manager Herman Franks had made a fortune in construction in California. Franks planned to back out of the Stadium deal, accept New Jersey's offer of the Meadowlands, make Willie Mays manager, and move the club. He offered CBS $12 million.

It was pathetic. In recent years other franchises, like the lowly Indians and even the expansion Seattle Pilots, had been sold for more. The Yankees were a fixer-upper, and no one was fooled.

But Burke put him off. He liked being part of the Yankees more than being part of CBS and wanted to be included in any proposed deal. Paley, who liked Burke, agreed. Burke's continuing involvement was a clear conflict of interest, but then that's often the case when-

On January 4, 1973, George Steinbrenner made the deal of a lifetime when he purchased the Yankees for $10 million, of which only $833,333.33 was his own money. Soon to start his fourth decade as owner, Steinbrenner has been one of the most controversial baseball executives in history.

grad, had been a track star in college, winning the national title in 220-yard low hurdles. The son more or less followed his father's path, attending military school and Williams College, where he too became a track star before joining the Air Force. He would go on to earn a master's degree in physical education from Ohio State, serve as a graduate assistant to the legendary football coach Woody Hayes, and become an assistant football coach at Northwestern and Purdue. Only 25, he was on track to become a head coach, but duty called. Steinbrenner's father wanted him to enter the family business.

That would prove to be the defining moment of his life: while Steinbrenner made his father's company thrive, he was clearly disappointed to be out of the game. As he earned his millions, buying American Shipbuilding and folding his father's company into the new venture, he started dabbling in sports. He bought the Cleveland Pipers AAU basketball team, joined the fledgling professional ABL, and outbid the NBA for the services of Ohio State star Jerry Lucas. The league folded, but Steinbrenner was hooked.

A lot of stocky guys in suits run companies. Only a few ever become famous. People buy sports franchises because they deliver celebrity, with the added benefit of turning one's heroes into employees. Steinbrenner liked making money, but he liked being a player more, and sports was a lot more exciting than building boats. He bought 11 percent of the Chicago Bulls, he bought a thoroughbred-racing stable, and he invested in the successful Broadway musical *Applause,* the touring show *George M.*, and several other productions. He had a lot in common with onetime Red Sox owner Harry Frazee, a theater impresario whose statement, "Baseball is essentially show business," was later aped by Steinbrenner, who said more definitively, "Baseball *is* show business."

In 1972 he thought he had a deal to buy the Cleveland Indians, but at the last minute Indians owner Vern Stouffer backed out. Now Indians GM Gabe Paul mentioned to Burke that the same guy might be interested in buying the Yankees. Burke was introduced to Steinbrenner, and they put together a deal.

It was a marriage of convenience, since each man needed the other to get what he wanted. They would be

ever a baseball team is sold. Franks' group even upped its offer to $14 million, but Burke kept stalling and shopping for another buyer who would cut him in.

Cleveland Indian president and GM Gabe Paul introduced Burke to one George Steinbrenner, a 42-year-old Great Lakes shipping magnate and CEO of the American Shipbuilding Company, which had a near-monopoly on grain-carrying container ships. While making money and making connections, he'd been floating around the fringes of the sports world for years.

Steinbrenner had grown up in suburban Cleveland, where his father, Henry, ran Kinsman Marine, a small but profitable shipping company. Henry Steinbrenner, an MIT

general partners, and a consortium of ten Steinbrenner acquaintances, best described by the Berra-ism "a group of rich millionaires," would be limited partners. They acquired the Yankees for $10 million in cash — $4 million less than what Franks' group had been willing to pay, and reportedly $6 million less than what CBS eventually spent for the franchise after buying out Topping and Webb. It was probably half the true worth of the franchise, particularly with the Stadium deal in place. Steinbrenner's initial investment — reportedly $833,333.33 — was a steal, a deal worthy of being made by Frank Farrell and William Devery.

The transaction was announced at Yankee Stadium on January 4, 1973. Burke would remain chief executive, and MacPhail and Houk would stay on. Steinbrenner promised to be an absentee owner. "My other interests, shipbuilding, horse racing, etc., keep me busy," he said. "I'd be silly trying to run a ballclub too." One could hardly help but notice at the press conference, however, that the "absentee" owner, looking like the president of the local Jaycees, was very much front and center as he mugged for the camera before the Yankee banner. But the New York press, dis-tracted by the recent news that Roberto Clemente's plane, in an attempt to deliver supplies to Nicaraguan earthquake victims, had gone down off the coast of his native Puerto Rico, gave little scrutiny to Steinbrenner. They took him at his word, although even a cursory examination of his past would have revealed that he had never been an "absentee" anything. His background was the family business, and in the Steinbrenner family business the old man had always been the real power. Now, for the first time in his life, it was George's turn.

No one since Jacob Ruppert has had more influence on the Yankee franchise than George Steinbrenner. At various times during his tenure — now stretching over three decades, the longest in Yankee history — he has been hated, vilified, mocked, berated, attacked, despised, reviled, ridiculed, and loathed, sometimes all at the same time, and often with good cause. But at the same time Steinbrenner has also been tolerated, occasionally liked, and

Bobby Murcer completes a 1973 Yankee Stadium home run trot and is greeted at the plate by Roy White (6) and Ron Blomberg (12). That year, Murcer batted .304 with 22 homers.

sometimes even loved by fans, because during his reign he made the Yankees matter again. The bottom line—and the one Steinbrenner himself has always cited—is that they have won under his stewardship, particularly in recent years. Steinbrenner deserves some credit for that, in spite of his many faults. New York is not a "Who do you know?" kind of town, but a city that looks for results. Many Yankee fans may think Steinbrenner is a jerk, but even they have to admit that he has been an effective jerk, and someone you'd rather have for you than against you.

But it has not always been easy to like the Yankees with Steinbrenner in charge, or to like Steinbrenner, for he has made himself the story too often. "The Boss"—the name he earned for his dictatorial management style, which is reminiscent of both "Boss" Tweed of Tammany fame and an organized crime boss—clearly loves being the owner of the Yankees and everything that entails: the power, the responsibility, and, in particular, the notoriety. At times he has seemed absolutely unwilling to share the spotlight with his players, managers, or other club employees. He has taken credit for successes that rightfully were the work of others, and he has distanced himself from failures that were clearly his own doing. He has demanded loyalty and yet tossed it away, paid homage to the Yankee tradition and at times trashed it and been an embarrassment— to himself, to the team he professes to love, and to the city the ballclub represents.

Nevertheless, from almost the first day he appears to have stumbled upon the same essential truth of the franchise that Ruppert recognized: the New York market provides the team with a tremendous advantage, giving it access to streams of revenue and publicity unavailable to other teams. When the Yankees fully exploit that advantage—especially when they put those benefits back into the team on the field—they win. Yet Steinbrenner has periodically forgotten the second half of the equation. The team's greatest success has come when Steinbrenner more or less leaves baseball matters to baseball people and focuses his efforts on the essential truth, the continued exploitation of all things Yankee in New York. In recent years he appears even to have learned a thing or two. His obituary has been written a hundred times, yet he has managed to survive, even thrive, in situations that would have caused others to say the hell with it and walk away.

On August 1, 1973, a long-simmering feud between the Red Sox and the Yankees, as well as between catchers Carlton Fisk and Thurman Munson, came to a boil at Fenway Park. In a failed squeeze play Munson barreled into Fisk, who dumped the Yankee on his head, then both exchanged punches in a bench-clearing brawl. This set the tone for the rival teams for the next decade and beyond.

And he has rarely hidden himself from view for long— Steinbrenner likes being seen and sits in full view. When he first came to New York, no one thought he had it in him. He was underestimated right from the start.

Mike Burke was the first to learn that being a "general" partner of Steinbrenner's meant that in general he'd be ignored. On January 10, when Steinbrenner unveiled the deal's limited partners, among whom were guys like GM executive John DeLorean and Steinbrenner's theatrical partner James Nederlander, Burke was stunned to learn that Gabe Paul was part of the group. Steinbrenner was already consolidating power.

Paul's involvement raised some interesting questions. Only a month before the Yankees had dealt four prospects

whom MacPhail called the organization's "crown jewels"—Jerry Kenney, John Ellis, Rusty Torres, and Charlie Spikes—to the Indians for the slugging third baseman Graig Nettles, thus ending the Rich McKinney era. Commissioner Bowie Kuhn looked into the deal and absolved Paul of any wrongdoing, but for the first time it caused some to look at Steinbrenner with eyebrows raised. This guy was slick.

Spring training had barely started when the organization was rocked by a story that made anything else going on secondary. In the off-season pitchers and close friends Mike Kekich and Fritz Peterson, in their terms, "swapped lives." Peterson moved in with Mrs. Kekich and her kids, and Kekich moved in with Mrs. Peterson and her brood.

Jaws dropped and journalists swooned. The story had already taken on a tinge more sad than tawdry, for the alliance between Kekich and Mrs. Peterson had already fallen apart, making everyone awkward. Still, the story dominated press coverage all spring. The old guard in the New York press pounded their fists over sexual liberation and announced the end of civilization. Dick Young thun-

dered that the two couples' insistence that they didn't hurt anyone was "the same self-centered rationale used by young dope-takers." Few were as understanding as Jim Bouton, the former pitcher who similarly had stood the town on its ear and become a Yankee pariah with the release of his landmark tell-all biography *Ball Four* a few years earlier. At the time a New York broadcaster, Bouton pleaded, "They're entitled to a private life." The organization agreed, at least publicly, and moved on.

Steinbrenner stayed relatively silent in the early days, trying to learn a lot by observing, although when he saw the shaggy Yankee haircuts on Opening Day, he wrote down the uniform numbers of the offending players (he didn't yet know their names) and ordered Houk to make them get haircuts. The manager delivered the announcement with a bemused smile amid chuckles in the clubhouse. But the hair got cut. And when Mike Burke realized he'd been outflanked and reluctantly stepped aside in late April, Graig Nettles asked, "Was his hair too long?"

Nettles solidified the Yankee infield and provided some power as the Yankee offense, taking advantage of the new designated hitter slot, filled by Ron Blomberg, proved surprisingly potent. They pulled into first place in June and hung there through July. Steinbrenner opened his checkbook and allowed MacPhail to buy veterans like Cleveland pitcher Sam MacDowell, and they added starting pitcher Pat Dobson in a trade with Atlanta. Entering August, the Yankees seemed on course to a division title. That all ended on an August evening in Boston.

The two clubs had exchanged bad vibes for several seasons, and the trade of Lyle and an emerging rivalry between Munson and Carlton Fisk, Boston's young star catcher, had only made matters worse. Fisk had edged out Munson in All-Star balloting and recently made the cover of *Sports Illustrated.* The proud Yankee catcher thought he was a better player. Every time Munson walked into the Yankee locker room he found another copy of the magazine surreptitiously placed in his locker. "I'm up to my ass in them," he said.

In the second game of the series, on July 31, Fisk tripped Roy White as he crossed home plate, causing him to miss it and be tagged out in the 5–4 Yankee win. The loss dumped Boston three and a half games back and into fourth place.

The next night Mel Stottlemyre nailed Fisk in the head with a second-inning fastball. The game was tied 2–2 entering the ninth when Munson opened the inning with a double and moved to third on an out. With one away, Houk called on shortstop Gene Michael to drop down a squeeze bunt.

Michael missed the ball as Munson charged home. Fisk tossed Michael aside and set himself to meet Munson. The two crashed like football players as Fisk put Munson out, then dumped him on his head in a move more appropriate to professional wrestling. Munson came up swinging and belted the bigger Boston catcher with a straight right under his eye. Fisk retaliated like a drunk in a poolroom, swinging back at Munson with the ball wrapped in his right hand.

Both benches emptied. Michael kept throwing haymakers from the back row. Both catchers were thrown out of the game. Fisk was the only combatant to be bloodied, with a mouse under his eye and a shallow cut down the side of his face. "I knew you were in a fight with Michael because your face was scratched," quipped Boston pitcher Bill Lee. The Yankees won the fight, but the Red Sox won the game, 3–2, scoring off Lyle in the bottom of the inning. The rivalry between the two teams that had been dormant for more than 20 years started smoldering again. It would provide a secondary drama to the events of the next few seasons.

The loss sent the Yankees into a tie with Baltimore for first place, and over the next month they fell back and out of the race. Steinbrenner started trying to tell Houk whom to play. By September the Yankees were reeling, and the owner was implicated in a scheme to make illegal contributions to the Nixon campaign. Public opinion, and the press, began to turn against Steinbrenner. He then started selling players, a none-too-subtle admission that the Yankees were done. As they played out the string, the Mets stole a division title with a record of only 82–79. Houk got the blame for the Yankee collapse.

The Yankees ended the season on September 30, closing down old Yankee Stadium to accommodate the scheduled renovation. In the final week of the season the Hall of Fame hauled away a ticket booth, a turnstile, and other memorabilia. Anticipating souvenir takers, the club had already removed the center-field monuments and a hoard of equipment scheduled to follow the Yankees to Queens.

The club hired extra security to head off bad behavior, but the crowd of 32,328 arrived at the Stadium in an ugly mood and packing wrecking tools. Disappointed at the late season collapse, banners urging the Yankees to fire Houk ringed the park.

The game was only a few innings old when it became clear that the souvenir hunters weren't going to wait. In the outfield and the bleachers fans turned their backs on the game and started demolishing the park. The Yankees took the lead over Detroit but lost it in the fifth. When Houk came to the mound to change pitchers, exuberant fans waved parts of seats over their heads like the angry mob they had become.

As soon as Mike Hegan flied out to end the 8–5 loss, 20,000 fans swamped security forces and stormed the field. The Yanks had plans for objects like the bases, but the mob had other ideas. First-base coach Elston Howard scooped up the bag for a scheduled presentation to Mrs.

Lou Gehrig, but he had to fight his way off the field, clutching the base like a fullback plowing through the line. Cops stood guard at home plate to make sure it went to Claire Ruth, but a fan stole second base, and third was nabbed by Detroit third baseman Ike Brown. Some 10,000 seats ended up being pulled loose. But those changes were cosmetic compared to the real upheaval about to commence in the front office.

Houk resigned after the game, breaking into tears as he told his players of his decision. "I think I'm doing the right thing," he said. He already disliked the owner for his interference and the way he seemed to tramp all over the Yankee tradition. Steinbrenner had tried to talk him out of it, but Houk wasn't buying his act. A week later he would become manager of the Tigers.

Elston Howard told the *Daily News,* "I'm ready. But are they?" There had long been speculation that Howard, who'd more than paid his dues, would become baseball's first black manager at the helm of the Yankees. Steinbrenner's presence made that seem even more likely. If one considered the American Basketball League a major league, Steinbrenner's coach of the Pipers, John McClendon, had been the first black head coach in the recent history of American professional sports. "I'd take it [the job] tonight," said Howard. "I've told Gabe Paul and Lee MacPhail I'm available." He'd also said the same thing to the Tigers. Howard had come close to becoming a big league manager once before, in 1968. Bill Veeck had tried to buy the Washington Senators and promised to hire Howard, but the purchase fell through.

But the Yankees weren't in any rush. "During the World Series we'll find out who's available," said MacPhail. As it turned out, he'd be leaving that job for someone else: MacPhail soon followed Houk out the door. He'd known he was a lame duck ever since the arrival of Paul. Joe Cronin was ready to retire as AL president, and MacPhail was offered the job. The page had finally been turned. The old Yankees were no more.

Steinbrenner once said that when he was a kid and the Yankees came in, it was "like the circus coming to town." Well, the circus was ready to begin, and Steinbrenner was about to take over. Paul was wise enough not to compete with the Boss for the center ring and stayed behind the

The All-Star battery of Thurman Munson (left) and Sparky Lyle helped lead the Yankees back to prominence. Munson made six All-Star game appearances before his death in a plane crash in 1979. Lyle saved 26 games and won 13 while capturing the Cy Young Award for the 1977 world champions.

scenes. He already seemed to sense that under Steinbrenner that was often the safest place to be. And as he once told a writer, "The great thing about baseball is that there's a crisis every day." Working for Steinbrenner made that a certainty. He got right to work, making what appeared to be a few minor deals, landing outfielder Lou Piniella from Kansas City.

The man Steinbrenner wanted apparently became available after the World Series. Oakland manager Dick Williams resigned after A's owner Charlie Finley, upset when second baseman Mike Andrews made two errors in the Series, tried to cut him.

Williams was baseball's reigning managerial genius, adept at navigating the dysfunctional clubhouse of the "Fighting A's." He would have been the perfect foil for Steinbrenner, but when the Yankees asked Finley for permission to talk to Williams, who technically was still under contract, the A's owner refused. He hadn't liked the way he'd been treated by the Yankees since the day he'd entered the league, and now was his chance at revenge.

Steinbrenner hired Williams anyway, holding a big press conference and shoving it in Finley's face. But outgoing lame duck AL president Joe Cronin and incoming prexy Lee MacPhail nixed the deal.

The Yankees kept Howard at arm's length and on January 3, 1974, finally hired former Pirate outfielder and manager Bill Virdon. "We had to do something," explained Gabe Paul. Elston Howard swallowed his pride and stayed on as coach.

With Steinbrenner's approval, Gabe Paul got going. Throughout the spring hardly a week went by without another deal. In March he worked a three-way trade with Detroit and Cleveland, landing outfielder Walt "No Neck" Williams, and he bought center fielder Elliott Maddox. Opening Day, a 6–1 win over Cleveland in the club's first game at Shea, didn't slow him down. On April 26, he traded four pitchers, Fritz Peterson among them, to his old club for first baseman Chris Chambliss and pitchers Dick Tidrow and Cecil Upshaw.

The press called it the "Friday Night Massacre," and Yankee players were stunned—they were winning, and they all got along. After Mel Stottlemyre beat the Rangers that night, he said, "It's the first time I ever won a game and felt lousy afterwards." Bobby Murcer added, "It means

they don't think we have a winning ballclub." Murcer was right, and he'd soon learn that "they" didn't like to be openly criticized.

Paul kept going, making ten more deals, mostly for cash, before the end of the season. The Yankees first swooned, falling to the cellar in July, then surged as the new players fell into place. They took over first place in early September as the Red Sox collapsed. Although Mel Stottlemyre blew out his shoulder, ending his career, Paul made up for it by adding players. Newcomers Elliott Maddox and Lou Piniella both hit .300 and keyed the Yankee offense, and Pat Dobson and Doc Medich both closed in on 20 wins.

The Yankees almost won it, and in any other year they would have. In September and October they won 20 of 31 games. But the Baltimore Orioles won 25 of 31, including a three-game sweep of the Yankees September 17–19. The Orioles, who swept Ralph Houk's Detroit Tigers at the end of the season, finished two games ahead of New York. "Houk let them win," bitched Steinbrenner later.

The pennant race was bittersweet for the Yankee owner. In August Steinbrenner had pled guilty to a felony charge over his campaign contribution and was fined $15,000. Baseball commissioner Bowie Kuhn suspended him for two years, excluding him from team offices and the clubhouse and supposedly barring his active involvement in running the Yankees until March 1976. Although he did stay out of the public eye, few people believed that Steinbrenner followed Kuhn's edict, not unlike a baseball manager thrown from a game who continues to manage from the dugout runway. Phones still worked, and there was little doubt that over the next two years the franchise did little without his approval.

Steinbrenner's suspension and the end of the season made little difference to Paul's shopping spree. Multitalented San Francisco outfielder Bobby Bonds had a down year and made too much money on a Giants ballclub that was rebuilding. When San Francisco offered him to New York straight up for Murcer, Paul jumped at the deal. Murcer was a fine player, and to Yankee fans a symbol of former glory about to be restored, but Bonds was a better player, albeit a far less popular one. Released from the chilly confines of Candlestick Park, there was no telling what he might accomplish. In New York there was some thought that for the first time since Mantle the Yankees had a superstar.

But a lot was never enough for the man whom everyone was accusing of trying to buy a pennant. After the 1974 season Charlie Finley missed a deferred payment to pitcher Jim "Catfish" Hunter. Only 27, in 1974 Hunter had won 25 regular season games, been chosen for the Cy Young Award, and picked up a win and a save in Oakland's World Series victory, the A's third consecutive world championship. All he did was throw strikes, relentlessly, on the corner, every fourth day without fail. Other pitchers had better stuff, but few were better pitchers.

Hunter himself seemed to be thoroughly unimpressed with his own talent. He stayed on an even keel and rarely got flustered, a quality that had served him well in the tempestuous Oakland clubhouse. In a game full of egos, the homespun Hunter seemed to be without one. In the '74 Series, after giving up two late home runs in his 3–2 defeat of the Dodgers in game three, Hunter brushed it off, saying, "I had some friends here from North Carolina, and they'd never seen a home run, so I gave 'em a couple."

But Hunter was no dummy. Finley's missed payment was a violation of his contract. The pitcher declared himself a free agent just before the start of the postseason, then saw his stock rise. When an arbitrator ruled in his favor on December 16, Hunter's services were available to the highest bidder. He was free to sign with any team in baseball, at any price he could get.

A new era in the history of the Yankees was about to begin.

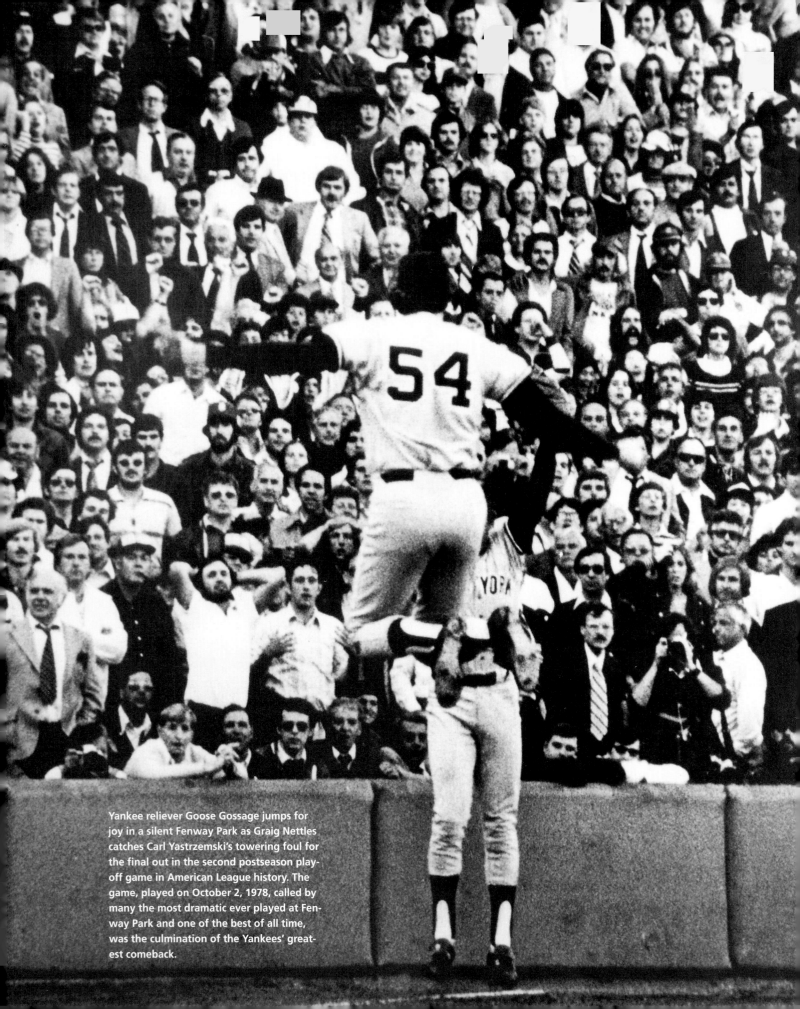

Yankee reliever Goose Gossage jumps for joy in a silent Fenway Park as Graig Nettles catches Carl Yastrzemski's towering foul for the final out in the second postseason playoff game in American League history. The game, played on October 2, 1978, called by many the most dramatic ever played at Fenway Park and one of the best of all time, was the culmination of the Yankees' greatest comeback.

1975–1978

START SPREADING THE NEWS

For a few short weeks in the winter of 1974–75 the most important place in the baseball world was not any ballpark but the office of lawyer Carlton Cherry in Ahoskie, North Carolina. For two weeks representatives of the wealthiest men in baseball descended upon Ahoskie like deer hunters at the opening of the season. But these men were after Catfish.

Nothing quite like it had ever happened. A handful of players had been granted free agency before, but none had ever been as fortunate as Hunter. His career was at its peak. He was easily the best pitcher in baseball, the rare ace who not only wins but also eats up innings and makes the rest of the staff better and stronger. The Major League Baseball Players' Association (MLBPA) was gaining strength and paying close attention. Hunter's price tag would transform baseball.

The way Major League Baseball operated would change more in the next few seasons than it had over the previous 75 years as players were granted limited free agency. For the first time, under some restraints, a number of players would be able to sell their services to the highest bidder. No team was swifter to react to these changes than the New York Yankees. While others withdrew in horror, hid their heads in the sand, or angrily pounded their fists and predicted doom for the game, the Yankees embraced the new era. They opened their wallets, took a place at the table, and turned the situation to their advantage. The clubs that hesitated or resisted were left behind to play catch-up.

Catfish Hunter provided the proof. The Yankees were the first team to comprehend what free agency meant. And in New York Hunter delivered added value, making the city Yankees territory again and putting the team on the back pages of New York's tabloids for the first time in a decade. That translated into ticket sales and TV ratings, both of which meant money.

Hunter gave Steinbrenner a chance to make good on a promise he'd made when he first bought the club: to deliver a championship within three seasons. Although Steinbrenner once claimed that "I am dead set against free agency. It can ruin baseball," he also told Gabe Paul never to "back off in money deals." Enlightened self-interest defined the franchise's approach to the many changes baseball would face over the next few seasons.

It took only days for the Yankees and the San Diego Padres to emerge as the final bidders, and only a few more for the Yankees to win their prize. They brought Hunter to New York for the official announcement on January 1, 1975, signing him to a four-year deal worth $3.75 million. He said all the right stuff, citing the Yankee tradition as one reason he'd signed with New York, and "the man on my left," head Yankee scout Clyde Kluttz, who'd originally signed Hunter for the A's back in 1965. "He never lied to me then, and he never lied to me now," said Hunter of Kluttz.

It was a new day in Yankee history. Hunter was the first Yankee widely acknowledged to be the best at his position in more than a decade. And as Maury Allen noted in the *Post,* "The baseball balance of power in this town has shifted dramatically from the Mets to the Yankees." It would prove to be even more than that. Free agency would eventually tilt the entire major league table back the Yankees' way.

But Hunter, on his way to 23 wins in 1975, could pitch only every fourth day. The Yankees fought Boston for first place into June, when they suddenly had to absorb a string of injuries. On June 7, Bobby Bonds tore cartilage in his knee. On June 11, Roy White tore a hamstring. On June 13, Elliott Maddox ruined his knee when he slipped on the perennially wet grounds at Shea; he would never be the same. And Lou Piniella's batting average tumbled more than 100 points as he battled a mysterious inner ear problem that took a year to clear up. When the Yankees went to Boston on June 26 for an important four-game series, Walt Williams, Rich Coggins, and Terry Whitfield were manning the Yankee outfield. The Red Sox had Jim Rice, Fred Lynn, and Dwight Evans. Wrote Joseph Valero in the *Post,* "Horrocious, a new word, best described the Yankees' recent exploits. The word, it must be noted, is derived from horrendous and atrocious. It is not related to ferocious." Boston took three of four, and the Yankees started to slide. By the end of July they were out of it.

Bill Virdon took the blame, but it was hardly his fault. When the Yankees lost three straight to Boston at Shea in late July, Steinbrenner, who was still allowed to attend games and watched from the stands, decided to make a change.

Since being traded from the Yankees to Kansas City in the wake of the Copacabana incident, Billy Martin had become something of a baseball gypsy. Away from New York his skills faded, and he had been repeatedly traded before being released by the Twins in the spring of 1962. He latched on as a scout and then third-base coach before beginning his managerial career in Denver in 1968 and taking over the Twins at the end of the season.

Jackie Robinson had once described Martin the player as "always thinking, always daring, always looking for a way to win." Martin took those qualities into the dugout. He had learned the game from Stengel, who in turn had learned it from McGraw, and McGraw from Ned Hanlon; Martin was thus the beneficiary of more than a century of baseball wisdom. He quickly became one of the most effective, inventive, and combative managers in the game.

The same pattern was repeated everywhere he managed. His team performed better than it had any right to for a year or two before Martin butted heads with management, then the team collapsed after he left. He led the

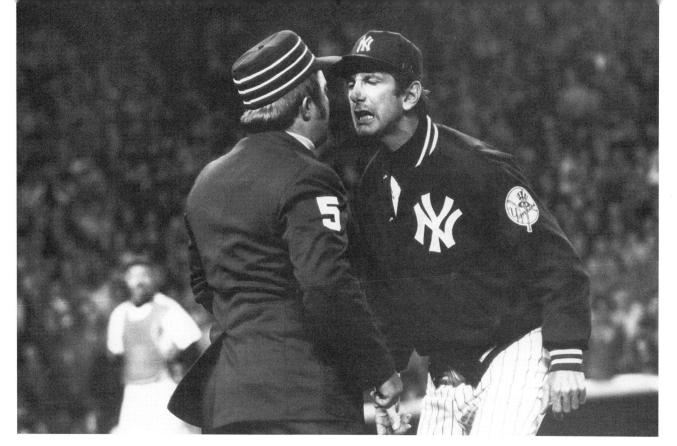

Billy Martin, here stating his case in the 1977 World Series, was named Yankee manager in 1975 after successful but tempestuous managerial stints in Minnesota, Detroit, and Texas. Jackie Robinson once described Martin as "always thinking, always daring, always looking for a way to win." He brought these assets and more to the Yankee dugout.

Twins to a division title but clashed with owner Calvin Griffith over his pitching choices during the Twins' playoff loss to Baltimore and fired himself. Hired by Detroit in 1971, Martin took the club from 79 to 91 wins in his initial season, then to a division title in 1972. Fired in midseason in 1973, Martin took over in Texas and the club went from 57 wins to 84 in 1974. Carl Yastrzemski later remarked that Martin "has had the ability to take mediocre teams and make them good"; in regard to the Yankees, Yaz added, "he has taken a good team and made them great."

But winning games wasn't enough for Martin—there were always other scores to settle. If there was no enemy in sight, he'd create one. Burning at the smallest slights, Martin had a small man's insecure and oversized ego, and he carried chips both real and imagined on his shoulders. He once said that "out of 25 guys there should be 15 who would run through a wall for you, two or three who don't like you at all, five who are indifferent, and maybe three undecided. My job is to keep the last two groups from

going the wrong way." His players played hard under him, yet over time they often did so in spite of, and not because of, their manager.

Winning emboldened Martin. While wildly popular with fans who appreciated his blue-collar style, and initially appreciated by players for his acumen and aggressive, "take no prisoners" style, Martin's act quickly wore thin. He did things his way, creating a team by making himself the only star. He pushed his team hard, particularly the pitching staff. One of the reasons he won was that he used his best pitchers as much as possible, with no thought of their longevity. Victory came at a price.

But the longer he stayed in one place, the harder he became to control and the more difficulty he had maintaining control. When he drank too much, as he often did, he couldn't handle it—alcohol unleashed the private demons he carried around his entire life and the thousand real and imagined slights he felt. Over and over again his on-field record was marred by ugly public incidents and physical confrontations. He often clashed and brawled with his own players, once punching out pitcher Dave Boswell and leaving him in need of 20 stitches. No one was exempt from his volcanic temper, not the opposition, umpires, coaches, the front office, or fans. On July 18, 1975, after a series of clashes with Rangers management—in one incident Martin had slapped the club's elderly traveling secretary—he was fired. He echoed Stengel when he left, charging that Texas owner Brad Corbett wanted a yes man, and "I'm no yes man."

In one sense, he was the last manager George Steinbrenner should have hired. In another, he was the perfect man for the job. Martin's fire impressed the owner, particularly when he compared Martin to the poker-faced Virdon. Martin reminded Steinbrenner of guys like Ohio State football coach Woody Hayes, who seemed able to inspire victory through will alone, a quality that Steinbrenner admired and hoped to emulate.

Besides, Martin validated Steinbrenner as a Yankee. He harked back to the era of Yogi, Mickey, Whitey, and Casey, tying Steinbrenner to the vaunted Yankee tradition. The owner was desperate to make that connection, for much of New York still viewed him skeptically as some kind of hick carpetbagger, as unhip and unsophisticated. At a time when President Gerald Ford had refused to bail out the city financially—leading to the famous headline "Ford to New York: Drop Dead"—Steinbrenner, by hiring Martin, reminded fans of the glory years.

Martin's availability made Virdon suddenly expendable. As soon as Martin accepted the Yankees' offer on August 1, Virdon was fired. Privately, Paul had tried to talk Steinbrenner out of hiring Martin—he could already foresee the inevitable clash between two such volatile personalities, each of whom liked to think he was completely in charge. Each thought he'd be able to handle the other.

Martin was reintroduced to New York on August 2, "Old Timers' Day" at Shea. As soon as Martin sprinted from the dugout, the crowd erupted in cheers, drowning out a smattering of boos in support of Virdon. A beaming Martin basked in the sound of his triumphant return. Fans loved him from the first instant. His combativeness mirrored New York's growing sense of itself as an embattled underdog tired of being pushed around and eager to resume its place at the top.

At first Martin was surprisingly low-key. He spent the rest of the season getting to know the players and evaluating talent, knowing that he'd be judged not on how the Yankees did the remainder of 1975 but on how they played in 1976. His only real clash came with Bobby Bonds, who challenged the manager after he questioned Bonds's desire to play. Martin didn't think Bonds was hurt.

But Martin was already grating against the confines of his role. He was only the manager. Paul controlled the roster and the farm system. Both knew, however, that Steinbrenner called the shots.

Yet Martin was not without influence, for he had Steinbrenner's ear, and the owner was thoroughly enthralled—Martin was the first big leaguer he really had a chance to hang out with. It was no coincidence that in the off-season Paul dumped several players Martin didn't want, including Pat Dobson and Bobby Bonds. In exchange he received outfielder Oscar Gamble, who destroyed right-handed pitching, the fleet California outfielder Mickey Rivers, and starting pitcher Ed Figueroa. The pieces of a new team were falling into place.

Paul made a final move on December 11, trading Doc Medich to Pittsburgh for problematic pitcher Dock Ellis, pitcher Ken Brett, and rookie second baseman Willie Randolph, a top prospect made expendable only because Pittsburgh already had Rennie Stennett, who was even better. But the deal was a risk. Medich was a known commodity, and Ellis, while talented, was outspoken and battling a drug and alcohol problem.

This Yankee team was built along the lines of one of Stengel's old clubs, featuring power, defense, and pitching, a few stars (Hunter and Munson), some valuable frontliners (Rivers, White, Nettles, Ellis, and Chambliss), key role players (Gamble, Piniella), and youthful promise (Randolph).

Martin won New York over in the second game of the season in Milwaukee. After the Yankees came back from a 6–0 deficit, the Brewers' Don Money cracked a walk-off, grand slam home run, and Milwaukee appeared to have won, 10–9.

But before Money even reached home Martin came charging out of the dugout. Martin, who missed nothing on the diamond, was the only man in the ballpark to have noticed that umpire Jim McKean had called time out just before Yankee pitcher Dave Pagan started his wind-up. McKean, thinking no one had seen him, intended to let the play stand. But Martin intimidated him into doing the right thing and calling back the home run. Money then flew out, and the Yankees won, 9–7, a victory snatched from defeat.

The win made Martin a legend. While Martin was more popular with the fans than with his players, not all of whom liked him, they respected his knowledge and played hard for him. Old Yankee fans started coming back, and younger fans who had never known the Yankees as winners turned out in droves. Attendance rose by more than 800,000 in 1976. And compared to what would take place over the next few seasons, 1976 was a cakewalk — the Yankees moved into first place early and stayed there, more or less comfortably, all year. Not that the season was without elements of controversy, but relatively speaking, New York hadn't seen anything yet.

When Steinbrenner's suspension ended in March, he returned to the fray and in only a few weeks found himself waist-deep in a battle with Kuhn again. Pitcher Andy Messersmith had successfully challenged a portion of the reserve clause and been declared a free agent, a judgment that shook baseball to its core and within a year would open the door for dozens of other players to become free agents as well. While other teams made speeches and denounced the ruling, the Yankees signed Messersmith for more than $1 million.

But when the MLBPA protested the deal for procedural reasons, the players' group was backed by Kuhn, who threatened to void the deal. The Yankees withdrew their offer but were clearly prepared to embrace a new age. The opening of newly renovated Yankee Stadium on April 15 provided an important, final element of their future success. At virtually no cost to the Yankees themselves, they now had what was essentially a brand-new facility, enabling them to more than double their attendance over the next few seasons, exploit the full financial potential of the New York market, and fuel a rise to prominence.

In their inaugural game at the new Stadium the Yankees defeated Minnesota, 11–4. The headline on the cover of the *Daily News* was prescient: "Yankees Like Bombers of Old."

Yet even as the Yankees staked their claim on first place in the AL East, they continued to try to improve. It has long been the trademark of Steinbrenner's Yankees that no lead is considered large enough; time and time again the Yankees have beaten the opposition to the punch and

The next championship era of Yankee baseball commenced the moment first baseman Chris Chambliss struck his playoff-winning home run against the Royals in the ninth inning of the fifth game of the 1976 American League playoffs. His excursion around the Yankee Stadium base paths proved difficult when thousands of fans poured onto the field.

added players to an already powerful team. In their willingness to take other clubs' problems — players who will soon become free agents — the Yankees acquire more depth than any other team. On the June 15 trading deadline in 1976, Paul engineered a deal with Baltimore. In exchange for Rudy May and several others, he landed pitcher Ken Holtzman, Doyle Alexander, and Grant Jackson. At any other time the trade would have been a blockbuster. But on this day it was a footnote.

A's owner Charlie Finley had seen the future and didn't like it. While the A's had slipped since winning three straight world championships from 1972 to 1974, they still had stars like Sal Bando, Joe Rudi, Vida Blue, Bert Campaneris, and Rollie Fingers. Finley knew that free agency would cost him plenty. Rather than be forced to pay high salaries in arbitration or watch his players leave him with nothing, he decided to sell them off and then rebuild. Long-time A's owner Connie Mack had used a similar strategy twice before.

Thurman Munson was the lone bright spot for the Yankees in the 1976 World Series as he hit Reds pitching for a .529 batting average. Despite Munson's heroics, the Yankees fell in four straight to the vaunted Big Red Machine.

The Yankees bought pitcher Vida Blue, one of baseball's great talents, for $1.5 million. In response, the Red Sox grabbed outfielder Joe Rudi and relief pitcher Rollie Fingers as aging owner Tom Yawkey, dying of leukemia, made one last grab for the world championship that had eluded him for 42 seasons. Three weeks earlier the rivalry between the two teams had intensified when Lou Piniella crashed into Fisk while trying to score in an 8–2 Yankee loss at the Stadium. Fisk came up swinging again, and in the 15-minute brawl that followed, Boston pitcher Bill Lee foolishly entered the fray and was dumped on his head by

Graig Nettles. Lee's pitching shoulder was dislocated, an injury that led him to call the Yankees "Steinbrenner's brownshirts" and "Nazis." A little over a week later the Yankees visited Boston and were pelted by all manner of debris from Fenway's rabid following, including ball bearings, golf balls, darts, and stones. In center field Mickey Rivers was the target of not only two cherry bombs but also vicious racial epithets from bleacher "fans" venting their ire in the racially charged city, which was still reeling from the fallout of enforced busing.

Bowie Kuhn, serving at the behest of baseball's owners, reacted by playing to his constituency. He voided Finley's fire sale, citing the "best interests of baseball." Steinbrenner roared in protest.

The Yankees' response was to keep winning. They took 12 of their next 14 games and surged to the division title, finishing with 97 wins, 10½ games ahead of Baltimore. Hunter, battling a sore shoulder that the Yankees kept a secret for most of the second half, slumped to only 17 wins, but Ed Figueroa won 19, Dock Ellis 17, and Alexander and Ken Holtzman combined for 19 more. On offense the Yankees demonstrated their most balanced attack in years, stealing 162 bases to go with their 120 home runs.

It was a time of relative calm before subsequent storms. Steinbrenner was satisfied, and Martin content. So far, by winning early and winning big, Martin had been able to keep the Yankee owner at bay. Not that Steinbrenner didn't try to interfere—at one point Martin became so exasperated at his midgame phone calls that he tore the phone out of the dugout—but in the end Steinbrenner gave credit to Martin, who signed a two-year contract in September to manage the club through 1978. With the postseason looming, however, Martin knew that anything short of victory would not be satisfactory.

In the upcoming American League Championship Series (ALCS) the Yankees faced the Kansas City Royals, the anti-Yankees. Less than a decade removed from expansion status, the Royals played in an antiseptic new stadium with no history or tradition, on artificial turf, which they exploited with speed, defense, and hitters who beat the ball onto the ground and then scooted around the bases as it shot through the gaps. The Royals were built from within, through the farm system. In comparison, the Yankees were mercenaries, the team the press had dubbed "the best team money could buy." That wasn't entirely true, for the core of the New York team had been built through Paul's savvy trades, but the national press was more comfortable creating a good guys versus bad guys story-line.

The two clubs were evenly matched and had played each other to a near-standoff during the season, Kansas City winning the series seven games to five, with half of their meetings decided by a single run. Despite their relative youth and lack of power, the Royals' speed made them competitive. They would be forced to do without injured outfielder Amos Otis, but they had stolen more than 200 bases, third baseman George Brett was the best young player in baseball, and manager Whitey Herzog had plenty of motivation to best New York. He'd been fired to make room for Martin in Texas.

But the Yankees were confident. When Lou Piniella learned that Kansas City had chosen swingman and former Yankee Larry Gura to pitch opposite Catfish Hunter in the opener, he quipped, "There's no way we can lose. We've got a $4 million pitcher going against a guy who was traded for [Yankee backup catcher] Fran Healy." Martin thought Gura pitched scared and had asked Paul to trade him earlier that spring. "If I had him here now, I'd get rid of him again," he said.

Although Hunter proved to be better than Gura in game one, a 4–1 Yankee win, the two clubs split the first four games of the series, setting up a game-five finale for the right to play Cincinnati's vaunted "Big Red Machine" in the World Series. Thus far Martin had squandered every advantage. He lost game two because he lost faith in reliever Sparky Lyle and stayed too long with Dick Tidrow, and in game four he pushed an ailing Hunter back onto the mound on three days' rest. Martin pushed the same button a second time in the final contest, calling on Figueroa on three days' rest to face Dave Leonard, ignoring Doyle Alexander and Ken Holtzman. Martin hadn't been in favor of the trade that landed him the two pitchers in the first place. Now, in the midst of the playoffs, he was playing the "I'll show you" game, determined to win without using either man just to make a point with Steinbrenner and Paul. Figueroa had outpitched Leonard in game two, lasting into the sixth while Leonard had been knocked out in the third, but Kansas City had won the game, and now Leonard had more rest.

It showed in the first inning as the Royals erupted for two runs, but the Yankees came back and took a 6–3 lead into the seventh. After Figueroa gave up a leadoff single in the eighth, Martin again ignored Lyle and chose to pitch lefty reliever Grant Jackson.

Pinch hitter Jim Wohlford greeted Jackson with a single, stilling a raucous Yankee Stadium crowd. That brought up George Brett, the reigning AL batting champion. He had already cracked seven hits in the Series.

At any point in Yankee history there often seems to have been one player who was designated the "Yankee killer," the one player who alone stood between the Yankees and total victory. Detroit pitcher Frank Lary was the first to earn the nickname, and in 1976 George Brett, beginning with his next at bat and lasting until his retirement, became the latest player to proudly wear that label. Brett had the added motivation of defending the honor of his older brother, Ken. Earlier in the season Ken Brett had been a member of the Yankee pitching staff, but Martin had buried him, using him only twice in the first six weeks before trading him away.

George Brett turned on a Jackson pitch and blasted it far and high around the pole and into the seats in right field, only his ninth home run of the season. As Phil Pepe noted in the *Daily News,* as Brett's blast fell to earth, "you could hear a pennant fall." The hit tied the game 6–6.

The Royals had a chance to win the game in the ninth. With two out, Tidrow gave up a single and a walk, bringing up Wohlford again with Brett on deck.

Wohlford bounced the ball to Nettles, who whipped the ball to Randolph covering second, but Al Cowens had been running with the pitch. More than 50,000 fans saw the throw come in and immediately thought that Brett would be coming to bat again.

But the second-base umpire raised his hand, calling Cowens out. Credit Martin for the call. The Yankee manager had so intimidated umpires, particularly in Yankee Stadium, that it seemed as if every close call went New York's way. Umpires would do anything to avoid the wrath of Martin, who was known to protest so long and so vehemently that umpires rued setting him off. The game remained tied.

Leading off for the Yankees in the ninth was Chris Chambliss, hardly the player New Yorkers wanted to see at the plate. Ever since he'd come to the Yankees in the "Friday Night Massacre," he'd been disappointing, hitting around .300 but supplying little power. He always seemed to be ending rallies.

Chambliss stood off to the side of the plate for a moment as Yankee public address announcer Bob Sheppard cautioned Yankee fans about throwing debris on the field. The game had already been halted several times as rolls of toilet paper, hurled from the upper deck, unfurled on the field.

He stepped into the batter's box at 11:13 P.M. on the evening of October 14 and looked out at Royals pitcher Mark Littell. Then, wrote Phil Pepe, on the first pitch out of Littell's hand, he "wound up as if he knew what was coming. He uncoiled out of his swing and when the sound of bat meeting ball reverberated throughout the Stadium, you knew the ball was gone, the game was over, the pennant was won."

Chambliss stood for a moment as he watched the ball streak into right field and then just over the fence for a home run. Just a few months before, when the new Yankee Stadium had first opened, there had been a chainlink fence atop the wall. Graig Nettles, a left-handed hitter like Chambliss, had complained to Martin, telling him it would cost the club some home runs. The Yankee manager had it removed. That decision delivered the Yankees their first pennant since 1964 — and has since assisted in several others.

Chambliss half leaped to first base, then seemed to react in horror as he saw first dozens and then hundreds of fans pouring out of the stands toward him. He halted his trot and took off like a halfback in the broken field, clutching his batting helmet, stopping, starting, and dodging around delirious fans, reaching second almost unimpeded, blasting his way to third while sending several bodies reeling to the side, then becoming lost on his way home, falling down and getting up, losing sight of the plate as it disappeared in a mass of humanity. He looked, wrote Dick Young, "like a man in a terrible dream, looking for a way home." Only the dream wasn't terrible. Baseball hadn't seen anything like it since Mazeroski's Series-ending blast in 1960. New York hadn't seen anything like it since Bobby Thomson sent Brooklyn home in tears in 1951. And Yankee fans had never experienced such a moment.

Chambliss was saved by some New York cops, who pulled him from the mob and into the clubhouse, and for a while there was some question about whether the run would count, for Chambliss had never touched home plate as the crowd descended on the field. But sometime later Chambliss, only half in uniform, was escorted back out to touch home. When Thurman Munson was asked whether the run should count, he said, "I saw 50,000 people touch home plate." Baseball agreed with the verdict of those 50,000. The Yankees were American League champions.

Martin was already thinking of Cincinnati and bursting with bravado. "We'll get that Red Machine wheel by wheel, axle by axle, if we have to. They're a good club, but we're the better club."

But the smug Reds, the defending National League champions and a team at their peak, had other ideas. The team was built around Joe Morgan, Johnny Bench, Tony Perez — three Hall of Famers — and Pete Rose, who would certainly have been inducted into the Hall if not for his personal troubles. The team included several other stars, like Dave Concepcion and George Foster, and a pitching staff deep in the back and strong enough in front, keyed by the most promising pitcher in baseball, young Don Gullett.

The Yankees didn't play badly, but the Reds played better. New York couldn't stop Johnny Bench, who hit .533, and while the Reds had no more success against Thurman Munson, who hit .529, Cincinnati swept to victory in four straight games. Martin came unglued in the final game, arguing every call, then blasting the umpires — whom, he complained, "don't get the assignment on merit" — and the influence of television, which had forced the Yankees to start the Series with only one day's respite after the ALCS.

The Reds weren't magnanimous in victory. Manager Sparky Anderson hated New York — he'd once asked, "Is New York America?" When a writer asked him to compare Munson and Bench after the Series, a smirking Anderson kicked sand in the Yankees' face when he said, "Don't embarrass anyone by comparing them to Johnny Bench."

But the Yankees were already plotting revenge, and the Reds were worried. Free agency was coming in the off-season, and salaries were rapidly escalating. The champion Reds knew it would be nearly impossible to keep their team intact. Steinbrenner fired a shot across the bow when he said, "We're going for number one."

Just a few weeks after the Series dozens of players were due to change addresses. Baseball scheduled a "reentry draft" to distribute negotiating rights to 24 free agents, with each team allowed to sign as many as three. A day later an expansion draft would stock new AL franchises in Seattle and Toronto.

The reentry draft was tailor-made for the Yankees, a team with a few holes and a large wallet. They wanted a shortstop—Fred Stanley had hit only .238 in 1976 and fielded poorly in the World Series—a right-handed bat in the outfield, and perhaps a pitcher. They drafted Baltimore infielder Bobby Grich with their first of nine picks, Baltimore outfielder Don Baylor with their second pick, and Reds pitcher Don Gullett with their third. With their sixth pick—almost as an afterthought, and at Steinbrenner's insistence—they also selected Baltimore outfielder Reggie Jackson, the flamboyant slugger who'd been the first player chosen in the draft, selected by the Montreal Expos. He'd starred with the Athletics before fleeing Charlie Finley's farm for one season as a hired gun in Baltimore.

Jackson was a classic slugger in the mold of Ruth and Mantle, a star who stilled the crowd with every at bat whether he hit a home run or struck out, and a player whose talent was matched only by his ego. Jackson had epitomized the swagger of the "Fighting A's." "We had a common bond," he once said. "Everybody hated [owner] Charlie Finley." Jackson loved being a star, loved the attention, loved being "the Man." "If I played in New York," he said in Oakland, "they'd name a candy bar after me." He knew what the city could do for him. His left-handed stroke was perfect for Yankee Stadium's short right-field porch, and the city provided the stage he craved.

Reggie Jackson was many things—a hot dog, a candy bar, the straw that stirs the drink, a star. No Yankee since Babe Ruth offered his combination of power and charisma, no Yankee delivered on both counts quite as often as Jackson, and no Yankee had more to do with taking a talented team and making it a championship team.

When Steinbrenner said after the draft that "Grich, Baylor, Gullet, and Jackson are the players we're most interested in," he wasn't speaking for everyone in the organization. Paul, and in particular Martin, didn't want Jackson. Paul felt the Yankees were too left-handed already, and Martin simply didn't care much for Jackson as a player. He

Slugger Reggie Jackson signed with the Yankees as a free agent prior to the 1977 season. It wasn't long before the three biggest egos in baseball—George Steinbrenner, Billy Martin, and Jackson—were making headlines with their brash, head-long styles. As a result, Jackson helped lead the Yankees to a long overdue world championship.

preferred A's outfielder Joe Rudi, described by one writer as "the most overrated underrated player in the draft." Like Munson, Rudi was tough and hard-nosed, the kind of player Martin liked. Jackson just didn't fit Martin's vision of the team. Knowing that Steinbrenner wanted him made Jackson even less desirable.

When the Yankees quickly signed Gullett, strengthening themselves as they simultaneously weakened the Reds, they instantly became the favorite to win the 1977 World Series. They next set their sights on Grich, but he signed with Gene Autry's Angels, along with Baylor and Rudi. Autry was showing signs that he was willing to outspend Steinbrenner.

That was a crown Steinbrenner was not yet willing to give up. Steinbrenner decided to go after Jackson, the draft's crown jewel. That decision opened the gates to what would soon be termed "the Bronx Zoo."

The Expos offered Jackson more money, an unheard-of (at the time) $4 million over five seasons. He listened because Dick Williams was managing Montreal and Jack-

son respected his former manager, but New York—and Steinbrenner—appealed to his vanity.

Steinbrenner, said Jackson later, "hustled me like a broad," and Reggie liked that. Jackson played the coquette on Steinbrenner's arm, and the Boss liked that. He wined and dined and sweet-talked Jackson over the course of several days as Reggie played hard to get, batting his eyes at the Expos and Padres and Orioles before the two finally consummated the relationship with lunch at 21, then a stroll down Fifth Avenue where everyone could see the evidence of their coupling. As Dick Young noted later, "While George's competition was offering nothing more than filthy lucre, George offered filthy New York—beautiful, big, bustling, exciting, pressurized, hurrying, unfunctioning, sexy, cultured, glamorous, filthy New York." Jackson tumbled for it. They worked out the basic details of

In 1977 Graig Nettles, shown here sliding into Boston catcher Bob Montgomery, not only coined the term "Bronx Zoo" to describe the Yankees, he also enjoyed his finest season as a pinstriper, socking 37 home runs with 107 RBIs.

their agreement on a piece of hotel stationery a few days later — a mash note that Steinbrenner later put on display in his house.

His prize cost him nearly $2.5 million for five years. The signing was officially announced on November 29 at a gala press conference, not at Yankee Stadium but at the Americana Hotel. Jackson and Steinbrenner were both beaming, and Reggie spoke at length about how important it was that "Steinbrenner dealt with me as a man and a person. . . . I feel like I'm a friend of his. . . . I've never felt wanted like that."

But the press conference was more notable for what it did not include — manager Billy Martin. Martin, who wore uniform number 1, was now clearly number two.

The three biggest egos in baseball would now try to occupy the same space in the same city and the same back pages of the New York tabloids. There had barely been room for Steinbrenner and Martin. With Jackson added to the mix, there wasn't room enough for all three. For the next few seasons Steinbrenner, Martin, and Jackson would often spend as much time and energy keeping score off the field as on, struggling for control and the affections of the public. The 1977 season and several seasons thereafter would play out like an extended serialized soap opera as questions of who loved whom, who hated whom, who was stabbing whom in the back, and why, often became more important than the game on the field. New York was enthralled. Fans couldn't look away. As former pitching coach and White Sox manager Bob Lemon commented, "It's like watching *Mary Hartman, Mary Hartman.* I can't wait to see what happens next."

The other Yankees became bit players in the larger psychodrama. Steinbrenner had asked Munson whether Jackson could help the team, and the catcher had encouraged the owner to sign him. But now that he had, neither Munson nor the rest of the Yankees were quite so sure that having Jackson on board was a good idea after all — they had egos too. Although Steinbrenner had assured Munson that he'd remain the highest-paid Yankee, and Munson had attended Jackson's press conference, he not only had been very much the third wheel but soon found out that his definition of "highest-paid" differed from Steinbrenner's. When Munson spoke, his caution reflected the discomfort of the rest of the team. "Let's put this into per-

spective," he said. "It's business . . . business, that's all," as if trying to convince himself that was all it was.

Munson predated Jackson, Martin, and Steinbrenner with the Yankees. He was their captain and, along with Roy White, one of only two men left on the team who had played for the club during the dark ages that had just ended. Munson had had a lot to do with the end of that era, as had Nettles, Lyle, Chambliss, Randolph, and others, but he could sense that his contributions were starting to be taken for granted as Martin and Steinbrenner fought to take credit for the reemergence of the franchise. Many other Yankees felt the same way. Their contracts, compared to Jackson's, suddenly made them feel a little unappreciated and a lot underpaid.

The problems started on the first day of spring training. Martin didn't like the press much to begin with, and he sure as hell didn't like it when they greeted Jackson like the second coming. The *Daily News* compared Jackson's arrival to "MacArthur returning to Corregidor, Armstrong landing on the moon, Gable coming back to the silver screen," etc., etc., etc. The club was tense all spring as Jackson, Martin, and Steinbrenner crept around and pushed each other's buttons while the rest of the team expressed their displeasure by showing up late and bitching about contracts and demanding to be traded. Every day was a new headline — "Ellis Wants Trade," "Nettles Walks Out," "Martin Bats Reggie Fifth," "Yanks Lose to Mets."

Gabe Paul, meanwhile, was still trying to get a shortstop and fill the few other holes the team had. Since signing Jackson and Gullett, he'd traded for veteran outfielders Jim Wynn and Paul Blair, making the club top-heavy with outfielders, and at least four minor league shortstops who were all Fred Stanley clones — reasonable fielders who couldn't hit. But Steinbrenner wanted a team of all-stars. White Sox shortstop Bucky Dent was available, but the mid-1970s was not an era of great shortstops. Martin was willing to go with what he had, but at Steinbrenner's insistence, the Yankees traded Oscar Gamble for Dent on April 5 and gave Steinbrenner his squad of all-stars. One scribe compared the Yankee lineup to the no-name roster of Opening Day opponent Milwaukee and concluded, "It hardly seems fair."

It wasn't. The Brewers torched Hunter and shut out New York 5–0. One day into the season and the Yankees were already in crisis.

A week later the Brewers shut out the Yankees again, and New York thumped into last place, 2–6. Jackson, not hitting, was batting sixth. Martin claimed he wasn't panicking, and Steinbrenner predicted the team would "turn it around and soon." The next day Martin allegedly had clubhouse attendant Pete Sheehy write down the names of the starting lineup on individual pieces of paper and place them in a cap, then told Reggie Jackson to pick the batting order at random. Jackson scoffed at that story later, saying, "If Billy says that's what I did, that's what I did." But Martin had used the strategy once before, when the Tigers were slumping.

It worked again, for some reason, even with Mickey Rivers hitting fifth. The Yankees won 14 of 16 as the lineup returned to normal and Paul dumped the disgruntled Ellis, who had sealed his fate by saying of Steinbrenner, "The man [Steinbrenner] wants the spotlight. . . . [H]e should stay up in his office, push his buttons, count his money, and stay the hell out of the locker room." He went to Oakland for Mike Torrez, and the Yankees moved into first place on May 7. It appeared as if the Yankees might actually survive each other.

The Orioles and Red Sox, however, refused to drop off. New York's grip on first place lasted only a few days as the three teams pulled away from the pack. Still, compared to what would follow, it was a time of relative peace — but not quiet, and that was the problem.

Two months before Jackson had given an interview to freelance writer Robert Ward, who was working on a story for *Sport* magazine. Jackson was his usually effusive, self-centered self, made even more so by the estrangement he felt from his new teammates. Among other things Jackson told Ward in the freewheeling interview:

You know, this team, it all flows from me. I've got to keep it all going. I'm the straw that stirs the drink. It all comes back to me. Maybe I should say me and Munson. But he really doesn't enter into it. He's so damned insecure about the whole thing. . . . Munson's tough, too. He's a winner, but there's nobody who can do for a club what I can do. There is nobody who can put the meat in the seats the way I can. That's just the way it is. Munson thinks he can be the straw that stirs the drink, but he can only stir it bad.

These statements — which Jackson later denied making — appeared in Ward's article, "Reggie Jackson in No-Man's Land," in the June edition. Advance copies reached the Yankee clubhouse on May 23, just as the Red Sox were coming to town. Jackson's teammates and the press seized on the "straw that stirs the drink" comment, and everything hit the fan.

Had they been closer readers, the controversy might well have been avoided, for in a careful reading of the story 25 years later, Jackson's muddy metaphor is nearly impenetrable. Whatever point he might have been trying to make is lost in his inability to articulate his feelings, for later in the story he also admits, "We already have a team leader. Thurman Munson." But few ballplayers reach the big leagues on the strength of their rhetorical skills — not even Jackson, who claimed to have an IQ in the genius range — and New York's reactionary press corps fanned the incoherent firestorm. In any other city 90 percent of what the players said would have been ignored and 90 percent of the rest never would have been reported, but in New York every word was a headline. And the Yankee organization was far behind the public relations curve, unable and unwilling to manage the growing feeding frenzy.

Jackson had never been popular with his teammates. Catfish Hunter epitomized their ambivalence when he once said that Jackson "would give you the shirt off his back. Of course, he'd call a press conference to announce it." Although appreciated for his talent, he didn't participate in the easy banter of the clubhouse, in part because of his own condescending, self-involved attitude, but also because of his teammates' jealousy over his contract, his talent, and his close relationship with Steinbrenner, whom his teammates didn't really trust, a perception Martin helped to fuel. Whatever small inroads Jackson had made during New York's recent hot streak were swept away, and he was instantly ostracized. Backup catcher Fran Healy became his only confidant.

Everyone needed to shut up, but no one did. Instead, they all spoke to each other in the papers, revealing as much by what they didn't say as by what they did. The line between the public and the private was lost on them all as the games became secondary. Oh yeah, and the Red Sox took two of three.

The Yankees played .500 baseball for the next three weeks, and Martin's job was ever more precarious. He seemed more interested in winning his way than in winning games as he stubbornly refused to bat Jackson fourth. In a season when one big explosion seemed to follow the next without a pause, it didn't take long for everything to come to a head again.

On June 17, the Yankees went to Boston for another critical series. They lost the first game 9–4 as the Red Sox crushed a sore-armed Catfish Hunter and crashed six home runs. The next afternoon, June 18, they were featured on NBC's nationally broadcast *Game of the Week*.

The rivalry between the Yankees and Boston, combined with the running soap opera in the Bronx, made the game must-see television. The Yankees didn't disappoint.

When Jackson came out of Arizona State, where he was a baseball All-American, he was considered a potential five-tool player, for he was blessed with both a strong arm and the speed of a running back. But over time Jackson had neglected his defense. He fell in love with the home run and set his sights on the glory of becoming a slugger and all that went with it, once saying, "Hitting taters [home runs] is better than sex." Although he wasn't a bad fielder, his glove didn't inspire confidence. He looked uncertain even when he wasn't, and sometimes he really was uncertain. Defense is mostly confidence anyway, and Jackson, for all his bravado, was basically insecure. He became overcautious in the field—more concerned with not screwing up than with making the play.

The Red Sox romped. In the sixth, with the score already 7–4 in favor of Boston and Fred Lynn on first base, slugger Jim Rice checked his swing and hit a soft fly into short right.

As video of the play shows clearly, Jackson was playing deep and started in for the ball at something less than full speed, as if expecting Willie Randolph to make the play. The ball fell between them, much closer to Randolph than Jackson. Even if Jackson had been running hard, he couldn't have made the catch—the ball landed a good 30 or 40 feet in front of him. But he fielded the ball cautiously, double pumped, and then made a bad throw to the infield, but to no one. Rice made second base on the bloop double as Lynn pulled into third.

YANKEE CY YOUNG AWARDS

1958	**Bob Turley**
1961	**Whitey Ford**
1977	**Sparky Lyle**
1978	**Ron Guidry**
2001	**Roger Clemens**

Martin popped out of the dugout and pulled Torrez in favor of Lyle. Then he motioned for Paul Blair to go to right field, telling Munson, "I'm gonna get that son of a bitch [Jackson] out of there."

Meanwhile, Jackson had retreated to the fence in front of the Yankee bullpen. He looked up and was incredulous as he saw Blair coming out to right field. Then he started sprinting in toward the dugout. Martin met him at the top step and went after Jackson, looking for a confrontation. The two started screaming at each other as coaches Yogi Berra and Elston Howard restrained Martin and Jackson retreated to the clubhouse. The great unblinking eye of television captured the whole thing. It was a mess. The Yankees were a joke. People were already writing books about it.

Over the next few days Martin's head seemed to be hanging over the chopping block—Jackson may have screwed up, but Martin had lost it. Steinbrenner fumed, Jackson pouted, Martin sneered, and Gabe Paul went back and forth between all parties, stomping on the flames. Boston swept the Yankees. Martin and Jackson talked. Martin called him "boy," and Jackson thought it was racial.

RIVALS

RICHARD A. JOHNSON

I am a sports fan and a native of Boston, a place where baseball is a pastime rivaled only by politics and civil corruption. Thank God for the comfort and entertainment provided by the Miracle Patriots, the Celtics and their 16 glorious banners, the Marathon, Rocky Marciano, Bobby Orr, the Kennedys, Boston cream pie, and real clam chowder.

Did I forget to mention the Red Sox? To Boston the Red Sox are the New York equivalent of the Jets, Knicks, and pre–Stanley Cup Rangers rolled into one and cubed by several factors, thwarted, almost always, by the Yankees. Over the years the relationship between the Red Sox and Yankees, both on and off the field, has resembled a series of theatrical productions as compelling as any seen on Broadway. However, the rivalry, like most shows born in Boston, has rarely possessed the legs or brilliance to make it in the Big City.

The *Concise Oxford Dictionary* defines rivalry as follows: "to vie with, be comparable to, seem or claim to be as good." It originates from the Latin word *rivus,* meaning "stream." The classical definition alludes to different parties being part of the same continuum.

But rivalries are nearly always molded by the weaker partner. The rivalry between the Red Sox and Yankees is sadly one-dimensional, primarily the result of the wishful thinking of the Boston press intent on making their cause echo the soulful lamentations of the Daughters of the Confederacy. It means more to us than you.

In New York the Red Sox elicit either a yawn or a chuckle when the rivalry is discussed. Boston chants "Yankees Suck" while New York responds with the succinct reminder, "Nineteen-eighteen." In Boston the rivalry is best remembered for those rare and memorable summers when pennant races were taken personally. Such campaigns were always marked by peripheral, private battles within the larger war—

Teddy Ballgame versus Joe D, Munson versus Fisk, Pedro versus Roger — and a handful of bench-clearing brawls. In Boston fans and sportswriters embrace the notion that winners don't necessarily always write history, for the Yankees' near total dominance of the Red Sox is often ignored or denied. Instead, we selectively celebrate skirmishes, fondly recalling the night Pudge walloped Piniella or the day Pedro outdueled Roger while somehow forgetting the result of the season in which these events took place.

For the past century the Red Sox have more than held up their lopsided end of this most celebrated rivalry. While the Yankees have won 26 world championships spread over eight of their first eleven decades, the Red Sox captured just five such championships in their first two decades. The last, of course, was their 1918 "title to end all titles" secured in a controversial World Series against the Cubs that concluded just two months prior to the end of "the war to end all wars." This Red Sox victory has assumed its rightful place alongside similarly misunderstood historical events in Boston, such as Paul Revere's famous ride. In recounting Revere's trek, poet Henry Wadsworth Longfellow said, "Hardly a man is now alive who remembers that famous day and year." So could it now be said of the Red Sox 1918 triumph.

Mention 1918 to any Red Sox fan and brace yourself for a windy repetition of the faux history that clings to the franchise like mildew. It is here that curses, numerology, astrology, and coincidence are woven in a motley tapestry that constitutes nothing less than a story seemingly determined by anything but the facts. Add to this mélange the self-appointed literati who identify with the team and whose excruciatingly weary prose assumes the mantle of myth and you readily understand why the franchise is nearly as despised as it is revered. Oh, to have a dollar for every time these scribes have mentioned Calvinism and Mister Yawkey and alluded to Boston and New York as Athens and Sparta.

While shouldering the burden of bad history, Red Sox fans often recoil when confronting the Yankees, specifically as that history relates to the true saga of the treasured but lopsided rivalry. From the barrens of the "Croney Island" Yawkey stewardship to the killshot exclamation point of the 1978 playoff game, the lows far outweigh the highs. By now you've probably already read of at least one Boston Massacre, several brawls, and the one and only time Boston bested New York in those infrequent seasons in which the two storied franchises battled each other to the wire. For the record, that took place in 1904, and in the end another New York franchise, the National League Champion Giants, stole Boston's thunder and declined to meet the American Leaguers in what would have been the defense of their first world championship. Little town blues indeed.

In many ways the rivalry burns as brightly (and predictably) as it did in the days over half a century ago when Yankee right fielder Tommy Henrich, as quoted in David Halberstam's *Summer of '49,* explained to Boston rival Johnny Pesky that while players from both teams drove Cadillacs, the Yankees bought theirs with their World Series shares whereas the Boston players were paid handsomely by owner Tom Yawkey, win or lose. For decades Yawkey was the most generous owner in baseball while outspending his rivals to no avail.

Several decades later Yankee magnate George Steinbrenner imitated Yawkey's spending habits while also capturing headlines amid the Sturm und Drang of nearly three decades of team stewardship. Ultimately he delivered the goods with six world titles capped by the Torre dynasty of the late nineties and early twenty-first century. And while Boston management has nearly matched the Yankees' nine-figure team payroll, the team mission statement merely calls for an attempt to field a championship-caliber team. Unlike their Bronx counterparts, who still price their bleacher tickets under $10, the Red Sox have achieved world championship status only with the highest ticket prices in major league history.

Since 1903 the true measure of any baseball season in New York is whether the Yankees win the World Series, and in Boston the true measure of seasonal success is merely how the Red Sox finish in relation to the Yankees. For Boston the World Series remains, in an era of pitcher-gobbling double-tiered playoffs, the unreachable star, the ever-impossible dream. That dream is made even more remote in an era of $100 million wild-card contenders. For decades Red Sox ownership has delivered teams of entertaining soloists like Jimmie Foxx, Ted Williams, Jackie Jensen, Dick Radatz, Carl Yastrzemski, Luis Tiant, and Pedro Martinez. The only truly great Boston teams, apart from 1967's "Cardiac Kids," are those known to purists from the Dead Ball Era. For Yankee fans that marks the two decade-long ice age before Ruth, Huggins, Gehrig, the Stadium, and all those pennants precipitated a lasting thaw.

In 1999 cartoonist Charles Schulz of "Peanuts" fame announced his imminent retirement. He received thousands of letters detailing just how he should end his half-century run. Most correspondents pleaded with Schulz to allow Charlie Brown to finally kick the football, eternally offered and always pulled away by Lucy, through the uprights. But Schulz realized that Charlie Brown, his "Everyman," the comic archetype for all underdogs, could and would never do so. Were he to succeed, he would cease to be.

And so it is with the Red Sox in regard to the Yankees and a world championship. The words "almost" and "never" assume an overriding importance in Boston's baseball vocabulary. In recent seasons, have the Red Sox ever toppled their rival? Almost. But will they win a world championship in the foreseeable future? Never.

Like their counterpart Charlie Brown, the entire identity of the Red Sox is forever defined and calculated by loss. In Boston next year always becomes this year and soon resembles last year. The proximity of New York as capital of the world and the Yankees as baseball royalty is a constant and vexing reminder of a multitude of unfulfilled dreams.

RICHARD A. JOHNSON is curator of the Sports Museum of New England and co-author of *Red Sox Century*.

Both men calmed down—a little—and agreed to disagree. An uneasy quiet descended over the team. The clubhouse became a morgue. Some players threatened to walk out if Martin was fired. Others threatened to walk out anyway. If the team had been able to vote the season over and finished and done with, they'd have done so by acclamation.

The Yankees promptly went to Detroit and lost two more. When Boston came to New York a week later, the Red Sox led by five and in the first game were one out away from making that six back when—boom—Randolph tripled, and then White homered off Bill Campbell to tie the game 5–5. Then Jackson won it with an eleventh-inning blast that probably saved Martin's job and maybe the season. The Yankees swept Boston and stayed alive.

The Yankees still had an all-star at every position and a friendly schedule the rest of the way, for they were nearly done with both the Red Sox and Baltimore. After the All-Star break Ron Guidry settled into the starting staff and made up for the sore arms of Hunter and Gullett. Jackson started hitting, and Martin even moved him into the cleanup spot on August 10. The headlines changed. The search for serial killer "Son of Sam" dominated the front page of the tabloids, and variations of the phrase "Yanks Win" took a permanent spot on the back page. On August 11, Phil Pepe wrote, "it was a weird kind of day for these Yankees. . . . Nobody popped off in the clubhouse. Nobody asked to be traded or sought an escape clause in his contract. The only thing to think about, or talk about, was baseball. Strange."

Maybe everybody was just exhausted, emotionally spent, leaving only the game to be played. At any rate, everybody more or less shut up. Guidry won 16 games, and Munson hit .308. Jackson led the team with 110 RBIs, including 49 in the final 50 games of the season, of which the Yankees won 40. "Team Turmoil" clinched the division title on October 1, and they all poured champagne over one another. Winning gave the club a measure of chemistry. Jackson claimed, "I'm a Yankee now." Martin said, "If somebody says winning isn't sweet, they're full of shit." They won 100 games and beat Baltimore by two and a half. And for the first time all season they were actually looking forward to playing ball.

In the ALCS they met up again with the Royals—a better club than the 1976 version, but so were the Yankees.

Kansas City pushed the series to the fifth game but couldn't win it because they couldn't hit Sparky Lyle late in the game. When Jackson slumped, Martin benched him in the final game. Jackson turned the other cheek, then knocked in a run with a pinch-hit single in the eighth to draw New York within a run of Kansas City. His replacement, Paul Blair, ignited a three-run ninth-inning rally that won the pennant for New York. The writers started penning the story of a season that had suddenly seemed to be turning into a fairy tale.

Yet everything that had happened until the World Series would just serve as a kind of crazy setup, for over the course of seven games the Sturm und Drang of the whole season would be compressed and repeated as the residents of the Bronx Zoo displayed all the behavior that had earned them that reputation in the first place. Somehow they almost managed to make the World Series seem insignificant.

Almost. For by October the Yankees seemed better able to channel their volatility into victory.

Their signing of Don Gullett had done its damage: the Reds finished second to the Los Angeles Dodgers in 1977. On paper, L.A. appeared to match up well with the Yankees, minus all the distractions. Dodger manager Tommy Lasorda claimed to "bleed Dodger blue," and his players appeared to have bought his act. Entering the Series, the Yankees' biggest threat was the Yankees.

They didn't even make it to the opening pitch before other stories began to dominate. Joe DiMaggio had been forced to wait for his tickets and left in a huff, giving the tabloids something to write about. But game one went according to plan—Sparky Lyle took over late and kept the Dodgers quiet until Paul Blair singled in Willie Randolph for a 4–3 Yankee win.

But Martin had a problem: he didn't trust most of his pitching staff. Apart from Guidry, Torrez, Tidrow, and Lyle, everyone was either coming off an injury or lying buried in Martin's doghouse. So when Martin passed over Ed Figueroa in game two in favor of Hunter, who'd been sidelined for more than a month, he left himself wide open.

Hunter was shelled, and Jackson walked through the open door, fuming, "How could he pitch him?" All bets were off. By the time the Yankees hit Los Angeles, Jackson and Munson were both complaining about their lousy tickets, Martin was telling Jackson to "play ball and stop

managing from the bench," and Munson was muttering that he only had "five more days of this," all but announcing he wanted a trade.

But Torrez and Guidry rendered these battles insignificant by shutting down the Dodgers to put the Yankees up three games to one and leaving open the possibility that the Yankees would return to New York as champions. Jackson even quipped that "they should give Billy Martin the Nobel prize for managing."

Of course, before game five *Time* magazine reported that Jackson had told Steinbrenner he wouldn't return in 1978 if the Nobel Prize nominee was still the Yankee manager. The Dodgers won 10–4, and now Martin told Ed Figueroa, who was already angry about not pitching game five, that he wouldn't pitch game six either. Figueroa wanted to quit. Although the Yankees were only one victory away from winning the world championship, they seemed just as close to complete and utter self-destruction. There was a distinct feeling that anything could happen and probably would, and that "anything" probably wasn't anything very good.

But all year long a handful of Yankees had more or less stayed out of the fray and, relatively speaking, just played, guys like Chambliss and Randolph, Piniella and Rivers, Torrez and Guidry and Lyle. No one seemed to be paying them much attention, but they'd been doing the things that win ball games all year long. While everyone around them lost their heads, so far in the Series they were still doing those things.

And Jackson, without much notice, was having a pretty good Series himself. He homered in both game four and in his last at bat in game five. In spite of everything, Jackson was a great hitter, and the Yankees needed him. They wouldn't have won the pennant if he hadn't stayed in the lineup, and in all likelihood they wouldn't win the Series without him either. Even Martin, deep down, knew that was true.

The morning before game six Steinbrenner tore up Martin's contract and gave him another one, good through 1979. Now all he had to do was win, for despite the new

Reggie Jackson is greeted by manager Billy Martin and a less-than-enthusiastic Thurman Munson (sixth from left) before the first game of the 1977 World Series at Yankee Stadium. The Yankees soon clinched their first world championship in 15 years as Jackson helped lead them to victory in six games.

contract, no one thought he'd keep his job if the Yankees blew a three-game lead in the World Series. His assurance that no such thing would happen came from the most unlikely source imaginable, and in a way that baseball had never seen before.

The Dodgers jumped ahead with two first-inning runs, but Chambliss got them back in the second when he jacked a two-run home run off Burt Hooten. Mike Torrez gave up a third run in the third and was on the ropes in the fourth, with Rick Monday on first, one out, and Steve Yeager at the plate.

Yeager drove the ball to deep left, over Lou Piniella's head. But Piniella played the carom off the wall perfectly, turned, and gunned the ball to Graig Nettles. Monday was out, and Torrez settled down.

Thurman Munson opened the fourth with a quiet single, bringing up Jackson. The last swing he had taken in the eighth inning of game five had gone over the fence for a home run. In an earlier at bat in this game, he had walked, the bat never leaving his shoulder.

The Dodger game plan against Jackson was to jam him and keep him from getting the fat of the bat on the ball. But Jackson was swinging the bat well, laying off the inside pitch, and crushing any ball that caught any portion of the plate. As Jackson said later, Hooten's first pitch "floated over the plate."

Jackson uncoiled in his inimitable way, his upper torso and shoulders turning square, both eyes straight ahead, the bat flying through the zone and hitting the ball flush, turning it around on a line into the first row of seats in right field. In a matter of seconds the Yankees led, 4–3. Jackson hit the dugout, where Billy Martin was the first to greet him and pat him gently on the cheek. Then Reggie, naturally, found the ever-present camera. He mouthed, "Hi, Mom," and held up a single finger.

The Dodgers saw their dreams of a comeback quickly disappear. Chambliss hit a flare that fell between shortstop Bill Russell and Dusty Baker in short left for a double, Nettles expertly moved him over, and Piniella brought him home with a fly ball. The lead was 5–3, and Torrez held on.

Jackson came up again in the fifth, one on, two out, with Elias Sosa on the mound in relief of Hooten. He threw one pitch—another one that floated over the plate.

Jackson hit rewind and play, hitting the ball again in a carbon copy of his last swing, another line drive to right and into the hands and roar of the crowd. New York went wild, and the Yankees led 7–3.

All across the city anyone listening on the radio stopped and got to a television. For Jackson would bat again and, well, in that season of insanity and improbability, you just knew what would happen next.

Jackson led off the eighth against knuckleballer Charlie Hough, and as Hough's first pitch floated across the plate, not dancing but spinning in a slow parabola, Jackson swung again, this time harder than before, reaching out for the ball and getting absolutely all of it, as if he were swinging against everything that had happened and was determined to send it all back *out* and away for good. The ball sailed high and deep into the night, majestic and bright against the blackness, far over the head of Dodger center fielder Rick Monday and into the empty black seats in center field.

Three pitches. Three swings. Three home runs and history as a host of Series records fell in one moment: Jackson's five home runs the most in a Series, his 25 total bases the most, his ten runs the most, his four consecutive home runs unmatched. As he rounded first, even Dodger first baseman Steve Garvey admitted to clapping into his glove. When he reached the dugout, it was "Hi, Mom," and three fingers.

The ninth went fast, and then it was over. Nettles and Munson converged on a leaping Torrez, and the rest of the team collapsed in a mob as the New York Yankees resumed their place atop the baseball world with their first world championship since 1962, ending a 15-year drought. And in the clubhouse celebration, for the first time all year long, players lingered, hung around and stayed, not in one big happy family but in knots of alliances and allegiances that seemed a little less permanent than before. "Billy Martin," said Jackson, "I love that man. There's nobody I'd rather play for." Even though nobody believed he meant it — as Dick Young commented, "Let me tell you about that huggin'. It's for TV"— it was still nice to hear after a season of unyielding stress.

But this was the Bronx Zoo. As the players cleared their lockers and wiped away the champagne, they were already looking ahead, and not entirely with optimism. "I don't know how I got through these final days," said Munson. "I don't think this club can win next year if these problems continue," added Piniella. For in addition to a championship ring, Jackson's performance and the Yankee victory also brought the team the assurance that next year would start with the same players and the same owner and the same manager and the same problems. In the end, after the champagne turned flat, all it meant was that business most unusual would continue.

In 1978 the more things changed the more they stayed the same. Steinbrenner kept collecting stars like Hummel figures. The club lost Mike Torrez to Boston but signed premier reliever Rich "Goose" Gossage, Andy Messersmith, and reliever Rawley Eastwick. The trade gave the team six or seven starting pitchers and three closers to go along with the rest of its embarrassment of riches, ensuring that even before the first pitch was thrown or a championship ring placed on a single finger half the team would be pissed off and clamoring to be traded. Sparky Lyle, who won the Cy Young Award for his efforts in 1977, was stunned by the acquisition of Gossage, and Munson in particular had had it. He wanted to be traded to Cleveland to be near his family. But the Indians didn't have anyone the Yankees wanted, and as Steinbrenner quipped, "He can't make it to the Hall of Fame from Cleveland." They were the unhappiest defending champions in the history of baseball.

Gabe Paul became the first casualty. The man most responsible for building the reigning champions had finally tired of the constant state of crisis and his increasingly uncomfortable place in the middle of the twisted orbits of Billy, Reggie, and George. He quit and went back to Cleveland. Al Rosen, the Indians' third baseman in the 1950s and Steinbrenner's childhood hero, took over as club president, with Cedric Tallis becoming general manager.

Standard Brands, a candy company, decided that Reggie Jackson did deserve his own candy bar and unveiled the "Reggie!" bar on Opening Day. When the fans threw the candy back onto the field, it somehow seemed symbolic. Last year was over.

In the first half of the 1978 season Ron Guidry was all that prevented the Yankees' total immolation. The little left-hander, with a devastating slider and a 95-mile-per-hour fastball that earned him the nickname "Louisiana Lightning," was almost perfect. Every fifth day he more or

In 1978 Ron Guidry enjoyed a career season by winning 25 games and losing only 3 for a gaudy winning percentage of .893. The little lefty had a devastating slider and a 95 mph fastball, which earned him the nickname Louisiana Lightning.

less guaranteed a Yankee victory. Good thing, because on the other four days all the Yankees had was a collection of sore arms in Hunter, Gullett, Messersmith, and Figueroa, one pouting long reliever in Lyle, and the untested arms of youngsters Ken Clay, Larry McCall, Jim Beattie, and Bob Kammeyer.

On June 17, Guidry demonstrated that he was no fluke. After warming up, Guidry told Sparky Lyle, "I've got nothing tonight." But after giving up a leadoff double to the Angels' Bobby Grich, Guidry's nothing became something. As he described it later, "I was throwing fastballs down the middle of the plate, but they couldn't hit it." His fastball was explosive, and made that much faster by his slider.

By midgame the crowd got into it. Each time Guidry got two strikes on a hitter, they started clapping and roaring for a strikeout, beginning a tradition that lasts to this day. After entering the ninth with 16 strikeouts, Guidry struck out the first two hitters to tie what was then the all-time record. He then had two chances to set a new major league mark, but Don Baylor singled and Ron Jackson hit into a force-out to end the 4–0 Yankee win. Eighteen strikeouts would have to be enough.

While Guidry was perfection on the mound, the Red Sox were perfection atop the AL East. Sox fans were giddy, already looking ahead to the World Series. Keyed by the power of Lynn and Rice, Yaz and Fisk, and the pitching of Dennis Eckersley and Mike Torrez, the Red Sox jumped into first place and pulled away as the Yankees bitched and moaned and stumbled. The two clubs met for the first time in mid-June, and the Red Sox took two of three, leading the *Times* to comment as the club left for Detroit that "as Billy Martin walked out of Fenway Park . . . he was headed to the states of Michigan and depression." The losses dropped the Yankees seven back in the loss column, and Martin was running out of time. Martin, said Rosen, "knows what happened to managers who are supposed to win and don't win." Red Smith noted that, "if the medical profession can't repair some sore arms quickly, Martin will be fired," and that while Rosen and Steinbrenner fiddled and the Yankees did a slow burn, "Billy Martin twists slowly, slowly in the wind."

He continued to twist for the next month as strange piled upon strange. He sent Munson and his aching knees to the outfield, *right* field, which bumped Jackson to DH and caused him to sulk. Pitching coach and Martin partisan Art Fowler was demoted and replaced by Clyde King. Steinbrenner and Martin even filmed a Miller Lite commercial together, waging a "less filling, tastes great" battle that ended with the owner telling the manager, "You're fired!"

That was looking ever more likely. Martin had already held the job longer than any other in his managerial career

Jackson follows through on the swing that just sent his third home run in a row into the October night to win game six of the 1977 World Series by a score of 8–4. In this, his first Series with the Yankees, Jackson hit .450 with 8 RBIs and a record-setting 5 homers and 10 runs.

and was well past the point where every other employer had lost patience with him. On July 17, the Yanks lost their 9th game in the last 11, with a 9–7 11th-inning loss to Kansas City. They fell to fourth place, 14 long games back of Boston. And that was the highlight of the game.

The Yankees should have won it, but Randolph made a ninth-inning error, and the bullpen blew a lead. In the tenth Munson led off with a single, bringing up Jackson.

Playing for the single run, Martin flashed the bunt sign to coach Dick Howser, who relayed it to Reggie, the first time all year the slugger had been asked to bunt. Jackson couldn't get the bunt down, and with one strike Martin called it off. But Jackson kept trying, ignoring Howser, and with two strikes popped out.

Martin went nuts, fined Jackson $12,500, and suspended him. "This guy's been doing this to me for a year and a half now," he said. "Nobody's bigger than the team." Jackson pled ignorance and went home to Oakland. That should have been the end of it, but on this team nothing was ever the end of anything.

The fact that the Yankees had started to win as the pitching suddenly got healthy was lost in the headlines. When Jackson rejoined the club, he was, for Jackson, relatively circumspect and spoke eerily of "the magnitude of me, the magnitude of the incident," sounding like Marlon Brando at the end of *Apocalypse Now.* While he regretted the trouble he'd caused, he refused to admit that he'd defied Martin.

When Martin read that, he went ballistic. While waiting to board a plane out of Chicago, he had a few drinks and then a few more. He collared a few reporters — Henry Hecht of the *Post,* Murray Chass of the *Times,* and AP's Frank Brown — and described Jackson as "like a guy getting out of jail and saying, 'I'm innocent,' after he killed somebody." Then Martin signed his own warrant. Steinbrenner and Jackson, he said, "deserve each other. One's a born liar, and the other's convicted."

Steinbrenner was ultrasensitive about his legal problems. One of the reporters immediately contacted him for his reaction. He sent Al Rosen to Kansas City on a fact-finding mission, and Rosen confirmed the reporters' tale.

Martin, in tears, resigned the next day, an emotional mess. He didn't have a choice. The fans hated to see him

The ever-combative Billy Martin confronted Reggie Jackson in this scuffle at Fenway Park during a nationally televised game. Martin would make one remark too many to the media, and he was eventually fired.

go, for they had sided with him in everything and always had, but as Mike Lupica wrote in the *Daily News,* "The further you were from Billy Martin the more charming he seemed. . . . The Yankees are better off without him." The *Post*'s Henry Hecht, Martin's least favorite writer, started his column: "It's four in the morning and I'm thinking how much I hate covering the Yankees." A lot of the Yankees felt the same way playing for the team.

The Yankees replaced Martin with his polar opposite,

low-key, grandfatherly Bob Lemon, who had been Martin's pitching coach in 1976 and had just been fired by the White Sox. "I think they can do it," he said of the team, "if I stay out of their way."

The real tragedy is that the Yankees already may have been on their way to mounting one of the greatest comebacks in baseball history, and Martin missed it. The pitching staff was finally healthy, and the Red Sox were beginning to be decimated by a series of injuries that would draw the two teams back toward one another and a final, unforgettable conclusion. Everything was suddenly going the Yankees' way. Lemon moved Munson back behind the plate and Jackson back to right field. And in another two weeks the New York newspapers would go on strike, making it almost impossible for anybody to blast anybody and have anybody pay attention.

Feeling the heat from fans, on Saturday, July 29, "Old Timers' Day," Steinbrenner seized the moment for one final crazed touch. Bob Sheppard first announced that Bob Lemon would be manager through 1979 and then become general manager. As the crowd booed, Sheppard continued: "The Yankees would like to announce at this time,

introduce and announce at this time, that the manager for the 1980 season, and hopefully for many years after, will be number one, Billy Martin."

The crowd went nuts as every jaw in the press box, the clubhouse, and the dugout hit the floor. Martin charged onto the field, doffed his cap, and took several curtain calls. No one knew what to say. Someone asked Joe DiMaggio what he thought. Never very quotable, DiMaggio spoke only a single word.

"Unbelievable," he said. And it was.

When the newspapers went on strike on August 9, Lemon did indeed stay out of his team's way, and in the relative silence of the strike they did it. Over the rest of the regular season the Yankees lost only 14 games. No games they played were any bigger than the ones at Fenway Park on September 7 through 10. The Red Sox still led New York by four games.

The Yankees came, they saw, and they conquered, beating the Red Sox in every possible way. In game one Torrez was matched against Catfish Hunter, who had undergone a successful shoulder manipulation procedure a few days before. He was pitching pain-free again.

The Yankees made his task easy as they collected 12 hits in their first 22 at bats and cruised to a 15–3 win. One Boston writer reported "how the touchdowns were scored." The next day the Yankees did it again, thumping Boston 13–2.

Ron Guidry put his 20–2 record up against Dennis Eckersley's 16–6 the next day, but after Guidry gave up two first-inning singles, that was it. Boston never got another hit as Guidry threw his slider over and over again to the same unhittable spot he'd been hitting all season. And in

Billy Martin addresses the press in his Yankee Stadium office after he suspended Reggie Jackson indefinitely for having missed three signs and bunting with two strikes. Both men deserved each other's ferocious company by dint of their passion for winning.

the fourth the Yankees scored seven two-out runs to make Guidry the first left-hander to start and win a game in Fenway in four years. Boston's lead was down to one.

"This is the first time," said former Yankee turned NBC announcer Tony Kubek, "I've seen a first-place team chasing a second-place team." Joe Gergen of *Newsday*, whose paper was providing many New Yorkers with their only print account of the season, chimed in: "The Yankees are a game behind and drawing away."

Game four brought down Boston manager Don Zimmer. He never recovered from the onus of passing over Luis Tiant to pitch rookie Bobby Sprowl. The Yankees won again, 7–4, to take over the lead and end what became known as the "Boston Massacre." The Red Sox had been outscored 42–9. "I pity them," said Sparky Lyle. Four days later the Yankees secured their position in New York when Guidry threw another two-hit shutout and the Yankees took two of three. With 14 games left, the Yankees led by two and a half.

The Red Sox proved more resilient than many expected, winning their last seven to keep pace, but the Yankees kept winning as well, even after losing Willie Randolph to a hamstring injury. When the Yankees lost the season finale in Cleveland, 9–2—with Hunter losing for the first time in two months—the two clubs ended the season in a tie, setting up a one-game playoff on October 2 at 1:30 P.M. in Fenway Park. New York and Boston, the rivalry at its peak for bragging rights forever. Before the game Carl Yastrzemski offered, "There should be no loser," but that was wishful thinking.

The Yankees were confident. Before the game even started, they sent their luggage ahead to Kansas City, anticipating the start of the ALCS. Torrez, with three days' rest, would pitch for Boston. Guidry, 24–3, but also pitching on only three days' rest, would go for the Yankees.

On a perfect autumn afternoon, both clubs went out quietly in the first. But Guidry, all 160 pounds of him, was finally starting to wear down after a season in which he had already thrown nearly 270 innings. His control was a little off, and in the second Yastrzemski pulled a drive down the right-field line and parked it in the stands.

Meanwhile, Torrez was getting stronger. The score was still 1–0 when Rick Burleson doubled off Guidry, was sacrificed to third, and scored on Jim Rice's 139th RBI of the season. Then Fred Lynn jerked a Guidry slider into right.

Piniella, a good hitter not known for his grace in the field, proved that a fielder's most important asset is his brain. He'd noticed that Guidry wasn't throwing quite as hard as usual and was playing Lynn unusually close to the line. Lynn's drive, which normally would have gone for extra bases, went right to him.

The score was still 2–0 at the top of the seventh. With one out, Chris Chambliss singled. Roy White, who had played for the Yankees when they finished last behind the Sox in 1966, followed with another hit. But Zimmer stuck with Torrez. He got Jim Spencer, pinch-hitting for Brian Doyle, to fly out.

Randolph's bad hamstring had left the Yankees short of infielders. Lemon wanted to pinch-hit for Dent, who was in the midst of a terrible slump, hitting only .140 in his last 20 games. But he didn't dare. If he did, he'd have to either move Nettles over or put in Paul Blair, who'd played all of four games at shortstop. Dent had to hit.

Torrez went right after him. He got ahead with a strike, then jammed Dent, who fouled the ball off his left foot. In any other game at any other point in the season, Dent might have left the game. A similar injury earlier in the season had knocked him out of the lineup. He grimaced and started hopping around on one foot as Yankee trainer Gene Monahan rushed to his aid.

While the trainer attended to Dent, Torrez stood on the mound. Mickey Rivers, on deck, picked up Dent's bat and noticed it had a small chip. Dent switched bats, going with a Roy White model, and after almost a five-minute delay stepped back in.

Torrez hadn't thrown a pitch during the delay. Now he threw one that no one in either city has ever forgotten.

He wanted to keep the ball down, but it was a little up and a little in, not unlike the pitch Ralph Terry threw to Bill Mazeroski to end the 1960 World Series. This pitch met a similar result.

Dent chopped down on the ball, as usual, but hit it out front. It went in the air to left, where Yastrzemski started drifting back, then stopped, stunned. The short little fly was over his head and up, up, up, up over the left-field wall, which seemed to shrink as Dent's little fly ball tucked into

the net. The Yankees led, 3–2, and Dent earned a new middle name from Boston fans.

Torrez lost it, walking Rivers, who stole second. Then Bob Stanley came on in relief, and Munson lined the ball off the left-field wall for a double, and now the lead was 4–2.

After Guidry gave up a leadoff single in the seventh, Lemon turned to Gossage, who shut the Red Sox down. Reggie Jackson came up in the eighth.

The previous year Graig Nettles had dubbed Jackson "Mr. October," intending it as an insult, because Jackson hadn't been hitting. His performance in the 1977 World Series had changed all that and turned the insult around. It was now October 2, and Jackson crushed the ball into the center-field bleachers to make the score 5–2.

Good thing, because Boston nicked Gossage for two runs in the eighth and threatened in the ninth. With Burleson on, Jerry Remy hit a soft line drive to right. Once again Lou Piniella was in the right place at the right time.

He completely lost the ball in the low sun that peers in on right field at Fenway Park in the autumn of the year, sticking out his arms in the universal sign for "I can't see it." But this was Boston, and these were the Yankees. Piniella stepped to his left, where he thought the ball was headed, and as it hit the ground just in front of him, he stuck out his glove and stabbed it. Burleson couldn't score.

Yaz, a dead fastball hitter, came up with two out and Burleson, representing the tying run, now on third. Yaz took a ball, then Gossage came in with a strike, a tailing pitch that exploded, leading Munson to ask Gossage later, "Where'd that extra foot come from?" The extra foot beat Yastrzemski. The ball popped into the air and fell into the glove of Graig Nettles, making the Yankees division champions and making the Red Sox, well, the Red Sox.

New York and Boston were the best two teams in baseball in 1978, and everything that came after, as exciting as it sometimes was, was anticlimactic. This had become the Yankees' year, and nothing was going to stop that. The ALCS and World Series unfolded like a predetermined script that gave all the overlooked Yankees a time to shine.

The Yankees faced Kansas City again in the playoffs, and after rookie Jim Beattie stepped up and beat the Royals in game one, the outcome appeared decided. George

Bucky Dent touches home plate and is greeted by teammates Chris Chambliss (left) and Roy White (right) in Boston after having socked one of the most infamous home runs in baseball history. His payoff game home run off former teammate Mike Torrez barely made it over the left field wall before settling into the Fenway net. The light hitting shortstop would continue his clutch play in the World series, winning MVP honors.

Brett's three home runs in game three were rendered meaningless when Munson's 430-foot, two-run homer in the eighth inning proved to be the difference in New York's 6–5 win. And in game four Graig Nettles and Roy White both homered to give Ron Guidry the only runs he needed in the 2–1 clincher.

For White, hitting a home run was particularly gratifying. He'd lost his starting job and hadn't even played in the 1977 World Series. In June the club tried to trade him to Oakland. When Lemon put him back in the lineup in September, White had responded by hitting .341. "I've had to prove myself over and over again through my whole career, and I had to prove myself again," he remarked. "The fact that I was able to prove myself this time gives

me a great deal of satisfaction." That was beginning to become the theme for the entire team.

The Dodgers were the Yankees' opponent in the World Series again, and for the first time in two months the Yankees came out flat, dropping the first game 11–5 and trailing in game two by a score of 4–3 entering the ninth inning. Jackson came to the plate with two out and two on — another situation made for Mr. October.

On the mound for the Dodgers was rookie fireballer Bob Welch, and his next nine pitches were among the most memorable in World Series history. Welch poured fastball after fastball over the plate, pitches Jackson called "aviation fuel, high-octane." Jackson worked the count to 3–2, fouling off fastball after fastball. But on the ninth pitch, with the runners going, Welch's rising pitch at the letters beat Jackson, and he fanned to end the game, sending the Dodger Stadium crowd home happy and sending the Yankees back to New York down two games to none.

It was the kind of defeat that many teams find impossible to overcome, but in this season of improbable comebacks the Yankees had one more, and they had Ron Guidry on the mound. Yet it was third baseman Graig Nettles who would prove to be the difference.

Although Nettles was one of the best third basemen in baseball, on this team of stars he was almost an afterthought. But every time the Dodgers threatened, he made another spectacular stop, stopping rallies in both the fifth and the sixth, robbing the Dodgers of extra-base hits, laying out at full extension, saving at least five runs. The Yankees won by four, 5–1.

Game four provided another unforgettable moment. Trailing 3–1 in the sixth, with Munson on second and Jackson on first, Piniella hit a sinking line drive to Dodger shortstop Bill Russell. He dropped it, then raced to second for the force-out and threw to first to get Piniella.

But Jackson was initially confused by the play. Thinking the ball had been caught, and then seeing that it hadn't been, he froze in the baseline as Russell stepped on second and threw to first.

As the throw came toward him, Jackson took a halfstep and stuck out his hip. The ball glanced off his backside and caromed into right field. As it did, Jackson spun his head toward first base, the kid caught in the cookie jar, as if to say, "It wasn't *my* fault."

It looked for all the world like intentional interference, particularly from where the Dodgers sat. But first-base ump Frank Pulli didn't see it that way. Munson scored to make it a one-run game, then doubled in the tying run in the eighth.

The Yankees won it in the tenth, Lou Piniella versus Bob Welch, with Roy White on second courtesy of a walk and a Jackson single. Piniella, a notorious bad-ball hitter, got the same pitch that Jackson had fanned on in game one, a high fastball. This time, however, the player they called "Sweet Lou" tomahawked it into right field, and the Yankees won, 4–3, tying the Series.

But they were already drawing away. Dent and Brian Doyle, who was filling in for Randolph and looked about 12 years old, combined for six hits in game five, and Munson knocked in five in the 12–2 rout. Back in L.A. the Yankees won game six in workmanlike fashion, winning behind Hunter 7–2 as Jackson provided the exclamation point with a long two-run homer in the seventh off Welch. Bucky Dent, with ten hits and eight RBIs, was named Series MVP, but it could have gone to Doyle — who hit .438 and said, "I feel like Cinderella"— to Jackson, who knocked in eight, to Nettles, who saved a half-dozen, or to White or Piniella or Gossage or just about anyone else. Comebacks are always team performances, and this team had come back, not just from being behind, but from being almost impossible to like.

The best team money could buy had finally become a team worth cheering for, and for a few brief weeks the Bronx Zoo became a place worth visiting.

For most of the 1980s, Yankee principal owner George Steinbrenner dominated the back pages of the New York tabloids with a variety of blowups and other headline-grabbing tirades. Still, for all his foibles, the man known to all as the Boss achieved greater fame than any shipping executive from Cleveland could have imagined.

1979—1995

DARKNESS AT THE EDGE OF TOWN

Winning back-to-back world championships, particularly the way the Yankees had won in 1978, should have served as a lesson in how to do things right. They weren't "the best team money could buy" anymore, but a team that had mounted one of the more incredible comebacks in the history of baseball. "God-damn," said Lou Piniella of the 1978 season after the World Series, "there was always an air of apprehension, we were always wondering what was gonna happen next." But over the final months of 1978 the air had cleared, and what happened next had been wonderful.

But any lessons learned were quickly lost. Over much of the next 15 years the Yankee organization—which usually meant the Boss, George Steinbrenner, and a coterie of the cowed yes men he employed—thought they had all the answers. Yet when the team failed to win, they were blind to the reason why. Their Yankees' inherent flaw was not the players or the manager, the pitching coach or the general manager, who was hitting or who wasn't, Yankee Stadium, the surrounding neighborhood, or any of the other myriad excuses later offered up. No, the buck stopped at the top, with Steinbrenner and the horrible organizational climate he perpetuated. The story of these seasons became the unending search for scapegoats and blame.

Steinbrenner thought the success of 1978 had been his doing. In fact, much of it had come in *spite* of his efforts: after Lemon was hired and the papers went on strike, the players could focus on the game and the Red Sox utterly collapsed. But Steinbrenner misread his role in what happened and used the 1978 championship season to justify his twisted style of costly micromanagement, which rapidly squandered an emerging dynasty. The pinstripes became a liability as free agents feared serving Steinbrenner in the Bronx. The Yankees would soon become something they had rarely been since before Babe Ruth — irrelevant. They would remain so for some time.

The downward spiral began with a tragedy, a precursor of even more painful events soon to follow. Only ten days after the Yankees won the world championship, manager Bob Lemon's son was killed in a traffic accident. A grieving Lemon turned inward, commenting later, "It's not that I didn't want to win, but when I lost, it didn't bother me as much."

In the off-season the organization again did what it could to garner all available talent. Gossage made Lyle, the Cy Young winner in 1977, a disgruntled luxury. On November 10, he was packaged and sent to Texas for minor league pitcher Dave Righetti, the best pitching prospect in baseball, and several others. The Rangers wanted to win now and thought Lyle might be the answer. As Nettles quipped, in only 14 months Lyle had gone from "Cy Young to sayonara."

Two weeks and $2 million more added Boston's Luis Tiant and the Dodgers' Tommy John to the roster, moves that both strengthened the Yankees and weakened the competition. As Carl Yastrzemski put it, "When they let Luis Tiant go to New York, they tore out our heart and soul." But the time when money and the chance to win a championship would be enough to convince players to come to New York would soon pass.

Only 12 days into the season some innocent horseplay turned the season around and flung the Yankees back into team turmoil. Goose Gossage needled the Yankees' powerful backup catcher and DH Cliff Johnson over his inability to hit him. The two traded barbs, then started scuffling, first in jest and then in anger. Gossage tore ligaments in his thumb. He missed the next 83 games.

As the club shuffled the staff, more injuries piled up. Hunter, Ed Figueroa, and Jim Beattie all developed sore arms. John pitched well, but Tiant struggled. Guidry went from great to very good, and even volunteered to pitch relief to make up for the loss of Gossage, but he wasn't unhittable anymore. Jackson tore a thigh muscle.

In June the Orioles vaulted way ahead, and Steinbrenner couldn't take it. With the Yankees 34–31, he pulled the trigger he couldn't resist. He fired Lemon and brought back Billy Martin early.

The fans were ecstatic at Martin's return, but the excitement didn't reach the clubhouse. Martin was supposed to get his act together in his year away, but he hadn't changed. In the off-season he'd punched out a sportswriter in Reno, Nevada. But Steinbrenner, who found Martin irresistible, would keep bringing him back, like the spouse in a bad marriage who believes the other one's promise that this time, *really,* he'll stop drinking, get a job, and quit running around. Martin's charm and fire, however, couldn't fix sore arms or heal torn ligaments. The Yankees continued to play the same kind of flat, uninspired baseball they had under Lemon. No amount of tinkering seemed to work.

Thurman Munson still wanted a trade to Cleveland, but his salary was too high, his knees too damaged, his arm too sore. He could still hit, but his power was gone. The last few seasons had worn him down, and Munson, a licensed pilot, flew home whenever he could. "I can fly to Canton in an hour," he said.

On August 2, Munson, a flight instructor, and a friend took off in his new, eight-seat twin-engine Cessna jet, lettered "NY15." Munson, still familiarizing himself with the more powerful plane, practiced touch-and-go landings. But on his last run the plane suddenly lost power and came down hard in a field short of the runway, nearly hitting some trees before crashing into a field and skidding 200 feet onto a road, where it burst into flames. Munson's companions escaped, but Munson was reportedly knocked unconscious on impact and wedged between his seat and the instrument panel. They tried to free him but had to retreat as the plane was engulfed by fire.

"The whole bottom fell out of the team," said Martin later. The catcher, whose legendary gruff exterior masked a man described by his friends as tender and caring, had been a fan favorite. He didn't act like a superstar. He was a regular guy, a tough player who got his uniform dirty, a throwback, and the heart of the team.

Yankee fans said good-bye to Munson the next night at the Stadium before their scheduled game against the Orioles. Munson's widow, Diane, insisted that the game be played. Eight Yankee starters trotted onto the field, leaving home plate unoccupied as catcher Jerry Narron stood on the top step of the dugout in deference to the absent Yankee captain. Cardinal Cook delivered a prayer, and Robert Merrill sang "America the Beautiful." Many Yankees broke into tears as Munson's picture was flashed up on the scoreboard for the expected moment of silence.

Without warning, the fans broke their silence and first started clapping, then cheering, then chanting, "Thurman, Thurman, Thurman," over and over again. They wanted to cheer for him one last time, and they did, turning the wake into a celebration of Munson's life. Then Luis Tiant, in the most difficult of circumstances, pitched perhaps the best game of his career, certainly his best as a Yankee. He gave up only one hit, a home run to John Lowenstein, as the Yankees lost 1–0. The next day Steinbrenner flew the whole team to Canton for the funeral, then back to New York to resume a season that one writer accurately described as "bordered in black."

Munson's death gave the team an unspoken excuse for underachieving; they ended the season in fourth place. Martin gave Steinbrenner an excuse to fire him in late October when he got into a brawl with a marshmallow salesman in a hotel bar in Minnesota. Martin pleaded innocent at first, but the man had to be hospitalized. Steinbrenner let Martin go, saying, "What if Billy killed the guy? How would it look, 'Billy Martin, Manager of the Yankees, Indicted for Murder?'"

He replaced Martin, who was soon hired by the Athletics, with former Yankee infielder and coach Dick Howser. Al Rosen also left, so Steinbrenner became club president and named former shortstop Gene Michael as general manager. As soon as the World Series ended, the Yankees got busy, trading kids for Seattle outfielder Ruppert Jones and some more kids and Chris Chambliss for pitcher Tom Underwood and catcher Rick Cerone, then signing veterans Bob Watson, Rudy May, and Eric Solderholm as free agents.

The strategy was telling. The loyalty of players like Chambliss wasn't valued, and Steinbrenner had no patience with young players. He expected them to produce instantly and blamed Yankee scouts when they didn't. The farm system was producing, but Steinbrenner was already demonstrating his tendency to dump kids for a collection of increasingly mediocre or soon-to-be-fading stars and spending his money on free agents who weren't worth the price and didn't fit.

Howser, who was secure enough to say no to the Boss, looked like the answer. He didn't let Steinbrenner get

On August 2, 1979, Yankee captain Thurman Munson died at the controls of his eight-seater twin-engine jet while landing near his home in Canton, Ohio. His hard-nosed play and clutch hitting endeared him to fans.

WAITING IN THE HALLWAY

Do Thurman Munson and Don Mattingly belong in the Hall of Fame?

The two Yankees are in select company—a club of two. Arguably the dominant, definitive Yankee during their individual tenures in pinstripes, Munson and Mattingly are not members of the National Baseball Hall of Fame, and neither seems likely ever to gain admittance.

Both men appear to fall short of the traditional statistical thresholds that often determine membership, for each had his career interrupted prematurely, Munson by his death in 1979 and Mattingly by a debilitating back injury that stripped him of much of his remarkable ability. But a compelling argument can still be made that each man belongs in the Hall.

Even when reduced to statistics, Munson holds up. In his 11-season career, Munson accomplished what only a handful of ballplayers have done: winning the Rookie of the Year Award in 1970, the league MVP Award in 1976, three Gold Gloves, and seven appearances on the All-Star team. Moreover, in three World Series Munson hit .373.

Munson compares favorably to the 12 catchers already in the Hall. His .292 career average places him sixth on the list, and he collected more hits than games played, a mark reached by only four other catchers. Similarly, Munson eclipses Roger Bresnahan, Roy Campanella, and Ray Schalk in doubles (229), Johnny Bench, Roy Campanella, and Ernie Lombardi in triples (32), and Roger Bresnahan, Rick Ferrell, Buck Ewing, and Ray Schalk in home runs (113), and he collected more RBIs than Bresnahan, Fer-

rell, or Schalk. All this despite playing in fewer games than all but three of his peers.

Munson's career can best be compared to those of two others—Roy Campanella and Carlton Fisk. Campanella was paralyzed in a car accident after ten seasons. Like Munson, he was named to the All-Star team seven times. "Campy" won three MVP Awards but in five World Series hit only .237. Campanella had a clear edge in power, but it was not as dramatic as one would think, given that Campy played in Ebbets Field and Munson at the Stadium.

But Munson matches up even better against Carlton Fisk, particularly when one considers only the nine seasons their careers overlapped. Munson was named to more All-Star teams (7–6) and won more Gold Gloves (3–1). Fisk was never named MVP and never played in the postseason. Moreover, most contemporaries considered Munson the better receiver by far. Fisk's election to the Hall stems from his dramatic World Series home run in 1975 and the cumulative impact of his 24 major league seasons.

Don Mattingly seems to fall short among other first basemen in the Hall, for after his first seven stellar seasons, his last six, by the numbers, tail off badly. Despite his MVP Award, batting title, and .307 batting average, he clearly doesn't compare with guys like Gehrig, Foxx, Sisler, and Carew.

Or does he? One school of thought holds that to gain admittance to the Hall a player must be the dominant player at his position for an extended period of time. By this logic, both Munson and Mattingly are worthy of admission. But perhaps an even better argument can be made for Mattingly. In the middle of the 1986 season the *New York Times* asked 417 major league players, "Including pitchers, who is the best baseball

player now active in the major leagues?" In an era that included George Brett, Rickey Henderson, Wade Boggs, Tony Gwynn, Tim Raines, and Roger Clemens, Mattingly won the poll with 13 percent of the vote. Excluding votes for pitchers, his peers thought even more highly of him—fully 30 percent of the players in the American League thought Mattingly was the best in the game, more than twice as many votes as Henderson collected.

It was just a poll, but so is voting for the Hall of Fame. One might argue that Mattingly wasn't the dominant player at his position for more than six or seven seasons, but how many players are? And for how many others is there definitive proof that at any time their peers considered them the very best in the game? That list grows ever shorter.

So why are Mattingly and Munson excluded? For years some have complained about a "Yankee bias" in the Hall, claiming that it is easier for a Yankee to gain election than it is for players from other teams. At one time that might have been true, but in recent years the reverse may well be true: a host of players with Yankee connections—Tommy John, Phil Niekro, and Goose Gossage, for example—have found election to the Hall nearly impossible. Apart from Phil Rizzuto's selection by the veterans committee and Reggie Jackson's election in 1993, the last Yankees to be voted into the Hall were Mickey Mantle and Whitey Ford—in 1974.

But there is some consolation for fans of both Munson and Mattingly. Both have been honored in Yankee Stadium's Monument Park with their own plaques, a far more exclusive club than the Hall of Fame.

under his skin, and once the Yankees started winning in May, he gave the Boss little excuse to do so anyway. Out from under Martin, Jackson responded with his best year ever, hitting .300 and cracking a league-best 41 home runs to key what was also the league's best offense, and John led the staff with 22 wins. Despite losing Graig Nettles for half the season to hepatitis and Ruppert Jones to shoulder surgery, the result was 103 victories, the most for the team since 1963 and fifth best in franchise history. As it turned out, they needed every one, because second-place Baltimore won 100.

But it wasn't enough. Under Steinbrenner, little is. Three failures would outweigh the 103 successes and render them immaterial. In the playoffs against the Kansas City Royals, the improving Royals finally cracked the Yankees. Gura beat Guidry, 7–2, in the opener, and Steinbrenner started sniping at Jackson, who went hitless, and Guidry for having the temerity to lose. When Jackson showed up at the park the next day unshaven, Steinbrenner ordered him to shave. The volcano was starting to sputter and steam.

In the eighth inning of game two, with the Yankees trailing 3–2 and Randolph on first, Bob Watson crashed a double to the left-field corner. Randolph stumbled between first and second, but third-base coach Mike Ferraro still sent him home. Outfielder Willie Wilson's throw missed the cutoff man, but George Brett, backing up the play, caught it and made a perfect spin and throw to nail Randolph.

Steinbrenner was livid, and fans all over the country caught him mouthing obscenities from the stands. The Yankees lost again, and Steinbrenner snarled, "My players didn't lose this one; my third-base coach did."

Predictably, the Yankees dropped game three as George Brett, the league MVP, crushed a three-run homer into Yankee Stadium's upper deck and the Royals completed the three-game sweep with a 4–2 win. Steinbrenner was anything but understanding. Somebody had to pay, and he decided it would be Ferraro.

But Howser didn't roll over and go along. When he told the press that he deserved "the courtesy of approving or disapproving the coaches," he signed his death warrant. At an uncomfortable press conference a month later Steinbrenner announced that Howser "has decided he will not

Not long after Thurman Munson's death, the Yankees bid farewell to right-handed starter Jim "Catfish" Hunter. After arriving from Oakland, Hunter helped reestablish the Yankee dynasty in the 1970s. In five seasons in New York, the five-time world champion won 63 games and taught the team how to win.

be returning to the Yankees next year." That was true only in the sense that Howser wouldn't agree to Steinbrenner's condition, which was to hire a new third-base coach. When the press asked Howser whether he'd been fired, he refused to comment. Steinbrenner kicked Gene Michael downstairs to the manager's office, making someone else general manager.

Under Steinbrenner, it was increasingly difficult to keep track of the various Yankee employees as third-base coaches, general managers, pitching coaches, and PR direc-

The 1980 Yankees seemed subdued and bewildered as they fell in three straight games to the Kansas City Royals in the 1980 American League Championship Series. Left to right: Bob Watson, Reggie Jackson, and Willie Randolph.

tors came and went and changed titles at the Boss's whim. Someone was always moving in, and someone else was always moving out, and three or four others were always trading places, according to Steinbrenner's mercurial will. From one season to another you couldn't tell the players without a scorecard, and from one day to the next you couldn't tell who was in the front office without looking at the latest press release.

Jackson's failure to come through in the ALCS sent Steinbrenner's eye wandering. Mr. October was 34 years old and entering not only the autumn of his career but the last year of his contract with the Yankees. Steinbrenner had been toying with the idea of signing him to another long-term contract, but his eyes had brightened at the prospect of free agent outfielder Dave Winfield, who had just completed his eighth season with the San Diego Padres.

Winfield was an immense talent, an incredible athlete, and a genuine five-tool player who had gone directly to the Padres from the University of Minnesota, where he also pitched and played basketball. He hadn't spent a day in the minor leagues and had emerged as one of the best all-around players in the game—an important distinction that Steinbrenner never quite seemed to grasp. Winfield wasn't Jackson, and he wasn't likely to lead the league in anything. Over the course of his career he led the league precisely once in any significant statistical category—RBIs in 1979. He was not a classic power hitter like Jackson. Winfield was a line-drive hitter with power who wasn't helped by the dimensions of Yankee Stadium in left. He could run but used his speed in the field and running the bases more than in stealing. But he did everything well. He could reach over the fence and catch balls that would otherwise be home runs, throw out runners from anywhere or keep them from running at all, take an extra base, or drive in the big run. He wasn't a product of statistics, but he could help win a game even when he went oh-for-four.

He was in his prime, and Steinbrenner wanted him. Winning 103 games and losing the Series was "like kissing your sister," he said. "It doesn't pack the wallop that kissing your girlfriend does." He courted Winfield just as he had Jackson, wining and dining him and even sending him midnight telegrams and mash notes.

Steinbrenner outbid both the Mets and Braves, stunning the baseball world by signing Winfield to a complicated ten-year contract that promised him a bonus, an annual base salary of $1.4 million, regular contributions to a charity foundation that Winfield intended to create, and a built-in, annual 10 percent cost-of-living increase.

Whoops. That was the kind of mistake the Boss usually fired guys for. Steinbrenner had miscalculated the value of that clause, which escalated the contract to a potential value of $23 million, and he didn't realize his mistake until Murray Chass wrote about it in the *Times*. Winfield's $23 million contract almost broke baseball's bank and gave the lie to the impression Steinbrenner's fellow owners were trying to make — that the game couldn't survive escalating salaries. It was hardly the message that baseball wanted to send on the precipice of a labor dispute.

Predictably, the money spent on Winfield caused others to grouse. Catcher Rick Cerone, who had filled in admirably for Munson but earned Steinbrenner's wrath by taking the owner to arbitration, commented, "Everyone knows we needed a right-handed starter. It's going to be awful hard to repeat as AL East champs without one." Hunter had retired at the end of 1979, his arm shot, and Gullett retired for the same reason at the end of the 1980 season. Luis Tiant had been a disappointment. Guidry, John, May, and Underwood were all left-handed, as was Righetti, who was just about ready.

Winfield and the Yankees overcame a slow start in 1981 by winning nine in a row to start June and move into first place, but then the season went on hold owing to a players' strike over the issue of free agent compensation. The strike lasted from June 12 to August 8 before the owners finally caved in and the players' union continued its unbeaten streak in labor battles, one still in effect today. To salvage the season, baseball instituted a bizarre split-season plan, like some kind of summer league for kids, naming first- and second-half champions and expanding the playoffs by one round to accommodate everyone and make some extra money. In effect, the Yankees had clinched their spot in the postseason on June 12.

Good thing, because the Yankees lost momentum during the strike and never got going again, following their 34–22 first half with a desultory 25–26 mark in the second. For Steinbrenner, the strike had deprived him of some time in the spotlight creating organizational apprehension, and he wasted little time once the season resumed. Gene Michael was canned. Billy Martin was still in Oakland, so Steinbrenner brought back Bob Lemon, putting the Yankees in the bizarre position of entering the playoffs with a different manager than the one who had been there when they clinched.

The only bright spots all year were Guidry, who led the league with 11 wins, and Righetti. The Yankees wisely sent Righetti to triple-A Columbus just before the strike. He returned to the majors in midseason form and instantly became one of the best pitchers in the league. Winfield did well, hitting .292 and leading the Yankees in a host of categories, but the owner expected his salary to guarantee a Triple Crown every year. Jackson, despite leading the team in home runs and RBIs, slumped to .237. Steinbrenner snapped, "He's killing us," leading everyone, including Jackson, to conclude that his days as a Yankee were just about over. Steinbrenner warned his club that they had to win the World Series — or else. He had two plans in mind, he said — one in the event that they won and another in the event that they didn't, intimating that under "Plan B" many players would have a different address in 1982.

The Yankees edged out Milwaukee in the first round, then swept Billy Martin's A's to win the pennant. In the World Series for the fourth time in seven seasons, they again faced the Los Angeles Dodgers.

But the Yankees didn't really belong there. They had made the playoffs only because of an exceedingly easy early schedule. The strike had skewed the entire season — missed games simply hadn't been played, the Cincinnati Reds, with the best record in baseball, didn't even qualify for postseason play, and in the American League Baltimore, Milwaukee, Detroit, and Oakland all had better records than the Yankees. The strike had also masked the Yankees' problems. Steinbrenner's strategy of trading kids for guys in their midthirties who didn't have much left was starting to catch up with him. He was trying to build through free agency rather than from within and using free agency to fill the holes.

The Yankees managed to beat the Dodgers in the first two games, then blew leads in three straight and lost all three by one run before the Dodgers romped to a 9–2 win in the finale. New York hadn't hit — Winfield was a woeful one for twenty-two. They were hurt by being forced to play without the designated hitter — Commissioner Bowie Kuhn's unsatisfactory solution called for the DH to be used in the Series only in alternate years — but they deserved to lose.

The lasting impression from the Series became not so much the Yankees' defeat as the stories it spawned. When Winfield finally got his first hit in game five, he stopped the game and asked to keep the ball as a souvenir, earning the ire of almost everyone, in particular fans, who viewed the request as selfish. He later claimed to have played the Series under a death threat, which was probably true, but crazies almost always threaten big stars before the Series. It sounded like an alibi. Similarly, after game five Steinbrenner claimed he had been smacked in the head with a beer bottle in the elevator of an L.A. hotel. The owner emerged with a swollen lip, a bruise, a cast on his left hand, and a press release that said, "The fifty-one-year-old owner responded with three punches, two rights and a left. Both men went down." But few believed his story, even after the *New York Post* produced a witness.

Steinbrenner wasn't through throwing haymakers. Fifteen minutes after the Series ended he released a statement: "I apologize to the fans of the New York Yankees everywhere for the performance of the Yankee team in the World Series." He neglected to apologize for his own.

In the off-season Steinbrenner kept throwing money at problems. Suddenly enamored with speed, he traded for Cincinnati outfielder Ken Griffey, whom the Reds couldn't afford to keep, and signed his teammate Dave Collins as a free agent. But at the same time the Yankees traded probably the best speed threat in the organization, minor league outfielder Willie McGee, to St. Louis for pitcher Bob Sykes. McGee would go on to become National League MVP and a perennial All-Star while Sykes did little in New York.

On January 22, 1982, Reggie Jackson said good-bye to New York and signed with the California Angels. In five seasons as a Yankee, Jackson had hit 144 home runs, helped

Superstar Dave Winfield was never a good fit in Yankee pinstripes, despite putting up numbers that helped him reach the Hall of Fame in 2001. In 1982 he sued the team for failing to meet its contractual obligation to make payments to his charitable foundation.

DAVE WINFIELD'S
EMPTY AFTERNOON

HOWARD BRYANT

It all seemed so forced and orchestrated, hardly a celebratory effort but one rife with pathos. The anecdotes, intended to soften a turbulent era, fell heavy and leaden, and the big man's once disarming bright smile now served only to further reveal the deep fault lines that still rumble so close to the surface. The resulting picture revealed all that remains unresolved between David Mark Winfield and the New York Yankees.

As much as pride is an asset to be relied upon and for adversaries to fear, it nonetheless is a sin, and perhaps more than any other day in his life it would betray Dave Winfield. More than greed for money or envy for the adulation that in New York would never be his, it was pride that put Winfield on the grass of Yankee Stadium this August day, wearing a metallic blue blazer over a black crewneck shirt, as always head and shoulders above the rest. Members of his family sat in a row of lawn chairs in between home plate and the foreboding, interlocked "NY" logo painted on the grass.

In front of a nearly empty Stadium, Dave Winfield stood at the podium smiling, reminiscing about the good times that came with playing in New York, in the 1980s, those days of complete chaos. Winfield's time was one in which managers were fired seemingly by the inning, talented offensive teams couldn't score enough to keep up with mediocre pitching, and team success was never the result of often-brilliant individual performances. Yet on Winfield talked, about the good times that even the most ardent archaeologist would have had difficulty discovering.

As it had done during his playing days in New York, the Yankee organization found a way to belittle Winfield. The ceremony was staged before an important game between the Yankees and the Seattle Mariners yet was scheduled more than three hours before game time, ensuring that only a smattering of fans would be in attendance. The event was not well publicized; thus, the early arrivals were likely to have come to watch Seattle phenom Ichiro Suzuki and Yankee stalwarts Bernie Williams and Derek Jeter take batting practice instead of to pay tribute to one of the most complete players in Yankee history. The result was the humbling experience of Winfield listening to practically only himself speak.

He was being honored by the Yankees, but it was not even for being a great Yankee. When he was inducted into Cooperstown a month earlier, Winfield had chosen to be counted not with the Yankees but with the San Diego Padres, a team devoid of a rich history like the Yankees' and the very one from which Winfield had fled for New York at the end of the 1980 season.

The gesture of wearing a Padres cap for enshrinement was more telling than any statement Winfield would utter about himself or the Yankees. It was the ultimate act of contempt for a place that he had been expected to conquer but that had left him mortally wounded, and for George Steinbrenner, the man who once had sought to make him king.

Yet there he stood on the grass, in a stadium of 56,000 seats that was less than a third full, accepting gifts—expensive collateral but not affection. The entire afternoon played much like Winfield's eight years in New York: grudging, edgy, bitter, slightly dishonest, and all assuaged by Winfield's broad smile and the belief held by both the Yankees and himself that money could make everything whole. Throughout the speech it was clear that Winfield had either completely deluded himself or was making a hideously courageous effort to muscle through words he couldn't have truly meant.

For the Yankees, "Dave Winfield Day" seemed more an obligation than a celebration, a defensive move meant to deflect the sure criticism that would have come had they completely ignored Winfield's Hall of Fame moment.

For his part, Winfield complied by refusing to talk about anything other than détente with the Yankees or even to acknowledge there was a reason for healing in the first place.

Steinbrenner, the man who organized the event, surely paid handsomely to end the Winfield chapter on a positive note, but he did not think enough of this special day to make a personal appearance or even record—as some, like Yogi Berra, did—a video greeting on the scoreboard.

That the Yankees were ambivalent about Winfield was hardly a surprise, for during his decade in New York mutual goodwill had been rare, and those seminal moments that transform very good athletes into legendary figures had been even rarer. Instead of championships there had been the haunting, forever echo of "Mr. May" after a forgettable World Series in which Winfield recorded but one hit in 22 at bats. In a city that celebrates only the ultimate victory, Winfield was further mocked by his own self-indulgence: after his lone single in that World Series loss to the Dodgers, Winfield had stood on first base, asking for the ball.

After the 1981 low, the Yankees would not make the postseason for 14 years, the longest drought in their history since their first World Series appearance in 1921. They would not compete in a prolonged pennant race until 1995, the year Winfield retired. If this was not truly Winfield's fault, he nevertheless shouldered as much of the blame as Steinbrenner did for overpaying for Ed Whitson not once but twice. During the weeks leading up to Winfield's Hall of Fame induction, there had been little real or energetic discussion of a career that was certainly worthy of baseball immortality. Winfield's considerable ability to play baseball, his dedication to the game, and his work ethic were beyond reproach. So were his numeric credentials: 3,110 hits, 465 home runs, 1,833 RBIs, named 12 times to the All-Star team.

He was the rare superstar who enjoyed playing defense, and had driven in a World Series–winning run in 1992 — as a member of the Toronto Blue Jays.

These statistics were true enough, but the compliments felt empty and lacking in passion, that quality with which real heroes are wreathed. Winfield had been, for much of his 22 years in the game, a great player. There have been few players who played baseball so completely, but he had never achieved that signature moment — so necessary for timelessness — and he had never in New York won a championship. After Winfield spoke and the game neared, the Yankees — unintentionally but nevertheless tellingly — ran a standard video clip, this one containing a quote from Winfield's old manager Billy Martin, who said in effect that only by playing on a championship team can a player become a "true Yankee."

It would be off the field where Winfield evoked passion, for nothing he accomplished on the field could ever exceed the seamy underworld drama that defined both him and the Yankees of that era. Drama for Winfield was not carrying a team through a summer, as DiMaggio had, or a fall, as Reggie Jackson had. Winfield's legacy began when Steinbrenner consorted with a known criminal to orchestrate a public campaign against him and wound up being suspended from baseball for it. The resulting bitterness between Winfield and Steinbrenner would in many ways represent the elusive, seminal moment that never occurred on the field.

But perhaps the most revealing detail about his day of celebration at Yankee Stadium that August afternoon was that after eight years in a Yankee uniform, 1,300 hits, 205 home runs, and 818 RBIs, only one of his Yankee teammates, team captain Don Mattingly, voluntarily appeared at the park that day. No one else from the Yankee teams of the 1980s — not Ron Guidry or Reggie Jackson, not Graig Nettles, Mike Easler, or Mel Hall — appeared at the Stadium

to watch Winfield be honored. It is this fact that best describes the volatile, unfulfilled Yankee career of Dave Winfield.

The legendary jazz trumpeter Miles Davis was notorious for hiring and firing musicians with little explanation. If asked why, his answers were vague at best. A sound didn't feel quite right. A transition was too harsh, maybe too gentle. Davis would say that he didn't hear "that thing," the intangible something that separates the good from the brilliant.

It is in this vein that New Yorkers talk about Dave Winfield. The Yankees at the end of the 1980 season were still considered a powerhouse. They were not the best team — Kansas City and Baltimore had bested them in recent years — but the memory of consecutive World Series titles in 1977 and '78 was still fresh in the public's mind. The free agent Winfield would usher in a new decade of Yankee dominance, as Jason Giambi is expected to do today. Everything should have been in place for a union of great achievements — a big man (observers marveled that at six-foot-six and 220 pounds he could play baseball), playing as the biggest star in the biggest city on the biggest baseball stage. Instead, "that thing" about Winfield never congealed. There was always something missing.

He was respected but not loved. Love both within the organization and among fans was reserved for Mattingly. Plus Winfield was black, and no black Yankee player has ever enjoyed the unbridled affection — the mandate of the people — that has always been reserved for whites. With the exception of Mattingly, the Yankees of the 1980s were the province of high-paid black players — Winfield, Rickey Henderson, Don Baylor — who did not win and were not the accommodating, easily likable black personalities that disarmed whites.

Winfield did not mingle with his teammates; he seemed to consider himself a cut above the banality of the locker room. "He was a great teammate . . . on the field," said Willie Randolph, the old Yankee second baseman and current Yankee coach. "He gave you 100 percent effort, but he wasn't the guy you hung out with. You didn't go to dinner with Dave." In many ways it was as if Winfield considered himself a corporation, with baseball merely the highest-profile section of his portfolio. To be considered only a baseball player was to accept the stereotypes that came with it and thus risk not being taken seriously as a businessman or intellectual.

Winfield could hit for power but was not a power hitter, and thus he would never have been Reggie Jackson. He hit 465 career home runs but never led the league in homers. Those titles were reserved for the game's other stars, such as Baltimore's Eddie Murray and Boston's Jim Rice and Mike Schmidt in Philadelphia. Worst of all, he was never the big-moment, boom-or-bust star like Babe Ruth and Jackson, for whom New York was made. Winfield's inability to compensate for the front-office tumult and weak pitching staffs to single-handedly push the Yankees into the postseason made him, in the piercing eyes of New York, the anti-Jackson, the nonwinner. The one time he carried the Yankees to the playoffs Jackson was still on the team, and Winfield, the heir apparent, failed miserably. Instead of accentuating what he was, New York had a way of always accentuating what Dave Winfield was not.

"None of this is fair, because say what you want, the guy busted his ass for this town." Jack O'Connell, secretary-treasurer of the Baseball Writers' Association of America and a longtime New York baseball writer, is talking now. He is Irish, but talks with an Italian flair. When he is excited, as he is when he talks about Winfield, he gesticulates passionately. "You look at these prima donnas today, and Dave Winfield wasn't one of them. He gave you everything he had every day, but he got off on the wrong foot with the Boss from the start, and George never forgave him for that."

The whole thing started over something called an escalator clause in Winfield's contract. Everything can be traced back to that contract signing, before Winfield even donned a Yankee uniform. Winfield was the crown jewel of the free agent market in 1980, and when the Yankees outbid Atlanta, Winfield would don pinstripes for an unprecedented 10-year contract worth some $16 million. Yet when Steinbrenner failed to realize that cost-of-living adjustments were included in the contract, he'd been had. In fact the contract was potentially worth $23 million over its life. Steinbrenner, livid and hoodwinked, vowed to get even. The next decade would be marked by Winfield's steady brilliance on the field and by various jousts with Steinbrenner over the legitimacy of his youth foundation off of it. Not only were Winfield's game-winning hits and steady defensive play secondary to Steinbrenner's lust for revenge, but so was the law. He hired a small-time criminal named Howard Spira, who once ran errands for Winfield, to gather information to discredit him and the foundation.

Steinbrenner himself sought FBI protection as Spira began extorting thousands from him. To free himself of Spira, Steinbrenner was forced to admit to having tried to destroy Winfield and was eventually banned from baseball.

Steinbrenner lost another public opinion round to Winfield, but Winfield's name as a community beacon took a severe hit when Steinbrenner portrayed the foundation as nothing but a front company for Winfield and his friends to spend the tax-exempt money meant for philanthropy. It was all so ugly and, in the opinion of most baseball people, impossible to heal.

When he was traded to California in 1990, Winfield moved on as a modern-day outfielder for hire. He won a World Series title with Toronto in

1992, avenging the misery of 1981 with a series-winning double against Atlanta. He went home to Minnesota and notched hit number 3,000 before giving in to age, too late, in Cleveland. The Indians released the 43-year-old after he hit just .191 and knocked in 4 runs in 46 games in 1995. It was over, and all that remained was the six-year waiting period to enter the Hall of Fame and the question of whether he would—despite a massive character defamation—enter the Hall of Fame as a member of the New York Yankees.

During the wait to be bronzed, Winfield drifted, as most retired players do. Carefully protecting his image, unable to be spontaneous, he was a disaster as a television analyst. Time neither sweetened nor softened his days with the Yankees, and as induction neared, it was clear that Winfield the baseball player—despite his abilities—had become something of a lost figure, a gifted player who didn't belong to any one club. His time with the most recognizable club—the Yankees—had left nothing but mutual scars, the specter of Howard Spira, and a populace that never truly accepted him. He had played for six teams, the first but certainly not the last modern superstar Hall of Famer to be so transient and unattached emotionally to a particular club. David Justice, the one-time Yankee outfielder, would speak for the modern player when he responded to the question, "Do you consider yourself a Yankee?" with the answer, "I consider myself a baseball player."

As Winfield's date with the Hall of Fame neared, a cynical belief emerged that Steinbrenner and the Yankees would throw enough money at him to bury past wounds, to alter the true history of his time in New York. Secretly, the two began to negotiate what clearly would have been a Faustian pact. Steinbrenner would welcome another Yankee into the Hall of Fame, another number retired to his monument, and Winfield would receive the cachet and financial perks that come with being a Hall of Fame Yankee.

Now here they were, the Yankees and Winfield, sitting at a folding table at Yankee Stadium, resting on the rubble of the 1980s, saying everything was all right. Bygones were now bygones. Unsurprisingly, the name Howard Spira was not mentioned once during this day, not even to express regret for those times and Winfield's survival of them. Mr. Steinbrenner's generosity, Winfield said with deference, made this great day possible. He has no regrets and can only remember, he said, "the great times of being a Yankee." And if he believed he was rising above the cacophony in this decades-old conflict with Steinbrenner, his pride again betrayed him into thinking the Yankees would accept him into the family, even as he was planning to reject them. Incredibly, he said he secretly believed the Yankees would relent and retire his number 31. He believed in this possibility even after electing to enter the Hall as a Padre.

A family member, perhaps finally tired of this empty afternoon, sat in the back of one of the press conferences grinding his teeth, hissing dissent, voicing what everyone was really thinking during this bizarre day. He was bitter about everything Winfield had endured as a Yankee and insisted that no one should ever forget that the man holding this day to honor Winfield had tried heartily to destroy his reputation. He said that the day was a nice one, but that Dave Winfield should never have allowed the Yankees and Steinbrenner to humiliate him once more by using his name to further their legend. They don't need him, true enough, for the Yankee legend is secure and continues to grow with each World Series victory. But Dave Winfield doesn't need the Yankees either. Because everyone expected Winfield to bow to Steinbrenner, the Yankee mystique, and its considerable marketing muscle, his surprising allegiance to the Padres seemed all the more attractive.

Still, that Dave Winfield allowed himself to stand in front of a largely empty stadium, in many ways humiliated again by the Yankees, suggests that the glass wall between him and the Yankees had damaged him more than he admitted. If his appearance was an attempt to call a truce or to extinguish a lingering bonfire once and for all and be the bigger man Steinbrenner could never be, he was certainly successful in this mission. Yet he may have achieved his victory at a very high price: it may have cost him his dignity. There was nothing — certainly not the 2001 Dodge Viper the Yankees gave him and the dozens of other gifts he accepted — that could erase the reality that his tenure in New York had been marked by workmanlike effort, high potential, and a result far short of success.

The family members gathered in an elevator, taking Winfield up to the luxury box where he would watch a playoff-style match between the Yankees and Mariners, a late-day thriller the Mariners ultimately won. Another family member noted that Winfield had remained unfailingly polite, having his day and in his own way winning a victory in this final confrontation by walking away from Steinbrenner, the Yankees, and New York, damaged but dignified in détente, and not fooled for a minute. That it will cost him countless dollars in memorabilia and endorsements to not be associated with Ruth, Gehrig, DiMaggio, and Jackson is nothing compared to the satisfaction that comforted Dave Winfield. It was the satisfaction of being the one person Steinbrenner's millions couldn't buy.

HOWARD BRYANT covers the Yankees for the *Bergen Record* and is the author of *Shut Out: A Story of Race and Baseball in Boston.*

In eleven seasons with the Yankees, Lou Piniella (right), shown here with Bobby Murcer, batted .295 and helped lead the team to two world championships and four pennants. He returned as manager in 1986. After being fired, he was later rehired to manage the team in 1988.

the team reach the postseason four times, and hit .400, with eight home runs in three World Series. Jackson would have preferred to stay, but Steinbrenner never made him an offer, a decision that the owner later regretted. For the last half of his contract, Jackson, at only $600,000 a season, had been a bargain. For it had been Jackson, for all his many faults, who had delivered on Steinbrenner's promise to win a championship and, as he had predicted, "put the meat in the seats." Not including the strike-shortened 1981 season, Yankee attendance had increased every year Jackson played in New York and reached a record 2.6 million in 1980. Broadcasting revenues had risen dramatically as well.

When the Yankees opened the 1982 season 6–8, Steinbrenner fired Lemon again and brought back Michael. It made no difference. Apart from Winfield, who changed his swing and belted 37 home runs—the most for any right-handed Yankee hitter other than Joe DiMaggio—and Dave Righetti, there was hardly a player on the team who hadn't already seen his best seasons. Jackson returned in an Angels uniform, hit a home run, and sparked the first

"Steinbrenner sucks!" chant in the Stadium. Trades were made solely for the sake of making trades, a shift of has-beens, with Watson, Dent, John, and others going and John Mayberry, Butch Wynegar, and Roy Smalley coming. The merry-go-round was beginning to spin at a dizzying rate.

And the Yankees' reputation was beginning to precede them. Players on other teams looked at the Yankees and saw only disarray. Over much of the next decade most top free agents steered away from New York completely or simply used the Yankees to ratchet up their price and then go elsewhere. Increasingly, the Yankees were forced to overpay for what talent they could attract and found themselves fleeced in trades, taking on other teams' problems and giving away the farm system. With each new acquisition, the organization seemed to be spinning its wheels, going nowhere except deeper into a rut.

Steinbrenner didn't help matters by publicly carping about Yankee Stadium and the surrounding area. The city already had a reputation as the crime capital of the world, and each time Steinbrenner and other Yankee officials carped about the safety of the South Bronx rather than the safety of the Stadium, the Yankees became a little less attractive to both fans and players. All they did was make a bad situation worse.

At each step the Yankees became a little more average. Griffey was all right, but Collins was awful. Gene Michael lasted only 86 games, then got the blame for the Yankees' .500 record. Clyde King, who'd been pitching coach in 1981 and then went upstairs, replaced him. The Yankees finished 29–33 under the third manager of the season, landing in fifth place, only a game ahead of Cleveland and Toronto, with a season record of 79–83.

No one was safe. Winfield had to sue to get the club to meet its payments to his foundation, beginning a long estrangement between the club and its best player, whom Steinbrenner regularly disparaged, causing the star to be viewed with more and more skepticism by fans. They never really warmed to Winfield. Steinbrenner always saw him in terms of what he was not instead of what he was. It wasn't Winfield's fault that the Yankees were old, overpaid, and, in the Boss's view, underachieving. But as the highest-paid member of the bunch, he took the blame.

The Oakland A's, under the special magic that Billy Martin always seemed able to conjure up in his first season with a team, had won the AL West in 1981. But his overworked pitching staff collapsed in 1982. Martin, who was hard enough to take when he was winning, was impossible when he was losing. When the A's let him go, Steinbrenner canned King and hired Martin on January 11, 1983, for the third time.

It was no charm. Buoyed by a few more free agents, good health, a few trades, and a few surprises, the Yankees improved in 1983 but were only briefly in the pennant race. On July 4, at Yankee Stadium, Dave Righetti provided one of the few highlights of the season.

He'd been knocking on the door of greatness since striking out 21 in a minor league game, and he was one of the few younger players of ability the Yankees had acquired since Steinbrenner purchased the club. They'd resisted the temptation to rush him. In 1983 he seemed ready to become a number-one starter, taking over as Guidry began to fade. He had already won nine games and was coming off his first career shutout. On a blisteringly hot day, before 41,077 fans, he overpowered Boston with a rising four-seam fastball and wicked slider. He faced Wade Boggs with two out in the ninth and a no-hitter on the line. Hitting .361 at the time, Boggs was not only one of the best hitters in baseball but one of the most difficult hitters to strike out.

Not to Righetti, however. He blew Boggs away on a 2–2 slider, then jumped and twirled in the air, a rare show of youthful exuberance on a team that had little of either. The no-hitter was the first by a Yankee in the regular season since Allie Reynolds in 1951, and the first in the Stadium since Don Larsen's perfect game in the 1956 World Series. Steinbrenner reminded everyone that it was his birthday.

Yet the season became better known for two meaningless incidents. On July 24, as the Yankees fought to keep the division-leading Baltimore Orioles in sight, they faced the Royals. Leading 4–3 in the ninth, the Yankees were killed once again by George Brett, who blasted a two-run home run off Gossage to put Kansas City ahead 5–4.

Martin had the Royals right where he wanted them. A few weeks earlier Graig Nettles had noticed that Brett treated his bat with pine tar beyond the 18-inch allowable limit. He recalled that an umpire had once taken a hit away from Thurman Munson and declared his bat illegal for just that reason, finding pine tar on the bat beyond 18 inches. Nettles told Martin. The manager filed the information away and waited.

Now he ran out on the field and explained to umpire Tim McClellan that the bat was in violation of rule 1.10 in the *Official Rules of Baseball,* and that according to rule 6.06(a), Brett was out. McClellan measured Brett's bat and agreed. His thumb shot up in the air, and the Yankees still led 4–3.

Brett rocketed out of the dugout, blind with rage, and charged into McClellan before being restrained by another umpire, George Brinkman. Brett was tossed out of the game, but Kansas City manager Dick Howser filed a protest.

Protests are rarely upheld in baseball, but that didn't stop league president Lee MacPhail. He ruled that the bat, not the batter, should have been tossed out, that the home run counted, and that the game would be replayed from that point. The replay happened on August 18, and the disgruntled Yankees treated it like a joke. Ron Guidry played center field and left-handed rookie Don Mattingly manned second base as the Yanks still lost 5–4.

Meanwhile, another equally bizarre incident took place. As he warmed up before the fifth inning in Toronto on August 4, a throw by Dave Winfield struck and killed a seagull, something he couldn't have done on purpose had he tried. Local authorities overreacted, and Winfield was escorted to a police station after the game, charged with cruelty to animals and forced to post bond.

Although charges were wisely dropped the next day, they illustrated what the Yankees had become: a team for which wins and losses were the sideshow to a larger circus. Martin, who'd battled umpires all year and been suspended in September, was fired again in December as his half-life as a Yankee manager kept getting shorter. Steinbrenner reached blindly into the past and named Yogi Berra the next Yankee manager. The club added Don Baylor and knuckleballer Phil Niekro by the usual route of free agency in 1984, but the real difference in 1984 was Don Mattingly.

One of the problems with the Yankees' fetish for free agents was that fans felt little connection to the players. Winfield, for all his skill, was viewed as a mercenary. Mattingly, by contrast, would fill a place that had been unoccupied since the death of Thurman Munson.

At first, Berra didn't want him and gave Roy Smalley a shot to win the first-base job in the spring, calling Mattingly his "swingman," which was another word for utility player, an approach almost certain to drive a young player to distraction. In Berra's mind, Mattingly was a singles and doubles hitter while Smalley was good for 20 home runs. Besides, Mattingly made only $75,000. Although he'd hit over .300 in every season in the minor leagues, he wasn't a big prospect — 489 players had been selected before him when he was drafted out of high school in 1979. Roy Smalley, on the other hand, had just signed a five-year deal worth $3.7 million for hitting 16 home runs in 1983.

But Mattingly crushed the ball all spring, and even Steinbrenner could already see he deserved to play. "Maybe we should give the job to Mattingly and let Smalley fight for the job," he said. The Boss was already starting to figure out he'd again overpaid for a player of deteriorating skills. By May Mattingly had hit his way into the lineup by merit. Incredibly, he became the first product of the farm system to earn a lasting spot in the starting lineup since Ron Blomberg played first base for much of 1972.

For the next decade Mattingly put up incredible numbers — particularly over the first half of his career — and provided much of the reason Yankee fans even bothered to stay Yankee fans. From 1984 through 1989 he averaged .325 with 27 home runs, 42 doubles, and 114 RBIs, winning a batting title in 1984 and an MVP Award in 1985, hitting home runs in ten straight games, and cracking six grand slams in 1987. Even better, he looked like he was trying and acted as if he cared.

That perception was genuine. In one late season game in 1992 against Detroit, with the Yankees trailing badly and already far out of the race, Mattingly singled off Frank Tanana, stretched it to a double, took third on a short fly to right, and then scored on a ground ball, creating a run purely on effort alone. Even players on opposing teams respected him. The Twins' Kirby Puckett dubbed him "Donnie Baseball."

In his four and a half years leading off for the Yankees, Rickey Henderson (sliding) enjoyed some of his finest seasons, scoring as many as 146 runs, batting .305, socking 28 homers, and stealing 93 bases. But his stint with the team came during a time the Mets ruled New York, and the Yankees were strictly "below the fold" material.

1979   [376]

1995

Mattingly seemed to understand his place on the club from the start—hitting close to .350 helped. He once said his stated goal was "not to be noticed," and one observer called him "all line drives and silence." He just wanted to play. He became the kind of team leader the Yankees have always favored, the one who leads by example. Young players were told to watch him as a living embodiment of the Yankee way.

At the same time Mattingly learned to stand up to Steinbrenner as he grew older, once saying, in a thinly veiled reference to the owner, "You come here and you play and you get no respect. They treat you like [bleep]. They belittle you and make you look bad in the media. After they give you the money it doesn't matter. They can do whatever they want. They think money is respect." That would have gotten anyone else canned. But Mattingly was bulletproof.

Like Munson, Mattingly was a player fans identified with. Standing only five-eleven and weighing 180 pounds, he left the impression that he succeeded only because of his work ethic. Like Munson and Piniella, Mattingly was viewed as a "grinder," a "real" Yankee. But the ambidextrous Mattingly was far more skilled than many thought. He was athletic enough to take balls at shortstop during practice and to play third in a pinch, and he had been recruited by Big Ten schools to play quarterback. Yet fans always saw Mattingly not so much as an athlete, like Winfield, but as a ballplayer somehow managing to do more than he should.

For the next few seasons the Yankees would be just close enough to first place for Steinbrenner to continue his ceaseless interference and tinkering, but not good enough to win. The statistical battles between Mattingly and Winfield would be of more interest than the ballclub's record. In 1984 Mattingly and Winfield battled each other for the batting championship until the final day of the season.

The reaction of the crowd that day was telling. Mattingly entered the last game trailing Winfield by a point and a half. The Yankee Stadium crowd cheered him wildly each time he came to bat, while Winfield was booed.

In his last at bat, Mattingly, with three hits already to his credit, slapped a fourth hit past second base off Detroit

Dave Winfield couldn't catch a break as a Yankee. George Steinbrenner vilified him as "Mr. May," implying he couldn't match "Mr. October," the departed slugger Reggie Jackson. In 2001 Winfield chose to be enshrined at the National Baseball Hall of Fame in Cooperstown wearing a San Diego Padres cap.

reliever Willie Hernandez, raising his average to .343 to win the title. Then Winfield, with only one hit for the day, stepped in for the last time and for the first time all day heard cheers. He pointed his bat at Mattingly in a salute, then grounded into a force play to finish at .340. As Mattingly left the field, he noticed that Winfield had been replaced by a pinch runner. He trotted over to him, and the two walked off arm in arm. But Winfield skipped his shower, dressed quickly, and left, saying to one teammate, "I'm getting the hell out of here." Later, as Mike McAlary wrote in the *Post,* Steinbrenner "felt compelled to take one last swipe at Winfield. 'Dave Winfield is a great athlete,' The Boss said, 'but I don't think he's the team player Mattingly is.'"

Apart from the day-in-day-out excellence of Mattingly and Winfield, the Yankees would often be one of the league's best offensive clubs over the next several seasons, winning between 85 and 97 games each season from 1984 to 1988 and accumulating baseball's best won-loss record in the 1980s. They never had enough pitching, however, to go over the top. Each season would play out in rough imitation of the last as the Yankees made coming close a new tradition.

Steinbrenner continued to throw baskets of money at players who didn't deserve it, as if salary alone could will a pitcher to win, a response to the Yankees' dilemma that was so comic it was almost tragic. Ed Whitson, who won 14 games for the NL champion San Diego Padres in 1984, became the most glaring example of this flawed approach. The Yankees signed Whitson, a good but not great pitcher, as a free agent to a five-year contract worth $4.4 million. A disaster from the very beginning, Whitson was overwhelmed by New York, and Steinbrenner only made it worse for Whitson by constantly carping about how much he was being paid. In the Stadium Whitson was jeered so unmercifully that the Yankees eventually had to stop pitching him in New York.

Whitson eventually clashed with Billy Martin, whom Steinbrenner brought back yet again in 1985. At the end of the year Whitson and Martin fought in a bar. When Whitson beat Martin badly, breaking his arm and fracturing his ribs, he provided the final evidence anyone needed that Martin's life was fully out of control.

One reason for the Yankees' annual pitching problem,

ironically, may have been the one steady performer over these seasons, Dave Righetti. In 1984 Steinbrenner discarded Gossage, who signed as a free agent with San Diego and had many more productive seasons. As a result, only one year after twirling a no-hitter and winning 14 games, Righetti was moved into the bullpen and turned into a closer. "Rags" immediately became one of the best in the game, but at the same time his absence left the starting rotation perennially thin. Guidry was getting older, Phil Niekro was already old, and no one else had stepped up to fill the breach. Young pitchers who later became very good, like Doug Drabek and Bob Tewksbury, were shipped out of the organization before they had a chance to adjust to the major leagues. The Yankee rotation was fleshed out instead by fading veterans like Rick Rhoden and Tommy John and by guys like Dennis Rasmussen, Bob Shirley, Joe Cowley, and Charlie Hudson, pitchers who would have been serviceable fourth or fifth starters but weren't suited to being at the front of the rotation. Meanwhile, Righetti pitched only 70 or 80 innings a year; he saved a lot of games, but as a starter he might have pitched 200 innings and been able to anchor the staff. In retrospect, putting him in the bullpen may have been a mistake.

But perhaps the worst thing about this era was the fact that it wasn't at all enjoyable—not for the players, not for the writers, not for the fans, not for anyone. Historically, it leaves little impression beyond Steinbrenner's shenanigans, Mattingly's day-in-day-out performance as the second coming of Stan Musial, and Winfield's exemplary play on the field. The team was known more for its managerial revolving door—Berra replaced by Martin in 1985, Martin by Piniella in 1986, Piniella by Martin in 1987, Piniella again in midseason, and so on. The character of the club was chaos.

The Mets ruled New York. With young stars like Dwight Gooden and Darryl Strawberry and solid veterans such as Keith Hernandez and Gary Carter, the Mets bumped the Yankees off the back page of the tabloids and became New York's dominant team. The almost invisible Yankees were strictly below-the-fold material.

Even the acquisition of A's outfielder Rickey Henderson in 1985 made little impact. The performance of Henderson—unquestionably the best leadoff man in baseball history—in the five seasons he played in New York was almost equal to that of any player in club history, yet he left hardly a ripple on the organization.

That response was partly due to Henderson's own self-involved personality and attitude toward the press, his teammates, and almost everything else outside what came to be known as "Rickey's World." Like a lot of other great ballplayers with a special skill, such as Ted Williams, Henderson was himself to a fault. His boyhood friend and fellow major leaguer Lloyd Moseby once commented, "He could strut before he could walk." In the words of one observer, the New York press found him "petulant, cocky, narcissistic — the embodiment of everything the press abhors."

But Henderson knew his role. "My job is to score," he said, and he did that and more, particularly when the Yankees were managed by Billy Martin, whom Henderson loved playing for. Across four and a half seasons as a Yankee, Henderson had some of the best seasons of his career, scoring as many as 146 runs, stealing as many as 93 bases, batting as high as .305, hitting as many as 28 home runs, knocking in as many as 72, and setting a host of team records. Henderson was the main reason Mattingly gained a reputation as an RBI machine, and he helped Winfield in the same way. Time and time again Henderson would get on first, steal second, and score on a hit as Mattingly or Winfield feasted on fastballs thrown by pitchers he'd made nervous.

But Henderson did a thousand things that drove people crazy. He was constantly late. Mattingly once quipped, when Henderson was making his usual late arrival, "At least he's consistent. That's what you want in a ballplayer — consistency." In the outfield he caught routine fly balls with a "snatch" catch, sweeping his glove at the ball, a move that was intended to be entertaining and flamboyant but that looked stupid and drove his managers nuts, because every once in a while he'd miss a catch that should have been routine. He was accused of being a hypochondriac, particularly in regard to his legs — within the organization he was known as "Hammy" for his obsession with the condition of his hamstrings. And when he did get hurt — as in 1987, when he missed extended periods of time with a pulled hamstring — the organization thought he was jaking it.

He got off to a slow start in 1989, and that was it. Like Winfield, he'd become a scapegoat. General manager du jour Syd Thrift thought Henderson was slipping and sent him back to Oakland. His exile marked the end of the Yankees' mini-revival. Beginning in 1989, they fell back further than ever.

The ultimate irony of the era is that the situation improved only when Steinbrenner was banned from acting as team owner. Not that the Yankees' record immediately improved — it did not — but the attitude of the organization began to change. In the relative quiet of Steinbrenner's enforced absence, New York slowly became a place where players wanted to play again. Yankee Stadium felt like a ballpark again instead of a set for a soap opera. Steinbrenner's suspension from baseball marks the point at which the current New York Yankees, the ruling dynasty of the game, began to emerge from the ashes.

Ever since he had signed Winfield and then discovered that he agreed to a contract he didn't understand, Steinbrenner had been sniping at Winfield. Late one day in the 1985 season, as it became clear that the Yankees weren't going to catch the division-leading Blue Jays, Steinbrenner stomped into the Yankee Stadium press box. With the Jays beating the Yankees down on the field, he loudly demanded, "Where's Reggie Jackson? I need Mr. October. All I have is Mr. May, Dave Winfield."

But his attacks went beyond verbal putdowns. Steinbrenner was galled by the money he had to pay Winfield and had been raising questions about his foundation. He forced an audit of the foundation, and according to Steinbrenner's attorneys, it revealed that in 1986 less than 20 percent of its funds actually went to charity; the rest was spent on overhead. This was a dismal record, to be sure, but not the whole story either.

Steinbrenner didn't stop at publicly embarrassing Winfield. A onetime gofer for the outfielder, a small-time gambler and wiseguy named Howard Spira, had been pestering Steinbrenner for years, promising him that he had the goods on Winfield. Now he wanted to be paid off.

Steinbrenner blanched, but Spira was nothing if not persistent, and according to Steinbrenner, whose story reportedly changed several times, Spira began couching his demands in veiled threats. In December 1990, Steinbrenner handed over $40,000, either for information already provided or because he thought that would put an end to it. But Spira upped his demands, and Steinbrenner eventually went to the FBI.

Spira had also been trying to sell his tale to the papers, which got wind of Steinbrenner's payoff and made it public. Baseball was touchy about anything related to gambling—Pete Rose had been banned by baseball for his troubles only a year earlier. Public disclosure of the payoff gave Commissioner Fay Vincent an excuse to mount his own investigation of the whole silly, stupid, sordid mess.

Steinbrenner wasn't in a position of strength—he'd been a thorn in baseball's side for years, and many of his fellow owners blamed him for starting baseball's out-of-control upward spending spiral. Beginning in 1987, the men who owned baseball illegally conspired to keep salaries down through collusion with one another; Steinbrenner had been a less than enthusiastic participant but hadn't gone against his brethren. He'd toed the line—barely—because the policy of collusion hurt the Yankees, leveling the playing field that their own self-interest demanded remain tilted their way. In the late 1980s, with Winfield, Mattingly, Righetti, and Henderson on board, the Yankees were one stud pitcher away from going over the top, but under the secret arrangement between owners, Steinbrenner was prevented from outbidding a player's original team. Faced with going to New York or staying elsewhere for the same money, most players had chosen elsewhere.

Spira's arrest provided baseball with an excuse to slap Steinbrenner down. Getting Steinbrenner made the commissioner look tough and was of some limited help in Major League Baseball's public relations battle with the players over labor issues. On July 30, 1990, Steinbrenner signed an agreement in which he agreed to accept a two-year period of ineligibility—the semantic equivalent of a suspension and an edict that Steinbrenner desperately wanted to avoid. He was vice president of the United States Olympic Committee and feared that an official suspension would cost him his post.

Steinbrenner's exile came just in time. Over the past two seasons, without the influx of free agents, the franchise had rapidly deteriorated under his watch. In 1988 Steinbrenner had brought back Billy Martin for an incredible fifth tour of duty, earning a "Ho-Hum, It's Billy V" headline from the *Daily News*. The Yankees didn't play

In 1988 Billy Martin returned to the Yankees as manager for an incredible fifth time, inspiring the *Daily News* headline "Ho-Hum, It's Billy V." Behind him, in his office, is a portrait of his mentor, Casey Stengel.

badly under Martin, but increasingly his life was slipping out of control. In late May he ended up in another fight in a bar, this time a topless one, and on June 23 Steinbrenner fired him for the final time, with the Yankee record at 40–28. He brought in Lou Piniella for a second tour of duty.

Injuries and age caught up with the club. After a late season pasting by Boston, the Yankees finished 85–76 for the season, only five games back of the division-winning Red Sox, but in fifth place.

That wasn't good enough. Piniella was canned, and the defections began in earnest. Willie Randolph, the only player left from the 1978 champions and an ultimate professional, and veteran pitcher Rick Rhoden fled as free agents for greener, calmer, and more soothing pastures, and disgruntled DH Jack Clark was traded. Steinbrenner hired Dallas Green, a tough disciplinarian who had driven the Phillies to a championship in 1980, as his new manager. But this was 1989, and the Yankees, who didn't have much to begin with, chafed under Green's militaristic approach. Winfield, still the best player on the team, missed the whole season after back surgery, and with him went what little chance the Yankees had.

The rest went when Rickey Henderson, batting only .247, was traded back to Oakland in midseason for a bunch of guys. He still led the league in runs, walks, and stolen bases. As usual, Steinbrenner kept trying to tell his manager how to do his job, and in August Green said in an interview with Philadelphia columnist Bill Conlin, "There's no hope that organization will be a winning organization with Steinbrenner running the show." Neither would there be with Green, who was almost immediately fired. The Yankee owner somehow resisted hiring Martin again, who was still employed by the Yankees as a scout, and went with Bucky Dent instead as the club finished fifth again.

On Christmas night that year Martin was killed in a car accident after spending the evening drinking in a bar, leaving a legacy as twisted as his own life. While he'd helped reinvigorate the franchise, he'd also played a big part in its collapse. Martin may well have been a most worthy successor to the lineage he represented — he should have made the Hall of Fame as a manager, like lesser talents Sparky Anderson and Tommy Lasorda. But he couldn't control himself, and the Yankees couldn't force him to change. Martin's heart was in the right place — he loved the Yankees, the uniform, and the tradition, and he loved being manager. Steinbrenner loved him for that, but it wasn't enough.

Bucky Dent didn't have a chance in 1990. Mattingly's back, which had been a cause of concern since he damaged a disk in 1987, started giving him real trouble, and on May 16, after word of Steinbrenner's relationship with Spira had leaked out, Winfield accepted a trade to California for ailing pitcher Mike Witt. As George Vecsey noted in the Times, "Ten years of being belittled by his owner were over." Like Jackson, Winfield would find a measure of redemption in California and prove to be a valuable player for several more seasons. Steinbrenner said the trade was a decision made by his "baseball people," a claim that fooled no one. Anytime a trade or signing hadn't worked, he'd blamed the same faceless, interchangeable "baseball people." Steinbrenner usually took credit only for the franchise's successes, which were becoming ever more rare.

Dent lasted only a few weeks into the season before he was fired. He should have been thankful, for New York's starting rotation consisted of Tim Leary, Dave Lapoint, Chuck Cary, and Andy Hawkins. Blech. Triple-A manager Stump Merrill took over, and the club tried to embark on a limited youth movement, but the minor league cupboard was virtually bare after years of trading away talent and losing top draft picks because of free agent signings. The club soon buried itself in last place. Reliever Lee Guetterman led the team with 11 wins, and Leary managed to lose 19. "The Yankees," said outfielder Luis Polonia, "are interested in only one thing, and I don't know what that is." No one did.

The season highlight took place on the evening of July 30, when the crowd at Yankee Stadium, informed of Steinbrenner's punishment, chanted gleefully, "No more George! No more George! No more George!" Limited partner Robert Nederlander took over. Steinbrenner was effectively banned from having anything to do with the operation of the team, although with his son Hank and son-in-law Joseph Malloy on the executive payroll, there was always the question of whether or not he followed that edict to the letter. Two days later Yankee pitcher Andy Hawkins provided a symbolic counterpoint, twirling a no-hitter yet losing 4–0 as the Yankee outfield dropped the ball. There'd been a lot of that going on recently.

Steinbrenner's absence finally gave the organization a chance to breathe. Under his oppressive reign, there had been no continuity, no plan, nothing but a series of Band-Aids slapped over major wounds. General manager Gene Michael became responsible for setting the franchise in a new direction.

There wasn't much to work with. In 1990, after six spectacular seasons, Don Mattingly's back gave out. He'd been carrying the team on it for so long that its collapse was almost inevitable. He'd spend the rest of his career as a diminished star, never again the player his peers once selected as baseball's best player in the New York Times poll. Second baseman Steve Sax and outfielder Jesse Barfield were bona-fide major league players, but only center fielder Roberto Kelly seemed to have much of a future. There was no young pitching, and without Steinbrenner, the Yankees weren't very active in the free agent market, which was starting to heat up in the wake of the owners' collusion and the resulting financial penalties levied on them. Under Merrill, the club won 71 games in 1991 and finished fifth. He was fired at the end of the season.

Meanwhile, Steinbrenner was rattling the bars of his cage, and baseball was starting to listen. Like it or not, having two lousy teams in New York was bad for business—the Mets had rapidly imploded after winning the world championship in 1986. The Yankees hired an organizational man, Buck Showalter, to take over as the new manager.

He wasn't the first choice. Michael had wanted to rehire Lou Piniella, but he was under contract to Cincinnati; besides, he told Steinbrenner, he was "tired of being fired." Showalter had been a good-hitting first baseman with no

power in the Yankee farm system before becoming a manager in the minor leagues, where he developed a reputation as someone who knew how to win and develop players. As Bill Madden cautioned in the *Daily News,* however, "everything in his resume and everyone who has watched him up close tells you that Buck Showalter can manage . . . [but] this is one lousy baseball team." The over-under on Showalter's survival was one season.

But he received some immediate help. After not spending money since Steinbrenner's suspension, the Yankees opened the vault again in the off-season, and with Steinbrenner gone, players began to consider New York as a des-

Left-hander Dave Righetti went from being touted as the successor to stopper Ron Guidry to becoming the next Yankee closer after Goose Gossage left New York following the 1983 season. In eleven seasons with the Yankees, Righetti was named American League Rookie of the Year in 1981, pitched a no-hitter in 1983 (on July 4 against the Red Sox), and set a then league record with 46 saves in 1986.

Until his appearance in the 1995 American League Championship Series against the Mariners, no Yankee had ever played so long and not appeared in postseason play as Don Mattingly. The player Kirby Puckett dubbed Donnie Baseball socked a homer in the wild card–clinching final regular-season game. Then, in the Division Series he batted .417 with 10 hits (including 4 doubles and a homer) and 6 RBIs, but the Yankees lost in five games to Seattle.

tination again. Attendance had dropped from 2.6 million in 1988 to under 2 million in 1991, but the Yankees weren't losing money. In December 1988, Steinbrenner had signed a long-term television pact with Madison Square Garden that promised to earn the Yankees $500 million over the next 12 years, the largest and most lucrative such contract for local rights in the history of the game. It guaranteed that the Yankees would be able to outspend everyone whenever they chose to. But if history teaches anything about the Yankees, it is that when they harvest the New York market and put the bounty back into the organization, they win. Steinbrenner had forgotten that tried-and-true strategy.

Falling attendance and a drop in TV ratings woke them up — Madison Square Garden expected some return for its investment. The Yankees slowly began to invest in themselves again. They wouldn't try to rebuild entirely through free agency, but while they waited for the farm system to mature, they had to lift the club to a certain level of respectability.

They signed infielder Mike Gallego and added third baseman Charlie Hayes in trade, but the big acquisition was slugger Danny Tartabull. He signed the biggest contract in team history, four years at more than $25 million, a move more symbolic than anything else, for Tartabull would eventually prove a disappointment. Signing him, however, gave Showalter the luxury of giving some playing time to some of the kids he'd managed in the farm system, like shortstop Andy Stankiewicz, outfielders Bernie and Gerald Williams, and Jim Leyritz. The Yankees still finished 20 games out of first in 1992, but they were a more likable team, one that finally seemed to offer hope of improvement.

Meanwhile, Steinbrenner petitioned for early reinstatement, and baseball caved in, allowing him to return on March 1, 1993. Before he did, the pace of rebuilding quickened. Third baseman Wade Boggs and pitchers Jimmy Key and Jim Abbott were added to the team. But the key may well have been the trade of Roberto Kelly for Paul O'Neill.

While Kelly had proven to be a valuable player, he hadn't quite become the star the Yankees envisioned. Increasingly, Gene Michael was making personnel decisions based as much on character and attitude as statistics and going with players who shared Don Mattingly's "nose to the grindstone" approach. They decided that young outfielder Bernie Williams was ready to take over in center, which made Kelly expendable, so they traded him to Cincinnati for outfielder O'Neill. Like the Yankees with Kelly, the Reds had expected more from O'Neill, and O'Neill, an Ohio native, might have suffered some from unrealistic hometown expectations, particularly after slumping from 28 home runs and 91 RBIs in 1990 to 14 home runs and 66 RBIs in 1992.

O'Neill, though more volatile than Mattingly, was similarly known as a "gamer," a guy who played hard all the time. Every at bat was a drama unto itself as O'Neill seemed mortally offended each time he made an out or an umpire called a strike. He fit the Yankees perfectly, in the mold of a Piniella or Mattingly. His swing was made for the Stadium, as he could pull line drives for power down the right-field line or spray hits the opposite way. In Mattingly's wake, he would set the tone for the team the Yankees would become. The next dynasty started the day he came to New York.

Steinbrenner returned on March 1, and everyone held their breath, wondering whether he'd allow the steady progress made under Showalter to continue. On his first day back a fan asked him, "Are you going to trade the best farm system in baseball for a 38-year-old pitcher and fire the best young manager in baseball?" That was precisely the question.

Had the Boss changed? No one was quite sure, but it became harder for him to argue with the decisions that had been made by his "baseball people," because most of the moves made during his exile had worked. Jimmy Key gave the Yankees a genuine number-one starter for the first time in almost a decade, and over the next two seasons he'd win 35 games. Boggs bounced back from a bad ending in Boston to hit over .300 again, and O'Neill flourished.

The club actually entered September in contention, and on September 4 it looked like everything might be lining up their way. Abbott, a left-hander who played with a malformed right arm due to a birth defect, threw a no-hitter against Cleveland, pulling New York to within one game of division-leading Toronto, and they moved into a tie the next day.

But they couldn't sustain it. Mattingly injured his wrist, Tartabull hurt his shoulder, and the Yankees suddenly had a hard time scoring runs. Toronto pulled away and won the division by seven games.

It wasn't all quiet in the South Bronx, but Showalter proved adept at not allowing Steinbrenner to do or say much that affected the players, and the Boss couldn't complain about the jump in attendance, which bounced all the way back up to nearly 2.5 million in 1993. That improvement was increasingly important to him, for like Jacob Ruppert, Steinbrenner found that the Yankees were becoming his primary business as his shipbuilding concern floundered.

In 1994 their improvement continued, helped considerably by realignment, which split each league into three divisions and added a wild-card playoff berth in each league, doubling the number of teams in the playoffs. The Yankees put virtually the same team on the field as in 1993, improved only by their own performances. Paul O'Neill entered July hitting .400, and Boggs wasn't far behind. Catcher Mike Stanley and Jim Leyritz supplied unexpected power, and Jimmy Key was almost unbeatable. Entering August, the Yankees were in command of the AL East and had the best record in the league.

Then baseball stopped. Players and owners were at loggerheads over the issue of a salary cap. "What might have been" became the Yankees' motto as the remainder of the season was canceled, robbing the team of the possibility of its first postseason appearance since 1981.

The stoppage was particularly painful to Mattingly. His aching back had robbed him of his power, and some were beginning to whisper that he had become a liability on a team that couldn't afford one. Most believed he was only hanging on in a vain attempt to make it to the postseason. No Yankee — ever — had played so long for the team without making a postseason appearance, and neither had any other active player in the major leagues. "I may never play again," he admitted as the strike lingered on. "Who knows what's going to happen over the winter?"

Very little happened over the winter that was very positive, for the Yankees or anyone else, as the strike extended into the spring. The Yanks, like every other big league team, engaged in the charade of forming a team of "replacement" players during spring training before the two sides finally agreed to resume business as usual. Still, the season was cut short by 18 games.

It almost cost the Yankees, for as the Red Sox jumped out to a fast start in 1995, the Yankees stumbled. Jimmy Key was lost to a torn rotator cuff, leaving free agent Jack McDowell as the Yankees' only established, healthy starter. The acquisition of premier closer John Wetteland turned out to have been critical. Nearly everyone slipped back from the numbers they'd put up in 1994. Mattingly returned to play one more season, and by midseason the Yankees were struggling.

Only Steinbrenner, it seemed, was back in prime form. He threw a fit in early July, dumping pitching coach Mark Connors for Nardi Contreras and sending an unmistakable shock wave through the clubhouse. Contreras became the 17th pitching coach in Steinbrenner's tenure — and the 36th time he'd made a change, as Steinbrenner tended to bring coaches back with the same regularity as managers. Showalter had to know that he was coming into focus under Steinbrenner's sights.

The wild card may have saved him. Even as the Yankees failed to gain ground on Boston, they remained in contention for the postseason because of the wild card. But they needed help to get there.

David Cone became available in mid-July. One of the game's best pitchers, Cone brought the added advantage of having already proved himself in New York, for he'd reached stardom as a Met. GM Gene Michael dickered back and forth with Toronto for weeks as the Blue Jays tried to pry prize pitching prospect Matt Drews or relievers Mariano Rivera or Bob Wickman from the Yankees, but Michael refused to budge, even as Steinbrenner grew more and more impatient. The baseball people had drawn a line in the sand — they weren't going to trade their top prospects or good young players for veterans anymore. Michael kept countering with a package of lesser talent but more bodies. The Blue Jays, who didn't want to lose Cone to free agency in the off-season and receive nothing in return, finally caved in and accepted the Yankees' offer on July 28. That same day the Yankees exchanged problems with Oakland, sending their failing slugger Danny Tartabull to the A's for their failing slugger Ruben Sierra. The deal was essentially a wash, but in the long run it freed the Yankees of some salary obligations, allowing them to sign Darryl Strawberry, the troubled Mets slugger who was resurrecting his career.

Like O'Neill, Cone seemed born to play for the Yankees. When the former Met left New York for Toronto in 1992, he had even retained his Manhattan apartment. Cone understood New York, and moreover, he liked it. "I can understand what the city can do for a team that's going good," he said upon his arrival. "I feel it already. I feel the excitement again." He thrived in the pressure and loved taking the mound knowing that everyone was watching him and everyone expected him to win. That's exactly what the Yankees expected.

He won his first start, beating Minnesota 4–2 to even the Yankee record at 42–42, then won his next three starts as well. The Yankees weathered a dismal road trip in mid-August, but Cone and rookie Andy Pettitte, who won nine games in the second half, helped key the Yankees' best September in more than a decade. They got dramatic in the last week as Pat Kelly crashed a game-winning two-run home run and the Yankees scored four ninth-inning runs to beat Toronto 4–3 on September 29. The Yankees won their last five to edge out California for the wild card.

Donnie Baseball was finally going to get his chance to win a ring. "We've been playing day-in-day-out for the last month," he said. "This is pure." He even cracked a home run in the season-ending clincher, only his seventh of the season, but an indication that if this was to be the end of his career, he planned to play it out to the end.

The Yankees had one day of rest before opening the playoffs against AL West champion Seattle, a scary team that featured baseball's best player, Ken Griffey Jr., and baseball's most frightening pitcher, Randy Johnson. But Johnson had been forced to pitch the final game of the season against California, as the Mariners won the division by only a single game. He'd thrown 150 pitches and wouldn't be available until game three of the best-of-five series. The Yankees, on the other hand, could use Cone in both game one and game five.

The Yankees pounded the Mariners 9–6 in the first game at the Stadium, then outlasted them 7–5 in 15 excruciating innings in game two as Jim Leyritz, some five hours after the game started, ended it with a dramatic two-run home run off Tim Belcher. At every opportunity the Yankee Stadium crowd had let Mattingly know how they felt about him. When he homered in game two, they chanted "Don-nie Base-ball" over and over. So far he was five for ten in the series. So much for being washed up.

But when the Yankees went to Seattle for game three and the game went inside Seattle's horrible Kingdome, the Mariners were a different team, and baseball was a different game. Johnson came back on three days' rest and gutted out seven strong innings in game three as the Mariners won 7–4. And then in game four the Mariners' Edgar Martinez knocked in seven runs in Seattle's 11–8 win. Mattingly went four for five in the contest, but New York's bullpen, particularly closer John Wetteland, couldn't stop the Mariners.

In game five Showalter put the ball and the game in David Cone's hands. "You get to pitch in front of 55,000 fans who hate you and hate New York," said Cone with a smile. He gave his manager his gutsiest, grittiest best. Fatigued after a long season that was getting longer every inning, he fought every hitter with every pitch, succeeding for most of 146 remarkable pitches. But in the eighth, with the Yankees leading 4–2, Tino Martinez hit one out of the park for a home run, and on pitch number 147 Cone walked in the tying run. When his pitch to Randy Knorr bounced in front of the plate, Cone slumped to his knees, completely spent, and Showalter finally turned to Rivera. The score was 4–4 entering the ninth.

In one of those rare baseball games in which neither team thought about tomorrow, both clubs let it all out, playing for right now, this minute, this pitch, this swing. Randy Johnson, 48 hours after pitching game three, came on in relief in the ninth, and the Yankees countered with their game-three starter, Jack McDowell. "There were guys out there willing to blow their arms out," said Cone later. "Those guys would have pitched all night."

The Yankees scratched a run off Johnson in the eleventh, but McDowell, who'd been shut down with arm trouble in September, was pitching from memory. Joey Cora and Ken Griffey singled, then Edgar Martinez doubled to left, scoring both men. New York's season ended as Griffey slid across the plate and the concrete walls of the Kingdome thundered.

Don Mattingly's final season ended in a knot of Mariners at home plate. He'd doubled with the bases loaded earlier in the game, collecting his final hit as a Yankee and knocking in his final run. He'd hit .417 for the series, leading the Yankees with ten hits and six RBIs, hitting four doubles and a home run as his power returned. Mattingly hit the ball better over the last five games than at any time over the last five years, and like Cone, he pushed himself to exhaustion. "I'll remember this game," he said to Jack Curry of the *Times* afterward. "There are games in high school we lost that I can still remember."

It had taken his entire career, but even as he was walking away from the game, putting down the burden of having played so long without ever playing in October, Mattingly had still delivered.

Across all those dark seasons he had carried the Yankees back.

After a breakout season in 1995, center fielder Bernie Williams maintained his brilliance in 1996, hitting .305 and driving in 102 runs. In the 1996 Division and League Championship Series he batted .467 and .474, respectively. He is shown here smashing a double at Camden Yards, in the Yankees' 13–5 victory on September 12, 1997.

Second place is not an option and that's fine. . . .
It means he's going to get you the players.

— JOE TORRE

1996–1997
TOP OF THE HEAP

Finishing second has always proven costly to employees of the New York Yankees.

Even in their glory years, finishing second had never been an acceptable option. Neither was it now, and if there's one enduring lesson of the Steinbrenner era, that's it. After Showalter took the Yankees to within one victory of the ALCS, Steinbrenner was unable to resist the many temptations that come with the appellation "Boss." The Yankees had finished second to the Mariners and second in the AL East. Buck Showalter paid the price.

Steinbrenner always had an excuse handy. This time it was Showalter's close friend and batting coach, Rick Down, and the expiration of the contracts for both Showalter and GM Gene Michael. Steinbrenner wanted Down replaced and made Showalter's proposed two-year contract dependent on the selection of a new batting coach. Michael was simply offered a pay cut.

Both men reacted as could have been predicted. Michael resigned and accepted a job as a scout, and Showalter refused to abandon his man. He turned down the offer. "I'm just disappointed in it all," he said. "Just say disappointed. I'm not trying to say anything else."

Five men turned down the GM job before Houston GM and former player Bob Watson accepted, a move many saw as a salve to quiet the media in the wake of the Showalter mess. No African American had ever served in the Yankee front office in such an important capacity. Watson, who'd been a member of the last pennant-winning Yankee team in 1981, was given the order and the means to remake the team. For the time being the move was critic-proof.

Many thought the Yankees would hire former New York Mets manager Davey Johnson to replace Showalter. Steinbrenner was in the midst of what one scribe called a serious case of "Met envy." He'd signed troubled slugger Darryl Strawberry in 1995, and he was now courting onetime pitching sensation Dwight Gooden. But Johnson wasn't the only former Mets manager available. When he decided to go to Baltimore, Steinbrenner adviser Arthur Richman brought up the name Joe Torre. Steinbrenner was enthusiastic.

Torre was a curious choice. Except for Bill Virdon and Bob Lemon, 11 of Steinbrenner's previous 13 managers had been employed by the organization before taking the manager's job. Torre was an outsider. A fine player with the Braves, Cardinals, and Mets, Torre had caught George Weiss's eye in the early 1960s, when Weiss offered the Braves $400,000 for him. Torre became Mets manager in 1977 but never had a winning record in five seasons. Hired by the Braves in 1982, he led them to the NL East title in his first season but left after 1984. His last managerial stint had come with the Cardinals, who had fired him midway through the 1995 season. He had never reached the World Series as either a player or a manager. In October, he was 0 for 4,100 games.

He was a usual suspect — safe, comfortable, and non-controversial, front-office oatmeal. In recent years his name had usually come up whenever there was an open managerial slot. The Yankees had even interviewed him for the GM job before they hired Watson, who'd once played for Torre in Atlanta. Torre was surprised when the Yankees called him back and offered him the manager's job — he was beginning to think that his time had passed.

When a writer later asked Watson, "Is this the old boy network?" he responded, "So be it."

Torre's record as a big league manager was decidedly mediocre — 894–1,003. But he was willing to accept the conditions of employment that Showalter wasn't — namely, Steinbrenner's coaching staff and the same two-year contract Showalter had turned down.

Yet there were elements of Torre's past that made him uniquely qualified for the job. A Brooklyn native who had grown up a Giants fan, he was comfortable with the city. He'd already worked for two of the more autocratic owners in baseball, the Cardinals' August Busch and the Braves' Ted Turner, so working for Steinbrenner didn't scare him. Torre already knew many members of the local media from his stint with the Mets, and he had spent several years on the other side of the line as a broadcaster for the Angels, so he understood how that game worked. And despite his run-of-the-mill record, Torre wasn't locked into one style of play. When his team could run, they ran. If they hit with power, they didn't. He didn't try to get players to do things they couldn't. Few others could have brought more to the table.

He accepted the job because he felt there was something still missing from his career — a World Series ring. He took the job knowing the Yankees had some talent and might give him a final chance to make it to the World Series. "This is a once-in-a-lifetime opportunity," he said. Wrong. It was a last-in-a-lifetime opportunity. If he failed in New York, his baseball career would probably come to an end.

He brought in a couple of his own people, most notably first-base coach Jose Cardenal and bench coach Don Zimmer, who joined third-base coach Willie Randolph and the new hitting instructor, Chris Chambliss. Mel Stottlemyre was the consensus pick as pitching coach. The press reaction to Torre ranged from lukewarm to hostile. One tabloid, noting his below-.500 record and failure with the Mets, welcomed him by dubbing him "Clueless Joe."

But Watson, not Torre, was in the hot seat first. The Yankees had a lot of off-season contract issues, and there was still the lingering question of Mattingly. His contract had expired, but he hadn't officially retired. He indicated that he'd sit out the 1996 season and then decide whether his back and his heart could take another year, perhaps with another team.

The Yankees didn't hesitate to replace him. They traded Sterling Hitchcock and prospect Russ Davis for Seattle first baseman Tino Martinez, who'd destroyed the Yankees in the playoffs, and reliever Jeff Nelson. The Yankees then let go good-hit, no-field catcher Mike Stanley. They traded for Colorado catcher Joe Girardi and outfielder Tim Raines, re-signed Cone, and added free agent Kenny Rogers, cutting loose McDowell.

Many of these moves came as something of a surprise to Watson. While Watson was in New York, Steinbrenner was running a virtual shadow management team at his office in Tampa. Watson sometimes found out about trades after they'd already been made. After signing Cone, he reported that there'd be no more big signings—that's what Steinbrenner had told him to say. Then the Boss signed Kenny Rogers. His credibility with the press suffered.

Nevertheless, the pieces more or less fell into place in spring training for Joe Torre as Watson more or less served as a buffer between Steinbrenner and Torre, who faced only one big question: Who would be his shortstop?

The position had been up for grabs ever since Bucky Dent played for the Yankees, filled by a series of etceteras, guys like Andre Robertson, Roy Smalley, Bobby Meacham, Wayne Tolleson, Alvaro Espinosa, Andy Stankiewicz, Rafael Santana, Randy Velarde, and, in 1995, veteran Tony Fernandez. None were the complete package, and none had been truly satisfactory—fielding but not hitting, hitting but not fielding, or not doing either and not staying healthy. For the first time in a long time, however, the Yankees thought they had the answer in their farm system.

Derek Jeter was born to be a Yankee. Like Ruth, Gehrig, DiMaggio, and Mantle, he was absolutely the right guy at the right position, arriving right on schedule as Mattingly was passing the torch and fans were looking for the next "real Yankee," the living embodiment of the franchise. The Yankees had changed and so had the city of New York, and Jeter was perfect for both. His multiracial background, which only a generation before might have been viewed as a liability, was now a positive in the increasingly multicultural city. Over the last decade or so Yankee Stadium

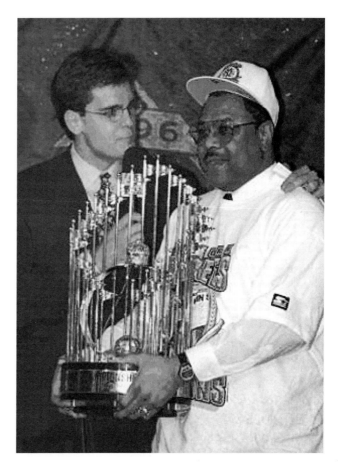

In 1996 Houston general manager and former Yankee player Bob Watson was hired to replace Gene Michael as Yankee general manager. No African American had ever been named to such an important position in Yankee management.

had become one of the most racially integrated ballparks in baseball, the crowd displaying every accent and shade of New York. Jeter, from day one, became the Yankees' "Everyman"—everybody's son, everybody's brother, everybody's dream boyfriend. Without even trying, he tapped into every chord of the Yankee mythos like no player since Mantle. He would add a few unmistakable new notes of his own, heralding a new age for the franchise. Jeter had it all, and from his first day he became the best shortstop in club history. The Yankees couldn't have invented him had they tried.

Jeter was born in New Jersey, and after moving with his family to Michigan at age four, he returned to spend each summer with his grandparents. His grandmother, Dot, was

a huge Yankees fan, and her obsession became his. His father had been a collegiate shortstop, and from the age of five Jeter told everyone he was going to grow up and play shortstop for the Yankees. Millions of kids have grown up with similar dreams, but when Jeter's came true, its fulfillment allowed untold numbers of fans to feel as if they were a part of his success.

Like Mantle, Jeter was identified by the organization as the Yankees' next star from the day they drafted him out of high school in 1991 with the sixth pick of the first round. The choice had been widely debated in the Yankee front office—they rarely had the opportunity to pick so high and needed an impact player, a sure thing. Pairing Jeter with 1990 number-one-pick pitcher Brien Taylor, the Yankees were building for the future. Later, when Taylor dislocated his shoulder in a fight, Jeter became even more important to the club's future. The last number-one pick to succeed with the Yankees had been Thurman Munson in 1968.

Jeter reminded Yankee scouts of a less powerful but more athletic Cal Ripken, whose size and power had revolutionized the shortstop position. Although some thought Jeter would eventually end up at third base, he made slow but steady progress through the Yankee farm system, hitting a little better and fielding a bit more consistently at each level. Moreover, he was smart and eager, confident but not overly cocky.

At the beginning of spring training Steinbrenner's advisers wrung their hands as they worried about whether Jeter was ready for the majors. He'd been error-prone in the minor leagues, and in a brief trial with the team in 1995 he'd been overmatched at the plate. But the Yankees also had a question mark at second—Pat Kelly would miss most of the year after shoulder surgery. Torre wanted to move incumbent shortstop Tony Fernandez to second base and make room for Jeter. If Jeter couldn't play, Fernandez could always move back to short and utility man Mariano Duncan could play second. But after Fernandez broke his elbow in the spring, Jeter was the only option at

Shortstop Derek Jeter, shown here in action against the Braves in the 1999 World Series, was born to be a Yankee. Like Ruth, Gehrig, DiMaggio, and Mantle, he was the right man for the right position at the right time. From the age of five, the New Jersey native told everyone he was going to grow up and play shortstop for the Yankees.

1997

short. Nothing he did made Torre regret the decision in the spring, even as Steinbrenner fussed and worried.

If anyone didn't understand the role that the Yankees expected Jeter to play, all they had to do was look at his uniform number — 2 — one of only two single-digit numbers that hadn't been retired. As a kid, Jeter had been steeped in Yankee history and hoped a single digit would be available when he made the team. It was, but giving out the number to a rookie was like making a reservation in Cooperstown 25 years in advance. Not since Mantle had a player faced such high expectations. None had ever made those expectations his life goal.

Jeter had been play-acting as the Yankee shortstop for years. He looked and acted comfortable from day one, answering any lingering questions over whether he was ready on Opening Day in Cleveland. In the second inning, with two out and Sandy Alomar on second, he ranged far back and made a spectacular over-the-shoulder catch of Omar Vizquel's pop-up that excited everyone but Jeter himself. No Yankee shortstop in recent memory would have come close to the ball, much less caught it. David Cone cruised after that, and Jeter added a solo home run off Dennis Martinez in New York's 7–1 win.

On May 2, the Yankees received a shock. After David Cone won his fourth game and lowered his league-low ERA to 2.03 with a 5–1 complete game win over Chicago, he complained of numbness in his hand. The problem had bothered him all spring but not really affected the way he pitched. But Yankee doctors insisted on an angiogram and found blood clots in his hand caused by an aneurysm in an artery in his shoulder. On May 10, Cone underwent surgery, and a vein was grafted from his leg to replace a small segment of the artery. His season, if not his career, appeared to be at an end.

All year long the closing of one door seemed to open another. Doc Gooden, despite pitching poorly all spring, had made the starting rotation, a decision for which Torre had been widely criticized. Then, in his first three starts of the year, Gooden had been lit up for 17 runs and pulled from the rotation. Had Jimmy Key pitched better after coming back from rotator cuff surgery, Gooden might well have been released.

But Cone's absence gave him another start, on May 14 against Seattle. Gooden almost asked out — his father was

scheduled for bypass surgery the next day. But as he said later, "Knowing my father, he would want me to pitch." Besides, he knew he might not get another chance in New York. Any chance of retribution and a positive ending to a star-crossed career was on the line.

Gooden was magnificent. Well, at least the results were. He pitched a gritty, 134-pitch no-hitter, winning 2–0. The final batter popped the ball into the air to Jeter, who made a routine catch. It wouldn't be the last time that the final out of a big game would end in his hands.

Gooden's teammates rushed to the mound and lifted him on their shoulders. The unlikely champion raised both arms and roared in a combination of relief and vindication. Although he knew he had wasted what should have been a Hall of Fame career, this win proved he could still pitch. He won seven of his next eight decisions.

Meanwhile, Torre kept tinkering with the lineup, particularly left field and DH, where Sierra, Tim Raines, and Gerald Williams all fought for playing time. Knowing his club was a little short of starting pitching and a little short on power, Torre installed a more aggressive, National League style of play — bunting, stealing, and using the hit-and-run, trying to get the early lead. Mariano Rivera was a revelation in middle relief, blowing hitters away with an overpowering fastball. Pairing Rivera with closer John Wetteland, Torre soon discovered that if the Yankees held a lead after six innings, the game was virtually over.

Other questions were rapidly answered. After a slow start, Tino Martinez relaxed and provided the power that had been lacking at first base. Andy Pettitte became the stopper, the most dependable pitcher on the staff, 13–3 for the season after a Yankee loss. Tim Raines and Mariano Duncan contributed far more than expected, and Bernie Williams continued his steady improvement.

The Yankees, it seemed, had been waiting for Williams for almost a decade. He had been the quintessential prospect with "tools" — a young player whose abundance of physical skill made up for his lack of experience and baseball instinct. He had been a project from the very beginning.

Born in Puerto Rico, Williams had lived in the Bronx as a baby before his parents returned to his birthplace. He grew up in a distinctly middle-class home as a protected, favored child who studied music and became a junior track star. Most scouts were far more interested in his friend and companion on the sandlots, Juan Gonzalez.

Scout Roberto Rivera liked Williams and compared him to Dave Winfield—someday. For now he was all legs and potential, yet so quiet he was nearly invisible to anyone but other scouts. The Yankees wanted him badly.

So the summer before Williams turned 17 and became eligible to sign a free agent contract, the Yankees came up with a plan. They "suggested" to his parents that they send their son to a baseball camp in Connecticut, explaining that he could start learning English and how to adapt to American culture. In reality, they wanted to hide him from other scouts and Williams rarely played ball that summer. Although the scheme was legal, it wasn't entirely ethical. Scouts are paid, however, to be resourceful. When Williams returned to Puerto Rico, the Yankees were the only team waiting on his doorstep. They signed him the day he turned 17.

Williams progressed slowly, struggling to harness his speed and turn his disparate skills into a fluid whole. His timidity worried the organization—teammates called him "Bambi" for his "deer in the headlights" look. But Williams's diffidence masked a serious approach and a drive for perfection. Torre challenged him to be great all the time, usually batting him in the star slots, third or cleanup. His play in the 1995 playoffs had showed what he could do, and Williams responded again in 1996. He began to fulfill his Winfield-esque destiny, becoming the team's best center fielder and best switch hitter since Mantle.

The Yankees hit stride in June and July, then pulled away. With a comfortable lead, they were expected by most observers to sit tight. But the loss to Seattle in 1995 had left an impression. That series, in which two games had gone to extra innings, had exposed New York's lack of depth and cost Showalter and Michael their jobs. By now Watson and Torre knew more about the team and enough about Steinbrenner to understand that enough was never enough and there was no such thing as too much. The Yankees added still more players to get them ready for the post-season. The organization would follow a similar approach in subsequent seasons, building one roster for the regular season, then adding to it for the postseason.

In 1995 Showalter hadn't trusted Darryl Strawberry in the field, and the Yankees hadn't picked up his contract in

RETIRED YANKEE NUMBERS

1	Billy Martin
3	Babe Ruth
4	Lou Gehrig
5	Joe DiMaggio
7	Mickey Mantle
8	Bill Dickey
8	Yogi Berra
9	Roger Maris
10	Phil Rizzuto
15	Thurman Munson
16	Whitey Ford
23	Don Mattingly
32	Elston Howard
37	Casey Stengel
44	Reggie Jackson

the off-season. One of the best raw talents ever to play the game, Strawberry became a star with the Mets but never reached his full potential because drugs and alcohol got in the way. His career appeared to have reached an end. No team in baseball would touch him.

But Strawberry, who had already hit bottom, was willing to start at the bottom again. He signed with the independent league St. Paul Saints, hitting 18 home runs in a little over six weeks. Steinbrenner insisted that he be signed. After he continued to hit in Columbus, on July 4, the Boss's birthday, Steinbrenner had Strawberry called up. "We didn't need him," said Watson, "but Mr. Steinbrenner wanted him."

Yet Strawberry did fill a void, providing pure raw power from the left side. Opposing clubs had to pitch around him even when he wasn't in the lineup. On July 13, in the middle of a four-game series with Baltimore, he broke out, hitting two home runs and knocking in five in a key doubleheader sweep. The Yankees went on to sweep the Orioles, the only team in the East that appeared able to mount a challenge.

Just before the trading deadline, the Yankees made another key trade. Torre hadn't been satisfied with Ruben Sierra's defensive play, and he pouted in the DH role. Detroit was looking to move right-handed slugger Cecil Fielder, who was becoming too expensive to keep. When the two teams worked out an exchange, the Yankees gained an equally potent bat from the right side. The two deals changed the nature of the team, making it far more explosive.

In August the Yankees inexplicably slumped. Their lead in the East, which had been as high as 12 games on July 28, started to shrink as both the Orioles and the Red Sox got hot.

David Cone returned to the staff on September 2 and provided the club with an immediate shot in the arm. He twirled seven no-hit innings against the A's before being removed because he'd reached his pitch count of 85. Cone was ecstatic afterward, saying, "If you can't enjoy this, something is wrong. When I heard the word 'aneurysm,' I didn't know if I'd pitch again."

But the Yankee lead kept shrinking. Steinbrenner was panicking and calling Bob Watson several times a day with suggestions, demands, and tirades. To his credit, he kept his outbursts relatively private. Since returning from his suspension, he'd been more or less able to restrain himself from blasting his team on the back page of the tabloids.

While the Boss fumed and the press railed against what the *Post* called "overzealous tinkering" and disruption of the club's "chemistry," Torre did something few Yankees managers since Stengel had had the confidence to do. Nothing. When the Boss called—and he did—Torre listened and then went on with the same methodical approach he'd used all year. He'd been around long enough not to worry too much about the specter of Steinbrenner looking over his shoulder. He knew that teams that collapse, like the 1964 Phillies or the 1978 Red Sox, generally do so because losing begets panic and managers start doing things out of the ordinary. Torre had the season in perspective. In midyear his oldest brother, Rocco, had passed away, and now his older brother Frank, who'd also played for the Braves, was hospitalized with heart trouble and awaiting a transplant. Compared to those events, baseball didn't matter very much. Torre's sense of calm permeates his ballclub to this day. Since he's been in charge, they've never panicked.

The slump ended as quickly as it began. The Orioles ran out of steam just as the Yankees, behind a series of standout pitching performances and clutch plays by a string of bench players such as rookie outfielder Ruben Rivera, won 10 of 13, including two key wins over both Baltimore and Boston. The Yankees won 92 games and finished four games ahead of the Orioles to win the AL East.

But under realignment, which made for six divisional champions and two wild-card champs, all that did was extend the season, making the Yankees one of eight remaining teams with a chance to win the championship. Actually doing so is now harder than ever before, for a team has to defeat three of baseball's best teams in consecutive series. None is harder than the first round, the only best-of-five series, where there is little margin for error.

Torre did have a chance to set his rotation before facing the AL West champion Texas Rangers in the Division Series. Although Andy Pettitte had led the league with 21 wins, David Cone was the acknowledged leader of the staff and drew the assignment in game one. The Yankees were heavily favored. The Rangers, keyed by league MVP Juan Gonzalez, had plenty of firepower, but their pitching staff was suspect.

The Yankee advantage lasted all of three innings. The Rangers ruined Cone's storybook comeback as Gonzalez hit a three-run home run and Dean Palmer followed with a two-run blast. Journeyman John Burkett shut down the Yankees, and as Steinbrenner reminded Torre afterward, the Yankees had to win three of four or else it would be 1997.

Torre, without panicking, managed differently in the postseason. Knowing that every game was huge, he became much more active. Slumping players no longer had the benefit of his patience. Torre reacted, and fast, knowing how quickly a game could get away and, with a single game, a series. He knew his club and knew he generally had many more bullets than the opponent. The Yankees could play matchup baseball all game long, and sooner or later the game would tilt in their favor. Torre didn't hesitate, for instance, in more or less platooning Hall of Fame certainty Wade Boggs and newcomer Charlie Hayes at third. Hayes had the better glove and was a more dangerous hitter than Boggs against lefties. Not all the participants liked his choices, but Torre went overboard to explain his decision-making process to everyone involved. Besides, it would be hard to argue with the results, and the team had been schooled in keeping any disagreements confined to the clubhouse. No one wanted to incite the newspapers and provide a distraction. They'd all seen that before.

Torre continued the strategy in the next three games. After using Strawberry as DH in game one, he went with Fielder in game two, and Fielder came through with an eighth-inning single to tie the game. As the Rangers threatened in the 12th, Torre exhausted his bullpen, using four pitchers. Then Jeter, who'd hit .350 in the second half, singled, went to second on a walk, and scored when Charlie Hayes — playing in place of Boggs — dropped a bunt that the Rangers' Dean Palmer threw away. The series was now tied.

Torre used a similar strategy in the next two games, and the Yankees emerged victorious. Jeter keyed a ninth-inning rally, and Mariano Duncan knocked in the winning run in game three; the Yankees then patiently chipped away at a four-run deficit to win game four. Juan Gonzalez hit five home runs in the series, but Bernie Williams held a coming-out party and cracked three of his own. He even started the final game comeback with a single and a brazen steal of second base off the Rangers' Pudge Rodriguez. And Jeter, whom many expected to show some jitters in his first postseason experience, was the coolest player on the field, hitting .412 and contributing in a host of little ways — taking the extra base, worrying the pitcher, slapping a great pitch for a bloop hit, making tough plays look easy.

Just before the 1996 trading deadline, Bob Watson exchanged troubled outfielder and DH Ruben Sierra for the Tigers' right-handed slugger Cecil Fielder. Fielder, shown here socking a two-run homer against the Orioles on September 19, 1996, added needed power to the Yankee lineup.

IT'S ONLY A GAME
IT'S MORE THAN A GAME

MOLLY O'NEILL

It ended softly. The ball left Bernie Williams's bat in the top of the ninth inning and, years later, sighed into Brian Giles's glove. One run down, two outs, and a pinch runner for my brother on second base. And it was over. The Yankees were no longer the defending world champions.

Nothing so decisive should be so gentle. Nothing so final should just fall from the sky. I stared at the television, then the telephone, and then I fell asleep.

Twelve hours later, I was balancing six grocery bags, running late, and edging toward a type-A episode when I shoved into a taxi. Even before I slammed the door, the driver asked if I'd followed the Yankees.

"Yes," I said.

"Paul O'Neill was amazing," said the cabby. "He's a hero."

Finally, my eyes felt hot. The traffic seemed trivial. For a few city blocks, nothing but baseball mattered.

The game is like a loose sweater around us — my five brothers and parents, assorted relatives, former classmates, childhood enemies and friends, forgotten loves, passing acquaintances, colleagues and cab-drivers. We are connected to one another because we are connected to something larger than ourselves.

In our family we tell stories, we don't really talk. We let baseball articulate the hopes and fears that we'd never consider confiding in each other. We weren't expecting the game to teach us about the limits of human effort. But it did.

The 1996 season confirmed everything we were raised to believe in. From the All-Star break until the final game of the World Series, my brother played in constant pain. At 33 years old, he'd been playing professional baseball for half his life. And all the tears and bruises and strains, the stuff of daily life in the sport, seemed to have consolidated into a throbbing, untreatable ache. Paul could hardly talk.

"Have you heard from Cheerful?" one brother asked me on the phone toward the end of the '96 season.

Ironic detachment is a thin membrane that gives us, in the family section behind home plate or in front of our individual television sets in Ohio, Florida and New York City, the fleeting illusion that the game is not our life story. But the pose never lasts. At the playoffs in Baltimore last year, my father and I groaned when my brother leaped and stretched over the right-field wall. "That hurt," Dad said. My brother caught the ball.

Paul would do anything for our father. The old-timer's baseball career ended in the minors. There was a war wound, lost time, and bad luck, then I appeared, followed by five brothers. Paul is the youngest.

Since the first time he stepped to the plate in a Class A game, Paul has been less a little brother, more a part of our father. The mythic part. The unrealized dream, repaired. To my father, the restoration is better than his own dream ever was. Last year, the scoreboard at Camden Yards paid him homage: "Paul's dad pitched in the California League in the late 1930s." My father didn't see it. He was watching Paul.

Besides, my father doesn't see or hear all that well anymore. His legs are bad. One of the places where they fixed his heart in a five-way bypass surgery ten years ago is 99 percent occluded, the doctor said.

My father said he felt fine. "I don't have another one of those darned operations in me," he told the doctor.

We worry with every cold and flu, but our visits and phone calls to him usually feel like batless swings. My father always says the same thing to me: "Feeling good, honey. You're doing great, honey. I'm real proud of you."

And then he refuses to get in a wheelchair unless one of us promises to hot rod him through the crowd. So we were relieved when he decided to stay at home in Columbus and watch the postseason on television this year.

I assume that like me in New York, my brothers watched with a phone on their laps. When I'd call after a poetic play, I'd sometimes hear the click of call-waiting. Usually on the nights we were winning.

Losing is too scary to contemplate. Losing anything is losing everything if you grew up in our family. In our house, if you lost, it was your fault, and if you won, you'd got lucky.

You don't talk about losing, not even as a remote possibility. If losing is inevitable, you don't talk at all. You focus. You pray. You breathe. You picture winning. This has never struck us as a harsh or merciless outlook. We saw ourselves as optimists. The 1996 Yankees proved our point of view.

This year changed everything. The Yankees with all their knotty seams brought out the ridges in our own lives. No one, least of all Paul, knew why the previous year's injuries-that-wouldn't-heal suddenly disappeared. I supposed his inarticulate worries shifted Dad-ward; I know that the rest of ours did.

Until the All-Star break, we still believed that determination makes dreams come true. In the second half, we started to suspect that after you get your dreams, you need another kind of fuel. We clung to scraps of evidence to the contrary, though.

When Paul's was the third of the back-to-back-to-back home runs in Game 1 against Cleveland, the phones went wild. When he hit a grand slam in Game 3, every number I dialed rang busy. And in Game 5 when, in the top of the fifth, Yankee walks and hits started to fracture the Indians' pitching, we rallied around everything we'd ever believed.

"What do you think?" I asked my father.

"I think they're going to win, honey," he said.

Between the telephone connection and his laryngitis, my father's voice sounded like the soundtrack of an old, battered film.

"Me too, Dad; they're going to win," I yelled.

But my father didn't hear me. I know now that he asked, "What'd you say?" On Monday night, however, I heard, "Big hooray."

I was still poised for the big hooray when my brother stepped into the batter's box, two outs, nobody on, top of the ninth, the Yankees down by a run. Paul hit a ball so hard off the outfield wall that even reaching second base didn't seem possible. But he ran against odds and launched into the base, headfirst. It was as if every ounce of fierce hope had lifted him, as if by sheer will a man can defy gravity and fate.

The next morning, my cabdriver said that my brother dived into that base and grabbed the bag and defied them, just defied them to tag him. The cabdriver railed against the team that didn't bring the ——ing run home. He said that my brother must be livid, crushed.

It would be several more hours before I talked to Paul, but I knew, even as the taxi spirited me uptown, that my brother didn't feel any of those things. The only thing that might have crushed Paul was seeing that determination only gets you to second base. If his heart was broken, it was by how softly a dream can end.

Later Paul would tell me: "I never played so hard in my whole life. I didn't want to stop playing. I wanted to keep playing and playing. But what are you going to do? That's the game. We lost."

But the lump in my throat had begun to fade before that. By the time the taxi pulled up to my building the morning after the game, I could talk again.

"Paul's my brother," I told the driver.

"Yeah, I know," the cabby said. "You were a passenger the day the Yankees traded for him. You were worried because he might not like New York and that your dad might be upset when Paul left Ohio. I felt connected to the Yankees every since."

Noted food columnist **MOLLY O'NEILL** is the author of *The New York Cookbook*. She lives in New York.

Such contributions have been Jeter's defining characteristic from the first day of his rookie year. Like DiMaggio, statistics don't tell his story; Jeter's all-around skill and uncanny awareness allow him to make subtle contributions that don't always show up in the box score. He rarely dominates a game with long hits, RBIs, or "can you believe that?" catches. Instead, the game seems to come to him. Time and time again he makes the nearly invisible decision or play that seems to tilt the balance. It's no accident that two of the more memorable plays of his career have been heads-up, acrobatic relay throws that completely changed the nature of postseason series. They epitomize what he brings to the field.

Wild-card champion Baltimore, which handily beat Cleveland in their Division Series, salivated at the opportunity to take another crack at the Yankees. They'd hit a record 257 home runs in what became known as "the Year of the Home Run." Even leadoff hitter Brady Anderson hit a remarkable 50. But for all their power, the Orioles had been ineffective against the Yankees, who hadn't lost a game at Camden Yards all year. In Baltimore the Yankees could match the Orioles' power as fly balls that fell short in the Stadium reached the seats. The season series had been marked by Yankee comebacks — a 13–10 Yankee win on April 30 after the Orioles had taken a six-run lead, a win the next night on a ninth-inning Tino Martinez grand slam that jump-started his season, and the rejuvenation of Darryl Strawberry in the sweep in mid-July.

The series opened in the Stadium, and the story went according to the script. The Orioles nicked and cut Pettitte early, but the gentle pitcher turned steel and hung on as the Yankees kept it close. Leading 4–2, the Orioles turned the game over to young fireballer Armando Benitez in the eighth to hold the door shut for closer Randy Myers.

But with one out, Derek Jeter came to bat in a situation he'd played out in his back yard a million times: game on the line and the Yankee shortstop up. Jeter hit a fly ball to right field, some 30 feet fair, toward section 31. Box 325. Row A. Seat 3.

Jeter took off running hard but kept his head up, knowing he'd hit the ball good but not knowing if he'd hit it good enough to go out. Baltimore right fielder Tony Tarasco, in for his defense and replacing Bobby Bonilla, was playing deep and toward the line against Jeter, protecting the lead.

He drifted back, placed his right arm on the wall, and reached up with his gloved left hand to make a routine catch. The ball was falling a foot short of a tie game.

And then it was gone. Six big guys and one 12-year-old kid jockeyed for position atop the wall to catch the potential tying home run. But the 12-year-old had his black fielder's glove for the reason all 12-year-old boys bring them to the ballpark, even when sitting in the upper deck 500 feet away. The kid beat everyone and reached out, level with the top of the wall, and swiped at the ball as it dropped from the sky.

He didn't catch it clean. The ball hit the heel of his glove, and he swept the ball back, trying to hold on, and a dozen pairs of hands tried to grab it as nearly 60,000 more were raised in applause and 60,000 pairs of eyes looked to umpire Richie Garcia, stationed on the right-field line to be in position for just such a play. He raised his right arm in the unmistakable circular motion that means "home run" and at this instant also meant a tie game.

Then another hand, Tarasco's, one finger pointed up, pointing to the mob atop the fence, and chaos.

Oriole manager Davey Johnson bolted onto the field as Jeter ran around the bases without looking back, then into the dugout. Johnson pled with Garcia, he pleaded and he cursed and cajoled, joined by Tarasco, who kept pointing and pantomiming the catch.

But there are no replays in baseball, and no crying either. The home run stood, even though Garcia admitted later that "after looking at it, no, obviously" it was not a home run. It was interference, a violation of section 3.16 of the *Official Rules of Baseball,* and Jeter should have been out. But what mattered was what Garcia had seen when it happened. "The way I saw it," he said, "I thought the ball was going out of the ballpark." No interference.

"It was a magic trick," said Tarasco later. "The ball just disappeared out of midair." The 12-year-old, Jeffrey Maier of Tappan, New Jersey, became the most famous Yankee fan of all time. He didn't know what had happened — his glove had been swept away in the frenzy, and while everyone was arguing on the field, he was trying to get his glove back. He didn't get the ball either. "I didn't mean to do anything bad," he said later. "I was just a 12-year-old kid trying to catch a ball."

Put it in the book. The game was tied and went into

extra innings. And as TV crews surrounded Maier and the crowd shouted "MVP, MVP, MVP"—for the kid—Bernie Williams hit the ball higher and farther and deeper, beyond any argument, to give the Yankees a 5–4 win and a one-game lead in the series.

After the game, when the camera found Jeter in the clubhouse, a voice asked him whether he had anything to say to Maier. Jeter's eyes opened wide, and with the smallest hint of a smile on his face, he said, "Attaboy . . . attaboy." He'd been that kid once.

Backup catcher Jim Leyritz joined the conga line of Yankee World Series heroes when he socked a game-tying three-run homer in the eighth inning of the fourth game of the 1996 World Series to lead the Yankees back from a 6–0 deficit.

The Orioles didn't cave and collapse, and as Maier experienced his 15 minutes of fame and the talking heads of the nation debated the extent to which one little boy had exposed our moral decay, the Yankees rolled. David Wells beat them in game two, but the Yankees shrugged off the defeat as Torre kept up what the *Post*'s Tom Keegan termed his "musical chairs strategy," benching Boggs in games two and three for Hayes, and O'Neill in game three for Strawberry. New York won game three when Oriole second baseman Roberto Alomar bounced a throw turning a double play early, and when third baseman Todd Zeile lost his grip on the ball, making a pump-fake in the eighth. Williams—he of allegedly no baseball instinct—broke for home when the ball rolled free to put the Yankees ahead, and they went on to win 5–2. Then the Yankees won games four and five easily, 8–4 and 6–4, cranking home runs out of Camden Yards every couple of innings as Williams, Fielder, O'Neill, and Leyritz each hit one and Strawberry cranked three. Jeter—who else?—squelched any thought of a Baltimore comeback in the finale. With two out in the ninth, he went deep into the hole to field Cal Ripken's grounder, then made a perfect throw to put him out as Ripken made a desperate headfirst slide. The Yankees were clearly the better team, and the win sent them to the World Series as American League champions for the first time since 1981, and sent Joe Torre there for the first time since he had watched brother Frank and the rest of the Braves fall to the Yankees in the 1958 Series. During that interim period he'd participated in 4,272 games as a player or a manager without ever playing a meaningful game in late October.

But as yet it all meant nothing, at least to Steinbrenner and much of New York, for the city had never celebrated pennants any more than it did second place. "There's nothing like being a winner in New York," reminded the Boss. "Nothing." That was the carrot now held out before the Yankees.

To reach it, they would have to beat the Atlanta Braves. Defending world champions and the NL pennant winner in four of the last five seasons, the Braves had achieved a level of dominance not seen in baseball since the Oakland A's of the early 1970s. With the world's best pitching staff in Greg Maddux, Tom Glavine, John Smoltz, and Steve

Avery, all the Braves needed was another world championship to secure their status as the team of the 1990s. The Braves, thought most observers, had learned to win in 1995 and would be nearly impossible to stop. In an interesting turnabout, that made the Yankees sentimental underdogs and rooting for the Braves like rooting for Microsoft. After falling behind the Cardinals in the NLCS three games to one, the Braves had swept to victory, beating St. Louis in the last three games by a combined score of 32–1. All the parts were working.

The same could not be said for the Yankees. Despite their pennant, they were damaged. Strawberry had fouled a ball off his foot in the final game against Baltimore and broken his toe, and Kenny Rogers wasn't pitching well. Tino Martinez and Boggs were mired in slumps.

The first two games in New York went according to plan—Atlanta's. A day of rain pushed the Series back. Andy Pettitte never made it out of the third inning in game one. The Braves' 20-year-old outfielder Andruw Jones was oblivious to history. When the Curaçao native looked at Yankee Stadium, which, Joe Torre had once said, "gives you chills," Jones shrugged his shoulders and muttered, "Some place." Then he hit two home runs someplace over the fence, and John Smoltz cruised to a 12–1 win. In game two Greg Maddux was his usual efficient self, throwing 82 pitches in eight innings of work to beat Jimmy Key 4–0. The good work of an entire season was about to come undone. The only news being spread in New York was on the kitchen floor to catch the mess that was the Yankees.

New York was headed south, and Steinbrenner and Watson were in full panic mode. But Torre, outwardly, remained calm. After game one he said, "We're going to Atlanta. Atlanta's my town. We'll take three games there, and win it back here [New York] on Saturday." That was like saying, "My best pitcher will suffer an aneurysm in May and return in September." Cone would start game three for New York, and Torre hoped for a six-inning game.

The manager played musical chairs again, stacking the lineup with right-handed bats against Tom Glavine, benching Martinez for Fielder, Boggs for Hayes, picking Strawberry over O'Neill, and hitting Tim Raines leadoff. Raines started the game with a single, and Torre had Jeter bunt him over. Then Williams knocked him in, and the

Yankees led for the first time. Cone hung in, nursed a 2–0 lead into the sixth, and then loaded the bases with one out. Torre came out to talk to him, and as Cone said later, "I did my best to lie. Apparently he believed me." Cone got out of the inning, giving up only a single run. The Yankees had gone 70–3 after leading in the sixth during the regular season, and Rivera and Wetteland turned the trick again, sandwiched around a standout performance by Graeme Lloyd. His late season acquisition had almost cost Watson his job: he showed up with a sore arm. But his arm had come back, and now he was suddenly unhittable. The Yankees won 5–2.

But the Yankees turned to Kenny Rogers in game four, and the skittish pitcher at first wouldn't throw strikes, then did, and McGriff hit one over the wall. Atlanta led 6–0 after five innings. No team had ever come back from such a large deficit in the Series since the 1929 Philadelphia A's.

The comeback started like most comebacks—one routine play unfolding in anything but a routine way. Jeter lofted a fly ball foul to right, but outfielder Jermaine Dye missed it as he tried to avoid colliding with the umpire. Given another chance, Jeter singled. Another hit and two errors made it 6–3.

The score held into the eighth, and the Braves went for the throat. For the first time all year, the first time in 77 appearances in 1996, Atlanta manager Bobby Cox chose to bring in his closer, Mark Wohlers, to start the eighth. He was unscored on in the postseason.

Charlie Hayes started the rally by dribbling a ball down the line that started to roll foul, then stopped on the line for a hit. Strawberry then singled, bringing up catcher Jim Leyritz, who was playing because, well, because Joe Torre was the manager. All season long he'd generally caught only when Andy Pettitte was pitching, but earlier in the game Torre, trying to spark a rally, had pinch-hit O'Neill for Girardi.

It couldn't have worked out better. Leyritz was nothing if not confident. His teammates called him "the King," not as a term of endearment but as a comment on the part-time player's inflated opinion of himself. He thought he should be playing every day and always had. Earlier in his Yankee career, after being informed that he was being sent down to Columbus, Leyritz, who'd disagreed with the move, had changed into his street clothes and jeered his team from the stands. But Leyritz did one thing very well—hit the fastball—and that had kept him a Yankee.

Wohlers had one of the best fastballs in baseball, topping out at 99 miles per hour. As much as Leyritz feasted on the pitch, Wohler's reputation rested on his ability to throw fastballs past fastball hitters. It was a mano a mano moment akin to that of Reggie Jackson against Bob Welch in the 1978 World Series.

Leyritz fouled the first 98-mile-per-hour pitch straight back, and Wohlers looked surprised. He then blinked first, shook off the fastball, and followed with two sliders off the plate. Now he was behind and *had* to come back with fastballs. Leyritz fouled two more straight back, and Wohlers blinked again. No more fastballs. He went back to the slider, a good one, and Leyritz just topped it foul down the third-base line.

The oldest adage in baseball is that a pitcher should never get beat with anything but his best pitch. The situation screamed for another fastball. But Wohlers blinked again and threw a slider. Leyritz could catch up to a slider, particularly one that just spun and hung over the plate.

Leyritz unwound. Gone. Tie game. Leyritz raised his arm in triumph as he toured the bases, stilling the crowd.

Now the Yankees had the edge and carried the game into extra innings. Torre went into overdrive. He loved playing without the DH, under National League rules, matching wits with Bobby Cox, his Atlanta counterpart. There was nothing to lose, everything to gain.

The game unfolded like a chess match, move and countermove, each manager planning three or four moves ahead. But Torre made sure he never quite exhausted his options. With the bases loaded in the tenth, Torre pinch-hit Boggs, the last nonpitcher left on the bench.

Boggs had forged a Hall of Fame career with his ability to do two things—work the count and hit ground balls through the infield. Over the last decade no man in the game had collected more hits and walks. In Boston he'd developed a reputation as a selfish player interested only in his stats, but he'd come to New York with one goal—winning the World Series. And now, even though he hadn't played all game and was only a part-time starter, like Torre he stuck with what had gotten him this far. He used the best eye in baseball to work a walk off Steve Avery in the most important at bat of his career. The run put the Yankees ahead, and they went on to score another to win the longest game in Series history, 8–6.

Leyritz's blast and Boggs's walk broke the Braves. Then, in game five, Leyritz convinced Andy Pettitte to keep going with a seldom-used two-seam fastball that rode away from the Braves' right-handed hitters and to eschew his usual pattern of throwing cutter after cutter in on their hands. The Yankee bullpen was spent, but the Braves never adjusted as Pettitte pitched into the ninth before Wetteland took over. Cecil Fielder doubled in one run off John Smoltz after Jermaine Dye and Marquis Grissom botched a fly ball, and that was all the Yankees needed as their defense proved supreme. Pettitte grabbed everything in reach. Leyritz made a spectacular stop of a 50-foot curveball in the seventh to stop a rally. Strawberry ran down Jeff Blauser's eighth-inning blast at the wall. With two down in the ninth and Chipper Jones on third, Wetteland put the winning run on with an intentional walk to Ryan Klesko. Bobby Cox pinch-hit Luis Polonia for Jermaine Dye with the game on the line.

The next few minutes were excruciating. Wetteland threw six high fastballs, and Polonia, like a cricket batsman, broke two bats and fouled all six off as Andy Pettitte sat on the bench, unable to watch, his head buried in his hands and a towel wrapped around his head. Then, on the seventh pitch, Polonia turned on the ball. Paul O'Neill, despite a painful hamstring, caught up to the long drive in the gap, reached out, grabbed it, and slapped his hand on the wall, affirming the last out of the 1–0 win, New York's eighth straight road win during the postseason. The Yankees returned to New York needing only one more.

The press had been falling all over itself searching for the single, ever-important "story line" to wrap the Series in a nice neat package. They'd tried several—the redemption of Strawberry, Torre and Boggs finally winning a Series, Key and Cone coming back from arm surgery, Williams emerging as a superstar, and so on. But no one story had really sufficed, for this was a Series and a team that no one individual dominated.

On the morning of the off-day before game six, the story wrote itself. Frank Torre got his heart transplant and came through the operation fine. All the Yankees had to do was follow the script the rest of the way.

Former Red Sox great Wade Boggs came to New York in 1993 in search of a world championship. In the most important at bat of his career, he worked a bases-loaded walk off Atlanta ace Steve Avery in the tenth inning of game four of the 1996 World Series to help carry New York to an 8–6 victory. Within a few days he drank champagne to celebrate the only world title of his Hall of Fame career.

Key and Maddux matched up again in a repeat of game two, and Torre, still not blinking, put Girardi back behind the plate. In the third they finally broke through. O'Neill, back in the lineup, doubled. Then Girardi, with 17 triples in eight big league seasons, drove one to deep center field. "When I got to third base," he said later, "I almost started crying." When Jeter and Williams singled, New York led 3–0.

Jimmy Key made it to the sixth, and with the score 3–1, the game belonged to the bullpen. Torre's work was done. "There was nothing I had to do anymore," he said. David Weathers, Lloyd, Rivera, and then Wetteland carried the ball into the ninth. The Braves nicked Wetteland for a run to send the crowd over the edge, leading Torre to comment later, "They had to test out the new heart." With the tying run at second base, Mark Lemke hit a foul ball to third that drifted into the crowd. Then he did it again, and Charlie Hayes caught it at the edge of the stands, and the Yankees were world champions for the first time since 1978.

The players swarmed the mound in a huge knot around Wetteland. It soon collapsed into a huge heap that player after player took turns climbing to the top and then floating on the backs of their teammates, floating and rolling back off and then on again and again, as the fans in the stands sang along with Frank Sinatra's signature rendition of "New York, New York." Top of the heap indeed.

Then the knot slowly untangled, and the whole team, led by Torre, jogged around the field. Boggs rode a police horse as New York's finest kept most of the fans off the field and in the stands, where they sang along with Sinatra over and over and over. Torre and Steinbrenner blubbered to each other in the clubhouse. The players said everything and nothing. It had all been said all season long. As Mariano Duncan had been saying all year, "We play, we win. Das it." It was.

As soon as the season ended it was time to begin anew for 1997, at least for Watson and the men behind the Tampa curtain who pulled most of the strings. In the era of free agency rosters rarely stay intact from one season to the next, and it was no different in the weeks and months following the World Series. The Yankees would have to retool for 1997.

The emergence of Mariano Rivera made closer John Wetteland expendable. Although Rivera had never been a closer, the Yankees thought his stuff and makeup made him perfect for the role, and he was many millions of dollars cheaper than Wetteland, who signed as a free agent with Texas.

Rivera, Jeter, and Pettitte were more important to the team than more highly paid stars, not just for the significant contributions they brought to the field but for the money they made. As young players with little leverage, their relatively small salaries freed money to be spent on others. And the Yankees, for all their unmatched resources, did have something resembling a budget. Steinbrenner didn't want to push the envelope too far. He didn't mind if the Yankees' payroll was at or near the top of the major league salary scale, but he was sensitive to criticism and

didn't want the Yankees to get all the blame for the escalation in the cost of everything related to baseball. When the Orioles, Red Sox, Marlins, Braves, and Indians pushed the ceiling up, however, Steinbrenner gladly rose to the new level.

When the Yankees signed super-sized David Wells of the Orioles, Key signed with Baltimore in a virtual swap of starters, but apart from that the Yankees were relatively inactive in the off-season. They did little beyond adding a few veterans, like reliever Mike Stanton, and bringing up some more kids from the farm, such as catcher Jorge Posada and pitcher Ramiro Mendoza.

They got off to a slow start in 1997. One of the problems for a veteran club is injury. The Yankees, plagued by injuries both big and small, struggled to get above .500 over the first two months of the season as Baltimore bolted out front. Strawberry hurt his knee and missed almost the entire season, and both Bernie Williams and Tim Raines battled recurring hamstring problems. Gooden got a hernia. Fielder had a bad hand. Rivera smoothly took over as closer, but the Yankees weren't the same team. Torre didn't have the same number of parts to play with, even after the Yankees picked up outfielder Chad Curtis and others in midseason.

All the while, one interesting sideshow was taking place. It was interesting both because there hadn't been many sideshows in recent years and because it was so minor compared to those of an earlier era that it was almost comical. Expensive too.

In 1995 Japanese pitcher Hideo Nomo secured his release, signed with the Dodgers, and was an immediate sensation. Before the 1997 season another Japanese hurler, Hideki Irabu, had tried to make a similar move. The San Diego Padres paid a couple of million dollars to Irabu's Japanese club for his rights.

But Irabu didn't want to play for the Padres. He wanted to play for the Yankees.

Dwight Gooden, here pitching against Cleveland on June 27, 1997, turned back the clock on his troubled career with six shutout innings as the replacement starter for David Cone in the fourth game of the 1997 divisional playoffs against the Indians. In the end, the Yankees lost games four and five to conclude a rare unsuccessful defense of a Yankee world title.

Right-handed pitcher Hideki Irabu arrived at Yankee Stadium from Japan in 1997 after rejecting the San Diego Padres for the bright lights of New York. Irabu is shown in the first inning of his first major league victory, a 10–3 win against the Detroit Tigers on July 10, 1997. In three seasons with the Yankees, Irabu went 29–20 with a hefty 5.40 ERA.

Steinbrenner got all excited. Irabu, so went the rumor, threw 100 miles per hour. Irabu was better than Nomo. Irabu was the best pitcher in the world. None of that was true, but it became clear that Irabu and his representatives were no dummies. They pitched him like a mail-order bride. By announcing his desire to play for the Yankees and no one else, he'd considerably raised the price on his services. Steinbrenner fell for him. If Irabu had to have the Yankees, well, the Yankees had to have Irabu.

But a lot of baseball people weren't all that enamored with Irabu, including GM Bob Watson. He was a little overweight, not very athletic, and slow to the plate, and although he had a good fastball and splitter, he didn't have very good command. In eight seasons in Japan he was only a .500 pitcher. But the Boss believed the hype. He had to have Hideki.

Perhaps that's why the Yankees had been relatively inactive earlier in the off-season: they were saving money for Irabu. The Padres held out and on April 22 finally let him go for $3 million and several prospects, including *Baseball America*'s two-time minor league Player of the Year, Ruben Rivera, Mariano's cousin. The Yankees inked the pitcher to a contract worth $12 million and sent him to the minors to work him into shape. He made his major league debut on July 10 in the Stadium against Detroit, welcomed by none other than New York Mayor Rudy Giuliani. It was hardly a fair test, for the Tigers were pretty awful, but Irabu struck out nine and gave up only two runs in 6⅔ innings.

Although he won his next start as well, it soon became clear that his fastball wasn't 100 miles per hour but 91 and pretty straight, that his splitter was inconsistent, and that there was a reason why Irabu had been a .500 pitcher in Japan. The mail-order bride wasn't a dog, but the fantasy had been much better than the reality. He was soon sent back to Columbus and ended the season 5–4 with an ERA of 7.09. He wasn't the answer to the Yankees' troubles, which turned dramatically worse on August 17.

Looking for his 13th win, as David Cone threw his warm-up pitches before the second inning of a game against the Texas Rangers, he abruptly stopped and made a slashing motion over his throat, like a master of ceremonies signaling the stagehands to bring down the curtain. He felt a sharp pain in his shoulder and couldn't roll the ball to the plate, much less throw. The Yankees put him on the disabled list.

That ended any chance they had of winning the division, and they limped home, unable to catch Baltimore, but earning a wild-card berth and the right to play Cleveland in the first round of the playoffs. Cone, after a month of rest and a series of cortisone shots, had been activated on September 20. Apart from Torre's faith and Cone's willingness to give it a shot — he said, "I'm just going to do the best I can" — there was little reason to think he was ready. But the Yankees were hoping, as Torre said, "to set the tone," for the move revealed both confidence and desperation. The Yankees were confident they could win but realized that they'd need to tap into the same kind of magic that had appeared so regularly in 1996. They seemed to be hoping that a Cone victory would leave the Indians prostrate before the notion of Yankee destiny.

But Cone had nothing. The Indians hit everything hard as he gave up five first-inning runs and left in the fourth trailing 6–1. While the bullpen did its job, the Yankees scratched back, and in the sixth, with the score 6–4, New York exploded. As Jack Curry wrote in the *Times,* "The first pitch soared into the upper deck in right field and tied the score. The second spiraled into the left field seats and gave the Yankees the lead. The third baseball soared over the centerfield seats to inflate the edge and transform Yankee Stadium into a rollicking baseball setting." Raines, Jeter, and O'Neill had homered in succession, and the Yankees held on to win, 8–6. To a man, the Yankees felt that they had "set the tone."

But the Indians weren't buying. They won game two as rookie Jaret Wright outpitched Pettitte, who was bothered by back spasms; for once, Torre's matchups seemed overmatched. But in game three O'Neill hit a grand slam and David Wells shut down the Indians in Cleveland as New York won, 6–1.

Gooden, called on to start game four because Cone couldn't, did his job, and the Yankee bullpen took over with two outs in the sixth, leading 2–0. They were already cuing up Sinatra back in New York when Sandy Alomar stepped in against Rivera in the eighth with a man on. Close observers noted that the situation was eerily similar to what Bobby Cox had done in the 1996 World Series — he turned to his closer an inning earlier than normal.

Rivera pitched smart, keeping the ball away from Alomar so that he couldn't pull it over the fence. But Alomar hit smart, going the other way and dropping the ball ten rows beyond Paul O'Neill's futile leap. The game was tied, and the tone was set.

The Indians, not the Yankees, would come back. In the ninth Marquis Grissom singled, went to second on a sacrifice, and scored the winning run when Omar Vizquel bounced a ground ball up the middle. In 1996 Jeter would have fielded it cleanly and made the out, but in 1997 it deflected off Ramiro Mendoza's glove to precisely the place Jeter had just abandoned as he reacted to the ball. It rolled into left center, and the series was tied.

The Indians took a 4–0 lead in the finale, and this time all the Yankee comebacks fell short. The Yankees lost — certainly one of the rarest phrases ever uttered in October. The knot in the middle of the field this time formed around Cleveland reliever Jose Mesa. It was the Indians who leaped and rolled atop the heap.

"You're running and running," said Torre afterward, trying to describe how he felt, "and all of a sudden there's a cliff." The Yankees weren't in free fall, but to a man they knew they had fallen off.

A victorious Scott Brosius rounds first base after hitting a three-run homer off Padre closer Trevor Hoffman, in game four of the 1998 World Series, to give the Yankees the lead and eventually the world championship. Brosius was acquired from Oakland in exchange for pitcher Kenny Rogers before the 1998 campaign. He subsequently enjoyed a career year, batting .300 with 19 homers and 98 RBIs.

1998–1999
TEAM OF THE CENTURY

As the groggy Yankees sauntered into Yankee Stadium the day after the loss to Cleveland to clean out their lockers, they were greeted by workmen painting over the words "World Champions" above the main entrance. A number of them also saw their pictures splashed over the *New York Post*. An after-hours wake held at a bar after the Yankee plane got in from Cleveland had been spiced with strippers and shot by a photographer. It looked worse than it was, but it added to the embarrassment of the loss.

Technically, the Yankees would retain their crown until October 26, when the Florida Marlins would win the World Series. But that was already yesterday, a ring in the back of a drawer that didn't mean anything at the moment.

It has been said that true perfection is achieved only by those who are prepared to destroy it. Well, the Boss never needed much of an excuse to make changes. Under George Weiss, the Yankees had to win because they were so poorly paid they needed the World

Series money to make ends meet. Under Steinbrenner, the Yankees were far better paid but had to win to ensure their security. The last time the Yankees had finished second, a couple of guys ended up on unemployment.

On the plane ride back Steinbrenner talked, and his brain trust — Mark Newman, Gordon Blakely, and Mark Connors — took turns nodding their heads, agreeing on the plan. There were decisions to be made and heads to roll, new contracts to be negotiated and a host of players to get signed for the upcoming season. Boggs had won his ring in 1995, and the end of his contract coincided with the erosion of his skills. Charlie Hayes had worn out his welcome, talking out of turn on a team that tried to stay as silent as possible. Boggs, Hayes, Cecil Fielder, and Kenny Rogers were all cast aside and relegated to history. That left a hole at third, and there was still one at second and at the top of the order, where Jeter struck out too much and his power was wasted.

On November 7, they agreed to pay half of Rogers' remaining salary to convince the A's to take him off their hands. He'd been nothing but a disappointment. Four days later the Giants took Hayes. The Yankees didn't lose much in the expansion draft to stock Arizona and Tampa Bay, and afterward they agreed to take A's third baseman Scott Brosius as the player named later in the Rogers deal. They knew Brosius could field, but there were questions about his bat — his batting average had fallen from .304 in 1996 to .203. He would be just one of several candidates to play third in 1998. Veteran Chili Davis signed as a free agent, adding power and filling the DH slot, and Strawberry and others were signed for another season.

The moves sent Bob Watson over the edge. He had the title but not the authority, and most of the changes took place without his input. In January he referred to Steinbrenner's "baseball people" as the "little voices that run around in his [Steinbrenner's] head." The Boss didn't think that was funny. Sick of it all, Watson resigned on February 3, his head held high. Steinbrenner was dismissive, saying, "Everyone knows I'm not easy to work for." Watson had been expendable since the day he was hired. Everyone was.

Assistant GM Brian Cashman replaced Watson. Cashman, who had worked for the Yankees since interning in the front office in 1986, was accustomed to the constant

On February 3, 1998, the Yankees named thirty-one-year-old Brian Cashman to replace Bob Watson as team general manager. Cashman, the second-youngest GM in major league history, had worked for the Yankees since starting a college internship in 1986 and had spent five seasons as assistant general manager under Gene Michael and Watson.

state of crisis and appreciative of being handed a GM job at age 31. Friends called him "Costanza" after the character on *Seinfeld,* but he was no caricature. Among the players, agents, and other front-office personnel around baseball, Cashman had a fine reputation and many friends. He was a guy other teams were comfortable dealing with. Despite his youth, he had earned the job.

But Steinbrenner wanted more. He was getting older and starting to entertain the idea of selling out or turning the team over to his kids. He was beyond the point where "wait till next year" was an acceptable answer to anything. *Every* hole had to be filled. A deal was already in the works for Twins second baseman Chuck Knoblauch. Cashman closed it, giving up some cash and four prospects, including future stars Christian Guzman and Eric Milton, to secure one of the best second basemen and leadoff hitters in baseball. He also avoided arbitration with key players like Pettitte and Williams, meeting them halfway, ensuring that everyone was under contract and relatively happy entering spring training. Any distractions were thus put off until the following fall.

Then George Steinbrenner, who'd alternately been the Yankees' biggest asset and worst enemy, finally got it right. After 25 years of ownership, he finally found his niche within his own organization. The Boss provided Torre with what he needed, then stayed more or less out of the way as Torre rolled the balls out on the field and let them play.

There wasn't a superstar on the team; neither was there a man who didn't contribute. A thousand pieces finally fell into place. The 1998 Yankees became a *team* in the truest sense, and by the end of the season everyone involved — even Steinbrenner — knew his place and came to realize that their cumulative achievement outweighed any individual contribution. That has always been not only the ideal standard in any team sport but part of the Yankee myth, and they have approached it more than any other team in baseball. But never more so than in 1998. The result was more wins in one season than any team has ever achieved in baseball history. This Yankee team transcended both its owner and its storied history to stand alone.

Spring training answered most remaining questions — a $72 million payroll could do that. Scott Brosius beat out Dale Sveum, Mike Lowell, and Luis Sojo to win the third-base job. He showed a good glove and was a better hitter than the Yankees had thought he would be. Cone was healthy. Raines, Strawberry, and Curtis all seemed satisfied sharing left field and filling in elsewhere. Even Irabu looked good, relaxed and in shape, and by the end of camp he fell into place behind Cone, Pettitte, and Wells. The Yankees, already favored to repeat as AL East champions, went only 15–12 in the spring, but they looked better than that. A lot better.

They started the season losing four out of their first five and suddenly looked a lot worse. Wells and Cone left their best stuff in Florida. Chili Davis hurt his ankle and was out of the lineup almost before he ever got in. Rivera blew a save and blew out his groin. They were the last team in baseball to hit a home run and after only five games were in fifth place, three and a half games behind Baltimore.

Torre was already under fire as Steinbrenner's impatience grew. The Boss reminded his team that they were behind the Tampa Bay Devil Rays. Cashman said, "Someday we'll look back on this and laugh," but he wasn't smiling when he said it.

The slow start was the best thing that could have happened, and the first of three or four events that would push the club to fulfill its potential. It is easy for vastly talented clubs to sleepwalk through a season, winning just enough to remain comfortable. It is much harder to fulfill destiny. Although a team can survive a bad streak in May or June or July or August, a slump in September can ruin an entire season and render October insignificant. It was early, but already every game mattered.

After the Yankees' fourth loss of the season, Torre reamed his team out. The next day he managed as if it were the first inning of game three of the playoffs and the Yankees were already down by two. They led 6–0 before David Wells even took the mound. But when he couldn't close the deal and allowed the Mariners back in the game, Torre pulled him. Mike Stanton, acquired in case something happened to Rivera, got out of a one-out, bases-loaded jam in the eighth with the score 11–7. Lucky number. The Yankees won 13–8 and moved into fourth place. The next day Irabu pitched the first decent game of the year by a Yankee starter, and Chad Curtis, third on the depth chart in left, hit a two-run homer in a 4–3 Yankee win. They moved into third place.

They won ugly in their home opener the next day, 17–13 over Oakland. It was ugly but sweet, because it was the type of game that good teams win because good teams don't quit, and this team was starting to learn that. Torre kept pushing, and the next day the Yankees used their speed against Oakland, stealing six bases to beat the A's again. Then Stanton saved his third game in a week, and all of a sudden the Yankees had won five in a row and were 6–5. The abyss had been avoided.

Then the roof fell in, literally. On April 13, just hours before they were scheduled to play the Angels in New York, a support beam fell in the Stadium, crushing a seat. The Stadium was closed for repairs, and the next game was hastily rescheduled at Shea. A home series against the Tigers was switched to Detroit while the damage was repaired.

In a scene reminiscent of junior high, the Yanks dressed at the Stadium, then rode the bus to Shea. They beat the Angels 6–3 as Strawberry slammed a home run at the scene of his former crimes, and they all rode back to the Stadium still in uniform, hot and sweaty and happy on the bus. It was silly, but it reminded them all a little of what baseball was like before the money and helped them come together as a team.

They took two of three in Detroit, then three straight in Toronto, taking over first place from the Red Sox on April 21 and returning to New York three days later with a record of 12–5. But Steinbrenner wasn't convinced. Even when they finished April 17–6, he said, "We haven't won anything." At 16–6, the Red Sox were staying close.

Despite 16 wins in 1997, David Wells hadn't really proven himself. The wide-body pitcher, who wore his heart on his sleeve and tattoos of his kids on his body, hadn't been a good fit. He loved the Yankees and even had the temerity to ask whether he could wear Babe Ruth's number 3, a major faux pas on the tradition-conscious club. But the Yankees and their fans did not yet love him, and for all his bluster, Wells was sensitive. Wells had crossed Steinbrenner in 1997, then broke his hand in the off-season and showed up at spring training bigger than ever. Wells reveled in playing the role of the California bad boy raised by bikers, but that attitude wasn't much appreciated, particularly when it had yet to be backed up by a performance worthy of his salary. He had all the stuff in the world but had never put it all together for an extended period of time. After throwing the occasional gem, he'd get sloppy and dribble wins down his chin. He was the quintessential "innings eater," but the Yankees expected more. "If there's one guy who has the ability to pitch a no-hitter every time out, it's Boomer," said Torre.

So far he was the weak link, and Irabu became the unlikely early season ace. On May 9, Wells spit up another big lead. When Torre came out to the mound to pull him, he rolled his eyes and tossed the ball in the air, showing up his manager and moping off the mound all the way to the dugout. His ERA was bigger than his waistline. Torre took him aside and did all the talking.

Wells was important to the Yankees. A team's top starters, like Cone and Pettitte, are expected to win. But the third and fourth starters often determine the fortunes of a team. If they perform above expectations, everything changes and good can become great. Irabu was doing his part to make that happen. Wells wasn't.

He pitched better in his next start, and as he warmed up in the Yankee Stadium bullpen on May 17 before facing Minnesota, pitching coach Mel Stottlemyre was almost speechless. Wells's stuff had never looked better. That happens to all pitchers sometimes, and they rarely know why. Sometimes it disappears on the long walk to the mound, but on this day Wells delivered it to the Twins.

He was perfect from the first batter as the Yankees backed him with four runs. Wells went to three balls on only four hitters, starting out Marcus Lawton 3–0 to lead off the seventh, and battling back from a 3–1 count to strike out always tough Paul Molitor to end the inning. The closest thing to a hit came in the eighth when Ron Coomer hit a hard one-hopper that Knoblauch knocked down before throwing him out by a step.

With a Beanie Baby crowd of 49,820 cheering madly, Wells faced Pat Meares needing only one more out for a perfect game. On Wells's 121st pitch and 79th strike, Meares lofted the ball to right. Wells raised his arm in the air and looked as if he were about to levitate, looking toward the dugout in disbelief, then back to O'Neill, watching the ball settle into his glove. Willie Banks and Darryl Strawberry lifted him to their shoulders and carried him from the field as he triumphantly waved his hat at the crowd.

The game marked the season as something special. The last perfect game pitched by a Yankee, also at the Stadium, had been Don Larsen's in 1956. Larsen and Wells had both attended the same San Diego high school, Point Loma. In the *Post,* Wallace Mathews recalled the words that Dick Young had written after Larsen's perfect game: "The imperfect man pitched the perfect game." They rang as true in regard to the fun-loving Wells as they had for the hard-living Larsen. Mathews added, "Magic surroundings breed magical happenings. Already the 1998 Yankee season holds the promise of magic." The victory lifted the Yankees' record to 28–9. By playing .500 the rest of the season, they'd finish 95–76, virtually guaranteeing a spot in the playoffs.

That's the only downside to quick starts—it's easy to relax and start to coast. But two days later against Baltimore, the Yankees received the only warning they'd need. After New York came from behind to take a 7–5 lead on Bernie Williams's eighth-inning three-run homer, Tino Martinez stepped in against Armando Benitez.

Several years before, immediately after giving up a grand slam, Benitez had clocked Martinez. Now he did so again, sending a fastball hard into the center of Martinez's back. As the first baseman folded in pain, Darryl Strawberry and a few other Yankees stepped out of the dugout and started barking at Benitez. Pitching inside after a home run is one thing, but drilling a guy in the back is another, for a hitter's first instinct on an inside pitch is to move away from the plate. Benitez appeared to have thrown behind Martinez knowing he'd hit him.

Then Benitez made his second mistake. He dropped his glove, spread his arms, and motioned for the Yankees to come get him if they dared. They did—all 25 of them.

For the next 15 minutes one big brawl and several small ones took place all over the field as Strawberry and Graeme Lloyd, racing all the way in from the bullpen, wreaked the most havoc. The main event even tumbled into the Orioles' dugout. Five players—Benitez, Strawberry, Lloyd, Jeff Nelson, and the Orioles' Alan Mills—were all tossed from the game, and Benitez was eventually suspended for eight games.

Baseball fights are inane, but like the bus trip to Shea, the battle served to bring the team even closer together. Tim Raines immediately homered to put the game away, and the Yankees went on to sweep Baltimore, burying them for good. From there they went to Boston, and after blowing the first game, they completely dominated the Red Sox, winning 12–3 and 14–4 to increase their lead over Boston to five games. The *Post*'s George King, who takes particular delight in tweaking Red Sox fans (he was excoriated in Boston after leaving Pedro Martinez off his 1999 MVP ballot), began his account of the 14–4 win by writing, "The AL East race is over," and announcing that the Yankees' magic number was 112. It was an outlandish statement, but in only a few more weeks King's prediction would be proven accurate as the Yankees added one final important piece to their lineup.

On December 26, 1997, legendary Cuban pitcher Orlando Hernandez defected from Cuba, escaping on a boat to Anguilla Cay before establishing residency in

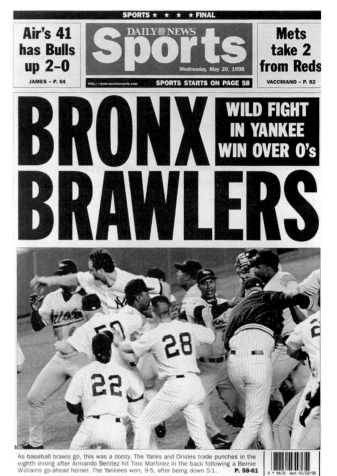

The 1998 Yankees came together on the night of May 19 when they brawled with the Orioles. Baltimore pitcher Armando Benitez first beaned first baseman Tino Martinez, then gestured to the Yankee dugout to come get him if they dared. They did.

Costa Rica to become a free agent. Over the past several seasons the defection of Cuban players had become common as the opportunity to become an instant millionaire and enjoy the fruits of freedom became ever more enticing and agents became ever more inventive in finding ways to get players off the island. Cuban authorities tried to stop the flow off the island by cutting back on international trips and punishing players they suspected of even thinking about leaving.

Orlando Hernandez was the best pitcher on the island. His father Arnaldo had been a pitcher whose flamboyant style earned him the nickname "El Duque." His son earned the right to his father's name with his performance on the Cuban National Team, for which he was 129–47.

But in 1996 Cuban authorities tossed Hernandez off the team and banned him from playing baseball anywhere. His younger half-brother Livan had already defected, and Cuban authorities believed Orlando was planning to do the same. He went from being a national hero to working as an aide at a psychiatric hospital for a miserable $8.75 a month.

After El Duque's escape, his agent, Joe Cubas, showcased him before scouts in Costa Rica. Most came away unimpressed. His fastball topped out just under 90 miles per hour — major league marginal. Although his motion, featuring his signature high leg kick, was deceptive, only a few clubs thought he would be more than an average major league pitcher. After factoring in the question of his true age — Hernandez claimed he was 28 even though his Cuban baseball card indicated he was at least four years older than that — interest in Hernandez was tempered.

But the Yankees saw the heart behind the arm. His athleticism and his feel for pitching, particularly given his enforced inactivity, impressed scout Lin Garrett. The Yankees outbid five other clubs and signed Hernandez to a four-year contract worth $6.6 million on March 7. He'd be worth every penny.

Determined not to rush him as they had done with Irabu, they allowed Hernandez to pitch himself into shape in the minors. He went 6–0 at triple-A Columbus in seven starts and earned a promotion in June as an emergency starter, filling in for David Cone after Cone was bitten on the hand by his mother's dog.

From the very beginning El Duque exhibited an unparalleled ability to rise to the occasion. In his first start on June 3, he pitched better than he had in Columbus, allowing only five hits in a 7–1 victory and ruining the plan to send him back to the minors. In his next start he went the distance and beat Montreal in an interleague game, 11–1. His performance put Torre in a quandary.

With the cheers of 49,820 "Beanie Baby Day" fans ringing in his ears, left-hander David Wells is hoisted aloft by teammates Willie Banks (left) and Darryl Strawberry after pitching a perfect game against the Minnesota Twins at Yankee Stadium. By sheer coincidence, Wells shared the same partying habits and the same alma mater (Point Loma High School in San Diego) as Don Larsen, who'd pitched the previous perfect game by a Yankee.

The addition of the Cuban national team's pitching legend Orlando "El Duque" Hernandez in 1998 solidified the Yankees' starting rotation. By June, New York possessed not only the best pitching in the majors but also the deepest rotation and bullpen in franchise history.

Cone's hand had healed. And fifth starter Ramiro Mendoza, after struggling early, was pitching well. But six starters gave him one too many. Fortunately, the Yankees still had an opening. Although Rivera was the designated closer for life, and Stanton, Nelson, and Lloyd created a sturdy bridge across innings seven and eight, long relief had been a problem. Mike Buddie and Willie Banks had already failed to keep the job, and Darren Holmes struggled. When Mendoza was shelled in his next start, he made the decision easy for Torre, who moved him into long relief. The move simultaneously gave the Yankees both the best starting rotation and the best bullpen in baseball. Every game became a six-inning contest again, sometimes even less.

They suddenly needed the help. Tino Martinez's back gave him trouble, and he slumped. Bernie Williams sprained his knee, and a rib injury knocked Jeter out for several weeks. The Yankees' three most productive players were out of the lineup, yet it made no difference. Chad Curtis took over in center, and super sub Luis Sojo slid into Jeter's spot. Strawberry was crushing the ball in tandem with Raines in left and at DH, while Brosius was cleaning up from the ninth spot. Despite all the injuries, the Yankees followed a 20–7 May with a 19–7 June as Pettitte, Cone, Wells, and El Duque combined for a 12–3 record with an ERA just over 2.00. They entered July at 56–20, ten games ahead of Boston, not only proving George King correct but making him appear a little conservative as they capped the month by taking five of six from the Mets and Braves in interleague play.

The Yankees wouldn't admit it publicly, but the season was over. The final three months would be spent only in pursuit of records and in preparation for the postseason. That provided its own minor drama.

One of the unexpected results of realignment has been that, in doubling the number of teams making postseason play, the number of teams thinking they might make it that far also doubles. With the approach of the July 31 trading deadline, every team over .500 still has a shot to win and believes it is only a player or two away. The price for that player goes up every day.

In 1998 that player was disgruntled Seattle pitcher Randy Johnson, "the Big Unit." His contract was up, and the Mariners felt they could no longer afford him. All month the Mariners entertained offers for the one available player who could tilt the balance.

With the luxury of thinking ahead to the postseason, Yankee GM Brian Cashman had to walk a fine line. While they were intrigued, the Yankees didn't really need Johnson. But they didn't want the competition, particularly Cleveland, to acquire him either.

A month-long game of liars' poker ensued that provided a portion of the excitement that the pennant race lacked. Mariner GM Woody Woodward, who'd once been New York's GM, dangled Johnson before all interested parties and strung everyone along. He hoped that, in the end, the Yankees' fear of seeing Johnson go to a competitor would force them into a deal they didn't want to make. He asked the Yankees for a package of top prospects. Plus Ramiro Mendoza. Or Irabu. Cashman wavered.

The Indians thought they had a deal, and with the deadline less than 24 hours away, the Mariners went back to the Yankees with a final request. Manager Lou Piniella had decided that he didn't want either Mendoza or Irabu. He wanted Pettitte.

Forget about it. Cashman said no, then held his breath, unsure what would be worse, seeing Johnson in a Cleveland uniform or finding a new job once the Boss found out.

But the Mariners miscalculated. The Indians got cold feet and withdrew their offer. In the end Johnson was traded out of the league to Houston. Cashman started breathing again.

August started like July. The Yankees were 76–27, 15 games up on Boston, and the news was only getting better. Everyone was getting healthy. Chili Davis returned to action in the middle of the month, adding a confirmed 100-RBI bat to the lineup. With boredom their only competition, the Yankees were now in a race with history. They kept pace with the latter and beat the former to death, reaching their high point on August 22 as they stormed from behind to beat Texas and former teammate John Wetteland 12–9 on Scott Brosius's two-out, three-run homer in the eighth. They were 94–32, and they were on pace to win 121 games. Comparisons to the '27 Yankees, Cincinnati's Big Red Machine, and other powerhouses from the past sounded out of place only because none of these predecessors seemed to belong in the same conversation with the '98 Yankees.

So the Yankees lost four straight, then won four straight, then lost five of seven. So what? Their lead continued to grow, and the attention of the baseball world turned elsewhere: Mark McGwire and Sammy Sosa were in their memorable race to break Roger Maris's home run mark. The Yankees treasured their temporary anonymity.

A few players cooled off, but in 1998 there was always an answer. Twenty-seven-year-old rookie Shane Spencer, a 28th-round draft pick with eight full years in the minors, had been on the shuttle between New York and Columbus

Outfielder Shane Spencer made the most of his rookie season in 1998, batting .373 in 27 games. His remarkable September caused the New York press to compare him with the fictional heroes Roy Hobbs and Joe Hardy. The former 28th-round draft choice had already spent eight full seasons in the minors before his Yankee debut as a 26-year-old rookie.

all year long as Torre played with the bottom of his roster, adding an extra pitcher when he needed one, adding an extra bat when he didn't.

Spencer had responded with a couple of big days, going five for five in one game, which only earned him another trip back down. But in a mild surprise, Torre called him back up on August 31, just in time to be eligible for the postseason roster. Still, Spencer was the last option in both left field and as DH.

When Strawberry started to slump in September, Spencer got to play a little. Then Strawberry was suspended for three games for taking part in a brawl after Toronto pitcher Roger Clemens beaned Brosius and Jeter. Spencer received a three-day invitation to the ball and played the Cinderella role to the hilt.

Beginning on September 18, through the end of the year, he was the best hitter in baseball. Joe Torre called him "Joe Hardy," after the character in *Damn Yankees* who sells his soul. The press called him "Roy Hobbs," after the Robert Redford character in the movie *The Natural.* But they were characters from fiction. Spencer was real.

On the 18th, he capped a seven-run ninth-inning comeback with his first major league grand slam. On September 22, he hit two more home runs. The next day he hit another, and the next day he hit another grand slam. Spencer hadn't hit this well in Little League. Torre and the rest of the Yankees were stunned. "I'm not sure what he is," the manager admitted. All he knew was that Spencer just kept hitting, everything — fastballs, curveballs, in and out, and up and down. All of it hard and a lot of it out of the park.

That's what Darryl Strawberry had been doing most of the season, cracking 24 home runs in less than 300 at bats. But beginning in July, he'd been bothered by a sharp pain in his side. He tried to ignore it, but it wouldn't go away and in September finally began to affect the way he swung the bat. As soon as the regular season ended, he would seek medical attention.

The Yankees finished with a flourish. After playing .500 ball for the first part of the month, they won their last seven, including David Cone's 20th win on September 26. With an 8–3 win over Tampa the next day, they finished the year with 114 wins against only 48 defeats, a franchise record and the most wins by a major league team during the regular season since the 1906 Cubs had won 116. The ballclub honored Joe DiMaggio before the finale, and Bernie Williams, with two hits in his first two at bats, finished with a .339 batting average to wrest the batting title from Boston's Mo Vaughn. Incredibly, while the Yankees led the league in virtually every significant batting and pitching category, Williams's batting title was the only major individual title claimed by any Yankee player — none had even been voted to start the All-Star game. They were just the best top-to-bottom team in history. Scott Brosius knocked in 98 runs from the ninth spot, and when Derek Jeter called him "our MVP," no one argued. On this team that was as true for the ninth hitter as for any other.

And Shane Spencer? In his final game the September MVP hit his eighth home run of the month, a rookie record, and his third grand slam of the season. Spencer's performance mirrored that of the Yankees in its spectacular, unexpected perfection. He hit .421 in September to finish at .373, with an ungodly slugging percentage of .910, better than Ruth in '21 or even Bonds in '01, one of the best months of hitting in baseball history. Put it this way: in September Spencer outslugged Mark McGwire, who set the new home run mark with 70.

All of which now meant nothing. Entering the postseason, the Yankees were 0–0, simply one of eight. They knew that if they lost now, that would become their story. The 114 wins would be forgotten, and Steinbrenner would probably revert to form and go nuts and clean house. They'd be viewed as a spectacular failure.

They faced potent Texas in the ever-dangerous best-of-five Division Series. But this time around Torre had few decisions to make — this team matched up everywhere, and the only shared spots were left field, DH, and catcher, where Jorge Posada split time with Joe Girardi. Torre won the series with a choice he'd made weeks ago when he set up his rotation and decided to throw his two left-handers at the Stadium, a tried-and-true strategy, saving right-handers David Cone and Orlando Hernandez for the smaller ballpark in Texas, where they'd be tough on slugger Juan Gonzalez.

Wells was thrilled with his assignment. After throwing his perfect game, he had flourished, going 18–4. "I want that opportunity," he said. "I want to be the hero, I want to be the goat." Wells, who was 4–0 in the postseason entering the game, got the better half of his wish and emerged an even more perfect 5–0 as he completely shut down the Rangers and sent Mel Stottlemyre's son Todd down to defeat, 2–0. In game two Andy Pettitte was nearly as good, winning 3–1 as Shane Spencer and Scott Brosius provided all the offense the Yankees needed with home runs.

The Yankees didn't miss Strawberry's bat, but they missed him. He stayed behind undergoing medical tests as they flew to Texas. They got the news as they arrived at the ballpark for an off-day workout.

Torre gathered the team together and told them that Strawberry had a malignant tumor on his colon. Cancer. One hundred and sixteen wins were temporarily made meaningless.

Fortunately, the team had a day to refocus, and Strawberry sent the ballclub a taped message before game three. It helped them to see him looking upbeat, and for the first time all year they went out and played for something more than the record books. Cone was magnificent,

pitching shutout ball for 5⅔ innings before a three-hour rain delay. When it ended, the pen took over, Shane Spencer kept dancing with the Prince and cracked another home run, as did Paul O'Neill, and the Yankees won, 4–0. Yankee pitching had held the Rangers to only 13 hits in three games.

Meanwhile, the Cleveland Indians, sans Randy Johnson, beat everybody but Boston's Pedro Martinez and dumped the Red Sox in four games to earn a place in the seven-game ALCS. Like the Rangers, the Indians, with Jim Thome, Dave Justice, and Manny Ramirez, had plenty of pop. But also like Texas, Cleveland's pitching was thin. The Yankees were expected to win easily. Justice moaned, "We don't have an advantage over them in any phase of the game."

In the midst of the Division Series against Texas, the joy of the Yankees' record-breaking 1998 season was diminished by the news that outfielder Darryl Strawberry had been diagnosed with a malignant tumor of the colon. He is shown here at Yankee Stadium, a month before his fateful medical exam.

Torre stuck with what got him there, and the Yankees bombed wanna-be Yankee-killer Jaret Wright in the first inning of game one and coasted to a 7–2 win behind Wells. Then the Indians finally provided the Yankees with a test.

This time around Torre wanted two lefties available for the middle games in Cleveland, so Cone started game two. He and Charles Nagy matched zeroes for most of the game, as New York's hitters couldn't adjust to Nagy's steady diet of off-speed pitches. With the score tied 1–1, both teams went to the bullpen, and each bullpen held.

With Cleveland's Enrique Wilson on first in the 12th, Travis Fryman bunted. Tino Martinez fielded the ball and threw to Knoblauch covering first, but the throw caromed off Fryman's back.

While 50,000 Yankees fans screamed at Knoblauch, he stood like a statue, pointing at the ground and arguing that Fryman had been out of the baseline and should have been called out. But as any Little Leaguer can tell you— GO GET THE BALL FIRST. While Knoblauch pled his case, Wilson and Fryman kept running. Wilson scored, and Fryman made it to third before the ball was retrieved. Rattled, pitcher Jeff Nelson gave up two more runs, and Cleveland walked off with a 4–1 win.

No one in New York enjoyed the result save for the headline writers at the tabloids—they termed it either "Brainlauch" or "Block-Head." Knoblauch, who hadn't performed up to the expected standard in 1998, didn't help matters by trying to talk his way out of it afterward before

Of course it's the money.

But it's not *only* the money. And that distinction makes all the difference.

Since 1903 the New York Yankees have been among the wealthiest teams in baseball, but it is incorrect to attribute all of their success to the size of their bank account. In fact, for most of their tenure atop the baseball world one or more other teams have had just as much if not more money than the Yankees. But no other team has spent it as wisely and as well.

Under Jacob Ruppert, the Yankees were probably the wealthiest team in baseball. But the personal resources of Tom Yawkey, who purchased the Red Sox in 1933, far outstripped those of the Yankees. For much of the next 45 years Boston's payroll was larger than that of the Yankees. The Milwaukee Braves of the late 1950s, Walter O'Malley's Dodgers in the 1960s, and the Cardinals of August Busch were all similarly capable of outspending the Yankees.

In recent years, under George Steinbrenner, the Yankees' financial advantage —much of it due to a series of lucrative

television contracts—has in general been more pronounced. At any given time during Steinbrenner's reign, however, there have been as many as a half-dozen other teams with similar resources— Ewing Kaufman's Kansas City Royals, Gene Autry's California Angels, and Ted Turner's Atlanta Braves, for example. It is interesting to note that from 1982 to 1993, despite the abundance of their resources, the Yankees won nothing. Since 1994 the Yankees have enjoyed a substantial advantage over "small market" teams, but other clubs have matched them in spending. In 2001 the Disney-owned Dodgers and the Red Sox both had payrolls virtually identical to New York's. The difference in wins and losses, however, was dramatic.

The truth is that the Yankees have done more with their money than other clubs. Many of their best players (Rizzuto, McDougald, Bernie Williams, Rivera) were acquired for virtually nothing. They have taken chances on players whom other teams shied away from (DiMaggio, Mantle, Strawberry, Orlando Hernandez), and

they have signed players to long-term free agent contracts that were bargains by the time they expired (Reggie Jackson, Dave Winfield, Tino Martinez).

The strength of the organization hasn't been limited to the field. The front office has done its job, creating in recent years a climate that players find attractive. While other clubs, such as the Red Sox and Rangers, have spent their fortunes on hitters, the Yankees have focused on pitching and poured their profits back into the farm system, ensuring a continuing stream of talent from which to draw.

Sure, money is important. Because of their wealth, the Yankees have been able to afford mistakes that might have crippled other teams (Ed Whitson, Danny Tartabull), but over a century their success has demonstrated that the price of mediocrity is even more costly. Consider this: since 1923 the Yankees have spent close to a billion dollars on salaries, making the average cost of each of their 26 world championships around $40 million. Their cost per world championship has been less than any other team in baseball.

finally giving up and admitting, "I screwed up the play." The Indians had stolen a win in the kind of game the Yankees usually won.

Confidence matters, and now the Indians believed. In Cleveland for game three they pounded Andy Pettitte for four home runs, catching Torre on his heels. He had to leave Pettitte in to get pounded while he got someone up and throwing in the bullpen. By then it was too late. Bartolo Colon blew fastballs by the Yankees, and the Indians won 6–1, making 114 wins look less impressive by the minute.

No one on the team was hitting the ball. In previous seasons Torre had responded to loss by turning to matchups, but with Strawberry out and Spencer hitting like a mortal again, his options were limited, and he stuck with what had worked all year long. The Yankees entered game four with the season on the line and an unknown commodity, El Duque, on the mound.

Hernandez had won 12 games during the year but at times had trouble with left-handed hitters, a Cleveland strength. To succeed he had to pitch inside and spot his breaking ball over. Otherwise, lefties pounded him. He hadn't pitched in 15 days, and there was no way of knowing how the layoff had affected him or whether the pressure would get to him.

But El Duque seemed either blissfully unaware of the pressure or wise beyond his years (however many that was). He dismissed thoughts of pressure, telling the press through an interpreter, "I've pitched big games before." After all, as Hernandez had noted earlier, "In Cuba, you win or you die."

This was nothing. After Paul O'Neill gave the Yankees a lead with a first-inning home run off former Yankee Dwight Gooden, El Duque was at his best against the Indians. He kept them off balance with pitches he seemed to pull out of the air — sidearm curves, three-quarter fastballs, and the occasional slider and change, all thrown to the perfect spot.

The Yankees tied the series with the 4–0 victory, leading Jeter to comment, "Duque is the whole story." The win was huge, perhaps the most important of the season. Hernandez himself put it best. "I had pressure," he said, "but no fear."

Neither did the Yankees, not with Wells and Cone scheduled to pitch the next two games. The Indians had missed their chance. The Yankees finally started hitting, and Wells coolly dispatched the Indians, 5–3, even taking time to pause in wonder at a long home run he gave up to Jim Thome, smiling and mouthing the word "Wow!" and then getting back to work. In game six the Yankees broke out to a six-run lead early, stopped an Indian rally in the fifth, then put Torre's six-inning rule into effect. Jeter broke Cleveland's back with a big triple, and Mendoza and Rivera closed the door on the Indians' season. The Yankees won 9–5.

The San Diego Padres prevailed over the Braves in the NLCS, provoking a yawn, since most observers expected a quick, brutal Yankee win over the Padres in the World Series. But you weren't supposed to say so.

Somebody forgot to tell David Wells the rules. Asked during an appearance on Howard Stern's radio show how many games it would take the Yankees to win, Wells responded, "Oh, five." He then added, "I'd like to wrap it up in four." That kind of bravado usually gets blown back in the face of the transgressor.

In game one the motivated Padres belted Wells and led 5–2 in the sixth inning, but this was New York's year and comebacks were becoming a trademark of Torre's team. The Yankees exploded for seven runs to get Wells off the hook as the slumping Knoblauch and Martinez — whom Buster Olney of the *Times* called "as popular as squeegee men a week ago" — both homered to account for all seven runs. San Diego's hopes in the Series had rested with starter Kevin Brown; there seemed little chance they could win unless Brown shut down the Yankees. He hadn't. The Padres were helpless.

Over the next three games the Yankees toyed with the Padres. San Diego led all of one inning as almost every Yankee got into the act. New York won 9–3, 5–4, and 3–0 behind Hernandez, Cone, and Pettitte. Scott Brosius hit two home runs in game three, knocked in six for the Series, and was named MVP. Rickey Ledee, a surprise starter in game one, hit .600. Jeter was in the middle of everything, and the bullpen gave up two runs. The four-game sweep, the Yankees' first in a World Series since 1950 and their 24th overall, gave the Yankees a final record of 125–50, a winning percentage of .714. Every Yankee fan in the world caught the significance of that — 714 is also Babe Ruth's career home run total.

Now the Yankees had the evidence. All year long they had stayed out of the debate over whether they were the greatest team of all time. But with the Series sweep and 125 wins, they finally allowed themselves to say publicly what they had thought all along. "I don't see how you can't say we're the greatest team ever," said Jeter. "We won 125 games. . . . We are unselfish and don't care who the hero is." Torre chimed in: "This team could influence how you put a team together down the road." Despite all the money Steinbrenner had spent over the years, this team was as much a product of scouting and the savvy management of its disparate parts as it was of contracts. The Yankees got more than their money's worth in guys like Scott Brosius, Joe Girardi, El Duque, Spencer, Curtis, Sojo, and Mike Stanton, who had all been picked up on the cheap. Only the Yankees had been wise enough to acquire them. The core of the team—Jeter, Williams, Pettitte, Rivera, and Posada—were all products of the farm system. And vets like Strawberry and Raines had willingly submitted to smaller roles in order to win. Only Cone, Wells, and Knoblauch qualified as high-priced mercenaries. Even so, Cone and Wells had thrived in New York like they would have nowhere else. One writer described their season accurately as "175 games, 125 wins, 0 excuses." The wonder is that they weren't even better, for no one on the team had a monster year. Chili Davis missed virtually the entire season, El Duque played only a little over half the season, and Knoblauch was a huge disappointment, neither hitting nor fielding as well as expected. Catcher Joe Girardi, for one, believed the Yankees could be even better in 1999.

New York fell all over itself celebrating the win, throwing the club a huge ticker-tape parade. But elsewhere reaction was subdued. The Yankees had been so dominant that their victory was expected. Television ratings for the Series reached an all-time low.

In their hometown, however, the Yankees' return to glory seemed to mirror a revival of the entire city as New York rode the wave of America's economic good times higher than anyplace else. Money was pouring into New York. Not only did the city never sleep, it never napped. Under mayor Rudy Giuliani, New York had embarked on a massive public relations campaign, clearing Manhattan of the dirt and the grime and the crime, along with the homeless, the hookers, the sex shops of Times Square, and

much of what had once scared away the tourists. Critics complained that Manhattan was being turned into some kind of urban theme park. Meanwhile, the city was rocked by a series of police brutality cases and other civil rights complaints, but those for whom the living was easy found these issues easy to ignore. Steinbrenner was politicking for a new ballpark, preferably in Manhattan, and for the first time the city seemed amenable to working something out. Giuliani himself was a huge Yankees fan, and he wasn't shy about basking in the team's reflected glory. They were New York's team now, as bright and brassy as the city itself.

The pressure to repeat as champions in 1999 began even before city sanitation workers had finished sweeping up after the parade. Although most people realized that another 114 wins might not be achievable, another 100 wins and another world championship seemed all but certain if Cashman and Steinbrenner could manage to keep the team intact—or improve it. Steinbrenner was starting to think of his legacy. In recent years it had become a cliché to describe him as having "mellowed." Not quite true, for no one was sure to what degree winning simply masked the same old George, but even if he wasn't quite a kindly old grandfather yet, neither was his name always paired with an epithet. Fans hadn't chanted "Steinbrenner sucks" in the Stadium in years.

Jeter was the Yankees' marquee player, but Bernie Williams was just as central to their success. When Williams hit, the Yankees won—always. The first player in baseball history to win a batting title, a Gold Glove Award, and a World Series ring in the same season was now eligible for free agency.

Williams was miffed that he hadn't been taken care of sooner, and Steinbrenner had apparently driven him away with a series of statements comparing him unfavorably to superstars such as Ken Griffey Jr., intimating that Williams wasn't worth their kind of money. Other clubs came to the opposite conclusion, recognizing that switch-hitting Gold Glove center fielders who can hit for power and average and go from first to third on singles are a pretty rare commodity. They were thrilled to find Williams available and took a page out of Steinbrenner's playbook: adding Williams to their own roster while subtracting him from New York's would serve a dual purpose. The Red Sox were the most active bidders, with Buck Showalter's Arizona Diamondbacks not far behind. Obsessed with topping the Yankees, Boston made Williams an offer in excess of $91 million.

The Yankees started looking elsewhere. Steinbrenner wined and dined Atlanta free agent Brian Jordan at the 21 restaurant, and the club even looked into signing problematic slugger Albert Belle, who was apparently willing to accept the five-year $60 million deal that Williams had turned down.

But at the same time, after giving every indication they would not, the club re-signed Scott Brosius and David Cone, a signal that sentimentality was now a part of New York's decision-making process. Steinbrenner had fallen in love with this group of players and with the notion of winning yet another championship with essentially the same team. That spelled dynasty, something few owners in professional sports have on their résumé.

That boded well for Williams, who felt the same way. He'd been a Yankee for life and decided that the level of comfort he found in the Yankee clubhouse wasn't guaranteed elsewhere at any price. At the last minute, just as the Yankees were preparing to sign Belle, both sides moved, and Williams signed with the Yankees on November 28 for seven years at $87.5 million. "I had to follow my heart," he said later. New York also decided to pick up Joe Girardi's option for one more season. The team and city that once had a hard time attracting players now had a hard time getting rid of them—everyone, save a few younger players pining for playing time, wanted to stay. Even more important, players from other teams now began to scheme for a way to get to New York.

The Yankees seemed content to enter 1999 with what they finished with in 1998. But that feeling lasted only until the beginning of spring training.

Roger Clemens left the Boston Red Sox as a free agent at the end of the 1996 season when general manager Dan Duquette claimed he was "in the twilight of his career." After dissing the Yankees, Clemens had put together back-to-back Cy Young seasons with the Toronto Blue Jays, winning his last 15 decisions in 1998. The Jays played in the AL East, however, and unless the city of New York migrated several hundred miles to the west, the Blue Jays were destined to spend another fall in front of the TV.

On October 24 the greatest Yankee team of them all rode through a blizzard of confetti in Manhattan's "Canyon of Heroes." Darryl Strawberry and his wife acknowledge the multitudes on their way to a ceremony at City Hall.

Clemens turned 35 in 1998. He still lusted after a World Series ring; the sting of the excruciating Red Sox loss in 1986 to the Mets hadn't fully abated, and his career was marred by a 1–2 record in six postseason starts. Boggs had gotten his ring in New York, and now Clemens was thinking about making a similar move. Earlier in his career he'd refused to entertain the notion of going to New York. But the Yankees' recent record and changing perceptions of the city made Clemens revisit the notion. The more he did, the more he liked it.

On July 18, 1999, "Yogi Berra Day" at Yankee Stadium, David Cone needed only 88 pitches to secure a perfect-game victory over the Montreal Expos. Among the spectators was Yankee perfect-game legend Don Larsen, who'd flown in to pay tribute to Berra.

On the precipice of spring training the Jays contacted Cashman and let him know that Clemens was available. When he heard that, Cashman reportedly admitted later, "it made my knees weak." The Yankees were already great. Add Clemens and there seemed to be no suitable adjective.

Of course, the Jays weren't going to give him away. They wanted the usual package of prospects and a starting pitcher—a good one—in return. They wanted David Wells, he of the 8–1 postseason record and 27–7 lifetime mark in Yankee Stadium.

Moreover, since pitching his perfect game Wells had emerged as one of the team's most popular players—not a teen idol like Derek Jeter, but a workingman's favorite like Bauer and Munson and Piniella had been, the guy you wanted to sit down and have a beer with. With Wells, if you knew where he hung out, you could actually do that.

Steinbrenner had always wanted Clemens. The certain Hall of Famer appealed to his vanity in the same way Reg-

gie and Winfield once had. Although the Boss was personally fond of Wells, sentimentality had its limits. The Yankees worried about his weight and long-term production, and he was no younger than Clemens. Steinbrenner gave Cashman the go-ahead, and in exchange for Wells, Graeme Lloyd, and infielder Homer Bush, Roger Clemens became a Yankee.

Wells was stunned. So were most Yankee fans, who vented on the talk shows for weeks. Wells had to go into hiding for a few days to get over it. "It was always my dream to be a Yankee," he said, "but I understand the business."

Clemens had never been a favorite in New York—like many other Boston players, his reputation was that of a selfish player concerned only with his statistics. Envisioning him in pinstripes was nearly impossible—he'd been vilified in New York in 1998 after beaning Brosius and Jeter. Fans had had the same problem with Wade Boggs. He'd eventually won them over, but only after hitting above .340 again and deferring to the "real Yankees" who preceded him on the club.

For all Clemens's talent, it was an awkward fit. He seemed diminished as a Yankee, overly cautious about not rocking the boat and about fitting in. "I just want to slide in the back door and get to work," he said. But by the end

of the spring that was the least of the Yankees' worries as they were hounded by a host of problems large, small, and symbolic. Joe DiMaggio died. Hideki Irabu showed up out of shape, and Steinbrenner called him a "fat toad." Darryl Strawberry, apparently healthy after surgery, started drinking again. And Joe Torre was diagnosed with prostate cancer. The Yankees seemed to have cornered the market on private tragedy played out in public. Fortunately, doctors caught the problem in time, but Torre would miss the beginning of the season. Bench coach Don Zimmer took over.

The Yankees seemed out of sync. Nothing came easy in 1999. Although they won 20 of their first 30 under Zimmer, they had to battle. Clemens, after a quick start, became inconsistent after he pulled a hamstring in late April. Torre returned on May 18, but the Yankees ground gears as Boston refused to fall back.

Jeter and Hernandez were keeping them afloat. The shortstop appeared ready to eclipse even the lofty expectations that surrounded him. Over the first half of the season he was arguably the best player in baseball. He hit outside pitches the other way and turned on the ball inside with power, all while displaying an impeccable batting eye that put him on base at least once in the first 53 games of the season. El Duque emerged as the staff ace as the

other starters scuffled or slid backward. Pettitte was so bad that the Boss wanted to trade him before being convinced by Cashman, Torre, and Stottlemyre that young, established left-handed pitchers are not exactly disposable. The Yankees were still good, but not close to great.

The only perfect moment of the regular season took place on July 18. After a long estrangement that stemmed from his firing as manager, Yogi Berra and George Steinbrenner had finally made up, and the Yankees decided to celebrate the occasion by holding "Yogi Berra Day." Don Larsen was a special guest.

Cone's patented "Laredo" slider was never better than it was that day against the Expos. The *Post*'s Joel Sherman was watching the game at home when he saw Cone strike out the side in the third. That convinced him that Cone had no-hit stuff, and he hustled over to the Stadium.

Despite a 33-minute rain delay after the third inning, it took Cone only 88 pitches to complete the 16th perfect game in baseball history. After Scott Brosius caught Orlando Cabrera's foul pop-up for the final out, Cone fell to his knees, hands on his head in disbelief. The Yankee scoreboard operator, taking note of the presence of the Larsen-Berra battery, flashed the Berra-ism "It's deja vu all over again" on the scoreboard.

The Yankees finally opened up some space in the pennant race in August and entered September with a 7½ game lead over Boston. But when the Red Sox swept the Yankees in midmonth to virtually clinch a wild-card spot and pull within 3½ of the Yankees, it was time to get serious.

Pedro Martinez had beat them 4–1 in the finale in a pitching performance so dominant that it would have been considered the best-pitched game of all time if not for Chili Davis's line-drive home run, New York's only hit. Seventeen Yankees went down on strikes. But Paul O'Neill placed it in perspective, saying, "The Red Sox didn't beat us. Pedro Martinez beat us." And he could pitch only once a week.

These were, after all, the Red Sox, an organization known for snatching defeat from the jaws of victory. Inexplicably, they decided to give up the chase and settle for the wild-card berth, turning to a six-man pitching rotation to protect Martinez's delicate right arm. The Yankees got hot and finished with 98 wins, 16 fewer than in 1998, but still four games ahead of Boston.

AL West champion Texas proved no match for New York in the Division Series. They went three and out as Hernandez, Pettitte, and Clemens gave up only a single run and Rivera was his usual perfect self — he hadn't given up a run since mid-July. Jeter and Williams provided the offense, and the Yankees won 8–0, 3–1, and 4–0. The win set up an ALCS matchup with Boston, the first October meeting between the two old rivals since the 1978 playoff game.

Boston entered the postseason physically diminished. Not only had Pedro Martinez pulled a muscle in his back, but shortstop Nomar Garciaparra was bothered by a banged-up wrist. A series of bizarre roster moves had left Boston short of pitching and almost everything else. Still, fatalistic Red Sox fans, who always fall for stories about curses and other fables instead of paying attention to the facts, clung to the belief that the Yankees would play this October below the standard they had set across a century.

Yogi Berra nailed it again, telling Bernie Williams before the series began, "We've been playing these guys 80 years; they can't beat us." That wasn't any Berra-ism, just a fact that Boston quickly learned still rang true. In games one

and two the Red Sox squandered leads and fell apart late as the Yankees won, 4–3 and 3–2. They got a chance to gloat in game three back in Boston as Clemens fell fast and early to Martinez, 13–1, but it was a temporary and hollow victory. Jeter silenced the Fenway Park crowd with a first-inning home run in game four, and Pettitte and the Yankees smacked down the Red Sox 9–2, leaving petulant fans throwing bottles on the field. Then Hernandez won 6–1 and sent the Sox off to spend the rest of October where they have spent it for the last 80-some years — sitting at home waiting for next year.

For much of the year all New York quivered over the possibility that the city might experience its first subway series since 1956. The Mets won the NL wild-card race, then beat Arizona in the Division Series. But in the NLCS they lost the first three games to Atlanta. The Mets didn't quit, but they finally fell to the Braves in the 11th inning of game six. The century, and the decade, would end with yet another New York–Atlanta World Series.

The press hyped the matchup, not inaccurately, as the battle for the title "Team of the '90s," for between them the two clubs had won eight pennants and three world championships in the decade. With a win, the Braves could shake off the impression that for all their talent they had never really fulfilled their promise. But the Yankees had a chance to make history: to win their 25th world championship, the second in a row and the third in the last four seasons. No team had won back-to-back titles since the 1977 and 1978 Yankees, and no team had won as many as three of four since the Oakland A's won three straight from 1972 through 1974. Winning now would be even more impressive, for the additional round of playoffs instituted in 1994 had made reaching the World Series exponentially more difficult than before. Repeating as champion would border on the miraculous.

But these Yankees needed no miracle or magic, nothing but nine innings and 25 players, day in and day out. All they needed now was four games to prove it.

The Series opened in Atlanta. Hernandez faced Greg Maddux in game one after Tom Glavine, suffering from a stomach virus, was scratched. As Joe Torre later said, El Duque "had the best stuff he had all year." Hernandez struck out the side in the first inning, and eight of the first eleven hitters. But the twelfth batter was Chipper Jones, and he hit the only mistake Hernandez made all game high and deep to right, just fair, for a home run. Meanwhile, Greg Maddux was equally dominant. The Braves' lead held into the eighth.

Scott Brosius, who already had two of the Yankees' three hits, singled to left to open the inning. Torre now had a decision to make. Hernandez was throwing a one-hitter and showing no signs of tiring. Torre could leave him in to sacrifice or call on a pinch hitter. He made the call for Strawberry.

The slugger had made it back after colon cancer but hadn't done much in limited opportunities. Yet his reputation was enough to make baseball's best control pitcher too cautious. Strawberry walked, bringing up Knoblauch.

Knoblauch was supposed to be the final piece of the Yankee puzzle, a Gold Glove and nonpareil leadoff hitter. Instead, he was a puzzle himself as he became inconsistent at the plate and a growing disaster in the field. Knoblauch fell victim to so-called Steve Blass disease, named after the onetime Pirate star who inexplicably lost his ability to throw the ball remotely close to where he wanted to. While Knoblauch made bang-bang plays fine, routine throws of 40 or 50 feet often either sailed into the stands or hit the ground 10 feet short of Tino Martinez.

To his credit, Knoblauch didn't run away from the problem, quit, or alibi. Torre stuck with him, hoping he'd turn it around because when Knoblauch got on base there were few better leadoff hitters in baseball.

In this World Series that part of his game returned. He bunted, and Atlanta first baseman Brian Hunter couldn't make a play. Jeter's single tied the game and chased Maddux. Left-handed reliever John Rocker entered, and Paul O'Neill, who'd struggled all year and was now playing with bruised ribs, showed his mettle by knocking the ball through the infield to put the Yankees ahead. New York went on to take a 4–1 lead. The bullpen, backed by Rivera, was perfect again, and the Yankees walked off with the win.

If Rivera isn't the best reliever in baseball history, that's only because he hasn't played quite long enough. But he is unquestionably the best reliever, if not the best pitcher, ever to appear in the postseason. He grew up helping his father fish and playing on the rough fields of Panama,

making gloves out of cardboard and batting with tree limbs. He didn't start pitching until he was 19, but scouts noticed him right away and he was signed by the Yankees. When Torre arrived in 1996, he was initially unimpressed; Rivera, despite ungodly minor league numbers, had what Torre called "a fastball that was very straight." But when he moved into long relief full-time, his fastball got faster and moved, flowing from his smooth delivery and then exploding on the corners. After being made the closer in 1997, Rivera became as predictable as "three strikes and you're out." In October he has been virtually untouchable.

Game two went according to plan. After Major League Baseball introduced the All-Century Team before the game, the Team of the Century took the field. Knoblauch started the game with a hit, and the Yankees singled Braves starter Kevin Millwood to death and scored three first-inning runs. David Cone, who'd slumped since his perfect game, secured his reputation as a big game pitcher by hurling seven innings of one-hit ball before turning the game over to Mendoza and Jeff Nelson. Rivera wasn't even needed to secure the 7–2 win.

Back in New York the Braves seemed ready to ruin the franchise's 200th World Series game, storming Pettitte and taking a 5–1 lead. But as they threatened to add to the lead, Girardi cut down Bret Boone trying to steal third, and reliever Jason Grimsley gave New York 2⅓ scoreless innings.

Under Joe Torre, Yankee comebacks — a product of the manager's personality and an abundance of talent, particularly in the postseason — have almost become predictable. Falling behind never seems to rattle the Yankees, for they know that if they can make it close late in the game, the bullpen will hold firm and give them a chance to win. The manager constantly reminds his club to remain patient and "think in small bites." They did so again. Chad Curtis homered in the fifth, and Tino Martinez in the seventh. Then, in the eighth, Chuck Knoblauch lifted the ball ever so slightly over the left-field fence, into outfielder Brian Jordan's glove and then back out again, for a two-run home run to tie the game.

Torre turned to Rivera, who shut the Braves out in the ninth and tenth. In the bottom of that inning Chad Curtis came up again. When Brosius had congratulated him after

Following the Yankees' second consecutive World Series sweep, in 1999, George Steinbrenner raises his fist in triumph while awaiting the presentation of the world championship trophy from baseball commissioner Bud Selig. Yankee manager Joe Torre (right) prepares for the ceremony in more subdued fashion.

his earlier home run, Curtis responded, "I want to hit one that matters." Now he had his chance, and now he did, slamming the ball into the Yankee bullpen for a walk-off home run and a 6–5 win. They were one game away from a dynasty.

Ever since Torre's arrival, it seemed as if every season had been tempered by some kind of private tragedy. In 1996 it was Frank Torre's heart transplant. In 1998 both Andy Pettitte's and Scott Brosius's fathers had been seriously ill, and Darryl Strawberry was diagnosed with cancer. This season had started with DiMaggio's death and Torre's cancer. In September Catfish Hunter died, as did Maury Brosius. Luis Sojo said his final good-bye to his father Ambrosio on October 22 and had to miss the first two games of the Series.

It was almost eerie, as if this most privileged franchise always had to be put to a larger challenge. But these Yankees were more than a collection of players, more than a product of money. They were tested again and again and passed each time, displaying qualities that can't be bought and sold on the free agent market, called up on command,

or credited to any single man. They understood, deeply, that while there were more important things than baseball, they were still a team with a job to do and they depended on each other. Perhaps they won so much because they came to understand what real loss was. Now, in the hours before game four, Paul O'Neill's father passed away.

Paul O'Neill will never make the Hall of Fame, but he is unquestionably a member of a more exclusive club, one that measures determination and value to the Yankees and made him perhaps the most beloved player on the team. Since arriving in New York, he had played every game as if it were his last, and he approached every at bat as if he might not have another. It was the way his father, a minor league ballplayer, had taught him. The son played the game the same way and would play game four that way as well.

In game four the Yankees pushed for the summit. Roger Clemens, looking for both acceptance and retribution, pitched the best game of his Yankee career thus far. In the third New York scored in typical fashion. Knoblauch started it with an infield hit, and Jeter moved him to third with a hit-and-run single. Williams walked, Tino Martinez singled off Ryan Klesko's glove, and when Posada singled, it was suddenly 3–0.

Torre wasn't taking any chances. In the eighth Knoblauch was replaced at second by Sojo. Knoblauch had done his job, leading the team with five Series runs. And Sojo, whose all-around contributions once led David Wells to describe him as "the most important guy on the team," was rewarded with the opportunity to protect the lead and be on the field for the final celebration. Clemens took a two-hitter into the inning—then, with two out, pulled a muscle covering first on Atlanta's third hit. Clemens tried to continue, but after he gave up another hit, Torre came and got him. As he walked off the field and turned the game over to Jeff Nelson, the crowd at Yankee Stadium gave him a standing ovation, finally accepting him. "I feel like a Yankee now," he said later. After Nelson gave up a single to make the score 3–1, Torre called on Rivera, who calmly dispatched Chipper Jones on a ground ball to Sojo.

Jim Leyritz, who'd returned to New York after a brief exile, capped the game in the bottom of the eighth with another home run, and Rivera took the mound in the ninth with victory in his right hand. It was October, and he was near automatic: the lowest ERA in postseason baseball history was about to go even lower, to 0.38. When the final out settled in Chad Curtis's glove in left field, the Yankees were champions again.

A quick celebration on the mound—termed a "happy scrum" by the *Times*—quickly evaporated into a group embrace around Paul O'Neill. He broke down as his teammates shielded him from the television cameras and allowed him to escape the field and grieve in private. In the clubhouse they sprayed some champagne but played no music out of respect to O'Neill, celebrating instead to the faint sounds that filtered in from the stands.

No team has ever accomplished what the 1998 and 1999 Yankees did. They became the first team to win the World Series in back-to-back sweeps since the 1938 and 1939 Yankees, and the first and only team to do so since realignment. In postseason play across two seasons they went 11–2 and 11–1, a combined 22–3 against the best competition baseball had to offer. They won six postseason series in a row and, since game three of the 1996 World Series, 12 straight Series contests.

The last game provided the exclamation point for a century of baseball that the Yankees claimed as their own. With their 25th world championship banner poised to rise above Yankee Stadium, the win was not a celebration of individuals but the culmination of the legacy of the team in the city of New York. "We are," said George Steinbrenner, "a tough team that depicts the town." Over the next two seasons both would be tested.

Mayor Rudolph Giuliani is embraced by Yankee manager Joe Torre during ceremonies on September 25, 2001, at Yankee Stadium honoring the victims of the World Trade Center terrorist attack.

In New York, normalcy means the Yankees in the World Series.

— NEW YORK MAYOR RUDY GIULIANI,
September 25, 2001

2000-2002
NEW YORK STORIES

Baseball in New York hadn't been this good in a long time. The 1999 season had been a wonderful tease that reminded both Yankees and Mets fans that it could get even better. Since the advent of interleague play, the rivalry between the two teams had been heating up, and New Yorkers dreamed of an October meeting, a subway series, a notion that had lain dormant since 1956.

To make that wish reality both clubs had some work to do. Baseball may have anointed the Yankees as the Team of the Century, but the competition was more determined than ever to start the next century with a new champion.

Despite the Yankees' back-to-back world championships, many outside New York believed that their time had passed. They were getting old. Chili Davis retired, and Strawberry slipped back into the grip of addiction, ending his career. Girardi went home as a free agent to Chicago. Every member of the starting lineup, save Jeter and Posada, was over 30.

Cone, Clemens, Knoblauch, O'Neill, Martinez, and Brosius all seemed to be falling off. In retrospect, it now appeared as if many Yankees *had* had career years in 1998.

The Yankees grappled with the question not only of what to do next but how to do it. The old answers weren't readily available. They couldn't deal away their veteran stars because they were being paid too much, and no one in the farm system was quite ready to contribute. The list of available free agents provided an obvious solution.

Cleveland and Boston had the Yankees in their sights, and each acquired a left-handed pitcher — Chuck Finley and Jeff Fassero, respectively — solely for his ability to match up against the Yankees in the playoffs. The Braves added bats, and the Mets re-signed catcher Mike Piazza and added pitcher Mike Hampton and others. Piazza thrived in New York, putting the Mets on the back page again and replacing Jeter in the gossip columns.

Boston, with pitcher Pedro Martinez and shortstop Nomar Garciaparra, became the chic pick of many to supplant New York — *Sports Illustrated* even picked the Red Sox to win the World Series. The Yankees got off to a fast start, however, and after beating Tampa Bay on May 9 in New York, the Yanks were a comfortable 22–9 and led Boston by four.

But the starting rotation proved unreliable, and they soon slipped back to the pack. Clemens continued to labor, and David Cone kept getting drilled. Knoblauch's throwing woes were frightening, and he wasn't getting on base. Martinez and O'Neill weren't driving in runs.

Even the rare positive outing turned out wrong. On May 28, Roger Clemens and Pedro Martinez met at the Stadium in a classic pitchers' duel with first place on the line. For the first time since he joined the Yankees, Clemens looked like the scintillating strikeout artist he had been for much of his career. When he struck out Trot Nixon early in the game and Nixon gave him a look, Clemens barked back, "That's a strike," and stomped around the mound, the King of the Hill again.

But with two out in the ninth, Nixon cracked a home run. Ballgame. Boston won 2–0 and took over first place.

The king of the hill was then rocked in his next two starts and went on the DL on June 15 with groin trouble. On June 28, after losing six of seven, the Yankees were 37–35, three games behind the surprising Blue Jays. A scout

summed up the team's problems for the *Post:* "Joe Torre always had a great bench and a deep pitching staff. Look at them now: no bench, a rotation that's one arm short, a lineup that's still one big bat short. They might still win it, but they're not special anymore." The Mets, on the other hand, looked special that year.

The Yankees decided to rebuild — not for next year, since under Steinbrenner next year is not an option, but for now. The Cubs' Sammy Sosa seemed to be available, but his cost didn't equal his potential return. Even a Steinbrenner budget had limits. Instead, they filled more holes for less money.

Cashman had been working the phones and was stunned to learn that Cleveland, looking to shed some salary, was willing to part with slugger David Justice. They didn't even want much in return, asking for Rickey Ledee, who starred in the 1998 World Series but hadn't done much since, and two minor league pitchers.

As Torre said later, Justice was "a perfect fit" for the Yankees — a big bat and potent veteran with postseason experience who didn't need to be the big star. He changed the complexion of the team, giving it a genuine home run threat in the middle of the order. Four days later Clemens came back off the DL and began to look like the pitcher the Yankees had traded for — "the Rocket," the intimidating, unstoppable force and power pitcher supreme. On July 7, the Yankees faced the Mets in interleague play and took three of four, spiced on July 8 by a Clemens fastball that struck Piazza on the side of the head and knocked him from the lineup.

The pitch caused a firestorm. Piazza had been seven for twelve against Clemens in his career, with three home runs. Piazza said afterward of Clemens: "I really can't say I have any respect for him." Clemens, as expected, admitted to pitching inside but claimed the pitch was an accident. Still, the purpose pitch delivered its intended message: for the rest of the season no one came to bat against Clemens without recalling the sight of Piazza lying dazed on the ground.

The Yankees needed that, because apart from Pettitte, the rest of the rotation was a shambles. El Duque was inconsistent and battling arm problems, and David Cone's fastball had no life, his slider no bite. He kept getting creamed. Torre showed remarkable patience and pitched

Cone every fifth day, but it hadn't been so painful watching a pitcher in pinstripes since Ed Whitson, and Cone deserved a better end.

The Yankees reluctantly accepted the fact that Cone might be done and dealt four top prospects for Cincinnati pitcher Denny Neagle, then picked up another big bat in Chicago's Glenallen Hill.

Now Torre had, as he put it, "a lot of little pieces that worked," as well as a lot of big pieces. Neagle gave them the extra arm and won five of his first seven. Hill shored up the bench and hit like Spencer had at the end of 1998, while Justice had the best half-season of his career.

As the season wound down, the Yankees kept picking up more valuable spare parts — Jose Canseco, Luis Polonia, Jose Vizcaino — and even brought back Luis Sojo, who'd signed with Pittsburgh. On September 13, Clemens won his seventh straight with a 3–2 win over Toronto. The Yankees, at 84–59, led Boston by 9 with only 19 games left.

Then the Yankees stumbled. They careened through the rest of the season, at one point trailing for an incredible 63 consecutive innings, losing 16 of 19, and looking like the worst team in baseball. Had the Red Sox not given up, they might have caught the Yankees, who won the division by only two and a half games at 87–74, the worst record of any of the eight postseason teams and only the ninth-best record in baseball. Finishing 94–68, the Mets won the National League wild card, second in the NL East behind Atlanta.

"I have a sense that what happened in the previous couple of weeks is not going to affect us," said Torre. That was the right thing to say, but the words rang hollow. The Yankees hadn't backed into the postseason, they had crawled. They were due to face the brassy and ballsy Oakland Athletics in the Division Series with little in their favor but history.

Torre had to manage again like he had in 1996, making use of matchups. He pulled Knoblauch and made him the occasional DH, installed Luis Sojo at second, and sent Cone, perhaps the best big game pitcher of his generation, to the bullpen.

The A's were oblivious. Number-four starter Gil Heredia outpitched Clemens in game one, and New York lost 5–3. All that stood between the Yankees and an apparently insurmountable two-game deficit was Andy Pettitte.

Catcher Jorge Posada was considered by many to have been the most valuable player of the 2000 Yankees. In a breakthrough season made difficult by his infant son's chronic illness, Posada handled an ever-changing roster of pitchers and hit .287 with 28 homers and 86 RBIs.

Since joining the Yankees in 1996, Andy Pettitte has been a given. While Cone and Wells and Clemens have garnered headlines, Pettitte has just kept winning, the one constant in the rotation. He has always won the game the Yankees needed most — coming back after being blown out in the first game of the 1996 World Series to win game five, winning the Series finale in 1998, stopping Boston after the Clemens blowout in the 1999 ALCS. "Forget what everyone says," said Oakland GM Billy Beane before the game. "He's the team's ace. Every time there's a must-win game . . ." The A's hadn't beaten him in three years.

Pettitte completed Beane's sentence, shutting down MVP Jason Giambi to even the series, and the Yankees went on to beat the A's in five games. They were the Yankees again, renewed in the cool October air. Meanwhile, the Mets got past the Giants in the NL Division Series.

The Yankees met the Mariners in the ALCS, and after Freddy Garcia shut them out in game one, Hernandez and Pettitte came back to win the next two. With Clemens scheduled to start game four, the whispers that he couldn't win big games had grown louder. He'd lost his only start in the Division Series and did not yet inspire confidence among Yankee fans.

It wasn't an entirely fair perception — Clemens had usually pitched well only to have his bullpen let him down. But his failures had been dramatic — losing his cool and being thrown from the game in the 1990 ALCS, and getting shelled by the Red Sox in the 1999 playoffs. Although the Yankees had won 28 of their last 33 postseason games, Clemens had three of those five losses.

As Clemens described it later, the ball was "flying out of my hand" in game four. The defining moment of the contest — and in fact of the entire postseason — came when Alex Rodriguez stepped to the plate with two out in the first inning. Two fastballs flew out of Clemens's hand toward A-Rod's head, and one of them sent him on his back.

While Rodriguez reacted with a wry smile, Mariner manager Lou Piniella and the rest of the Seattle bench exploded. "It's mind-boggling how a guy can go corner to corner and then miss up and in," said Rodriguez. A-Rod struck out, and before the game was done, Clemens punched out a total of 15, giving up only a single hit, a seventh-inning double to Al Martin that glanced off Tino Martinez's glove. The Yankees won 5–0. Although Seattle came back to win game five, Justice and Williams keyed a

Andy Pettitte was the Yankees' most consistent starter in their latest dynasty. Before the 2000 playoffs, Oakland general manager Billy Beane told a reporter, "He's the team's ace. Every time there's a must-win game . . ."

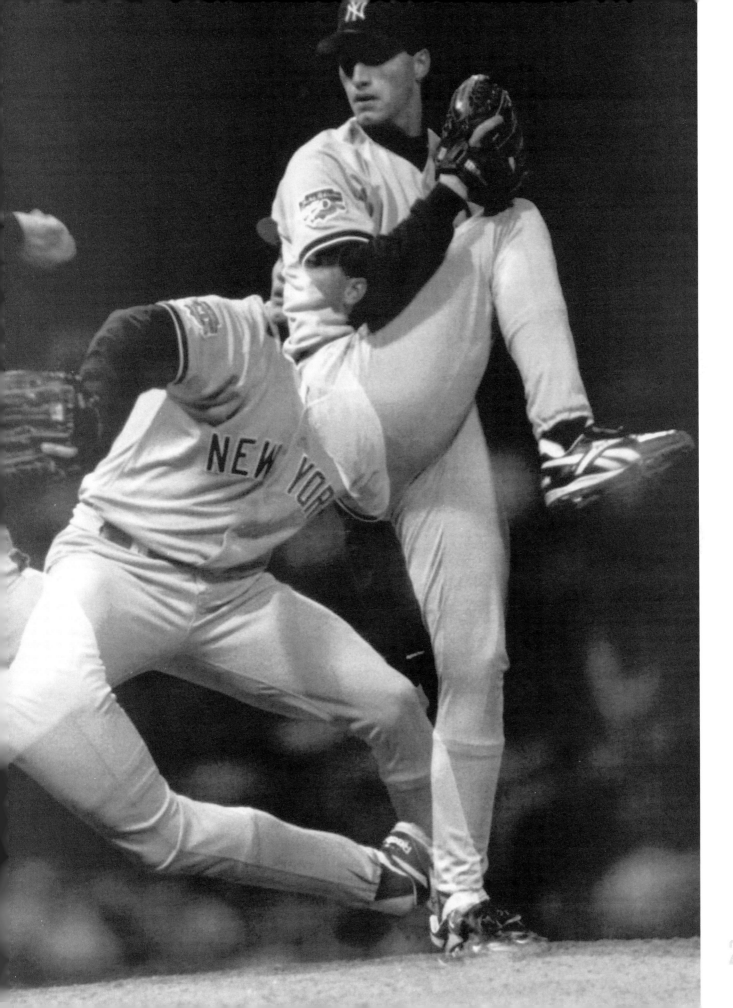

2002

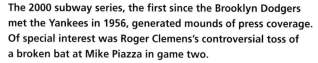

The 2000 subway series, the first since the Brooklyn Dodgers met the Yankees in 1956, generated mounds of press coverage. Of special interest was Roger Clemens's controversial toss of a broken bat at Mike Piazza in game two.

comeback in game six, and the Mariners went down to Hernandez for the second time.

The Mets did their part, knocking off St. Louis in the NLCS, and the subway series was a reality. The number 7 train from Queens and the number 4 from the Bronx, with a change at Grand Central. Two at the Stadium followed by as many as three at Shea, and potentially two more back at the Stadium.

Since 1956 the cost of a subway token might have risen from 15 cents to $1.50, but one thing hadn't changed: baseball was once again the number-one topic of conversation in all five boroughs as all New York seemed to pause. Hats, T-shirts, jackets, and pennants were for sale on every corner—some of it even legal and authorized—as Mets or Yankees garb became de rigueur. The tabloids reserved the front and back pages of the newspaper for the matchup, pushing other news, such as the presidential race and the recent terrorist bombing of the USS *Cole,* far inside—out of sight and out of mind. Terrorism was of some concern— after all, the eyes of the sporting world would all be focused on one place. The *Daily News* reported that, according to Giuliani, "extra cops will be deployed at the World

Series games due to the specter of terrorism—not out of fear of warfare between Mets and Yankee fans."

Rudy Giuliani beamed—he'd promised New York a subway series when he first ran for mayor seven years before, and the event gave the city an opportunity to show itself off and bask in the attention like no place else could or would. Although Steinbrenner remained relatively quiet, the Yankees knew that while winning the subway series would offer the greatest prize, the Boss would make losing insufferable. As George King quoted Paul O'Neill in the *Post,* for the Yanks it was: "Lose, and it's underground." That was pretty clear from the sign King noted on the wall of the batting cage deep inside the Stadium: "Yes, we do hate the Mets and Red Sox." But the Yankees watched what they said, at least to the press. They didn't want to provide any more motivation to the Mets.

That wasn't the case in Queens. The Mets made it clear that they hated the Yankees, particularly Clemens. When the press brought up the beaning of Piazza, they didn't shy away. Piazza called it a "cowardly act," and Todd Zeile said, "It is *not* ancient history."

The city was alive with baseball. The Yankees were on top and always had been, while the Mets still enjoyed playing the underdog. The Yankees were all business, the Mets more emotive. The Mets were on the way up, the Yankees on the way down. Yankee heroes were legends like Ruth,

DiMaggio, and Mantle. The Mets were still part Stengel and "Marvelous Marv" Throneberry. The Yankees were the last century, the Mets the next. It was the "Pride of the Yankees" versus the "Miracle Mets." Most of it was hype, because both clubs were among the richest in the game, but New York loved a good debate.

The only relief came when the Series started on October 21. Game one: Andy Pettitte versus Al Leiter. The Mets thought Torre was gutless for saving Clemens for game two. That decision ensured that he wouldn't pitch in Shea later and bat in front of the hostile crowd. But Torre's idea was to win, and Clemens's record in the Stadium was much better than elsewhere. Torre also didn't think his club needed the circus that would surely surround a Clemens appearance in Queens. He was more worried about beating Leiter. The onetime Yankee phenom, who had done for the Mets what Cone did for the Yankees, loved the pressure of being a number-one starter in New York. It would be Leiter's white heat, wearing every pitch on his sleeve, against the steely resolve of Andy Pettitte.

In the first few innings neither team was particularly sharp. But Leiter was on, and he overmatched the Yankees early. Pettitte kept working his way out of trouble, and the Mets kept helping him with one costly baserunning mistake after another. The gaffes kept the Mets from scoring, and the game entered the sixth scoreless.

Then, with Met rookie Timo Perez on first, Todd Zeile turned on a Pettitte fastball. The ball soared deep to left, and Zeile went into a home run trot. Timo Perez turned spectator and jogged to second.

The ball came down in left in front of longtime Yankee fan Jack Nelson near the intersection of sections 30 and 32. He resisted the urge to reach out and pluck the souvenir from the sky, and it struck the padded wall just short of the top and bounced back onto the field. Zeile, arm raised in premature triumph, looked to the umpire for the home run signal. None came. He started running harder. So did Perez, who had just rounded second.

But in left field David Justice was already running hard. He fielded the carom, whirled, and threw home. The ball tailed badly, heading toward the line.

Derek Jeter had moved out to take the cutoff, but as soon as he saw the throw go wide, he took off in a sprint, catching the ball on the fly while running toward the stands. In one motion he jumped and spun and threw home, just as he did after fielding a grounder in the hole.

The ball reached Posada on one bounce, one stride ahead of Perez, who slid into the tag. Out. For the fourth time bad baserunning had cost the Mets. Of course, few other shortstops would have had either the presence of mind or the athleticism of Jeter to make such a play, but it still cost the Mets a run.

The Series turned on the play, even though the Mets came back to lead 3–2 after the Yankees took a 2–0 lead in the sixth. The theme of lost opportunities would be the Mets' story line. Rivera held the Mets at bay, and Paul O'Neill, all determination, fought off ten pitches in the bottom of the ninth before walking. The Yankees went on to load the bases before Knoblauch, as DH, hit a sacrifice fly to tie the game. Then, in the 12th, José Vizcaino slapped

Second baseman Alfonso Soriano enjoyed a superb rookie season in 2001, capped by his two dramatic home runs in the World Series. He is shown after hitting the first of the pair, a game-winning two-run homer in game four at Yankee Stadium. In game seven, his eighth-inning homer gave the Yankees a short-lived lead.

a pitch into left, and the Yankees won the longest World Series game in history, 4–3, making bartenders happy all over New York.

Game one may have been the artistic success of the Series, but game two got all the attention. The Rocket was in launch mode and struck out the first two Met hitters before going to 1–2 on Piazza.

Clemens rode a fastball in on the hands, and Piazza fought it off, breaking his bat in half. The handle stayed in his hands and the rest of the bat went spinning toward Clemens as the ball bounded foul.

Clemens fielded the bat-head, thinking it was the ball, and then rejected it, pitching it sidearm hard into the ground toward the first-base line. As he did, a clearly confused Piazza started to run, slowed, then started up again and nearly ran into the bat.

What others saw was Clemens fielding the bat-head, glimpsing Piazza, and, in a moment of madness, deciding to take out his adversary with a well-timed toss.

It was a strange and scary moment as everyone waited, wondering whether a brawl was about to happen. Piazza did a slow burn, then started toward Clemens, arms spread wide, snapping, "What's your problem? What's your problem?" Clemens was already asking the umpire Charlie Relaford for a ball, and the umpire moved in between the two stars. "I thought it was the ball," Clemens kept saying. No one was thrown out, and no one fought, but no one forgot the episode either.

The bat had barely stopped rolling and this was the biggest story imaginable in the middle of what was already one of the biggest New York stories ever. Talk shows and tabloids prepared to take over.

The only thing certain is that the incident took the Mets out of the game, and perhaps the Series. In the bottom of the inning Mike Hampton struggled with his control, and the Yankees jumped ahead 6–0. Clemens made it through eight innings, and although the Mets stormed back with five ninth-inning runs, once the lead got down to one, Rivera abruptly ended the game.

Forty-eight hours of pure media frenzy followed, answering no questions and coming to no conclusions, churning the story over and over as the game tape of the incident was analyzed like the Zapruder film. Was Piazza right to be pissed? Should Clemens have thrown the bat? Those questions were easy. But was it intentional? That answer was more complicated.

Neither Roger Clemens nor any other pitcher can think that fast — the time from when the ball left his hand to when he threw the bat was less than two seconds. A bat flying out toward a pitcher is a moment of pure adrenaline. Instinct says it's a baseball, and when it's not, the next reaction is, it doesn't belong here. By the time any of those thoughts entered Clemens's brain, the bat was out of his hands and it was too late. That should have been the end of the story.

But this was New York, and it wasn't the end. Neither Clemens nor Piazza had the good sense to let it go. Baseball also seemed unable to decide precisely what had happened. Clemens was fined $50,000 over the incident but not suspended, which he undoubtedly would have been if Major League Baseball had been certain of his intent.

The Mets were all bluster and no bite afterward, and the end result was that the incident left them distracted and intimidated, while the Yankees stayed focused and won. Almost lost was the fact that by the time fans took the number 4 and 7 trains to Shea Stadium two days later for game three, the Yankees were ahead two games to none. Even better, they had the inscrutable El Duque, 8–0 in the postseason, on the mound. The Yankees were looking for their 15th straight Series win, and when Hernandez struck out the side to start the first, it looked like a short night for the Mets. But Steve Reed and four relievers proved better, and the Mets emerged with a 4–2 victory.

Then Jeter made his usual momentum-stopping appearance at the start of game four, homering on the first pitch of the game to snap the Mets off at the ground. But not until the fourth inning did the game reach the point of no return. With the Yankees nursing a 3–2 lead, Neagle was laboring. Torre had toyed with the idea of giving the start to David Cone — he still wanted to believe that in the big game, on the large stage, Cone's heart and head could override his arm. But as Torre mulled over the decision, Cone let him off the hook and took one for the team, saying he could pitch in relief.

Mike Piazza came up to bat in the fifth against Neagle. Torre didn't like the matchup and called on Cone. He worked quickly, going inside with his first pitch, then away with the next two, and then back inside. Piazza popped up to end the threat, and Cone left for a pinch hitter the next inning. It was fitting for his Yankee career, if it had to be over, to end in the Series. The six-inning rule held again, and the Yankees won 3–2 to put the Series on the brink.

Al Leiter was all guts and guile for the Mets in game five, but so was Pettitte. Manager Bobby Valentine stuck with Leiter despite the fact that he'd given up solo home runs to both Bernie Williams and Jeter, the eventual Series MVP. He took the mound in the ninth with nearly 130 pitches under his belt and the score tied 2–2.

He'd struck out the last two hitters in the eighth, and now he struck out the first two in the ninth, bringing up Posada. The Yankee catcher had slowly evolved into one of the best-hitting catchers in baseball. He came through with a typical Yankee at bat, exhausting Leiter over nine pitches before working a walk. Leiter visibly sagged as Posada jogged to first.

On pitch 141, Brosius singled, bringing up Luis Sojo, probably the most emblematic Yankee of them all. A player whose limited set of skills nevertheless played an important role on the team, Sojo provided defense and the ability to get the bat on the ball, as well as a habit of collecting more than his share of big hits. He knew his role.

He did it again, slapping Leiter's first pitch up the middle, an eight- or ten-bouncer into center field. Posada scored, and when the throw got away, so did Brosius. It was 4–2 and time to bring on Rivera.

Torre has said that after Rivera gave up the losing home run to Cleveland in 1997, he "did nothing but grow from that time on," evolving from a thrower to a pitcher. In the postseason Rivera changes the game.

The subway series ended with Rivera versus Piazza, speed versus power, a long drive to left center and Bernie Williams drifting back and the ball dying in his glove. In the Yankee clubhouse, the players chanted, "Three-peat, Three-peat," over and over again.

It did not seem possible for it to get much better. As Bernie Williams later said about playing the Mets, "It really made us feel like we were playing for something other than the World Series." He was right. They were playing for New York, something that was soon to take on even greater meaning.

Change was inevitable. Cone was a free agent and left for Boston, looking for a new start. Jeff Nelson, looking for a larger role and a lot more money, signed with Seattle.

But in this free agent market, Nelson and Cone hardly registered. Alex Rodriguez, Manny Ramirez, and Mike Mussina were three names that promised to change whichever team signed them. Everyone knew that at least one of them would probably land in New York.

With Jeter, the Yankees had no need for A-Rod. Ramirez was more intriguing. One of the top power-hitting outfielders in the game, the Dominican native grew up in Washington Heights, near the site of the old Hilltop Grounds. Ramirez and the Yankees made sense. A right fielder, he could move into Paul O'Neill's slot, provide a power bat, and play in his hometown.

But the Yankees never made a play for Ramirez. Under Cashman, the club has focused primarily on pitching. Mussina had anchored the Orioles for a decade, winning 147 games. The Yankees schmoozed him, starting with a personal chat with Joe Torre. Mussina wanted a ring and found the call of the Bronx irresistible. Soon after, the *Post Sports Weekly* featured a cover story that called the Yankee starting rotation "The Best Ever." Maybe not, but if everyone stayed healthy, the perception wasn't far off.

The only other change came in spring training. Knoblauch's throwing woes continued, and he was moved to the outfield, opening the way for Alfonso Soriano, a shortstop and designated future star. The Yankees turned him over to coach Willie Randolph to make him into a second baseman.

The 2001 season unfolded not unlike 2000. The Yankees got out fast and then sagged. El Duque was hammered before undergoing toe surgery that would sideline him until late August. Justice got off quick, then was slowed by a groin injury. Paul O'Neill hit a bunch of home runs early, then looked like he was playing one year too long. Knoblauch couldn't get on base. Jeter and Brosius both scrambled. And after going through their annual personal tragedy in 2000 when Mel Stottlemyre periodically had to leave the club to receive cancer treatments, in 2001 Bernie Williams's father became gravely ill. Torre allowed Williams to leave the club and take as much time as he needed. After several weeks he returned, clearly distracted, and then left again when his father passed away on May 18. In early June his batting average hovered around .200. In the meantime, the Red Sox had been riding Manny Ramirez's bat to an early lead. For the first two months of the season he seemed to have a lock on the Triple Crown, staying on pace to hit close to .400 with over 60 home runs and knock in 160. And Mussina? He struggled.

All the Yankees had was Roger Clemens, Andy Pettitte, and Mariano Rivera. In 2001, the soon-to-be 39-year-old Clemens was almost enough by himself.

He seemed rejuvenated by his performance the previous October and bounced back to resume the form that had already won him a record five Cy Young Awards. When he pitched well, Yankee wins were automatic. And when he didn't pitch well, the Yankees scored runs behind him and won anyway. He was a classic stopper who anchored the staff and set a sterling example for others with his work ethic. Pettitte even credited Clemens's off-season exercise regimen with helping him add three or four miles per hour to his fastball.

Clemens kept the Yankees close while they waited for Mussina to hit stride and for everyone else to get healthy. Kids like Ted Lilly and Randy Keisler tried to fill the void as fourth or fifth starters, but the bullpen was overworked and held together by string. Meanwhile, the Boston Red Sox, despite losing another player to injury every other week, just kept winning. They were gaining confidence, and the Yankees worried about falling too far behind.

The Yankees put together a streak just before the All-Star game and put some pressure on Boston, which finally showed some signs of cracking in the second half. They pulled ahead in mid-August and slowly started pulling away. With El Duque and Justice back and Mussina finally pitching well again, September was beginning to look like a good month.

They were a contender, but no longer the league favorite. The AL West Seattle Mariners were modeled after the 1998 Yankees, a smooth machine fueled by Japanese import Ichiro Suzuki. The Oakland A's, after a poor start, were surging and seemed a certain bet for the wild card. For the Yankees, it was the division title or nothing.

"There's something about Boston that scares me," said Joe Torre. The Yankees faced the Red Sox in a three-game set in Fenway Park beginning on August 31, the first of

With five Cy Young Awards, Roger Clemens dominated the American League once again in 2001 with a 20–3 record. His efforts garnered a sixth Cy Young and almost certain enshrinement in the Baseball Hall of Fame.

seven scheduled games between the two clubs in the next eleven days. Even though the Yankees now led by a full five games, with a sweep the Red Sox could make it a pennant race again. Sox fans recalled the Yankees near-collapse at the end of the 2000 season with relish.

But across three days the Yankees beat Boston in excruciating fashion. In the first game Clemens ran his record to 18–1, his 14th win in a row, as Posada cracked a late home run. The next day El Duque was at his mesmerizing best, beating Boston and Pedro Martinez 2–1 when Bernie Williams hit his second straight ninth-inning home run and increased New York's lead to seven. Boston's scribes dusted off their usual September screeds. The *Globe*'s Dan Shaughnessy moaned, "The Yankees have crushed the spirit of New England again. It's September, it's baseball, and the story never, ever changes." The Yankees had never squandered a seven-game lead in September and weren't about to start.

Mike Mussina capped it off the next day. Pitching opposite Cone, who'd regained much of his stuff in Boston,

The Yankees dropped the first two games of the divisional playoffs against the Athletics. Nevertheless, manager Joe Torre and general manager Brian Cashman found reason to smile as the two watched batting practice on the eve of the pivotal third game, in Oakland.

Mussina dominated, taking a perfect game to the last out, before losing it when Boston's Carl Everett fisted a clean hit into center. Mussina settled for a one-hit, 1–0 shutout, striking out 13.

The Yankees have broken New England's heart innumerable times over the years, but this was the worst. The Yanks departed from Boston with a comfortable eight-game lead, leaving the Red Sox in ruins, collapsed in their wake. Boston GM Dan Duquette, who had fired manager Jimy Williams a few weeks earlier, new manager Joe Kerrigan, and CEO John Harrington were instantaneously vilified.

On the evening of September 10, all New York looked to Yankee Stadium, where Clemens, pitching against Boston again, looked to stretch his winning streak to 15, win his 20th game, and rub it in against the club that had considered him "in the twilight of his career." On that same day

Steinbrenner's YankeeNets Corporation, the parent company he'd created that owned a majority interest in the Yankees as well as the NBA Nets and NHL New Jersey Devils, formed its own cable network, Yankee Entertainment and Sports (YES), and was immediately profitable, as 40 percent of the company was sold to investors for $345 million, guaranteeing that for the foreseeable future the financial health of the franchise would continue unabated.

But it rained in New York that night, causing the game to be canceled and robbing New York of the most anticipated game of the year. Clemens's start was pushed back to the following day, September 11, 2001.

As no one will ever be able to forget, 12 hours after the cancellation, Clemens's winning streak, the pennant race, the baseball season, and virtually everything else in New York City and much of the world ceased to be important anymore. The two towers of the World Trade Center were pierced by hijacked commercial jets manned by terrorists, lit like candles, and then fell to the ground in what was immediately termed the Pearl Harbor of our generation. Nearly 3,000 were killed.

Beat writers became war correspondents in a heartbeat. Firefighters became gravediggers, and heroes emerged from ash. Chuck Knoblauch watched the conflagration from his penthouse. Roger Clemens, who had a good friend whose mother-in-law was in one of the planes, immediately left the city and drove back to Texas with his wife to be with his kids. So did Tino Martinez. Yankees called Yankees to make sure everyone was all right. All across the rest of the nation, everyone else who had any connection at all to New York City reached out in similar fashion as the nation tried to put its collective arms around itself and hold close. Baseball and other matters faded to black in the smoke and dust that covered the city like a shroud.

Commissioner Bud Selig postponed the games that night and for the next week, the longest non-labor-related stoppage since World War I caused the 1918 season to be cut short by a month. At week's end the Yankees gathered together at the Stadium again, working out, touching base with one another, glad to be alive. The first practice was cut short by a moment of prayer as the club gathered on its knees in the middle of the diamond. George Steinbrenner gave $1 million to the World Trade Center Foundation.

Like everyone else in New York, the Yankee players were

stunned and uncertain about what to do and how to react. Modern ballplayers live in glass towers of their own and are no more proficient at dealing with such an out-of-scale tragedy than anyone else. But they recognized their public role, and when the club organized a trip to the Javits Center to meet with families still looking for loved ones, manager Joe Torre and a contingent of players that included Bernie Williams, Derek Jeter, and Paul O'Neill accepted the responsibility of that role. They felt awkward about it—who were they, at a time like this, anyway? What could they offer to those who had lost so much? But they went, not so much as ballplayers as New Yorkers, offering quiet words of comfort and encouragement because that's all anyone had to give at such a time. In the following weeks their involvement expanded to include charity work to help raise funds for the families of the victims.

After a week baseball continued, as it always has, in a world where someone is always throwing a ball and someone is always catching it. Baseball's capacity to go on, particularly in New York City, was unabashedly symbolic of the ability of New Yorkers to live on in a city whose heart was broken in a world gone suddenly mad. Baseball provided a place of green and order and quiet where little else seemed that way, where wins and losses were clear, bombs were home runs, and the faces of strangers neither pasted to light poles nor weeping made them friends. In its own small way, with the Yankees on the field again, the sight of Yankee Stadium was as friendly and welcoming as a Little League field tucked away in the corner of a city park, a place where friends welcome friends, kids play and laugh and run, and no one worries about the score, because at times that really is the least important thing about the game and this was one of those times.

On September 17, when the Yankees finally resumed their season in Chicago, the most welcome words of all were, "Play ball." And so the season continued, irrevocably changed for this city and its team. Most of what baseball had become in recent years just didn't mean as much, at least for a while. Contracts were irrelevant, and winning and losing became secondary to the activity of simply playing ball again. Baseball was more of a game than it had been in a long time—less important in the ways that had mattered before, and more important in the ways everyone had forgotten about.

Clemens picked up his 20th win and record-tying 16th victory in a row on September 19, beating the White Sox. The club returned to New York on September 25 for its first home game after the tragedy, with a chance to clinch and Clemens in search of consecutive win number 17. But that wasn't the story.

In an understated ceremony before the game, the Yankees honored the fallen and the members of the New York Police and Fire Departments and Port Authority Police who had lost their lives on September 11. During a 20-second moment of silence, the Stadium was more still than at any time in its history. Branford Marsalis played "Taps," and the Harlem Boys Choir sang "We Shall Overcome." During the national anthem, the players stood on the field, each one paired with a police officer, firefighter, or EMT worker; the stands were sprinkled with rescue workers and National Guardsmen taking a rare break from their grim task.

Clemens took the mound and struck out the first Tampa Bay hitter, but he lost the game, and the Yankees didn't clinch until later. No celebration was appropriate, and the players remained subdued. Yankee Stadium, as much a public building as any in New York, later hosted an interfaith prayer service as a memorial to the victims of the attacks. The Yankees played win-one-lose-one baseball for the rest of the regular season as Paul O'Neill nursed a broken foot, Jeter a pulled hamstring, and Brosius a broken hand.

Few gave the Yankees a chance against Oakland in the Division Series. Since starting 8–18, the A's had compiled the best record in baseball, better even than that of the Seattle Mariners, who won 116, topping the mark set by the 1998 Yankees. The A's had rebounded to win 102 games and remained dominant in the second half. Their starting pitching was untouchable, and they had won their last 17 games at home.

Home-field advantage and experience were all the Yankees had in their favor, and no one was quite sure whether either was of much help anymore. The events of September 11 still cast a pall over all things New York, and the Yankees' vaunted "experience" seemed like a euphemism for age, less important than pure raw talent.

Nothing seemed settled when the series started. One fan held a sign before game one that read, "If Ever a City

Needed a Parade . . . ," but that seemed a remote hope. The crowd was subdued, and the Yankees were curiously sluggish. Clemens limped off the mound with a bad hamstring in game one as Mark Mulder and the A's beat the Yankees 5–3, and the next day Tim Hudson shut them down completely as the A's beat Pettitte 2–0. In Las Vegas the odds of a Yankee world championship dropped to 30–1. "Inevitably," wrote Buster Olney in the *Times,* "there will be an October when the Yankees do not win the World Series, when their ageless stars break down and pressure finally buckles them. Inevitably there will be an October without a parade. This might be that October."

Derek Jeter was the only Yankee playing well. Before the team left for Oakland, Torre reminded everyone, "What we need to do is go on a three-game winning streak and hope momentum comes our way." Scott Brosius called

game three "the 'mustest' of must wins." No team had ever come back to win a five-game series after losing the first two games at home. Torre started wearing one of Yogi Berra's "It Ain't Over Till It's Over" caps, with a Port Authority police emblem stitched on the side. All the Yankees had left, like their city, was faith and heart.

All anyone will remember about the next game in Oakland—about the whole series really—is that in the seventh inning the Yankees were nursing a 1–0 lead over Tim Hudson, courtesy of a Jorge Posada home run on the only mistake Hudson had made all night. Then Mike Mussina, who had been equally magnificent, was staggered. With two outs, Jeremy Giambi singled. Terrence Long followed with a double into the right-field corner. Shane Spencer dug the ball out and threw toward home. But his throw was too strong, sailing over the heads of both Alfonso Sori-

THE DYNASTIES' DYNASTY

The Golden Age is now.

From 1936 through 1939 Joe McCarthy's Yankees won four straight World Series. Casey Stengel's Yankees of 1949 through 1953 won a record five World Series in a row. These two clubs have long been considered the two greatest dynasties in baseball history. But from 1996 through 2001 Joe Torre's Yankees, with five pennants in six seasons and four world championships, have set a standard that no team may ever approach again. Unless, of course, Torre's club surpasses itself.

Compared to Torre's team, the McCarthy and Stengel dynasties had it easy. While they had to defeat seven clubs to win the pennant, once that was done, only the best-of-seven World Series remained. McCarthy's dynasty was rarely pressed during the regular season. In winning four World Series with a combined record of 16–3, they were barely tested: the Giants (twice), Cubs, and Reds hardly provided a challenge. Stengel's Yankees faced better competition. Boston, Detroit,

and Cleveland each gave them hard battles for the pennant, and apart from the 1950 Phillies, the Giants and Dodgers provided a stiff test in the World Series. Still, Stengel's Yankees managed to win 20 games and lose only 8 in five World Series.

Torre's Yankees have had it much harder. Winning the AL East or wild card has given the club nothing but the opportunity to continue play against seven teams that have already been tested over the course of a season. All are capable of winning.

Consider their competition. In the 1996 and 1999 World Series, the Atlanta Braves featured three of the game's best pitchers in Greg Maddux, Tom Glavine, and John Smoltz. The 2000 Mets had the added motivation of playing for the bragging rights of the city. In divisional and championship series play, the Yankees have had to beat the 2001 Seattle Mariners, winners of an incredible 116 games, and the 2001 A's with their 102 victories. The Indians and Rangers, whom these Yankees have faced several times in divisional playoffs, may be short on pitching but are among the most potent teams in recent baseball history.

Yet Torre's club has still managed to win not only four of six possible world championships, but 14 of 16 playoff series. Realistically, given the grueling nature of the schedule, the Yankees should have won one, or perhaps two titles. But four? In the postseason Joe Torre's Yankees have exceeded their already extraordinary regular season standard, going an incredible 53–18, or .746.

Yankee fans have never had it better. These are the good old days.

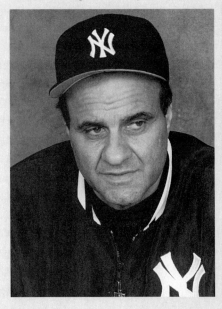

ano, in cutoff position in short right, and Tino Martinez, backing him up near first base as the second cutoff man. As the ball sailed over their heads and died, so did all hope for the Yankees.

Then, wrote Olney later, "Superman swooped down and saved the day." But this Superman didn't wear an "S" on his chest. He wore a "2" on his back. In a moment of pure inspiration, Derek Jeter, from absolutely nowhere, raced across the diamond, caught the ball on the dead run, and shoveled the ball backhanded to Posada as he careened far into foul ground. Posada gloved the ball and swiped at Giambi behind his back, tagging him out, popping the Athletics' balloon, turning the series, saving the day, changing everything—taking the game and the series from where it was headed and bringing it back, back to New York.

It was breathtaking, pure artistry, transcendent.

Jeter used another adjective. Routine. He said the play was something he practiced. "I work on those things," he said. "You win a lot of games doing the little things. . . . I was where I was supposed to be." He calmly explained that his job on the play was to act as the cutoff man in the event of a throw to third, then to track the ball and be the backup man if a throw to the plate eluded both cutoff men. Joe Torre said the same thing.

Routine? Oakland manager Art Howe admitted, "I don't have a clue why he was involved in that." Routine? Even the other Yankees had to laugh. "You don't practice the old run-toward-the-dugout-and-make-a-backhand-flip-to-the-catcher play," said Scott Brosius. Like so much else in this strange autumn, the play was beyond words or precedent. No one had ever seen it before. Earlier that day, in the first inning of the Seattle-Cleveland divisional contest, Mariner right fielder Ichiro Suzuki had similarly overthrown both cutoff men on a play to the plate. The ball bounded away into foul territory, and no one, absolutely no one, asked, "Where was the shortstop?" As Luis Sojo said, "You're not ever going to see that play again. A shortstop making that play from behind first base, in foul territory."

Only if you are Derek Jeter and you have been playing shortstop for the Yankees in big games since the age of five, imagining yourself all over the field making great plays time and time again. Willie Mays's famous catch of Vic Wertz's drive to center field in the 1954 World Series

has long been considered baseball's greatest defensive play, but neither Mays's catch nor any other play under consideration compares to the play made by Jeter. Most great defensive plays are primarily the product of effort and genes. All Mays did was outrun a baseball—beautifully and elegantly and unforgettably, to be sure—but that's what outfielders are supposed to do. Jeter's play was as far beyond instinct as it was belief—not one single great play, but five or six strung seamlessly together, each equally inspired, accented by poetic timing that both changed the game and brought joy. For not only did Jeter make what all baseball now knows as simply "the Play," he was the only person *anywhere* who saw the play before it even happened, reacted, then realized in the slender instant as he caught the ball with the play behind him that, "if I had spun around, he would have been safe." The chance of making any single portion of the play was small enough, but the chance of doing each step in sequence, in a perfect marriage of planning and execution, with the intended result, is infinitesimal. The game simply came to Derek Jeter, and he took it. He often does.

Give Posada some credit too. He believed, for he stayed at home plate even as the ball was arcing awry, ready to take the impossible throw after the implausible snag, and he then made the incredible tag as Giambi didn't slide and the ball and the glove found the back of his calf with his right foot frozen an inch above the plate. As Posada made the tag, Jeter even had the presence of mind to swoop back toward home in case Giambi knocked the ball free.

Routine? As routine as a miracle.

The 1–0 New York win broke Oakland. In the Yankee clubhouse afterward Luis Sojo snapped, "That's it, that's it! They had their chance! Yankees in five!" The Yankees surged to a 9–2 win in game four, then dragged Oakland back across the country to Yankee Stadium for the finale. Yogi Berra and Phil Rizzuto shared first pitch duties, and Rizzuto mimicked "the Play," sending the crowd into a frenzy. In the first two games, like the Yankees, the fans had been on their heels, distracted and worn. Now they were swept along, caught up by the game, on their feet from the first pitch.

It was a classic Yankee win, the kind that Joe Torre's team always seemed to produce. They first fell behind as Clemens hung in, then clawed back, playing nearly perfect fundamental baseball while the A's didn't catch the ball, didn't throw it, and didn't run the bases. And Jeter again, in the middle of everything, a double here, a sacrifice fly there, an unforgettable headlong tumbling dive into the stands along third to catch an uncatchable ball. Routine. The crowd chanting "Der-ek Je-ter! Der-ek Je-ter!" so loud that afterward players said they could feel the ground shake. Then Mariano Rivera at the end, and most amazing of all, a celebration again in New York. Joe Torre escorted Rudy Giuliani out onto the field to join the players, and a million smiles wreathed a city that needed each and every one.

Yankee Stadium was back to normal.

The disconsolate A's were crushed. "You can't give them an inch," said second baseman Frank Menechino. "They'll take four." Added Jason Giambi, "They hibernate, man. They hibernate till the postseason."

And Jeter, a player Joe Torre described as someone who "thinks cool in hot situations," was the reason why, clearly and without argument even from the A's. As Jason Giambi noted, "If he's not there, if he's just standing around like every other shortstop in the world, who knows what would have happened?"

The win set up a dream ALCS matchup against the Seattle Mariners. Using the 1998 Yankees as a model, under ex-Yankee Lou Piniella the Mariners had shed themselves of superstars Randy Johnson, Ken Griffey, and Alex Rodriguez and built a team that had won 116 games — two more than the 1998 Yankees and tied with the 1906 Cubs for best of all-time. The Yankees entered the series fully cognizant of the fact that they could protect the legacy of the 1998 team only by dumping the Mariners.

The Yankees were a machine in the first two games in Seattle, taking quick leads, holding on, and then handing the ball and the game to Rivera for safekeeping. Although Lou Piniella vowed after game two, "We are going to be back here for game six," at the Stadium for game three the Yankees seemed poised to put the Mariners away. Bernie Williams cracked a two-run home run off current Yankee-killer Jamie Moyer in the first, and El Duque was sharp.

But he began to tire in the fourth, and in the fifth, with two on and two out, Bret Boone lofted a short fly to left. Knoblauch ran and ran and ran, dove, and caught the ball, only to have it bounce from his glove.

The floodgates were open, and the Mariners poured through, winning 12–3 and giving the Yankees their worst postseason beating since Clemens lost to Boston in 1998. Perhaps, it seemed, there was something to those 116 wins after all.

But in games four and five, Yankee Stadium spoke again. The fans had lifted the team on a cushion of sound over the Athletics, and they treated the Mariners in the same fashion. For five innings Roger Clemens, still fighting his balky hamstring, and Mariner starter Paul Abbott walked a sagging tightrope, each pitcher shaky and straining but neither quite falling, Abbott walking eight but giving up no hits in five innings, and Clemens giving up only one.

Both clubs gave the ball to the bullpen in the sixth, with the game still scoreless, and each held firm. Then, in the eighth inning, Bret Boone, with two out, popped the ball over the left-field wall off Ramiro Mendoza to put the Mariners six outs away from fulfilling Piniella's prediction.

But the Yankees answered. Bernie Williams tied the game in the bottom of the inning with a home run off Arthur Rhodes, and Torre gave the game to Rivera again. Rivera threw three pitches in the top of the ninth, got three outs, and now the Mariners knew they would have to face him at least two innings more. They hoped their closer, Katsohiru Sasaki, would engender the same fear in the Yankees.

He did not. Scott Brosius, whose only purpose in life seems to be to provide big hits late in postseason games for the Yankees, reached base on an infield single. That brought up Alfonso Soriano, the rookie who had made the unlikely journey from the Dominican Republic to Japan as a 17-year-old, playing in the Japanese minor leagues and watching Sasaki play on television. Soriano oozed potential, but he'd also fallen asleep earlier in the playoffs, watching a home run that did not make it over the fence and forgetting to cover second.

One pitch made him a Yankee legend. Sasaki left a fastball up, and Soriano struck it hard and deep to right center, over the leaping Mike Cameron and into the stands, to the same place where Jim Leyritz struck his dramatic 15th-inning home run in the 1998 playoff, the feeling the same as when Chris Chambliss hit the home run to beat

Kansas City in 1976, and the sound of the crowd "a seismic shake," according to Howard Bryant of the *Bergen Record,* as New York rose as one and Soriano, arms raised, collapsed into the Yankees massed at home.

Broken, the Mariners went down quickly in game five, Pettitte beating Aaron Sele 12–3. The 2001 Seattle Mariners suddenly became a footnote while for the Yankees and New York the baseball season would stretch into November and the city would receive still another chance to stand together and celebrate.

While the Yankees were fully aware of what winning the World Series might mean for New York, they went out of their way to make certain they did not trivialize the deaths of so many by turning it into a sports metaphor wrapped in the flag. As Joe Torre said, "We're not trying to use this." Jeter added, "There's no way us coming out here can help heal this city or heal the country." Nevertheless, he admitted, "it makes people feel better." That's all they could hope for and everything they could do and exactly what New York needed—a few hours to forget and feel better.

The four-year-old Arizona Diamondbacks were built for the postseason, for a short Series. Their model was the 1997 Florida Marlins, another new franchise mortgaged to the hilt for one shot at instant history. Arizona owner Jerry Colangelo didn't care how much money he lost, and by spending big on expensive mercenaries, he had already guaranteed that his club, already some $200 million in the red, would lose $20–30 million for the season. Fronted by aces Curt Schilling and Randy Johnson and buoyed by veterans like Mark Grace and Luis Gonzalez, the Diamondbacks were an experienced crew that wasn't likely to be intimidated. "Aura and Mystique," said Schilling before the start of the Series in Arizona, "are the names of two dancers in a nightclub."

He forgot to mention Destiny, but after the first two games, she seemed to be wearing a Diamondback uniform. Mussina pitched his first bad game in a month in the opener, while Schilling, who had already won three postseason games and was politicking to pitch three times in the Series, was magnificent. He gave up a single first-inning run, then nothing more, leaving the game after seven innings to save his arm for game four and winning 9–1.

Derek Jeter became baseball's first Mr. November as he socked a game-winning homer to lead off the 12th inning in game four of the 2001 World Series at Yankee Stadium. His blast came in the midst of a one-for-fifteen series slump.

When Randy Johnson trumped him the next night, shutting out the Yankees in a performance so dominant it seemed impossible he could ever be beaten, the brilliant run that had delivered the Yankees past Oakland and Seattle and over all baseball since 1996 seemed spent, their string of 11 consecutive postseason series wins about to end. Clinging to clichés and hoping Roger Clemens's heart was stronger than his hamstring, the Yankees flew back from Phoenix, a city named after the legendary bird that rose from the ashes to live again, to New York, a city that was doing just that.

With a tattered flag recovered from the World Trade Center rippling in the breeze in center field and Yankee

Scott Brosius celebrates his game-tying ninth-inning home run against the Diamondbacks in game five of the World Series, on November 1, 2001. The blast provided a fitting end to his four seasons as a Yankee and capped his major league career.

Stadium at its raucous best, the Yankees also rose again. As President George W. Bush looked on, Clemens teetered early and was saved only when he picked Craig Counsell off first and when Jorge Posada nailed Steve Finley in a strikeout–throw-out double play. Clemens settled down, giving up only a single run in the fourth after Posada staked him to a 1–0 lead with a second-inning home run.

Meanwhile, the Diamondbacks' Brian Anderson kept the Yankees off balance. But his teammates, particularly catcher Damian Miller, had a hard time catching the ball in the swirling wind, forcing Anderson to get extra outs. In the sixth Shane Spencer stopped a rally with a diving catch in left, and in the seventh Scott Brosius put the Yankees up by two with a soft hit to left that Luis Gonzalez let drop, Bernie Williams scoring from second to make the score 2–1.

Rivera came on, as always, and the game raced to an end. He recorded the final out on a ground ball to Jeter at 11:59 P.M. to give the Yankees the win and a chance in the Series. Then the clock struck twelve, and it was Halloween.

Clemens's standout performance and Rivera's expected spectacular one forced Arizona's hand. Diamondback manager Bob Brenly decided to bring back Curt Schilling in game four on three days' rest, a decision that lit up the airwaves for the next day. Torre stayed the course as usual, sticking with El Duque.

But Torre also did something else. He tweaked his batting order and lineup, leaving Shane Spencer in left, moving Jeter to leadoff and Paul O'Neill to second, playing matchup baseball again, putting each man in the right place at the right time.

For much of the game it made no difference. Schilling was, incredibly, even better and more efficient than before, but Spencer sliced a rare mistake into the stands in right to give the Yankees a 1–0 lead. Mark Grace then answered with an upper-deck shot off El Duque in the fourth. But Hernandez, growing stronger as the game went on, kept pace with Schilling. In the fifth, after Tony Womack doubled and moved to third, Luis Gonzalez lofted a ball to left, and this time Spencer needed no help from Derek Jeter with his throw. He hit Posada on one hop, perfect, and the catcher — so often overlooked for his defense — made another great stop, spinning and tagging Womack, first with his empty glove and then with the ball half out of his bare hand, and then as he fell turning his palm up to keep the ball from falling out. The game remained tied.

El Duque finally tired in the seventh, and in the eighth a single by Gonzalez and a long double by Erubiel Durazo put Arizona ahead. Moments later, with the infield in, Arizona went ahead when Jeter's throw home went to the wrong side of the plate. With six outs to go, Arizona led 3–1. The Yankees, with only three hits off Schilling, were down and nearly out.

But Brenly pulled a shocker, removing Schilling after only 88 pitches — his last a 98-mile-per-hour fastball that punched out Justice — to save him for a potential game seven, as if he didn't expect to put the Yankees away before then. Submarining closer Byung-Hyun Kim struck out the side in the eighth — all on 3–2 counts — and the game entered the bottom of the ninth with the Yankees still down 3–1.

Jeter tried to bunt for a hit but was thrown out by Matt Williams. Then, with the Who's "Baba O'Riley" wailing, the crowd gave Paul O'Neill his now-obligatory ovation. It was an open secret that the Yankee right fielder, age 38, who had said earlier that "I'm tired of waking up in the morning and finding out what doesn't work," would retire after the Series.

But not tonight, not yet, for Paul O'Neill would play hard to the end. He punched the ball into left field for a single, giving the Yankees a chance. Tino Martinez stepped to the plate, the tying run.

Kim threw one pitch, and Martinez swung. And time stopped.

It was high, it was deep, and it was gone.

And as Martinez's blast dropped over the fence in right center, the Stadium moved again, and what was beyond belief was made real. The game was now tied, remarkably, incredibly, improbably, 3–3, the first time in the World Series since 1947 — Lavagetto versus Bevens — that a team had come back after trailing by two in the ninth. Everything suddenly seemed tilted New York's way.

Kim wiggled out of the inning after the Yankees loaded the bases, and then Torre gave the ball to Rivera in the tenth. Thirteen pitches and three broken bats later and it was time — midnight and November, a month for veterans and Thanksgiving. Derek Jeter stepped in against Kim.

Since taking his tumble into the stands against Oak-land, Jeter, limping and wrapped and ending each game packed in ice in the clubhouse, had slumped. He was only one for fifteen in the Series and hadn't gotten the ball out of the infield. The rest of the Yankees weren't doing much better.

But Jeter's childhood dreams had included all of this, every imagined possibility, and he was now the veteran, and it was his month. He'd stayed loose all game, joking with Torre, reminding him that his contract expired at midnight, and asking bench coach Don Zimmer whether he was going to take over. As he prepared to step to the plate to lead off the 12th inning, he went up to his manager — still "Mr. Torre" to Jeter — and told him, "You've only got five minutes."

Then Jeter stepped to the plate. He took a ball low, and then fouled two pitches. The next two drifted wide, and Jeter watched, then stood in, 3–2, bat held high. Kim wound up and threw again . . .

. . . and they all came pouring out — the Yankees from their dugout, the hoarse cheers of fans — when Jeter swung and created another incredible memory for New York, a snapshot of a state of mind that New York needed and pleaded for like no place else. The ball sliced off his bat to right, just long enough, just high enough not to need the help of Jeffrey Maier or any other pair of hands into the stands and out of time and into the arms of history. Jeter raised his right arm and ran open-mouthed around the bases — his first walk-off home run ever — then disappeared, lost in the pinstriped mass that always seems to mean the same thing at the end of the year, something almost beyond words, that on this night meant a 4–3 Yankee win and much, much more. Even "cathartic" seemed too small a word to explain the feeling.

Somehow, incredibly, the Yankees were still playing baseball in November, and Sinatra was singing again. But only moments after striking the home run, while standing on the field being interviewed, Jeter was already warning, "This game means nothing if we lose tomorrow." The player they were calling "Mr. November" was right, and he was already starting to regroup, focusing on what lay ahead, anticipating what might come next.

But not even Jeter could foresee that. Game five unfolded in rough approximation of game four, an extended, improbable setup. Arizona starter Miguel Batista kept

New York's virtually hitless wonders off balance all night. Mike Mussina, much better than in game one, was similarly successful, but in a five-minute span in the fifth inning Steve Finley and Rod Barajas both homered and put Arizona ahead 2–0. The Yankees threatened in both the seventh and eighth, but each rally ended short, the first with a fly ball by Brosius, the second with a fly by Martinez. In the top of the ninth the crowd seemed resigned to defeat, cheering Paul O'Neill wildly in what seemed to be his last appearance in the Stadium, calling him out in right field with a syncopated "Paul O-Nee-ul, Paul O-Nee-ul" chant. When the Diamondbacks went down, he entered the dugout and tipped his hat, a good-bye that seemed symbolic, a farewell not only to the game and the season but to the era that in many ways began the day he joined the team.

The ninth inning began with the Diamondbacks poised on the dugout steps for the second night in a row and closer Byung-Hyun Kim on the mound. Yankee fans tried to muster a cheer, but voices still hoarse from the night before had lost their thunder.

Only ten minutes shy of midnight Jorge Posada woke them up with a sharp double to right, the first hard-hit ball for New York since Jeter's home run earlier that morning. Perhaps Kim, who'd thrown 62 pitches the night before, was weakening.

But Spencer grounded to third, and Knoblauch, who'd pinch-run for Justice in the eighth, struck out. All that stood between the Yankees and a 3–2 deficit in the Series was Scott Brosius.

Everyone watching thought about it, but no one dared put words to the thought. Not even Brosius. The 1998 World Series MVP said later that he thought only of trying to hit the ball hard.

He took a ball. Then, with one swift swing, he took the ball, and the game, and sent it up where all could see it, white against the black of night growing small. He raised his arm, and the Stadium moved and heaved again and spoke with one voice as the ball crashed into the stands in right. For the second night in a row, with two out in the ninth inning, when hope lay dormant, another Yankee rose to the occasion. The score was tied, 2–2.

The Yankees almost won it then, loading the bases afterward before Spencer struck out, then turned to Rivera again. He broke three bats on thirteen pitches in the tenth, but Mike Morgan shut down the Yankees as well.

In the eleventh Rivera, working his third night in a row, proved relatively human, giving up two singles, a sacrifice, and an intentional walk to load the bases with Reggie Sanders coming to bat.

Torre, he admitted later, rolled the dice. He brought the infield in at the corners but left Jeter and Soriano at normal depth, hoping for a bang-bang double play.

But Sanders hit a rocket, and the sharp sound said "base hit."

But there was Soriano, horizontal, diving to his right, with the ball in his glove.

And on the game went. Grace grounding out to Brosius to end the inning, the Yankees going down in order again, then Sterling Hitchcock setting down Arizona in the 12th and Albie Lopez coming on in relief for the Diamondbacks in the bottom of the inning, the tension excruciating, night turning into morning again.

Fundamentals won it. Knoblauch hit his first pitch into center for a single. Brosius bunted his third pitch for a sacrifice, bringing up Soriano. He took two balls, then fouled one off, then swung again.

The ball sliced into right field, landed, and bounced once, then twice away from Reggie Sanders, who scooped it up and turned and fired home. Knoblauch, running hard, saw third-base coach Willie Randolph, who had only two runners thrown out at the plate all year, waving him home.

The ball hit short of the plate and careened off Barajas as Knoblauch slid, bounding free.

Then it all poured forth once more. Clemens picked up Soriano. Knoblauch leapt in the air.

In 1951, following Bobby Thomson's home run, long considered the most dramatic moment in baseball history, Red Smith had written: "Now it is done. Now the story ends. And there is no way to tell it. The art of fiction is dead." Over the course of two improbable mornings, playing baseball in a month and at a time unlike any other, with three home runs and one solid single, the Yankees killed off nonfiction too and created a whole new genre, a place where "back to normal" meant the incredible, where the implausible became routine, and where nothing seemed impossible for this city and this team.

"I can't be surprised," said Torre afterward. "It just happened the day before." Perhaps Yogi had been right all along. It really *wasn't* over till it was over. It *was* déjà vu all over again.

Yet it was not the end of the World Series, even though after these three days in New York the World Series somehow seemed a lesser championship than the victory the Yankees had just earned. The end would come in Arizona, where the Diamondbacks fashioned their own version of the implausible.

In game six the Diamondbacks, noticing that Pettitte was tipping his pitches, exploded early. The Yankees, who had yet to really hit in this Series, were shut down by Johnson again. The Diamondbacks cracked out a World Series record 22 hits to beat the Yankees 15–2 and send the World Series into a seventh game.

Joe Torre's Yankees had never been forced to a game seven before, but it seemed a fitting end to a remarkable postseason. The past six weeks had been one long grind, the ultimate test, and game seven would be their final trial.

The finale matched Clemens and Schilling. Schilling described it as akin to "an essay contest against Hemingway," the student taking on the master. A decade before, when Schilling was an unaccomplished pitcher of unfulfilled potential, he approached Clemens and asked for advice, expecting perhaps a pat on the head and a tip on

how to grip the split-finger fastball. Instead, he received an hourlong lecture as Clemens berated him for his attitude and approach and challenged him to make the most of his ability. The conversation turned his career around. Now, before game seven, despite pitching on three days' rest for the second consecutive start, he guaranteed an Arizona win, saying, "If I get the ball, we'll win the World Series."

Some still intimated that Clemens couldn't win big games, but after Clemens's victory in game three, Joe Torre had said, "For a pitcher as great as Roger has been, he's had to defend himself. I don't think he'll have to defend himself again."

In game seven Clemens, at age 39 the oldest game-seven starter in Series history, rendered the point moot. The student was magnificent, but the teacher refused to break. While the Yankees barely touched Schilling, Clemens kept Arizona at bay, time and time again making the pitch he needed to.

But in the sixth inning Steve Finley singled, and then Danny Bautista roped a long double to center. Jeter made

Derek Jeter shakes off a twisted ankle in the final agonizing moments of the seventh game at Bank One Ballpark. Despite their heroic postseason defense of the world title, epitomized by Jeter's all-around brilliance, the Yankees fell to the devastating one-two Diamondback punch of Schilling and Johnson.

Paul O'Neill contemplates the Diamondbacks' victory celebration. He later told the *Daily News* columnist Filip Bondy, "A lot of people would say they want to be in the other locker room right now. I don't want to be in the other locker room. I want to be right here." O'Neill retired after the game.

a remarkable relay and threw him out at third, but Arizona led, 1–0. Schilling seemed to have the only run he might need. But in this season, the Yankees, trailing late, also seemed to have Arizona right where they wanted them.

Jeter led off the seventh with a single, then Paul O'Neill collected his second hit of the game. Williams moved Jeter over with a ground ball, and as rain began to spit down, Tino Martinez singled to right. Jeter scored easily, and the game was tied.

Incredibly, Arizona manager Bob Brenly stuck with Schilling. After the Yankees went out, Schilling led off the eighth inning, striking out, then took the mound in the bottom of the inning. And on pitch 95, Alfonso Soriano sent it over the wall for yet another reality-defying late-game home run, the hero for the moment, the Series MVP in waiting. The Arizona crowd was silent. Randy Johnson came in and got out of the inning. The Yankees led 2–1, and their 38th world championship was only six outs away, held in the capable right hand of Mariano Rivera.

He struck out the side in the bottom of the eighth, according to plan, and after Johnson dispatched the Yankees, Rivera took the mound in the ninth, as close to post-season perfection as any pitcher in history. With 27 postseason saves in 28 opportunities, his only blemish — like the single wrong stitch in a Persian rug — was the 1997 home run he had given up to Sandy Alomar.

As he took the mound, the writers had already started to write the story to end all stories, Soriano was voted Series MVP, and the TV guys started draping the lockers with plastic for the expected champagne bath. George Steinbrenner stopped them and made everyone leave, not taking anything for granted. The entire Series — in fact, the entire postseason for New York and the Yankees — had been based on the improbable and the impossible. Both happened again, in the most unbelievable way of all.

Perhaps the Yankees were finally spent, their emotional reservoir depleted, exhausted by the strain of one more comeback, one more game, and one more inning with no margin for error. They felt confident with the ball in Mariano Rivera's hand, looking for his 15th straight postseason save. But not even Rivera can control the ball once it leaves his fingers.

Mark Grace, jammed, singled soft to center to start the inning. Then the pitcher, with one error to his credit in his career, made his second, losing his grip on Damian Miller's bunt and throwing the ball into center field. He fielded a second bunt and got a force-out at third, then Tony Womack tied the game with a slap double down the right field line.

Now the season that wouldn't end raced to the finish. Rivera hit Craig Counsell with a pitch to load the bases, and with Luis Gonzalez up, this time Torre brought the infield in to cut off a run at the plate.

Rivera made the pitch he wanted, his cutter boring in on Gonzalez's hands, breaking his bat — the second of the inning. But Gonzalez fought it off, and the broken bat delivered a hit, this time breaking hearts as well. The ball flared softly into center, out of even Jeter's miraculous reach, and the game was over. For the first time in his career, Jeter ended the season on the field watching another team celebrate a world championship. The previous weeks receded like a dream.

In many ways it was incredible that the Yankees made it as far as they did. They never hit in the entire Series, somehow squeezing 3⅝ wins out of a .183 batting average and only 14 runs, while Arizona scored 37. In the end they depended too much on the infallibility of Rivera—and a sudden dependence on miracles.

But in New York and around much of the country, the 2001 World Series is not likely to be remembered for what the Diamondbacks achieved. It was the Yankees who made the Series and the postseason special and memorable. The D-Backs' story still seems fleeting, especially given their financial reality, perhaps already past due.

But the Yankees, even in defeat, were eloquent and more enduring. In New York the lasting memory of this World Series will not be that the Yankees lost, although they did, on the scoreboard and in the record books. Instead, after a season like no other in their remarkable history, the 2001 Yankees will be remembered for something more: for what they gave their city, for the moments they won back from despair. Their story will continue.

Some things will change, as Paul O'Neill and Scott Brosius head off to retirement and others sign bigger contracts or are traded elsewhere. The Yankees have already changed, because their recent ability to recognize the need to change is an element of their continuing success. But they are also still the same, for by now they also seem to have learned which parts of their past to retain and honor.

No other team in baseball can match their tradition, but no team is better at living up to their tradition than the Yankees. No other team has their history, and no team makes more history. The Yankees are different, and the difference is New York: no team has ever gotten more from its city, or given more back to it, than the Yankees.

These Yankees demonstrated that difference like no Yankee team ever before. At the end of the World Series, in his first few moments as a former ballplayer, Paul O'Neill summed it up perfectly, telling Filip Bondy of the *Daily News:* "A lot of people would say they want to be in the other locker room right now. I don't want to be in the other locker room. I want to be right here."

Despite losing the World Series, in their incredible, extended October that stretched into November, the Yankees accomplished something no other Yankee team has touched. Over the course of three incredible weeks, they transcended their own history. For even as they lost, these Yankees somehow still won, and they made it clear that there is something about this team and this franchise beyond wins and losses. For the first time in decades, rooting for the Yankees was not like rooting for U.S. Steel—it was like rooting for *us.* They weren't just "the best team money could buy." They were the best team they could be, squeezing everything possible out of a season. They weren't the Bronx Zoo—they were a national treasure.

These Yankees—O'Neill and Brosius, Martinez and Jeter, Posada, Williams, Pettitte, Rivera, and the others—managed by Joe Torre and owned by George Steinbrenner, set a standard as a *team* because they played their best when it mattered most. For three amazing weeks the way they played the game—not perfectly, but always passionately—allowed the "national pastime" to do what it does best and made that title true again as baseball briefly pushed the real world aside. For a few moments the Yankees made something else matter, not just for New Yorkers but for much of the entire country. Losing a World Series was a small price to pay for that. And while that loss may signal the end of an era, it may also mark the beginning of a new one. These are the Yankees, after all, and George Steinbrenner still doesn't like to finish second and quickly proved it, signing free agents Jason Giambi, David Wells, Steve Karsay, and Rondell White, and filling every imaginable hole. But for the Yankees and for their city, the phrase "wait till next year" has rarely meant either failure or regret.

Over the last 100 years the New York Yankees have won 38 pennants and 27 world championships. More often than not, they have shown just how the game of baseball is supposed to be played. Ruth, Gehrig, DiMaggio, Mantle, Mattingly, Jeter, and dozens of other players impossible to forget have worn their uniform. Yankee Stadium has been their stage. The very definition of a dynasty, they have created the collective memories that make friends of strangers, given their city a face, and displayed its heart and soul.

In New York, at the end of the first Yankees Century, "next year" is a declaration of faith.

APPENDIX A
YANKEES CENTURY TEAMS

Comparing baseball players across eras is as impossible as selecting an All-Star team from the most successful franchise in major league history. To make our selections meaningful, we've created two rosters: the first for players, managers, and executives prior to 1945, and the second from the post–World War II era to the present. The prewar team honors a total of 25 players, two executives, and two managers. The post–World War II squad honors 30 players, two executives, and two managers.

Years as a Yankee and significant career statistics for those years are presented for each player through 2001.

PRE-WORLD WAR II (1903-1944)

MANAGERS

Miller Huggins (1918–1929): 6 AL pennants, 3 World Series Titles
Huggins inaugurated the first Yankee dynasty while compiling a regular season won-lost record of 1,067–719 (.597).

Joe McCarthy (1931–1946): 8 AL pennants, 7 World Series Titles
McCarthy's tenure spanned both the Ruth and DiMaggio eras; his teams compiled a won-lost record of 1,460–867 (.627).

EXECUTIVES

Ed Barrow (general manager, 1921–1938; club president, 1939–1944)
Barrow can be considered the architect of the modern Yankees.

Jacob Ruppert (owner, 1915–1938)
Ruppert built both Yankee Stadium and the Yankee tradition as the team won ten pennants and seven world championships under his stewardship.

INFIELD

1B **Lou Gehrig** (1923–1939): .340, 493 HR, 1,995 RBI
Gehrig, the "Iron Horse," established the long-standing record for consecutive games played with 2,130 and, with Babe Ruth, formed the greatest one-two batting punch in major league history.

1B **Hal Chase** (1905–1913): .284, 494 RBI, 248 SB
The slick-fielding first baseman was considered by his peers to be one of the game's great players. A fine batter and fan favorite, Chase ruined his reputation through his involvement in gambling.

2B **Tony Lazzeri** (1926–1937): .293, 169 HR, 1,154 RBI
One of the first middle infielders with power, the California native helped lead the team to five world championship titles and six pennants.

2B **Joe Gordon** (1938–1943, 1946): .271, 153 HR, 617 RBI
Gordon took over for Lazzeri in 1938, helping the club win three world championships and capturing American League MVP honors in 1942.

SS **Frank Crosetti** (1932–1948): .245, 98 HR, 649 RBI
A team player and consistent gloveman with a knack for sign-stealing, Crosetti was an invaluable member of eight pennant winners. He also served as a Yankee coach from 1947 to 1968.

SS **Kid Elberfeld** (1903–1909): .268, 257 RBI, 117 SB
The "Tabasco Kid" was one of the toughest players of the Dead Ball Era and a fan favorite at Hilltop Park.

3B **Red Rolfe** (1934–1942): .289, 69 HR, 526 RBI
As Joe McCarthy's leadoff man, Rolfe scored 100 or more runs seven years in a row while anchoring third base for six pennant winners.

3B **Frank Baker** (1916–1922): .288, 48 HR, 375 RBI
"Home Run" Baker brought veteran leadership to the fledgling dynasty and helped secure the Yankees' first pennants in 1921 and 1922.

3B **Joe Dugan** (1922–1928): .286, 22 HR, 320 RBI

"Jumping" Joe Dugan arrived from Boston in 1922 and took over from Frank Baker as the regular third baseman. Dugan was considered one of the best-fielding third basemen of his time.

OUTFIELD

RF **Babe Ruth** (1920–1932): .349, 659 HR, 1,971 RBI

The best player in baseball history was also the best drawing card. Yankee Stadium will always be known as "the House That Ruth Built" in tribute to his talent and role in helping to shape the Yankees' winning tradition.

CF **Joe DiMaggio** (1936–1942, 1946–1951): .325, 361 HR, 1,537 RBI

The "Yankee Clipper" was the consummate winner, helping the club capture ten pennants and nine world championships while playing with an unmatched combination of grace and power.

CF **Earle Combs** (1924–1935): .325, 1,866 H, 1,186 R

The speedy Kentucky native not only patrolled the expanse of Yankee Stadium's center field but also was a superb hitter and table-setter for Ruth and Gehrig.

LF **Bob Meusel** (1920–1929): .311, 146 HR, 1,005 RBI

Although known for the strength of his throwing arm, Meusel was also one of the first home run hitters in the game. He usually played left field in an outfield that also featured Ruth and Earle Combs.

RF **Tommy Henrich** (1937–1950): .282, 183 HR, 383 RBI

Dubbed "Old Reliable" by broadcaster Mel Allen, Henrich played on eight pennant winners and seven world champions.

RF **"Wee Willie" Keeler** (1903–1909): .294, 206 RBI, 118 SB

One of the greatest bunters in baseball history, Keeler gave the young franchise instant credibility. He led the Yankees in batting average their first three seasons.

OF **William Franklin "Birdie" Cree** (1908–1915): .292, 332 RBI, 132 SB

Cree was a solid four-tool player. In 1911 he hit .348, with a slugging percentage of .513, both Yankee single-season records until broken by Babe Ruth in 1920.

RF **George Selkirk** (1934–1942): .290, 503 R, 576 RBI

Babe Ruth's replacement forged a consistent career, batting over .300 for five seasons. He played for six pennant winners and five world champions.

CATCHERS

Bill Dickey (1928–1946): .313, 202 HR, 1,209 RBI

Dickey played in eleven All-Star games and for nine American League pennant winners, which included eight world championships. Along with Mickey Cochrane and Josh Gibson, he was one of the greatest catchers of his generation.

STARTING PITCHERS

RHP **Red Ruffing** (1930–1942, 1945–1946): 231–124, 3.47 ERA, 1,526 K

Ruffing was one of the great power pitchers of the era and helped New York win seven pennants while batting .269 with 36 career homers. Ruffing pitched a team record 261 complete games.

RHP **Jack Chesbro** (1903–1909): 128–93, 2.58 ERA, 169 CG

A pioneer of the spitball, in 1904 Chesbro won 41 games, still the all-time major league single-season record.

RHP **Bob Shawkey** (1915–1927): 168–131, 3.12 ERA

Shawkey was successful in both the Dead Ball and Lively Ball Eras as he helped establish the Yankee dynasty.

RHP **Waite "Schoolboy" Hoyt** (1921–1930): 157–98, 3.48 ERA, 156 CG

Hoyt helped lead the Yankees to five pennants in ten seasons. In five World Series Hoyt was 6–3, allowing only 14 earned runs in 77⅔ innings.

LHP **Lefty Gomez** (1930–1942): 189–101, 3.34 ERA, 28 SHO

Gomez was a stalwart of seven pennant winners and six world champions. In World Series competition from 1936 to 1939, Gomez was 5–0 with a 3.46 ERA.

LHP **Herb Pennock** (1923–1933): 162–90, 3.54 ERA, 164 CG

Pennock was a perfect 5–0 in six World Series and was at his best in the heat of a pennant race or World Series.

RELIEF PITCHERS

RHP **Wilcy Moore** (1927–1929, 1932–1933): 36–21, 3.31 ERA, 35 SV

One of the first great relievers in baseball history, Moore won 19 and saved a league-leading 13 games for the legendary 1927 champions.

RHP **Johnny Murphy** (1932, 1934–1943, 1946): 93–53, 3.54 ERA, 104 SV

Manager Joe McCarthy called Murphy his "pennant insurance"; he led the American League in saves or relief victories for seven straight seasons while helping to lead New York to pennants in seven of eight seasons from 1936 to 1943.

POST–WORLD WAR II (1945–2001)

MANAGERS

Casey Stengel (1949–1960): 10 AL pennants, 7 World Series Titles
Always colorful and quotable, Stengel was the master of platooning. He learned his baseball from John McGraw, who learned the game from Ned Hanlon in the 1890s.

Joe Torre (1996–): 5 AL pennants, 4 World Series Titles
Brooklyn native Torre has made the Yankees into baseball's first dynasty since Stengel's championship team of the 1950s.

EXECUTIVES

Dan Topping and **Del Webb** (1945–1966)
The odd couple of socialite Topping and developer-visionary Webb were stewards of the Stengel-Houk championship eras.

George Steinbrenner (1973–)
"The Boss" grabs headlines, pennants, and world championships with an equal measure of passion and deliberation.

INFIELD

1B **Don Mattingly** (1982–1995): .307, 222 HR, 10 Gold Gloves
The best Yankee to have never played for a world champion was also the most complete first baseman of his era.

1B **Tino Martinez** (1996–2001): .279, 175 HR, 654 RBI
After Don Mattingly retired, Martinez took over. In six seasons he helped the club win four world championships. No Yankee fan will ever forget his dramatic game-tying home run with two outs in the 9th inning of game four of the 2001 World Series.

2B **Willie Randolph** (1976–1988): .275, 251 SB, 1,731 H
Randolph was a consistent and soft-spoken professional during the "Bronx Zoo" era and helped the team win back-to-back world championships in 1977 and 1978.

2B **Billy Martin** (1950–1957): .262, 449 H
Known as "Casey's Boy," Martin was a fiery addition to five world champions. His World Series heroics included a 12-hit .500 performance in 1953.

IF **Gil McDougald** (1951–1960): .276, 112 HR, 1,291 H
McDougald was the most versatile player on eight Yankee pennant winners, playing second, third, and shortstop with equal skill.

3B **Graig Nettles** (1973–1983): .253, 250 HR, .964 FA
For over a decade Nettles led the Yankees with his power and slick fielding. His glovework in the 1978 World Series is legendary.

3B **Clete Boyer** (1959–1966): .241, 95 HR, .968 FA
Boyer was the hot-corner magician of five Yankee pennant winners. Batting .318 in the 1962 World Series, he won game one with a seventh-inning homer.

SS **Derek Jeter** (1995–): .320, 725 R, 1,199 H
All Jeter does is win games by every way possible. He is possibly the first six-tool player in baseball, as his unmatched baseball instincts provide an extra dimension.

SS **Phil Rizzuto** (1941–1956): .273, 1,588 H, .967 FA
Ty Cobb named "the Scooter" as one of only two major league players (Stan Musial was the other) who would have been a star in his day. Perhaps the most beloved figure in team history, the former shortstop broadcast Yankee games for five decades.

OUTFIELD

CF **Joe DiMaggio** (1936–1942, 1946–1951): .325, 361 HR, 2,214 H
The only member of both the pre- and postwar teams was the most complete player of his era.

CF **Mickey Mantle** (1951–1968): .298, 536 HR, 2,415 H
Mantle's combination of speed and power made him the perfect replacement for Joe DiMaggio. He led the Yankees to 12 pennants in 18 seasons.

CF **Bernie Williams** (1991–): .305, 207 HR, 896 RBI, 1,629 H
Williams has patrolled the Yankee outfield with style and grace while hitting in the middle of the batting order for the recent dynasty.

CF **Rickey Henderson** (1985–1989): .288, 326 SB, 513 R
Baseball's greatest leadoff hitter spent five seasons in his prime as a Yankee.

LF **Roy White** (1965–1979): .271, 1,803 H, 964 R
Dignified and consistent, White was the Yankees' best player from 1965 through their championship seasons of the late 1970s.

RF **Reggie Jackson** (1977–1981): .281, 144 HR, 461 RBI, 661 H
"Mr. October" restored glamour to Yankee Stadium by helping to lead New York to back-to-back world championships in 1977 and 1978.

RF **Roger Maris** (1960–1966): .265, 203 HR, 797 H
Maris's 61 home runs in 1961 will always be one of the game's landmark performances. He was named MVP in both 1960 and 1961.

RF **Paul O'Neill** (1993–2001): .303, 185 HR, 858 RBI, 1,426 H
O'Neill won the AL batting title in 1994, hitting .359. He was a fan favorite at the Stadium, appreciated for his unmatched intensity.

OF **Dave Winfield** (1981–1990): .290, 205 HR, 1,300 H
Winfield made eight All-Star appearances as a Yankee while winning four Gold Gloves and driving in 100 or more runs for five consecutive seasons.

CATCHERS

Yogi Berra (1949–1963): .285, 358 HR, 2,148 H
Berra won three MVP Awards and helped to lead the Yankees to 14 pennants and 10 world championships.

Elston Howard (1955–1957): .279, 161 HR, 1,405 H
Howard, the first African-American player in franchise history, was a superb catcher who supplanted perennial All-Star Yogi Berra behind the plate.

Thurman Munson (1969–1979): .292, 113 HR, 1,558 H
The heart and soul of three pennant winners and two world champions was a superb clutch performer who captured the 1976 AL MVP Award.

STARTING PITCHERS

RHP **Allie Reynolds** (1947–1954): 131–60, 3.30 ERA, 1,700 IP
The ever-versatile Reynolds was adept as both a starter and a reliever. In eight seasons he helped to lead the Yankees to six world championships.

RHP **Mel Stottlemyre** (1964–1974): 164–139, 2.97 ERA, 1,257 K
The best Yankee starter to never pitch for a world champion, Stottlemyre won 20 or more games for New York three times.

RHP **Jim "Catfish" Hunter** (1975–1979): 63–53, 3.58 ERA, 993 IP
Hunter helped revive the Yankees' winning tradition. In five seasons he helped to lead New York to three pennants and two world championships.

LHP **Whitey Ford** (1950–1967): 236–106, 2.75 ERA, 1,956 K
Known as "the Chairman of the Board," Ford was the ultimate World Series performer. He helped capture six world titles in eleven visits to the Series.

LHP **Ed Lopat** (1948–1955): 113–59, 3.19 ERA, 1,497 IP
The "Junkman" was an integral member of the pitching staff that helped the Yankees capture five consecutive world championships from 1949 to 1953.

LHP **Ron Guidry** (1975–1988): 170–91, 3.29 ERA, 1,778 K
A three-time 20-game winner for the Yankees, Guidry had his best season in 1978, when he won the Cy Young Award with a won-lost record of 25–3.

RELIEF PITCHERS

LHP **Joe Page** (1944–1950): 57–49, 3.44 ERA, 76 SV
In 1947 Page was a major factor in the Yankee world championship, winning 14 games while saving 17. His five-inning relief appearance in the seventh game of the World Series saved the season for New York. In 1949 he was even better, winning 13 and saving 27.

LHP **Albert "Sparky" Lyle** (1972–1978): 57–40, 2.41 ERA, 141 SV
In the Yankees' 1977 world championship season, "Sparky" Lyle captured the Cy Young Award with a won-lost record of 13–5 with 23 saves.

RHP **Rich "Goose" Gossage** (1978–1983, 1989): 533 IP, 512 K, 151 SV
The most intimidating reliever of his era, Gossage saved the 1978 playoff game against the Red Sox.

RHP **Mariano Rivera** (1995–): 533 IP, 419 K, 215 SV
His postseason record is the best of any reliever in history. Rivera led the American League with 45 saves in 1999 and 50 in 2001.

APPENDIX B

THE YANKEE RECORD

Year	W	L	Finish	+/-	Manager	Highest Batting Average	Most Hits	Most Home Runs	Most RBIs	Most Wins
1903	72	62	4th	-17	Griffith	Keeler, .318	Keeler, 164	McFarland, 5	Williams, 82	Chesbro, 21
1904	92	59	2nd	-1½	Griffith	Keeler, .343	Keeler, 185	Ganzel, 6	Anderson, 82	Chesbro, 41†
1905	71	78	6th	-21½	Griffith	Keeler, .302	Keeler, 169	Williams, 6	Williams, 60	Chesbro, 20
1906	90	61	2nd	-3	Griffith	Chase, .323	Chase, 193	Conroy, 4	Williams, 77	Orth, 27
1907	70	78	5th	-21	Griffith	Chase, .287	Chase, 143	Hoffman, 5	Chase, 68	Orth, 14†
1908	51	103	8th	-39½	Griffith, Elberfeld	Hemphill, .297	Hemphill, 150	Niles, 4	Hemphill, 44	Chesbro, 14
1909	74	77	5th	-23½	Stallings	Chase, .283	Engle, 137	Chase, Demmitt, 4	Engle, 71	Lake, 14
1910	88	63	2nd	-14½	Stallings, Chase	Knight, .312	Chase, 152	Cree, Wolter, 4	Chase, 73	Ford, 26
1911	76	76	6th	-25½	Chase	Cree, .348	Cree, 181	Cree, Wolter, 4	Hartzell, 91	Ford, 22
1912	50	102	8th	-55	Wolverton	Chase, Daniels, .274	Chase, 143	Zinn, 6	Chase, 58	Ford, 13
1913	57	94	7th	-38	Chance	Cree, .272	Cree, 145	Sweeney, Wolter, 2	Cree, 63	Fisher, Ford, 11
1914	70	84	6th	-30	Chance, Peckinpaugh	Cook, .283	Cook, 133	Peckinpaugh, 3	Peckinpaugh, 51	Caldwell, 17
1915	69	83	5th	-32½	Donovan	Maisel, .281	Maisel, 149	Peckinpaugh, 5	Pipp, 58	Caldwell, 19
1916	80	74	4th	-11	Donovan	Baker, .269	Pipp, 143	Pipp, 12†	Pipp, 99	Shawkey, 23
1917	71	82	6th	-28½	Huggins	Baker, .306	Baker, 154	Baker, 6	Baker, 68	Mogridge, 16
1918	60	63	4th	-13½	Huggins	Baker, .306	Baker, 154	Baker, 6	Baker, 68	Mogridge, 16
1919	80	59	3rd	-7½	Huggins	Peckinpaugh, .305	Baker, 166	Baker, 10	Baker, 78	Shawkey, 20
1920	*95*	*59*	*3rd*	*-3*	*Huggins*	*Ruth, .376*	*Pratt, 180*	*Ruth, 54†*	*Ruth, 137†*	*Mays, 26*
1921	*98*	*55*	*1st*	*+4½*	*Huggins*	*Ruth, .378*	*Ruth, 204*	*Ruth, 59†*	*Ruth, 171†*	*Mays, 27†*
1922	*94*	*60*	*1st*	*+1*	*Huggins*	*Pipp, .329*	*Pipp, 190*	*Ruth, 35*	*Ruth, 96*	*Bush, 26*
1923	**98**	**54**	**1st**	**+16**	**Huggins**	**Ruth, .393**	**Ruth, 205**	**Ruth, 41†**	**Ruth, 131†**	**Jones, 21**

Year	W	L	Finish	+/-	Manager	Highest Batting Average	Most Hits	Most Home Runs	Most RBIs	Most Wins
1924	89	63	2nd	-2	Huggins	Ruth, .378†	Ruth, 200	Ruth, 46†	Ruth, 121	Pennock, 21
1925	69	85	7th	-30	Huggins	Combs, .342	Combs, 203	Meusel, 33†	Meusel, 138†	Pennock, 16
1926	*91*	*63*	*1st*	*+3*	*Huggins*	*Ruth, .372*	*Ruth, 184*	*Ruth, 47†*	*Ruth, 146†*	*Pennock, 23*
1927	**110**	**44**	**1st**	**+19**	**Huggins**	**Gehrig, .373**	**Combs, 231†**	**Ruth, 60†**	**Gehrig, 175†**	**Hoyt, 22†**
1928	**101**	**53**	**1st**	**+2½**	**Huggins**	**Gehrig, .374**	**Gehrig, 210**	**Ruth, 54†**	**Gehrig, Ruth, 142†**	**Pipgras, 24†**
1929	88	66	2nd	-18	Huggins, Fletcher	Lazzeri, .354	Combs, 202	Ruth, 46†	Ruth, 154	Pipgras, 18
1930	86	68	3rd	-16	Shawkey	Gehrig, .379	Gehrig, 220	Ruth, 49†	Gehrig, 174†	Pipgras, Ruffing, 15
1931	94	59	2nd	-13½	McCarthy	Ruth, .373	Gehrig, 211†	Gehrig, Ruth, 46†	Gehrig, 184†	Gomez, 21
1932	**107**	**47**	**1st**	**+13**	**McCarthy**	**Gehrig, .349**	**Gehrig, 208**	**Ruth, 41**	**Gehrig, 151**	**Gomez, 24**
1933	91	59	2nd	-7	McCarthy	Gehrig, .334	Gehrig, 198	Ruth, 34	Gehrig, 139	Gomez, 16
1934	94	60	2nd	-7	McCarthy	Gehrig, .363†	Gehrig, 210	Gehrig, 49	Gehrig, 165†	Gomez, 26†
1935	89	60	2nd	-3	McCarthy	Gehrig, .329	Rolfe, 192	Gehrig, 30	Gehrig, 119	Ruffing, 16
1936	**102**	**51**	**1st**	**+19½**	**McCarthy**	**Dickey, .362**	**DiMaggio, 206**	**Gehrig, 49**	**Gehrig, 152**	**Ruffing, 20**
1937	**102**	**52**	**1st**	**+13**	**McCarthy**	**Gehrig, .351**	**DiMaggio, 215**	**DiMaggio, 46†**	**DiMaggio, 167**	**Gomez, 21†**
1938	**99**	**53**	**1st**	**+9½**	**McCarthy**	**DiMaggio, .324**	**Rolfe, 196**	**DiMaggio, 32**	**DiMaggio, 140**	**Ruffing, 21†**
1939	**106**	**45**	**1st**	**+17**	**McCarthy**	**DiMaggio, .381†**	**Rolfe, 213†**	**DiMaggio, 30**	**DiMaggio, 126**	**Ruffing, 21**
1940	88	66	3rd	-2	McCarthy	DiMaggio, .352†	DiMaggio, 179	DiMaggio, 31	DiMaggio, 133	Ruffing, 15
1941	**101**	**53**	**1st**	**+17**	**McCarthy**	**DiMaggio, .357**	**DiMaggio, 193**	**Keller, 33**	**DiMaggio, 125†**	**Gomez, Ruffing, 15**
1942	*103*	*51*	*1st*	*+9*	*McCarthy*	*Gordon, .322*	*DiMaggio, 186*	*Keller, 26*	*DiMaggio, 114*	*Bonham, 21*
1943	**98**	**56**	**1st**	**+13½**	**McCarthy**	**Johnson, .280**	**Johnson, 166**	**Keller, 31**	**Etten, 107**	**Chandler, 20†**
1944	83	71	3rd	-6	McCarthy	Stirnweiss, .319	Stirnweiss, 205†	Etten, 22†	Lindell, 103	Borowy, 17
1945	81	71	4th	-6½	McCarthy	Stirnweiss, .309†	Stirnweiss, 195	Etten, 18	Etten, 111†	Bevens, 13
1946	87	67	3rd	-17	McCarthy, Dickey, Neun	DiMaggio, .290	Keller, 148	Keller, 30	Keller, 101	Chandler, 20
1947	**97**	**57**	**1st**	**+12**	**Harris**	**DiMaggio, .315**	**DiMaggio, 168**	**DiMaggio, 20**	**Henrich, 98**	**Reynolds, 19**
1948	94	60	3rd	-2½	Harris	DiMaggio, .320	DiMaggio, 190	DiMaggio, 39†	DiMaggio, 155†	Raschi, 19
1949	**97**	**57**	**1st**	**+1**	**Stengel**	**Henrich, .287**	**Rizzuto, 169**	**Henrich, 24**	**Berra, 91**	**Raschi, 21**
1950	**98**	**56**	**1st**	**+3**	**Stengel**	**Rizzuto, .324**	**Rizzuto, 200**	**DiMaggio, 32**	**Berra, 124**	**Raschi, 21**
1951	**98**	**56**	**1st**	**+5**	**Stengel**	**McDougald, .306**	**Berra, 161**	**Berra, 27**	**Berra, 88**	**Lopat, Raschi, 21**

Year	W	L	Finish	+/-	Manager	Highest Batting Average	Most Hits	Most Home Runs	Most RBIs	Most Wins
1952	**95**	**59**	**1st**	**+2**	**Stengel**	**Mantle, .311**	**Mantle, 171**	**Berra, 30**	**Berra, 98**	**Reynolds, 20**
1953	**99**	**52**	**1st**	**+8½**	**Stengel**	**Woodling, .306**	**McDougald, 154**	**Berra, 27**	**Berra, 108**	**Ford, 18**
1954	103	51	2nd	-8	Stengel	Noren, .319	Berra, 179	Mantle, 27	Berra, 125	Grim, 20
1955	*96*	*58*	*1st*	*+3*	*Stengel*	*Mantle, .306*	*Mantle, 158*	*Mantle, 37†*	*Berra, 108*	*Ford, 18†*
1956	**97**	**57**	**1st**	**+9**	**Stengel**	**Mantle, .353 †**	**Mantle, 188**	**Mantle, 52†**	**Mantle, 130†**	**Ford, 19**
1957	*98*	*56*	*1st*	*+8*	*Stengel*	*Mantle, .365*	*Mantle, 173*	*Mantle, 34*	*Mantle, 94*	*Sturdivant, 16*
1958	**92**	**62**	**1st**	**+10**	**Stengel**	**Howard, .314**	**Mantle, 158**	**Mantle, 42†**	**Mantle, 97**	**Turley, 21†**
1959	79	75	3rd	-15	Stengel	Richardson, .301	Mantle, 154	Mantle, 31	Lopez, 93	Ford, 16
1960	*97*	*57*	*1st*	*+8*	*Stengel*	*Skowron, .309*	*Skowron, 166*	*Mantle, 40†*	*Maris, 112†*	*Ditmar, 15*
1961	**109**	**53**	**1st**	**+8**	**Houk**	**Howard, .348**	**Richardson, 173**	**Maris, 61†**	**Maris, 142†**	**Ford, 25†**
1962	**96**	**66**	**1st**	**+5**	**Houk**	**Mantle, .321**	**Richardson, 209†**	**Maris, 33**	**Maris, 100**	**Terry, 23†**
1963	*104*	*57*	*1st*	*+10½*	*Houk*	*Howard, .287*	*Richardson, 167*	*Howard, 28*	*Pepitone, 89*	*Ford, 24†*
1964	*99*	*63*	*1st*	*+1*	*Berra*	*Howard, .313*	*Richardson, 181*	*Mantle, 35*	*Mantle, 111*	*Bouton, 18*
1965	77	85	6th	-25	Keane	Tresh, .279	Tresh, 168	Tresh, 26	Tresh, 74	Stottlemyre, 20
1966	70	89	10th	-26½	Keane, Houk	Howard, .256	Richardson, 153	Pepitone, 31	Pepitone, 83	Peterson, Stottlemyre, 12
1967	72	90	9th	-20	Houk	Clarke, .272	Clarke, 160	Mantle, 22	Pepitone, 64	Stottlemyre, 15
1968	83	79	5th	-20	Houk	White, .267	White, 154	Mantle, 18	White, 62	Stottlemyre, 21
1969	80	81	5th*	-28½	Houk	White, .290	Clarke, 183	Pepitone, 27	Murcer, 62	Stottlemyre, 20
1970	93	69	2nd	-15	Houk	Munson, .302	White, 180	Murcer, 23	White, 94	Peterson, 20
1971	82	80	4th	-21	Houk	Murcer, .331	Murcer, 175	Murcer, 25	Murcer, 94	Stottlemyre, 16
1972	79	76	4th	-6½	Houk	Murcer, .292	Murcer, 171	Murcer, 33	Murcer, 96	Peterson, 17
1973	80	82	4th	-17	Houk	Murcer, .304	Murcer, 187	Murcer, Nettles, 22	Murcer, 95	Stottlemyre, 16
1974	89	73	2nd	-2	Virdon	Piniella, .305	Murcer, 166	Nettles, 22	Murcer, 88	Dobson, Medich, 19
1975	83	77	3rd	-12	Virdon, Martin	Munson, .318	Munson, 190	Bonds, 32	Munson, 102	Hunter, 23†
1976	*97*	*62*	*1st*	*+10½*	*Martin*	*Rivers, .312*	*Chambliss, 188*	*Nettles, 32†*	*Munson, 105*	*Figueroa, 19*
1977	**100**	**62**	**1st**	**+2½**	**Martin**	**Rivers, .326**	**Rivers, 184**	**Nettles, 37**	**Jackson, 110**	**Figueroa, Guidry, 16**
1978	**100**	**63**	**1st**	**+1**	**Martin, Lemon**	**Piniella, .314**	**Munson, 183**	**Jackson, Nettles, 27**	**Jackson, 97**	**Guidry, 25†**
1979	89	71	4th	-13½	Lemon, Martin	Jackson, Piniella, .297	Chambliss, Randolph, 155	Jackson, 29	Jackson, 89	John, 21

Year	W	L	Finish	+/-	Manager	Highest Batting Average	Most Hits	Most Home Runs	Most RBIs	Most Wins
1980	103	59	1st	+3	Howser	Watson, .307	Jackson, 154	Jackson, 41†	Jackson, 111	John, 22
1981	*59*	*48*	*1st/6th*	*—*	*Michael, Lemon*	*Winfield, .294*	*Winfield, 114*	*Jackson, Nettles, 15*	*Winfield, 68*	*Guidry, 11*
1982	79	83	5th	-16	Lemon, Michael, King	Mumphrey, .300	Randolph, 155	Winfield, 37	Winfield, 106	Guidry, 14
1983	91	71	3rd	-7	Martin	Griffey, .306	Winfield, 169	Winfield, 32	Winfield, 116	Guidry, 21
1984	87	75	3rd	-17	Berra	Mattingly, .343†	Mattingly, 207†	Baylor, 27	Mattingly, 110	Niekro, 16
1985	97	64	2nd	-2	Berra, Martin	Mattingly, .324	Mattingly, 211	Mattingly, 35	Mattingly, 145†	Guidry, 22†
1986	90	72	2nd	-5½	Piniella	Mattingly, .352	Mattingly, 238†	Mattingly, 31	Mattingly, 113	Rasmussen, 18
1987	89	73	4th	-9	Piniella	Mattingly, .327	Mattingly, 186	Pagliarulo, 32	Mattingly, 115	Rhoden, 16
1988	85	76	5th	-3½	Martin, Piniella	Winfield, .322	Mattingly, 186	Clark, 27	Winfield, 107	Candelaria, 13
1989	74	87	5th	-14½	Green, Dent	Sax, .315	Sax, 205	Mattingly, 23	Mattingly, 113	Hawkins, 15
1990	67	95	7th	-21	Dent, Merrill	Kelly, .285	Kelly, 183	Barfield, 25	Barfield, 78	Guetterman, 11
1991	71	91	5th	-20	Merrill	Sax, .304	Sax, 198	Nokes, 24	Hall, 80	Sanderson, 16
1992	76	86	4th	-20	Showalter	Mattingly, .288	Mattingly, 184	Tartabull, 25	Mattingly, 86	Perez, 13
1993	88	74	2nd	-7	Showalter	O'Neill, .311	Boggs, 169	Tartabull, 31	Tartabull, 102	Key, 18
1994	70	43	1st	+6½	Showalter	O'Neill, .359†	O'Neill, 132	O'Neill, 21	O'Neill, 83	Key, 17†
<u>1995</u>	<u>79</u>	<u>65</u>	<u>2nd</u>	<u>-7(wc)</u>	<u>Showalter</u>	<u>Boggs, .324</u>	<u>B. Williams, 173</u>	<u>O'Neill, 22</u>	<u>O'Neill, 96</u>	<u>Cone, 18</u>
1996	**92**	**70**	**1st**	**+4**	**Torre**	**Duncan, .340**	**Jeter, 183**	**B. Williams, 29**	**Martinez, 117**	**Pettitte, 21†**
<u>1997</u>	<u>96</u>	<u>66</u>	<u>2nd</u>	<u>-2(wc)</u>	<u>Torre</u>	<u>B. Williams, .328</u>	<u>Jeter, 190</u>	<u>Martinez, 44</u>	<u>Martinez, 141</u>	<u>Pettitte, 18</u>
1998	**114**	**48**	**1st**	**+22**	**Torre**	**B. Williams, .339†**	**Jeter, 203†**	**Martinez, 28**	**Martinez, 123**	**Cone, 20**
1999	**98**	**64**	**1st**	**+4**	**Torre**	**Jeter, .349**	**Jeter, 219†**	**Martinez, 28**	**B. Williams, 115**	**O. Hernandez, 17**
2000	**87**	**74**	**1st**	**+2½**	**Torre**	**Jeter, .339**	**Jeter, 201**	**B. Williams, 30**	**B. Williams, 121**	**Pettitte, 19**
2001	*95*	*65*	*1st*	*+13½*	*Torre*	*Jeter, .311*	*Jeter, 191*	*Martinez, 34*	*Martinez, 113*	*Clemens, 20*

wc: AL wild card

Bold denotes AL pennant winner and world champions
Italic denotes AL pennant winner but defeated in World Series
Underline denotes defeated in ALCS (LCS 1995)
† denotes league leader

* Divisions were established in 1969;
all subsequent finishes are for the AL East.

TOTAL (through 2001): 8,674 wins, 6,629 losses, .567

POSTSEASON RECORD

26 world championships, 38 AL pennants, 10 AL East titles, 2 wild cards
World Series (through 2001): 128 wins, 84 losses, .604
Division Series and ALCS (through 2001): 54 wins, 28 losses, .659

INDEX

Page numbers in italics refer to illustrations.

Aaron, Hank (Henry), 210, 219, 249, 269
Abbott, Jim, 385
Abbott, Paul, 448
Alcohol (drinking)
    and McCarthy, 196, 200, 202
    as baseball's secret, 266
    and Mantle, 288, 306
    and Martin, 331
Aldridge, Vic, 131
Alexander, Doyle, 333, 334, 335
Alexander, Grover Cleveland, 118–19, *119*, 134
Allen, Bernie, 319
Allen, Johnny, 29
Allen, Maury, 298, 330
Allen, Mel, 173, 284
Allyn, Arthur, 297
Alomar, Roberto, 402
Alomar, Sandy, 394, 409, 454
Alou, Felipe, 290
Alou, Matty, 291
Alston, Walt, 256
Amaro, Reuben, *312*
American Association (early years), 8
American League
    and 1903 New York, 3–4
    beginning of, 4
    coexistence with NL attained by, 8
    as unlevel playing field, 24
    schism among owners of ("Insurrectos" vs. "Loyal Five"), 74, 79, 81, 82
    1961 expansion of, 278
    See also Major League Baseball
American League Championship Series. *See at* Playoff series, AL
American League Park. *See* Hilltop Park
Amoros, Sandy, 256, 260
Anderson, Brady, 401
Anderson, Brian, 450
Anderson, John, 35
Anderson, Sparky, 336, 382
Andrews, Mike, 326
Angus, Sam, 21
Anson, Cap, 24
Antitrust legislation, baseball's exemption from, 297
Aparicio, Luis, 272
Appling, Luke, 166
Arizona Diamondbacks, in 2001 World Series, 449–51
Arnold, Dorothy (wife of Joe DiMaggio), 189

Arroyo, Luis, 168, 279, 288
Ashburn, Richie, 232
Astor, William Waldorf, 96
Atlanta Braves
    in 1996 World Series, 402–5, 446
    financial resources of, 422
    in 1999 World Series, 428–31, 446
Auker, Elden, 180
Austin, Frank, 227
Austin, Jimmy, 56, 58
Autry, Gene, 338, 422
Avery, Steve, 402–3, 404, *405*
Avila, Bobby, 255

Bagby, Jim, Jr., 181
Bahnsen, Stan, 317, 318
    as Rookie of Year, 244
Baird, Tom, 210
Baker, Dusty, 348
Baker, Frank "Home Run," 57, 68–69, 70, 71, *77*, 78, 88, 96, 99, 101, 103, 456
Baker, Newton, 74
Ball, Neal, 47
Ball, Phil, 72
Ball Four (Bouton), 323
Baltimore Orioles
    original, 4, 8
    in 1996 playoffs, 401–2
Bancroft, Dave, 125
Bando, Sal, 333
Banks, Ernie, 210, 219–20, 276
Banks, Willie, 414, *417*, 418
Barajas, Rod, 452
Barber, Red, 221, *279*, 309–10
Barber, Steve, 284
Barfield, Jesse, 382–83
Barnes, Frank, 232
Barney, Rex, 221
Barrow, Ed, 93–94, 138, *201*, 295, 456
    as Tiger manager, 21
    as Red Sox manager, 77, 83
    and Ruth, 87, 88
    becomes Yankee GM, 93–94
    and deals with Boston, 96
    and 1922 acquisitions, 102
    and players' misbehavior, 103
    and Ruppert over Huston, 104
    Pipgras and Pennock acquired by, 104
    in post-1925 rebuilding, 116, 117, *118*
    1929 plans of, 141
    and manager after Huggins, 143, 144
    and McCarthy, *144*, 200
    and 1932 season, 149

in deals with Yawkey, 155
and Ruth's hopes for managership, 157
1936 deals of, 164
as president after Ruppert, 172, 199
and Gehrig's illness, 173
and WWII loss of players, 188
and Holmes-Hassett trade, 189
Etten acquired by, 192
and MacPhail as owner, 199, *201*
Yankee demeanor stressed by, 202
resignation of, 206–7
Barry, Jack, 57, 77, 83
Barstow, Rogers L., Jr., 14
Baseball
    as good for country (WWI), 74
    medical risks in playing, 142
    and war, 187–88
    "Massachusetts game" of, 205
    and alcohol, 266
    Molly O'Neill's experience of, 398–400
    See also Major League Baseball
Baseballs
    continued use of (first years), 18
    livelier version of (1920s), 86
Base Ball Writers Association of America (BBWAA), 211
Batista, Miguel, 451–52
Bauer, Hank, 227, 232, *238*, 240, 247, 252, 257, 260, 266–67, 270, 271–72, 273, 426
Bautista, Danny, 453
Baylor, Don, 337, 338, 350, 370, 375
Beane, Billy, 436, *436*
Bearden, Gene, 223, 225
Beattie, Jim, 349, 355–56, 360
Beazley, Johnny, 191, 193
Beggs, Joe, *170*
Behrman, Hank, 213
Belcher, Tim, 387
Bell, Hi, 118
Belle, Albert, 425
Bellinger, Clay, 27
Bench, Johnny, 243, 336, 362
Bender, Chief, 57
Benitez, Armando, 401, 415, *415*
Bennett, Eddie, *127*
Bentley, John, 108
Berkow, Ira, 251
Bermuda, spring training in, 60
Berra, Yogi, 209, *221*, 242–43, 459
    as MVP, 154, 243
    and Dickey, 164, 227, 243
    and 1947 MVP voting, 211
    in 1947 World Series, 212, 213, 214

and Weiss's trades, 216
and Yankee look, 219
in 1948 season, 222
in 1949 season, 227, 229
in 1950 season, 230
in 1950 World Series, 233
in 1951 season, 239
in 1952 season, 242
and proposed DiMaggio-Williams trade, 243
in 1952 World Series, 245
in 1953 World Series, 247
and Stengel years, 252
and Howard, 253, 255
in 1955 season, 255, *257*
in 1955 World Series, 256
in 1956 World Series (perfect game), 260, 261
and Howard, *266*
in Copacabana brawl, 266–67
in 1957 World Series, 270
in 1958 season, 271
in 1960 season, 275
in 1960 World Series, 276, 277
in 1961 season, 279
as manager, *286*, 295, 296–97, 298, 375, 376, 379
quoted, 287
in 1962 season, 288
in 1962 World Series, 290
on Koufax, 293
malaprops of, 295–96
as "special field consultant," 302–3
and Martin as manager, 332
as coach, 341
and Dave Winfield Day, 369
uniform number of retired, 395
and Yogi Berra Day, 426, 427
on Red Sox as rivals, 428
and "It Ain't Over Till It's Over" caps, 446
in 2001 playoff ceremonies, 447
Bevens, Floyd Clifford "Bill," *212*, 212–14, 222, 451
Black, Joe, 244
Black players
    and Yankees, 172, 199, 210–11, 219–20, 226–27, 232, 245–46, 264, 278, 292, 295, 311, 370
    Jackie Robinson, 208, 210
    increased numbers of (1950s), 254
    on Cardinals, 299
    See also Negro Leagues baseball
Blacks
    and Ruth, 87, *141*, 153, 210
    protest demonstrations by (1945), 199

and multiracialism of Yankee
  fans, 391
Black Sox scandal, 92, 93, 119–20
Blackwell, Ewell, 244
Blair, Paul, 339, 341, 345, 355
Blakely, Gordon, 412
Blanchard, Johnny, 277, 279, 307
Blauser, Jeff, 404
Blomberg, Ron, *321,* 324, 376
Blue, Vida, 333, 334
Bodie, Ping (Francesco Pezzolo), 73,
  74, 76, 78, 87, 88, 90, 91, 116,
  117
Boggs, Wade, 294, 362, 375, 385,
  397, 402, 403, 404, 405, *405,* 412,
  425, 426
Bonds, Barry, 284, 420
Bonds, Bobby, 326–27, 330, 332
Bondy, Filip, *454,* 455
Bonham, Ernie "Tiny," 29, 185, 190,
  190, 191, 193, 196, 206
Bonilla, Bobby, 401
Boone, Bret, 429, 448
Borowy, Hank, 193, 196, 200
Borton, Baker, 61
Boston Americans (Boston team
  prior to adoption of "Red Sox"),
  4, 9, 21, 24, 25, 27, 28–29,
  32–37, 205
Boston Braves, 58
  Ruth plays for, 158, 162
  in 1948 World Series, 223
  Stengel as manager of, 224, 248,
    250
  See also Milwaukee Braves
"Boston Massacre," 209, 354
Boston Red Sox
  as Yankees' alter ego, xx
  Babe Ruth on, 71, 75, 76, 77–78,
    83
  allied with Yankees, 77
  and sale of Babe Ruth, 81
  as trading partner, 92
  and Fenway Park, 97
  Yawkey as owner of, 155 (*see also*
    Yawkey, Thomas A.)
  wealth of, 161
  farm system of, 177
  and World War I, 188
  postwar surge of, 201, *204,* 206
  in 1946 World Series, 203
  as Yankee rivals, 205–6, 342–44
    (*see also under* New York Yan-
    kees)
  racism of, 210
  McCarthy as manager of, 222,
    223, 224, 229, 232
  Berra considered for manager of,
    295
  Johnson on, 342
  ticket prices of, 344
  payrolls of, 422
  in 1999 playoffs, 428
Boston Red Sox fans, and Ruth,
  83, 89
Boswell, Dave, 331
Boudreau, Lou, 181, 223
Bouton, Jim, 287, 292, 293, 296,
  299, 301, 307, 311, 323
Boyer, Clete, 264, 273, 276, 285,
  293, 301, 311, 312, 458
Branca, Ralph, 212, 213, 221, 239

Brenly, Bob, 450, 451, 454
Bresnahan, Roger, 24, 362
Brett, George, 335, 356, 362, 363,
  375
Brett, Ken, 332, 335
Brinkman, George, 375
Broaca, Johnny, 155
Brock, Lou, 220, 299
"Bronx Zoo," 338, *338,* 345, 348,
  357, 455
Brooklyn Dodgers
  and Garvin, 28
  attendance for, 60
  vs. Yankees, 76
  in 1941 World Series, 184–85
  and MacPhail, 197
  and Jackie Robinson, 210
  in 1949 World Series, 229–30
  1950s as triumphal age of,
    235–36
  in 1951 playoff, 239
  in 1952 World Series, 244–45
  in 1953 World Series, 247, 252
  Stengel as manager of, 248, 249
  constituency of (1950s), 253
  in 1955 World Series, 255–57, *257*
  in 1956 World Series, *258,*
    258–61
  as Yankees' competitors (late
    1950s), 263–64
  move to Los Angeles, 269
  See also Los Angeles Dodgers
Brosius, Scott, 412
  as Gold Glove winner, 294
  in 1998 season, 413, 418, 419, 420
  in 1998 playoffs, 421
  in 1998 World Series, *410,* 423
  as acquired cheaply, 424
  re-signing of, 425
  beaned by Clemens, 426
  in 1999 season, 427
  in 1999 World Series, 429
  illness of father, 430
  in 2000 season, 434
  in 2000 World Series, 442
  in 2001 season, 442, 445
  in 2001 playoffs, 446, 447, 448
  in 2001 World Series, 450, *450,*
    452
  retirement of, 455
Broun, Heywood, 59, 61, 67
Brown, Bobby, 227, 232, 233, 239,
  242
Brown, Charlie, 344
Brown, Ike, 325
Brown, Kevin, 423
Brown, Skinny, 284
Brush, John, 9, 10–11, 21, 28, 43,
  54, 56
Bryant, Howard, 373, 449
Buddie, Mike, 418
Buhl, Bob, 269
Bulger, Bozeman, 123
Burde, Bill (Cree pseudonym), 52
Burdette, Lew, 239, 269, 270, 271,
  272
Burke, Mike, 309, 310, 311, 316,
  316, 319, 322, 323
Burkett, John, 397
Burleson, Rick, 355
Burns, George (Boston player), 105
Busch, August, 390, 422

Bush, "Bullet Joe," 29, 72, 102–3,
  112
Bush, Donnie, 124, 125, 132, 143
Bush, George W., 450
Bush, Homer, 426
Byrd, Harry, 252
Byrd, Sammy, 149, 157
Byrne, Tommy, 223, 224, 227, 255,
  256, 259, 270, 271

Cable television, 297
Cabrera, Orlando, 427
Caldwell, Charlie, 113
Caldwell, Earl, 223
Caldwell, Ray, 68, 71, 76
California Angels, resources of, 422
California League, 47, 48
Cameron, Mike, 448
Camilli, Dolph, 184, 185
Campanella, Roy, 229, 242, 244,
  246, 247, 254, 255, 256, 260, 362
Campaneris, Bert, 333
Campbell, Bill, 345
Canfield, Richard, 14
Cannon, Jimmy, 218, 281
  quoted, 263
Canseco, Jose, 435
Cantillon, Joe, 53, 54
Captain of team
  importance of (1910), 54
  Gehrig named as, 162, *164*
Cardenal, Jose, 390
Carey, Andy, 245, 252, 254, 259,
  260
Carey, Max, 249
Carter, Gary, 379
Cary, Chuck, 382
Casey, Hugh, 185, 213, 214, 221
"Casey at the Bat," and 1923 Series,
  107
Cashman, Brian, 412, *412,* 413, 419,
  424, 426, 427, 434, 442, *444*
Cater, Danny, 318, *318*
CBS, as owners of Yankees, 277,
  297, *299,* 306, 308, 319, 321
Cepeda, Orlando, 290
Cerone, Rick, 361, 365
Chambers, John, 295
Chambliss, Chris, 326
  as Gold Glove winner, 294
  in 1976 season, 332
  in 1976 playoffs, *333,* 335–36,
    448–49
  and Yankee resurgence, 339
  in 1977 World Series, 347, 348
  in 1978 playoff game, 355
  traded, 361
  as hitting coach, 390
Chance, Dean, 297
Chance, Frank, 58, 60–62, 72
Chandler, Happy, 208, 211, 227,
  236, 265
Chandler, Spud, 29, 154, 191, 193,
  193, 195, *195,* 201, 210, 212–13,
  309
Chapman, Ben, 144, 148, 152, 157,
  166, 189, 232
Chapman, Ray, 91, 92, 96
Chartak, Mike, 199
Chase, Hal (Harold Homer), xx,
  40–41, *43,* 46–47, 57–58, 138, 456

in 1905 season, 43
in 1906 season, *41,* 44, 45
and divisions in Yankee team, 46
in 1907 season, 47
and Elberfeld as manager, 48
in 1909 season, 49, *51*
in clash with Stallings, 53–55, *55*
as manager, 55, 56, 57, *57,* 58, 59
and Chance, 60–61
and New York City, 61, 76
and Pratt, 72
Chass, Murray, 352, 365
Cherry, Carlton, 329
Chesbro, Jack, 8, 16, *22,* 138, 457
  in 1903 season, 18, 19, 20, 21
  in 1904 season, *22,* 24, 25, 26, 27,
    28, 29, *29,* 30–31, 32, 32–33,
    35, 35–37, 39
  quoted, 23
  after 1904 season, 26, 39, 40
  and spitball, 26, 41, 44
  in 1905 season, 41, 43
  in 1906 season, *41,* 44, 45, 46
  as drinker, 43
  after 1906 season, 47
  in trade offer from Boston, 47
  in 1907 season, 47
  last big-league victory of, 48
  in 1909 season, 49
  end of career for, 49
Chicago Cubs, 44, 57, 67, 172, 343
Chicago White Sox
  and AL raiding of NL, 4
  in 1904 season, 28
  in 1906 season, 44, 45
  bid for Ruth by, 87
  and 1920 season, 91
  and Black Sox scandal (1919), 92,
    93, 119–20
  and 1932 World Series, 152–54
  black players on (1950s), 254
Cimoli, Gino, 276
Cincinnati Reds, 177, 285, *334,* 336
Clark, Jack, 382
Clarke, Horace, 308, 315, *315*
Clarkson, John, 27
Clarkson, Walter, 27, 33
Clay, Ken, 349
Clemens, Roger, 425–26
  Chesbro compared with, 25
  as Cy Young winner, 341
  in poll on best players, 362
  with Toronto, 420
  acquired by Yankees, 426
  in 1999 season, 427
  in 1999 playoffs, 428, 436, 448
  in 1999 World Series, 430, 431
  and 2000 season, 434
  in 2000 playoffs, 435, 436
  seen as big-game loser, 436
  in 2000 World Series, 438, *438,*
    441
  in 2001 season, 443, *443,* 444, 445
  and terrorist attacks, 444
  in 2001 playoffs, 446, 447, 448
  in 2001 World Series, 450, 452,
    453
Clemente, Roberto, 276, 277, 321
Cleveland Indians
  and AL raiding of NL, 4
  in 1914 season, 62

Cleveland Indians (cont.)
  and Yankee trade, 67, 70
  Ban Johnson's interest in, 79
  in 1948 season, 223, 224
  in 1954 season, 236, 252
  black players on (1950s), 254
  Steinbrenner almost purchases, 320
  and Gabe Paul's suspect trade, 322–23
  and 1997 playoffs, 408–9
  in 1998 playoffs, 421
and Yankee playoff achievements, 446
Clift, Harland, 157
Coates, Jim, 277
Cobb, Ty, 40, 52, 57, 70, 99, 111, 120, 121, 122, *229*
Cochrane, Mickey, 138, 148, 149, 167, 243
Coggins, Rich, 330
Colangelo, Jerry, 449
Coleman, Jerry, 227, 229, 232–33, 239, 242, *254*, 255, *258*, 269, 271
Coleridge, Samuel Taylor, quoted, 3
Collins, Dave, 366, 374
Collins, Eddie, 57, 68, 70, 91, 96, 99, 121, 143, 147, 222
Collins, Jimmy, 33, 47, 69
Collins, Joe, 245, 252, 256, 271
Collins, Pat, 117, 122
Collins, Rip, 102
Colon, Bartolo, 423
Columbus Clippers, xx
Combs, Earle, 109, *153*, 457
  and Meusel, *102*
  in 1924 season, 111
  in 1925 season, 113
  purchase price of, 117
  in 1927 season, 126, 127
  in 1927 World Series, 134
  and 1928 World Series, 135
  in 1929 season, 140
  and Joe McCarthy, 144
  in 1932 World Series, 154
  in 1934 season, *153*, 157–58
  retirement of, 162
  at Lou Gehrig Appreciation Day, 176
  as "table-setter," 179
Comiskey, Charles, 8, 79, 92, 265
Concepcion, Dave, 336
Cone, David, 386
  in 1995 playoffs, 387
  in 1996 season, 391, 394, 396
  in 1996 playoffs, 396–97
  and 1996 World Series, 403, 404
  and 1997 playoffs, *407*, 408–9
  in 1997 season, 408
  in 1998 season, 413, 417, 418, 420
  as top starter, 414
  in 1998 playoffs, 420, 422, 423
  in 1998 World Series, 423
  as high-priced mercenary, 424
  re-signing of, 425
  perfect game of (1999), 427
  in 1999 World Series, 429
  and 2000 season, 434–35
  in 2000 playoffs, 435
  in 2000 World Series, 441–42
  with Boston, 442, 443
Conlin, Bill, 382

Connery, Bob, 117
Connors, Mark, 386, 412
Conroy, Wid, 8, 16, 35, 37, 44, 47
Contreras, Nardi, 386
Cook, Cardinal, 361
Cooke, Dusty, 144
Coomer, Ron, 414
Cooper, Mort, 195
Cooper, Walker, 195
Copacabana incident, 266–67, 330
Cora, Joey, 387
Corbett, Brad, 332
Cosell, Howard, 271
Counsell, Craig, 450, 454
Coveleski, Stan, 100
Cowens, Al, 335
Cowley, Joe, 379
Cox, Bobby, 403, 404, 409
Cox, John, 264
Crane, Sam, 19, 20, 56, 61
Cravath, Gavvy, 86
Crawford, Sam, 57, 99
Cree, Birdie (William Franklin), xx, 49, 51–52, 53, *53*, 57, 60, 69, 138, 457
Criger, Lou, 26, 32, 33, 36, 37
Croker, Richard, 5, 11, 67
Cronin, Joe, 177, 207, 222, 297, 325, 326
Crosetti, Frank, *74*, 146, 147, 162, 163, 164, 177, 178, 189, 195, 247, 456
Crowder, Enoch B., 73
Cubas, Joe, 417
Cuccurullo, Cookie, 206
Cullen, Jack, 306
Cullenbine, Roy, 191
Cullop, Nick, 70
Curry, Jack, 387, 409
Curtis, Chad, 407, 413, 418, 424, 429–30, 431

Dahlgren, Babe, 169, 175, 176
Daley, Bud, 298
Damn Yankees (musical), 257, 420
Dandridge, Ray, 210
Daniel, Dan, 123, 126, 179, 211
Dark, Al, 290, 291
Davenport, Dave, 70
Davis, Chili, 412, 413, 419, 424, 428, 433
Davis, Curt, 184
Davis, Lefty, 8, 16, 19, 20
Davis, Piper, 226
Davis, Russ, 391
Dawson, Ed, 94
Dead Ball Era
  and Keeler, 18
  and Chase, 40
  baseball parks built for, 97
  Stengel in, 226
Cobb on players of, *229*
Dean, Dizzy, 172
Deering, John, 21
Delahanty, Ed, 20, 151
DeLorean, John, 322
DeMaestri, Joe, 273
Dempsey, Jack, 128
Dent, Bucky, 339, 357, 374, 382, 391
  1978 playoff home run of, 355
Depression, 148, 158, 161

World War II as end of, 191–92
  in Mantle's background, 237
Derringer, Paul, 177
Designated hitter, 323–24, 366
Detroit Tigers, 4, 21
Devens, Charles, 146–47
Devery, William S. "Big Bill," *9, 13, 14–15*, 19, 20, 63, 277
  and new ballpark construction, 18
  and Yankees' 1903 season, 20, 23
  and Hughes-Tannehill trade, 27
  and Brush, 28
  and 1904 closing series, 32, 39
  in Yankees 1904 success, 39
  players sold by, 43
  and NY logo, 49
  insolvency of, 58, 62
  and Wolverton as manager, 59
  "Yankees" name chosen by, 59
  and Chase, 61
  and Chance, 61, 62
  and Ruppert, 65
  and Steinbrenner, 321
Devine, Joe, 162
Devormer, Al, 103
Dickey, Bill, 140, 164, 457
  in 1930 season, 144
  Devens's memories of, 147
  in 1936 season, 164, 166
  Berra tutored by, 164, 227, 243
  DiMaggio outpolls, 166
  on 1937 All-Stars, 167
  in 1937 season, 169
  in 1938 season, 170
  in 1939 season, 177
  in 1940 season, 178
  at Gehrig funeral, 179
  in 1941 World Series, 185
  in 1942 season, 189
  in 1943 season, 193
  in 1943 World Series, 195, *195*
  WWII service of, 195
  as accompanied by other greats, 201
  as manager, 202, 203
  retirement of, 209
  as one of greatest catchers, 243
  on Mantle power, 258
  uniform number of retired, 395
DiMaggio, Dom, 180, 192, 201, *204*, 206, 223, 224, 227–28, 238, 242
DiMaggio, Joe, xix, 160, 161, *163*, *204, 230*, 455, 457, 458
  as Italian American, *74*
  as home run leader, 75
  as RBI leader, 90
  and Yankee Stadium, 97
  as batting champion, 129
  and Gehrig, *149*, 151, 165, 166, 167, 176, 177
  as MVP, 154, 211
  Yankees' discovery and acquisition of, 159, 162–64, 422
  and Ruth, *160*, 165, 166, 168, 169
  and press, 163, 164, 168
  in 1936 season, 164–65
  in 1936 World Series, *163*, 166–67, 182
  made center fielder, 166
  in 1937 season, 168

on 1937 All-Stars, 167
  in 1937 World Series, *167*, 169
  public image of, 168–69
  in 1938 season, 169–70, 172
  in 1939 season, *170*, 172, 173, 175, 177
  nicknamed "Clipper," 173
  in 1940 season, 178
  in 1941 season, 179–81, 182
  hitting streak of, 179–81, *182*
  and Williams, 180, 182, 188, 224
  in 1941 World Series, 185
  in 1942 season, 188, 190
  marriage of (first), 189, 192
  in 1942 World Series, 191
  WWII service of, 192, 196, *197*, 200
  and 1945 season, 200
  in 1946 spring tour, 200
  in 1946 season, 201, 202, 203
  in company of other great players, 201
  as 1946 World Series spectator, *202*
  on McCarthy, 203
  MacPhail offers to trade for Vernon, 207
  in proposed trade for Williams, 207, *207*, 243
  bone-spur injury and surgery of, 208–9, 223, 226, 227
  and Berra, *208*
  in 1947 season, 209–10, 211
  in 1947 World Series, 211, 212, 213, 221–22, *222*
  Rickey on, 222
  in 1948 season, 223–24
  and Stengel, 227, 230, 232, 236, 250
  in 1949 season, 227–29
  considers retiring, 230
  in 1950 season, 230, 232
  in 1950 World Series, 232
  and Yankee reemergence, 233
  retirement contemplated by, 236
  and Mantle, 237
  in 1951 season, 238, 239
  in 1951 World Series, *238*, 240
  retirement of, 242
  during Stengel years, 252
  at 1961 World Series ceremonies, 285
  monument to, 317
  1977 World Series snub of, 345
  on Martin's reinstatement, 353
  and Winfield, 374
  uniform number of retired, 395
  Jeter compared with, 401
  honoring of (1998), 420
  death of, 427, 430
DiMaggio, Vince, 162
Dinneen, Bill, 29, 33, 36, 37, 47, 103, 130
Dinsmore (in DiMaggio trade), 159
Ditmar, Art, 264
Dobson, Pat, 324, 326, 332
Doby, Larry, 210, 227, 243, 252, 254
Doerr, Bobby, 177, 189, 201, 229
Donahue, Jiggs, 58
Donald, Atley, *186*
Donatelli, Augie, 270
Donovan, "Wild Bill," 67, 68, 71, *72*

Dougherty, Patsy, 27, 29, 32, 33, 36, 37, 39, 43
Douglas, "Shuffling" Phil, 100, 101
Down, Rick, 389
Downing, Al, 226, 292, 293, 306, 307
Doyle, Brian, 355, 357
Doyle, Joe, 44, 45
Drabek, Doug, 379
Drebinger, John, 127, 191
Dressen, Charlie, 206, 208, 213
Drews, Matt, 386
Dreyfuss, Barney, 132
Drysdale, Don, 292, 293
Duffy, Hugh, 94
Dugan, "Jumping" Joe, 89, 102, 103, 105, 108, 113, *114,* 116, 122, 126, 135, 138, 140, 457
Dukes, Tom, 295
Duncan, Mariano, 392, 394, 397, 405
Dunn, Jack, *93,* 149
Dunn, James, 70
Duquette, Dan, 425, 444
Durante, Sal, 285
Durazo, Erubiel, 451
Duren, Ryne, 168, 267
Durocher, Leo, 138, 140, 141, 184, 197, *202,* 206, 208, 229, 238
Durst, Cedric, 120, 132, 134
Dye, Jermaine, 403, 404

Earnshaw, George, 148, 149, 151
Easler, Mike, 370
Eastwick, Rawley, 349
Ebbets Field, 208, 264
Eckersley, Dennis, 350, 354
Edwards, Bruce, 213
Edwards, Doc, 307
Egan, Dave, 224, 225
Ehmke, Howard, 105
Elberfeld, Norman "Kid," 21, *45,* 456
   in 1904 season, 25, 32, 33, 36, 37, 39
   and Chase, 40
   in 1906 season, 44, 45, *45*
   and divisions in Yankee team, 46
   in 1907 season, 47
   as manager, 48
   in 1909 season, 49
   Cree compared with, 51
   Wolverton compared with, 59
   as unremembered in 1920s, 138
Ellis, Dock, 332, 334, 340
Ellis, John, 323
Emery ball, of Russ Ford, 49, 86
Ennis, Del, 232
Erskine, Carl, 244, 247
Espinosa, Alvaro, 391
Essick, Bill, 162
Ethnic identification
   by fans in early years, 24
   See also Italian-American players
Etten, Nick, 75, 90, 192, 193, *195,* 196, 199, 201
Ettinger, Jerry, 53
Evans, Dwight, 330
Everett, Carl, 444
Ewing, Buck, 362
Expansion draft, 337

Fan interference, in 1996 playoffs, 401
Fans, Yankee. *See* Yankee fans
Farm system, 148
   of Cardinals, 148
   of Red Sox, 177, 210
   of Dodgers and Giants, 264
   of Yankees, 148
   and Weiss, 149, 155, 161, 216, 219, 270
   Ruppert's wisdom in, 172
   during World War II, 188
   and black players, 210, 220
   weakening of, 278, 293, 311
   and Steinbrenner's mistakes, 361
   1990s maturing of, 384
   emphasis on, 422
   core of 1998 team from, 424
   See also Scouting system, Yankee
Farrell (in trade for DiMaggio), 159
Farrell, Duke, 32
Farrell, Frank, *9,* 10, *10, 13,* 14, 19, 63, 277
   and gambling, *10,* 14, 46
   and Devery, 15
   and new ballpark construction, 18
   and Yankees' 1903 season, 20, 23
   and Hughes-Tannehill trade, 27
   and Brush, 28
   and 1904 closing series, 32, 39
   and Yankees 1904 success, 39
   players sold by, 43
   and 1907 expectations, 47
   and Stallings as manager, 48–49
   and Stallings-Chase conflict, 54, 55
   and first subway series, 54, 56
   insolvency of, 58–59, 62
   "Yankees" name chosen by, 59
   and Chase, 61
   and Chance, 61, 62
   Yankee franchise sold by, 63
   and Ruppert, 65
   and MacPhail, 197
   and Steinbrenner, 321
Fassero, Jeff, 434
Federal League, 62, 66, 68, 69
Feller, Bob, 188, 192, 239, 266
Fenway Park, 97
   and Babe Ruth, 76
and pitchers, 96, 289, 354
as unique, 104
Fernandez, Tony, 391, 392
Ferraro, Mike, 363
Ferrell, Rick, 362
Ferrell, Wes, 162
Ferris, Hobe, 33, 36
Fewster, Chick, 88
Fielder, Cecil, 396, 397, *397,* 402, 403, 404, 407, 412
Figueroa, Ed, 332, 334, 335, 345, 347, 349, 360
Fingers, Rollie, 333, 334
Finley, Charles O., 278, 297, 306, 307, 326, 327, 333–34, 337
Finley, Chuck (pitcher), 434
Finley, Steve, 450, 452, 453
First base position, and Chase, 40
Fisher, Jack, *283,* 285
Fisher, Ray, 68
Fisk, Carlton, *322,* 324, 350, 362

Fitzsimmons, Freddie, 184
Five-tool player
   DiMaggio as, 163
   Winfield as, 364
Fixed games
   1907 suspicion of, 47
   Black Sox scandal, 92, 93, 119–20
   suspicion of (1926 World Series), 120
   1919 plan for, 120
   speculation on in 1927 Series, 134
   See also Gambling
Flatiron Building, *2, 3,* 4, 48, 137
Fletcher, Art, 141, 143, 175, 196
Flood, Curt, 220, 299
Florida Marlins, 411, 449
Forbes Field, 132
Ford, Gerald, 332
Ford, Russ, 49, 51, *52,* 53, 56, 57, 59
Ford, Whitey, xx, *230, 254,* 459
   in 1950 season, *230,* 237
   in 1950 World Series, *230,* 233
   in service, 237
   in 1953 season, 246
   in 1953 World Series, 247, 252
   during Stengel years, 252, 253
   in 1955 season, 255
   in 1955 World Series, 256
   in 1956 season, 259
   in 1956 World Series, 259
   in 1957 season, 266, 267
   as exempt from discipline, 267
   in 1958 season, 271
   in 1961 season, 279, 288
   in 1961 World Series, 285
   in 1962 season, 288, 289
   Stengel's vs. Houk's use of, 288, 289
   in 1962 World Series, 291, *291*
   in 1963 season. 292
   in 1963 World Series, 293
   and Berra as manager, 296
   in 1964 season, 301
   in 1964 World Series, 301
   in 1965 season, 307
   in 1966 season, 309, *310,* 311
   as ERA leader, 309
   retirement considered by, 311
   retirement of, 314
   and Martin as manager, 332
   as Cy Young winner, 341
   in Hall of Fame, 362
   uniform number of retired, 395
Fortner, Joseph, 130
Foster, George, 336
Fowler, Art, 350
Fox, Nellie, 272
Foxx, Jimmie, 135, 138, 148, 149, 166, 177, 189, 258, 344
Franks, Herman, 319–20, 321
Frazee, Harry, 82–83
   in deal with Athletics, 72, 73
   and Ban Johnson, 74, 76–77, 79, 82, 83, 87
   and 1918 success, 76
   and Mays trade, 78
   and Robert Wagner, 79
   and sale of Babe Ruth, 81, 82, 83, 87, 88
   and Barrow, 94, 96

Pipgras and Pennock traded by, 104
   in World War I, 188
   and Steinbrenner, 320
Frazier, Walt "Clyde," 251
Free agency, 329–30
   and Hunter, 327, 329, 330
   and Messersmith decision, 333
   and Finley, 333
   and 1976 Reds, 336
   shifting rosters under, 405
   and Yankees, 330, 333, 336, 374
   and black ballplayers, 220
   Catfish Hunter signed, 330
   and reentry draft, 337
   Steinbrenner's misuse of, 361, 365
   and fans, 375
   inactivity (early 1990s), 383
   and farm system, 384
   and Bernie Williams, 424–25
   and vacancies after 2001 season, 455
Free agent draft, 307
Free agent draft of minor leaguers, 295
Freedman, Andrew, 4, 5, 7–8, 9–10, 11, 13, 18, 20, 21, *22,* 67, 68
Freeman, Buck, 33, 36, 86
Frick, Ford, 123, 126, 265, 283, 284
"Friday Night Massacre," 326, 336
Friend, Bob, 276, 277
Frisch, Frankie, 100, 101, *107,* 107–8
Fryman, Travis, 422
Fuchs, Emil, 158, 249
Fullerton, Hugh, 117
Fultz, Dave, 16, 19, 21, 24
Furillo, Carl, 213, 247, 255, 260

Galehouse, Denny, 224
Gallagher, Joe, *170*
Gallego, Mike, 385
Gallico, Paul, 123, 126, 130, *131,* 134
Gamble, Oscar, 332, 339
Gambling
   and Farrell, *10,* 14, 46
   and 1907 Yankees, 46–47
   and Chase, 55, 57
   prevalence of (1918), 77
   and Black Sox scandal, 92, 93
   and World Series, 101–2
   by Ruth, 102
   and 1926 World Series, 119–20
   and 1919 season game-fixing plan, 120
   Pete Rose affair, 120, 381
   and MVP voting, 211
   and Steinbrenner's relationship to Spira, 381
   See also Fixed games
Gandil, Chick, 120
Ganzel, John, 16, 18, 37, 40
Garagiola, Joe, 296
Garcia, Freddy, 436
Garcia, Mike, 243, 244
Garcia, Richie, 401
Garciaparra, Nomar, 428, 434
Garrett, Lin, 417
Garvey, Steve, 348
Garvin, Ned, 28, 29, 32
Gaston, Milt, 122

Gedeon, Joe, 188
Gehrig, Eleanor (wife), 173, 176,
    324–25
Gehrig, Lou, xix, 109, *114*, 138, *149*,
    151–52, 176–77, 455, 456
    and Hal Chase, xx
    as home run leader, 75
    as RBI leader, 90
    and Yankee Stadium, 97
    as thirteen-year-old, *109*
    consecutive-games streak of,
        113, 168, 173, 176
    in 1926 season, 116, 117, 120
    and Ruth, *120*, 121, 122, 126–27,
        130, *149*, 151, 152, 155, 158,
        162, 167, 176, 276
    in 1927 season, 120, 121, 122,
        123, 126, 127, 129, 131
    as batting champion, 129
    in 1927 World Series, 134
    in 1928 season, 135
    quoted, 137
    in 1929 season, 140
    and Shawkey as manager, 144
    in 1930 season, 144
    Devens's memories of, 146, 147
    in 1931 season, 148
    in 1932 season, 149, 151
    and DiMaggio, *149*, 151, 165,
        166, 167, 176, 177
    four-homer game of, 149, *149*,
        151
    in 1932 World Series, 152, 154
    as MVP, 154, 166, 167
    in 1933 season, 155
    in 1934 season, 157, 158
    wins Triple Crown, 158
    in 1935 season, 162
    named team captain, 162, *164*
    and press, 164, 173
    in 1936 season, 166, *173*
    in 1936 World Series, 166, 167
    as older player, 167, *173*
    on 1937 All-Stars, 167
    off-the-field life of, 168
    in 1937 season, 169
    in 1937 World Series, 169
    in 1938 season, 169, 170, 172
    stoic compliance of, 169
    and 1938 World Series, 172
    illness of, 172–73, 175, 176
    Appreciation Day for, *175*, 176
    death of, 179
    in company of other great play-
        ers, 201
    monument to, *214*, 317
    and Mantle, 236, 258
    uniform number of retired, 395
Gehringer, Charlie, 166
Gergen, Joe, 354
Giambi, Jason, 370, 436, 446, 447,
    448, 455
Gibbs, Jake, xx
Gibson, Bob, 220, 299, 301, *301*
Gibson, Norwood, 29
Giles, Brian, 398
Gilhooly, Frank, 70
Gilks, Bob, 117
Gilliam, Jim, 256, *260*
Gilmore, James, 62
Gionfriddo, Al, 213–14, 221
    1947 World Series catch by, *221*

Girardi, Joe, 391, 403, 405, 420, 424,
    425, 429, 433
Giuliani, Rudy, 408, 424, *432*, 433,
    438, 448
Glavine, Tom, 402, 403, 428, 446
Gleason, Jackie, 293
Globe Theatre, and Yankee Sta-
    dium, 97
Gloves worn by players, 58
Gomez, Lefty (Vernon), 148, 152,
    155, 164, 165, *167*, 167–68, 169,
    172, 180, 184, 226, 309
Gonzales, Juan, 395, 397, 420
Gonzalez, Luis, 449, 450, 454
Gooden, Dwight, 379, 390, 394,
    407, *407*, 409, 423
Gooding, Gladys, 261
Goodman, Irval, 177
Goodman, John, 130
Gordon, Joe, 169, *170*, 456
    as MVP, 154
    in 1938 season, 172
    in 1939 season, 172, 173, 177
    in 1940 season, 178
    in 1941 season, 179
    in 1941 World Series, 184, *184*,
        185
    in 1942 season, 190
    in 1943 season, 193
    in 1943 World Series, *193*, *195*
    WWII service of, 195, 196, 201
    traded for Reynolds, 206, 216
Gordon, Joseph (team president),
    11, 18, 19, 32
Goslin, Goose, 111, 166
*Gospel According to Casey: Casey Sten-
    gel's Inimitable, Instructional, Histor-
    ical Baseball Book, The* (Berkow and
    Kaplan), 251
Gossage, Rich "Goose," 168, *328*,
    349, 355, 357, 360, 375, 379, *383*,
    459
Grabowski, Johnny, 120
Grace, Mark, 449, 450, 452, 454
Graham, Charlie, 163, 164
Graham, Frank, 123
Gray, Sam, 129
Grba, Eli, 275
Great Lakes Naval Station team,
    196
Green, Dallas, 382
Greenberg, Hank, 157, 169, 189–90,
    258
Greenwade, Tom, 226, 236
Gregg, Hal, 213
Grich, Bobby, 337, 338, 349
Griffey, Ken, 366, 374
Griffey, Ken, Jr., 387, 424, 448
Griffith, Calvin, 331
Griffith, Clark, *14*, 16
    acquired from White Sox, 8
    in 1903 season, 18, 21
    and 1904 season, 24, 25, 29,
        32–33, 35, 36, 37, 39
    and Hughes, 27
    and Chase, 40
    and 1905 season, 41
    and 1906 season, 44, 45
    and 1907 season, 47
    trading after 1907 season, 47
    and 1908 season, 48
    resigns as manager, 48

Grim, Bob, 168, 244, 253, 270
Grimes, Oscar, 199, 201
Grimsley, Jason, 429
Grissom, Marquis, 404, 409
Groat, Dick, 276, 277
Gross, Milton, 291, 292, 302, 309
Grove, Lefty, 25, 121, 127–28, 129,
    177, 189
Guetterman, Lee, 382
Guidry, Ron, 459
    as Gold Glove winner, 294
    as ERA leader, 309
    as Cy Young winner, 341
    in 1977 season, 345
    in 1977 World Series, 345, 347
    in 1978 season, *349*, 349–50, 354
    in 1978 playoff game, 354, 355
    in 1978 World Series, 356
    in 1979 season, 360
    in 1980 playoffs, 363
    and 1981 season, 365
    and Dave Winfield Day, 370
    in 1983 season, 375
    decline of, 379
    and Righetti, *383*
Gullett, Don, 336, 337, 338, 345,
    349, 365
Gumpert, Randy, 238
Gura, Larry, 335, 363
Guzman, Christian, 412
Gwynn, Tony, 362

Haddix, Harvey, 277
Hadley, Bump, 164
Hadley, Kent, 273
Haines, Jesse, 118
Halberstam, David, 220, 343
Hall, Mel, 370
Hall of Fame, and Yankees, 362
    Yankee Stadium memorabilia in,
        324
    Munson and Mattingly fit for, 362
Hamey, Roy, 278, 279, 292, 293, 295
Hamner, Granny, 232
Hampton, Mike, 434, 441
Haney, Fred, 272
Hanlon, Ned, 226, 330
Hanna, W. B., 130
Harper, Harry, 96
Harrington, John, 444
Harris, Bucky, 121, 206, 213, 214,
    223, 224
Harris, Lum, 285
Harrison, James, 121, 122, 123, 126
Hartzell, Roy, 58
Hassett, Buddy, 188–89, 191, 192
Hatten, Joe, 213
Hawkins, Andy, 382
Hayes, Charlie, 385, 397, 402, 403,
    405, 412
Hayes, Tom, 226–27
Hayes, Woody, 320, 332
Healy, Fran, 335, 340
Hecht, Henry, 352
Heffner, Don, *157*
Hegan, Mike, 324
Heilmann, Harry, 99
Heimach, Fred, 140
Held, Woodie, 265, 267
Henderson, Ricky, 189, 362, 370,
    376, 379–80, 382, 458

Henie, Sonja, 197, *198*
Henrich, Tommy, 169, *204*, 457
    in 1938 season, 172
    in 1939 season, 172
    in 1941 season, 180
    in 1941 World Series, 185
    WWII service of, 190–91
    and 1947 season, 209
    in 1947 World Series, 213, 221
    Rickey on, 222
    in 1948 season, 223
    in 1949 season, 227, 228, 229
    on Yankees vs. Red Sox, 343
Heredia, Gil, 435
Hernandez, Arnaldo, 415
Hernandez, Keith, 379
Hernandez, Livan, 417
Hernandez, Orlando "El Duque,"
    415, 417
    in 1998 season, 418, *418*
    in 1998 playoffs, 420, 423
    and Yankees' smart decisions,
        422, 424
    in 1999 season, 427
    in 1999 playoffs, 428
    in 1999 World Series, 428–29
    in 2000 season, 434
    in 2000 playoffs, 436, 438
    in 2000 World Series, 441
    in 2001 season, 442, 443
    in 2001 playoffs, 448
    in 2001 World Series, 450–51
Hernandez, Willie, 379
Herzog, Whitey, 335
Higbe, Kirby, 184
High, Andy, 240
High, Hugh, 68, 70
Hill, Carmen, 131, 134
Hill, Glenallen, 435
Hiller, Chuck, 291, *291*
Hilltop (American League) Park, *7*, *16*,
    19, 19–20, 21, *25*, *43*, *46*, 59, 60
    construction of, 11, 13–14, 18
    Opening Day at, *13*
    rented to Columbia U. (1904), 32
    subway opened to, 41
Hitchcock, Sterling, 391, 452
Hoag, Myril, 157, 166
Hoak, Don, 276
Hoblitzell, Dick, 75
Hodges, Gil, 244, 245, 255, 260
Hodgson, Claire (later Mrs. Claire
    Ruth), 116, 140, 162
Hoffman, Danny, 47
Hoffman, Trevor, *410*
Hogg, Billy, 45
Holmes, Darren, 418
Holmes, Tommy (player), 188–89,
    189
Holmes, Tommy (writer), 301
Holtzman, Ken, 333, 334, 335
Home runs
    in Dead Ball Era, 18
    Yankee leaders in, 75
    Yankees recognize potential of,
        75
    and Babe Ruth, 75, 78, 86,
        128–31, *131*, 423
    proliferation of, 86
    by Ruth and Gehrig (1927), 122
    Mantle's tape-measure home
        runs, 246, *247*, 257–58

Maris's record for, *279, 280,* 280–85, 288
McGwire-Sosa race for, 419
Hooper, Harry, 47, 77
Hooten, Burt, 348
Hoover, Herbert, and Ruth's salary remark, 143
Hopkins, Paul, 129
Hornsby, Rogers, 118, 119, *119,* 144, 179
Horween, Arnie, 146
Hough, Charlie, 348
Houk, Ralph, 278, *290*
    as Tiger manager, 325, 326
    as Yankee manager, 278, 279, *290*
    in 1961 season, 279
    in 1962 season, 288, 289
    and Ford, 289
    in 1962 World Series, 290, 291
    and 1963 World Series, 292, 293
    and Yankees of 1960s, 293, 295
    as Yankee general manager, 295, 308
    and players vs. Berra, 296
    racial remarks by, 298
    and acquisition of Ramos, 298
    and Berra's end as manager, 302–3
    do-nothing approach of, 306
    and 1965 slide, 307, 308
    and Keane, 308, 309
    Lee MacPhail compared with, 317
    as Yankee manager (second stint), 309, 316, *316*
    under Steinbrenner, 321, 323
    in 1973 season, 324
    resignation of, 325
Howard, Elston, 232, 253–55, *266,* 459
    as MVP, 154
    in 1955 World Series, 256
    in 1957 World Series, 270
    in 1958 season, 271
    in 1960 season, 275
    in 1961 season, 279, 288
    on Ford, 288
    as one of two black players, 290
    as Gold Glove winner, 294
    in 1964 season, 298
    in 1965 season, 307
    retirement considered by, 311
    in 1966 season, 311
    breaks up no-hitter (1967), 314
    traded to Boston, 314
    as Yankee coach, 324–25, 326, 341
    and managership, 325
    uniform number of retired, 395
Howard, Frank, 293
Howe, Art, 447
Howell, Harry, 16, 18, 19, 24
Howser, Dick, 352, 361, 363–64, 375
Hoyt, Waite "Schoolboy," 29, 96, 100, 101, 107, 121, 122, 123, 132, 134, 135, 140, 144, 168, 457
Hubbell, Carl, 166, 167, 169
Hudson, Charlie, 379
Hudson, Tim, 446
Huggins, Miller, *64,* 71–72, *78, 89,* 100, 456

precarious position of, 88–89, 101
in 1920 season, 91
and Barrow, 94
and Ruth, 87, 88, *89,* 99, 103, 108, 113, 116, *120,* 155, 162
and 1922 acquisitions, 102
and Yankee players' misbehavior, 103
in 1922 World Series, 104
and Ruppert-Huston dispute, 104
Ruppert endorses for 1924 season, 108
and Mays, 108
and Gehrig, 113
in post-1925 rebuilding, 116
and Wilcy Moore, 121
in Lardner's essay, 125
and 1927 World Series, 128, 132, 134
and 1929 season, 140
illness and death of, *140,* 141–42
McCarthy contrasted with, 145
Gehrig on, 176
monument to, *214,* 317
Hughes, Long Tom, 24, 25, 27
Hughson, Tex, 189, 196, 229
Hunt, Marshall, 123
Hunter, Billy, 253, 264
Hunter, Brian, 429
Hunter, Catfish (Jim), 327, *363*
    pursuit of, 329, 330
    in 1976 season, 332, 334, 335
    in 1977 season, 339, 341, 345
    on Reggie Jackson, 340
    in 1977 World Series, 345
    in 1978 season, 349, 353, 354
    in 1979 season, 360
    retirement of, 365
    death of, 430
Huston, Tillinghast L'Hommideau, 62–63, 66, *66,* 67, 68, 69, 277
    and Yankee financial losses, 68
    and Speaker deal, 70
    in World War I, 70, 71
    and hiring of Huggins, 71, 72
    and Frazee, 74, 87
    at end of World War I, 77
    and Ruth, 85–86, 88
    and Huggins, 88, 101, 104
    and 1919 World Series shares, 88–89
    and Barrow, 94
    and Yankee Stadium, 96
    and players' misbehavior, 103
    leaves Ruppert as sole owner, 107
Hyland, Robert, 158

Inside (scientific) baseball, 18, 19, 101, *229*
"Insurrectos, the," 81, 82, 93
Irabu, Hideki, 407–8, *408,* 413, 414, 417, 419, 427
Irvin, Monte, 210, 244, 254
Irwin, Arthur, 62
Italian-American players
    on Yankees, 74, 76, 117, *160,* 162
    scarcity of (1926), 116

bias against (other clubs), 162
WWII backlash against, 190
Izenberg, Jerry, 314

Jackson, Grant, 333, 335
Jackson, Joe, 70, 87, 91, 92, 99
Jackson, Reggie, 337–38, 366, 374, 459
    and Chase, 40
    as home run leader, 75
    and Ruth, 87
    and Robinson, 311
    in reentry draft, 337
    and Martin, *337,* 337–38, 339, 341, 347, 352, *352, 354*
    and Steinbrenner, *337,* 338–39, 340, 347, 363, 364, 374, 380
    Yankees' hiring of, 338–39
    in 1977 season, 340, 341, 345
    ostracized after interview, 340
    defensive uncertainty of, 341
    in 1977 playoffs, 345
    in 1977 World Series, xx, 345, 347, *347,* 348, *350*
    and "Reggie!" bar, 349
    in 1978 season, 350, 352, 353
    in 1978 playoff game, 355
    in 1978 World Series, 182, 356, 357, 404
    in 1979 season, 360
    in Hall of Fame, 362
    in 1980 season, 363
    in 1980 playoffs, 363, *364*
    and Winfield, 364, 370, 371, *378*
    in 1981 season, 365
    with Angels, 366, 374
    and Dave Winfield Day, 370
    uniform number of retired, 395
    long-term contract of, 422
Jackson, Ron, 350
James, Bill, 57
Javier, Julian, 299
Jazz Age and Roaring Twenties, 72–73, *78,* 138
Jennings, Hugh, 53
Jensen, Jackie, 237, 242, 344
Jeter, Derek, 391–94, 401, 455, 458
    and Cree, 51
    and Ruth, 87
    as black player in Yankee system, 220
    as Rookie of Year, 244
    and crowd at Dave Winfield Day, 369
    in 1996 playoffs, 397, 401, 402
    in 1996 World Series, 403, 405
    small salary of, 405
    in 1997 playoffs, 409
    and top-of-order spot, 412
    in 1998 season, 418, 420
    on Brosius, 420
    on El Duque, 423
    in 1998 playoffs, 423
    in 1998 World Series, 423
    on 1998 team record, 424
    as farm system product, 424
    as marquee player and idol, 424, 426
    beaning by Clemens, 426
    in 1999 season, 427
    in 1999 playoffs, 428

in 1999 World Series, 429, 430
and gossip columns, 434
in 2000 World Series, 440, 441, 442
in 2001 season, 442, 445
in response to terrorist attack, 445
in 2001 playoffs, 446, 447, 448
in 2001 World Series, 449, *449,* 450, 451, 452, *453,* 453–54
Jimenez, Elvio, 295
Johanson, Ingemar, 272
John, Tommy, 360, 362, 365, 374, 379
John Paul II (pope), in Yankee Stadium, 97
Johnson, Arnold, 264, 273, 278
Johnson, Ban, xix, 4
    and birth of Yankees, *2,* 3, 4, 5, 7–11, 13, 14, 18, 62
    Yankees backed by, 16
    and ejection of Elberfeld and Griffith, 44
    Yankees' reaction to edicts of, 46
    and speculation on fix (1907), 47
    and Stallings' sign-stealing, 53
    and Stallings-Chase conflict, 54–55, *55*
    Chance acquired through, 60
    and Ruppert-Huston ownership, 62, 63, 65, 66, 67, 68
    and Eddie Collins to Chicago, 68
    and Baker to Yankees, 69
    and Speaker deal, 69–70
    and grabbing Huggins from St. Louis, 71–72
    and law degree, 72
    WWI proposals of, 73, 73–74
    and Frazee, 74, 76–77, 79, 82, 83, 87
    trades reviewed by, 76
    and Mays acquisition, 78–79, 88
    dissatisfaction with, 79
    end of reign of, 79, 81, 93
    and cancellation of Polo Grounds lease, 91
    and threatened boycott over Mays, 92
    and Lasker Plan, 93
    and Pie Traynor deal, 94
    trading deadline imposed by, 103
    on 1922 World Series, 103
    and gambler at 1926 World Series, 120
Johnson, Billy, 193, *195,* 209, 213, 227, 229
Johnson, Cliff, 360
Johnson, Davey, 390, 401
Johnson, Randy, 387, 418–19, 448, 449, 450, 453, *453,* 454
Johnson, Richard A., 344
Johnson, Roy, 164, 165
Johnson, Walter, 48, 60, 61, 69, 111
Jones, Andruw, 403
Jones, Chipper, 404, 429, 431
Jones, Fielder, 44
Jones, Nippy, 270
Jones, Ruppert, 361, 363
Jones, "Sad Sam," 102–3, 170
Joost, Eddie, 211
Jordan, Brian, 425, 429
Jorgensen, Spider, 213

Judge, Joe, 111, 127
Justice, David, 372, 421, 434, 435, 440, 443, 451, 452

Kaat, Jim, 362
Kaese, Harold, 211, 224
Kahn, Jim, 170
Kahn, Roger, 245
Kamm, Willie, 116
Kammeyer, Bob, 349
Kansas City Athletics
   as de facto Yankee farm club, 220, 264
   Yankees become equivalent of, 311
Kansas City Royals
   in 1976 playoffs, 334–36
   in 1977 playoffs, 345
   in 1978 playoffs, 355–56
   in 1980 playoffs, 363, 364
   financial resources of, 422
Kaplan, Jim, 250, 251
Karsay, Steve, 455
Kaufman, Ewing, 422
Keane, Johnny, 303, 306, 307, 308, 309
Keegan, Tom, 402
Keeler, Wee Willie, 15, 18, 457
   Johnson's signing of, 8
   in 1903 season, 19, 20, 21
   in 1904 season, 24, 32, 33, 36, 36, 39
   and Chase, 40
   in 1905 season, 43
   in 1906 season, 45
   in 1907 season, 46, 47
   Farrell wants as manager, 48
   in 1908 season, 48
   and Cree, 51
   hitting streak of, 180, 181
Keeler's Hollow, 19, 20, 20, 21, 36
Keisler, Randy, 443
Kekich, Mike, 323
Keller, Charlie "King Kong," 172, 177, 184, 185, 190, 191, 193, 195, 195, 209, 210, 227
Kelley, Joe, 4
Kelly, George, 101
Kelly, Pat, 386, 392
Kelly, Roberto, 383, 385
Keltner, Ken, 180–81
Kemp, Abe, quoted, 161
Kenney, Jerry, 323
Kerrigan, Joe, 444
Key, Jimmy, 385, 386, 394, 403, 404, 405, 407
Key Largo (movie), quote from, 411
Kieran, John, 85, 108, 123, 126, 127, 128, 130–31, 144, 158, 175
Killebrew, Harmon, 276
Killilea, Henry, 24
Kim, Byung-Hyun, 451, 452
Kinder, Edward, 138, 139
King, Clyde, 350, 374, 375
King, Edward, 142
King, George, 415, 418, 438
Kleinow, Rod, 36, 37
Kleskow, Ryan, 404, 430
Klimkowski, Ron, 314
Kluttz, Clyde, 330
Knickerbocker, Billy, 166

Knoblauch, Chuck, 412, 422–23, 423, 424, 429, 430, 434, 440, 442, 444, 448, 452
Knorr, Randy, 387
Koenig, Mark, 114, 116, 117, 122, 126, 127, 130, 135, 140, 141, 144, 152
Konstanty, Jim, 232, 233
Koppett, Leonard, 267, 288, 289–90
Kosco, Andy, 314
Koufax, Sandy, 25, 292, 293
Kramer, Jack, 222–23, 223–24, 226
Kremer, Ray, 131, 132
Krichell, Paul, 109, 147, 179, 219, 236
Kubek, Tony, 265, 293
   as Rookie of Year, 244
   in 1957 season, 267
   in 1957 World Series, 270
   in 1958 season, 271
   in 1960 season, 275
   in 1960 World Series, 276–77
   in service, 287
   in 1962 World Series, 291
   in 1963 season, 292
   in 1963 World Series, 293
   in 1964 season, 298
   and 1964 World Series, 299
   in 1965 season, 307
   retirement of, 310
   on 1978 pennant chase, 354
Kucks, Johnny, 259, 261, 266, 267, 272
Kuenn, Harvey, 290
Kuhn, Bowie, 323, 326, 333, 334, 366
Kuzava, Bob, 245

Labine, Clem, 247, 260, 261
Labor relations, and Weiss, 216–17, 218, 230, 252
LaChance, Candy, 33, 36
La Guardia, Fiorello, 208
Lajoie, Napoleon, 40, 99
Landis, Kenesaw Mountain, 93, 102, 103, 124, 148, 188, 249
Landridge, Vic, 125
Lane, Frank "Trader," 273
Lannin, Joseph, 82, 83
Lapoint, Dave, 382
Laporte, Frank, 58
Lardner, Ring, 123, 125, 134
Larsen, Don, 253
   in 1955 World Series, 256
   perfect game of (1956 World Series), 259–61, 375, 414, 417
   in 1957 World Series, 270
   in 1958 World Series, 271–72, 272
   traded to A's, 273
   with San Francisco, 290
   and Wells, 414, 417
   at Cone's perfect game, 426, 427
Lary, Frank, 335
Lary, Lyn, 138, 141
Lasker Plan, 93
Lasorda, Tommy, 345, 382
Latin players, and Yankees, 172
Lavagetto, Cookie, 212, 214, 221, 451
Law, Vern, 276
Lawrence, Jack, 100
Lawton, Marcus, 414

Lazzeri, Tony, 114, 116–17, 169, 456
   as Italian American, 74, 116
   and Barrow's rebuilding, 118, 138
   in 1926 World Series, 119
   in 1927 season, 122, 123, 126, 127
   as base stealer, 126
   in 1927 World Series, 134
   in 1928 season, 135
   in 1929 season, 140, 140
   Devens's memories of, 146
   in 1931 season, 148
   in 1932 World Series, 154
   popularity of, 162
   as power hitter, 164
   in 1936 season, 166
   in 1936 World Series, 166
   in 1937 World Series, 167, 169
   as older player, 167
   released by Yankees, 169
   at Lou Gehrig Appreciation Day, 176
   in company of other great players, 201
Leary, Tim, 382
Ledee, Rickey, 423, 434
Lee, Bill, 324, 334
Leiter, Al, 439, 442
Lemke, Mark, 405
Lemon, Bob, 339, 352–53, 355, 356, 360, 365, 374, 390
Leonard, Dave, 335
Leonard, Dutch, 76, 120
Lewis, Duffy, 76, 77, 78, 87, 91
Leyritz, Jim, 385, 385–86, 387, 402, 402, 403–4, 431, 448
Lieb, Fred, 58, 61, 104, 123, 203
Lieber, Hank, 166
Lilly, Ted, 443
Lindell, Johnny, 193, 195, 196, 201, 209, 212, 213, 227, 229
Lindsay, John, 305, 319
Linz, Phil, 287, 296, 298, 301
Lisenbee, Hod, 129
Littell, Mark, 336
Little, Jimmy, quoted, 235
Lloyd, Graeme, 403, 405, 415, 418, 426
Loes, Billy, 245
Loftus, Tom, 18
Logan, Johnny, 270
Lombardi, Ernie, 177, 362
Lonborg, Jim, 314
Long, Dale, 277
Long, Danny, 40
Long, Herman, 16, 19, 21
Long, Terrence, 446
Lopat, Eddie, 216, 217, 222, 223, 227, 244, 252, 309, 459
Lopez, Al, 243, 275
Lopez, Albie, 452
Lopez, Hector, 272, 273, 290
Los Angeles Dodgers
   in 1963 World Series, 292–93
   in 1977 World Series, 345–48
   in 1978 World Series, 356–57
   in 1981 World Series, 365–66
   large payrolls of, 422
"Lou Gehrig's disease," 176
Louis, Joe, and 1939 Yankees, 177
Lowe, Bobby, 151
Lowell, Mike, 413
Lowenstein, John, 361

"Loyal Five, the," 81, 82, 102
Lucas, Jerry, 320
Lumpe, Jerry, 269, 272
Lupica, Mike, 352
Lyle, Sparky (Albert), 318, 318–19, 325
   as saves leader, 168
   and Yankee–Red Sox rivalry, 324
   in 1976 playoffs, 335
   and Yankee resurgence, 339
   as Cy Young winner, 341, 349
   in 1977 season, 341
   in 1977 playoffs, 345
   in 1977 World Series, 345, 347
   and acquisition of Gossage, 349
   in 1978 season, 349, 354
   traded, 360
Lynn, Fred, 330, 341, 350, 355

McAlary, Mike, 379
McAvoy, Thomas, 13
McCall, Larry, 349
McCarthy, Joe, 144, 144–45, 148, 186, 203, 456
   Devens's memories of, 147
   and Ruth, 148, 155, 157, 158
   and 1932 season, 149
   and 1933 season, 155
   names Gehrig captain, 162, 164
   and pitching staff, 164
   on Murphy, 165
   and 1936 World Series, 167
   and 1938 season, 170, 172
   in 1939 season, 170, 177
   and Gehrig's illness, 173, 175, 176
   and Lou Gehrig Appreciation Day, 176
   in 1941 season, 179
   at Gehrig funeral, 179
   in 1941 World Series, 185
   in 1942 World Series, 191
   and WWII circumstances, 191, 193, 195
   illness of, 195–96
   and MacPhail, 199–200, 202
   Yankee demeanor stressed by, 202
   becomes alcoholic, 202
   resignation of, 202
   as Red Sox manager, 222, 223, 224, 229, 232
   and Houk, 279
   dynasty of, 446
McClellan, Tim, 375
McClendon, John, 325
McConaughty, J. W., 48
McCovey, Willie, 290, 291–92
McDermott, Mickey, 238
McDonald, Arch, 173
McDougald, Gil, 237, 237, 242, 458
   in 1951 season, 237, 239
   as Rookie of Year, 237, 242, 244
   and Weiss's contract arguments, 252
   open-mindedness of, 254
   in 1955 World Series, 256
   in 1956 World Series, 259
   in 1957 season, 266
   and injury to Score, 266
   in 1957 World Series, 270
   in 1958 season, 271

in 1958 World Series, 272
in 1960 season, 273
in 1960 World Series, 277
absence of critical, 306
acquired cheaply, 422
McDowell, Jack, 386, 387, 391
MacDowell, Sam, 324
McFarland, Herm, 16
McGann, Dan, 24
McGee, Willie, 366
McGeehan, W. O., 79, 89, 99, 104,
119, 123, 131, 134, 135
McGinnity, "Iron Man" Joe, 4
McGovern, Artie, 116
McGowan, Bill, 214
McGraw, Bob, 78
McGraw, John, 4, 21, 24, 32, 33, 57,
57, 62
and Huggins, 72, 78
and 1921 World Series, 100, 101
and 1922 World Series, 103
and Ruth, 107, 108
death of, 149, 151
Stengel taught by, 226, 330
McGriff, Fred, 403
McGuire, Jim "Deacon," 37
McGwire, Mark, 258, 284, 285, 419,
420
McInnis, Stuffy, 57, 58
McKean, Jim, 332
McKechnie, Bill, 135, 158
McKinley, Bill, 255
McKinney, Rich, 318, 319, 323
McNally, Mike, 96
McNamee, Graham, 118
MacPhail, Larry, 197, 198, 198–99,
201, 203, 206, 222, 277
as Dodgers' executive, 173, 197
and McCarthy, 199–200, 202–203
and Ladies Day, 202
and proposed trade of Williams
for DiMaggio, 207
on black players, 208, 210
and Rickey, 208, 211
players antagonized by, 209
retirement of, 222
and Harris, 224
and Stengel, 224–25
and Berra offer, 243
MacPhail, Lee, 218–19, 264–65, 311,
316, 316, 317, 321, 324, 325, 326,
375
McQuinn, George, 207, 209, 213,
221
Mack, Connie
Cree signed by, 52
and 1911 A's, 57
and Home Run Baker deal, 68,
69, 71
and 1927 season, 121
with Shawkey, 143
financial pressures on, 148, 149
and receding fortune of A's, 155
selling and rebuilding strategy
of, 333
Mack, Ray, 181
Madden, Bill, 383
Maddox, Elliott, 326, 330
Maddux, Greg, 402, 403, 405, 428,
429, 446
Magee, Lee, 68, 69
Maglie, Sal, 259, 260

Mahaffey, Leroy, 151
Maier, Jeffrey, 401–2, 451
Maisel, Fritz, 69, 70, 189
Major League Baseball
antitrust exemption of, 297
changing structure of (1960s), 306
divisional system in, 316
and free agency, 329–30
collusion among owners in, 381,
383
realignment in, 396, 418, 431
and All-Century Team, 429
in aftermath of terrorist attacks,
445
See also Baseball
Major League Baseball Players'
Association (MLBPA), 329, 333
Malloy, Joseph, 382
Malone, Pat, 168
Manhattan Field, 7
Manley, Effa, 210
Mann, Arthur, 131
Mantilla, Felix, 270
Mantle, Mickey, xix, 253, 262, 279,
312, 314, 455, 458
and author's childhood, xx
as home run leader, 75
and Ruth, 87
as RBI leader, 90
as batting champion, 129
as MVP, 154
and Stengel, 236–37, 238,
250–51, 258, 275
Yankees' discovery of, 236–37,
422
in 1951 camp, 237
and press, 237, 246, 314
demoted during 1951 season,
238–39
after recall in 1951 season, 239
speed of, 239–40
in 1952 season, 242, 244
in 1952 World Series, 245
as great white hope, 246
tape-measure home runs of, 246,
247, 257–58
in 1953 World Series, 247
in 1954 season, 252
in 1955 season, 255
and 1955 World Series, 256, 257
in 1956 season, 257–58
in 1956 World Series, 260
in Copacabana brawl, 266–67
as exempt from discipline, 267
in 1957 season, 267, 269
in 1957 World Series, 270
in 1958 season, 271
in 1959 season, 272, 273, 273
and 1960 pay cut, 273
in 1960 season, 275, 276
and Ruth's home run record, 276
in 1960 World Series, 276, 277
in 1961 season, 279, 280, 281,
283, 284, 288
and 1961 World Series, 285
in 1962 season, 288
in 1963 season, 292
in 1963 World Series, 293
as Gold Glove winner, 294
in 1964 season, 296, 296, 298, 299
and Berra as manager, 296, 298
in 1964 World Series, 301

decline of, 302
in 1965 season, 307
in 1966 season, 309, 311
as relic, 310
retirement of, 311, 312, 314
Murcer compared to, 311, 312,
315
moved to first (1967), 312
in 1968 season, 312
and Mickey Mantle Day, 316–17
monument to, 317
and Martin as manager, 332
in Hall of Fame, 362
and Jeter, 392, 394
uniform number of retired, 395
injuries and illnesses of, 288,
289, 298
osteomyelitis, 239
right knee torn, 239, 242, 288
speed diminished by, 239–40, 288
and neglect of health, 242, 246,
288
knee surgery, 252
"shin splints" (cut shin), 253, 267
ripped hamstring, 255, 288
Stengel on, 275
broken foot, 292
jammed knee, 298
and retirement, 314
Mapes, Cliff, 227, 229
Marberry, Firpo, 121, 165
Marciano, Rocky, 342
Marichal, Juan, 290, 291
Maris, Roger, 279, 459
and author's childhood, xx
as home run leader, 75
as RBI leader, 90
as MVP, 154, 288
Weiss's acquisition of, 220, 273
Cannon on, 263
in 1960 season, 275, 276
in 1960 World Series, 276, 277
and 1961 lineup, 279
1961 home run record of, 279,
280, 280–85, 288
in 1961 World Series, 285
in 1962 season, 289
in 1963 season, 292
as Gold Glove winner, 294
in 1964 season, 298
absence of critical, 306
in 1965 season, 307
in 1966 season, 309, 311
retirement considered by, 311
with St. Louis, 312
uniform number of retired, 395
Marquez, Luis, 227
Marshall, George C., 196
Martin, Al, 436
Martin, Billy, 225, 237, 242, 330–32,
458
and Artie Wilson, 227
in 1951 season, 237
and 1952 World Series, 244, 245
in 1953 World Series, 247
in 1955 World Series, 256
in 1956 World Series, 258, 260
in Copacabana brawl, 266–67,
330
in 1957 season, 267
traded, 267
quoted, 329

as Oakland manager, 365,
374–75
and Dave Winfield Day, 370
and Stengel, 381
as Yankee scout, 382
death of, 382
as Yankee manager, 332, 382
and Steinbrenner, 330, 332, 337,
339, 347, 350, 352, 353, 361,
381, 382
in 1976 season, 332, 334
and Gura, 335
in 1976 playoffs, 335
and umpires, 335, 336
in 1976 World Series, 336
and Jackson, 337, 337–38, 339,
341, 347, 352, 352, 354
in 1977 season, 339, 340, 341, 345
and Munson, 339, 361
in 1977 playoffs, 345
in 1977 World Series, 331, 345,
347, 347, 348
in 1978 season, 350, 352
resignation of, 352, 352
reinstatement of (1978), 353
returns early (1979), 360
fired after Minnesota brawl, 361
hired back (1983), 375
and Brett pine-tar protest, 375
fired (1983), 375
hired back (1985), 379
in fight with Whitson, 379
replaced by Piniella (1986), 379
hired back (1987), 379
replaced by Piniella (1987), 379
and Henderson, 380
hired back (1988), 381, 381
replaced by Piniella (1988), 381
Martin, Hersh, 199
Martinez, Dennis, 394
Martinez, Edgar, 387
Martinez, Pedro, 344, 415, 421, 428,
434, 443
Martinez, Tino, 387, 391, 394, 401,
403, 415, 415, 418, 422, 423, 429,
430, 434, 436, 444, 447, 451, 452,
454, 458
Martyn, Bob, 267
"Massachusetts game," 205
Mathews, Eddie, 269, 270, 276
Mathews, Wallace, 414
Mathewson, Christy, 25, 27, 43, 56,
57, 213
Mattingly, Don, xx, 362, 375–76,
378, 387, 455, 458
as RBI leader, 90
as batting champion, 129
as MVP, 154
as Gold Glove winner, 294
monument to, 362
at Dave Winfield Day, 370
love for, 370
in 1983 season, 375
in 1984 season, 375, 378–79
work ethic of, 378, 385
as 1980s highlight, 379
and Henderson, 380
back gives way, 382
and postseason play, 384
and O'Neill, 385
in 1993 season, 385
and 1994 season, 386

Mattingly, Don (cont.)
  in 1995 season, 386
  in 1995 playoffs, 387
  and 1996 season, 390–91
  and Jeter, 391
  uniform number of retired, 395
May, Jakie, 152
May, Rudy, 309, 333, 361, 365
Mayberry, John, 374
Mays, Carl, 78–79, 91–92
  as percentage leader, 29
  in 1919 season, 77
  and Ruth's politicking, 83
  in 1920 season, 89, 91
  in fatal beaning incident, 91, 92
  in 1921 season, 96, 100
  in 1921 World Series, 100, 104
  and Ruth's barnstorming tour,
    101, 102
  in fights with Devormer, 103
  in 1922 World Series, 103, 104
  sold to Reds, 108–9
  in Cincinnati, 111
  as saves leader, 168
Mays, Willie, 210, 219, 238, 239,
  244, 246, 252, 254, 255, 276, 290,
  291, 314, 319, 447
Mazeroski, Bill, 277, 336, 355
Meacham, Bobby, 391
Meadows, Lee, 131
Meares, Pat, 414
Medich, Doc, 326, 332
Melton, Cliff, 169
Mendoza, Ramiro, 407, 409, 418,
  419, 423, 429, 448
Menechino, Frank, 448
Mercer, Sid, 176
Merchant, Larry, 319
Merrill, Robert, 361
Merrill, Stump, 382, 383
Mesa, Jose, 409
Messersmith, Andy, 333, 349
Metheny, Bud, 195, 199
Meusel, Bob, 90, 102, 457
  as RBI leader, 90
  and Ruth, 96, 99–100, 121, 122
  speed of, 99
  in 1921 World Series, 101
  and Ruth's barnstorming tour,
    101, 102, 102
  and Yankee Stadium left field,
    104
  in 1923 World Series, 107, 107,
    108
  and 1925 season, 113
  in 1926 season, 117
  in 1926 World Series, 119, 120
  as base stealer, 126
  as outfielder, 126
  in 1927 World Series, 134
  in 1928 season, 135
  in 1928 World Series, 132
  in decline, 138
  in 1929 season, 140
  release of, 143
  at Lou Gehrig Appreciation Day,
    176
Meusel, Emil "Irish," 107
Michael, Gene, 324, 361, 364, 365,
  374, 382, 385, 386, 389, 391, 395
Mikkelsen, Pete, 295
Miksis, Eddie, 214, 221

Miljus, 134
Miller, Damian, 450, 454
Miller, Elmer, 100
Miller, Marvin, 217
Mills, Alan, 415
Millwood, Kevin, 429
Milnar, Al, 182
Milton, Eric, 412
Milwaukee Braves, 269
  in 1957 World Series, 269–70
  in 1958 World Series, 271
  payroll of, 422
Milwaukee Brewers, in 1981 play-
  offs, 365
Minor league teams
  of Yankee organization, 148–49
  See also Farm system
Minoso, Minnie, 254
Mitchell, Dale, 260
Mitchell, Fred, 146, 147
Mize, Johnny, 228, 229–30, 245
Mogridge, George, 77, 91
Molitor, Paul, 414
Monahan, Gene, 355
Monday, Rick, 348
Money, Don, 332–33
Montgomery, Bob, 338
Moon, Sun Jung, 97
Moore, Earl, 193
Moore, Johnny, 153
Moore, Terry, 190, 191, 193
Moore, Wilcy, 117, 120, 120–21,
  122, 123, 126, 128, 132, 134, 135,
  138, 140, 155, 165, 168, 309, 457
Morgan, Joe, 336
Morgan, Mike, 452
Morgan, Tom, 237, 264
Moriarty, George, 47
Moschito, Ross, 306
Moseby, Lloyd, 380
Moyer, Jamie, 448
Mulder, Mark, 446
Munson, Diane, 361
Munson, Thurman, 317, 325, 339,
  361, 362, 459
  as MVP, 154
  as Rookie of Year, 244
  as Gold Glove winner, 294
  in brawl with Fisk, 322, 324
  in 1976 season, 332
  in 1976 World Series, 334, 336
  on Chambliss playoff home run,
    336
  and Rudi, 338
  and Reggie Jackson, 339, 340
  in 1977 season, 345
  in 1977 World Series, 345, 347,
    347, 348
  and 1978 season, 348–49, 350,
    352, 353
  dissatisfaction of (1978), 349
  in 1978 playoff game, 355
  in 1978 playoff series, 356
  in 1978 World Series, 357
  death of, 360–61, 361
  monument to, 362
  and pine tar on Brett's bat, 375
  Mattingly fills place of, 375
  work ethic of, 378
  as number-one pick, 392
  uniform number of retired, 395
  Wells compared with, 426

Murcer, Bobby, xx, 294, 308, 311,
  312, 315, 321, 326, 374
"Murderers' Row," 78, 114, 131
Murphy, Johnny, 155, 157, 165, 168,
  193, 458
Murphy, Morgan, 53
Murray, Eddie, 371
Murtaugh, Danny, 276
Musial, Stan, 191, 229, 379
Mussina, Mike, 442, 443, 444, 446,
  449, 452
MVP voting, strange 1947 results
  in, 211
Myers, Randy, 401
My Fifty Years in Baseball (Barrow), 87
Myth, as Yankee way, 154

Nagy, Charles, 422
Narron, Jerry, 361
National Commission, 74, 91, 93
National League
  and advent of AL, 4
  forced to come to terms by John-
    son, 8
  expansion of, 278–79
  See also Major League Baseball
Neagle, Denny, 435, 441
Nederlander, James, 322
Nederlander, Robert, 382
Negro Leagues baseball, 148, 173,
  208, 210, 226, 229, 236, 246
Nehf, Art, 100, 108
Nelson, Jack (fan), 440
Nelson, Jeff, 391, 415, 418, 422,
  429, 431, 442
Nelson, Rocky, 277
Nettles, Graig, 323, 323–24, 458
  as home run leader, 75
  as Gold Glove winner, 294
  in 1976 season, 332, 334
  on Stadium fence, 336
  in 1977 season, 338
  and Yankee resurgence, 339
  in 1977 World Series, 348
  in 1978 playoff game, 328, 355
  on Jackson, 355
  in 1978 playoff series, 356
  in 1978 World Series, 356–57
  on Lyle, 360
  in 1980 season, 363
  and Dave Winfield Day, 370
  and Brett's pine tar, 375
Neun, Johnny, 203
Newcombe, Don, 229, 256, 258
New England, Yankees as favorites
  in Italian sections of, 117
Newkirk (in trade for DiMaggio),
  159
Newman, Mark, 412
Newsome, Bobo, 212, 213
Newton, Doc, 46
"New York Americans," 8
New York City, xx, 3, 4–5, 86
  corruption in, 5, 14
  as temptation, 46
  as stage, 61, 158
  and Ruth, 76, 86, 136
  1920s changes in, 137
  as Yankee market, 149, 172, 271,
    322, 384
  in 1950s, 235–36

  changing demographics in
    (1950s), 240, 264
  1960s and 1970s troubles of,
    305–6, 332
  Reggie Jackson lured by, 338
  newspaper strike in, 353, 360
  and Cone, 386
  resurgence of in Giuliani years,
    424
  and terrorist attack, 444–45
New York Giants, 3, 21
  and McGraw, 4
  and Freedman, 7
  in competition with Yankees, 21,
    23–24, 25, 27, 35, 44, 62, 91,
    211, 263–64
  and 1904 season, 28
  in 1905 World Series, 43
  and Mathewson, 43
  as establishment team, 76
  and cancellation of Yankees'
    Polo Grounds lease, 91
  in 1921 World Series, 100
  in 1922 World Series, 103
  in 1923 World Series, 107–8
  and 1924 season, 111
  in 1936 World Series, 166–67
  in 1937 World Series, 169
  and Lou Gehrig Appreciation
    Day, 176
  1950s as triumphal age of,
    235–36
  in 1951 playoff, 239
  in 1951 World Series, 239–40
  and Berra, 243
  in 1954 World Series, 252
  constituency of (1950s), 253
  move to San Francisco, 269
  See also San Francisco Giants
New York Mets
  Stengel as manager of, 248, 290,
    295, 308, 439
  popularity of, 290, 295, 299, 310
  in Shea Stadium, 299
  as competition for Yankees, 302,
    317, 330, 376, 379
  1969 and 1973 championships
    of, 314, 324
  and New York market, 319
  deterioration of, 383
  and Steinbrenner's "Met envy,"
    390
  in 2000 World Series, 438–42
New York Mutuals, 5
New York Yankee fans. See Yankee
  fans
New York Yankees, xix–xx, 446, 455
New York City's relationship to, xx
  birth of, 2, 3, 4, 5
  initial names of, 8, 18
  "Yankees" becomes name,
    18–19, 59
  and Hal Chase, 40
  pinstripe uniforms of, 59, 59
  early reputation of, 67
  and Babe Ruth, 82, 87, 158 (see
    also Ruth, Babe)
  attitudes toward, 101
  institutional arrogance of, 101,
    270–71, 310
  1927 team as greatest, 115–16,
    123, 126

numbers put on uniforms of, 140
farm system of, 148–49, 161, 216, 219, 422 (see also under Farm system)
and New York market, 149, 172, 271, 322, 384
myth in popular view of, 154
wealth of, 161
unsentimental personnel decisions of, 169
and black players, 172, 199, 210–11, 219–20, 226–27, 232, 245–46, 264, 278, 292, 295, 311, 370
and Gehrig, 177
scouting system of, 178, 216, 219, 242, 243
and World War II, 188
victory demanded of, 191
under MacPhail's management, 199, 200, 203, 209
and typical Yankee, 219, 315
1950s as triumphal age of, 235–36
replacements for great players found by, 236, 242
constituency of (1950s), 253
owners of, 277 (see also individual owners)
Mets more popular than, 299
1960s decline and collapse of, 301–2, 304, 306–7, 310
as resting on savior-stars, 311
and free agency, 330, 333, 361, 365, 374 (see also under Free agency)
and Steinbrenner organizational climate, 359–60, 364, 382
and Hall of Fame, 362
postseason drought of (1982–1994), 369
Mattingly as example for, 378
current dynasty of, 380, 385, 446
postseason rosters different from regular-season rosters of, 395
1998 team as best in history, 413, 419, 420, 424
as benefiting from wealth, 422, 424
and YankeeNets Corporation, 444
and terrorist attack, 444–45
consecutive-postseason-series string of, 450
need for change recognized by, 455
All-Century teams of, 456–59
year-by-year record of, 460–63
Red Sox as rivals of, 155, 204, 205–6, 342–44
and DiMaggio vs. Williams, 182
and 1946 season, 201, 202
and 1947 season, 209, 210
and 1948 season, 223–24
in 1949 season, 227–29
in 1950 season, 230, 232
and Fisk-Munson brawl, 322, 324
in 1978 playoff game, 328
and Piniella-Fisk brawl, 334
in 1978 season and playoff, 350, 353–55
and payrolls, 422

and Bernie Williams, 424–25
in 1999 season and playoffs, 428
in 2000 season, 434, 435
and sign on Stadium batting cage, 438
in 2001 season, 443–44
New York press corps. See Press corps of New York
Niarhos, Gus, 222
Niekro, Phil, 362, 375, 379
Night games, MacPhail institutes, 197
Niles, Harry, 47
Nixon, Trot, 434
Nixon, Willard, 238, 255
No, No, Nanette, 82
No-hit games
    by Pearson, 170
    by Jones, 170
    Bevens' near miss (1947 Series), 212–14, 221, 451
    by Reynolds, 238, 239
    Larsen's perfect game (1956 Series), 259–61, 375, 414, 417
    by Righetti, 375
    by Hawkins, 382
    by Abbott, 385
    by Gooden, 394
    Wells's perfect game, 414, 417
    Cone's perfect game, 426, 427
Nomo, Hideo, 407
Norbett (in trade for DiMaggio), 159
Noren, Irv, 242, 255, 264
Norfolk Naval Training Station team, 196

Oakland Athletics
    in 1981 playoffs, 365
    in 2000 playoffs, 435–36
    in 2001 playoffs, 445, 446
O'Connell, Jack, 371
O'Connell, Jimmy, 116
O'Connor, Jack, 16
O'Dell, Billy, 290
O'Farrell, Bob, 119, 119
Official Record Book, and Maris vs. Ruth home run record, 283
Official Rules of Baseball, on fan interference, 401
Oliva, Tony, 297
Olivo, Chi Chi, 311
Olney, Buster, 423, 446, 447
O'Loughlin, Silk, 44, 45, 45, 49
O'Malley, Walter, 264, 422
O'Neill, Harry, 188
O'Neill, Molly, 400
O'Neill, Paul, 129, 385, 430, 459
    Molly O'Neill (sister) on, 398–400
    in 1996 playoffs, 402
    in 1996 World Series, 403, 404, 405
    in 1997 playoffs, 409
    in 1998 season, 414
    in 1998 playoffs, 421, 422
    on Red Sox and Martinez, 428
    in 1999 World Series, 429, 431
    death of father, 430, 431
    and 2000 season, 434
    in 2000 World Series, 440
    Ramirez as prospective successor to, 442

in 2001 season, 442, 445
    in response to terrorist attack, 445
    in 2001 World Series, 450, 451, 452, 454, 454, 455
    retirement of, 451, 452, 454, 455
O'Neill, Steve, 232
Orr, Bobby, 342
Orth, Al, 19, 27, 28, 29, 32, 39, 41, 41, 44, 45, 46, 47, 49
Osborn Engineering Company, 94, 96, 97
Otis, Amos, 335
Owen, Brick, 145
Owen, Mickey, 184, 185
Owners of New York Yankees, 277. See also individual owners

Pacific Coast League, 40, 41, 59, 116, 159, 161
Pagan, Dave, 332
Page, Joe, 168, 202, 213, 222, 227, 229, 459
Paley, William, 319
Palmer, Dean, 397
Pappas, Milt, 284
Parent, Fred, 33, 37
Parnell, Mel, 229
Partee, Roy, 226
Paschal, Ben, 113, 122
Pasqual, Camilio, 257
Patterson, Arthur, 168
Patterson, Floyd, 272
Patterson, Red, 218, 246
Paul, Gabe, 320, 322–23, 325–26, 326, 330, 332, 333, 335, 337, 339, 340, 341, 349
Paul VI (pope), in Yankee Stadium, 97
"Peanuts," and Red Sox, 344
Pearson, Monte, 164, 169, 170, 172, 173, 177
Peckinpaugh, Roger, 61, 62, 87, 90, 91, 100, 102–3, 180
Pemberton, James, 199
Pennock, Herb, 29, 108, 111, 125, 132, 134, 135, 138, 140, 155, 457
Pepe, Phil, 335, 336, 345
Pepitone, Joe, 287, 292, 293, 294, 296, 298, 306, 308, 309, 312, 314, 316
Perez, Timo, 440
Perez, Tony, 336
Perry, Scott, 89
Person, Monte, 29
Pesky, Johnny, 154, 189, 201, 343
Peterson, Fritz, 308, 312, 317, 323, 326
Pettitte, Andy 435–36, 436
    in 1995 season, 386
    in 1996 season, 394, 396
    in 1996 playoffs, 401
    in 1996 World Series, 403, 404
    as low-paid star, 405
    in 1997 playoffs, 409
    in 1998 season, 413, 418
    winning expected of, 414
    as asking price for Johnson, 419
    in 1998 playoffs, 421, 423
    in 1998 World Series, 423
    as farm system product, 424

in 1999 season, 427
    in 1999 playoffs, 428
    in 1999 World Series, 429
    illness of father, 430
    in 2000 season, 434
    in 2000 playoffs, 435, 436
    in 2000 World Series, 439–40, 442
    in 2001 season, 443
    in 2001 playoffs, 446, 449
    in 2001 World Series, 453
Pezzolo, Francesco. See Bodie, Ping
Philadelphia Athletics
    and AL raiding of NL, 4
    in 1903 season, 20–21
    and 1910 World Series, 57
    1915 rebuilding of, 68
    See also Kansas City Athletics
Philadelphia Phillies
    in 1950 World Series, 230, 232–33
    black players absent from, 232
Piazza, Mike, 243, 434, 438, 438, 441–42
Pierce, Billy, 275, 290
Piercy, Bill, 101, 102, 102
Pinelli, Babe, 260
Pine-tar incident, 375
Piniella, Lou, 374
    acquired from Kansas City, 326
    in 1975 season, 330
    in 1976 season, 332
    in 1976 playoffs, 335
    in 1977 World Series, 347, 348
    on Yankee problems (1977), 349
    in 1978 playoff game, 355
    in 1978 World Series, 357
    on events of 1978 season, 359
    work ethic of, 378
    as Yankee manager, 379, 381
    in Cincinnati, 383
    and O'Neill, 385
    as Seattle manager, 419, 436, 448
    Wells compared with, 426
Pinstripe uniform, 59, 59
Pipgras, George, 121, 122, 126, 132, 135, 140, 152, 155
Pipp, Wally, 68, 70, 71, 75, 78, 87, 89, 90, 92, 103, 109
    and beginning of Gehrig's consecutive-game string, 113, 175
Pittsburgh Pirates
    Ban Johnson's attack on, 8
    in 1903 World Series, 24
    in 1927 World Series, 124–25, 131–34
    in 1960 World Series, 276–78
Plank, Eddie, 57
Players' League, 8
Players' strike (1972), 319
Players' strike (1981), 365
Players' strike (1994–1995), 386
Players' union. See Major League Baseball Players' Association
Playoff game (1978, vs. Boston), 354–55
Playoff series, AL (1976), 333, 334–36
Playoff series, AL (1977), 345
Playoff series, AL (1978), 355–56
Playoff series, AL (1980), 363, 364
Playoff series, AL (1981), 365
Playoff series, AL (1995), 387

Playoff series, AL (1996), 396–97, 401–2
Playoff series, AL (1998), 420–23
Playoff series, AL (1999), 428
Playoff series, AL (2000), 435–36, 438
Playoff series, AL (2001), 445–49
Podres, Johnny, 247, 256, 258, 293
Polo Grounds, 3, 7, 25, 59
    Yankees play in, 60, 62, 68, 75
    and Babe Ruth, 76, 88, 104, 223
    and pitchers, 96
    and Yankee Stadium, 104–5
    bad condition of (1950s), 264
    Mets play in, 290
Polonia, Luis, 382, 404, 435
Posada, Jorge, 407, 420, 424, 430, 435, 440, 442, 443, 446, 447, 450, 450–51, 452
Powell (in trade for DiMaggio), 159
Powell, Jack, 24, 25, 27, 27–28, 29, 32, 33, 35, 41, 43
Powell, Jake, 166, 169
Power, Vic, 219, 232, 245, 252
Powers, Jimmy, 272
Pratt, Del, 72, 73, 78, 87, 94, 96
Press corps of New York
    and Ruth, 85, 139, 154, 163, 168
    during 1927 season, 115–16, 123, 126
    and DiMaggio, 163, 164, 168
    and Gehrig, 164, 173
    and Weiss, 218
    and Stengel, 225, 265
    and Mantle, 237, 246, 314
    and players' indiscretions, 246
    new and more critical generation in, 267, 281, 285
    and Maris home run record, 280, 281, 284
    and Berra, 295
    and Yankees' demise, 314
    and "life-swapping" episode, 323
    and Reggie Jackson, 340
    and Henderson, 380
    and Torre, 390
Priddy, Jerry, 178, 179, 189
Prohibition, 96, 113; end of, 138
Puckett, Kirby, on Mattingly, 376, 384
Pulli, Frank, 357
Puttman, Ambrose, 27, 32

Quinn, Jack, 56, 102, 129

Racism
    of Red Sox, 210
    of Weiss, 219–20
    and Houk vs. Al Dark, 291
    of Boston fans, 334
    See also Black players
Radatz, Dick, 344
Radio
    Yankee games on, 173, 192, 319
    MacPhail embraces, 197
    and Giants or Dodgers fans, 264
Raft, George, 202
Raines, Tim, 362, 391, 394, 403, 407, 409, 413, 415, 418, 424
Ramirez, Manny, 421, 442, 443

Ramos, Pedro, 258, 298, 299, 307
Randolph, Willie, 332, 335, 339, 341, 345, 347, 352, 354, 355, 357, 363, 364, 371, 381, 390, 442, 452, 458
Rankin, W. R., 48
Raschi, Vic
    and 1950 season, 29
    as Italian American, 74
    and Weiss, 217, 218, 252
    and 1948 season, 223
    as strikeout leader, 226
    in 1949 season, 227, 229
    in 1949 World Series, 229
    in 1950 World Series, 232
    in 1951 season, 238
    in 1951 World Series, 240
    in 1952 World Series, 244, 245
    during Stengel years, 252
    sold to Cardinals, 252, 253
Rasmussen, Dennis, 379
Rawlings, Jimmy, 101
Realignment, 396, 418, 431
Red Sox. See Boston Red Sox
Reed, Steve, 441
Reentry draft, 337
Reese, Harold "Pee Wee," 196, 197, 213, 244, 255, 256
Reese, Jimmy, 138
Reichardt, Rick, 306
Reiser, Pete, 184, 184–85, 212, 214
Relaford, Charlie, 441
Relief pitching (bullpen)
    Griffith as pioneer in, 41
    Huggins's use of, 100, 121
    by Marberry for Washington, 121, 165
    by Murphy, 165
    Berra's misuse of, 297
    and Righetti, 379
    Rivera best at, 429
Remy, Jerry, 355
Rennie, Rud, 123, 131, 184, 213, 232, 246
Repoz, Roger, 295, 306, 311
Reuther, Dutch, 117–18
Reynolds, Allie, 459
    as win-percentage leader, 29
    acquired from Cleveland, 206, 216
    and 1947 World Series, 213
    in 1948 season, 224
    as strikeout leader, 226
    in 1949 season, 227, 228
    in 1949 World Series, 229
    in 1950 season, 230
    in 1950 World Series, 232, 233
    no-hitters of (1951), 238, 239, 375
    in 1951 World Series, 240
    in 1952 season, 244
    in 1952 World Series, 245
    in 1953 World Series, 247
    during Stengel years, 252
    retirement of, 253
    as ERA leader, 309
Rhoden, Rick, 379, 381
Rhodes, Arthur, 448
Rice, Grantland, 70, 99, 108, 118, 123, 132
Rice, Harry, 144
Rice, Jim, 330, 341, 350, 355, 371
Rice, Sam, 111

Richardson, Bobby, 182, 265, 267, 271, 275, 277, 285, 292, 293, 294, 301, 310–11, 315
Richman, Arthur, 390
Rickey, Branch
    as Cardinals president, 71, 148
    on luck, 189
    and MacPhail, 197, 208, 211
    and Jackie Robinson, 208
    on 1947 Yankees, 222
    and Negro Leagues, 229
Righetti, Dave, xx, 74, 168, 244, 360, 365, 374, 375, 379, 383
Ripken, Cal, Jr., 109, 284, 392, 402
Rivera, Mariano, 429, 459
    as saves leader, 168
    in negotiations over Cone, 386
    in 1995 playoffs, 387
    in 1996 season, 394
    in 1996 World Series, 403, 405
    in 1997 season, 407
    in 1997 playoffs, 409
    in 1998 season, 413, 418
    as acquired without great cost, 422, 424
    in 1998 playoffs, 423
    in 1999 playoffs, 428
    in 1999 World Series, 429, 431
    in 2000 World Series, 440, 441, 442
    in 2001 season, 443
    in 2001 playoffs, 448, 448
    in 2001 World Series, 450, 451, 452, 454, 454–55
Rivera, Roberto, 395
Rivera, Ruben, 239, 396, 408
Rivers, Mickey, 332, 334, 340, 347, 355
Rizzuto, Phil, xx, 178–79, 458
    as MVP, 154, 229, 230
    in 1941 season, 179, 180
    and DiMaggio at end of streak, 181
    draft deferment of, 189
    in 1942 season, 190
    WWII service of, 191, 196, 201
    in 1947 season, 209
    in 1947 World Series, 214
    and Banks, 219–20
    in 1949 season, 227, 229
    and Cobb on Dead Ball Era, 229
    in 1950 season, 230
    in 1951 season, 239
    in 1952 season, 244
    in 1954 season, 253
    and Howard, 254
    in 1955 World Series, 256
    release of, 266
    on Maris home run chances, 276, 281
    in Hall of Fame, 362
    uniform number of retired, 395
    as acquired without great cost, 422
    in 2001 playoff ceremonies, 447
Roberts, Robin, 232
Robertson, Andre, 391
Robertson, Gene, 141
Robinson, Aaron, 209, 216, 222
Robinson, Bill, 311
    quoted, 305
Robinson, Earl, 285

Robinson, Eddie, 252
Robinson, Jackie, 208, 211–12
    and Ben Chapman, 144, 232
    in 1947 season, 210
    and Weiss, 219
    in 1952 World Series, 244, 245
    on Yankee prejudice, 246
    and talent of black players, 254
    and racist words, 255
    and 1955 World Series, 255, 256
    in 1956 World Series, 258
    in 1956 World Series, 259–60, 260, 261
    on Martin, 330, 331
Robinson, Wilbert, 71, 126
Rocker, John, 429
Rodriguez, Alex, 436, 442, 448
Rodriguez, Ivan "Pudge," 243, 397
Roe, Preacher, 229
Rogers, Kenny, 391, 403, 410, 412
Rohr, Billy, 314
Rolfe, Red, 146, 147, 157, 161, 164, 167, 178, 180, 185, 189, 201, 456
Roosevelt, Franklin Delano, 188, 196
Root, Charlie, 147, 152
Rose, Pete, 120, 336, 381
Rosen, Al, 252, 349, 350, 352, 361
Rosenthal, Harold, 232, 256
Roth, Braggo, 103
Roth, Mark, 37
Rowe, Schoolboy, 157
Royal Rooters, Boston, 37
Rudi, Joe, 333, 334, 338
Ruel, Muddy, 87, 92, 94, 96
Ruffing, Red, 29, 144, 145, 152, 155, 164, 169, 173, 177, 178, 178, 184, 191, 192, 196, 226, 457
Runyon, Damon, 108, 123
Ruppert, George (brother), 172
Ruppert, Jacob, 62–63, 65–68, 89, 172, 277, 456
    mansion of, 60
    and Ban Johnson, 63, 67, 68, 76, 79, 87
    Huggins hired by, 64
    quoted, 65
    Steinbrenner compared with, 66, 321, 385
    and Ruppert brewery, 66–67, 69
    and Yankee financial losses, 68
    initial player acquisitions of, 68–69
    and Speaker deal, 70
    takes sole command, 70
    and hiring of Huggins, 71, 72
    and Ruth, 75–76, 85–86, 87–88, 157, 157, 158, 172
    Mays acquired by, 78–79
    and Frazee vs. Johnson, 82
    and 1919 World Series shares, 88–89
    and Barrow, 94
    and Yankee Stadium, 96, 97
    and players' misbehavior, 103
    and Huggins after 1922 Series, 104
    becomes sole owner, 107
    after 1923 Series, 108
    Yankees saved by cash of, 116
    and 1927 World Series, 134
    diminished finances of, 138

and manager to succeed Huggins, 143, 144
Devens on, 147
in deals with Yawkey, 155
death of, 172
Gehrig on, 176
MacPhail contrasted with, 197, 208
winning as sole aim of, 199
and McCarthy, 200
Yankee demeanor stressed by, 202
decisive changes made by, 295
Yankees as wealthiest team under, 422
Ruppert, Jacob, Sr., 66
Ruppert heirs, as owners, 172, 199, 277
Rush, Bob, 272
Russell, Allen, 78
Russell, Bill, 348, 357
Russo, Marius, 184–85, *186*, 195
Ruth, Babe (George Herman), xix, *84*, 85–87, *99*, *117*, *136*, 138, 158–59, 455, 457
and Birdie Cree, xx
Yankees' acquisition of, xx, 75–76, 81–82, 83, 87–88
and Donovan, 67
with Red Sox, 71, 75, 76, 77–78, 83
and Ruppert, 75–76, 85–86, 87–88, 157, *157*, 158, 172
and New York City, 76, 86, *136*
importance of to Yankees, 82, 87, 158
and press, 85, 139, 154, 163, 168
and Huggins, 87, 88, *89*, 99, 103, 108, 113, 116, *120*, 155, 162
and blacks, 87, *141*, 153, 210
in 1920 season, 89–91, 92
as RBI leader, 90
in movies, *93*, 120
and Dunn, *93*, 149
and Meusel, 96, 99–100, 121, 122
and Yankee Stadium, 97, 104
in 1921 season, 99, 100
in 1921 World Series, 100, 101
barnstorming tour of, 101–2
in 1922 season, 103
in 1922 World Series, 103–4
in 1923 season, 105
in 1923 World Series, *107*, 107–8
in 1924 season, 111
in 1925 season, 112, 113, 116
in 1926 season, 117, *117*
in 1926 World Series, 118, 119, *119*
salary of, 120
and Gehrig, *120*, 121, 122, 126–27, *130*, *149*, 151, 152, 155, 158, 162, 167, 176, 276
in 1927 season, 121, 122, 123, 126, 127, 128–31, *131*
home run trot of, 130
in 1927 World Series, 132, 134
in 1928 season, 135
in 1928 World Series, *132*, 135
decline of, 138, 154–55
in 1929 season, 140
managership sought by, 143, 157, 158
and Shawkey as manager, 144
in 1930 season, 144
umpire-baiting of, *145*
Devens's memories of, 146, 147
"called shot" by, 147, 153–54, 246, *247*
in 1931 season, 148
and McCarthy, 148, 155
in 1932 season, 149
final major league pitching appearance of, *151*
in 1932 World Series, 152
in 1934 season, 155, 157
released by Yankees, *157*, 158
barnstorming tour of (1934), 158
with Boston Braves, 158, 162
and DiMaggio, *160*, 165, 166, 168, 169
Yankees after departure of, 161, 162
at Lou Gehrig Appreciation Day, 176
in Japanese soldiers' taunt (quoted), 187
in company of other great players, 201
and New York–Boston rivalry, 206
and Babe Ruth Day, 209
death and funeral of, 223, *225*
Stengel on, 249, 258
and Mantle, 258, 314
Frick as ghostwriter for, 265, 283
Maris on, 284
and Yankee style of play, 306
monument to, 317
and Reggie Jackson, 337
Winfield contrasted with, 371
uniform number of retired, 395
Wells asks to wear number of, 414
achievements of: home run record (season), 75, 130–31, *131*, 280, 281, 283, 285; diversity of, 99; as batting champion, 129; consecutive-score-less-innings record, 288; lifetime home run total, 423
personal characteristics of: misbehavior, 76, 83, 102, 103, 104, 139; and potential knifing incident, 88; lavish spending, 102; criticism of and amends for misbehavior, 104; illness (1925), 112, 273; as drinker, 112–13; rehabilitation program (1925), 116
performance for photographers, *128*
at orphanage, *134*
popularity, 139, *141*
Ruth, Claire (previously Claire Hodgson), 116, 140, 162, 325
Ruth, Helen, 116, 138–39, *139*

Sain, Johnny, 168, 239, 269, 297
St. Louis Browns
and AL raiding of NL, 4
as wartime champions (1944), 196
St. Louis Cardinals

Huggins from, *64*, 71
in 1926 World Series, 118–19
in 1928 World Series, *132*, 135
minor league teams of, 148
in 1943 World Series, *186*, 193, *193*, 195
in 1942 World Series, 190–91
in 1964 World Series, *296*, 299, 301–2
Keane from, 303
large payrolls of, 422
Sanders, Reggie, 452
San Diego Padres, in 1998 World Series, 423–24
Sanford, Fred, 226
Sanford, Jack, 290
San Francisco Giants, 290
in 1962 World Series, 290–92
as racially integrated, 291
Santa Ana Air Base team, 196
Santana, Rafael, 391
Sasaki, Katsohiru, 448
Sawyer, Eddie, 232
Sax, Steve, 382–83
Scarborough, Ray, 244
Schaap, Dick, 305
Schalk, Ray, 125, 362
Schang, Wally, 72, 96, 101, 102, 113
Schilling, Curt, 449, 450, 451, 453, *453*, 454
Schmidt, Mike, 371
Schoendienst, Red, 270
Schulz, Charles, 344
Schumacher, Hal, 169
Scientific (inside) baseball, 18, 19, 100, *229*
Score, Herb, 255, 266
Scott, Everett, 102, 113
Scouting system, Yankee, 178
under Weiss, 216, 219
and McDougald, 242
and Berra, 243
See also Farm system
Seattle Mariners
in 1995 playoffs, 387
in 2000 playoffs, 436, 438
season-wins record set by, 445, 448
in 2001 playoffs, 446, 448–49
Selbach, Kip, 37
Sele, Aaron, 449
Selig, Bud, *430*, 444
Selkirk, George, 161, 162, 164, 166, 169, 177, 178, 192, 457
Seminick, Andy, 232
Seventh Air Force team, 196
Sewell, Joe, 147, 148
Seymour, Harold, 54, 57
Shallock, Art, 238
Shannon, Paul, 83
Shantz, Bobby, 264, 267, 276, 277, 294, 309
Shaughnessy, Dan, 443
Shawkey, Bob, 68, 70, 73, *73*, 78, *82*, 87, 88, 91, 101, 105, 143, *143*, 144, 145, 168, 309, 457
Shea, Spec, 210, 212, 213, 221, 222, 225, 242
Shea Stadium, 299, 319
Sheckard, Jimmie, 125
Shecter, Leonard, 267, 285, 291, 295, 296

Sheehy, Pete, 340
Sheldon, Rollie, 307
Sheppard, Bob, 336, 353
Sheridan, Jack, 35, 37
Sherman, Joel, 427
Shirley, Bob, 379
Shocker, Urban, 71, 112, 120, 121, 135
Shor, Toots, *202*, 218, 293
Shore, Ernie, 76, 78, 88
Shotton, Burt, 213, 214, 221, 229
Showalter, Buck, 383, 385, 386, 387, 389–90, 395, 425
Siebern, Norm, 271, 273, 294
Sierra, Ruben, 386, 394, 396, *397*
Sign-stealing (other than by players)
by Stallings, 52–53, *55*, 57
made illegal, 53
and Giants' 1951 victory, 239
Simmons, Al, 138, 148, 151, 166; quoted, 115
Simmons, Curt, 232
Simpson, Harry, 267
Sisler, Dick, 232
Sisler, George, 180
Skinner, Bob, 277
Skowron, Bill "Moose," 252, 254, 255, 256, 271, 275, 276, 277, 279, 292
Slaughter, Enos, 154, 191, 193, 203, 259, *260*
Smalley, Roy, 374, 376, 391
Smith, Charlie, 312
Smith, Edgar, 179, 180
Smith, Hal, 277
Smith, Red, 200, 202, 206–7, 209, 214, 222, 223, 224, 233, 245, 248, 256, 276, 278, 281, 285, 350, 452
Smith, Reggie, 311
Smith, Saint John, 147
Smith, Wendell, 208
Smoltz, John, 402, 403, 404, 446
Snider, Duke, 244, 245, 246, *247*
Snyder (Giants catcher), 108
Sojo, Luis, 413, 418, 424, 430–31, 435, 442, 447
Solderholm, Eric, 361
Somers, Charles, 67, 70
Soriano, Alfonso, *440*, 442, 446–47, 448–49, 452, 454
Sosa, Elias, 348
Sosa, Sammy, 284, 419, 434
Sousa, John Philip, at Yankee Stadium opening, 105
Spahn, Warren, 248, 269, 270, 271, 272
Spalding's Official Base Ball Guide, quoted, 115
Sparrow, Harry, 93
Speaker, Tris, 40, 52, 69–70, 79, 99, 100, 120
Spencer, Jim, 355
Spencer, Shane, *419*, 419–20, 421, 423, 424, 446, 450, 452
Spikes, Charlie, 323
Spinks, J. G. Taylor, 71
Spira, Howard, 371, 372, 380–81
Spitball, 37
and Chesbro, 26, 37, 41, 44
and Russ Ford, 49
outlawing of, 86
of Lew Burdette, 270

Sporting News, 71
Sprowl, Bobby, 354
Stafford, Bill, 290, 291, 297
Stahl, Chick, 36
Stainback, Tuck, 191
Stallard, Tracy, *283,* 285
Stallings, George, *38,* 48–49, 52–55, *55,* 57, 58
Stankiewicz, Andy, 385, 391
Stanky, Eddie, 213, 214, 221
Stanley, Bob, 355
Stanley, Fred, 337, 339
Stanley, Mike, 385–86, 391
Stanton, Mike, 407, 413, 418, 424
Steffens, Lincoln, 15
Steinberg *New Yorker* cover, 236
Steinbrenner, George, 277, *320,*
        320–22, 325–26, 343, *358, 458*
    and Ruppert, 66, 321, 385
    and MacPhail, 197
    and Gabe Paul, 322–23
    and shaggy haircuts, 323
    and illegal campaign-contribu-
        tion charge, 324, 326
    and black players, 325
    and Dick Williams as manager,
        326
    suspension of (over campaign
        contributions), 326, 330, 333
    and Martin, 330, 332, *337,* 339,
        347, 350, 352, 353, 361, 381,
        382
    and free agency, 330, 336, 361,
        365
    and Jackson, *337,* 338–39, 340,
        347, 363, 364, 374, 380
    and Munson's dissatisfaction,
        339, 349
    Ellis on, 340
    and 1977 season, 340, 341
    1978 signings by, 349
    bumper sticker against, 359
    and post-1978 atmosphere,
        359–60, 364, 374, 378, 379,
        382
    becomes club president, 361
    trading young players for veter-
        ans as policy of, 361, 365
    and Howser's leaving, 363–64
    and Winfield, 364–65, 369, 370,
        371, 372, 373, 374, 376, *378,*
        379, 380–81, 382
    and 1981 World Series, 366
    suspension of (over association
        with Spira), 370, 371, 380–81,
        382, 385
    and Mattingly, 378
    and Whitson, 379
    and Yankees' spending, 381, 405,
        407, 422
    and "baseball people," 382, 385,
        412
    television pact signed by, 384
    reinvestment strategy forgotten
        by, 384
    and coaches, 386
    "Met envy" of, 390
    and Strawberry, 390, 396
    and Jeter, 394
    as continually pushing for depth,
        395
    and Torre, 396, 413

    and 1996 World Series, 403, 405
    and Irabu, 408
    after 1997 Series, 412
    and Wells, 414
    new ballpark sought by, 424
    and Bernie Williams, 424
    and Clemens, 426
    and Irabu, 427
    and Berra, 427
    and 1999 World Series, *430*
    on 1999 team, 431
    YankeeNets Corporation of, 444
    9/11 donation of, 444
    and 2001 World Series, 454
    attitudes and practices of: inter-
        fering with managers, 324,
        325, 334, 378; after 1978
        championship, 360; and
        improvement in his absence,
        380, 382; second place unac-
        ceptable, 389, 411–12, 455;
        intruding on Watson as GM,
        391, 396, 412; pennants alone
        meaningless, 402; newfound
        restraint (1998), 413; postsea-
        son victory demanded, 420;
        mellowing, 424; impatience,
        434
Steinbrenner, Hank (son), 382
Steinbrenner, Henry (father), 320
Stengel, Casey (Charles Dillon),
        224–26, *234,* 248–51, 458
    as Giant (1923 World Series),
        107, 108
    in Lardner's essay, 124
    and Rizzuto, 178–79
    on Holmes, 189
    as Braves manager, 224, 248, 250
    Stengelese and aphorisms of,
        243, 248, 250, 278, 295–96
    as Mets manager, 248, 290, 295,
        308, 439
    as Yankee manager, 224, 225,
        226, 278
    and press, 225, *265*
    in 1949 season, 227, *228,* 229
    and DiMaggio, 227, 230, 232,
        236, 250
    platooning by, 227, 230, 239, 252
    in 1949 World Series, 230
    as 1949 Manager of the Year, 230
    in 1950 season, 230, 232
    as shield for Weiss, 232
    and Yankee reemergence, 233
    and Mantle, 236–37, 238,
        250–51, 258, *275*
    in 1951 season, 237, 238, 239
    in 1952 season, 242
    on home run production, 242–43
    and Berra, 243
    and Yankee edge, 244, 252, 278
    in 1952 World Series, 245
    racism of, 255
    in 1955 season, 255
    in 1955 World Series, 256, *257*
    in 1956 World Series, 259
    on deal with A's, 265
    on late-1950s prospects, 265, 271
    and punishment for Copacabana
        brawl, 267
    and Martin-Simpson trade, 267
    in 1957 World Series, *270*

    and 1958 World Series, 271, 272
    retirement considered, 272
    and 1959 season, 273
    and Maris, 273, 276
    in 1960 season, 275
    and 1960 World Series, 277
    retirement of, 278
    and false impression about suc-
        cess, 279
    and Ford, 288–89
    decisive changes made by, 295
    and Berra, 295
    and Martin, *381*
    uniform number of retired, 395
    dynasty of, 446
Stennett, Rennie, 332
Stephens, Vern, 222–23, 227
Stern, Howard, 423
"Steve Blass disease," 429
Stirnweiss, George "Snuffy," 129,
        189, *192,* 193, 196, 201, 209, 213,
        254
Stobbs, Chuck, 239, 246
Stock market crash (1929), 143
Stoneham, Charles, 91, 264
Stoneham, Horace, 269
Stottlemyre, Mel, 297, 315, 459
    as hopeful prospect, *289*
    in 1964 season, 297, *301*
    in 1964 World Series, 299, 301,
        301
    in contrast to late-1960s players,
        306
    in 1965 season, 307, *307*
    as untouchable, 311
    in 1967 season, 312–13
    in 1970 season, 317
    in 1973 season, 324
    in 1974 season, 326
    as pitching coach, 390, 414
    and Pettitte, 427
    cancer of, 442
Stottlemyre, Todd, 421
Stouffer, Vern, 320
Strand, Paul, 116
Strawberry, Darryl
    with Mets, 379, 396
    Yanks' signing of, 386, 390, 422
    released and re-signed, 395–96
    in 1996 season, 396, 401
    in 1996 playoffs, 397, 402, 403
    in 1996 World Series, 403, 404
    hurt in 1997 season, 407
    in 1998 season, 412, 413, 414,
        415, *417,* 418, 420
    suffers from colon cancer, 421,
        421, 430
    in 1998 playoffs, 423
    as submitting to smaller role,
        424
    in parade, *425*
    in 1999 season, 427
    in 1999 World Series, 429
    slips again into addiction, 433
Stricklett, Elmer, 26
Strike by players (1981), 365
Strike by players (1994–1995), 386
Strunk, Amos, 72
Sturdivant, Tom, 259, 261, 267, 272
Sturm, Johnny, 179, 188, 189
Subway series
    first (1910, second-place Yankees

        vs. second-place Giants), 54,
        55–57, *57*
    1921 (Giants-Yankees), 100
    1922 (Giants-Yankees), 103–4
    1923 (Giants-Yankees), 107–8
    1936 (Giants-Yankees), 166–67
    1937 (Giants-Yankees), 169
    1941 (Dodgers-Yankees), 184
    1947 (Dodgers-Yankees), 211–14,
        221–22
    1949 (Dodgers-Yankees), 229–30
    1951 (Giants-Yankees), 239–40
    1952 (Dodgers-Yankees), 244–45
    1953 (Dodgers-Yankees), 257,
        252
    1955 (Dodgers-Yankees), 255–57,
        257
    1956 (Dodgers-Yankees), *258,*
        258–61
    1999 prospects of, 428, 433
    2000 (Mets-Yankees), *438,*
        438–42, 446
Sullivan, Big Tim, *9,* 10, 14
Sullivan, Ed, 126
Sullivan, Haywood, *307*
Sullivan, Sport, 120
Summer of '49 (Halberstam), 343
Summers, Bill, 155
Sunday baseball, 86
Suzuki, Ichiro, 27, 369, 443, 447
Sveum, Dale, 413
Sykes, Bob, 366
Syndicate system, 7, 264

Tabasco Kid, Elberfeld as, *45*
Taborn, Earl, 227
Tallis, Cedric, 349
Tammany Hall, 5, 9, 10
    and Freedman, 5, 11
    and construction of ballfield, 11,
        13–14
    Farrell's "retirement" from, 16
    and subway, 24–25
    Farrell's and Devery's depend-
        ence on, 58, 65
    and Ruppert, 67, 87–88
    and construction of Yankee Sta-
        dium, 96
Tanana, Frank, 376
Tannehill, Jess, 8, 11, 16, 18, 21, 24,
        27, 29
Tarasco, Tony, 401
Tartabull, Danny, 385, 386, 422
Taylor, Brien, 392
Taylor, Harry, 213
Taylor, John I., 32
Tebbetts, Birdie, 229
Television
    and Weiss, 218
    in 1952 World Series, *240*
    and Yankee constituency, 253
    and Giants or Dodgers fans,
        264
    and New York sportswriters,
        267
    cable, 297
    and Martin on World Series
        schedule, 336
    Steinbrenner's deal with, 384,
        422
Tenney, Fred, 58

Terrorism, and 2000 World Series, 438

Terrorist attack on World Trade Center, 444–45

Terry, Bill, 179

Terry, Ralph, 265, 267, 272, 277, 289, 291, 292, 293, 297, 298, 355

Tewksbury, Bob, 379

Texas Rangers
  in 1996 playoffs, 396–97
  in 1998 playoffs, 420–21
  in 1999 playoffs, 428
  and Yankee playoff achievements, 446

Thayer, Ernest L., 107

Thomas, Al, 123

Thome, Jim, 421, 423

Thomson, Bobby, 239, 336, 452

Thormhalen, Hank, 91, 96

Thrift, Syd, 380

Throneberry, Marv ("Marvelous Marv"), 265, 271, 439

Thurman, Bob, 227

Tiant, Luis, 344, 354, 360, 361, 365

Tidrow, Dick, 326, 335, 345

Tolleson, Wayne, 391

Toney, Fred, 100

Topping, Dan, 197–98, 198, 199, 201, 277, 458
  and proposed Williams-DiMaggio trade, 207, 207
  and MacPhail's retirement, 222
  and Harris firing, 224
  and Stengel as manager, 226, 273, 278
  talks DiMaggio out of retiring, 230
  and race issue, 232
  on Vic Power, 245
  and Arnold Johnson, 264
  and 1959 season, 272
  status quo approach of, 278
  and Berra as manager, 295, 302–3
  and Houk as general manager, 295
  and sale to CBS, 297, 298, 299
  and bidding for quality players, 306
  and Yankees' 1965 weakness, 308
  CBS buyout of, 309, 321

Topping, Dan, Jr., 309, 311

Torre, Frank, 396, 402, 404, 430

Torre, Joe, 390, 458
  Stengel compared with, 244, 278
  quoted, 389
  and Jeter, 394, 448
  and Bernie Williams, 395
  and Steinbrenner, 396, 413
  sense of calm of, 396
  postseason style of, 397
  in 1996 playoffs, 397, 402
  and 1996 World Series, 402, 403, 404, 405
  on Yankee Stadium, 403
  in 1997 season, 407
  in 1997 playoffs, 408–9
  in 1998 season, 413, 417, 419–20
  on Wells, 414
  on Spencer, 420

in 1998 playoffs, 420, 422, 423
on 1998 team record, 424
prostate cancer of, 427, 430
in 1999 season, 427
in 1999 World Series, 428, 429, 430, 431
and Rivera, 429, 442
and Yankee comebacks, 429
with Giuliani at ceremony, 432
in 2000 season, 434–35
in 2000 World Series, 441
and Mussina, 442
on Red Sox (2001), 443
in 2001 playoffs, 444, 446, 447, 448
in response to terrorist attack, 445
dynasty of, 446
and 2001 World Series, 449, 450, 451, 452, 453, 454
on Clemens, 453

Torre, Rocco, 396

Torres, Rusty, 323

Torrez, Mike, 340, 341, 345, 347, 348, 349, 350, 353, 354, 355

Townsend, Jack, 20

Trail, Chet, 295

Traynor, Pie, 94, 131

Tresh, Tom, 244, 287, 289, 292, 294, 299, 307, 312

Trimble, Joe, 267, 276, 281, 285, 292

Tunney, Gene, 128

Turbeville, George, 165

Turley, Bob, 253, 255, 259, 261, 272, 276, 341

Turner, Jim, as saves leader, 168

Turner, Ted, 390, 422

Tweed, William M. "Boss," 5, 322

Uhle, George, 100

Underwood, Tom, 361, 365

Unglaub, Bob, 27

Uniform numbers, retired, 395

Uniforms, New York
  in first season, 18
  interlocking NY design on, 49
  pinstripes on, 59, 59

Union, players. See Major League Baseball Players' Association

Upshaw, Cecil, 326

Valentine, Bobby, 442

Valero, Joseph, 330

Van Wyck, Robert, 15

Vaughn, Mo, 420

Vecsey, George, 382

Veeck, Bill, 197, 227, 273, 325

Velarde, Randy, 391

Ventura, Robin, 455

Vernon, Micky, 207

Vick, Sammy, 73, 94, 96

Vidmer, Richards, 123, 126, 127, 135, 153, 169, 177, 185

Vila, Joe, 11, 44, 46, 47, 48, 53, 101, 103–4, 119–20, 123

Vincent, Fay, 381

Virdon, Bill, 276, 326, 330, 332, 390

Vizcaino, Jose, 435, 440–41

Vizquel, Omar, 394, 409

Voigt, David, 79

Wagner, Honus, 8, 40, 243

Wagner, Robert (N.Y. supreme court justice), 79

Walberg, Rube, 129, 148

Walker, Dixie, 165, 212, 213

Walker, Harry, 203

Walker, Jimmy, 104, 137

Walsh, Christy, 116, 139

Walsh, Ed, 45, 48

Walsh, Ed, Jr., 181

Waner, Lloyd, 131

Waner, Paul, 131

Wanninger, Pee Wee, 113, 116

Ward, Aaron, 91, 101, 103, 105, 113, 116

Ward, Robert, 340

Warhop, Jack, 56

Warneke, Lon, 152

Warp, Harold, 153–54

Washington Senators, 3, 20, 27

"Was There Ever a Guy Like Ruth?" (Kieran), 130–31

Watson, Bob, 361, 363, 364, 374, 390, 391, 391, 396, 403, 405, 408, 412, 412

Weatherly, Roy, 192

Weathers, David, 405

Webb, Del, 198, 198, 199, 201, 207, 277, 458
  and MacPhail's retirement, 222
  and Harris firing, 224
  and Stengel as manager, 226, 278
  and race issue, 232
  hit by foul ball in 1955 Series, 256
  status quo approach of, 278
  Modesto team owned by, 291
  and sale to CBS, 297, 298
  and bidding for quality players, 306
  sells share in Yankees, 308, 321

Webb, Mel, 211

Weiss, George, 148–49, 155, 216–20, 270
  and farm system, 149, 155, 161, 210, 216, 219, 270
  and WWII loss of players, 188
  and Holmes-Hassett trade, 189
  and black players, 211, 232, 245, 246, 254, 278
  Lopat acquired by, 216, 222
  and players' pay, 217, 230, 252, 411–12
  players' attitudes toward, 217, 252
  and MacPhail's retirement, 222
  becomes general manager, 222
  and Harris firing, 224
  and Stengel, 224–26, 250
  Sanford and Partee acquired by, 226
  Mize acquired by, 228
  and Yankee reemergence, 233
  and DiMaggio's contemplated retirement, 236
  sees players as products, 242
  and threat of trade, 252

trades for Turley and Larsen, 253
and Arnold Johnson, 264
and punishment for Copacabana brawl, 267
and trade for Simpson, 267
retirement considered by, 272
trades for Maris et al., 273
retirement of, 278
decisive changes made by, 295
Houk contrasted with, 307
and Torre, 390

Welch, Bob, 356, 357, 404

Wells, David, 402, 407, 409, 413, 414, 417, 418, 420–21, 422, 423, 424, 426, 431, 455

Werber, Billy, 139, 155

Wertz, Vic, 447

Wettelend, John, 168, 386, 387, 394, 403, 404, 405, 419

Wheat, Zack, 121

Whitaker, Steve, 311

White, Bill, xx, 220, 299

White, Ernie, 191

White, Roy, xx, 308, 316, 321, 324, 330, 332, 339, 345, 355, 356, 357, 459

White, Stanford, 14

White Construction Company, 96, 97

Whitfield, Terry, 330

Whitson, Ed, 369, 379, 422, 435

Wickman, Bob, 386

Wife-swapping episode, 323

Wilhelm, Hoyt, 284–85

Wilhoit, Joe, 180

Williams, Bernie, 388, 394–95, 458
  as batting champion, 129
  as black player in Yankee system, 220
  as Gold Glove winner, 294
  and crowd at Dave Winfield Day, 369
  and Showalter, 385
  Yankees' acquisition of, 395, 422
  in 1996 playoffs, 397, 402
  in Molly O'Neill's account, 398
  in 1996 World Series, 403, 404, 405
  in 1997 season, 407
  and 1998 season, 413, 415, 418, 420
  as farm system product, 424
  and Steinbrenner, 424
  re-signed as free agent, 424–25
  in 1999 playoffs, 428
  in 1999 World Series, 428, 430
  in 2000 World Series, 442
  father's illness and death, 442–43
  in 2001 season, 443
  in response to terrorist attack, 445
  in 2001 playoffs, 448
  in 2001 World Series, 450, 454

Williams, Cy, 105

Williams, Dick, 326, 338

Williams, Gerald, 385, 394

Williams, Jimmy, 16, 19, 20, 32, 33, 36, 39, 47

Williams, Jimy, 444

Williams, Joe, 123, 153, 209–10

Williams, Ken, 103

Williams, Matt, 451

Williams, Stan, 292, 297
Williams, Ted, *204*
   in 1939 season, 173
   as Hall of Famer, 177
   hitting streak of, 180
   and DiMaggio, 180, 182, 188, 224
   in 1941 All-Star game, 180
   .406 average of (1941), 182
   WWII service of, 192
   vs. Yankee counterparts, 201
   in proposed trade for DiMaggio, 207, *207*, 243
   in 1947 season, 209
   and 1947 MVP voting, 211
   in 1949 season, 227, 229
   in 1951 season, 238, 239
   and Mantle, 258
   and Yankee–Red Sox rivalry, 344
   self-involvement of, 380
Williams, Walt "No Neck," 326, 330
Williamson, Ned, 86
Wills, Maury, 293
Wilson, Artie, 226–27
Wilson, Enrique, 422
Wilson, Willie, 363
Wilson, Woodrow, 61
Wiltse, Hooks, 56
Winfield, Dave, 364, *366*, 368–73, *378*, 459
   as Gold Glove winner, 294
   and Jackson, 364, 370, 371, *378*
   signing of, 364–65
   and Steinbrenner, 364–65, 369, 370, 371, 372, 373, 374, 376, *378*, 379, 380–81, 382
   in 1981 season, 365
   contract of, 365, 371
   in 1981 World Series, 365–66
   in 1982 season, 374
   seagull killed by throw of, 375
   fans' view of, 378
   in 1984 season, 378, 379
   as 1980s highlight, 379
   and Henderson, 380
   as scapegoat, 380
   and 1989 season, 382
   traded away, 382
   Bernie Williams compared to, 395
   long-term contract of, 422
Winter, George, 24
Witt, George, 382
Witt, Mike, 382
Witt, Whitey, 103, 105, 109, 111
Wohlers, Mark, 403, 404
Wohlford, Jim, 335
Wolverton, Harry, 59, *59*
Womack, Dooley, 308
Womack, Tony, 450, 454
Wood, Barry, 146
Wood, Joe, 25, 120
Woodling, Gene, 227, *230*, 233, 247, 252
Woodward, Stanley, 168
Woodward, Woody, 419
World Series
   and gambling, 101–102
   Yankees enter fresh, 184, 290
   Ford's record in, 289
   and Yankee dynasties, 446
World Series (1903), 24
World Series (1904), hopes for dashed by Giants, 27, 28, 32, 343

World Series (1905), 43
World Series (1918), 188, 342
World Series (1919), and Black Sox scandal, 92, 93, 119–20
World Series (1921), 100–101
World Series (1922), 103–4
World Series (1923), 107, *107*–8
World Series (1926), 118–19
World Series (1927), 131–34
   Lardner's essay on, 124–25
   and myth of demoralizing Yankee batting practice, 131
World Series (1928), *132*, 135
World Series (1932), 152–54
World Series (1936), 166–67
   and DiMaggio, *163*, 166–67, 182
   Murphy in, 165
World Series (1937), 169
World Series (1938), 172
World Series (1939), 177
   Murphy in, 165
World Series (1941), 184–85
World Series (1942), 190–91
World Series (1943), *186*, 193, *193*, 195
World Series (1946), 203
   and Pesky, 154
World Series (1947), *204*, 211–14, 221–22, 451
World Series (1948), *204*
World Series (1949), 229–30
World Series (1950), *230*, 232–33
   and Weiss on salaries, 218
World Series (1951), *238*, 239–40
World Series (1952), *240*, 244–45
World Series (1953), 247, 252
World Series (1954), 252, 447
World Series (1955), 255–57, *257*
World Series (1956), *258*, 258–61
World Series (1957), 269–70
World Series (1958), 271
World Series (1960), 276–78
World Series (1961), 285
World Series (1962), 290–92
World Series (1963), 292–93
World Series (1964), *296*, 299, 301–2
   Yankees' black opponents in, 220, 299
World Series (1976), *334*
World Series (1977), 345–48
   Martin in, *331*, 345, 347, *347*, 348
   Jackson in, 347, 348, *350*
World Series (1978), 356–57
   Jackson vs. Welch in, 356, 404
World Series (1981), 365–66
World Series (1986), and Clemens, 425
World Series (1996), 402–5, 446
   and Boggs, 404, *405*
   and Yankee strategy in 1997 playoff, 409
World Series (1998), 423–24
World Series (1999), 428–31, 446
   Jeter in, *392*
World Series (2000), 438–42
World Series (2001), 449–55
World Trade Center, terrorist attack on, 444–45
World War I, 70–71, 72, 73, 187, 188
   exemption proposals for, 73, 73–74

World War II, 185, 187, 188, 191–92
   military baseball teams in, 196
   and claims by blacks, 199
Wright, Jaret, 409, 422
Wyatt, Whit, 184
Wynegar, Butch, 374
Wynn, Early, 275
Wynn, Jim, 339

Yankee Entertainment Sports Network (YES), 444
Yankee fans, 76
   Italian-American, *74*, 76, 117, *160*, 162
   and Ruth, *84*, 85
   and DiMaggio, 166
   change in demographics of, 264
   and departure of Giants and Dodgers, 271
   vs. Mets fans, 290
   defection of, 310, 374
   and Mattingly, 376, 378
   as multiracial (1990s), 391
   cool toward Clemens and Boggs, 426
Yankee Game of the Week, 308
"Yankee killer," 335
Yankees. *See* New York Yankees
Yankee Stadium, 96, 97, 104, 105, *105, 111*
   site of, *60, 81*
   construction of, *94*, 97, 104
   and pitchers, 96
   and Ruth, 97, 104
   renovation of, 97, *111*, 172, 319, 324
   varied activities in, 97, 148
   opening of, 104, 105
   during 1923 World Series, *112*
   as costly, 138
   Negro Leagues as users of, 148, 208
   and right-handed hitters, 169
   Ruppert's wisdom in, 172
   MacPhail, Topping, and Webb as owners of, 199
   bleachers of (1947), *214*
   stars' monuments in, *214*, 317, 362
   sale-lease arrangement for, 264
   smallest crowd in (1966), 309
   deteriorating neighborhood of, 310, 317
   deterioration of (1970s), 317
   mob vandalizes on eve of renovation, 324–25
   reopening of, 333
   Torre on, 403
   emergency repair of, 413–14
   prayer service in (2001), 445
Yankee uniform numbers, retired, 395
Yastrzemski, Carl, 314, *328*, 331, 344, 350, 354, 355, 360
Yawkey, Thomas A., 155, 172, 177, 206, *207*
   Barrow supported by, 87
   as wealthy owner, 161
   quoted, 205
   as rumored purchaser of Yankees, 206

   and proposed trade of Williams for DiMaggio, 207, *207*
   McCarthy hired by, 222
   and 1949 pennant celebration, 228
   and Berra, *286*, 295
   player purchases from Finley attempted, 334
   generosity of, 343
   and Boston payroll, 422
Yeager, Steve, 348
Young, Buddy, 232
Young, Cy, 24, 25, *25*, 29, 33, 35, 48, 213
Young, Dick, 265, 267, 270, 272, 277, 278, 281, 283, 284, 293, 295, 302, 314, 323, 336, 338, 348, 414

Zachary, Tom, 130, 138, 140
Zarilla, Al, 229
Zeider, Rollie, 61
Zeile, Todd, 402, 438, 440
Zimmer, Don, 256, 354, 355, 390, 427, 451

Prepared by Automobile Club of New York, 1952
© AAA. Used by permission.